HIDDEN MEXICO

Adventurer's Guide
to the Beaches and Coasts

"Fascinating."   *Los Angeles Times*

"Loaded with data."   *Philadelphia Inquirer*

"Very comprehensive."   *New Orleans Times-Picayune*

"Searches out little-known islands and secluded shores."
San Francisco Examiner

"An authoritative guide to the country's coastline. Unlocks the secrets of Mexico's beaches."   *Denver Post*

"Excellent. This well-written, carefully thought out volume would serve as a model for future guidebooks."   *Oceans*

Hidden Mexico

*Adventurer's Guide
to the Beaches and Coasts*

Rebecca Bruns
**with Dave Houser, Jean Pierce Postlewaite and
Eleanor S. Morris**

Executive Editor   Ray Riegert

Ulysses Press
Berkeley, California

Published by: Ulysses Press
Sather Gate Station
Box 4000–H
Berkeley, CA 94704

Library of Congress Catalog Card Number 89-50596
ISBN 0-915233-16-9

Printed in the U.S.A. by the George Banta Company

10 9 8 7 6 5 4 3

Production Director: Leslie Henriques
Managing Editor: Lindsay Mugglestone

Editor: Judith Kahn
Senior Research Associate: Jan Butchofsky
Illustrator: Rob Harper
Cover Designer: Bonnie Smetts
Research Assistant: Claire Chun
Index: Sayre Van Young

Cover Photography: Front cover photo by Chuck O'Rear/West Light; right back cover photo by Bill Ross/West Light; left back cover photo by Ed Simpson

Notes from the Publisher

An alert, adventurous reader is as important as a travel writer in keeping a guidebook up-to-date and accurate. So if you happen upon a great restaurant, discover a hidden locale, or (heaven forbid) find an error in the text, we'd appreciate hearing from you. Just write to:

Ulysses Press
Box 4000–H
Berkeley, CA 94704

* * *

Throughout the text, hidden locales, remote regions, and little-known spots are marked with a star (★).

* * *

More and more sea and wildlife is disappearing from the earth. In Mexico, as in other developing countries, trade regulations are not as restrictive as in the United States. Many products for sale in the marketplace have been made from endangered species. Think twice before you buy. Products fashioned from hides, shells, feathers or teeth may come from endangered species. By avoiding such purchases you not only save the earth's natural resources but also avoid the risk of being fined or having your goods seized by government inspectors.

* * *

It is our desire as publishers to create guidebooks that are responsible as well as informative. The danger of exploring hidden locales is that they will no longer be secluded.

We hope that our guidebooks treat the people, country and land we visit with respect. We ask that our readers do the same. The hiker's motto, "Walk softly on the Earth," applies to travelers everywhere...in the desert, on the beach, and in town.

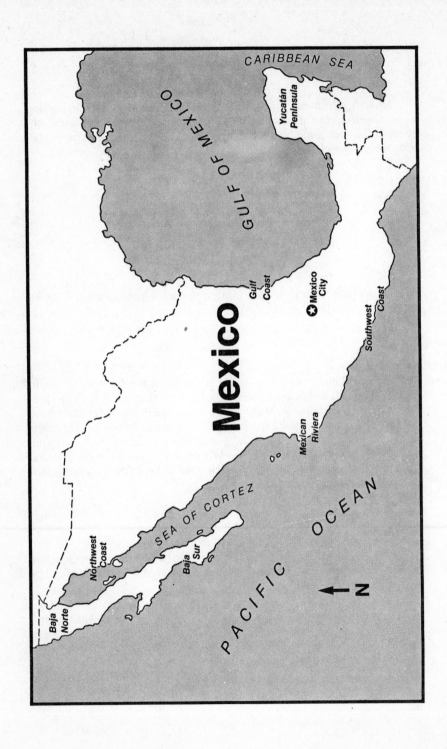

Preface

To many travelers, Mexico seems like an exotic dream representing all things magical. It is Indian culture, ubiquitous folk art, a jumble of vivid markets. Ancient history stalked by the ghosts of Aztec kings and Mayan gods. A living frontier, with noisy cantinas and men sporting bristling moustaches and dusty sombreros. A fiesta of fireworks, cockfights, fancy dancing, hot chilies and tequila. And, of course, this country beckons us as a tropical paradise, with beaches as seductive as the people's smiles and as lovely as bittersweet Mexican ballads.

Hedonists, beware! Once you set foot on Mexican sand, the luxurious coast can get under your skin and you'll never be satisfied until you go back. Then you may become one of those people who rush off to Mexico at every chance, lured by the lifestyle, the heat, your own favorite beach and all those legendary spots you have yet to see.

About 20,000 miles of roads—good, bad and almost unmentionable—were covered to bring you the best secrets of Mexico's coasts. Anyone with a sturdy standard car can retrace this route, and will no doubt find undisturbed beaches still waiting to be discovered.

Some may wonder if this book about the coasts of Mexico is geared exclusively toward camping or low-income travel. Not at all. Ten months in both homespun hamlets and sequin-streaked discos went into shaping a guide for everyone, naturalists and night owls, scavangers and sybarites alike. The book's guiding light, however, was distinct: Where is the adventure and the magic?

Selected details on everything from shopping to snorkeling take you to the heart of Mexico's coastal areas—the cities, villages and undeveloped regions. The satellite principle is used—that is, beach listings are connected, whenever possible, to the nearest sizable town that can serve as a base of operations. This way you can explore the wilds by day, enjoy mariachis at night and take a hot shower every morning.

Besides being an expansive, diverse country geographically, Mexico and its ways can be downright confusing to the newcomer. Street names sometimes change in the middle of a block. Appointments often are not kept. Phones may not work. Cars race maniacally through stoplights that don't change. But what often strikes visitors as anarchy is simply a reminder that they are experiencing a culture whose customs, laws and unspoken traditions are quite different from their own. The purpose of this book is to translate the unfamiliar into understandable nuggets of information that lead you through the chaos unscathed.

Step-by-step, *Hidden Mexico: Adventurer's Guide to the Beaches and Coasts* guides you through every phase of your Mexican journey. Chapter

One tells how to prepare for your trip, from procuring a tourist card to scanning a calendar of fiestas, to dealing with traditions south of the border, such as *mordida* (literally, "the bite," or the country's notorious "sanctioned" bribes) to confronting the sometimes-befuddling address system. Chapter Two gives important information about driving in Mexico and enjoying the outdoors—camping, fishing and boating, tropical flora and fauna. You'll also find a unique sand-quality scale for judging beaches. Chapter Three delves into Mexican history, the Spanish language (with a compendium of useful terms) and Mexican culture.

The last seven chapters explore beaches, villages and resorts in each coastal area: Baja Norte, Baja Sur, the Northwest Coast, the Mexican Riviera, the Southwest Coast, the Gulf of Mexico and the Yucatán Peninsula.

Each chapter is divided into three parts. When you want to find a rental car, hotel or restaurant, check out the "Easy Living" section. "The Great Outdoors" segment covers recreational activities, beaches and trailer parks. The last section, "Travelers' Tracks," returns to the beaten path and leads to sightseeing, shopping and entertainment spots.

Throughout the text, especially enticing hidden locales and remote regions are marked with a star (★).

Putting this book together has been a fascinating discovery. I hope it helps enrich your own visit to Mexico.

Now, *vámanos a la playa*—let's go to the beach!

CONTENTS

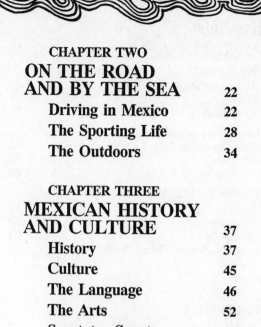

MAPS

SPECIAL FEATURES

CHAPTER ONE

Preparing for Your Trip
Where, When and How To Go

Where to Go

Where to go is determined by what you want to do. Whether it's lounge in the sun or chase a black marlin, Mexico has a coast for it, usually with much more than beach life to offer.

Baja Norte provides a great entree into the wilds of the Mexican desert. Many visitors come down to shop for bargains in Tijuana; others venture along the fine surfing beaches from Rosarito to Ensenada, lunching on lobster and octopus. Nightlife and seafood are Ensenada's strong points. But for a real taste of the desert, San Felipe offers dunes, the towering Sierra San Pedro Mártir and vast beaches on the Sea of Cortez. You can also enjoy quail-hunting in San Quintín, fishing and exploring jagged islands around Bahía de los Ángeles, and wandering through a cactus forest in the central desert.

Baja Sur is more the chic vacationland, best known for its swank hotels in Cabo San Lucas and big-time sportfishing off the Capes. Some of the world's most enchanting desert beaches line the Sea of Cortez between La Paz, Baja's loveliest city, and San José del Cabo. There's also wonderful camping around Mulegé and Bahía Concepción, superb whale-watching around Guerrero Negro, prime windsurfing off Los Barriles and surfing along the savage Pacific around Todos Santos.

Mexico's **Northwest Coast** repeats much of the arid scenery of Baja, although its Sea of Cortez beaches aren't nearly as spectacular. One exception is Puerto Peñasco, site of some beautiful dunes. You can collect fine ironwood carvings of marine and desert animals around Bahía Kino, home of the Seri Indians. Or you can skin-dive off the islands around San Carlos, the resort linked to Guaymas. And don't miss the hair-raising train ride through the Sierra Madre from Los Mochis.

Probably the part of coastal Mexico everyone knows best, the **Mexican Riviera** combines glittering resorts with tiny fishing villages slumbering amid bougainvillea and palms. Here some of the best hidden beaches on

1

the Pacific await you off bumpy dirt roads, especially around San Blas, Rincón de Guayabitos, Barra de Navidad and the state of Michoacán. For swimming, boating, shopping and nightlife, you'll be hard-pressed to find resorts that can outdazzle sporty Mazatlán, picturesque Puerto Vallarta, rugged Manzanillo, dual-faceted Ixtapa-Zihuatanejo (blending highrises with village charm) and glamorous Acapulco.

The **Southwest Coast** provides several great getaways, primarily the former vagabond town of Puerto Escondido, now a burgeoning little resort. These days vagabonds head for drowsy Puerto Ángel and wild beaches down to Salina Cruz. Soon the nearby hamlet of Santa Cruz Huatulco will be the center of a snazzy tourist development called Bahías de Huatulco situated along a string of virgin coves with jewel-like water. Many say it will be the next Cancún.

The eastern coast along the **Gulf of Mexico** takes you to the sites of some of Mexico's earliest Indian and Hispanic history. You'll see the flying pole dancers of Papantla and the ruins of El Tajín, the overgrown house where Spanish explorer Hernán Cortés lived, and the massive stone Olmec heads in Villahermosa. The rowdy port of Tampico and the markets of Matamoros add touches of color, but the highlight of this coast is festive Veracruz, with the biggest port, best coffee and most energetic marimba music in Mexico—a must for anyone who loves tropical towns.

The fascinating **Yucatán Peninsula** needs a lifetime of visits. The Mayan ruins alone could fill many vacations, not to mention the caves and *cenotes*, or natural wells, scattered throughout the lowland jungle. Mérida, a colonial city made for romance, is alive with folkdancing and ballads. Colorful sights such as the area's flocks of pink flamingos and the old walled city of Campeche await travelers to the Gulf. For beach life, the Mexican Caribbean fulfills just about every dream of paradise, from the tranquility of Isla Mujeres to the opulence of Cancún to the heart-stopping beauty of rustic beaches in Tulúm and beyond. Snorkeling is unparalleled in these crystalline waters, and skin divers flock to the lovely island of Cozumel to marvel at one of the world's greatest reefs.

See the chapter introductions for more detailed information about each of these main coastal areas.

When to Go

SEASONS

Mexico, like most of the tropics, has just two seasons: rainy and dry. Generally, rain falls and temperatures rise during summer and autumn months, from June through October: the least expensive time to visit coastal Mexico. That leaves November to May as the high and dry season—literally, the time when prices shoot up as much as 40 percent or more, in response to the crowds rushing down to enjoy the perfect balmy weather. Be aware that Christmas, New Year's and Easter pack the resorts wall-to-wall and the beaches towel-to-towel, sometimes with sky-high prices. I usually find the off-season pleasantly uncrowded, wonderfully economical and seldom unbearably hot—at the worst, requiring two swims a day instead of one.

Mexico, on the metric system, measures temperature in degrees Celsius. (To convert Celsius to Fahrenheit, multiply by 9, divide by 5 and add 32. For example, 26° Celsius—the average temperature in Acapulco during the winter—equals 79° Fahrenheit.) The regional climates of the seven beach zones in this book are as follows (with temperatures given in Fahrenheit readings):

Baja Norte has a climate resembling that of southern California, but drier, with even less rain. Winters often require a jacket, with temperatures sometimes dropping into the low 50s. Summers bring heat waves that can top 100° on the Sea of Cortez, causing many places to close. The Pacific Coast tends to be cooler and more overcast.

Baja Sur is considered subtropical desert, quite arid yet subject to balmy sea breezes and cool winter evenings. The temperature seldom goes below the 60s but may leap into the 100s in the summer—a dry heat with little humidity. Here, too, the Pacific Coast may be considerably cooler than the Sea of Cortez.

Northwest Coast temperatures resemble those of Baja Norte—chilly winters, blazing summers—especially hot up north around Guaymas. Rainfall here is more frequent, though irregular, sometimes coming in gusty storms even in the spring.

The **Mexican Riviera** is blessed with warm tropical weather year round. Winter nights rarely drop below 65°—shirtsleeve weather—with perfect, rain-free days in the 70s and 80s. Frequent showers and high humidity occur during summer, when the mercury may zoom into the 90s.

The **Southwest Coast** climate follows that of the Riviera, with northerlies often blowing across the Gulf of Tehuantepec. Hot, stagnant air hovers along the Mar Muerto.

The **Gulf of Mexico** area is known for its muggy temperatures in the 70s and 80s, with severe summer humidity. Up north, in the desert terrain bordering the United States, sparse rain falls more often in the winter than summer. South of Tampico rainfall increases (evident in the lush green landscape), often accompanied by a chill season of *nortes*, or brisk northerly winds, from September through March.

The **Yucatán Peninsula** can be suffocatingly hot and humid in its inland jungles during the summer, while its Gulf and Caribbean coasts often stay comfortably cooled by trade winds. Drenching rain falls sporadically between May and October. The mercury shoots into the 90s with dips into the 80s. Hurricanes occasionally blow in from July to October.

CALENDAR OF EVENTS

You may plan your visit around a certain holiday or festival and join in the spirit that has led Mexicans to say, "There's a fiesta going on somewhere in Mexico every moment." Writers from Octavio Paz to Alan Riding have described the fiesta as a vital liberation from solitude, stoicism and the restraints of poverty, whether the occasion celebrates a religious or patriotic event, a birthday or a wedding. Here are the most important events of the Mexican coastal areas:

JANUARY

January 1: **New Year's Day** is celebrated all over Mexico as a national holiday.

January 6: **Day of the Three Kings** is the traditional time for exchanging Christmas gifts in Mexico.

FEBRUARY

February–March (varying dates): **Pre-Lenten Carnival** brings an explosion of music, dance and fireworks to most coastal towns, notably Ensenada, La Paz, Mazatlán, Acapulco, Veracruz and Mérida. Mazatlán and Veracruz have the biggest bashes.

February 2: **Día de Candelaria** is celebrated throughout Mexico by dancing, processions, bullfights, and the blessing of candles and seeds.

February: **Días de Charros** brings Matamoros and Brownsville together in a seven-day rodeo.

MARCH

March–April: **Semana Santa** (Easter Week) is Mexico's biggest holiday season, with Passion plays, music and dance in the squares. There's a general exodus of city folk for the sea or lakeshore, where they picnic and camp.

Mid-March: *Brujas* (witches) gather for a **annual conference** around Lake Catemaco in the state of Veracruz.

March 21: The **birthday of Benito Juárez**—a 19th-century president and Mexican hero—is a national holiday.

APRIL

Early April: The **spring festival** celebrating the founding of Tampico is this city's answer to Carnival.

April–May: The **Newport (California)–Ensenada Yacht Race** is among the world's biggest.

MAY

May (varying dates): The **Tecate–Ensenada Bicycle Ride** is a mammoth parade of wheels in Baja Norte.

May 1: **Labor Day** is a nationwide holiday featuring parades.

May 3: The **Feast of the Holy Cross** is marked nationwide.

May 5: The famous **Cinco de Mayo** national holiday commemorates the defeat of the French at the Battle of Puebla in 1862.

May 15: The **Feast of San Isidro**, patron saint of rain and livestock, is celebrated all over Mexico.

May–June: **Corpus Christi Day** occasions blessings of children all over the country; with colorful festivities take place in Papantla, where the flying Totonacs perform their pole dance.

JUNE

June (varying dates): **Festival de Primavera** jams the streets of Rosarita Beach and features five- and ten-kilometer runs.

June (varying dates): The **Baja 500**, little brother of the famous Baja 1000 race, sends hot-rodders and dune buggiers across the desert.

June: The **Regatta Amigos** is a sailboat race from Galveston to Veracruz.

JULY

July 16: Ciudad del Carmen in Campeche honors its patroness, **Nuestra Señora del Carmen**, with a big citywide fiesta.

AUGUST

August 15: **Assumption Day** is celebrated nationwide.

SEPTEMBER

September 14: **Charro Day** honors cowboys all over Mexico.

September 15: Every major *zócalo* in Mexico re-enacts **El Grito**, the cry of independence from Spain dating back to the era of Father Hidalgo in 1810. Music, dancing and fireworks follow.

September 16: **Independence Day** is a major holiday, when banks, government offices and other establishments close down.

September 27–October 14: **Cristo de las Ampollas** (Christ of the Blisters) in Mérida honors a sacred cross immune to fire. See the "Sightseeing" section in Chapter 10.

OCTOBER

October 12: **Día de la Raza** (Columbus Day) is a national holiday.

October 31: **Halloween** takes place in many Mexican towns with pumpkins, trick-or-treat and costumes.

NOVEMBER

November 1–2: **All Souls' Day** and **Día de los Muertos** (Day of the Dead) are Mexico's unique Indian-Christian tributes to death. Sugar skulls, altars, papier-mâché skeletons and toy coffins fill the streets of cities where strong Indian traditions survive.

November (varying dates): The **Baja 1000**, the biggest offroad race in the world, has variable starting points on the peninsula.

November 7–30: **Feria de la Nao de China**, named for the legendary galleon *Nao de China*, is an annual fair in Acapulco commemorating the port's 16th-century trade link with the Orient.

November 20: The **anniversary** of the beginning of the Mexican Revolution of 1910 is a national holiday.

DECEMBER

December 12: The **Feast of Our Lady of Guadalupe**, patroness of Mexico, inspires parades, dancing and music nationwide.

December 16–25: The week before **Christmas** features a warm round of family gatherings, *posadas* (parades re-enacting the journey to Bethlehem), *piñata*-breaking parties and religious festivities around the country.

December 28: **All Fool's Day** resembles April Fools' Day.

FISHING TOURNAMENTS (International)

Sportfishing plays such a big part in Mexican coastal life that tournaments are held all year round, both in major resort areas and small fishing villages. For exact dates, contact a Mexican government tourism office. Here's a general rundown of cities and states:

January: Barra de Navidad, Jalisco; Acapulco, Guerrero.

March: Tampico, Tamaulipas.

April: Cozumel, Quintana Roo; Tampico, Tamaulipas.

May: Zihuatanejo, Guerrero; Veracruz, Veracruz; San Blas, Nayarit; Tampico, Tamaulipas.

June: Loreto, Baja Sur; Cabo San Lucas, Baja Sur; Mazatlán, Sinaloa; Rancho Buena Vista, Baja Sur; Tampico, Tamaulipas.

July: Guaymas, Sonora; Tampico, Tamaulipas; Ciudad del Carmen, Campeche; Coatzacoalcos, Veracruz.

August: La Paz, Baja Sur; Ensenada, Baja Norte; Tampico, Tamaulipas.

September: Tampico, Tamaulipas.

October: Rancho Buena Vista, Baja Sur.

November: Manzanillo, Colima; Cabo San Lucas, Baja Sur; Puerto Vallarta, Jalisco; Manzanillo, Colima; Acapulco, Guerrero.

December: Acapulco, Guerrero.

How to Go

TRANSPORTATION

Traveling to Mexico **by car** is convenient and generally safe. It's a good idea to check maps and determine distances ahead of departure so you can arrive at your destination before nightfall. Driving on the road after dark or spending the night in your car may invite danger—don't do either. For those with trailers or RVs, trailer parks abound, especially in northern Mexico. (See Chapter 2 for important information about preparing your car for the trip, auto insurance, car permits and petroleum problems.)

Commercial airlines fly frequently between the United States and Canada and coastal Mexico. These include United, American, Continental, Northwest, Delta, Alaska, Resorts and the three Mexican airlines— Aeroméxico, Mexicana, and Aero California. During special events, holidays and the November-to-May high season, make flight reservations at least two weeks to a month in advance. Air delays are common, late departures and arrivals frequent. Major airports charge an airport departure tax of about $10. Charter flights are a popular alternative during the high season, especially to Mexican Riviera resorts. Generally, baggage allotment is one carry-on bag, plus two bags for cargo storage. Check with the airline for its exact baggage restrictions.

Going **by bus** is the cheapest mode of transportation. Tickets are sold at the stations for cash, on a first-come, first-served basis. During the high season or big holidays (Christmas and Easter), buy tickets well in advance. A good system of first- and second-class buses connects nearly every pinprick on the map.

Sometimes there is not a great deal of difference between these classes, although first-class usually means air-conditioning, a toilet on board and comfortable, less crowded seating, while second-class may put you in a dilapidated schoolbus that feels like an oven on wheels with seat springs exposed and chickens in the aisles. Riding a back-country Mexican bus, with its radio blaring, a daredevil driver at the wheel and religious decor all over the dash, can rival the wildest theatre.

Trains are a novel and economic alternative. The government-owned Mexican National Railway (Ferrocarriles Nacionales de México) has recently added new routes and upgraded services, now providing more special features like dome viewing cars and express trains. Like buses, train seating comes in first-class (which may include air-conditioning and berths) and second-class (coach only, more crowded and hot). Tickets may be booked in the United States through a travel agent or bought directly at the train station.

Cruise ships offer glamour and comfort, stopping in many of Mexico's ports. The cruise industry is booming in Mexico, especially along the Mexican Riviera. Luxury liners go to Ensenada, Cabo San Lucas, Mazatlán, Puerto Vallarta, Ixtapa-Zihuatanejo, Acapulco, Puerto Escondido, Cozumel and Cancún. See the "Transportation" section of each chapter for names and addresses of the various lines.

Ferries ply the Sea of Cortez and the Pacific Ocean in overnight journeys between Baja California and the mainland, carrying both passengers and vehicles. To ship your vehicle aboard a ferry requires a car permit, available at any border crossing or from an office of the **Registro Federal de Vehículos** at any of the ferry's port cities. For a car permit, current registration papers and proof of your citizenship are required. Advance reservations for your vehicle and on-board accommodations should be made at ferry offices. Even to ticket-holding travelers, passage cannot be guaranteed at any time because commercial vehicles take priority. Be patient. Ferry accommodations include salon class (reclining seats, not reserved), tourist class (berth with bunk), cabin class (berth with bath) and special class (a suite, not offered on all ferries).

AT THE BORDER—PERMITS, ENTRY CARDS AND LICENSES

All American and Canadian citizens who plan to visit the interior of Mexico are required to have a tourist card. All tourist cards are free. Single-entry cards are valid for 90 days. The multiple-entry card is valid for 180 days. Naturalized citizens of the U.S. and Canada and citizens of other countries need a valid passport and visa (check with the nearest Mexican consulate for exact entry requirements). No tourist cards are required for visits up to 72 hours to towns along the U.S. border and to Baja California north of Maneadero (Mexico Highway 1) and Mexicali (Mexico Highway 5). You can obtain a tourist card at a Mexican government tourism office in the United States or Canada (see the list under "Getting Ready" in this chapter), from Mexican automobile insurance stations, at the border, or from a travel agency or airline if you buy an airline ticket. You must present proof of citizenship (a birth certificate, passport or voter's registration card; a driver's license won't do).

Carry this proof of citizenship with you to Mexico. The law also requires that you carry your tourist card with you at all times. To stay beyond the time specified on your card, you must leave Mexico and reapply upon re-entering. No matter what anyone at home tells you (including the Mexican Tourist Office), once you're in Mexico the renewal process can tie you up in red-tape for days. So if you're planning to stay awhile, spare yourself the frustration and go for the 180-day limit the first go-round.

For driving in Mexico, your American or Canadian driver's license is valid. If you're bringing your own car, you'll need a car permit and auto insurance (see Chapter 2 for details).

If you plan to hunt or fish in Mexico, see the "Recreation" section of Chapter 2 for information about obtaining special licenses.

AT THE BORDER—REGULATIONS AND CUSTOMS

Passing across the Mexican border from the United States is usually not very difficult—often you're waved through, no tourist cards checked, no questions asked. (Red tape is more likely to occur when you re-enter the United States.) At worst, Mexican customs officials may routinely check your tourist card, your car permit if you're driving and your luggage. Minimize border problems by dressing neatly and having documents at hand.

Each visitor to Mexico is allowed to bring in 110 pounds of luggage, 100 cigars, 200 cigarettes (one carton), one still camera, one motion picture camera and 12 rolls of film for each camera (these regulations are seldom strictly enforced). You may not bring plants, fruit or flowers across the border. If you want to bring a pet, you must have a certificate signed by a U.S. veterinarian verifying that the animal is in good health.

Strict regulations govern the transport of firearms into Mexico. If you intend to do any hunting, make sure you have the necessary permits (see Chapter 2 for further information).

American visitors returning from Mexico may bring home $400 worth of purchases duty-free. Anything over this amount is subject to a ten percent tax on the next $1,000 worth of items. Save your purchase receipts in case officials question their value. You are allowed just one liter (or quart) of liquor. Sportfish, shrimp and any seafood that can be legally caught in Mexico can be brought across the border and should be declared.

Canadian visitors are affected by different rules. Those who have been outside Canada at least 48 hours may bring back $100 (Canadian dollars) worth of goods duty-free, any number of times in a year. For trips of seven days or more, Canadians may bring back $300 (Canadian dollars) worth of goods duty-free, one time per year. Residents of Canada may bring back no more than 1.1 liters of liquor. Anything over the allotted amount is subject to a 20 percent tax. For more information, write the Canadian Department of External Affairs (125 Sussex Drive, Ottawa, Ontario K1A 0G2; 613-996-9134).

Warning: *Pirata* (pirated copies of copyrighted articles, such as records, computer programs, cassettes and books) are being produced in Mexico for a fraction of what their cost would be if produced in the U.S. Transport of these unauthorized items is strictly prohibited.

Most fresh foods (except seafood) and all items made from any part of an endangered species—such as the sea turtle, crocodile, black coral or ocelot—are not allowed into the United States and will be confiscated. Ancient artifacts, such as pre-Columbian statues or colonial art, cannot be exported and will also be confiscated at the border if found in your possession. All archaeological finds are considered national treasures and the property of Mexico. For more details, write U.S. Customs (1301 Constitution Avenue, Washington, D.C. 20229; 202-566-8195), the U.S. Fish and Wildlife Service (Department of the Interior, Mailstop 1111, Arlington Square, 18th and C Street NW, Washington, D.C. 20240; 202-343-9242) or TRAFFIC, World Wildlife Fund and the Conservation Foundation (1250 24th Street NW, Washington, D.C. 20037; 202-293-4800).

To avoid confiscation of prescribed drugs, label them carefully and bring along a doctor's certificate or prescription.

If you want to mail goods home from Mexico, you may send items of less than $50 duty-free to a particular address (but not your own) as often as every 24 hours. Mark the parcel "Unsolicited Gift—Value Under $50" and enclose a sales receipt.

Customs checks at the U.S. border can be stringent or swift, depending on how suspicious your paraphernalia looks. I came home with my dusty Toyota packed to the ceiling and they called out the dogs to sniff my tires, stuck mirrors under the car and had me remove every last empty Coke bottle for inspection. Meanwhile, people with neat, orderly cars whizzed through.

Getting Ready

WHAT TO WEAR AND PACK

The tropics encourage traveling light. Don't bring a great deal of luggage, and keep your clothing to a minimum. Cotton sportswear, casual dresses and slacks, T-shirts, shorts, sandals, swimsuit, sunglasses, a light sweater or jacket for those breezy tropical Decembers—what else do you need? Some glittery get-up for resort nightlife, a heavier jacket for northerly climes if you're going during winter months, long pants if you plan to be crashing through the bug-bitten jungle, good walking shoes for taking in sights, an umbrella if you go during the rainy season.

If you are visiting remote fishing villages, keep your clothing modest so as not to offend the locals: no hot-pants, string bikinis, tight tops or other suggestive outfits (which are definitely acceptable in Acapulco). Nudity is frowned on; in fact, it is against the law. If you want to sunbathe in the buff, find a very private place to do so. Never visit a church in shorts; signs at the entrance of many cathedrals announce (always in English), "NO SHORTS, STAY OUT!" Women should always have the respect to wear a skirt and men should wear a shirt.

When it comes to toiletries, Mexican towns carry almost everything you'll find at home, often at lower prices: toothpaste, deodorant, shampoo, soap, bug repellent, skin creams, shaving cream and batteries (buy the expensive ones, the cheapest kind don't work). Items like tampons, camera film and imported suntan lotions cost a bit more than north of the border but are widely available in larger towns. The selection of film, however, isn't great—go well-supplied. Bring snorkeling and fishing gear, some good books (most Mexican newsstands sell only bodice-rippers and spy thrillers in English) and an extra pair of eyeglasses.

If you are bringing a bicycle, bring all extra equipment and parts.

HEALTH PRECAUTIONS

No inoculations are necessary to travel in Mexico. Cases of hepatitis, malaria, typhoid and other tropical diseases do occur but seldom afflict travelers. To be on the safe side, you might want to get a tetanus shot and a typhoid booster.

It is always a good idea to pack a first-aid kit, including: insect repellent, aspirin, band-aids, cold tablets, vitamins, motion sickness tablets, prescription drugs you use, iodine or alcohol for disinfecting wounds, antibiotic ointment, water purification tablets, sunscreen, lip balm and diarrhea medicine. Anyone with a medical condition should consider wearing a Medic Alert identification tag, which identifies the problem and gives a phone number to call for more information: contact Medic Alert Foundation International (P.O. Box 1009, Turlock, CA 95381; 800-344-3226).

The illness most people encounter is *turista*, or diarrhea, due to food and drink carrying unfamiliar strains of bacteria (see "How to Beat Moctezuma's Revenge" in this chapter). For this and other mild health problems, Mexico's many pharmacies (*farmacias*) dispense excellent medicines, most (including antibiotics) without a doctor's prescription.

For good medical care, there are hospitals, clinics, dentists and other services available in Mexico, including the Red Cross. Private facilities are generally better-funded than public ones and tend to offer superior care. Visits to doctors are relatively inexpensive, and hotels can usually recommend English-speaking physicians. If you carry health insurance, find out before you depart how applicable it is in Mexico.

For true emergencies, a San Diego-based service called **Critical Air Medicine** (619-571-8944) provides air ambulances to anywhere in Mexico.

For bug bites, lime juice takes the itch out, disinfects your wounds and acts as a repellent, too. Limes (limones) are sold in every village. An ointment called *andantol*, sold in pharmacies, also helps reduce itching. Clean bug bites *daily*. Use an antiseptic on bad bites to avoid infection.

Scorpions (*alacranes*) are most prevalent in desert areas like Baja. Their bites are rarely fatal for adults, but can be perilous for children. The bite tends to cause swelling and increased heartbeat as toxins enter the bloodstream. The best remedy: pack the bitten area with ice, lie down, relax and have someone contact a doctor.

Stingrays camouflage themselves in the sand along the Sea of Cortez and can deliver a wicked puncture with their stingers. Avoid being stung by shuffling your feet in the sand as you enter the water to scare stingrays away. Stingray wounds cause painful swelling. See a doctor at once.

Stinging jellyfish are most prevalent in the Pacific and the Caribbean during the summer. Their sting causes a burning rash. Immerse the affected area in ice water or apply ammonia mixed with water to reduce the sting.

(Text continued on page 14.)

How to Beat Moctezuma's Revenge

Some say it's in the water, maybe in the air. Or could it be in the chilies, the sauces, the fork prongs? Look out, it's lurking under every plate and napkin—Moctezuma's Revenge! The defeated old Aztec emperor laughs in his tomb each time a gringo groans and doubles over with his curse, also known as *turista*, diarrhea, the trots, the squats or the runs.

But roll over, Moctezuma, there are ways to beat you yet.

First of all, not everybody gets sick in Mexico. Second, some go to ridiculous lengths not to. ("Let's not eat anything in Mexico except boiled beef and bananas, Harry.") But still they get sick. Sensible preventive medicine is the best defense:

Avoid drinking tap water or ice made from tap water (commonly used in restaurants), and don't brush your teeth with tap water. Ask if your hotel has *agua purificada* (purified water). Most good-sized hotels provide bottled water in the rooms if their running water isn't potable.

Eat street food with discretion. Fruits with peels, like oranges, and nuts with shells, such as peanuts and coconuts, are pretty safe bets. Meat, seafood, peeled fruit used in drinks and candies on which flies have taken their siestas are more risky. However, a lot of the food from stalls—tacos, *tortas* (sandwiches), *licuados*, *elotes* (shucked corn)—is delicious and very well prepared. Be the judge and take your chances.

Drink bottled liquids whenever possible. Bottled mineral water (*agua mineral*), sodas, fruit drinks, all sorts of beer and soft drinks are plentiful.

Go easy on the experimentation. Piling *huevos rancheros* on top of *ceviche* on top of a mango *licuado* on top of *huachinango a la Veracruzana*, topped off by flaming flan and a *coco loco*, is asking for a firecracker in your stomach.

If you're doing your own cooking, wash foods with purified water or water containing iodine (available at pharmacies).

I don't advocate avoiding half the food in Mexico, foregoing the wonderful fruit juices or missing out on spicy dishes you've never heard of—you're here to dip into the unknown, *verdad?* If you do get a bellyache, try these remedies:

Lomotil, the stopper-upper. Use sparingly. Not a cure, it's a morphine derivative, inducing a kind of intestinal paralysis. Stop the dosage as soon as symptoms disappear. It's available in Mexico and at home.

Paragoric, Kaopectate, Kaomycin and Pepto-Bismol help keep the cramps down. Diodoquin, Mexaform, Streptomagnum and Donamycin are stronger over-the-counter cures available in Mexican drug stores. For diarrhea with a fever, you can take Septra or Bactrium if you are not allergic to sulfa drugs. But remember that prolonged use of any antibiotic is not good for your immune system.

Manzanilla (chamomile) tea, popular in Mexico, soothes the stomach and often works wonders. Papaya restores the digestive tract.

Light, easy-to-digest foods like toast and soup keep your strength up. Lots of nonalcoholic liquids—any kind—prevent dehydration.

Rest and relaxation will help your body heal faster than if you run around sick and wear yourself down further.

See a doctor if the diarrhea persists beyond five days or if you have a high fever.

WOMEN TRAVELING ALONE

Women alone do not ordinarily face great threats in Mexico if they follow some simple precautions. In fact, Mexican families are often very protective, adopting solo travelers for outings or offering meals and assistance, welcoming you into the family. If you steer clear of cantinas and undesirable company, the worst you can expect is a lot of male attention. If you're not interested, just ignore the advances completely, don't make eye contact and dress modestly.

TRAVELING WITH CHILDREN

Bringing your children can be an advantage in Mexico, where the family is the revered cornerstone of society. Mexicans adore children and are used to dealing with them in hotels and restaurants. Disposable diapers, baby food and medicines are widely available in bigger towns, but many hotels do not have cribs or babysitting services. A few hints on bringing along your child:

Remember to get a tourist card for your child. Children traveling with only one parent must have notarized permission from the other parent (or divorce papers, guardianship document or death certificate, if applicable), authenticated at a Mexican consulate. Minors traveling alone must have a notarized letter of permission signed by both parents or guardians.

Prepare a junior first-aid kit with baby aspirin, thermometer, vitamins, diarrhea medicine, sun block, bug repellent, tissues and cold medicine.

Pack extra plastic bags for dirty diapers, cloth diapers for emergencies, a portable stroller and papoose-style backpack, a car seat if you plan to use a car, easy-to-wash clothes, swimsuits, a life jacket, beach toys and picture books relating to Mexico.

Try to plan a flight during your child's nap time. Bring everything you need on board—diapers, food, toys, books, and extra clothing for kids and parents alike. It's also helpful to carry a few new toys, snacks and books as treats if boredom sets in.

Pace your trip so your child can adapt to the changes. Don't plan exhausting whirlwind tours, and keep travel time at a minimum. Seek out zoos, parks, aquariums, plazas, outdoor entertainment and short excursions to amuse your child. Mexico's marketplaces are more fascinating to some children than museums.

TRAVELING FOR THE DISABLED

Disabled travelers can enjoy Mexico with the proper planning. Because Mexican establishments and transportation systems offer few provisions for the disabled, such as wheelchair access, you may need the help of a good travel agent to track down an airline, hotel and other facilities to suit your situation.

For more information, contact the **Society for the Advancement of Travel for the Handicapped** (SATH) (26 Court Street, Brooklyn, NY 11242; 718-858-5483); **Travel Information Center** (Moss Rehabilitation Hospital, 12th Street and Tabor Road, Philadelphia, PA 19141; 215-329-5715); **Mobility International USA** (P.O. Box 3551, Eugene OR 97403; 503-343-1284); or **Flying Wheels Travel** (143 West Bridge Street, P.O. Box 382, Owatonna, MN 55060; 800-533-0363). Or consult the comprehensive guidebook *Access to the World—A Travel Guide for the Handicapped* by Louise Weiss (Holt, Rinehart & Winston).

OLDER TRAVELERS

Mexico, particularly up north, is becoming a retirement haven where senior citizens from El Norte often spend the winter and spring, or settle all year round. Because of the temperate climate, easy lifestyle, friendly people, low cost of living, cultural activities and proximity to the United States, many older travelers are drawn here.

Be extra careful about health matters. Bring any medications you use, along with the prescriptions. Consider carrying a medical record with you—including your current medical status, medical history, your doctor's name, phone number and address. See that your insurance covers you south of the border.

Ask your travel agent about hotel, transportation and other discounts for older travelers in Mexico. For those who are 60 or over, an agency called **Elderhostel** (80 Boylston Street, Suite 400, Boston, MA 02116; 617-426-7788) provides educational programs for seniors in Mexico. The programs cover Mexican history, folk art and archaeology. For more information about escorted tours in Mexico, contact the **American Association of Retired Persons Travel Service** (AARP) (5855 Green Valley Circle, Culver City, CA 90230; 213-496-2277).

MEXICAN GOVERNMENT TOURISM OFFICES
NORTH OF THE BORDER

The following offices in the United States and Canada provide tourist cards, maps and information about travel in Mexico: in Chicago—70 East Lake Street, Chicago, IL 60601 (312-563-2786); in Houston—2707 North Loop W, Suite 450, Houston, TX 77008 (713-880-5153); in Los Angeles—10100 Santa Monica Boulevard, Suite 224, Los Angeles, CA 90067 (800-262-8900); in New York—405 Park Avenue, Suite 1002, New York, NY 10022 (212-755-7261); in Washington, D.C.—1615 L Street NW, Suite 430, Washington, D.C. (202-659-8738); in Montreal—1 Place Ville Marie, Suite 2409, Montreal PQ H3B 3M9 Canada (514-871-1052); and in Toronto—181 University Avenue, Suite 1112, Toronto, Ontario M5H 3M7 Canada (416-364-2455).

Nearly every major U.S. and Canadian city also has a Mexican consulate, available for general travel inquiries. American and Canadian consulates in Mexico also provide information about **legal aid** and lawyers; these consulates are listed in the address and phone directories at the end of each area chapter.

How to Deal With...

ACCOMMODATIONS

Accommodations in Mexico come in several forms: hotels, which are modern, full-service and the most expensive; motels, which are more modest, generally smaller and less costly; *casas de huéspedes* (guest houses), which may be part of someone's home or plain, no-frills inns; and pensiones, which are budget inns favored by families, often in the heart of downtown, sometimes in older buildings, always plain.

Mexican hotels in popular resort areas sometimes raise their rates on weekends. During the high season (November to May) and holidays, many hotels hike up their rates and offer the American Plan (rates include three meals a day), insuring a captive audience for their in-house restaurants. During the off-season, they may switch to the less expensive European Plan (room only). Be sure to check on this if you book a hotel in advance.

Reservations are crucial during the high season and holidays, when the scramble for rooms can be fierce. *Confirm* your reservation, preferably in writing, before you go. If the hotel reneges (hotels typically overbook during holidays to make sure they are filled if any parties fail to show), make a complaint to the local tourist office and swift action is likely to be taken. Many hotels demand a two-day (but sometimes up to 30-day) cancellation notice before refunding your deposit. Check on cancellation policies at the outset, and remember that cancellation by mail can be fiendishly slow.

For travelers on a shoestring, a government-run chain of youth hostels offers clean, cheap, dormitory-style accommodations in tourist towns across Mexico. For a list of locations, write: **Agencia Nacional de Viajes de la Comisión Nacional del Deporte**, Glorieta del Metro Insurgentes, Local C-11, Colonia Juárez, Delegación Cuauhtémoc, C.P. 06600 México, D.F., México.

HOTEL AND RESTAURANT PRICE CATEGORIES

This book's hotel and restaurant listings range from budget to ultra-deluxe, with an emphasis on middle-range establishments. Hotels are rated as follows: *budget* facilities have rooms for less than $40 per night for two people; *moderate* hotels are priced between $40 to $70; *deluxe* facilities offer rates from $70 to $120, and *ultra-deluxe* have accommodations at prices above $120.

Restaurants are rated as follows: *budget* restaurants usually cost $7 or less for dinner entrees; *moderately* priced restaurants range between $7 and

$14 at dinner and offer pleasant surroundings and a more varied menu; *deluxe* establishments tab their entrees above $14, featuring sophisticated cuisines, plush decor and more personalized service; and *ultra-deluxe* restaurants generally price above $20.

THE ADDRESS SYSTEM

Confused by the street names and directions? Remember that in Mexico, few places are neatly laid out. Maps may disagree, spellings may differ, streets may even have various names—or no name at all.

In coastal towns, the *malecón* (waterfront walkway) is a common point of reference. So is the *zócalo* (town square).

Numbers always follow street names, as in Calle Alvaro Obregón 59. Often no street number is given, or the address will read Calle López Mateos s/n (*sin número* = without number). That means you're on your own. An address reading "Calle 5a y (and) Calle 10a" indicates cross streets. *Entre Avenida Héroes y Paseo Juárez* means between Avenida Héroes and Paseo Juárez. The abbreviations *Ote.* (*Oriente*) and *Pte.* (*Poniente*) stand for east and west, respectively. An *a* after a number (*3a* or *5a*) indicates numerical ranking, as in *tercera* (third) or *quinta* (fifth). Km. stands for kilometer (six-tenths of a mile), usually appearing on roadside markers with a number, as in *Km. 9*. The common catch-all address, widely used in small towns, is *Domicilio Conocido* (Known Address)—which means everybody in town should know where to point you.

CAR RENTALS

Rental cars are widely available at airports along the Mexican coasts, eliminating the need for your own insurance and car permits. Advance reservations are wise if you're traveling during the high season. Anyone 25 years or older, with a credit card, can order a car in advance via one of the larger companies and have it waiting in Mexico. Renting a car inside Mexico requires your tourist card, driver's license and a credit card (or cash deposit) for collateral.

MONEY, EXCHANGE RATES AND BANKS

The steep inflation that crippled the Mexican economy throughout the 1980s has at last begun to stabilize, but this situation can change at any time. Furthermore, the sales tax (IVA Tax) now stands at 15 percent, which affects tourists virtually everywhere. Shops, restaurants and hotels crave greenbacks but they usually give you back pesos in change. (The $ sign is also used in Mexico for pesos.) But be smart and protect your vacation by carrying traveler's checks, for which you get a solid rate of exchange at almost any check-cashing outlet. Well-known brands like American Express and Bank of America are easiest to cash and quickest to replace if lost or stolen. Canadian traveler's checks and currency can pose problems in this regard; some banks will not cash them. Keep in mind that many villages have no banks, and those that do sometimes run out of cash. In some villages it is impossible to cash traveler's checks.

Most Mexican banks are open at 9 a.m., close between noon and 2 p.m., and reopen until 6 p.m., Monday through Friday. They often have specified hours, which vary from bank to bank and day to day, for exchanging foreign money. Your tourist card or passport are often needed for identification. In lieu of banks, *casas de cambio* (money exchange houses) give good rates and sometimes quicker service; every sizable town has its share. Airport exchange counters usually give good rates, too.

Credit cards are accepted in resort towns, although many hotels and deluxe resorts are requiring cash or travelers' check payment only. Many establishments frown on American Express because of its stiff fees to them. Mastercard and Visa are the most popular foreign cards in Mexico. But an American Express card does let you buy additional travelers' checks and cash personal checks at its Mexican branch offices.

If you need a financial transfusion while on the road, money transfers can be made via Western Union (*usually* taking one day) or via any big bank at home through one of its Mexican affiliates (which is more secure but can take as long as five working days). Check to see if your bank provides this service.

TIPPING

Propinas (tips) are completely personal, but the 15 percent rule applies in Mexican restaurants as elsewhere. Tip bellboys, porters, chambermaids and anyone who renders extra service the equivalent of at least 50¢ to 75¢. Taxi drivers do not expect a tip. Gas station attendants deserve one (25¢ to 50¢) if they wash your windows, check your oil or put air in your tires. Children often assault your car at stoplights or outside restaurants, madly cleaning your windows or begging to watch your car for a tip. Fire-eaters, musicians, jugglers, magicians and clowns perform in public places for tips. Even a 100-peso coin is much-appreciated. What's a little extra money when you're getting paradise?

BRIBES

Mexico is famous for *mordida*, "the bite," a piece of the action, a bribe. In a tit-for-tat game of favor-granting, palms are greased throughout society, from the upper echelons of government to the humblest traffic cop. But as a traveler, you should consider such "customs" cautiously, weighing the pros and cons.

And, although such incidents are rare, you may find yourself in a situation where a bribe is demanded, as in, "Give us $100 or we'll take you to jail for drunken driving." Or, "A new tourist card will cost you $10," when in fact it's free. You can politely refuse to meet such demands and ask to see the *jefe* (boss) if trouble persists. Some towns have tourist attorneys if you should face any standoffs.

SIESTAS AND BUSINESS HOURS

One of the more famous Latin traditions is the siesta, a midday break lasting two or three hours, when establishments close while workers go home and eat. Between 1 p.m. and 4 p.m., or 2 p.m. and 5 p.m., you won't get much shopping done. Later, shops reopen. Most shop hours are from 9 a.m. to 1 p.m., then from 4 p.m. to 7 p.m. In big resort towns, some shops stay open all day and don't close till 9 p.m.

BARGAINING

In Mexico, haggling is a form of street theatre. Merchants in the traditional markets expect bargaining as part of the sale. Often their starting price will be two or three times higher than what they'll settle for. Cut their bid in half and start bargaining from there. Appear disinterested, doubtful, insulted or pained as you haggle. Drift away and watch the vendor call a lower bid. But if you reach a good ballpark figure, don't quibble over nickels and dimes. So the vendor got an extra 50¢! You got a great deal.

Bargaining is very rare in resort shops and boutiques or any store that uses fixed prices (*precios fijos*). Don't be shy, however, about asking the price of an item, then naming a figure you'd be more willing to pay. I got a great leather bag in Tijuana that way, for half the asking price.

Note: To avoid buying fake silver, look for the numerals .925 stamped on the item. Authentic silver in Mexico bears this mark (although a few merchants are now using illegal stamps to mark goods that are not real silver). Also, make sure that leather goods are 100 percent leather, not plastic or cardboard with a thin leather exterior.

TAKING PHOTOS

This can be a sensitive issue, especially among the locals. Indians and others often resent being gawked at and tracked with snapping cameras. I have even seen villages with signs on the outskirts forbidding the use of cameras beyond the town limits. One way to avoid invading the privacy of others is to politely ask if a photo would be all right. Some natives have gotten wise to the photomania and request money in return for a pose. A little courtesy can vastly improve the relations between tourists and locals.

PUBLICATIONS IN ENGLISH

U.S. magazines, newspapers and paperback books can be found in the larger Mexican resorts, at newsstands, department stores and gift shops in big hotels. The *Mexico City News*, a daily English-language tabloid published in Mexico City, provides general coverage of local and world events and is the most widely available English publication in Mexico. Cities like Acapulco and Cancún are oases of foreign print media; you can usually find the *New York Times* and the *Los Angeles Times*. The selection of books in English is generally limited to romance novels and fat, glitzy best-sellers.

METRIC CONVERSION

Mexico uses the metric system. Conversions are as follows: one mile = 1.6 kilometers; one pound = .45 kilos; one gallon = 3.8 liters; and 32° Fahrenheit = 0° Centigrade (freezing). ·

TIME ZONES

Most of coastal Mexico—the majority of the West Coast, the Gulf of Mexico and the Yucatán—is on Central Standard Time. The exceptions are the states of Sonora, Sinaloa and Baja Sur, which operate on Mountain Standard Time, and Baja Norte, which operates on Pacific Standard Time (using Daylight Savings Time from early April to late October).

MAIL

Mail deliveries to and from Mexico are slow and unreliable. Most postcards and letters eventually make it to their destinations, but packages are less secure. Always use air mail, and send important deliveries by registered mail.

While on the road, you can receive mail in Mexico at the main post office in any city via **Lista de Correos** (similar to General Delivery in the United States). Use this address: Your name, *Lista de Correos*, Name of City, State, México. The post office holds *Lista de Correos* mail for only ten days, then returns it to the sender. For more security, American Express offices throughout Mexico hold mail for cardholders.

TELEPHONES

Calling into Mexico can be a frustrating experience. Access codes differ depending upon your long-distance carrier.

Likewise, telephones in Mexico can drive you crazy. Some hamlets may have no phone at all, others change phone numbers with maddening frequency. Many establishments in Mexico do not have phones, partly because of the expense, partly because service is erratic. Most Mexican phone numbers contain five or six digits, but some far fewer, depending on the size of the town.

Casetas de larga distancia are public outlets for calling long-distance. The process can take hours if the international operators are tied up, as they often are. Calling from your hotel is much more convenient (though the service charge may be more expensive) because you can relax in your room until the hotel operator places your call. You will save money by calling collect (*por cobrar*) and on weekends or after 11 p.m. If you want to make your own call from a public phone (good luck finding one that works, half of them don't), here are some key numbers to remember: long-distance operator in Mexico: 02; international operator (English-speaking): 09;

prefixes for dialing direct to the United States and Canada: 95 (station to station) and 96 (person to person). Following the above numbers, dial the area code and number you wish to reach.

In Mexico, you answer the phone by saying *bueno*, not *hola*.

ELECTRICITY

Electric currents are the same in Mexico as in the United States: 110 volts, 60 cycles, compatible with all American portable appliances.

LAUNDRY

Your wash can be taken care of at your hotel (often quite costly) or at an inexpensive laundromat, found in all big cities. Drop-off laundromats (the best kind) have your clothes ready the next day, all washed and folded. Coin-operated laundries often use American dimes or quarters. In tiny towns, village women will often wash your clothes for extra cash. Dry cleaners (*tintoreras*) are found in all major towns.

SAFETY

Travelers from the United States may have a mistaken notion of Mexico as a dangerous place—largely a result of distorted media images. You may be surprised to find yourself feeling much more at ease in a Mexican city than you do at home. The reason is simple: the crime rate is lower here than north of the border.

But every country has its thieves, and camera-toting tourists are a natural target. Use common sense: guard your valuables and money. Keep your traveler's check receipts in a safe, inaccessible place. Don't leave wallets and cameras lying on the beach while you go for a swim or sitting on a café table while you go to the bathroom. Always lock your hotel room and your car. Park it in an enclosure at night. Don't leave radios, gifts, cassettes and other temptations visible inside.

Don't tempt fate by wandering around dark back streets at all hours. And if you're camping out, avoid lonely roadside stops or completely barren beaches unless you're with a group. Rule of thumb: exercise the same caution you use at home.

DRUGS

Possessing, using and exporting drugs are serious crimes in Mexico that can land you in jail. To make matters worse, Mexico operates under the Napoleonic Code, which presumes the accused guilty until proven innocent. Foreigners found guilty are not allowed bail, trial by jury or parole. Prison sentences for possession may run from 7 to 15 years. Although marijuana is grown in Mexico and is certainly available in the tourist centers, along with other drugs, it's wise to ignore hissing salesmen and stay clean.

CHAPTER TWO

On the Road and by the Sea

Driving in Mexico

Having a car during your Mexican travels can open up new vistas and double the excitement of your trip. The advantages of driving to Mexico in your own car—freedom of movement and familiarity of vehicle—should be carefully weighed against the problems: bad gas, hard-to-get parts, punishing side roads, expensive insurance, unfamiliar traffic rules and unpredictable driving styles. Renting a car can alleviate some difficulties, though rentals can be steep. Whichever method you choose, there is no better way to discover the real Mexico than by driving through it. The following information will help you prepare for most eventualities on the road.

PERMITS AND INSURANCE

You must register your car for a permit to drive south of the border zone in mainland Mexico. Car permits are not required in Baja California. Car permits are valid for 90 days and can be renewed by Mexican immigration officials. The permit is valid only for the person in whose name the vehicle is registered; this means you must accompany anyone else who drives your car. Registration can be routinely handled at the border or at registration offices (*registro de vehículos*) in towns with ferry terminals (cars leaving Baja for mainland Mexico must be registered first). A valid American or Canadian registration card, proof-of-ownership papers and proof of citizenship are needed to get a Mexican car permit, which is free. Permits for RVs are also mandatory, obtained just as car permits are.

It is against the law to sell your vehicle in Mexico, principally because the government does not want less expensive gringo vehicles competing on the market with higher-priced vehicles manufactured in Mexico. You must leave Mexico with the vehicle that you entered in.

Mexican auto insurance should be purchased before you cross the border, since American and Canadian car insurance is not valid in Mexico. Full coverage is recommended. Rates drop with the length of your stay. Many mom-and-pop outlets sell car insurance inside Mexico and at the border. Three of the best firms north of the border are the **American Automobile Association** (AAA, with branches in every state), **Sanborn's Mexican Insurance Service** (P.O. Box 1210, McAllen, TX 78502; 512-682-3401) and **Instant Mexico Auto Insurance Service** (223 Vía de San Ysidro, San Ysidro, CA 92073; 619-428-4714).

CAR PREPARATION

Before leaving for Mexico, get your car ship-shape so it can weather the dust, gravel roads, potholes and mediocre gas south of the border. Check the tires, radiator, engine, transmission, shock absorbers, brakes, horn and lights. For long trips, consider a diagnostic check-up by AAA or a mechanic; a tune-up is a must.

If your car has a catalytic converter (a required smog-control device on post-1975 models), have it removed before venturing on a long trip. Leaded gas—often the only kind you can buy in Mexico—will destroy the converter, which can result in serious performance problems. Since it is illegal to remove a catalytic converter in the United States, have the job done at a big Mexican border town, where there are many excellent, inexpensive mechanics. Have your car's timing adjusted, too, to adapt to the tropical weather.

WHAT TO BRING ALONG

Mexican garages stock parts only for American-made cars and foreign brands manufactured in Mexico, most commonly Datsuns, Volkswagens and Renaults. If your Toyota, Honda, Subaru, Saab or Volvo breaks down in Mexico, you may have to order parts from afar and wait weeks for their arrival. Obviously, you can't lug a whole new engine with you, but on fairly long trips be prepared for basic emergencies by bringing the following:

Parts: Spare tire, fan belt, gas filters, oil filters (many sizes aren't available in Mexico), rubber tubing, air filters, fuses, extra gas cap, spark plugs, points and distributor cap.

Gear: Flares for emergencies, a set of tools, rope and chains for towing, tire jack and pump, flashlight, tire pressure gauge, gallon gas can, jumper cables, small shovel to dig out of sand, brake fluid, transmission fluid, motor oil (several extra quarts), extra water mixed with antifreeze for your radiator and octane booster or gas additive. Hide **spare keys** in a magnetic box in your roadster's chrome underbelly.

AUTO CLUBS AND MAPS

If you belong to an auto club, find out if it is associated with any Mexican clubs. If so, you may qualify for certain travel benefits from the **Asociación Mexicana Automovilística** (AMA, Colonia Roma Apartado Postal 24-486, 06700 México, D.F., México; 588-9090) or the **Asociación Nacional Automovilística** (ANA, Edificio ANA, Calle Miguel E. Shultz

140, Apartado Postal 1720, 06470 México, D.F., México; 705-1757). Both sell road maps. Mexican consulates and Mexican tourist offices may supply free maps, but the **American Automobile Association** provides probably the best Mexican maps available, plus guide booklets for its members. You may also contact the **American Map Company** (46-35 54th Road, Maspeth, NY 11378; 718-784-0055) for individual maps of Mexican states.

CAR MAINTENANCE

Reduce the risk of breakdowns by checking your tires, radiator and oil regularly in Mexico. Have your oil, gas filter and air filter changed at least every 3,000 miles—dust in the air plus water and impurities in the gas can clog your system. Clean the water out of your gas tank every four or five times you fill the tank by tossing in a quart (or liter) of cane alcohol, available at Mexican drugstores and liquor stores. Have your battery and brakes checked every time you get a tune-up, about every 6,000 miles. Auto repair labor is cheap and reliable in Mexico, so why scrimp? To find a good mechanic, inquire at the local tourist department or your hotel.

MEXICAN GASOLINE

Low in octane and often mixed with water and impurities, Mexican gas has been known to give tourist cars their own kind of Moctezuma's Revenge: carburetors and gas filters flooded with water, fouled spark plugs, engine knocks and pings, no pickup. This gas does no car any good, but your car *will* run on it. You have no choice anyway: Pemex (Petróleos Mexicanos) produces all the petrol and owns all the gas stations in Mexico.

The three kinds of gas in Mexico are *Nova* (80 octane, leaded, in a blue pump, available all over), *Extra* (87 octane, unleaded, in a silver pump, limited availability especially as you head south) and *Diesel* (in a red pump, usually available). *Extra* costs the most, going for a bit more than unleaded gas in the United States. Octane booster can be brought from home to give your buggy some pep, but this gets expensive. Or you can try the Mexican *aditivo* (additive), not very effective, from my experience.

Tanks are filled by the liter (3.78 liters equals a gallon). When driving long stretches, top off your gas tank at every opportunity. Stations can be miles apart, and you can't count on the next station having the type of fuel, or quantity, you need. Most station attendants are honest but some will take advantage of your ignorance and overcharge you. Make sure the pump registers all zeros before the nozzle is in your tank, then multiply the final figures by the cost of gas per liter. Pemex accepts cash only.

MEXICAN ROADS AND REGULATIONS

Mexico's main road system consists of good two-lane paved highways. Most are narrow and without shoulders. But the highways far surpass the American image of the unnavigable Mexican road; that portrait better fits many side roads, or *brechas*, leading out to beaches.

Technically, the speed limit seldom tops 60 miles per hour (100 kilometers per hour), but rarely is this enforced. Mexicans often go 80 or 90 mph, and more if their vehicle can do it. All speed limit and mileage signs are in kilometers.

Short white posts appear along the roadside, marking the number of kilometers between major destinations, as in "Km. 4." Sometimes these numbers serve as an establishment's only address, as in "Restaurant Don José, Carretera Internacional (International Highway), Km. 87."

PECULIARITIES OF MEXICAN DRIVERS

Some claim Mexicans drive with a gusto bordering on the suicidal. In fact, bus drivers, truck drivers and taxi drivers may stand guilty as accused, but most Mexicans are very skillful drivers.

Mexicans don't take rules of the road as seriously as do most people north of the border. Don't be too surprised if you see a Mexican driver go up a one-way street the wrong way, make a U-turn in a busy thoroughfare, coast through a red light if nobody's coming or drive over a sidewalk to pass another car. And they rarely turn down anyone who needs a lift. Mexican vehicles bulge with people, like little fiestas on wheels—four generations of family members stuffed into an old Chevy, 40 workers in the back of a pick-up, etc. All this is done with a flair and nonchalance that may look like insanity. Luckily, the person behind the wheel usually has a great deal of driving skill.

You may notice frequent little crosses and shrines dotting the Mexican roadside. Each marks a traffic fatality. It is a Latin custom to erect these shrines in commemoration of the dead and as a warning to others. But if you fear Mexican drivers, let me point out that during my ten-month research journey in Mexico, my car was struck twice, both times by tourists.

ACCIDENTS AND DRIVING AT NIGHT

Don't drive at night—it's truly dangerous. Mexicans sometimes drive with broken lights or don't bother to use lights at all. Animals stray into the road and lie down on the warm asphalt; if you hit a cow head-on, say goodbye to your car. Assaults occur on occasion at night. Visibility is terrible and roads are poorly marked, with vague lines and no reflectors.

If you have an accident that isn't serious—a fender-bender or nick to your door—drive on. Otherwise, you may stand accused of being the perpetrator and, guilty or not, may drown in red tape before you ever get to the ocean. For serious accidents, contact the police and file a report with your Mexican insurance company to recoup your losses. Be aware that Mexican authorities will hold you and your car, guilty or not, until payment of damages and claims.

Highway Signs

 Stop

 Yield Right-Of-Way

 Dip

 Two-Way Traffic

 Traffic Circle

 Trailer Camp

 Airport

 Hospital

 Mechanic

 Ferry

 Restrooms

 Slippery Road Loose Gravel

 Steep Hill

 Landslide Area

 Bumps

 Narrow Bridge

 Maximum Weight (Metric Tons)

 No Pedestrians

 Parking Limit

One-hour Parking

No Parking

Horizontal Clearance

 Vertical Clearance

 Signal

 R.R. Crossing

 Cattle

 School Crossing

 Men Working

 Inspection

 No Trucks

 No Left Turn

 No U Turn

 No Passing

 Use Right Lane

 No Bicycles

 Keep Right

 Do Not Enter

 Pedestrians Keep Left

 Speed Limit

 Continuous Turn

ROAD SIGNS IN SPANISH	DESCRIPTIONS IN ENGLISH
TOPES	Speed Bumps
UN SOLO CARRIL	One Way Bridge
PAVIMENTE DERRAPANTE	Pavement Slippery
PROHIBIDO SEGUIR DE FRENTE	Do Not Enter
VADO	Dip

THE GREEN ANGELS

Los Ángeles Verdes, or the Green Angels, are a marvelous invention of the Mexican government: bilingual (Spanish- and English-speaking) mechanics who roam the main highways in green trucks between 8 a.m. and 8 p.m. (some areas have 24-hour service), on the lookout for motorists in distress. They provide free repair service and first aid, plus gas and oil at cost. To signal that you need assistance, pull over as far as possible off the road and open the hood of your car.

PARKING

Bigger towns have meters and parking problems like anywhere else, but Mexican police sometimes take extreme measures to deal with illegal parking: they remove your license plate, forcing you to come to the station to pay your fine. Wherever there are parking lots, it's worthwhile and usually inexpensive to use them. At night, your car should never be parked on the street unless the area is bright and too busy to attract a burglar. Always lock your car, wherever you park it.

HITCHHIKING

It's legal and fairly common to hitch south of the border. Villagers often stand on the roadside to wave down passing trucks. Mexicans, in their neighborly way, do tend to stop for stranded travelers. But hitchhiking anywhere can be dangerous and is more so in Mexico, where most roads have no shoulders for cars to pull over. It's also dusty, hot and really unnecessary since buses are so cheap.

The Sporting Life

CAMPING

By no means the organized activity that it is up north, camping in Mexico takes place in a handful of national parks and trailer parks and along scores of peaceful beaches. All beaches in Mexico are public by law, but a good bit of beachfront land is connected to private property—hotels, homes, *ejidos* (community-owned Mexican land)—which the owners may consider off limits for camping. When in doubt, check with the facility nearest the spot you're interested in. For camping in national parks, no permit is necessary.

Unsettled Baja makes the best campground, with its wild, empty beaches and dunes. Camping is also good along the central and southern West Coast beaches, particularly in between the big resorts in areas around Rincón de Guayabitos, Barra de Navidad, the state of Michoacán, Puerto Escondido and south to Salina Cruz. The Caribbean has splendid camping beaches south of Cancún, which grow less crowded the farther south you go. Camping is not as attractive along the Gulf of Mexico, but beaches like

Playa Paraíso near Villahermosa and Playa Tecolutla near Papantla are beautiful exceptions.

For further camping information, write to **Club Monarca de Acampadores** (Apartado Postal 31-750, 45050 Guadalajara, Jalisco, México) or pick up *The People's Guide to Camping in Mexico* by Carl Franz (John Muir Publications).

Insects are likely to share your Mexican campsite. Bug spray, mosquito nets and insect coils can help make camping enjoyable. Locals burn coconut husks to smoke out bugs. Bug attacks are worst at dawn and sunset.

Other basic camping equipment may include a sleeping bag, dropcloth, tent, water container, collapsible shovel for burying trash (few beaches have trash cans), a tarp, first-aid kit, small stove and cooking gear, ice chest, bucket, jacket for evenings, flashlight, knife, matches and toilet paper. Remember to burn your toilet paper and carry out any trash you don't bury. It can be disposed of at a city dump (*basurero municipal*).

SWIMMING

Mexico's diverse waters—four seas, numerous lakes and countless lagoons—offer visitors some of the world's most pleasurable swimming. Lakes and lagoons generally resemble placid swimming holes, where you can soak and relax. But the oceans, with their erratic currents and powerful waves, contain hidden pitfalls that can be avoided with a little awareness.

Keep in mind that waves can be deceptive. They come in varying sets: one set may consist of seven small waves, followed by seven big ones; or seven big waves followed by one calm swell; or a series of small waves overshadowed suddenly by a big, angry swell. If you get caught in a wave about to crash you onto the shore, try to roll up and tumble with it rather than thrash against it. Remember that waves grow bigger and more surly during the full moon. Stay alert and never turn your back to the sea.

Surfing and body-surfing are sports of skill practiced in often-treacherous waves. Familiarize yourself with the techniques and take a few lessons in beginners' waters before you try anything bigger.

Rip currents threaten open sections of the Caribbean. These currents can be spotted by their ragged-looking surface water and foamy edges. If you get caught in one, don't struggle against it; instead, swim parallel to the shore to free yourself from its inexorable pull toward the open sea.

Be careful in waters full of coral reefs. Coral edges are jagged and can make nasty cuts. Consider wearing rubber thongs in the water to protect your feet. Treat any cuts with alcohol and an antiseptic.

Stingrays and stinging jellyfish may strike in the Sea of Cortez or along the Pacific (see Chapter 1 for advice on what to do if stung). Spiny sea urchins may inflict wounds that should be well-cleaned and disinfected with lime juice or hydrogen peroxide.

Above all, when you go swimming, use common sense in judging safety conditions. Strong surf, steep dropoffs at the tideline, whirlpools and eddies around cliffs all signal danger. If in doubt, don't go. Avoid swimming alone.

Beware of sunburn, the trickiest ailment of the tropics. Tan slowly and use plenty of sunscreen on sensitive areas: lips, nose, shoulders, even the tops of your feet.

Nude sunbathing is against the law in Mexico. Travelers get away with it on deserted beaches, where no one can be offended, but remember that Catholic traditions reign here and Mexican families find flagrant nudity disrespectful. Be discreet.

FISHING AND BOATING

Sportfishing is terrific off every coast. To fish in Mexico you must have a license, easily obtainable in any coastal town at the local **PESCA** (fish) office or from major sportfishing companies and resorts. A license can be obtained in advance from Mexican insurance stations at the border. Harpooning is illegal. It is also against the law to kill sea turtles or take their eggs. To protect its rarer sea treasures, the Mexican government prohibits visitors from taking certain species. Check on the latest restrictions when you apply for a Mexican fishing license.

Boating is delightful everywhere—from Ensenada to Tampico. Regattas and sailboat races are plentiful, and many fine harbors and marinas skirt each of Mexico's coasts. Boat owners sailing Mexican waters or transporting their boats into Mexico need a permit, obtained from a Mexican consul.

SURFING AND SKIN DIVING

In the "Beaches" section of each area chapter there is information about surfing, snorkeling and diving in that area. Surfing is best along the Pacific coast of Baja and the West Coast of the Mexican mainland. Windsurfing is hot along Bahía Concepción and the southern tip of Baja and almost anywhere along the West Coast and the Caribbean. For diving, the Mexican Caribbean ranks among the best spots in the world; the West Coast and Baja have some outstanding skin-diving sites as well.

HUNTING

Hunting can be very good along the Mexican coastline, especially for fowl—quail, geese, ducks, doves, pigeons. Bigger game, such as rams and deer, inhabit the mountainous interior and lowland jungles. As rich as the wildlife is, the red tape behind hunting in Mexico can be nearly prohibitive. You need permits and licenses to carry guns across the border, hunt, bag certain species and export game back to the United States or Canada. These documents are obtained through complex, time-consuming procedures. There are also strict rules about when, where, what and how much you can hunt. I strongly advise that you avoid the official government agency,

Secretaría de Desarrollo Urbano y Ecología (SEDUE) (located in most major cities throughout Mexico); instead, make arrangements before you go, through private SEDUE-approved agencies like the **Mexican Hunting Association** (3302 Josie Avenue, Long Beach, CA 90808; 213-421-1619). Mexican consulates can also arrange for hunting licenses.

HORSEBACK RIDING

This sport is an especially popular activity in northern Mexico, with facilities available in nearly every major resort. You will find horses for rent around Ensenada, the Capes region of Baja, the San Carlos area, Mazatlán, Puerto Vallarta, Manzanillo, Ixtapa-Zihuatanejo, Acapulco and parts of the Yucatán. Puerto Vallarta has a comical sport called "donkey polo," with riders on burros playing polo using brooms. For a true adventure, you can explore the Sierra Madre's Copper Canyon and environs by horse. (See Chapter 6 for further information.)

TENNIS

All luxury resorts and many small hotels come with tennis courts. Most large towns also have public courts and private clubs open to visitors. Tournaments, instructions and equipment rentals are offered by the more modern outlets. For more details, contact the **Federación Mexicana de Tenis** (Avenida Durango 225-301, México, D.F., México; 514-3759.)

GOLF

Every major resort town features one or two good golf courses for tourist use. Some are located at a specific hotel and open only to its guests; others are open to the public. Private country clubs with golf courses are usually open to visitors as well.

DUNE BUGGYING AND DESERT CYCLING

Along the dunes and beaches of Baja and the Northwest Coastal Desert, people of all ages participate in the dune buggy craze and drive big-wheeled cars and cycles, often at breakneck speeds, through the desert sand. Although many enjoy the sport, a warning is in order. Buggying and cycling are ecologically harmful, since they plow up tons of sand (thus killing turtle eggs), disturb wildlife with the roar of unmuffled engines and displace natural vegetation needed to hold dunes in place.

Not only are these sports a threat to the environment, they are a threat to people. All-Terrain Cycles (ATCs), those three-wheel cycles for rent at several beach resorts, in particular, have been shown to be unstable and potentially dangerous, sometimes causing death or debilitating injuries to drivers. See that you receive full instructions in how to operate the vehicle if you rent one. Driving at reasonable speeds, with only one person to a vehicle, can also help prevent accidents.

(Text continued on page 34.)

Marine World, Mexico

Besides hundreds of fish species in the Pacific Ocean, Sea of Cortez, Caribbean Sea and Gulf of Mexico—the four seas surrounding Mexico—a fascinating menagerie of marine mammals, seabirds and aquatic creatures teems around offshore archipelagoes or plies the channels of the deep.

Each coastal region in Mexico has its specialties. You may encounter stealthy stingrays, massive shrimp and 1,000-pound marlin along the Sea of Cortez, a fisherman's paradise. There are giant conches with edible flesh. Prisms of tropical fish flash amid the Caribbean reefs, a mecca for skin divers. Along the West Coast, you may witness swordlike barracudas slicing through the Pacific or gangly octopi and graceful manta rays gliding along the ocean floor. Languid sea turtles, an endangered species, and tiger sharks prowl the cloudy waters of the Gulf of Mexico.

Along every part of the coast, oysters encrust mangrove roots in lagoons, clams sleep under blankets of bubbly goo in mudflats and *langostinas* (crawfish) laze in the rivers that flow to the sea.

The waters surrounding Baja California are the richest in sealife. Some travelers come down exclusively to watch the pods of gray whales. Every winter, in the world's greatest migration, they journey from the Bering Sea to the warm lagoons on Baja's Pacific coast, where they bear their young in protected coves. On the other side of the peninsula, blue whales, fin whales, humpbacks and dolphins frolic in the Sea of Cortez. (See "Whale-Watching in Baja" in Chapter 5.)

Many species of birds and big marine animals cluster around Baja islands. Experts say these rocky isles are among the least spoiled on earth, with an almost untouched ecology. Their peaks still look as jagged as erupted rock at the dawn of time.

Remote Isla Guadalupe off the northwest coast of Baja, where seals and sea elephants were once massacred for their hides, has been set aside as an ecological preserve for a reviving sea elephant population. Isla Espíritu Santo and La Partida, near La Paz, are home to a sea lion rookery. Ruby-toned Sally Lightfoot crabs and enormous starfish wink in the tidepools and undersea gardens around nearby Isla Cerralvo.

An abundance of fish and a lack of land predators make Baja islands ideal nesting grounds for sea birds. Gulls and pelicans coat every islet with guano and sail along the tides, hunting for fish. Funny, awkward brown- and blue-footed boobies, which nest on remote islands like San Pedro Mártir, dive-bomb into the sea for their dinner or catch flying fish in midair with their slate-blue beaks. There is even a breed of coastal bat on Sea of Cortez islands and shorelines that impales its prey on its talons, a style of natural spearfishing.

Isla Tiburón, the biggest West Coast island, has a huge population of land tortoises ambling along its shores. This desert island, which stands closer to the Mexican mainland than to Baja, was the original home of the Seri Indians. Today, the Seris live in coastal villages around Bahía Kino, commemorating their attachment to the sea with superb wooden carvings of porpoises, sailfish, marlin, shells and sharks.

The Outdoors

TROPICAL FLORA AND FAUNA

From half-a-dozen kinds of palm trees to over 70 species of orchids, Mexico overflows with a profusion of exotic plant life. Bougainvillea, hibiscus, jasmine, plumeria, gardenias and flowering jacaranda trees flood the lush West Coast, Yucatán and Gulf Coast with fragrance and color. Even the harsh desert terrain of the Northwest and Baja is alive with succulents and over 100 varieties of cacti, many existing nowhere else in the world.

The agave cactus of the Yucatán, yielding henequen fibers for rope, garnered fortunes for 19th-century landowners and is still grown today. Also in the Yucatán, the ceiba tree, representing the tree of life, is held sacred by Mayas and never cut down.

Along the swampy edges of West Coast and Yucatán lagoons, mangroves thrive, as do stands of bamboo, ferns and cypresses. Fruit trees are ubiquitous; oranges, limes, grapefruit and bananas brighten the roadsides and fields of the West Coast and Yucatán. Less familiar breeds like papaya, grown to hothouse proportions, and *tamarindo*, rarely found north of the border, multiply at a feverish rate all over. Likewise, you could practically live on the fruit of the coconut palms edging beaches from Mazatlán to Matamoros.

Mexican markets reflect this abundance in heaping produce stands and vivid flower stalls, which sometime sell edible blossoms. Other stalls offer herbs and seasonings, such as fresh chamomile, cilantro, basil, mint, rosemary, *jamaica* (dried hibiscus, used to make a refreshing drink), vanilla beans, sesame seeds, *nopalitos* cacti and dried chili peppers.

The animal life of the Mexican tropics is equally diverse. Lagoons and estuaries are the haunts of doves, ducks, geese, egrets and herons. The Gulf of Mexico on the northern Yucatán coast is home to immense flocks of pink flamingos, and the Yucatán's lowland jungles hide keel-billed toucans and noisy parrots.

The Yucatán, in fact, may have the country's most exotic cross section of fauna: spotted ocelots that look like mini-jaguars, needle-nosed coatimundis, yard-long iguanas, sunning themselves on Mayan ruins, spider monkeys (commonly kept as pets), peccaries (also called *javelinas* or musk hogs) and the rare bulb-nosed manatee (a disappearing marine species, also called the sea cow).

Elsewhere, inland mountains shelter wild goats, rams, deer, mountain lions and jaguars (called *tigres*). The whole West Coast is invaded by bug-eyed geckos (tiny, likable lizards that make a clucking sound and dart across hotel walls everywhere). Butterflies swirl like confetti through jungles and fields in the tropical climes of the West Coast and Yucatán. Bats and swallows take refuge in caves, rocky caverns and the moist, dark passages of Yucatán ruins.

DESERT LIFE

Some envision the desert as a blank slate, when in truth its residents simply keep a low profile for the sake of self-preservation. It takes a tough breed of wildlife to endure the desert wilderness. Rattlesnakes, rams, wild pigs, goats, bobcats, raccoons, gray foxes and jackrabbits roam the canyons and mountains. Long-tailed roadrunners, lean coyotes, wheeling frigate birds, armadillos, quails, vultures and numerous lizards inhabit the desert. Sometimes animals show up in the most unexpected places, like the scarlet cardinals and brown scorpions nesting inside dried cacti.

The hardy cactus rules the desert flora of northern Mexico, particularly Baja California. For a rundown on the sprawling cactus dynasty, see "Baja's Prickly Circus" in Chapter 4.

SHELLS

Better-known beaches have all been picked clean, but many offbeat Mexican beaches are still thick with shells: turritellas, butterfly (tellin) clams, venus clams, murex snails, keyhole limpets, cowries, olives, scallops, whelks, moon snails, conches, tulips, coral, colored stones, starfish and sand dollars.

Points and islands are great places to shell hunt because they protrude into the passing current and catch the best of the booty before the tides hit the mainland shores.

The "Beaches" section in each chapter includes information on shell hunting.

SAND QUALITY SCALE

It's usually the sand that makes (or breaks) the beach. Throughout the "Beaches" section in each chapter, sand is rated according to a 1-to-10 quality scale. The lowest end of the scale, from 1 to 3, means the sand belongs to the mud family and the beach is chiefly marsh. Sand grades 4 to 6 should be in a pepper shaker or in a dust pan. Grade 7 and above sand shakes down like this:

Grade 7: Respectable cornmeal facsimile, good enough to bring back to the hotel in your shoes.

Grade 8: Hearty, full-bodied stuff you can roll in, bury yourself in, put in a child's sandbox and build sandcastles with.

Grade 9: Elegant, clean, artistic sand sometimes seen in sculpted dunes. It is often blended with glittery minerals or thickened by crystallized grains.

Grade 10: Satin-soft, pure white and always cool. The sand of the gods, the magic grains in which poet William Blake saw a world. Only Caribbean sand qualifies for this rating. The Sandman gets his here.

CHAPTER THREE

Mexican History and Culture

History

PRE-AZTEC CIVILIZATION

The earliest Mexican *indígenas* (indigenous people) wandered across the Bering Strait some 30,000 years ago, drifting south through what is now Canada and the United States into the deserts and rainforests of ancient Mexico. Slowly over succeeding millennia these populations introduced agriculture, irrigation, textiles and pottery. Eventually came religion, the gods and the ritual of human sacrifice. Then, out of the steamy jungles to the far south where the spotted jaguar roams, rose the first great civilization of Mesoamerica.

The village-dwelling Olmecs thrived from 1000 to 400 B.C. They settled in the area that is today Tabasco and Veracruz and spread into parts of Chiapas. From a Stone Age survival-level existence, these innovators spawned the beginnings of a controlled, creative civilization. They dug canals, fashioned jewelry and weapons, designed a calendar, invented a form of glyph writing, built ceremonial centers and created impressive carvings. Their 40-ton sculptures were chipped from stones rolled as far as 100 miles from the mountains to the coast—a mystery of transportation archaeologists still cannot fathom.

We know the Olmecs today chiefly for these enormous sculpted basalt heads, which combine negroid and catlike features. Scholars speculate that these facial characteristics point to a race with some Negroid traits and simultaneously to their reverence for the jaguar. Worship of this great cat was the focal point of the Olmec religion.

Olmec culture had a strong influence on the tribes that came after them—specifically the Zapotecs, Mixtecs and Toltecs. These and other cultures flourished in this part of the world before the advent of the Aztecs. Although little is known about the day-to-day life of these people, they launched an era of city-states all over Mexico, with remnants still in existence today: Monte Albán, El Tajín, Zempoala and, in the Valley of

Mexico, the magnificent, far-reaching Teotihuacán, whose fabulous ruins can be visited from Mexico City. As these centers grew, the most sophisticated culture of all was gradually moving up through Guatemala toward the Yucatán.

THE MAYAS

The Mayas first settled in Mexico sometime after 300 B.C. Although their origins are obscure, their culture flourished for over a thousand years and gave Mexico probably its most advanced society, a remarkable race of inventors, priests and artists. At a time when the Roman Empire was being overrun by barbarian invaders in Europe, the Mayas were constructing pyramids and temples, painting murals, studying the stars, making complex mathematical calculations, organizing two calendars and discovering agricultural and medical concepts the Roman world had not yet conceived..

For a long time historians thought the Mayas were a gentle race of stargazers, worshipping rain gods and a pantheon of hundreds of other deities. But recent studies show the Mayas were also a barbaric race, practicing human sacrifice, torture, mutilation and ritual games in which the heads of losers were sometimes used as balls. Their bizarre beauty rites included head-binding to produce sloping foreheads, drilling teeth for inlays and inducing crossed eyes in babies.

For reasons still not known, Mayan culture slid into decline around 900 A.D. The great cities were rather abruptly abandoned. Warlike Toltecs from the north invaded the Yucatán, imposing their militant lifestyle on remaining ceremonial centers and introducing the cult of Quetzalcoatl, the plumed serpent.

Ironically, legends surrounding Quetzalcoatl would one day lead to the undoing of an even more advanced civilization. The serpent-god, according to tradition, had been tricked into drinking *pulque* (cactus liquor) and making love to his sister, thus breaking a strict taboo. In shame, Quetzalcoatl exiled himself from his kingdom. But the fair-skinned Quetzalcoatl vowed to return in a specific future year. The prophesy of Quetzalcoatl's return was to have a profound impact on the tribes that the Toltecs left behind in central Mexico—specifically the mighty Aztecs.

AZTEC RULE

For generations before settling in the Mexico Valley, the Aztecs (also known as the Méxicas) were a nomadic tribe. One legend says they came from seven caves to the north, another that they originated in the mysterious land of Aztlán. In the midst of an unlikely swamp in central Mexico, the Aztecs saw a sign their prophets had foretold: an eagle perched on a cactus, eating a snake—today, the emblem on the Mexican flag. Honoring legend, the Aztecs laid down their bundles and built their empire in the middle of Lake Texcoco, the site of present-day Mexico City.

In just two centuries, from 1300 to 1519 A.D.—the year Spanish conquistador Hernán Cortés arrived—the Aztecs created a glamorous,
prosperous megalopolis, the island city of Tenochtitlán. The world's biggest
city in its day, it had bridges and aqueducts, causeways and floating islands,
mighty pyramids, running water, a massive market, a rich merchant class,
lavish gardens and as many as 300,000 residents.

But the temples also ran with blood from constant human sacrifices
and feasts on the victims' flesh. These offerings of blood were intended
to satiate and revitalize the gods who kept the universe in motion. Battles
called "flowery wars" were staged to capture prisoners who were sacrifi-
cially offered to the ruthless war god Huizilopochtli. The Aztecs also raided
neighboring tribes for victims and forced them to pay taxes and obeisance
to the Aztec king, Moctezuma. The Aztecs' stranglehold on their neighbors,
along with their reverential superstition about the return of the pale-skinned
Quetzalcoatl, proved their undoing. By the time the Spanish arrived, the
Aztecs' enemies were eager to overthrow their hated masters.

THE SPANISH CONQUEST

The Spanish conquest of Mexico surely ranks as one of the most brazen
and sensational epics in history. Captain Hernán Cortés, a short, cocky man
in his mid-30s, landed on the Gulf Coast with a pitiful army of 500 men
in 1519, fully intending to conquer this unexplored land for the king of Spain
and win power and gold for himself. Inland and on the shores waited
hundreds of thousands of Indians, whose impulse was to attack. But through
luck, firearms, horses (which the Indians had never seen), sheer nerve, un-
flinching religious faith and brilliant guile, Cortés defeated his adversaries.

He had a genius for manipulation. Out of one side of his mouth, he
buttered up Moctezuma's couriers with flattering messages to their king,
while out of the other he plotted against the Aztecs with promises and praise
to their enemies. Town by town, Cortés gradually won the restless Indians'
friendship with the help of his Indian interpreter, Doña Marina, known as
Malinche (today a word synonymous with betrayal in Mexico).

The Indians were amazed by Cortés' flame-spouting cannons and
spirited horses, which they at first mistook as being half-man, half-animal.
The Spaniards in turn were struck dumb by the gory sacrifice and can-
nibalism that dominated every village; even the gold and impressive towns
they encountered did not make up for the hardships and threats of their mission. To prevent any attempt at mutiny, Cortés burned his own galleons.
It was either fight or die gruesomely on the sacrificial slab. Given these
alternatives, Cortés and his ragged army battled their way over the mountains, all the way to the throne of Moctezuma.

The great Aztec emperor was one of history's fatally indecisive rulers.
Unable to determine whether the fair-skinned, bearded Cortés was Quetzalcoatl come back or a greedy foreigner aiming to overthrow his kingdom,

Moctezuma handled the invaders alternately with lies and kindness, sometimes planning a total massacre, other times delivering golden gifts and warm welcomes. Even after the Spaniards entered Tenochtitlán and arrested him on his own turf, imprisoning him in their guest quarters, Moctezuma could not decide whether or not Cortés had the divine right to do so. Moctezuma's priests and other Aztec leaders, angered by the audacity of the intruders, finally revolted. In the scuffle, Moctezuma was killed, though precisely how is unclear. A famous first-hand account of the battle, *The Conquest of New Spain* by Bernal Díaz, one of Cortés' soldiers, reports the Aztec ruler was felled by flying stones hurled by Moctezuma's own people. Cortés himself barely escaped the capital. Thousands of his allies and men were killed or later sacrificed by the Aztecs.

While Cortés licked his wounds and rebuilt his army at a distance, Tenochtitlán fell under the scourge of a smallpox epidemic brought on by an afflicted Spanish soldier. Corpses piled high in the Aztec capital. The new emperor, Cuauhtémoc, attacked Cortés furiously. But when Cortés' renewed battalions invaded, cutting off water and food to the crippled city, Tenochtitlán crumbled. In 1521, Cortés proclaimed the empire New Spain.

COLONIAL ERA

The conquistadors razed the proud kingdom to the ground, mindlessly destroying every fragment of Aztec art and culture. With the fallen stones of temples and palaces, the Spanish began building their colonial empire— or rather, enslaved Indians did so. These natives had fought to throw off Aztec tyranny only to be harnessed for labor under their new lords for the next three centuries: erecting churches, missions and monasteries for the Catholic friars, building haciendas, tilling fields and working in mines—in short, forging a powerful colony whose silver and gold passed directly into Spanish pockets.

The indigenous people had no rights, no land, no leaders. Even their customs and beliefs were banned and Christianity forced upon them. Colonial Mexico became an open playground for missionaries and opportunistic Spaniards. The conquerors lived in aristocratic grandeur, with balls, bullfights and native servants.

STRUGGLE FOR INDEPENDENCE

Centuries of cruel and unjust Spanish rule roused *indígenas*, mestizos (those with mixed Spanish and native blood) and Creoles (pure-blooded Spaniards born in Mexico) to rise up and demand autonomy. These disparate peoples were second-class Mexican citizens, never accorded the rights and status of pure-blooded Spaniards born in Spain, the despised *gachupines*. Of the three angry castes, the Creoles fumed with the most discontent.

The unrest was aggravated by turmoil in Europe. First, the French Revolution of 1789 gave the people of New Spain hope for their own independence. Then, Napoleon Bonaparte attacked Spain and King Charles IV abdicated in 1808, replaced by Napoleon's incompetent brother. The antagonized Mexicans refused to recognize the new king. After years of bowing to Spain, would they now be expected to kiss the feet of the French?

Father Miguel Hidalgo y Costilla, a Creole priest from the northern village of Dolores, decided to take action. He plotted with a local captain, Ignacio Allende, to stage a coup in nearby San Miguel (today San Miguel de Allende). The rebellion was launched in December, 1810, with Hidalgo's famous *el grito Dolores* (the cry of Dolores) from his pulpit: *"Mexicanos, viva México!"*

Battles broke out throughout central Mexico, and Hidalgo's army grew. He stood for equality among Mexicans and redistribution of land to the workers—widely popular demands. But in the end, both Hidalgo and Allende were captured and shot, and the revolt momentarily fizzled. José María Morelos picked up the torch but was also executed. Agustín de Iturbide, a mestizo brigadier general, joined forces with remaining rebels, authored a peace treaty with Spain and was declared the emperor of Mexico. At last the Spanish were ousted. But chaos reigned and Iturbide abdicated. His successors drafted a constitution in 1824, and the first president of the Mexican Republic, General Guadalupe Victoria, was elected.

Despite the struggle, independence brought few changes to the difficult lives of most Mexicans, and no real peace. Dictators followed on each others' heels like shuffled cards; land conflicts continued; the church and military clashed. The figure who best characterizes this shaky period is General Antonio López de Santa Anna, who boomeranged in and out of the presidency 11 times. The one-legged Santa Anna is notorious for having lost half of Mexico's territory to the United States in the Mexican-American War. Texas, New Mexico, Arizona and California all belonged to Mexico until 1846 when United States forces invaded Mexico to battle for the Lone Star State and eventually seized all four territories. The peace treaty after the Mexican-American War gave Uncle Sam all four states for $15 million.

As the young Mexican Republic suffered through its early identity crises, there emerged a growing split between wealthy conservatives and poor liberals. This division eventually widened and erupted into civil war. The emerging liberal leader was Benito Juárez, a Zapotec Indian lawyer who became Mexico's first *indígena* president in 1858. He ranks among the country's greatest heroes (nearly every town has a street named after him), establishing railroads, an educational system and industrial developments.

Initially, with the government bankrupt, Juárez halted all payments on foreign debts. The French jumped at this excuse to invade, but were soundly beaten at Puebla on May 5, 1862—the occasion for the Cinco de Mayo holiday celebrated yearly.

The French, however, bounced back. They captured Mexico City and routed Juárez. With the support of Mexican upper-class conservatives, Napoleon III of France implanted the idealistic Archduke Maximilian and his wife Carlota of Austria as puppet emperor and empress of Mexico in 1864. With no grasp of Mexican politics, Maximilian made many enemies during the next three years. In the end, Napoleon abandoned him to be executed by the Juárez forces. Juárez returned to power until 1872.

A mestizo general under Juárez named Porfirio Díaz grabbed control next and did not let go for 35 years. A ruthless dictator, he censored the press, controlled schools, permitted graft and encouraged foreign exploitation of Mexico's resources. His presidency did, however, mark Mexico's longest period of peace in its first hundred years of independence. The economy boomed as outside investments poured in from the United States and Europe, bringing industry and modernization to the young republic. Those who prospered, of course, were the upper and middle classes. Once again, the deprived Indians remained at the bottom of the heap.

MEXICAN REVOLUTION

Although Díaz planned to rule until he died, in 1907 he let slip to an American newsman that he was considering retirement. Out of the resulting political furor burst a potential successor, reformist Francisco Madero, who had come from a wealthy Creole family in northern Mexico. Madero financed a political party called the *Anti-reeleccionistas*—those who opposed the reelection of Díaz. The dictator hastily exiled Madero and rigged the next elections in his own favor. Undaunted, Madero rounded up allies to stage an explosive rebellion.

The era that followed was the bloodiest since the war for independence from Spain. During the Mexican Revolution, waged from 1910 to 1920, over a million people died. At the same time, the revolution gave birth to more Mexican legends than any other modern period.

Two characters of the revolution rode straight out of history into folklore: Pancho Villa (real name: Doroteo Arango), a hell-raising cattle rustler from Chihuahua who shaped his roughshod band of cowboys into a guerrilla army; and Emiliano Zapata, the silent Indian with a handlebar moustache whose rebel troops sacked the southern haciendas to protest for land reform.

While Villa is often thought of as the ultimate revolutionary hero, he was actually flashy and power hungry, with a cruel streak, often more dedicated to self-aggrandizement than to the principles of the revolution. Zapata, on the other hand, was much more the genuine insurgent, the brooding freedom fighter deeply tied to the land and sympathetic with the peasants, battling for land reform and an end to the prejudices out of which Mexico was born. Both men became instant heroes. Through their marauding armies, Díaz was toppled and Madero took over.

Madero restored some of the basic freedoms Díaz had destroyed: freedom of the press, free elections, worker's unions. But he neglected to restore land to the Indians and for all his honesty and good intentions brought few real improvements. He, too, was overthrown and murdered. The revolutionary leaders bickered among themselves over power—all but Zapata, who did not seek rank for himself. Yet, with seeming inevitability, as the revolution raged on, Zapata was shot and killed by a treacherous government emissary.

This succession of assassinations that haunted Mexican history can be traced back to the same thirst for wealth and power that drove Hernán Cortés. As Mexico labored to establish itself as a nation, leader after leader would fall under a murderer's bullet, only to be replaced by another glory seeker or well-meaning individual.

Venustiano Carranza, the governor of Coahuila and an active *revolucionista*, emerged from the revolution as the new president. The war-torn nation, nearly bled dry, eagerly hailed the new constitution he signed in 1917, still in effect today. It established a presidential republic with 31 states, the United Mexican States (*Estado Unidos Mexicanos*), and it included rights for workers, a minimum wage, restoration of peasant land, equal rights for women and free education. With this new rudder to steer by, the Mexican Republic set a course for the present era.

MODERN MEXICO

Unfortunately, the wily Carranza, rather than enforcing the constitution, ushered in the era by trying to skip the country with all of Mexico's treasury money in tow. He was murdered en route to Veracruz.

In 1927, the *Partido Revolucionario Institucional* (PRI), or Institutional Revolutionary Party, rose from the ashes of the revolution as a champion of land reform. PRI has towered over Mexican politics ever since, so much so that the party has never lost a major election. Opposing parties exist, but PRI's arm-twisting control is so overwhelming that Mexico is considered a one-party democracy.

The young party really flexed its muscles in 1934, when President Lázaro Cárdenas nationalized the booming oil industry and expropriated all foreign-owned oil fields. This was part of his massive land reform program, in which 49 million acres were divided into *ejidos*—communally owned property where Mexicans can settle and work for their own profit.

Although Mexico took back its oil from outsiders, World War II brought in fresh waves of foreign investment, particularly by big automobile and food firms, which spurred industrialization and boosted the economy. Mexico was now primed to steam ahead toward its full potential. But in its eagerness, the republic overspent on commercial and cultural development, and by the mid-1970s, Mexico was foundering. In 1980, the peso took a nosedive, oil prices plummeted and the national debt ballooned into a nightmare of impossible interest payments.

With inflation skyrocketing, Mexico's new leaders have inherited some brutal problems. Not the least of these remains widespread poverty, especially among Indians.

Modern presidents since 1970—Luis Alvarez Echeverría, José López Portillo, Miguel de la Madrid Hurtado—have worked to develop Mexico as a leading Third World nation and tourist center while trying to stem inflation, build the oil industry, buoy agriculture, and deal with immigration issues.

The question of illegal aliens and border conflicts with the United States remains controversial and unresolved. Some call the flow of undocumented workers into border states like California and Texas a kind of poetic justice, a reclamation of the lands America snatched from Mexico over 100 years ago. To many Mexicans without jobs, *El Norte* represents an economic safety valve where, with luck, they may escape the curse of poverty. Despite American laws and border patrols, undocumented immigrants continue to pour across the border.

At its southern border, Mexico is also coping with illegal immigration—a huge influx of Guatemalan refugees left homeless after the Guatemalan army destroyed hundreds of native villages.

The devastating 1985 earthquake in Mexico City and Hurricane Gilbert in the Yucatán in 1988 added a blow to the already financially weakened nation and ushered in a tough period for *la república*. But the nation that sprang from the Mayas and Aztecs, that gave birth to Hidalgo, Juárez and Zapata, has shown the will and spirit to endure. As one Mexican writer observed, Mexicans have a genius for survival.

ECONOMY

Despite its poverty and astronomical inflation, Mexico enjoys a strong position among developing countries. In mining, it is the world's greatest producer of silver and is likewise rich in barites and antimony, sulphur, lead, bismuth and copper.

Industry has expanded, especially in electronics and textiles and in manufacturing autos, such as Volkswagens. Hydroelectric and thermal power stations produce all the country's electricity, and a new nuclear power plant—Mexico's first—is located on the Gulf Coast. Agricultural development is slow, suffering a shortage of funds, fertilizers and irrigation. However, new federally funded water-drilling projects are boosting agricultural development in many areas.

Tremendous investments and efforts have gone into bolstering Mexico's oil industry, concentrated around Veracruz, Tabasco and Chiapas. With proven reserves of more than 60 billion barrels, Mexico is one of the world's leading sources of oil, although inflation and dropping oil prices have hurt the market.

Mexico's biggest bid for profits these days is tourism. Now considered the number one industry, tourism brings in several billion dollars per year from over five million visitors. New tourist sites are being developed to create instant revenues and jobs and put a dent in the country's massive foreign debt.

THE MARKETPLACE

When the Spanish conquistadors arrived at the great Aztec capital of Tenochtitlán, one of the things that impressed them most was the immense, exciting market of Tlatelolco. The tradition of big Indian markets (*tianguis*, more commonly called *mercados*) has stayed alive in Mexico to this day. Usually the market is located in the center of town. A maze of indoor-outdoor stalls, it overflows with produce, meats, cheeses, flowers, clothing, bird cages and more in a noisy disarray. Items sold at the market are almost always cheaper than their equivalents in department or grocery stores. This is where the locals shop, socialize and seek bargains.

Culture

THE PEOPLE

Mexicans are fiercely nationalistic, loyal, and proud of their culture. In spite of their poverty, Mexicans are remarkably generous. For their countrymen they provide a free educational system (83 percent of the populace is literate, according to government statistics). Similarly, travelers may find complete strangers stopping to help them. Big families will sometimes take in foreign visitors and treat them like royalty—feeding and entertaining them and taking them along on outings.

Don't be disturbed if someone calls you a *gringo*. No malice is intended; the term is simply part of the endless Mexican lexicon of *apodos* (nicknames). As a people, Mexicans exude affection. They shake hands at every opportunity—a chance to exchange a reassuring touch on meeting and parting. Mexicans consider a blunt and forthright manner to be crude; they would usually rather tell a white lie than chance hurting someone's feelings.

The family unit holds together this nation of 84 million people. Some ten million are Indians, still the lowest class, facing prejudices from both mestizos and pure-blooded Spanish.

The difference between the typical Mexican's idealized view of the world and the reality most Mexicans live in, points to the gap between Mexico's two major classes, the very rich and the very poor. Although there is a growing middle class, the rift between these economic extremes grows like the national debt and the Mexican birthrate (26 births per 1,000 habitants, second only to Kenya).

This birthrate reflects the continuing importance of the large family. While Mexican families are not quite as big as they once were, many men still measure their masculinity by the number of their children; and, often for religious reasons, many women don't use birth control (though the pill is widely available).

The cult of masculinity, or *machismo*, still reigns supreme in Mexico. No feminist movements have even put a dent in the old double standard, which allows men the right to roam (married or not) while women (married or not) are expected to stay home and behave like ladies. Except perhaps in the bigger cities, a woman is supposed to be a virgin when she marries. *Machismo* is an integral part of the social fabric, and nowhere else in the world are men more self-consciously men and proud of it.

Many Americans are fascinated but confused by the Latin mentality, the intense emotions, the outbursts of sentimentality and the rites of courtesy. To understand this country, it helps to grasp Mexican values, which are neither materialistic nor optimistic. They are in many ways the reverse of Anglo values. Family and tradition rate much higher in Mexico than personal gain or success. To eat a good meal, make love, or laugh with the family far outrank a job promotion. Mexico's tragic history has touched the populace with an instinctive fatalism: life must be taken a day at a time, borne with fortitude and resilience; and whenever possible, the steam can blow off in fiestas, bullfights, soccer, music and dance.

Here lies a paradox: the irrepressible Latin gaiety that can seem so uplifting to the outsider is in many ways a protest of defiant joy in the face of unbearable obstacles. Mexico's passionate songs and religious zeal well up from a struggle between despair and rebellion. Those impassioned coyote cries of woe and shrill whistles of cheer in Mexican songs are a good-humored release of joy and sorrow. In the darkest moment, a Mexican will smile and find wry humor in the situation. Their Day of the Dead even pokes fun at death, with papier-mâché skeletons in gaudy costumes.

As Mexican novelist Carlos Fuentes said, Mexico is "a country far more intricate and challenging to the North American mind than anything in Europe; a country at times more foreign than anything in Asia." What luck for *norteamericanos* that this intriguing country should be just next door.

THE LANGUAGE

So many Mexicans are bilingual, especially in resort areas, that English-speaking visitors can usually sail smoothly through Mexico without knowing a word of Spanish. But a traveler does not live by English alone. To really know a country is to know its language. Even a smattering of Spanish will open doors, light up eyes and elicit warm smiles as will nothing else. You're speaking their lingo—it's a sign of respect and a way of belonging. The more you know, the more your travels bloom: you can understand popular songs, catch headlines on the street, eavesdrop, get better prices in the market and, best of all, make friends.

It's helpful to study Spanish before you leave home, then amplify your studies by devouring newspapers, comic books (they plaster every street stall), subtitled movies and television once you get to Mexico. Listen to Latin radio to build your fluency. And speak up—don't be afraid to sound like a three-year-old. You'll inevitably stumble over verb forms, masculine and feminine nouns and adjectives, the confusing use of the formal *usted* vs. the informal *tu*. Talk right past the mistakes. What you want to do is communicate ideas, which does not require perfect grammar. Mexicans love being addressed in their own language, and they are unfailingly congenial regardless of your blunders.

Unlike English, Spanish is spoken just as it is spelled—a rule so universal that you need only know the principles of pronunciation to read aloud a text correctly. You may even be able to spell words just from the way they sound. With accented words, just place an emphasis on the part that is accented. The letter "ñ" indicates a gentle "nya" sound, as in *niño* (neen-yo) or *cabaña* (kah-ban-yah). Double r's are rolled off the tongue with an elegant trill for words like *ferrocarril*, but few non-natives can pull this off without a lot of practice. Here's a rundown on basic vowels and consonants to get you started:

Vowels: *A*—pronounced *ah* as in *father*; *E*—pronounced *eh* as in *get*; *I*—pronounced *ee* as in *ski*; *O*—pronounced *oh* as in *bold*; *U*—pronounced *oo* as in *boot*.

Consonants: generally pronounced the same as in English. The exceptions are as follows:

C—pronounced like *s* before *e* or *i*, as in *cerca (sehr-kah)* or *cigarro (see-gah-roh)*. Otherwise, it sounds like *k*, as in *camino (kah-mee-noh)*.

G—pronounced like *h* before *e* and *i*, as in *general (heh-neh-ral)* or *giganta (hee-gan-tah)*. Otherwise, it sounds like a hard *g*, as in *get*. One notable exception is the town *Guaymas*, pronounced *Why-mas*.

H—always silent, as in *habla (ah-blah)*; *J*—pronounced like *h*, as in *José (Ho-seh)*; *LL*—pronounced like *y*, as in *llanta (yan-tah)*; *QU*—pronounced like *k*, as in *que (keh)*; *Z*—pronounced like *s*, as in *zapato (sah-pah-toh)*.

CUISINE

Travelers who think Mexican food consists chiefly of tacos and burritos dipped in chile sauce are in for a delightful surprise when they visit this Latin country. Mexicans believe their cuisine to be equal to the finest French food. The blending of Indian spiciness and Spanish heartiness has produced dozens of unexpected dishes, bursting with calories and flavor.

(Text continued on page 52.)

GENERAL TERMS AND PHRASES

Hello - *Hola*
Goodbye - *Adiós, Hasta la vista*
Yes - *Sí*
No - *No*
Good morning - *Buenos días*
Good afternoon - *Buenas tardes*
Good evening - *Buenas noches*
How are you? - *¿Cómo está usted?*
Fine, thank you - *Bien, gracias*
You're welcome - *De nada*
Please - *Por favor*
Thank you - *Muchas gracias*
My name is... - *Me llamo...*
Do you speak Engish? - *¿Habla usted inglés?*
I don't speak Spanish - *No habla español*
More slowly, please - *Más despacio, por favor*
I don't understand - *No comprendo*
What did you say? - *¿Cómo dice?*
Repeat, please - *Repita, por favor*
Could you spell it? - *¿Podría usted deletrearlo?*
Please write it down - *Por favor, escríbalo*
Excuse me - *Perdóneme*
May I - *Con permiso*
I'm sorry - *Lo siento*
What time is it? - *¿Qué hora es?*
It is one o'clock - *Es la una*
It is ten thirty - *Son las diez y media*
I'm in a hurry - *Tengo prisa*
Where? - *¿Dónde?*
How? - *¿Cómo?*
When? - *¿Cuándo?*
What? - *¿Qué?*
Why? - *¿Por qué?*
Who? - *¿Quién?*
Where is? - *¿Dónde está?*
How far? - *¿A qué distancia?*
How long? - *¿Cuánto tiempo?*
What does this/that mean? - *¿Qué quiere decir esto/eso?*

How much does it cost? - *¿Cuánto cuesta?*
I don't want to spend more than... - *No quiero gastar más de...*
Very expensive - *Muy caro*
Can you help me? - *¿Puede usted ayudarme?*
Very kind of you - *Muy amable*

NUMBERS

1 - *uno*	5 - *cinco*	9 - *nueve*
2 - *dos*	6 - *seis*	10 - *diez*
3 - *tres*	7 - *siete*	100 - *cien*
4 - *cuatro*	8 - *ocho*	200 - *doscientos*

HOTEL PHRASES

Can you recommend a hotel? - *¿Puede recomendarme
    un hotel?*
Can you recommend another hotel? - *¿Puede recomendarme
    otro hotel?*
I need a single room - *Necesito un cuarto sencillo*
    a double room - *un cuarto doble*
Is there air-conditioning? - *¿Hay aire acondicionado?*
    parking? - *estacionamento?*
    running water? - *agua corriente?*
    hot water? - *agua caliente?*
    a private toilet? - *servicios particulares?*

RESTAURANT PHRASES

Breakfast - *Desayuno*
Lunch - *Almuerzo*
Dinner - *Comida*
Supper - *Cena*
I'm hungry - *Tengo hambre*
    thirsty - *sed*
Are there any restaurants near here? -
    ¿Hay algunos restaurantes cerca de aquí?
May I have a menu, please? - *¿Puedo ver la carta, por favor*
What do you recommend? - *¿Qué me aconseja?*
I'd like... - *Quisiera...*
    eggs - *huevos*
    fish - *pescado*
    meat - *carne*
    chicken - *pollo*

I'd like more - *Quisiera más*
The check, please - *La cuenta, por favor*

BANKING PHRASES

Where is the bank? - *¿Dónde está el banco?*
When does the bank open? - *¿A qué hora abren el banco?*
  close? - *cierran?*
Open - *Abierto*
Closed - *Cerrado*
Where's the currency exchange office? -
  ¿Dónde está la oficina de cambio?
re can I cash a traveler's check? -
  ¿Dónde puedo cobrar un cheque de viajero?
I'd like to cash a traveler's check -
  ¿Quiero cobrar un cheque de viajero
I lost my traveler's checks - *He perdido mis cheques de
  viajeros*

GETTING AROUND

What is the address? - *¿Qué es la dirección?*
Where is the main square? - *¿Dónde está el zócalo?*
  a telephone? - *un teléfono?*
  the bus stop? - *la parada de autobús?*
  the train station? - *el estación de ferrocarril?*
  the airport? - *el aeropuerto?*
Where is the bathroom? - *¿Dónde están los servicios?*
How far is it to...? - *¿Qué distancia hay hasta...?*
Can you tell me the way to...? - *¿Puede indicarme el camino a...?*
How do I get to...? - *¿Cómo puede ir a...?*
Can you show me on the map? - *¿Puede enseñarme en el mapa?*
Where's this? - *¿Dónde está esto?*
Go straight ahead - *Siga derecho*
Turn to the right - *Vuelta a la derecha*
  to the left - *a la izquierda*
Where does this road lead? - *¿A dónde conduce esta camino?*
Highway - *Carretera*
Road - *Camino*
Street - *Calle*
Avenue - *Avenida*
Corner - *Esquina*

Block - *Cuadra*
Left side - *Lado izquierdo*
Right side - *Lado derecho*
North - *Norte*
South - *Sur*
East - *Este*
West - *Oeste*

AT THE BEACH

Where is the beach? - *¿Dónde está la playa?*
Is it safe for swimming? - *¿Se puede nadar sin peligro?*
Are there dangerous currents? - *¿Hay alguna corriente peligrosa?*
I'd like to hire a boat - *Quiero alquilar una lancha*
Can we camp here? - *¿Podemos acampar aquí?*
Is that road in good condition? - *¿Está en buen estado aquel camino?*

PHRASES FOR CAR CARE

Where is the nearest gas station? - *¿Dónde está la gasolinera más cercana?*
I need a mechanic - *Necesito un mecánico*
   a tow truck - *una grúa*
I have run out of gas - *Se me acabo la gasolina*
Fill up the gas tank - *Llene el tanque de gasolina*
   the radiator - *el radiador*
Give me five liters - *Deme cinco litros*
Check the oil - *Vea el aceite*
   the tires - *las llantas*
Please tune the engine - *Por favor, deponer al punto el motor*

PHRASES FOR EMERGENCIES

Help! - *¡Socorro!*
Call the police - *Llame a la policía*
Get a doctor - *Llame a un doctor*
I'm ill - *Estoy enfermo(a)*
My child is ill - *Mi niño(a) está enfermo(a)*
Danger - *Peligro*
Fire - *Fuego*
Look out! - *¡Cuidado!*
My wallet has been stolen - *Me han rebado mi cartera*
Leave me alone, please - *Déjeme tranquilo(a), por favor*

The staples of Mexican cooking have always been corn and beans, traditionally used to make tortillas and *frijoles* (mashed beans). To pick up the flavor, Mexicans season dishes with chilies in 80 varieties, from the hot *jalapeño* to the fiery *habañero*. From these come *salsa picante* (hot sauce), placed on every table next to the salt and pepper shakers and liberally used on nearly every standard dish. Tomatoes also play a big part in garnishings and sauces.

While Tex-Mex chile con carne does not exist as such in Mexico and few places serve burritos, there are *sincronizadas* (flat ham and cheese in a soft tortilla), *sopes* (soft corn shells filled with ham, beans, cheese and lettuce), *chiles rellenos* (stuffed mild chili peppers), *caldos* (thick broth), *menudo* (tripe), *carne asada* (broiled beef), *guacamole* (creamed avocado), *huevos rancheros* (fried eggs soaked in hot sauce on a tortilla), *huevos a la Mexicana* (eggs scrambled with chilies and tomatoes), *chilaquiles* (tortilla strips in cream) and hosts of other delicious classics of Mexican cookery.

Wine is not Mexico's strong point, though a decent vintage, Santo Tomás, is bottled in northern Baja. Every region in Mexico, however, produces *cerveza* (beer), in *clara* (light) and *obscura* (dark) brews, among the world's best.

Meals close with coffee. Ask for *café de olla* for brewed coffee, *café con leche* for hot milk with coffee, and *café con crema* for coffee with cream.

Mexico's customary eating style focuses on hearty meals by day and light repasts at night. *Desayuno* (breakfast) is early and substantial (most hotels stop serving breakfast by 11 a.m.). *Almuerzo* or *la comida* (lunch) starts at 2 p.m. and, depending on the spread, may go on through siesta; it is traditionally the biggest meal of the day. *Cena* (dinner) often doesn't begin until 9 p.m. or later.

For a closer look at some spirited Mexican specialties, see "Exotic Taste Treats" in this chapter.

The Arts

RELIGION AND ARCHITECTURE

Until this century, art and religion were inextricably intertwined in Mexico. Priest-kings ruled the ancient tribes; gods of rain and war were worshipped; and the great Quetzalcoatl (called Kukulkán by the Mayas) was revered as god of the arts, agriculture and science. Obeisance was paid to these gods in human sacrifices, and they were glorified in bas-reliefs and murals.

Early Olmec society revered its jaguar-gods by sculpting giant heads with jaguar mouths. Teotihuacán, the massive ceremonial center outside

Mexico City, remains a tribute to the Indians' gift for monumental architecture. The Mayas built over 100 ceremonial centers in the Yucatán and farther south. Beautiful realistic figurines from the island of Jaina off Campeche accompanied the dead to their graves. Of the Maya's fine murals, the best remain at Bonampak.

Unfortunately, Spanish destruction of the Aztec empire was so thorough that we can only guess at Aztec talents. Their worship revolved around massive, somber pyramids caked in sacrificial blood. At each conquest, they assimilated gods of the conquered tribe into their own pantheon.

From the rubble of the Aztec empire, the Spanish erected grand monuments to Catholicism. In these churches, monasteries and missions, a unique, ultrabaroque Mexican architecture emerged throughout the colonial era, combining Romanesque, Renaissance, Gothic and Islamic elements. The *indígenas,* who converted to Christianity under pain of death, supplied the manpower to build these castles to the Christian God.

In 1531, an Indian peasant named Juan Diego reported a miraculous appearance by the brown-skinned Virgin of Guadalupe. He claimed to have seen her just at the temple site of the Aztec goddess Tonantzín. A shrine was built and this mestizo virgin became the patroness of Mexico. Out of respect for the virgin and from their association of suffering with redemption, Indians crawl for miles to visit her basilica.

By the 18th century, Mexican church facades, altars and ceilings were erupting with foliage, blossoms, angels and rosettes in the so-called Churrigueresque style. A stable period under Porfirio Díaz brought forth many grandiose public buildings imitating European designs. Today's architecture tends to mirror styles in vogue north of the border and abroad.

THE FINE ARTS

The most innovative creative art form since the revolution has been Mexico's great murals.

In pre-Hispanic times, murals decorated many religious buildings. The tradition faded after independence, but in the 1920s the post-revolutionary government began commissioning murals for public buildings in hopes of creating a new sense of national identity. Their program succeeded on a grand scale.

Diego Rivera, David Siqueiros and Clemente Orozco splashed Mexican edifices with vehement political statements about the Spanish conquest, rebellion, land reform and war, capturing the restless spirit of Mexico. Their fiery colors, bold design and outspoken revolutionary flair have inspired critics to acclaim Mexican murals the best in the world. Rufino Tamayo and Juan O'Gorman are among the modern masters who have kept the mural tradition alive.

(Text continued on page 56.)

Exotic Taste Treats

A sauce with 30 ingredients, from chilies to chocolate? Skulls made from sugar? A liquor with a worm in the bottle? These and many other unusual palate pleasers await you in Mexico. Mexican cuisine rarely does things by halves, and each part of the country kicks in its own concoctions to bolster the Latin passion for drama—even at the dinner table.

The choco-chili *mole* sauce, concocted by the Aztecs and enhanced by a 16th-century Spanish nun in Puebla, is poured over turkey, in a dish entitled *mole poblano* or *mole de pavo*—a culinary tour de force which may take days to prepare. Sugar skulls and bread bones are made all over Mexico to celebrate the Day of the Dead (*Día de los Muertos*) in early November. The worm-in-the-bottle *mezcal*, brewed in Oaxaca from the maguey cactus, proves its potency with the first shot.

Along the coast, succulent fish recipes abound. Believing much seafood to be an aphrodisiac—particularly oysters, clams, *cuatate* (lagoon catfish), turtle (and turtle blood)—Mexicans prepare it breaded, broiled, barbequed, fried and *al diablo* (with hot sauce). From Veracruz comes *huachinango a la Veracruzana*, one of the all-time great fish dishes: red snapper smothered in tomatoes, onions, olives and capers. *Pan de cazón*, from Campeche, blends baby shark with layers of spicy tortillas. *Ceviche* is Acapulco's own sushi salad: raw white fish soaked in lime juice with diced onions, chili, seasonings and tomatoes.

Mexicans are equally enthusiastic carnivores, skillful at bringing out the best in meat. *Carne a la tampiqueño*, from Tampico, combines thin broiled beef with beans, cheese, guacamole and chilies: a good all-round Mexican standard. *Pozole*, originating in Jalisco, pulls together a sumptuous garden in a thick corn and pork stew, with onion, oregano, avocado and lettuce. *Salpicón de venado* features cold shredded venison tossed with radish, cilantro and orange juice—a modest introduction to the scintillating world of Maya-based Yucatán cooking.

In Yucatán, your taste buds will tingle to the tang of *sopa de lima* (chicken and lime broth), *cochinita pibil* or *pollo pibil* (pork or chicken slathered in tomatoes and zingy *achiote* paste, cooked in a banana leaf) and *huevos motuleños* (fried eggs heaped with tomato sauce, ham, onions, peas and a fried banana).

To conclude your feast, you may want an after-dinner drink. Every region in Mexico features a unique cocktail or liquor: *Xtabentum*, an anise-flavored liqueur made from Yucatán flowers and honey; *Damiana*, a reputedly aphrodisiac herb liquor made in Sinaloa and Baja; *Rompope*, a rum-spiced egg-nog-type drink, concocted in Michoacán and Guerrero; *Kahlua*, the famous coffee liqueur first made in Guadalajara; and *pulque*, the original Aztec cactus drink, yeasty and milky, made in central Mexico. Tequila (order *anejo*, or aged, if you drink it straight) is universal.

Salud and *buen provecho!*

CRAFTS AND FOLK ART

Some two million people in Mexico earn their living creating folk art. The range of crafts in every medium, from glass to lacquerware, is staggering. Some objects are religious, others simply decorative, while many are utilitarian. The majority of these collectibles—pottery, blankets, baskets, hammocks—sprang from a need, then became an art form. Different villages and areas produce their own particular specialties. All the big resorts have complete selections of handicrafts, including government-run shops with fixed prices called FONART, although the prices are generally lowest in the place where the item originated.

MUSIC AND DANCE

If you've always pictured Mexico with music pouring from every balcony and full-skirted dancers sashaying in every square, you won't be disappointed when you come here. Guitar-strumming minstrels and foot-stomping dances are as much at home in Mexico as tortillas and toreadors. From influences as disparate as Afro-Caribbean rhythms, Germanic polkas, Spanish fandangos and Aztec chants, a fantastic mix of sounds and fancy footwork has emerged.

In pre-Hispanic times, narrative songs dedicated to the gods were accompanied by the percussive *huehuetl* and *teponaztli*, types of hollowed logs, along with rattles, flutes, conch shells and bones. Music and dance were such an important part of religious rituals that men were employed to serve as temple musicians. Through the language of music, the Indians became absorbed into the Catholic Church, learning chants, building organs and composing songs for the mass.

Spanish galleons brought string music from abroad, and the Gulf Coast imported rhythms from the Mediterranean, Arabia, Africa and the Caribbean. The melting pot bubbled (and still does) with danceable beats like the tango, rumba, bolero and *danzón*. Perhaps the best-known tropical sounds to surface from this blend are the breezy Cuban tunes played on the marimba, a type of large xylophone.

Mariachi music, a symbol for the spirit of Mexico, took its name from the French word for marriage (*mariage*), describing musicians who played at weddings. Some say the name dates to 1867, when the French-appointed Emperor Maximilian was overthrown by Benito Juárez. Initially plainly dressed *campesinos* with guitars, the mariachis began to jazz up their acts with elaborate *charro* outfits and trumpets in the 1920s. Today, mariachis can be found in every resort along the coast—the best in the state of Jalisco—and are hired by lovesick swains to serenade their *novias* (sweethearts) in the wee morning hours.

Another well-loved form of music is the *corrido*, derived from Spanish chivalric ballads. The storytelling *corridos* sing of heroes and villains, rivalries and heartbreaks, politics and revolution. More than songs, *corridos* were once a news medium in an era without radio or television, often relating important events and gossip. During the revolution from 1910 to 1920, the *corrido* glorified the exploits of Pancho Villa.

In the mid-19th century, the far north adopted accordions for country-and-western *norteña* music, still popular along the border today. Old World waltzes, mazurkas and polkas were transformed into exotic village folk dances. The bolero, or romantic ballad, became the basis for most popular songs you now hear on Mexican radio, dripping with emotion, nostalgia and intense melancholy.

Tropical music, a loose term for anything with a Caribbean accent, is the happiest music in Mexico. Always upbeat and snappy, celebrating life's little pleasures and making light of its rude twists, these tunes sport the irresistible beat of bongos, rattles, marimbas and guitars.

Like the music, Mexican folkloric dances had their roots in pagan Indian celebrations, such as dances to the gods of light and darkness. After the conquest, these dances were integrated into Catholic ritual, so that a dance to the Aztec goddess Tonantzín became one honoring the Virgin of Guadalupe. Folk dancing, like the music it accompanies, developed specific styles in each region. You have only to happen upon a fiesta to see colorful costumes, and traditional choreographic displays.

Some of the better known dances are the classic *jarabe tapatio* (hat dance) of Guadalajara, the graceful *huapango* and sassy *bamba* of Veracruz, the more sedate *jarana* of Yucatán (in which dancers perform with bottles of beer on their heads), the *baile venado* (deer dance) done by the northwest Yaqui Indians to prepare for the hunt, the comical *baile viejito* (dance of the little old men) from Michoacán, and the spectacular flying dance of *Los Voladores* (The Fliers) of Papantla, who swing from a tall pole and look like flying birds. If you have a chance to attend a *ballet folklórico* presentation, you'll be mesmerized by a flamboyant cross section of Mexico's finest regional dances, each unique in costumes, music and personality.

LITERATURE

Like much Latin American writing, Mexican literature is often richly surreal, earthy and tough, full of passion, folklore and pain. Unfortunately, translations are limited, but a good place to begin is with well-known modern authors like Carlos Fuentes, Octavio Paz and Juan Rulfo, whose works are available in English.

Mexico's literary heritage is older than any in North America—the first book ever printed in the Western Hemisphere was published here in 1539. Although most written records and painted books (codices) of the early *indígenas* were destroyed by the Spanish conquistadors, the Mayas created their great *Popul Vuh* (*Book of the Counsel*) and their *Books of Chilam*

Balam (about religion, medicine, astrology and history) in 1554, after the conquest; these still exist today.

The most outstanding literature produced during colonial times came from the pen of Latin America's greatest colonial poet, Sor Juana Inés de la Cruz. This 17th-century Mexican nun and early feminist devoted her life to intellectual pursuits.

Partly because Spanish edicts forbade the export of novels to its distant colony, Mexicans were largely unaware of this literary form and no novels were written in Mexico until 1816, when *El Periquillo Sarmiento (The Itching Parrot)*, by Joaquín Fernández de Lizardi, was published.

From the mid-19th century to the start of the Mexican Revolution, there was an explosion of political poetry. But not until the turbulent revolution of 1910 did Mexican literature really flower. Novels like Mariano Azuela's *Los de Abajo (The Underdogs)* and Martín Luis Guzmán's *La Sombra del Caudillo (The Shadow of the Dictator)* captured peasant hardships and the ruthless ways of dictators and politicos during the revolution.

Later, Octavio Paz and Juan Rulfo produced powerful works that explored the solitude of the Mexican psyche. Carlos Fuentes, Mexico's greatest living novelist, began turning out books that penetrated modern Mexican life.

At the same time, scores of foreigners fascinated with Mexico have written essays, stories or novels set south of the border: D.H. Lawrence, Aldous Huxley, Ray Bradbury, Graham Greene, Jack Kerouac, Oscar Lewis, Jack London, Malcolm Lowry, John Steinbeck, Tennessee Williams and the mysterious B. Traven, to name a few.

Spectator Sports

BULLFIGHTS

The bullfight (*corrida de toros*), sometimes interpreted by foreigners as an act of cruelty to animals, is not for everyone. Yet it is one of the great national spectacles of Mexico, and better than any other sport it captures the bravado, passion, color and pomp of the country.

Imported from Spain a few years after Cortés conquered Mexico, the bullfight today can be seen in every major town. Many small ones have bullrings (*plazas de toros)* as well. Along the Mexican coastline, bullfight season runs from November through March, although some resorts, like Acapulco, stage fights year round. During the high season, great matadors from both Mexico and Spain fight the most challenging bulls (*toros bravos*). During the low season, novices (*novilleros*) try their hand in the ring. The best place to watch from is the shady side of the stands, so ask for tickets in *la sombra* (the shade).

Generally, each *corrida* features six bulls and three matadors. The ceremony begins with the *desfile*, the parade of matadors, *bandarilleros* (lancers on foot), *picadors* (lancers on horseback), various assistants and a team of mules to drag the dead bull away. After these players enter the ring and take their places, the bullfight continues in three acts, called *tercios* (thirds).

Those who enjoy bullfights see them as great pageantry, a theatrical presentation with a life-and-death struggle. The bulls, bred on special farms to fight, are seen as opponents equal to the matadors in skill. A fierce bull is applauded by Mexicans but almost never leaves the ring alive.

What does the bullfight mean? Some interpret it as a ritual sacrifice, or a symbolic battle between man and nature, even a flirtation between man and woman (in which the matador, with his decorative costume and silken cape, plays a female role). Perhaps more than anything, as one authority described it, the bullfight is a rendezvous with death, for both man and bull, and an attempt to outwit it.

SOCCER

With an obsession dating back to the pre-Hispanic days when losers of ritual ball games lost their heads, the Mexicans take soccer (called *futbol*) very seriously. Soccer stars, along with champion bullfighters and balladeers, are Mexico's most popular heroes. Children play soccer everywhere and professional games are held in stadiums all over the country. Check with a Mexican consulate or at the tourist office in any given Mexican town for the nearest pro soccer games.

CHARREADAS (RODEOS)

Sometimes considered the only indigenous national sport, *charreadas* are spectacular rodeos performed by *charros*, or Mexican cowboys. The custom originated at big haciendas in northern Mexico, where mounted *rancheros* developed fancy riding, roping and herding tricks with the cattle. At today's *charreada*, costumed horsemen and horsewomen enter the *lienzo charro* (rodeo ring) to present their acts to the festive backdrop of mariachi music and folk dancing. *Charreadas* are held all year round, usually on Sundays.

JAI ALAI

Featured in Tijuana and Mexico City, jai alai or *frontón* (which means "the merry fiesta") originated in the Basque provinces of Spain over two hundred years ago and has changed very little since then. Jai alai resembles an extremely fast-paced racquetball game, using a cupped basket. Balls are pitched at white-hot speed against a wall, caught in the basket-glove and hurled back at the wall. Parimutuel betting adds to the thrill and excitement.

BASEBALL

Baseball (*béisbol*) has many fans all over Mexico and two outstanding professional leagues. The season runs from March to September.

CHAPTER FOUR
Baja Norte

Baja lovers will tell you the peninsula is somehow different—friendlier, safer, slower, *más tranquilo*. Some call it the forgotten piece of Mexico. Without question, Baja California is one of the last great frontiers for travelers.

This narrow land mass juts out for over 800 arid, sparsely settled miles—the world's longest peninsula, bathed by the thunderous waves of the Pacific to the west and the crystalline Sea of Cortez (or Gulf of California) to the east. Across this sea steam overnight ferries connecting southern Baja with mainland Mexico, about 100 miles—seemingly worlds—away.

The peninsula is divided into northern and southern states, Baja Norte and Baja Sur, which share a similar geography and climate. Baja's southernmost tip lies in the Tropic of Cancer and offers sultry temperatures in the summer. This area is subject to sudden tropical storms called *chubascos*, striking from August to October with winds of up to 150 miles per hour. More often, gentle sea breezes soften the dry desert heat and keep the nights balmy. Winters can be cool up north, but rainfall on the peninsula is rare.

Desert terrain dominates the landscape—pale, flat expanses of dust and sand, ridged with interior mountain ranges whose 10,000-foot peaks swirl with snow, while the coast stays dry and barren. Aside from its vineyard-rich northern valleys, much of Baja strikes the eye as a moonscape, sweepingly empty and clean, grand and solitary.

Yet that solitude stirs with subtle life: birds, reptiles, flowering cactus, coyotes, crabs and secretive clams, not to mention 800 species of fish in its waters. So many stars are visible in its skies that the government has built an observatory in the northern San Pedro Mártir mountains to take advantage of Baja's middle-of-nowhere clarity. And the desert has an added boon for bug-haters: with minimal vegetation and water, Baja doesn't breed those buzzing little Draculas that plague much of the tropics.

This wilderness draws droves of nature lovers and outdoors people. They drive their dune buggies in the Baja 1000, the world's premier cross-country off-road race. They watch gray whales that migrate from the icy Bering Strait each winter to bear their young in warm Baja lagoons. They explore the peninsula's steamy sands for the ruins of California's oldest Spanish missions and the southern Sierras for cave paintings of mysterious origin. They come because Baja still has the feel of the American Southwest of the late 1800s, when cowboys roamed the range.

As rugged as it remains, Baja has certainly entered the 20th century. The modern horse is the pickup truck, a macho status symbol, the more chrome overhead road lights the better. Until recently, driving the peninsula's lonesome trails was for hardened adventurers only. Today, anyone can drive from one end of Baja to the other along the Transpeninsular Highway. This thousand-mile asphalt ribbon, completed in 1973, has opened the wilds to a steady flow of RVs and jeeps jammed with surfboards.

With the traffic have come the amenities, like the chic hotels packing the coast around Cabo San Lucas. But Baja fans swear the ultimate way to experience this area is by camping out, with a cactus-husk bonfire for cooking and warmth. Mazes of tortured back roads (many suitable only for 4-wheel drive) lead to nearly limitless virgin beaches ideal for camping. As for scare tales of Baja's bandidos, scorpions and menacing wilderness, I must confess I feel safer in Baja than in San Francisco. Baja dwellers are among Mexico's most hospitable people, drawn closer by their struggle against the elements and a history of hardships.

The peninsula's earliest inhabitants left few traces of their civilization aside from scattered, remote cave paintings. The three ruling tribes when the Spanish arrived in the 16th century were the southern Pericues and Guaycuras and the northern Cochimies—polygamous hunters and fishermen with no written language. Less than 500 pure-blooded descendants of these Indians survive today in northern Baja. Like most Mexicans, Baja's approximately three million inhabitants (concentrated in the north) are *mestizos*, people of mixed indigenous and Spanish blood, whose culture reflects many foreign influences.

Legends of opulence lured the first colonizers to Baja. A Spanish novel called *The Adventures of Esplandián*, popular in the early 1500s, described an idyllic Pacific isle where a Queen Calafia, decked out in pearls and gold, ruled a race of beautiful Amazons. Those tales intrigued Hernán Cortés, conqueror of mainland Mexico. In 1535 he sailed to what is now La Paz and founded a small colony there. As history tells it, all of California came to be named for the mythical island he sought. But Baja proved too unforgiving and dry for greedy Cortés. Two years of failure sent him hightailing back to the mainland.

He was succeeded by a string of explorers who struggled to tame the arid land. Among them were English and Dutch pirates who lurked in the peninsula's southern coves and preyed upon treasure-laden galleons bound for Acapulco. In an indirect way, their looting inspired the settling of Baja.

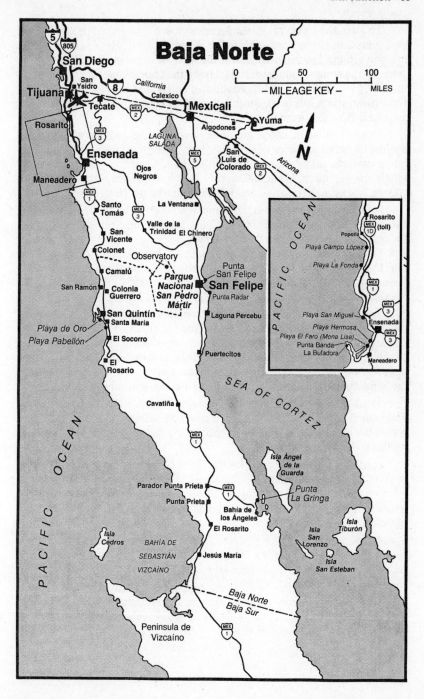

Baja Norte

– MILEAGE KEY –

0   50   100   MILES

San Diego
5
805
San Ysidro
California
Tijuana
8
Calexico
Tecate
Mexicali
2
Yuma
Rosarito
Algodones
3
LAGUNA
SALADA
San Luis de
Colorado
5
Arizona
Ensenada
Ojos
Negros
2
Maneadero
Santo
Tomás
1
La Ventana
San
Vicente
3
Valle de la
Trinidad
El Chinero
Colonet
Observatory
Camalú
Parque
Nacional
San Pedro
Mártir
Punta
San Felipe
San Ramón
Colonia
Guerrero
San Felipe
Punta Radar
San Quintín
Santa María
Laguna Percebu
Playa de Oro
Playa Pabellón
El Socorro
El
Rosario
Puertecitos
SEA OF CORTEZ
Cavatiña
1
Isla Ángel
de la
Guarda
Punta
La Gringa
Parador Punta Prieta
1
Punta Prieta
Bahía de
los Ángeles
Isla
Tiburón
El Rosarito
Isla
San
Lorenzo
Isla
Cedros
BAHÍA DE
SEBASTIÁN
VIZCAÍNO
Jesús María
Isla
San Esteban
PACIFIC OCEAN
Baja Norte
Baja Sur
Peninsula de
Vizcaíno
1

PACIFIC OCEAN

Rosarito
1D
(toll)
Popotla
Playa Campo López
Playa La Fonda
1
3
Playa San Miguel
Ensenada
Playa Hermosa
Playa El Faro (Mona Lisa)
3
Punta Banda
La Bufadora
Maneadero

To stem the pirate raids, the Spanish crown established protective settlements on the Baja coast. This led to the founding of Baja's first Catholic mission around Loreto in 1697. For the next 70 years the Jesuits built missions up the spine of southern Baja, laying the cornerstones for whole communities with schools, crude roads and cultivated land. Franciscan and Dominican friars followed, forging a chain of over 30 missions that linked Baja and Alta California.

Most of those missions are gone now, like the Indians who rebelled against the strict morality of Christianity even as they succumbed to devastating diseases introduced by Spanish soldiers. Over the years many other outsiders—English, French, Chinese, Dutch, Germans, Japanese and, of course, *norteamericanos*—have left their marks on Baja.

As a result of the Mexican-American war of 1846, with battles at Mulegé, La Paz and San José del Cabo, the United States absorbed the former Mexican territories that are now California, Arizona, New Mexico and Texas, though Baja remained Mexican. The discovery of gold in the late 1800s brought a brief era of prosperity to the northern peninsula, followed by increasing cultivation of its valleys. In 1952, Baja Norte earned Mexican statehood. Southern Baja followed in 1974.

Today, Baja's main industry is tourism. Its coastline is a growing retirement playground for older Americans. Condos are mushrooming and gringos are snapping up real estate packages down south. Dollars are almost as widely used as pesos. Some people jokingly wonder if Baja will be the next star on the American flag. Baja lovers only pray the peninsula keeps the wild streak that has always been its richest natural resource.

Most travelers enter Baja at Tijuana, Mexico's largest border town, nicknamed "the world's most visited city." More than 95,000 people pour across the border daily, principally to shop the downtown markets that have replaced the red-light strip.

Northern Baja's first good Pacific Coast beaches are at the homely little town of Rosarito, just south of Tijuana. About 60 miles down lies Ensenada, a brawny port city and growing resort on Bahía de Todos Santos. Though short on fabulous beaches, the town abounds in excellent seafood and nightlife.

Across a lonely stretch of desert, the small fishing resort of San Felipe on the Sea of Cortez claims 20 miles of northern Baja's best dunes and beaches, aswarm with Mad Max-style dune buggies.

Back on the Pacific, well south of Ensenada, the drab town of San Quintín is a minor mecca for quail hunters and fishermen. About 200 miles east on the Sea of Cortez, rustic Bahía de los Ángeles drowses on a neon-blue bay afloat with jagged islands where sportfishing is king.

Easy Living
Transportation

ARRIVAL

BY CAR

You may cross the border into Baja at any of six points: Tijuana (near San Diego, California); Otay Mesa (a new crossing near the Tijuana Airport); Tecate; Mexicali (near Calexico, California); Algodones; and San Luis (near Yuma, Arizona). The most heavily used border crossing is at Tijuana, especially in the late afternoons when day-trippers are returning to the States after a shopping spree. Try the Otay Mesa crossing instead, and leave before noon to avoid a long line-up here, too. The least-used, quickest border crossing is at Algodones farther east.

The **Transpeninsular Highway** (Mexico Highway 1, officially named Carretera Transpeninsular Benito Juárez) runs for over 1,000 miles from Tijuana to the tip of the peninsula at Cabo San Lucas. It is well marked and generally in very good condition, although shoulders are narrow or non-existent. Gas is widely available, but unleaded (*extra*) becomes harder to find as you head south. Sudden rainstorms (during winter months up north) can cause washouts in arroyos marked by *vado* (dip) signs and can make travel risky on unpaved side roads. Check with the American Automobile Association (AAA) for timely road reports on Baja.

The best part of the Transpeninsular Highway is the new 68-mile four-lane toll (*cuota*) road—**Mexico 1-D**—between Tijuana and Ensenada; it's smooth, fast and well traveled. The old Tijuana–Ensenada free (*libre*) road—**Mexico 1**—meanders past scenic coastal communities. The Transpeninsular Highway connects all towns in this chapter except San Felipe, for which you use **Mexico 3** (proceeding 130 miles southeast from Ensenada to join southbound **Mexico 5**).

BY AIR

The busiest commercial airport in Baja Norte is Tijuana's bustling Aeropuerto Internacional Abelardo L. Rodríguez, six miles east of the downtown area near the U.S. border.

Three airlines currently serve **Tijuana**: Aeroméxico, Mexicana and Aero California.

Taxis go from the airport to downtown Tijuana and nearby destinations. There's also daily van service to Ensenada and back.

BY BUS

The most exciting way to see Baja is overland, whether by car or bus. You can enter Mexico via **Greyhound Bus** (619-239-9171) and continue south all the way down the peninsula aboard various inexpensive Mexican buses. All major destinations in this section are reachable by bus except

Bahía de los Ángeles. Some Baja buses have no central station in a town but simply stop on the highway to let off or pick up passengers.

Among the better Baja bus lines are **Tres Estrellas de Oro** (serving Tijuana, Ensenada, San Quintín), **Transportes Norte de Sonora** (serving San Felipe only) and **Transportes de Baja California** (serving Tijuana and Ensenada).

Northern Baja bus depots and information numbers are as follows: **Tijuana,** Central de Autobuses de Tijuana (Avenida Río del Mar en route from town to the airport, 86-90-60); **Ensenada** depot (Calle 11a and Avenida Riveroll, 8-66-77); **San Felipe** depot (Calle Zihuatanejo across from El Puerto Bar); **San Quintín,** two stops—one on Transpeninsular Highway at Colonia Lázaro Cárdenas and one at Café Don Lupe.

An inexpensive and entertaining way to reach the Mexican border is via the **San Diego Trolley** (619-233-3004), affectionately called the "Tijuana Trolley," which leaves from downtown San Diego at regular intervals. Be prepared to walk or taxi into downtown Tijuana from the border.

Also consider the **Green Tortoise** (Box 24459, San Francisco, CA 94124; 415-821-0803), a New Age company with a fleet of funky buses. Each is equipped with sleeping platforms allowing travelers to rest as they cross the country. The buses stop at interesting sightseeing points en route. The Green Tortoise, an endangered species from the '60s, travels to and from Baja with service to mainland Mexico. Schedules are flexible; one-week to three-week and longer round-trips are available.

BY BOAT

Two cruise lines make frequent runs to Ensenada—**Admiral Cruises** (800-327-0271) and **Norwegian Cruise Lines** (800-327-7030).

CAR RENTALS

Cars can be rented in Tijuana and Ensenada—your last chance for wheels until you get as far south as Loreto. The Tijuana airport has a line-up of rental booths, including **Hertz** (83-20-80), **Avis** (83-23-10), **Amca** (83-16-44), **Budget** (83-29-05), **National** (82-44-33) and **Dollar** (83-18-61). In Ensenada, try **Hertz** (8-21-01), **Ensenada** (8-18-96) and **Scorpio** (8-32-85).

BICYCLING AND MOTORBIKING

Cycling around Ensenada or down the Tijuana–Ensenada free road can be fun. Both bike and motorbike rentals can be arranged at **Tourist Information** (Avenida López Mateos 1306, Ensenada; 6-37-18).

PUBLIC TRANSPORTATION

In Tijuana, inexpensive buses cruise the main streets, such as Avenida Constitución and Avenida Revolución. Taxis are also plentiful and reasonable.

City buses are unreliable in Ensenada. You're better off taking taxis.

Hotels

TIJUANA HOTELS

Coincidental with the city's rapid growth and changing face, Tijuana's hotel industry is undergoing a cataclysmic shift. Big-name chains such as Raddison and Fiesta Americana have arrived on the scene, the latter with a 32-story tower, larger and more extravagant than all but a few properties in neighboring San Diego. Liveable hotels in the budget and moderate price range, however, remain scarce.

The best-located downtown hotel is the landmark **Hotel Caesar** (Avenida Revolución and Calle 5a; 85-16-66), with a famous restaurant that is reportedly the birthplace of the Caesar salad. Its overpriced rates buy you a bed with a velveteen spread in one of 75 musty, carpeted rooms. Opened in the 1950s, the hotel seems to flaunt its age with campy plastic rose bouquets and gaudy gold-leaf mirrors. Moderate.

Jai Alai fans will love **La Villa de Zaragoza Hotel** (Avenida Madero 1120; 85-18-32), a 42-room courtyard hotel directly behind the Frontón Palacio. Tile and stucco, clean and simple—a Mexican variation on Motel 6. Rooms are carpeted, air-conditioned and have phones and television. There is a small patio bar and restaurant. Moderate.

Symbolic of the "new" Tijuana, the 110-room **El Conquistado** (Boulevard Agua Caliente 1777; 86-20-10) will surprise you with its handsome colonial elegance and modern conveniences. Cobbled patios, handpainted tiles, lush plantings and custom-furnished suites suggest a private hacienda. Ideally located, it offers a pool, jacuzzi, restaurant, bar and disco. Moderate to deluxe.

The towering 422-room **Fiesta Americana** (Boulevard Agua Caliente 4500; 81-70-00, reservations: 800-343-7825), deserves mention as Tijuana's premier deluxe hotel. Modern to the hilt and offering all the amenities you'd expect in any big hotel, the 32-story Fiesta Americana can swaddle you in a fancy suite; feed you in four different restaurants; slake your thirst in its three bars; dance your legs off in its showy disco; take your *dinero* in a galaxy of exclusive shops; exercise your triceps in its gym; and satisfy your late-night craving for cheesecake with its 24-hour room service. Deluxe.

ROSARITO TO ENSENADA HOTELS

The old **Rosarito Beach Hotel** (Boulevard Benito Juárez, Km. 27.5, Rosarito; 2-11-06), a rambling villa-style inn, overlooks the Pacific at the southern end of Rosarito. Built in the glamorous 1920s, this 155-room hacienda attracted guests such as King Farouk, Orson Welles and Lana Turner. A Baja landmark, it is the peninsula's oldest resort hotel still in operation and a wonderful repository of Mexican art and craftsmanship. Dominating the grand old lobby with its massive arches and decorative tile are the dramatic scenes of Mexican muralist Matías Santoyo. Old rooms have been completely upgraded with new carpet, furnishings, bathrooms, telephones and televisions. A modern condo-style wing contains 80 suites, all with kitchens and beautiful ocean views. The sprawling complex includes a huge dining room, three bars, a disco, shopping arcade, pool, tennis courts and a health club. Even with all the improvements and additions, no Baja hotel better evokes the magic of Old Mexico. Room rates remain moderate.

Speaking of magic, just one mile down the road stands the seaside **Motel Castillos del Mar** (Tijuana–Ensenada free road, Km. 29; 2-10-88), designed in the style of a Moorish castle. Although maintenance has slipped of late, the place still has loads of character—a brick exterior highlighted with bougainvillea, caged doves and a snug bar with a pot-bellied stove. The large rooms are wonderful hideaways with balconies, beamed ceilings and saloon-style doors in the showers. Suites come with fireplaces. Deluxe.

Of all the romantic lodgings along this strip, my favorite is the deceptively humble **La Fonda** (Tijuana–Ensenada free road, 37 miles south of Tijuana; from the Tijuana–Ensenada toll road take La Misión–Alisitos exit, reservation address: P.O. Box 268, San Ysidro, CA 92073). This '60s-era pink-brick inn, known for its fine hacienda restaurant, stands back from a cobblestone drive leading into a compound of red-tiled roofs and banana trees. No two bedrooms here are alike. Older rooms have hand-painted romantic proverbs over the beds, palm-thatched trim around the ceilings and pastel balconies overlooking the prettiest beach between Rosarito and Ensenada. Newer rooms resemble caves, reached via spiral stairs, with built-in hearths and all-glass showers facing the sea. There is no place else quite as personal as this in all of Baja. Moderate.

Hidden within a splashy real-estate development, **Villas By The Sea at Bajamar** (Transpeninsular Highway, Km. 77.5; 8-24-18, reservations: 800-522-1516), offers a dozen rental units. The finest one, with sweeping ocean views, is called Villa Mar, a three-bedroom, split-level palace that will comfortably accommodate three couples or a very large family. Connecting is a cozy one-room *casita* with a full kitchen that rents separately. Deluxe to ultra-deluxe.

Most stunning of all the new properties on the booming Baja Norte coast is **Las Rosas** (Transpeninsular Highway, two miles north of Ensenada; 4-43-20, reservations: 800-522-1516). Stylishly contemporary in peach and aqua tones, this lovely 32-room layout is set on a dramatic rock formation overlooking Ensenada Bay. Las Rosas makes up for the lack of beach with its spacious sun terrace, swimming pool and romantic seaside jacuzzi. Designer-furnished rooms and suites all feature bayfront balconies, air-conditioning and cable television. Just off the soaring atrium lobby are gift shops and an elegant bar and restaurant. A gym and sauna round out the facilities. Well worth the deluxe rates.

ENSENADA HOTELS

In popular Ensenada, medium-range hotels are on the rise. Low-budget hotels are harder to find. One of the best is the little 15-room **Hotel Carioca** (Transpeninsular Highway, one mile north of Ensenada). Nothing to write home about, its tidy, sparsely furnished rooms have private baths and open onto a patio and pool overlooking the bay. Catch here is that hot water is available only two hours in the morning and evening. Budget.

Creature comforts await you at the 58-room **Misión Santa Isabel** (Avenida Castillo at Avenida López Mateos; 8-36-16). This whitewashed inn, simulating an old mission, occupies a courtyard with prominent arched entrance. Inside there's parking, a key-shaped pool, restaurant and bar. The tile-brightened hallways connect two floors of attractive rooms with beamed ceilings, colonial furniture and views of the distant hills. Moderate.

A few blocks away is one of Ensenada's better hotels, the three-story **Hotel La Pinta** (Avenida Floresta and Boulevard Los Bucañeros; 6-26-01). Part of a privately owned chain, this hotel provides Mexican flavor in slick American packaging. The courtyard encircles a quiet pool, with adjoining disco and restaurant. The 52 large, comfortable rooms have televisions, air-conditioning and gold-paned windows. Moderate to deluxe.

For Las Vegas-style luxury *à la Mexicana*, check out the **El Cid** (Avenida López Mateos 993; 8-24-01), Ensenada's biggest downtown hotel. Even the simplest of its 52 rooms comes with wet bar, shag carpet, color television and mega-bed. The suites hold a boudoir ambience, with jacuzzis and acres of mirrors. Spanish-style restaurant and bar and authentic antique swords in the lobby (El Cid's very own?) all add up to a pretty flashy piece of old Andalusia. Deluxe.

SAN FELIPE HOTELS

For its size San Felipe has a wide selection of hotels.

The cheapest habitable accommodations in town are to be found at the **Chapala Motel** (Avenida Mar de Cortez 142; 7-12-40). The best rooms are upstairs facing the street, with balconies and a view of the sea. They're breezy and fresh but feel a bit bare for lack of decor. Budget.

Two blocks down on the right, you'll pay a bit more for the slightly fancier **El Capitan Motel** (Avenida Mar de Cortez 298; 7-06-57). Rooms are off the street, offering a little more peace and quiet. It has a pool, rare at the price. Budget.

Moving up the scale and down the street, the 105-room **Motel El Cortez** (Avenida Mar de Cortez, end of paved road; 7-10-55) is the best beachfront family hotel in town, with cabañas, rooms and suites. The small air-conditioned cabañas open directly onto the sand. The family-sized rooms, with high arched ceilings, are so immense you could park a dune buggy in front of the dresser. The comfy two-room suites also front the beach. There's a pool, restaurant and two bars with superb sea views. Moderate.

San Felipe's deluxe hotel is the **Castel San Felipe** (Avenida Misión de Loreto 148; 7-12-84), several miles from the downtown area. This self-contained resort, part of Mexico's cushy Castel chain, is set on lovely tropical beachfront. At your disposal are two pools, tennis courts, restaurant and bar. The 185 modern rooms in chilly blues and grays probably contain more phones and televisions among them than all the rest of town.

SAN QUINTÍN HOTELS

Unpretentious, two-story **Motel Chavez** (Transpeninsular Highway, Km. 294), with its huge, dusty parking lot and small adjacent bar, resembles a truck-stop motel. But the rooms are sparkling clean, neat and pretty, with carpets and firm double beds. Budget.

Two rough-hewn motels that cater to sportsmen are the **Old Mill Motel** (reservation address: Apartado 90, San Quintín, Baja California Norte) and **Ernesto's Resort Motel** (reservation address: 2319 South Corning, Los Angeles, CA 90034). These off-the-beaten-track motels stand side by side on Bahía de San Quintín several miles off the Transpeninsular Highway along the same labyrinthine sand road that leads to the old English cemetery and the Old Pier Restaurant. Both have rooms designed like hunters' cabins, with metal frame beds, funky kitchenettes, cement floors and kerosene lamps (electricity is limited out here). The Old Mill Motel features pieces of machinery from an old English grist mill, and the motel owners have a fascinating collection of photos from the era of that mill. Moderate.

Getting back to civilization, the comfortable 58-room **Hotel La Pinta** (off the Transpeninsular Highway about nine miles south of San Quintín and 2.5 miles west on the paved road marked with La Pinta signs) occupies a remote spot on windswept Playa Santa María like a lonely fortress. Completely equipped with café and bar, the hotel is fairly self-sufficient. The spacious rooms are colonial in decor, with balconies facing the sea. Moderate.

BAHÍA DE LOS ÁNGELES HOTELS

The **Casa Díaz** (across from the Pemex station) is the somewhat faded vestige of a proud old motel. The facility has a half-dozen charmingly ramshackle beach bungalows with a million-dollar view of the bay and another row of clean but sparsely furnished rooms adjacent to the main compound. Budget.

The more comfortable and higher-priced 50-room **Villa Vitta Hotel** (reservation address: Jimsair, 2904 Pacific Highway, San Diego, CA 92101; 619-298-4958) dominates the only street in town. This attractive hotel is truly an oasis in the wilderness, with a pool, restaurant-bar, air-conditioning and jacuzzi. The rooms are ample, some with sitting areas and kitchens and a casual grab bag of furnishings. Budget to moderate.

Restaurants

TIJUANA RESTAURANTS

Next to shopping, Tijuana's favorite tourist sport is eating. Avenida Revolución is the principal restaurant strip.

One of the premier Mexican restaurants in town and one of the oldest, the attractive **Bol Corona** (Avenida Revolución 520; 85-25-13) used to be a bowling alley. The plaque on the door says this historic spot dates back to 1934, though the interior is now every inch a glossy modern café, with padded booths and countertop coffee-bar. Though the wait can be long, the food is very tasty, from the 17 kinds of burritos to the many other Mexican specialties. Budget to moderate.

A spot not to miss, for both food and atmosphere, is **Tía Juana Tilly's** (Avenida Revolución 701; 85-60-24), next to the Jai Alai Palace. There's an awning-covered outdoor-café (open only in the afternoon) and a carpeted dining room with paraphernalia crowding the ceiling, a trademark of Carlos Anderson restaurants throughout Mexico and part of the frenetic bazaar-mood of Tijuana. The amusing menu has scores of eccentric dishes and a witty blurb comparing women to tacos and men to cucumbers. Moderate.

The clever and uniquely atmospheric **Guadalajara Grill** (Calle Diego Rivera 19 at Paseo de los Héroes; 84-20-43) is worth getting off the beaten track to discover. Pop in here in the evening and you'll think you've stepped back in time to a turn-of-the-century Mexican town plaza complete with adobe haciendas, hanging laundry and flickering gas lamps. Mariachis roam the courtyard and with the mood so set, you're bound to enjoy the routine menu of Mexican seafood, steak and chicken. If not, you can always find a spot at the 45-foot-long bar where you can toss down shooters and imagine you're watching cockfights in the simulated arena. Moderate.

Similar in concept, though more modern and less imaginative is the nearby **Hacienda El Abajeño** (Boulevard Sánchez Taboada and Avenida Antonio Caso; 84-27-91). Sprawled around a courtyard patio with a flower-draped fountain, this popular restaurant and cantina is abuzz with special happenings every night of the week: happy hour and mariachis nightly, ballet *Folkloricos* on Fridays, and an exquisite Sunday brunch. Beautifully presented dishes include such regional favorites as beef filet Tampiqueña style, *mole poblano*, filet *tapado* and Jalisco barbequed goat. Moderate.

ROSARITO TO ENSENADA AREA RESTAURANTS

The many restaurants along the Tijuana–Ensenada free road excel in seafood.

One of the absolute seafood heavens of this coast is Puerto Nuevo (Tijuana–Ensenada free road, Km. 44.5, south of El Pescador, turnoff at "New Port" building). This dusty fishing community consists of about two dozen restaurants specializing in lobster. Amid this wonderful excess of choices, where to begin? Start at what's rumored to be the original restaurant, the white, family-style **Puerto Nuevo No. 1.** This old establishment, dating back to the 1960s, has a sprawling dining room, open kitchen and Viking-sized meals of lobster, soup, rice, french fries and frijoles. For sheer volume and price (moderate), that's hard to beat. A classier, and pricier, **Puerto Nuevo II** next door has a fireplace and more upscale ambience.

But for more personal atmosphere I prefer **Restaurant Chela** (Calle Chinchorro), tucked on a side street, with Diego Rivera posters and a mother-of-pearl shrine to the Virgin of Guadalupe in the wall. Besides lobster, this restaurant serves fresh abalone, homemade cheesecake and superior margaritas. Budget to moderate.

One of the oldest establishments on the coast is the well-preserved wooden **Halfway House** (Tijuana–Ensenada free road, Km. 53), marking the halfway point between Tijuana and Ensenada. Inside, you slip back to an era of wooden dance floors and reminisce by an old jukebox full of Latin favorites. Live piano music sparks special occasions, and a fireplace crackles with fog-melting fires. Breakfasts are extra good. Hotcakes, omelettes and all sorts of seafood are served. Budget.

For a seductive and delicious evening, treat yourself to dinner at **La Fonda Restaurant-Bar** (La Fonda Hotel, Tijuana–Ensenada free road, Km. 66 or La Misión–Alisitos exit from the toll road). The restaurant, perched above a long white-sand beach, features a triple-entree special and an old Mexico charm you will dream about for days. Around a blazing hearth decked with a whale's weathered rib, dozens of elegant dark-wood tables steam with superb wild quail, fried scallops, succulent lobster and sinful mountains of homemade lemon pie. Nightly mariachi music and weekend bands coax diners onto the compact dance floor. The vine-trellised outdoor patio is ideal for breakfast, lunch or sunset snack. Moderate, and worth every penny.

ENSENADA RESTAURANTS

Ensenada is filled with juicy lobster and abalone.

The cheapest, most savory meal in town is a fistful of fish tacos, sold on street corners all over town. The **Fish Market** (on the service road off Boulevard Costera and Avenida Macheros) is jammed with little stalls serving some of the best. Mexicans eat them for breakfast and wash them down with warm soft drinks. Great *ceviche* too!

Bahía de Ensenada (Avenida Riveroll 109; 8-10-15) is a lively downtown seafood restaurant with formica tables and nightly serenades. As mariachis swing in and out, blaring on their horns, you can order lobster burritos, breaded squid and albacore caught fresh daily by the restaurant's own boats. Budget to moderate.

Settle in under the brick arches at **Casamar** (Boulevard Lázaro Cárdenas 987; 4-04-17) and feast on some of Ensenada's best and freshest seafood. A favorite among locals and *turistas* alike since 1975. There's fish, lobster, abalone, squid, clams, mussels and ten different shrimp dishes. Service is *pronto* and prices mostly moderate.

A more formal atmosphere awaits you at the perennially popular **El Rey Sol** (Avenida López Mateos, between Avenida Alvarado and Avenida Blancorte; 8-17-33). Once your eyes adjust to the dark, you'll catch the French theme—both in the decor, notable for the French oils hanging about, and on the menu. There's *escargots de Bourgogne*, chicken cordon bleu, chateaubriand *bouquetière*, shrimp *medaillons*, quail à la crème and the house's own homemade French pastries. Gourmet fare at deluxe prices.

Ensenada's premier restaurant is **La Cueva de los Tigres** (one mile south of Ensenada off the Transpeninsular Highway; at Playa Hermosa, watch for sign; 6-64-50). Perched above the beach and boasting a smashing view, the air-conditioned Tigers' Cave has classy dark decor set off by floods of natural light. One entire window is crammed with awards earned by the Cave's cuisine, especially its renowned abalone with crab sauce. Squid steak, lobster, quail and various meats are also on the menu. Lunch and dinner only. Deluxe.

SAN FELIPE RESTAURANTS

San Felipe is famous for its big, plump shrimp and clams.

Without doubt the most unusual eatery in town is the outdoor **Clam Man's Restaurant** (two blocks west of the Pemex station on Calzada Chetumal). It's a haphazard personal museum of whale bones, hand-carved statues, picnic tables, fishing nets, kittens, kids and a big blackened hearth made famous by the late "Clam Man" himself, Pasqual Cruz Guerrero, who steamed, barbequed and fried tasty Sea or Cortez butter clams well into his 80s—serving them with a patented spiel that would have you believe clams are the greatest thing for the human sex drive since hormones. The clams are as good as ever—even without the sales pitch. Budget.

Conventional dining at its best comes with live Lawrence Welk-type organ music at **George's** (Avenida Mar de Cortez Sur 336; 7-10-57). This is the neighborly *in* spot for retired Americans who call San Felipe home at least part of the year. The broad polished floor is edged in candle-lit leatherette booths. The food, ranging from steaks to seafood, is excellent. Moderate.

San Felipe's best food and liveliest atmosphere can be found at **El Nido** (Avenida Mar de Cortez Sur 348; 7-10-28). This fancy steak-and-seafood house, handsomely appointed in brick and tile with a dark-beamed ceiling, offers a wide range of steaks, lobster, shrimp and fish broiled over mesquite wood. You can also order frog's legs, quail and dangerous strawberry margaritas. Moderate to deluxe.

Concealed within the upscale Mar del Sol RV Campground south of town, **La Misiones** (Avenida Misión de Loreto 130) has become a favorite for family dining, especially among the RV crowd. Sans theme of any kind, the decor is simple, bordering on spartan. To be sure, the kids won't knock over any objets d'art. The menu is rather sparse as well, listing less than a dozen steak and seafood entrees, topped by the house specialty, seafood crepes. Meals are well-prepared, however, and promptly served. Moderate.

SAN QUINTÍN RESTAURANTS

It's slim pickings out here, but you won't go hungry.

Your best bet is **El Alteño** (Transpeninsular Highway, next to the cinema). Somewhat bare but clean and friendly, this little roadhouse features locally caught seafood and Mexican dishes. Toss in cocktails and mariachi music and the place becomes almost festive. Loyally patronized by both locals and vacationing *gringos*. Moderate. Closed from July to September.

An alternative is the rather remote **Muelle Viejo** (Old Pier) **Restaurant** (off the Transpeninsular Highway at the turnoff for "Muelle Viejo," go about 1.5 miles along the sand road). Situated on Bahía de San Quintín, this homey blue restaurant is decorated with china knickknacks and stares out at the remains of the old pier in the bay. Seafood dominates the menu, and the margaritas are tops. Lunch and dinner, sometimes breakfast. Budget to moderate.

BAHÍA DE LOS ÁNGELES RESTAURANTS

"LA Bay's" newest restaurant is **Guillermo's**. Housed in a whitewashed two-story building on the main drag, fronted by the town's only gift shop, this enterprise offers a cheery decor with eight oilcloth-covered tables (more on the bayfront patio) and a small bar. Local seafood and Mexican specialties are tasty and nicely prepared. Moderate.

At the northern edge of town sits **Las Hamacas Restaurant,** an easygoing café with a brick-arched patio, slow service and a view of the bay from the main street. The varied menu includes lobster, fried fish, Mexican specialties and omelettes—a good place for breakfast on your way out of town. Budget.

The Great Outdoors
The Sporting Life

CAMPING

Camping along the coasts of northern Baja can be a pleasure. Trailer parks and campsites are plentiful. Rosarito has a free campsite in the middle of town, and there's a **KOA Campground** north of town (San Antonio exit off the Tijuana–Ensenada toll road). The Rosarito tourist office (2-10-05) has more local information.

It's chilly in northern Baja from November to March or April, so tents and warm sleeping bags are advised.

Also, Mexican police along the Rosarito-to-Ensenada route have a penchant for singling out American vans for impromptu drug checks.

For camping supplies in Ensenada, try the sporting goods shop **La Popular** (Avenida Ruiz 150; 8-19-86) or the **Astra Shopping Center** (Transpeninsular Highway south of town).

SWIMMING

Many northern Baja beaches have steep drop-offs and strong currents, so be careful when you swim. The water in winter is often around 55 degrees all the way down to Bahía de los Ángeles—too chilly for swimming without a wetsuit—and rough. From April on, it warms up and gets smoother. Watch out for stingrays in the Sea of Cortez.

There's also a pollution problem around Rosarito and Ensenada. Stick to beaches several miles away from those towns.

FISHING AND BOATING

The fish are really jumping in Ensenada's Bahía de Todos Santos: yellowtail and white sea bass during the summer, opaleye and golden fin croaker all year round. The city likewise teems with sportfishing operations. Most are located at Federalson Sportfishing Landing. Some of the big ones are **Gordo's Sportfishing** (Sportfishing Landing #5; 8-35-15), **Ensenada Clipper Fleet** (Sportfishing Landing, 8-21-85), **Pacific Anglers Fleet** (Sportfishing Landing #2; 4-08-65) and **Fritz's Boat House** (Sportfishing Landing #4; 4-02-94).

At San Felipe, the Sea of Cortez is rich with bass, corbina, triggerfish, yellowtail, halibut and tortuaba. You can hire a *panga* (16-to-24-foot skiff) at **Ruben's Trailer Park** (north end of town off Avenida Mar de Cortez and Golfo de California) and at **Playa de Laura Trailer Park** (south end of Avenida Mar de Cortez). For extended cruises, 65-foot boats are rented by **Tony Reyes Fishing Tours** (7-11-20) and 85- to 105-foot boats are available at **Baja Fishing Tours** (7-10-92 or 800-992-7744 for reservations).

In San Quintín, bottom-fishing in both the open sea and Bahía de San Quintín yields rock cod, platefish, yellowtail, black sea bass and many others. Isla San Martín just off the coast is good for sportfishing. You can rent *pangas* with guides at the **Old Mill Motel** and **Ernesto's Resort Hotel**, both located on the sandy track leading off the Transpeninsular Highway in San Quintín. Take the turnoff at the "Muelle Viejo" sign and continue several miles to the bay.

Trout fishing is excellent in lagoons in the Sierra San Pedro Mártir to the east. Clams can be found at El Socorro and Playa San Ramón, two rocky beaches to the north and south of San Quintín. From April to August, during the full moon, grunion are plentiful at most local beaches. For the best times to go grunion-running, check tidal charts for this area.

In Bahía de los Ángeles, the same kinds of fish are biting as in San Felipe, plus there are lobsters, scallops, clams, oysters and mussels close to shore. Fishing *pangas* can be rented right on the beach in front of the Casa Díaz cabañas.

SURFING AND WINDSURFING

Surfers flock to the beaches from Rosarito to Ensenada for the long smooth waves that never seem to break. Surfing gear can be bought in Ensenada at **San Miguel Surf Shop No. 1** (Avenida López Mateos and Calle Alvarado) and **San Miguel No. 2** (Avenida Ruiz 1).

SKIN DIVING AND SNORKELING

The Punta Banda area south of Ensenada, located out toward La Bufadora, is one of northern Baja's few popular diving sites. For more information and equipment rentals check out **Elmo's Dive Tours** (Avenida Ruiz 4-2; 4-06-37).

HUNTING

There's a Spanish saying that portrays Baja as the *tierra de no hay, mar de mucho* (land of little, sea of a lot)—but in fact northern Baja's mountainous interior is filled with wildlife, including quail, doves, ducks, geese, deer, jackrabbits, wild goats, pigs, rams and mountain lions.

HORSEBACK RIDING

Horseback riding is very popular from Rosarito to Ensenada. For horse rentals check at El Faro (or Mona Lisa) Beach south of Ensenada; at Estero Public Beach south of Ensenada off the Transpeninsular Highway; and at San Miguel, a small community nine miles north of Ensenada off the Tijuana–Ensenada toll road.

GOLF

Two fine 18-hole courses are situated in northern Baja: the **Tijuana Golf and Country Club** (Boulevard Agua Caliente near the Toreo de Tijuana Bullring, Tijuana; 86-14-02) and the country club at **Bajamar**

Baja's Prickly Circus

The Baja peninsula is the ultimate cactus garden, with over 100 species, the majority of which are found nowhere else in the world. Used for firewood and fence posts throughout the region, these spiny denizens of the desert range from the 80-foot cardon cactus to one-inch succulents.

Most have adapted to the harsh aridity with accordion-like stems that expand and contract with the intake and use of precious water. Their needles are an evolved defense against roaming animals (many hothouse cactus don't produce thorns). Yet for all their armor, they can be quite beautiful—many burst forth with tender yellow and magenta blossoms in late spring, and they decorate the landscape with their curious shapes year round.

The best place to view Baja vegetation is the heart of the central desert, between El Rosario and Bahía de los Ángeles, where years may pass without a drop of rain. Just south of the Arroyo del Rosario along the Transpeninsular Highway, the landscape explodes into a spiny jungle. First come the zany cirios (also called boojum tree after a Lewis Carroll character). Just outside Cataviña, huge graffiti-splashed boulders stand alongside mammoth cardons, and you can roam through forests of chollas, ocotillo, prickly pear and fat-limbed elephant trees, a world of barrel cactus and century plants, galloping cactus with thorny, sinuous tentacles and old man cactus with whiskery needles. Some quilled trees form walk-through arches by burying their heads in the ground, and flowering bushes splash the roadside with color.

This is the Baja of our dreams, only better.

(Tijuana–Ensenada toll road, Km. 77.5). For reservations, call 619-263-0079 in San Diego or 8-22-20 in Ensenada).

TENNIS

There are tennis courts for rent north of Ensenada at **Bajamar** (Tijuana–Ensenada toll road, Km. 77.5; 8-38-38); in Ensenada itself, at the **Baja Tennis Club** (Calle San Benito 123-A). Free public courts are in Ensenada at **Campo Sullivan** (Avenida Ciprés and Calle Diamante).

Beaches

ROSARITO TO ENSENADA BEACHES

This 60-mile corridor of Pacific beaches combines powdery, grayish sand—about a four on a scale of ten—and often-rocky shores. The loveliest of some dozen beaches:

Playa Rosarito—This broad, clean, silvery beach follows the length of Rosarito village and its main business drag. A continuation of unattractive Playa Tijuana farther north, this beach has much prettier landscaping and is wide open except for one fenced section fronting a resort hotel.

Facilities: All amenities in Rosarito. *Camping:* Permitted in non-fenced areas and trailer parks. *Swimming:* Swim with care. Drownings have been reported here because of the undertow. There may also be some pollution. *Surfing:* Good here, plus Baja Malibu to the north and Km. 38.5 (Rancho Cotal) to the south. Best during the summer. *Fishing:* Good for everything from barracuda to croaker.

Getting there: In Rosarito, via any east-west road.

Playa Campo López or **Media Camino** (Cantamar Dunes) (★)—The only large sand dunes near Ensenada, and they are beauties, are fenced off along the road but quite accessible via the seaside Mexican settlement of Ejido Primo Tapia. The shabby *ejido* (communal village) rests in the foothills of the dunes, which rise spectacularly at a bend in the road and continue in undulating ivory hills along the sea for several miles. Hang gliding fans enjoy this site as a pushoff point. The thick white beach at the base of the dunes is great for roaming and rolling. One of northwest Baja's most romantic, surreal landscapes.

Facilities: Small stores in the village behind the dunes, with public bathrooms nearby. *Camping:* Permitted for a fee. Be sure you get a receipt to avoid problems with unauthentic fee collectors. *Swimming:* Safe for good swimmers. *Surfing:* Hot surfing hangout to the south at Km. 55.

Getting there: Take the Tijuana–Ensenada free road south of Cantamar until you spot the dunes. Then, turn right onto a sand road near the *llantera* (tire shop) sign, which marks the beginning of the *ejido*. This road curves left toward the beach, taking you out to where you can park. The dunes run from Km. 47 to Km. 52 along the old road.

Playa La Fonda—This dreamy, satiny beach running alongside the old La Fonda Hotel is the prettiest stretch of silver sand north of Ensenada. Far from the lights of either Tijuana or Ensenada, this beach is superb for star-gazing or long walks in the shallow tide.

Facilities: Hotel, restaurant-bar and bathroom. *Camping:* Good just south of La Fonda Hotel. *Swimming:* Safe and pleasant. *Surfing:* Fair; better to the south at La Misión.

Getting there: At Km. 66 on the Tijuana–Ensenada free road or off La Misión–Alisitos exit from Tijuana–Ensenada toll road. Enter beach around La Fonda Hotel.

Playa San Miguel—Although the beach here is rocky and fairly small, it is pleasant for picnicking and building midnight bonfires. A favorite surfer's beach, it's a stone's throw from Ensenada and a popular getaway spot for sunbathing and camping.

Facilities: Trailer park/camping area with showers and restrooms on the beach, restaurant and store in village. *Camping:* Tent and trailer camping, RV hookups. *Swimming:* Too rocky for comfort. *Surfing:* One of the top spots north of Ensenada. Right-point breaks attract lots of boards.

Getting there: In San Miguel off Tijuana–Ensenada toll road, just after the last toll booth).

ENSENADA BEACHES

With no beaches in town, you're limited to the rather mediocre beaches south of Ensenada. The two best:

Playa Hermosa—This dusty salt-and-pepper sand beach curves for a mile or so along Bahía de Todos Santos with *palapa* umbrellas for sunbathers and a good view of Ensenada. Beyond the tide line is a burnt-out wrecked ship stuck in the sand on its side, against which the waves crash with ghostly grandeur.

Facilities: Nearby restaurant. *Camping:* Okay. *Swimming:* Safe, but check with locals on pollution. *Surfing:* Best around Isla Todos Santos in the bay. *Fishing:* Very good; boats for rent in Ensenada.

Getting there: Follow Transpeninsular Highway one mile south of Ensenada and turn right onto sand road at sign for Cueva de los Tigres. Road leads directly to beach.

Playa El Faro or **Playa Mona Lisa**—This beach with interchangeable names is given much less play than nearby Estero Beach, yet it is cleaner, more attractive, quieter and nicer smelling (having no nearby stagnant estuary waters like its neighboring beach). The sand is vast, pewter-colored and barren, with a striking vista of rocky Punta Banda to the south.

Facilities: Bathrooms at the beach motel and grocery store. *Camping:* A per-vehicle fee is charged. *Swimming:* Safe conditions, but check on the pollution level. *Fishing:* You can snag corbina, bonita, croaker and more.

Getting there: Take Transpeninsular Highway four miles south of Ensenada, turn right at the Estero Beach sign, continue to dirt road and turn right opposite sign for Estero Beach, bear left at the fork and enter El Faro Motel directly on beach.

SAN FELIPE BEACHES

These beaches, the best in northern Baja, have thick, grainy, full-bodied sand—about an eight on the Sand Quality Scale—and beautiful, clean water.

Northern San Felipe Beaches—For about 20 miles north of San Felipe, there's a string of rustic solitary *campos* along the beach. With names like "Campo Pee Wee" and "Pop's Place," these camps are clearly *norteamericano* hangouts. Reached via long narrow sand tracks off the main highway, many have only rudimentary shelters and are often uninhabited. The main attractions here are cactus, sea and beach in a runway of wild, lonely sand stretching north and south as far as the eye can see. *Campos* charge a small access fee—usually a few dollars a day.

Facilities: None. Amenities in San Felipe. *Camping:* Fabulous for escapist camping. *Swimming:* Good. *Snorkeling/diving:* Good around offshore Isla Conzag. *Fishing:* Excellent. Clamming is good, too—the beach in front of Campo Los Compadres has abundant butter clams.

Getting there: Sand turnoffs along Mexico 5 north of San Felipe lead to some dozen *campos*, all on a beautiful beach.

Playa San Felipe—From Punta San Felipe to Punta Radar to the south, the beach along Bahía San Felipe follows the contours of the town and continues in a six-mile belt of snowy shore along a sheltered cove. Extreme tidal shifts expose great ballrooms of sand where you can walk out among colonies of pelicans, grounded skiffs and treasure troves of sand dollars.

Facilities: All amenities located in San Felipe. *Camping:* Best in the designated camping spots. *Swimming:* Safe, clean, lovely water with calm waves. *Windsurfing:* Good. *Fishing:* Excellent. Boats for rent in the town.

Getting there: In San Felipe off Avenida Mar de Cortez.

Southern San Felipe Beaches (★)—South of Punta Radar along the 54-mile unpaved road to Puertecitos are two dozen small settlements and *campos* situated on isolated white beaches. The farther south you go, the more secluded and ideal the beaches are for bathing au naturel. The rosy crags of the Sierra San Pedro Mártir loom behind this boundless shore and the desert into which it disappears.

Facilities: None. Occasional designated camping spots. *Camping:* Excellent. If you opt for a *campo* rather than the open beach, there may be a small camping fee. *Swimming:* Excellent. Many shallow stretches founs amid sandbars. *Windsurfing:* Good. *Fishing:* Excellent. *Shell-collecting:* Great, especially around Punta Estrella and Laguna Percebu. Sand dollars and clam shells galore.

Getting there: For standard cars, the only route is Puertecitos road, a poor but passable gravel road that splits after Km. 25 into two roads—one of graded gravel (washboard), the other of smoother sand. Both will give your car delirium tremens. All turnoffs at *campo* signs lead to the beach.

SAN QUINTÍN BEACHES

These so-so beaches have that dusty, grayish sand indigenous to the northern Pacific. The area's nicest beaches:

Playa de Oro—Located near the Cielito Lindo Hotel south of town, this beach features gentle sand dunes that ripple down to the shore and swerve west for miles to Punta Azufre. Wind-blown Playa de Oro merges with Playa Santa María to the east, forming a continuum of shoreline ideal for solitary camping. (Frequent windstorms make camping less than comfortable in winter.)

Facilities: Trailer park with bathrooms and showers. Restaurant in nearby hotel. *Camping:* Very good; trailer park fee. *Swimming:* Strong current, safe only for good swimmers. *Fishing:* Trowel out pismo clams by the bucketful. *Shell-collecting:* At Punta Azufre to the west.

Getting there: Take Transpeninsular Highway south through San Quintín to the La Pinta Hotel turnoff, continue past La Pinta and follow signs to Cielito Lindo Hotel and Trailer Park.

Playa Pabellón—The prettiest beach in the San Quintín vicinity, Playa Pabellón combines soft hilly dunes and silver sand in a secluded setting on the open sea. Extending for some five miles both north and south, this empty beach is tailor-made sheltered camping.

Facilities: Trailer park with bathrooms and hot showers. Other amenities are about five miles north in Santa María. *Camping:* Very good behind protective dunes. Per-vehicle fee at trailer park; also protected by windbreaker barricades. *Swimming:* Safe for good swimmers. Strong current. *Surfing:* None here, but good surfing starts about eight miles south at El Socorro. *Fishing:* Good surf-fishing and pismo clamming. *Shell-collecting:* Sand dollars.

Getting there: Off Transpeninsular Highway about 15 miles south of San Quintín and three miles past Santa María. Turn at Km. 15 at RV campground sign, go one mile on dirt road to beach.

BAHÍA DE LOS ÁNGELES BEACHES

Playa Bahía de los Ángeles—Right in the heart of the village, this series of minibeaches at the foot of the Casa Díaz cabañas and Guillermo's Trailer Park gives you just enough room to roll over and tan the other side. The view of the craggy offshore islands helps make up for missing beach space.

Facilities: All amenities are within walking distance. *Camping:* Permitted, but you'd better have a compact tent. *Swimming:* Good, but watch out for stingrays. *Surfing/windsurfing:* Pleasant windsurfing in the bay. *Snorkeling/diving:* Around Isla Coronado, Isla Pioto and Isla La Ventana in the bay. *Fishing:* Excellent.

Getting there: In Bahía de los Ángeles.

Punta La Gringa (★)—This uninhabited spit of rocks and sand, by far the nicest beach on the bay, juts out into the water about eight miles north of Bahía de los Ángeles and looks out toward tiny Isla Smith. Its only residents are nomadic RV-dwellers and scallop divers living in makeshift shacks. Because of the landscape, this beach gets lots of afternoon sun.

Facilities: None. *Camping:* Secluded but the shores are grainy. *Swimming:* Good. *Snorkeling/diving:* Excellent around the offshore islands. *Surfing/windsurfing:* Good windsurfing, but no waves for surfing. *Fishing:* Excellent.

Getting there: Take the road from Bahía de los Ángeles north toward airport, follow sandy fork opposite airport road; continue for several miles until sugar-white sand signals your arrival.

Trailer Parks

Except where noted, all parks have full hookups and bathrooms.

ENSENADA TRAILER PARKS

Scores of trailer parks line the Rosarito–Ensenada coast. Those listed below are among the best.

A deluxe RV park, **Baja Ensenada** (Km. 72 off the toll road north of Ensenada), boasts acres of concrete and pavement plus such niceties as tennis courts.

San Miguel Village (eight miles north of Ensenada off the toll road) has good out-of-town beach camping on a rocky shore.

California RV Park (five miles north of Ensenada on the toll road across from the Pemex station, Km. 102) is a little city of trailers near the sea.

Estero Beach Trailer Park (eight miles south of Ensenada off the Transpeninsular Highway) is part of the Estero Beach Hotel.

La Jolla Beach Camp (eight miles southwest of town on the road to La Bufadora) is more remote, with no electric hookups.

SAN FELIPE TRAILER PARKS

San Felipe's parks are full of gossip and satellite dishes.

The best of them is the **Mar del Sol** (Avenida Misión de Coreto 130), which has a pool, jacuzzi, hot showers and laundry facilities, plus some of the town's best restaurants.

Others are **Club de Pesca** and **Ruben's Trailer Park**. Club de Pesca (at the end of Avenida Mar de Cortez Sur; 7-11-80) is backed by steep dunes. Ruben's (just off Avenida Golfo de California past the baseball stadium) is one of San Felipe's oldest, with a fine seafood restaurant.

SAN QUINTÍN TRAILER PARKS

Posada Don Diego (off the Transpeninsular Highway, Km. 276, north of San Quintín in Colonia Guerrero), with everything from restaurant to laundry, is a small world unto itself.

Campo de Lorenzo (several miles off Transpeninsular Highway on a well-signed dirt road at the south end of town; reservations: 714-946-6692) is a park catering to fishermen and divers. Full compliment of *pangas* and guides.

Cielito Lindo Trailer Park (off Transpeninsular Highway south of San Quintín, turnoff for La Pinta Hotel) enjoys a secluded beachsite with restaurant-bar at a nearby hotel.

Honey's RV Campground (Transpeninsular Highway, Km. 15) is a new trailer park on a beautiful, isolated beach.

BAHÍA DE LOS ÁNGELES TRAILER PARKS

Guillermo's Trailer Park is right on the sea in the middle of Bahía de los Ángeles, with a scrap of beach out front.

Travelers' Tracks
Sightseeing

TIJUANA

Fast-growing Tijuana, with about two million people, was born with the founding of the international border along the Río Tijuana in 1848. It made its name in the early 1900s, offering prostitution, gambling, drinking and other racy entertainment that attracted crowds from the north. Even after the Mexican government outlawed gambling in the 1930s and reformers passed laws aimed at cleaning up the rest, Tijuana remained the big bad border town.

It's grown considerably tamer since those days, and although still congested, the city caters to the family trade with an emphasis on shopping. Just a mile across the narrow **Río Tijuana**, which runs through town, red-brick **Avenida Revolución** forms the axis of all the downtown tourist action. Despite its tacky appearance—the shabby hotels, loud upstairs discos, streetcorner burros dyed to look like zebras—Avenida Revolución has many fine restaurants and shops. Just up the street is the striking Moorish-style **Jai Alai Palace** (also known as Frontón Palacio, Avenida Revolución between Calle 7a and Calle 8a; 85-16-12 or 619-282-3636 in San Diego), finest headquarters of jai alai in Mexico. Bilingual commentary and parimutuel betting accompany the fast-paced nightly games.

Avenida Revolución curves southeast into Boulevard Agua Caliente, home of the city's oldest bullring and the race track, both dating back to the 1920s. Famous matadors from Mexico and Spain appear regularly from May through September at the **Toreo de Tijuana** (Boulevard Agua Caliente) and the grand **Plaza Monumental** (or Bullring by the Sea, off the toll road to Ensenada). For information and tickets, visit the box office (Avenida Revolución 815; 85-22-10 or 619-231-3554 in San Diego). Tijuana's famous **Caliente Racetrack** (Boulevard Agua Caliente; 81-78-11 or 619-231-1919 in San Diego) is the scene of jam-packed weekend thoroughbred races, with pari-mutuel betting. On weekdays greyhounds replace the horses at the track.

Several different *charro* grounds host exciting *charreadas* (rodeos) on Sunday afternoons from May through September. Call the Tijuana Tourist Bureau (84-05-38) for information.

Running parallel to Boulevard Agua Caliente is the more grandiose Paseo de los Héroes, a tree-lined avenue traversing a series of monument-studded traffic circles. Changes in Tijuana's once-derelict character are evident here, especially in the futuristic **Centro Cultural Tijuana** (Paseo de los Héroes and Calle Mina; 84-11-11; admission). This giant moon-shaped building houses a theatre with daily films in English about Mexican destinations and a museum with a tale-telling exhibit ("Mexican Identities") about the nation's history and culture.

For a look at the tired remains of the legendary **red light district** (Zona Norte or Zona Roja), head to Calle Coahuila and Avenida Constitución on the fringe of the shopping quarter.

ROSARITO TO ENSENADA

Two roads lead south from Tijuana to Rosarito and Ensenada: an old coastal road (*libre* or free) and a parallel four-lane toll road. The free road hugs the shore for some 40 miles, wandering past interesting little communities of ramshackle cafés, lighthouses, surfing spots and rugged beaches. The newer toll road cuts through mountainous terrain and presents some loftier spectacles. From the toll road, at Km. 84, take the "Mirador" turnoff (*mirador* means "lookout") and feast your eyes on the panoramic vista to the south—**Bahía de Todos Santos,** a curving bay where sheer cliffs descend to the water, and **Isla Todos Santos,** a lone island 12 miles offshore.

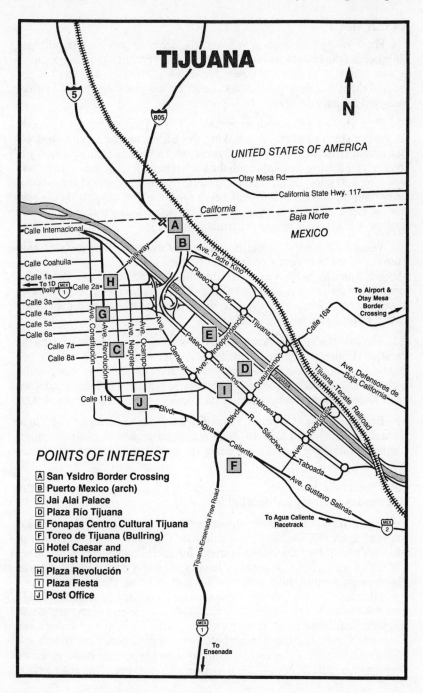

TIJUANA

N

UNITED STATES OF AMERICA

Otay Mesa Rd
California State Hwy. 117
California
Baja Norte
MEXICO

5
805

Calle Internacional
Calle Coahuila
Calle 1a
To 1D (toll) MEX 1
Calle 2a
Calle 3a
Calle 4a
Calle 5a
Calle 6a
Calle 7a
Calle 8a
Calle 11a

Ave. Padre Kino
Paseo de
Ave. Constitución
Ave. Revolución
Ave. Negrete
Ave. Ocampo
Ave. General
Paseo de los
Ave. de Independencia
Ave. Tijuana
Calle 16a
Ave. Cuauhtémoc
Héroes
R. Sánchez
Ave. Rodríguez
Taboada
Ave. Gustavo Salinas
Blvd. Agua Caliente
Blvd.
Tijuana-Tecate Railroad
Ave. Defensores de Baja California

To Airport & Otay Mesa Border Crossing

To Agua Caliente Racetrack

MEX 2

Tijuana-Ensenada Free Road

MEX 1
To Ensenada

POINTS OF INTEREST

A **San Ysidro Border Crossing**
B **Puerto Mexico (arch)**
C **Jai Alai Palace**
D **Plaza Río Tijuana**
E **Fonapas Centro Cultural Tijuana**
F **Toreo de Tijuana (Bullring)**
G **Hotel Caesar and Tourist Information**
H **Plaza Revolución**
I **Plaza Fiesta**
J **Post Office**

ENSENADA

For a lovely introduction to Ensenada, drive up into the **Chapultepec Hills** behind the city (turn off Avenida Ryerson, carefully avoiding potholes as you ascend, and follow the *mirador* arrows). From the top you can see the harbor, Bahía de Todos Santos, Punta Banda to the south and half the backyard laundry in town.

Start your morning with an excursion to the lively, pungent **Mercado de Pescas** (Fish Market), overlooking the harbor on the service road off Boulevard Costera and Avenida Macheros. Ensenada's main industry is commercial fishing. Stroll through the bins of hefty San Quintín clams, tuna weighing 100 kilos, delicate pink croakers, frozen scallops and the massive savory shrimp of San Felipe—all going for a fraction of what they would cost up north. For a treat try a chunk of barbequed tuna with a squeeze of lime or a fish taco with all the trimmings.

Wash it all down with a little wine at the cavernous **Bodegas de Santo Tomás** (Avenida Miramar 666; 4-08-66), the oldest and biggest winery in Mexico, founded in 1888 in the nearby village of Santo Tomás. Scheduled tours take you into the heady-smelling cellars where some 500,000 cases of wine are produced every year from 25 varieties of grapes grown in the fertile valleys around Ensenada.

The spirits also once flowed freely in the beautiful seaside **Riviera del Pacífico** (Boulevard Lázaro Cárdenas at Avenida Riviera). Built as a plush hotel-casino in the 1920s, this pearly-white mini-Monte Carlo was popular with the Hollywood gang before gambling was outlawed in Mexico a decade later. Now it's a convention center. Its shadowy old bar is open for drinks.

Ensenada's newest pride, **Plaza Cívica** (also known as "The Three Heads") on Boulevard Costero, is an oceanside park with giant sculptures commemorating Mexican heroes Bento Juárez, Miguel Hidalgo and Venustiano Carranza.

Contact the local tourist office (6-37-18) for information on colorful **charreadas** (rodeos) and **bullfights**.

Ensenada's other outdoor attractions are well worth a day's excursion south of town. Follow the Transpeninsular Highway to the settlement of Maneadero and take the marked turnoff for La Bufadora. The road curves out onto a slim finger of desolate land crowned by rocky **Punta Banda**. To reach its summit, hike or take a 4-wheel drive up the unnamed rocky 1.5-mile road (a righthand turn about six miles along the La Bufadora road.) You can enjoy the ultimate view of Ensenada and the bay from here. Backtrack and continue along the paved road to the tip of the peninsula and Ensenada's most celebrated natural wonder: **La Bufadora** (The Blowhole). This natural geyser is formed by in-rushing waves as they crash against a deep crevice in the rocks and spray the air with rainbows. The spout is best during high tide. The site is surrounded by small seafood restaurants and a phalanx of curios stalls.

SAN FELIPE

The three-hour drive from Ensenada to San Felipe along Mexico 3 leads through miles of lonely desert, a boneyard for the bleached remains of junked cars. The arid mountains and plains radiate a dusty pastel light reminiscent of Georgia O'Keeffe's desert paintings of nearby New Mexico.

The turnoff onto Mexico 5 takes you past miles of rustic beach camps. Almost out of nowhere, the imposing, 50-foot **San Felipe Arches** straddle the entrance into the fishing resort of San Felipe. In some ways the arches reflect the monumental stature of the **Sierra San Pedro Mártir**, Baja's highest mountain range. These 10,000-foot pinnacles ripple down the coastline past sleepy Puertecitos, an escapist community of expatriates 54 miles south of San Felipe via rough unpaved roads.

On more modest Punta San Felipe, a headland on the bay flanked by a lighthouse and a rusty shipyard, stands the **shrine of the Virgin of Guadalupe** (just off of Avenida Mar de Cortez). This hilltop altar provides a great view of Bahía San Felipe and the cove and village.

SOUTH OF ENSENADA

Backtracking to Ensenada from San Felipe, you can proceed south on the Transpeninsular Highway toward San Quintín. Just north of Colonia Guerrero and 80 miles south of Ensenada, a dirt road (marked San Telmo/Observatorio) climbs east to the chilly, rugged **Parque Nacional San Pedro Mártir**, Baja's biggest national park. The steep two-hour drive takes you into dense forests of Jeffrey pines, through occasional patches of snow, and up to a 9,000-foot-high government observatory basking in the clear alpine air, with camping spaces nearby.

SAN QUINTÍN

About 125 miles south of Ensenada, the lush **San Quintín Valley** appears, extending from Colonia Guerrero south to Santa María, irrigated and ripe with fields of every vegetable from snow peas to brussels sprouts. Locals say this land is as rich as California's San Joaquin Valley, but to visit the plain-Jane town of San Quintín, you'd never know it.

Various sand roads lead off the Transpeninsular Highway to tranquil **Bahía de San Quintín**, where scant traces of the San Quintín's early English settlers still remain. They came in 1890 to mine for gold and farm for wheat, but lack of water spoiled their dream. All that's left is a sun-bleached cemetery of weathered crosses in the sand just south of the Old Pier Restaurant, and the pilings of a former pier poking forlornly out of the bay.

BAHÍA DE LOS ÁNGELES

From San Quintín, the Transpeninsular Highway passes the seaside town of El Rosario, site of the first Dominican mission built in 1774. The highway then cuts inland and across the peninsula via a fascinating cactus jungle en route to Bahía de los Ángeles about 180 miles away. This region offers southbound visitors their first look at the giant cardón cactus and the bizarre "boojum" (*Cirio*) trees. These comical trees, relatives of the spindly ocotillo, have tall trunks tapered at the tops and covered with thin, whiplike limbs. They adorn the dry hillsides by the thousands and no two are alike. Near Cataviña, Highway 1 enters a spectacular boulder-strewn rock garden area called **Las Vírgenes**, a marvelous natural wonder, now protected as a national park.

Bahía de los Ángeles is so small that buses do not stop here and there is no bank, but this village has one of the most vivid views of the Sea of Cortez in Baja. The town is all dusty languor, like a sleeping lizard, while the sea gleams a shocking, electric blue against the arid hills. The primeval **offshore islands** definitely merit a boat trip. These 12 floating mountains loom over the bay with prehistoric grandeur and swarm with dolphins, seabirds, seals, whales and sea turtles. You half-expect Godzilla to rear up next to a guano-covered rock, swatting away pterodactyls. The biggest islands are 42-mile-long Isla Ángel de la Guarda (farthest offshore, the second largest island in the Sea of Cortez), Isla Coronado, Isla Piojo, Isla La Ventana and Isla Cabeza de Caballo. At sundown, this area is bathed in an unearthly golden light that turns the island pinnacles into heaps of embers shimmering in the ice-blue sea. It's breathtaking.

Shopping

The entire peninsula of Baja California is a duty-free zone, making imported goods cheaper here than in the United States or Canada.

TIJUANA SHOPPING

Border towns are notoriously expensive, Tijuana most of all. Mixed in with the downtown bargain basements are pricey department stores, packed with imported goods, and sleek shopping malls. The best buys are in blankets, leather, designer fashions, Mexican glassware and ceramics, quantity items like tiles and wrought iron, and custom-made furniture.

Let's go on a shopping spree down Avenida Revolución. Starting around the Jai Alai Palace and heading up toward Calle 1a, our first stop is at **Tolan** (Avenida Revolución 1111; 88-36-37). Specializing in Mexican folk art and hand-carved colonial-style furniture, this enormous shop is stocked with clothing, ceramics, glassware and black pottery. Marvelous browsing.

Tucked in the courtyard of a no-name arcade, **La Fuente** (Avenida Revolución 921 10; 85-92-13) has one of Tijuana's finest selections of Mexican masks and artisans' crafts.

Across the street is probably the town's best leather goods store, though not necessarily its cheapest. The **Leather Factory** (Avenida Revolución 1042; 85-47-20) stocks gorgeous jackets, multicolored purses, skirts, pants, and belts, everything custom-made from top-grade supple leather. Good place to haggle.

"Fight smog and buy a horse," is the motto at a Wild West leather emporium two blocks down. **El Vaquero** (Avenida Revolución 802; 85-52-36) specializes in rawhide boots and saddles.

An expensive selection of French perfume, Waterford crystal and European fashions glitters under the roof of the glamorous import warehouse **Sara** (Avenida Revolución 1004; 88-22-12).

Duck into the lace-draped **Villa Colonial** (Avenida Revolución 517) where vendors display handmade lace, embroidered clothing and Mexican blankets.

Toward Calle 2a, you can escape the brassy avenida at **Plaza Revolución**, an indoor mall full of jewelry stores and craft boutiques like **Galerías Fernanda** (Local PB8 and PB9, street level; 85-22-42), specializing in Nativity figurines.

Selected handicrafts from the state of Mexico are featured at **Casart** (Paseo de los Héroes and Calle Mina; 84-11-11), a gift shop inside the Centro Cultural Tijuana.

On the other side of busy Avenida Independencia stands giant **Plaza Río Tijuana**, with its supermarket, cinemas and boutiques crammed with elegant souvenirs. Across Paseo de los Héroes is snazzy **Plaza Fiesta**, Tijuana's leather-sole heaven.

Tijuana's newest shopping extravaganza is the brightly colored 263-store **Pueblo Amigo** (Vía Oriente and Paseo Tijuana, Zona del Río). This rambling complex, reminiscent of the pueblos of Central Mexico, offers a variety of shops and services including a carnival complete with clowns. Get yourself some comfortable shopping shoes; there's a lot of ground to cover.

ENSENADA SHOPPING

Easy-going **Avenida López Mateos**, the main shopping promenade, has good buys in leather goods (jackets from Oaxaca for one-fifth the going rate in the United States), ceramics, crafts and wrought iron.

One of the finest local selections of Mexican folk art fills several rooms at the government-run **Centro Artesanal Fonart** (Avenida López Mateos 1306; 6-15-36).

Asin (Avenida López Mateos 797; 8-29-80) is a tiny shop offering a fine selection of duty-free perfumes and quality gifts.

There's leather galore at **Raquel's Leather Boutique** (Avenida López Mateos 775-B; 8-11-55), with wall-to-ceiling shelves of clothing, belts, wallets and purses. If you can't find it here, move on to the next leather palace in line, **Old Joe's** (Avenida López Mateos 755; 8-11-55), crowded with sandals and bags.

The exquisite gold and silver jewelry will turn your head at **Artes Bitterlin** (Avenida López Mateos 1000; 8-17-33), also featuring sculptures and stonework, and at **La Mina de Salomón** next door (Avenida López Mateos and Avenida Blancarte; 8-17-33).

La Casa del Abuelo Zen (Calle Ruiz 108; in a gallery of shops below Las Margaritas Restaurant) is the best bet in Ensenada for quality, custommade cowboy boots.

For a full dose of kitsch from all over the world, wander through the cuckoo clocks and Venus de Milo figurines at **Estero Beach Imports** (Estero Beach Resort south of town; 6-62-44). If you can't decide on something Old World, try the import shop's tropical branch, **Estero Beach Mexican Shop** (Estero Beach Resort south of town; 6-62-44).

SAN FELIPE SHOPPING

Stores and stalls along **Avenida Mar de Cortez** and downtown side streets make up San Felipe's shopping zone. The main items for sale are fireworks, ironwood animal sculptures, sombreros and sunhats, and whimsical shell sculptures of dune buggies.

Nightlife

The nighttime party mood swings into high gear on weekends in Tijuana and Ensenada, attracting waves of tourists to overflowing discos. South of this border belt the nights close early.

TIJUANA NIGHTLIFE

Flashing lights and throbbing music transform Avenida Revolución from a shopper's promenade into a tawdry discoland after 9 p.m. The downstairs shops close and the upstairs discos open—at least ten of them. Two of the best are **Viva Zapata** (Avenida Revolución between Calle 5a and Calle 6a; 88-29-93; weekend cover), featuring photos of Emiliano Zapata and Pancho Villa, and **Tequila Circo** (Avenida Revolución and Calle 3a; 85-02-75) with confetti-scattered carpets and big-top tent on the ceiling to match its disco-circus chaos.

Sip a margarita and listen to serenading mariachis at **Tía Juana Tilly's** (Avenida Revolución 701; 85-60-24), the popular *tourista* hangout, next to the Jai Alai Palace. Or check out the nearby sister establishment, **Tijuana Tilly's Fifth Avenue** (Avenida Revolución and Calle 5a).

Outside the downtown district, several discos draw crowds. The multi-level **Disco Splash** (Francisco Javier Mina 3, Zona del Río; 84-21-19) features bubbling lucite columns in day-glo colors and splashing ultraviolet dance floor lights. Sundays are reserved for non-drinking teens.

If bigger is better, the more glamorous giant disco **OH!** (Paseo de los Héroes 50, in Plaza Río Tijuana) is always packed to its video-lit rafters. Nobody loves a light show more than the modern-day Mexican, and you, too, will be amazed at the sophisticated **Club Baccarat** (Boulevard Agua Caliente 4500, in Fiesta Americana; 81-71-00). In all seriousness, this state-of-the-art club received an International Lighting Design Award, the first, but probably not the last, awarded to a disco in Mexico.

ENSENADA NIGHTLIFE

Hussong's (Avenida Ruiz 113; 8-32-10), the most disreputable saloon in Baja, is a place you ought to visit at least once. Founded in 1892 during Ensenada's gold-rush era, this cantina slaked the thirst of countless rowdies and dreamers who flooded the pioneer city when gold was discovered at nearby Real de Castillo. Today it's still rowdy, with sawdust on the floor and disintegrating murals on the walls. Police stand guard to keep the mayhem at a minimum. If the world-famous margaritas don't make the mark, try Hussong's own bottled brew.

Across the street is the new **Papas & Beer** (Avenida Ruiz and Calle Prima Altos; 4-01-45), a popular, two-floor video disco for the younger crowd. Huge baskets of french fries, potato balls and potato skins are served, in keeping with its name (*papas* means "potatoes").

My personal favorite is **Tortilla Flat** (Terminal de Pesca Deportiva; 8-25-86). A local hangout, this disco-bar features live rock and Latin tunes, with a quiet glass patio at the back of the club dangling out over the starlit harbor.

Another romantic sanctuary is **Sarape's Bar** (Boulevard Costera and Avenida Blancarte; 8-16-06). The beamed ceiling and dim-lit seating around a colonial fountain create an Old Mexico mood, enhanced by background ballads and serenading mariachis.

The best live entertainment in town can be found at **La Pinta Disco** (at Hotel La Pinta, Avenida Floresta and Boulevard Los Bucaneros; 6-26-01). This classy circular cubbyhole has a bar, dance floor and excellent Mexican musicians.

SAN FELIPE NIGHTLIFE

San Felipe is swimming in bars—about half-a-dozen, not counting the back-alley cantinas.

For the daring and the curious, **El Puerto** (Calle Zihuatenejo, across from the bus station) is the oldest and one of the raunchiest bars in town, dating back to the 1940s. It is frequented by Mexican fishermen and aging ladies-of-the-night. There's often good Latin music and dancing, with an occasional strip show. Women should go accompanied.

By comparison, the Americanized **Miramar** (north end of Avenida Mar de Cortez 315; 7-11-92) is bland and tame, with a jukebox, cable television and slippery dance floor. Here and at the more refined **Plaza Club Ladies Bar** next door (Avenida Mar de Cortez; 7-12-36), the tourists gather to boogie to Top-40 tunes and watch television sports.

Baja Norte Addresses and Phone Numbers

TIJUANA

Bank—Bancomer, Calle Constitución between Calle 4a and Calle 5a
Consulates—American Consulate, Calle Tapachula 96 (81-74-00);
 Canadian Consulate, Calle German Gedovius 5-202 (84-04-61)
Laundry—Lavamática Campestre, Avenida Agua Caliente near Hotel
 Fiesta Americana
Medical Service—85-81-91
Money exchange outlet (Casa de Cambio)—Booth in front of Caesar's
 Hotel, Avenida Revolución and Calle 5a (88-37-74)
Police—Calle 8a and Avenida Constitución (85-70-90; emergency phone 134)
Post Office—Calle 11a and Calle Negrete (85-77-93)
Tourist Attorney—Attorney for the Protection of Tourists, Centro de
 Gobierno Z. R. 22000 (84-21-38)
Tourist Office—Paseo de los Héroes, Edificio Paseo Héroes, Oficina #2
 (84-05-37). There's also an information booth at Avenida Revolución
 and Calle 4a

ENSENADA

Bank—Banco Internacional de Baja California, Avenida Juárez and
 Avenida Gastelum
Hospital—Avenida Ruiz and Calle 10a (8-65-55)
Laundry—Lavamática Blanca, Centro Comercial Limón Bahía (6-25-48)
Medical Emergencies—Avenida Obregón 318-2 (8-25-50)
Police—Avenida Obregón 259 (6-43-43 or 134 for emergencies)
Post Office—Avenida López Mateos and Calle Floresta
Tourist Information—Two offices: Avenida López Mateos 1306 (6-37-18)
 and Avenida Blancarte 128 (8-24-11)
Tourist Attorney—Attorney for the Protection of Tourists, Avenida
 López Mateos and Avenida Espinoza, next to tourism office
 (6-36-86)

SAN FELIPE

Bank—Banco Internacional and Bancomer, both on Avenida Mar de Cortez

Hospital— Clinical Escareño, Calzada Chetumal (7-13-70)

Laundry—Laundromat on Calzada Chetumal near Avenida Mar de Cortez

Police—Calle Bermejo near Calle Ensenada (7-10-21)

Post Office—Avenida Mar de Cortez across from Chapala Motel

Tourist Attorney—Attorney for the Protection of Tourists, Avenida Mar de Cortez and Calle Manzanillo (7-11-55)

Tourist Information—Office in back of El Marino Liquor Store, Avenida Mar de Cortez and Calzada Chetumal (7-11-83)

SAN QUINTÍN

Bank—Banco Internacional, off Transpeninsular Highway behind the small Pemex station and plaza

Post Office—Transpeninsular Highway, Km. 297, across from Restaurant El Alteño

CHAPTER FIVE
BAJA SUR

Southern Baja is, some feel, the peninsula's better half. Seekers of sun and outdoor adventure will certainly agree. While more-populous Baja Norte toils with industry and agriculture, Baja Sur plays. It has the most beautiful beaches and swankiest hotels, the lushest date-palm oases, the best-preserved ancient cave art, the premier whale-watching sites, the top sportfishing and windsurfing and the loveliest sunsets on the peninsula. All this without a swelled head. Prices are quite affordable in all but the ritziest zones.

The climate draws admirers, too. Balmy, bright winters and springs into which little rain ever falls sweeten the Sea of Cortez resorts; weather tends to be cooler on the Pacific. Summers are so hot, the saying goes, that lizards carry twigs around in their mouths to stand on when they stop to rest in the desert. But coastal breezes relieve much of that sting, and there are occasional hurricanelike *chubascos* from August through October.

Although most of the Baja Sur interior rolls out flat as a griddle, especially in the barren Vizcaíno Desert and the dusty, irrigated Magdalena Plain, chains of awesome mountains heave up along the coast. The regal, brick-raw Sierra de la Giganta rears up behind Loreto, and the lusher Sierra de la Laguna soars to 7,100 feet along the southernmost tip of the peninsula. As you head into the shady oases communities of San Ignacio and Mulegé, the ubiquitous cactus begins to blend with increasing numbers of palm trees and shrubs to form subtropical pockets in the desert.

The Baja Peninsula, originally believed by the Spanish to be an island, actually broke off from the Mexican mainland some 30 million years ago along the San Andreas Fault, which burrows under the Sea of Cortez and all the way up California to San Francisco. More recently, about 10,000 years ago, nomads drifted south into Baja and settled along the coasts. In the sierras between Santa Rosalía and Mulegé, their cave paintings still cover the roofs and walls with animals and images that date back perhaps 500 years before the coming of the Spanish.

Come they did, in search of gold and pearls. But the first discoverers sailed into La Paz purely by chance—they were a group of mutinous Spanish sailors, part of an expedition sent by Hernán Cortés, on the run after murdering their captain. Fortún Jiménez, who led the mutiny, was later massacred by Baja Indians when he and his men tried to rape the native women.

In 1535, Cortés himself tried to colonize the La Paz area, but so many of his fellow colonists starved to death that he gave up and sailed back to the mainland. It took the faith of the Jesuits to conquer unruly Baja. Father Juan María Salvatierra established a permanent settlement at Loreto in 1697, and his order set about civilizing the peninsula. For the next 132 years, the Jesuits, Franciscans and Dominicans governed in Baja and laid the groundwork for most major towns that exist today.

During the Mexican-American War of 1846-1848, the United States invaded southern Baja in hopes of annexing the peninsula along with the rest of Alta (or upper) California. Only a narrow negotiating concession kept Baja California within Mexican territory when a peace treaty was signed.

Over the years, cut off from mainland politics, Baja developed its own hardy, roughneck lifestyle, often attracting fugitives and shady opportunists. Foreign settlers moved in to colonize and build industries, such as the French mining concern at Santa Rosalía. But in 1933, President Lázaro Cárdenas snatched back all foreign-owned lands in Mexico under a nationalization mandate, returning Baja to Baja Californians. And in 1974, lovely Baja Sur became Mexico's 30th state.

This vivid vacationland gets off to a leisurely start with Guerrero Negro, a plain little Pacific Coast town at the edge of the Vizcaíno Desert where the state of Baja Sur officially begins. A mammoth salt production plant here churns out tons of salt per day, but the real attraction is watching whales congregate in two nearby coves.

Across the peninsula on the Sea of Cortez, the colorful town of Santa Rosalía hovers on the edge of a windy seaside plateau. You'll notice immediately that this town was once a mining center—it is surrounded by hills that have been gouged and slashed for ore. Much more appealing are the downtown wooden houses with close-set verandas and overgrown alleys, installed by the French-owned mining company that built most of Santa Rosalía in 1885.

To the south, the pretty little oasis town of Mulegé, resting in a date-palm forest, introduces southern Baja's first good camping beaches along Bahía Concepción.

After Mulegé, the dusty sportfishing resort of Loreto about 90 miles south is a disappointment. Despite its historic background as Baja's oldest settlement, Loreto—with its crumbling *malecón* and drab beaches—lacks

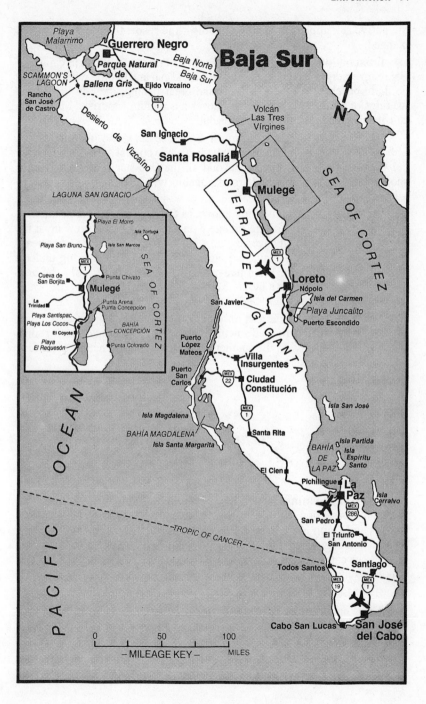

Playa Malarrimo

Guerrero Negro

Baja Norte
Baja Sur

Baja Sur

Parque Natural de Ballena Gris

SCAMMON'S LAGOON

Ejido Vizcaíno

Rancho San José de Castro

Desierto de Vizcaíno

Volcán Las Tres Vírgines

San Ignacio

Santa Rosaliá

LAGUNA SAN IGNACIO

Mulegé

SEA OF CORTEZ

SIERRA DE LA GIGANTA

Playa El Morro

Isla Tortuga

Playa San Bruno

Isla San Marcos

SEA OF CORTEZ

Cueva de San Borjita

Punta Chivato

Mulegé

La Trinidad

Punta Arena
Punta Concepción

Playa Santispac
Playa Los Cocos

El Coyote

BAHÍA CONCEPCIÓN

Playa El Requesón

Punta Colorado

Loreto

Nópolo

Isla del Carmen

San Javier

Playa Juncalito

Puerto Escondido

Puerto López Mateos

Villa Insurgentes

Puerto San Carlos

Ciudad Constitución

Isla Magdalena

Isla San José

BAHÍA MAGDALENA

Isla Santa Margarita

Santa Rita

BAHÍA DE LA PAZ

Isla Partida

Isla Espíritu Santo

El Cien

Pichilingue

La Paz

Isla Cerralvo

San Pedro

El Triunfo

San Antonio

PACIFIC OCEAN

TROPIC OF CANCER

Todos Santos

Santiago

Cabo San Lucas

San José del Cabo

0   50   100

– MILEAGE KEY –   MILES

N

the native sex appeal to become the big-time resort the government has planned.

From out of the parched desert south of Loreto, La Paz, the capital of Baja Sur, emerges like a breath of fresh air. Clean and balmy, with beautiful northern beaches, gorgeous sunsets and great fishing, the city has all the makings of a top seaside resort yet never has a glut of tourists. Many now call it the finest city on the peninsula.

About a three-hour drive south, San José del Cabo introduces Los Cabos (The Capes)—the hotel-saturated, 20-mile coastal strip from San José del Cabo to Cabo San Lucas. Beyond all the five-star hotels and T-shirt shops, San José remains a charming pueblo with meandering streets and a broad shady plaza.

Cabo San Lucas, commonly known as Cabo, is the hottest destination in Baja. Once a sleepy fishing village with a cannery, Cabo grew up at the rim of a lovely protected cove beyond which the Sea of Cortez rushes head-long into the Pacific. Today, that old hamlet is fast disappearing under a veneer of tourist chic. With heavenly beaches and arguably the best sportfishing in Baja, plus a fabulous primitive setting at the tip of the penin-sula, Cabo San Lucas just can't lose.

North of Cabo San Lucas on the Pacific, the moist green oasis town of Todos Santos offers limited amenities but serves as headquarters for some of the wildest beaches on the southern peninsula, favorite haunts of surfers.

Easy Living
Transportation

ARRIVAL

BY CAR

The **Transpeninsular Highway** (Mexico Highway 1) connects all towns in this section, except for a short stretch where **Mexico 19** connects La Paz and Cabo San Lucas to Todos Santos. Both highways are well marked and in good condition. Occasional downpours in the fall and winter months can cause temporary washouts. Gas is usually available in all towns, although unleaded (*extra*) gas can be hard to find.

BY AIR

Three commercial airports operate in Baja Sur: Loreto International Airport, La Paz International Airport and Los Cabos International Airport (for San José del Cabo and Cabo San Lucas).

Resorts Airline serves **Loreto's airport.** The **La Paz airport** is served by Aeroméxico, Mexicana Airlines and Aero California. The **Los Cabos**

airport has flights via Aeroméxico, Mexicana Airlines and Continental Airlines. The bidding war is on, however, and several more airlines will be serving Los Cabos in the near future.

Taxis and vans wait at all three airports to transport you to your hotel or nearby areas.

BY BUS

There's daily bus service to and from all southern Baja towns. The two main bus lines in these parts are **Tres Estrellas de Oro** and **Autobuses Aguila**.

Bus depots can be found in the following towns:

Guerrero Negro: The station is located at the entrance to town next to Cuartos Rita.

Santa Rosalía: Tres Estrellas de Oro (22-01-50) is found on the Transpeninsular Highway south of Pemex station; Autobuses Aguila (2-03-74) is at Calle 3a and Calle Constitución.

Mulegé: The station is located on Transpeninsular Highway near entrance to town.

Loreto: The depot for Tres Estrellas de Oro is at Calle Salvatierra.

La Paz: Tres Estrellas de Oro and Autobuses Aguila (2-30-63) can be found at Calle Jalisco and Calle Ortiz while Autotransportes La Paz (2-21-57) is located at Calle Degollado and Calle Prieta.

San José del Cabo: Tres Estrellas de Oro and Autobuses Aguila (2-02-00) are located at Calle Doblado 605 while Autotransportes La Paz (2-03-11) is found at Calle Zaragoza and Niños Héroes.

Cabo San Lucas: The depot is found across from the marina near the Giggling Marlin Hotel and Restaurant on Avenida Lázaro Cárdenas.

Todos Santos: The depot is on Avenida Colegio Militar at the Santa Mónica Restaurant.

BY BOAT

Luxury cruise ships make frequent stops in Cabo San Lucas. Some of these lines include **Admiral Cruises** (800-327-0271), **Carnival Cruise Lines** (800-327-9501), **Cunard Line** (800-528-6273), **Holland America Line** (800-426-0327) and **Princess Cruises** (800-421-0522).

There's also **ferry service** to and from the mainland of Mexico between Santa Rosalía and Guaymas, La Paz and both Topolobampo and Mazatlán. At press time Cabo San Lucas–Puerto Vallarta service was suspended but rumored to be restarting (with additional service from La Paz to Puerto Vallarta). Several classes of overnight accommodations are available.

In Santa Rosalía, tickets for Guaymas are sold at the **Maritime Building** (Transpeninsular Highway south of downtown; 2-00-13). Service is less crowded than out of La Paz.

In La Paz, tickets for Topolobampo and Mazatlán are purchased at the **Ferry Building** in town (Calle Altamirano and Héroes de la Independencia; 5-11-56). Ferries use the terminal at Pichilingue, 17 miles north of La Paz. This is a very busy crossing. Make advance reservations.

In Cabo San Lucas, tickets and information are available at the **Muelle Marítimo** in the marina (3-00-79). Advance reservations advised.

Before boarding the ferry, you must have your tourist card or visa stamped, then obtain a car permit at the local vehicle registration office **(Registro Federal de Vehículos)**.

CAR RENTALS

Cars can be rented in Loreto by contacting the Presidente Hotel (3-07-00). The airports serving La Paz, San José del Cabo and Cabo San Lucas all have rental booths. In La Paz, the airport booths include **Budget** (2-10-97), **Avis** (2-18-13), **Hertz** (2-53-00), **Auto Renta Sol** (2-45-45) and **Auto Servitur** (2-56-59). At Los Cabos airport, you'll find **Budget** (2-04-14), **Hertz** (2-03-75) and **Avis** (3-06-80). In Cabo San Lucas, there's a **Hertz** office at the Hacienda Hotel (3-01-17).

BICYCLING AND MOTORBIKING

The many coastal roads in the southern peninsula make wonderful biking routes. For bicycle, moped and Honda rentals in La Paz, see **Viajes Palmira** (Avenida Alvaro Obregón, across from Hotel Los Arcos; 2-40-30). For bike rentals near San José del Cabo, check at **Costa Azul Rentals** (Transpeninsular Highway, four miles south of San José; 20-9-38). For moped, scooter and bicycle rentals in Cabo San Lucas see **Chubasso's** (22 Boulevard de la Marina; 3-04-04).

PUBLIC TRANSPORTATION

In La Paz, municipal buses operate along the *malecón*, with regular service from the corner of Avenida Obregón and Avenida Cinco de Mayo to the Pichilingue ferry terminal. Taxis in all Baja cities are widely available.

Easy Living
Hotels

GUERRERO NEGRO HOTELS

The **El Morro Hotel** (Boulevard Emiliano Zapata en route into town) is a favorite of both whale watchers and local laborers. The quiet rooms adjoin the parking area. Each is a clean, screen-doored crackerbox with double beds and a light in the shower so you can watch the Baja dust go down the drain. Budget.

The only thing resembling luxury out here is the **Hotel La Pinta** (Transpeninsular Highway, Km. 5). In the shadow of the futuristic eagle monument, La Pinta stands all by its lonesome self in the desert several miles north of town. Its 33 rooms are large and comfortable. Moderate.

SAN IGNACIO HOTELS

Nestled in a grove of palms, **Hotel La Pinta** (Transpeninsular Highway, 1.2 miles south at the San Ignacio turnoff) is one of the more attractive of the chain's Baja hotels. Its 28 rooms ring an open courtyard with a pool and, for additional recreation, there's a volleyball net out back. The restaurant and bar provide a view of the surrounding date palms. Moderate.

SANTA ROSALÍA HOTELS

My local favorite is the 24-room, tropical **El Morro Hotel** (Transpeninsular Highway, Km. 1.5; 2-04-14), a mile south of town. Built from chiseled stone, the hotel and its restaurant-bar rest on a flowery terrace jutting out over the sea. Its ritzier rooms have ocean views, and some have patios. More modest rooms are well lit, tile-floored and comfortable. Budget.

Up in the residential area amid authentic French colonial houses, you can bed down with local history at the graceful **Hotel Francés** (Calle 11 de Julio 30, Colonia Mesanorte; 2-08-29). This century-old guest house, renovated in 1983, is one of the most unusual hotels in Baja. With an old locomotive parked out front, fine interior woodwork, cloth-covered walls, ample balconies and verandas, the Francés is a fascinating architectural specimen. Its public areas, however, have the cold and barren feeling of an old museum. Budget.

PUNTA CHIVATO HOTELS

On this secluded point between Santa Rosalía and Mulegé stands a newly renovated mini-resort with one of the most beautiful settings in all of Baja. **The Hotel Punta Chivato** (Transpeninsular Highway, Km. 156, ten miles east on a dirt road; 3-01-88, reservations: 706-853-0188 for direct radio-phone contact), built in the 1960s as a desert hideaway for fly-in fishermen, has been restored to a new level of elegance. Stone and stucco villas (34 now with more on the way) line a rocky point overlooking Bahía de Santa Inés. They have stone fireplaces, sunken tiled tubs and arched windows with dramatic sea views. There's a pool and a spacious restaurant and bar fronted by a patio flanked with palms. A 4,000-foot landing strip and RV campground round out the facilities at this superlative resort. Fishing, diving, snorkeling and windsurfing are favorite pastimes here, but kicking back and enjoying the idyllic beauty and warm sun comes a close second. Moderate.

MULEGÉ HOTELS

For low, low prices with a bit of history, you can't beat the century-old **Hotel Hacienda** just off the town plaza (Calle Madero; 3-00-21). The worn rooms, rather shabbily furnished, surround a shade-filled courtyard used by guests for reading and relaxing. Four of the rooms have kitchenettes. Budget.

Just up the block is the cheerful **Las Casitas Hotel** (Calle Madero 50; 3-00-19). Its eight air-conditioned rooms have garden-style furniture and kerosene lamps in case the town's electricity dies. Parrots and umbrella-shaded tables brighten the central courtyard, adjoining a lovely restaurant. Budget.

Tranquility and a spectacular view of Mulegé's river and palm groves are yours at the 21-room **Hotel Vista Hermosa** (Camino al Faro or Lighthouse Road; 3-02-22), only five minutes from town. This lovely hilltop complex of low buildings and red-tile roofs contains a pool, elegant restaurant and tasteful, large rooms with air-conditioners, double beds and tile floors. Gracious management. Moderate.

Directly across the river, cloistered among the palms, is the 52-room **Hotel Serenidad** (Transpeninsular Highway, exit two miles south of Mulegé; 3-01-11). Long popular with the pilot set (the airport is next door), this well-maintained hideaway is an ideal overnight sanctuary for terrestrials as well. Old hacienda atmosphere. Some rooms have kitchens, woodburning fireplaces and king-sized beds. The restaurant and bar are legendary in these parts. Moderate.

LORETO HOTELS

There are few budget accommodations here since Loreto caters to game fishermen who expect to pay American rates.

If you're really down on your dollars, you can go to the 17-room **Hotel Salvatierra** (Calle Salvatierra; 3-00-21), a bland but tidy motel with air-conditioning located near the entrance to town. Budget.

Your best find in Loreto may be the **La Fiesta Bungalows** (Beachfront on Boulevard López Mateos at Fernando Jordan; 3-00-29, reservations: P.O. Box 131, Loreto, Baja Sur, Mexico). Problem is there are only two of these picture-postcard, thatched-roofed units, situated on the grounds of a private home. They're large enough, however, for a family and feature full kitchens, queen-sized beds, tiled floors and air-conditioning. Quality furnishings plus nice extras such as hammocks and barbeque grills. Budget.

For comfort, you'll be in good shape at the 49-room, beachfront **Hotel La Pinta** (Fraccionamiento Madero, northern end of town; 2-00-25). The premises, facing the nicest section of Loreto's city beach, hold every convenience: pretty pool and patio, sitting room with television and fireplace, and an attractive restaurant. Every room has a balcony and Spanish-style furnishings. Moderate.

Baja Sur's resorts begin getting bigger and slicker at the 250-room **Presidente** (Boulevard Misión de Loreto, on Playa Nópolo, five miles south of town; 3-07-00, reservations: 800-472-2427), a sprawling, self-contained seaside resort. International standards prevail here from the huge pool (with swim-up bar) to the classy restaurant and to the rooms as well—carpeted, air-conditioned and richly furnished. Sports activities galore (sailing, windsurfing, water skiing, scuba diving and fishing) flourish on the well-groomed beach. Ultra-deluxe rates, with meals and activities included.

LA PAZ HOTELS

The old **Hotel Yeneka** (Calle Madero 1520; 2-46-88), downtown's best low-cost inn, has 20 clean rooms uniquely furnished with closets, lamps, doors and all trimmings made from *palo de arco*, a bamboo-like wood. Located several blocks off the beach, the fan-cooled rooms open onto an antique-strewn courtyard—complete with resident pet monkey. Budget.

The colorful **Pensión California** (Calle Degollado 209; 2-28-96) also is easy on your cash flow. Its courtyard is a pack rat's dream, crammed with paintings, maps, masks, turtle shells, Aztec statues and the accumulated souvenirs of 20 years. In your high-ceilinged room, with its cement floor, ceiling fan and simple armoire, you may find an infant Jesus painted on the plaster wall. Budget.

Moving up the scale, the 56-unit **Hotel Gardenias** (Avenida Aquiles Serdán 520 Norte; 2-30-88) is the prettiest hotel in town for your money. Located several blocks off the *malecón*, its gardens extend from the parking lot to the pool and patio. Its big, attractive rooms have phones, air-conditioning, two double beds and roomy baths. Budget.

If you'd rather be in the heart of the action, stay at the busy **Hotel Perla** (Avenida Alvaro Obregón 1570; 2-07-77), the cheapest hotel on the *malecón*. Its spartan older accommodations include scuffed furniture and tired beds, while the newer upstairs rooms have a fresh upbeat mood, with blond-wood trimmings, big windows and enough light switches for a light show. All have phones and air-conditioning. Moderate.

Perhaps the most popular bayfront hotel, with a good blend of services and colonial elegance, is the three-story **Hotel Los Arcos** (Avenida Alvaro Obregón 498; 2-22-44). The 130 cushy rooms give you carpeting, air-conditioning, color televisions, phones, servibars and balconies suspended over the patio and pool. Moderate. If you prefer more privacy, rough-hewn bungalows with the same luxuries are available at the nearby **Cabañas de los Arcos** (Calle Mutualismo between Calle Nicolás Bravo and Calle Rosales; 2-22-97). Moderate.

Toward the southern end of town, a lovely hacienda-by-the-sea is half hidden by blossoming grounds. The **Hotel La Posada** (Playa Sur and Calle Nuevo Reforma; 2-40-11) is an idyllic 25-unit retreat with fireplaces in all its rooms. Moderate.

BAHÍA DE LOS MUERTOS TO CABO PULMO HOTELS

This coastal stretch south of La Paz and north of San José del Cabo contains an off-beat brigade of comfortable, sports-oriented, remote hotels. All have private airstrips and are accessible by often-rough roads. None has a local phone, and communication takes place by radio. All operate on the American plan, including three meals per day, in their rates. Many close for the month of September each year due to heat, humidity and the danger of the *chubascos* (hurricanes). All have loads of character and out-of-the-way, unhurried charm.

The **Hotel Las Arenas** (off Highway 286 south of San Juan de los Planes, 40 miles southeast of La Paz, reservations: P.O. Box 3766, Santa Fe Springs, CA 90670; 800-352-4334 in California, 800-423-4785 outside California) is a paradise for beachcombers. The big, wind-swept rooms with balconies look out on miles of gorgeous empty beach fronting Bahía de la Ventana. Deluxe.

The **Hotel Punta Pescadero** (off Transpeninsular Highway 10 miles north of Los Barriles on a terrible road, not for wide vehicles or faint-hearted drivers, reservations: P.O. Box 1044, Los Altos, CA 94022; 800-346-2252 in California, 800-426-2252 outside California) is an ideal romantic hideaway. Clinging to a precipice called Punta Pescadero, this remodeled hotel mixes spectacular views with an intimate air. Rooms have private terraces and fireplaces with wood placed at your door. Deluxe to ultra-deluxe.

The **Rancho Buena Vista** (off Transpeninsular Highway south of Los Barriles, reservations: P.O. Box 673, Monrovia, CA 91016; 818-303-1517, 800-258-8200) is a hacienda-style fishing resort well suited to families. One of the oldest of Baja's coastal resorts, the Buena Vista has bright, air-conditioned rooms with patios and verdant, tropical grounds rolling down to a long, beautiful beach. Deluxe to ultra-deluxe.

Rancho Leonaro (off Transpeninsular Highway south of Buena Vista, reservations: The Entrepreneur Center, 910 Grand Avenue #114, San Diego, CA 92109; 619-270-6400) is a 350-acre dude ranch on Bahía de las Palmas with facilities for fishing, hunting and horseback-riding along a fabulous beach. Guests bed down in spacious thatched quarters with queen-sized beds and ocean-front patios. Deluxe.

Hotel Punta Colorada (off Transpeninsular Highway, La Ribera exit, four miles south on the coastal road to the signed entry, reservations: P.O. Box 2573, Canoga Park, CA 91306; 818-703-1002), calls itself "The Roosterfish Capital of the World." This old, bungalow-type hotel, the most rugged and homey of Baja's fishing resorts, features large, air-conditioned rooms on a rise overlooking a point with a stony beach. Deluxe.

El Rincón (off Transpeninsular Highway, La Ribera exit, several miles south of Punta Colorada on the coastal road, reservations: Peter Wirth, Casa de Sierra Nevada, Hospicio 35, P.O. Box 226, San Miguel de Allende, Guerrero, Mexico; 465-2-04-15) is a bed-and-breakfast-style guesthouse on a smashing beach. The suite-sized rooms invite long stays with their vibrant Mexican decor, solid furnishings and terraces with glorious views. Moderate to deluxe.

SAN JOSÉ DEL CABO HOTELS

San José has two hotel zones: downtown, with few good choices, and beachfront, with high-priced resorts.

At the 12-room, family-run **Hotel Colli** (Calle Hidalgo) your bottom dollar buys a small, neat room with ceiling fan, simple decor and, if you're lucky, sliding glass door opening onto a streetside balcony. Budget.

Best deal downtown is the **Hotel Posada Terranova** (Calle Degollado between Calle Zaragoza and Calle Doblado; 2-05-34). Newly converted from an old two-story family home, this five-room charmer has a patio restaurant and bar attached. Rooms are simple, comfortable and spotless. The Tolentino family goes out of its way to make you feel at home. One upstairs room has a kitchen. Budget.

Along the belt of swank tourist hotels (Zona Hotelera), there's one humble place you might overlook. **Brisa del Mar Trailer Park and Motel** (three miles south of town off Transpeninsular Highway) has a row of quiet, comfortable motel rooms in a bungalow-style building half hidden by the trailer sites, pool and restaurant that dominate the grounds. Budget.

If the town's few budget hotels are full, you can dip into your ice cream money for an upscale pad at the **Posada Real** (Zona Hotelera; 2-01-55, reservations: Pan American Hotels International, P.O. Box 2776, Chula Vista, CA 92012; 800-678-7244). Its 150 rooms go all out on bed space, phone, television, air-conditioning and sea views. Deluxe.

SAN JOSÉ DEL CABO TO CABO SAN LUCAS HOTELS

The 20-mile corridor from San José del Cabo to Cabo San Lucas is studded with deluxe hotels. The two most distinctive:

The **Hotel Palmilla** (five miles south of San José off the Transpeninsular Highway, reservations: 800-542-6082 in California, 800-854-2608 outside California) is clearly Baja Sur's finest resort. Beautifully landscaped with swaying palms, this villa-style hotel on Punta Palmilla could not be more Old Mexico. The large rooms shine with colorful handicrafts, hand-carved furniture and painted tiles; they include open hearths and small refrigerators. Patios look out to sea over a superb, sheltered beach. The lobby is alive with the squawk of parrots and macaws. A life-sized chess game stands next to the tennis court, and the chapel has blessed many weddings. Full American plan from November through May at ultra-deluxe rates; European plan the remainder of the year at deluxe rates.

One of the cape's most elegant and popular hotels, the **Twin Dolphin** (Transpeninsular Highway, seven miles north of Cabo San Lucas; 3-02-56, reservations: 1625 West Olympic Boulevard, Suite 1005, Los Angeles, CA 90015; 213-386-3940) is a modern 50-room hotel, rather spare and strikingly contemporary in design, with landscaped rock gardens. This uncluttered style extends to the air-conditioned rooms and suites, all with balconies, some with fireplaces. A sophisticated, well-executed Baja cave-painting motif decorates the grounds. American plan. Ultra-deluxe.

CABO SAN LUCAS HOTELS

Amid Cabo's top-dollar joints are scattered economy hotels. The bottom of the barrel is the **Hotel Marina** (Paseo La Marina and Calle Guerrero; 3-00-30), offering compact, comfy rooms surrounding a pool and patio. Moderate. The colonial-style **Hotel Mar de Cortez** (Avenida Lázaro Cárdenas; 3-00-32, reservations: 800-248-9900) puts you right downtown in one of 72 big, air-conditioned rooms with balconies. Moderate.

If you've come to party in style, hang your sombrero at the 112-room **Hotel Hacienda** (Playa Medano, turnoff at sign near Pemex station; 3-01-17, reservations: 800-421-0645). Right on Cabo's liveliest beach, the Hacienda bustles with poolside barbeques and nightly mariachi music. The air-conditioned rooms are adorned with beautiful wood furniture made at the hotel, cozy writing nooks, balconies and cheerful rose-marble bathrooms. Deluxe to ultra-deluxe.

The Sheik of Araby would have headed straight for the Moorish-looking **Hotel Solmar** (Playa Solmar; 3-00-22, reservations: 213-459-9861). Situated on Baja's southernmost beach, the Solmar's molded low white buildings crouch among vast sands that stretch to the pounding Pacific. The hotel has a tennis court, and its 67 air-conditioned rooms face the sea, with balconies and colonial-style decor. Deluxe.

Next door and overlooking Cabo's busy harbor, **Finisterra** (Domicilio Conocido; 3-00-00, reservations: 800-347-2252) is something of a landmark here at Land's End. A masterpiece in natural stone, tile and mahogany, this 104-room resort is well-managed and maintained. It has a beautiful pool and sun terrace, health club, restaurant, and the area's best fleet of fishing boats. Deluxe.

TODOS SANTOS HOTELS

The only true hotel in town is the colonial-style **Hotel California** (Calle Juarez, next to the Pemex station; 4-00-02). This 16-room hideaway has been extensively renovated and now sports a lovely brick patio and solar-heated swimming pool surrounded by bougainvillea. Red-tiled stairways lead to several floors of tidy rooms with handmade Mexican pine furniture and newly plumbed bathrooms. A small restaurant and bar have been added as well. Moderate.

The charming **Todos Santos Inn** (Calle Obregón 17) is like an ancient Latin townhouse. Decorated throughout with antiques and original beams and bricks, this marvelous 125-year-old building was restored from near ruin by its live-in *norteamericanos* proprietors. They lovingly outfitted three rooms with well-preserved wood furniture (including beds with gauzy mosquito nets) and turned the house into a bed-and-breakfast inn. Moderate.

Restaurants

GUERRERO NEGRO RESTAURANTS

No place else in this area comes close to the **Malarrimo Restaurant-Bar** (Boulevard Emiliano Zapata, en route into town). Named for the remote beach north of Guerrero Negro, the restaurant is strung with nets and floats and glass balls. Soft music accompanies breakfast, lunch and dinner, including breaded scallops, Spanish-style octopus, abalone steak and other delicacies of the sea. Budget to moderate.

For even less expensive fare, fill up at the rambling **Mario's Restaurant-Bar** (Boulevard Emiliano Zapata, next door to the El Morro Hotel). This simple stop-in has wobbly Spanish-style chairs and tables, a bar and the town's only disco. The menu offers omelettes, seafood and all sorts of Mexican plates. Budget.

SANTA ROSALÍA RESTAURANTS

For a fish dinner that would feed a family of four, try the attractive seaside **Restaurant El Morro** (Transpeninsular Highway one mile south of town, in the El Morro Hotel; 2-04-14). This rough-hewn stone restaurant, with a cozy bar and expansive dining hall, dishes out generous servings of mouth-watering seafood and Mexican dinners. Budget.

Down toward the ferry terminal, you can also enjoy an inexpensive meal at the beachfront **Balneario Selene** (Transpeninsular Highway, across from the Pemex station; 2-06-85). Order a T-bone steak, *almejas* (snail cocktail), or oysters, or step into the north wing of this odd little restaurant and sample the town's only Chinese cuisine. Budget.

That big thatched-roof structure you'll see rising up from the harborfront is Santa Rosalía's popular **Palapa Mauna Loa** (Transpeninsular Highway, below the copper smelter; 2-11-87). Oddly enough you'll find some of Baja's best pizza and spaghetti (plus traditional steak and seafood dishes) served up in this tropical setting. Budget.

MULEGÉ RESTAURANTS

The **Restaurant Patio El Candil** (Calle Zaragoza) draws you into its sun-speckled, shadowy patio at the end of the entry passage. Excellent breaded shrimp, Mexican meals and breakfasts are served outdoors at simple picnic tables. Budget.

Warmth and camaraderie go with the chow at **Paco & Rosy's** (Transpeninsular Highway, well-signed turnoff about a mile south of town).

The rustic old *palapa*, nestled in a clump of palms beside the river, opens for dinner each night at "sex o'clock" according to Paco, who says he's switched from steaks to Chinese cuisine because of the skyrocketing cost of beef. Most evenings turn into a party—Paco strumming with hurricane force on his guitar and his guests dancing up a storm. Budget.

Mulegé's larger hotels all host weekly Mexican fiestas with buffet dinners and mariachi music. The most lip-smacking of these fiesta meals is served in the king-sized dining room of the hacienda-like **Hotel Serenidad** (off the Transpeninsular Highway, several miles south of Mulegé). Moderate. Buffet servers ladle out tamales, enchiladas, chile rellenos, tacos, guacamole, chips and beans while mariachis serenade at the tables and a fire flickers in the hearth. If you like your parties smaller, **Las Casitas Hotel** (Calle Madero 50; 3-00-19) hosts a cozier buffet with minstrels at its colorful restaurant-patio and cool bar. Moderate.

The casual **Restaurant Azteca** at the Hotel Terraza (Calle Zaragoza; 3-00-09) and the gracious restaurant at the **Hotel Vista Hermosa** (Camino al Faro—Lighthouse Road) should not be ignored, either. Both serve good food at budget-to-moderate prices.

BAHÍA CONCEPCIÓN RESTAURANTS

Several good outdoor restaurants serve the beach communities along the Bahía Concepción.

Playa Santispac, the most popular beach south of Mulegé, has an open-air *palapa* café with down-to-earth chow and prices. **Ana's Restaurant & Bakery** (on the beach) is one of two bakeries in the Mulegé area. Ana's has become a local institution, operated by the industrious Mariana Ríos Aredondo. It produces a procession of cookies, pastries, rolls and fruit cakes that disappear as fast as she turns them out. Her adjoining patio restaurant is an extension of her kitchen, serving steaks, chicken, fish, tacos and other Mexican dishes. Budget to moderate.

The other bakery is at the **Villa María Isabel RV & Trailer Park** (Transpeninsular Highway, 1.5 miles south of Mulegé). While Ana's goods are distinctly Mexican, these (baked by a New York-trained chef) taste unmistakably gringo: golden loaves of French and rye, grainy bran muffins, coffee cakes so rich they'd make Sara Lee crawl under a rock. Moderate.

LORETO RESTAURANTS

For breakfast, grab a tiny leather-covered chair and chow down with a cactus omelette (*huevos con nopolitos*) at the *palapa*-style **Café Olé** (Calle F. Madero 14; 3-04-96). All sorts of egg dishes, hamburgers and Mexican plates are on the slate at this quick-stop, al fresco eatery. Budget.

For more formal dining with a little candlelight thrown in, pay a visit to the spacious thatch-roofed **Cesar's Restaurant** (Calle Emiliano Zapata and Calle Benito Juárez; 3-02-03). The walls of stone and lofty ceiling recall some old exotic pavilion. The waiters treat you like royalty and meals are all delicious: spaghetti, seafood, steak, crepes suzette. Moderate.

My best meal in Loreto came from the casual, sandy-floored **Restaurant Playa Blanca** (Calle Hidalgo and Calle Madero; 3-04-28), which resembles an oversized fisherman's shack. Adorned inside with picnic tables and the huge spine of a killer whale arched across the ceiling, this seafood house serves hefty American-style meals with baked potato and warm buttered bread. I recommend the succulent garlic-spiced crab. Budget to moderate.

LA PAZ RESTAURANTS

For an out-of-this-world seafood soup, check out the simple **Restaurant Puerto Balandra** (Calle Rosales and Calle Altamirano), five blocks off the *malecón* in the suburbs. Just as the walls and ceilings swim with crabs and starfish, so too your soup will teem with shrimp, crab, scallops, clams, octopus, fish and oysters in a spicy broth that will open your pores. Breakfast and lunch only. Budget to moderate.

Without doubt, *número uno* for morning coffee or afternoon tea is the big, wide-open, bayfront **La Terraza Restaurant** (Avenida Alvaro Obregón 1570; 2-07-77), next door to the Hotel Perla. As a meeting place and happy hunting ground, La Terraza attracts both upper-class Mexicans and tourists. Many people gather for a drink here or at the attached bar to watch the famous La Paz sunsets over the bay. As for meals, the chef's salads are okay, but most of the entrees are overpriced and not very good. Instead, have breakfast here—they turn out terrific *huevos rancheros* and omelettes. Budget to moderate.

For cuisine and class, La Paz's best restaurant may well be the **Bermejo** in the Hotel Los Arcos (Avenida Alvaro Obregón 498; 2-27-44). It's a white-napkins-and-grand-piano type of place, with fresh roses on the table and a salad bar, but its chief asset is plain old good cookin'. You may choose from lobster in garlic sauce, seafood fetuccine, filet mignon and the taste treat of the house—the seafood platter for two, served in a big split-level terra-cotta dish with hot coals on the bottom to keep the mound of lobster, shrimp, clams and scallops piping hot. Moderate to deluxe.

Two other notable seafood restaurants (why eat anything else while on the Sea of Cortez?) are **Las Brisas** (Avenida Alvaro Obregón and Héroes Colegio Militar at the north end of town) and **La Paz-Lapa** (also known as Carlos y Charlie's) (Avenida Alvaro Obregón and Calle Marqués de León; 2-60-25). Both are big *palapa*-style bayfront outfits with generous menus and wandering mariachis. Locals seem to favor the simple, quiet Las Brisas, but I prefer La Paz-Lapa for its setting directly on the beach, superb sunset view, frosty margaritas, delicious garlicky vegetable appetizers (*zanahorias*) and friendly waiters. Both moderate to deluxe.

SAN JOSÉ DEL CABO RESTAURANTS

Andremar (Boulevard Mijares 34; 2-03-74) sets you in a sunny, multilevel garden ideal for an outdoor brunch. Good French toast, eggs and *licuados*, plus seafood meals and Mexican food are dished out under the palms. Budget to moderate.

Steakabo Charcoal House (Calle Hidalgo, next to the Aeroméxico office) offers an intimate, candlelit atmosphere and some of the best mesquite-grilled beef in town. Moderate.

When you get downright desperate for a big, juicy hamburger, straddled with homemade french fries, stop in at **Pancho & Lefty's** (Boulevard Mijares, just south of City Hall; 2-02-66). Run by Texans who honor the tradition of good, hearty eatin', this popular new *palapa*-style restaurant also serves seafood, steaks and Mexican dishes; but its burgers are the region's best. Budget to moderate.

If money is no object, check out **Damiana** (Boulevard Mijares 8; 2-04-99) or **Da Giorgio's** (Transpeninsular Highway, 2.5 miles south of San José), two somewhat overpriced but snazzy restaurants. Damiana, divided between a dim indoor bar with pigskin chairs and a garden of towering palms aglow with lamplight, serves excellent seafood, meats and Mexican dishes. Da Giorgio's, an elegant Old World quasi-manor up on a hill, specializes in rich, nongreasy pizzas (the combination pizza is a world unto itself), with a good salad bar. Both deluxe.

CABO SAN LUCAS RESTAURANTS

Restaurant prices have skyrocketed in Baja and nowhere is the trend more evident that in Cabo. Deluxe prices are the rule nowadays at most upper-crust resorts and you'll be hard-pressed to find quality food anywhere at less than moderate figures.

Tucked away on a side street en route to Medano Beach, the unassuming **Rey Sol** (across from Marina Sol Condominiums) is noted for its outstanding breakfasts and seafood. Its elevated veranda-like dining space, shaded by overhanging trees, is backed by a polished bar and a grinning mustachioed carving of the sun. Try the savory chicken tacos and tender abalone. Budget to moderate.

The latest craze in Cabo is mesquite-grilled steak and seafood and the two most popular restaurants serving such fare are **Paty's** (Los Niños Héroes and Calle Zaragoza; 3-07-99) and **Flor Guadalajara** (Avenida Lázaro Cárdenas; 3-01-34). Both have open-air patios, mariachi music and big barbeque pits emitting the tantalizing aroma of sizzling Sonora beef, lobster, shrimp and ribs. Dinner only at Paty's. Moderate to deluxe.

The two favorite *palapa* restaurants down on lively Medano Beach are **El Delfín** and **Las Palmas**. Both are known for their fresh, savory seafood and great ringside seats for people-watching amid the bronzed beach bunnies and yachtsmen. Las Palmas has a bit more panache, El Delfín a tad more action. Moderate to deluxe.

Locals repeatedly told me the best food in town is hiding out not at some five-star bayside bistro but at the dusty **El Faro Viejo Trailer Park** (Calle Abasolo and Calle Morales, a half-mile inland from downtown Cabo San Lucas). The circular bar and comfortable dining area, drenched in shadows in the center of the park, attract long waiting lines. Moderate.

TODOS SANTOS RESTAURANTS

It's not the most likely place in the world to find a genuine French restaurant so, understandably, **Le Bistrot** (Calle Juarez; 4-01-84) has this little farming village abuzz. The owners have painstakingly restored the old brick paymaster's office from a 19th-century sugar plantation and now serve such Gallic specialties as quiche Lorraine crepes, steak à la bernaise and chocolate mousse to an enthusiastic throng of visitors and locals. Moderate.

The Great Outdoors
The Sporting Life

CAMPING

Beach camping is excellent in Baja Sur, especially during the late winter and spring when the weather is balmiest. Summers can get very hot, and winters may warrant a down-filled sleeping bag.

For general camping supplies in La Paz, try **La Perla de La Paz** (Calle Arreola and Calle 21 de Agosto); in San José del Cabo, try **Supermercado Aramburo** (Calle Zaragoza); and in Cabo San Lucas, try **Supermercado Aramburo** (Calle Morelos and Calle 20 de Noviembre).

SWIMMING

The swimming in Baja Sur's many placid bays is wonderful. The wilder, open seas of the Pacific call for caution. The water stays chilly, even down south, until around March or April, but the fierce sun warms you up. Protect yourself from the rays. The first time I came to Baja, my companions and I all got blistered feet and had to guard our skin by wearing socks.

FISHING AND BOATING

The Bahía Concepción is alive with *cabrilla*, snapper, triggerfish and hundreds of others. *Pangas* for fishing and exploring can be rented at Punta Arena and Playa Santispac south of Mulegé. Fishing trips can also be arranged at most hotels in Mulegé. Check with **Jorge Yee's Tackle Shop** (across from the Pemex station in Mulegé) to rent cruisers and equipment.

(Text continued on page 114.)

Whale-Watching in Baja

Every winter they migrate down by the thousands from the frigid Bering Sea near Alaska to the tropical waters of Baja California's lagoons to breed and bear their young. California gray whales, nearly hunted to extinction by greedy whalers as recently as the 1940s, have made a remarkable comeback. From January to March, you stand a good chance of seeing them splashing and spouting off the Pacific shoreline of western Baja. From the east side of Baja on the Sea of Cortez, other kinds of whales can be seen—humpbacks, killer whales, blue whales.

Laying eyes on the biggest creature on earth, in the flesh, is a special thrill. Grays are 50-foot, 40-ton leviathans. Of course, what you're likely to see may only hint at this bulk: the roll of a mottled gray back or the flip of a blue-black fluke, a staggering 12 feet across. These dimensions, coupled with whales' romantic reputations as indomitable Moby Dicks and gentle giants, can make whale-watching an unforgettable adventure.

The three Baja lagoons where whales tend to congregate are Scammon's Lagoon, Laguna de San Ignacio and Bahía Magdalena. Farther north, whale spouts are visible from La Bufadora lookout on Punta Banda near Ensenada. One of the best and most accessible whale-watching sites is on Laguna Guerrero Negro (Estero de San José), about five miles south of Guerrero Negro at the end of a washboard road. This spot is reputed to be a favorite mating ground for grays.

Parque Naturel de Ballena Gris (Gray Whale Natural Park) on Scammon's Lagoon is another excellent, though more remote, whale-watching spot. The turn-off is about five-and-a-half miles south of Guerrero Negro at Km. 110 on the Transpeninsular Highway, marked as Laguna Ojo de Liebre. Drive for about 15 miles over sandy washboard, periodically marked with little whale signs, (don't get stuck in soft sand!), and you will arrive at a beachy area on the lagoon where you can camp or hire native *pangas* for a close-up look. If you're lucky, you'll see the spouts going like fountains. Binoculars help. In a nearby channel nicknamed "The Nursery," mother whales shelter their newborn from the dangers of the deep.

Captain Charles Scammon, for whom the lagoon is named, ruthlessly slaughtered the babies and mothers when he discovered this breeding ground in 1837. Now, according to authorities in Guerrero Negro, no whale-watching boats are permitted here.

If you want to watch whales by boat, go south to Laguna de San Ignacio, where fishermen will take you out among Baja's friendliest whales. Mothers and calves have been known to swim up and nuzzle the boats or let their noses be stroked. From the oasis town of San Ignacio, a rough road runs southwest for about 50 miles to the lagoon, a trip requiring a truck or other high-clearance vehicle. If you lack transportation, stop by the **Cooperativa Laguna de San Ignacio** (Calle Juárez 23, just off the town plaza in San Ignacio), a company that transports fishermen out to the lagoon every day.

Farther south, at the sleepy port of San Carlos on Bahía Magdalena, you can also hire a boat for a close-up look at whales off Isla Magdalena and Isla Santa Margarita. Check at the Hotel Las Cabañas out on the point south of town past the landing strip. Some say the whale watching is even better (and less expensive) at the fishing village of Puerto López Mateos, about 30 miles north of San Carlos on a side road off Mexico 22. Boat owners will happily haggle for the chance to show you the whales that pass through narrow Boca de Soledad.

If you miss these opportunities to see whales, inquire about whale-watching trips out of La Paz at **Viajes Lyesa**, a travel agency located in the Hotel Gran Baja (Calle Rangel; 2-46-80).

A unique, two-week whale-watching cruise called **Special Expeditions** (720 Fifth Avenue, New York, NY 10019; 212-765-7740) takes adventurers around the Baja peninsula to both the Sea of Cortez and the Pacific.

To arrange other Baja whale-watching trips from north of the border, contact **Baja Expeditions** (P.O. Box 3725, San Diego, CA 92103; 619-297-0506), offering trips out of La Paz; and **Baja Adventures** (16000 Ventura Boulevard, Suite 200, Encino, CA 91436; 800-345-2252), with trips to Laguna de San Ignacio.

Loreto's best-known outdoor activity is sportfishing. You can nab yellowtail, *dorado*, marlin, sea bass and sailfish, especially in winter. *Pangas* line the beach, for rent at half the going rate in Cabo San Lucas. Check with the **Sociedad Cooperativa La Loreteña** (Playa Loreto right in town; 3-00-72). For cabin cruisers, check at the sportfishing center at the **Hotel Misión de Loreto** (Avenida López Mateos 1; 3-00-48). Fishing tournaments are sponsored by the **Presidente** (Boulevard Misión de Loreto, on Playa Nópolo; 3-07-00).

Sailors and fishermen should note the new yacht harbor and marina at **Puerto Escondido** (15 miles south of Loreto off the Transpeninsular Highway). The boat landing and anchoring facility are operational but the complex remains under construction and is far from being completed.

The southernmost peninsula is the best-known sportfishing paradise in Baja. Some say the biggest marlin (300 to 500 pounds) can be caught out of La Paz, but blue marlin weighing over 1,000 pounds have been wrestled in off the cape. Peak marlin season extends from February to November, but gamefishing is generally great year-round.

For sportfishing in La Paz, try **Velez Fleet** (Los Arcos Hotel, Avenida Alvaro Obregón; 2-27-44), **Operadora de Viajes Sud California** (Avenida Alvaro Obregón 1665-3; 2-83-82), **Viajes Coromuel** (Avenida Alvaro Obregón at Los Arcos Hotel; 2-27-44). For boating excursions, try **Aventuras Turísticas Calafia** (Calle Yucatán 2013; 2-58-37).

Pangas and guides are available for rent at **Pangas Fishing** (Los Arcos Hotel, Avenida Alvaro Obregón; 2-27-44). Just north of San José del Cabo, you can rent *pangas* at nearby **Puebla La Playa**. Major hotels between San José and Cabo can arrange trips in larger boats.

Big hotels like the **Solmar** (3-00-22) and the **Finisterra** (3-00-00) in Cabo San Lucas have some of the best local fleets, with fishing information booths in their lobbies. Another good source for anglers is **Cabo Sportfishing** (3-04-40).

SEA KAYAKING

Southern Baja waters are fine for this strenuous but exciting sport. Alaska-base **Ageya Kayak Routs** (P.O. Box 141506, Anchorage, AK 99514; 907-248-7140) offers kayak trips from 7 to 14 days departing from Loreto. On the Pacific side of the peninsula they venture to the islands and estuaries in Bahía Magdalena. **National Outdoor Leadership School** (P.O. Box AA, Lander, WY 82520; 307-332-6973) gives a Baja sea-kayaking course from November through March on the Sea of Cortez.

SKIN DIVING

Diving in Baja Sur gives you the opportunity to see manta rays, octopus, seals, dolphins, whales, plus tropical and game fish galore. The best time of year to dive is from May to November, when the water is warm—up to 95° in August.

Equipment rentals and trips around Bahía Concepción are available at the **Mulegé Dive Shop** (Calle Madero 45, Mulegé).

On Loreto's municipal beach there's a scuba and snorkeling information and equipment booth near the fishing pier and small lighthouse. Also check at the **Presidente** (Boulevard Misión de Loreto, on Playa Nópolo; 3-07-00).

For La Paz diving trips and equipment rentals, check at **Baja Diving & Service** (Calle Independencia 107-B; 2-18-26) or **Deportiva La Paz** (Calle Obregón 1680; 2-73-33).

You can rent equipment and find out about trips out of Cabo San Lucas at **Cabo Acuadeportes** (Playa Medano in front of the Hotel Hacienda; 3-01-17), which offers diving instructions for novices, **Amigos del Mar** (near the Cabo San Lucas marina; 3-00-22) and **Fantasía Diving** (at Hotel Pamilla, five miles south of San José off the Transpeninsular Highway).

SURFING AND WINDSURFING

The east side of southern Baja is generally too calm for surfing but breezy enough for some excellent windsurfing.

In La Paz, **La Concha Beach Resort** (Carretera Pichilingue, Km. 5; 2-65-44) has equipment rentals.

Vela Highwind Center (125 University Avenue, #40, Palo Alto, CA 94301; 415-322-0613) offers one week and longer windsurfing packages in Los Barriles from November to March. You can also rent sailboards at the **Playa Hermosa Hotel** right on Playa Los Barriles. In Cabo San Lucas, try **Cabo Acuadeportes** (Playa Medano in front of Hotel Hacienda, 3-01-17) for board rentals.

HUNTING

Hunting along the Baja Sur coast revolves around ducks, geese, doves and quail. Hunting trips can be arranged through most major hotels and resorts.

GOLF

The sprawling **Campo de Golf Los Cabos** (located in the Zona Hotelera, one mile south of San José del Cabo) is a popular, well-manicured course. Tee times are arranged through major hotels in the Los Cabos area including Posada Real (Zona Hotelera; 2-01-55) and Hotel Palmilla (five miles south of San José del Cabo off the Transpeninsular Highway).

TENNIS

The **Loreto Tennis Center** at the Presidente near Loreto (Boulevard Misión de Loreto, Playa Nópolo; 3-07-00) has lighted courts, as do most of the deluxe hotels in the Los Cabos area.

Beaches

GUERRERO NEGRO BEACHES

Guerrero Negro is surrounded by marshy ground and salt evaporating ponds. There are no good beaches reachable by conventional car.

Playa Malarrimo—Adventurous owners of 4-wheel drives can try this remote beach on the Vizcaíno Peninsula, the famous repository of driftwood, bottles, crates, nets and debris from shipwrecks and plane wrecks—tons of sea litter swept onto its long, wild shores by a strong Pacific current. Many treasure hunters have come and gone, taking part of Malarrimo with them.

Facilities: None.

Getting there: About 45 miles south of Guerrero Negro, turn off the Transpeninsular Highway at Ejido Vizcaíno. Proceed about 70 miles to Rancho San José de Castro, take the turnoff shortly past this ranch and continue about 25 miles on poor road to beach.

SANTA ROSALÍA BEACHES

Santa Rosalía has several narrow black sand beaches, the result of nearly a century's worth of slag dumped into the sea from the coastal copper refinery. Some better ones:

Playa El Morro—Next to El Morro Hotel, this rocky beach looks out at a little lighthouse on a rock and at the town of Santa Rosalía in the northern distance. Large, mottled rocks in subtle earth tones cover the beach. A sandy road continues from this beach to a secluded one sometimes called **Playa Hanky-Panky.**

Facilities: None. *Camping:* Good. *Swimming:* Lovely. A small seawater lagoon just off the beach makes a nice wading pool for children. *Snorkeling:* Around offshore rock with lighthouse.

Getting there: Off Transpeninsular Highway at sand road descending to sea just south of El Morro Hotel, Santa Rosalía.

Playa San Bruno—About 15 miles south of Santa Rosalía on the fringes of the catatonic village of San Bruno, you'll find a surprisingly attractive mile-long stretch of beach with powdery grayish sand dunes, a handful of *palapa* shacks and a cove of date palms waving their heads out toward Isla San Marcos.

Facilities: A camping area called **Costa Serena** rents one-room palm-leaf huts at low rates. Bathrooms; hot showers. Groceries are in San Bruno. Careful of the bugs that live in the thatched roofs of huts. *Camping:* Good. Small fee. *Swimming:* Good. *Diving/snorkeling:* Around Isla San Marcos. *Windsurfing:* Good. *Fishing/boating:* Good around Isla San Marcos and Isla Tortuga. Boats for rent from local fishermen.

Getting there: Located in San Bruno.

Punta Chivato (★)—This offbeat point of land is one of Baja's prettiest destinations, preserved from tidal waves of tourism only by its twisting washboard road and shortage of facilities. However, standard cars can make the road trip, and many RVs do so regularly. Punta Chivato's relative isolation gives it the feel of an island, with 25 miles of white sand curving around both its northern and southern shores. Its gorgeous views and quietude have captivated a handful of *norteamericanos* who are colonizing the point.

Facilities: Restaurant, cold showers nearby. *Camping:* Very good, for a fee. *Swimming:* Good all around the point. *Snorkeling:* Good around offshore islands. *Windsurfing:* Good along sheltered shoreline. *Fishing/boating:* Very good. *Pangas* for rent at the house. *Shell-collecting:* A wealth of lovely shells.

Getting there: Take Transpeninsular Highway to marked turnoff some 25 miles south of Santa Rosalía. Proceed on sand road for about 12 miles to beaches.

MULEGÉ TO BAHÍA CONCEPCIÓN BEACHES

The pearly beaches along the 33-mile-long Bahía Concepción face spectacular multihued waters of blue, turquoise and jade green, glimmering by night with phosphorescence that streaks the forms of leaping fish like fireworks. The beaches have good, full, grainy sand—about a seven out of ten—but tend to be rather narrow. Still, their beauty attracts swarms of campers. For the most hidden beaches, take a boat out to Punta Concepción on the bay's protective peninsula and explore its eastern shore. There are dozens of premier beaches waiting to be explored; many are unmarked. Closer to home, from north to south along the bay you will find:

Punta Arena—This pretty, half-mile-long beach is also commonly called "Raul's Beach" after one of its permanent residents. Some travelers rent huts along this beach from October to May, escaping north when the summer temperature skyrockets. Being more settled than the other beach camps, Punta Arena is also less fiesta-frantic and more relaxed.

Facilities: Pit toilets. *Camping:* Good, for a small fee. *Swimming:* Wonderful. *Snorkeling:* Pleasant. *Windsurfing:* Outstanding. Punta Arena is rated by sports magazines as a top spot for beginners. *Fishing/boating:* Offshore islands and hidden beaches can be explored by boat from here. Skiff rentals along the beach. *Shell-collecting:* Good, small shells.

Getting there: About ten miles south of Mulegé off Transpeninsular Highway at marked turnoff onto long sand road.

Playa Santispac—This is the most popular Bahía Concepción beach, an RV heaven, though not as attractive as many others, with rather hard, gritty sand. It does have good anchorage (surrounding islands form a protected cove), a seaside lagoon with natural hot springs, and places to eat. It also has a slightly rowdy reputation as the partying beach of the bay.

Facilities: Toilets; restaurants. *Camping:* Excellent, for a small fee. *Swimming:* Great. *Snorkeling:* Pleasant. *Windsurfing:* Good. *Fishing/boating:* Boats for rent.

Getting there: About ten miles south of Mulegé past Punta Arena, take marked turnoff from Transpeninsular Highway.

Playa Los Cocos—For peace and quiet, complete with improved bathroom facilities and friendly campers, this is a good choice. The white sand extends for about half-a-mile with numerous lean-to *palapas* at the campsites. Even more private is the shell-strewn, empty beachlet around the rocky northern tip.

Facilities: Toilets. *Camping:* Very good, for a fee. *Swimming:* Very good. *Snorkeling:* Pleasant. *Windsurfing:* Good. *Shell-collecting:* Good around the northern tip.

Getting there: About 12 miles south of Mulegé just past Playa Santispac, turn off Transpeninsular Highway at palm tree sign.

Playa El Coyote (★)—This is my favorite Bahía Concepción beach for many reasons: its privacy, panoramic view, pillowy sand, the exquisite hues of its water, its cliffs and, not least of all, its trees—the only beach on the bay with natural shade.

Facilities: Shower. Also, a stone pool was built below the beachside cliffs to trap warm waters bubbling out of the rocks into the sea—another attempt at a hot tub, though not as successful as the one at Playa Santispac. *Camping:* Wonderful. Fee charged. *Swimming:* Lovely. *Snorkeling:* Good around cliffs northeast of beach. *Windsurfing:* Good.

Getting there: About 20 miles south of Mulegé off Transpeninsular Highway past Rancho El Coyote, turn at palm tree sign and continue along rocky coastal road to beach.

Playa El Requesón—This beach has the distinction of being attached to its own island. Windswept and open, far from the madding crowd along the rest of the bay, El Requesón feels like some farther shore in a romance novel. A wide sandbar connects it to bushy Isla Requesón and separates the bay from an inlet forming a glassy lagoon. The sandbar is walkable and driveable at low tide, but beware of wet sand sucking your tires in.

Facilities: None. *Camping:* Good. *Swimming:* Good. *Snorkeling:* Good around island. *Windsurfing:* Good.

Getting there: About 26 miles south of Mulegé past El Coyote, turn off Transpeninsular Highway at sign.

LORETO BEACHES

The beaches around Loreto are overrated. **Playas de Loreto**, the municipal beaches extending five miles north of town, tend to be dusty and rocky. **Playa Nópolo**, the site of the looming Presidente Hotel 15 miles south of town, consists of a neatly combed patch of imported white sand fronting the hotel and a larger section farther south around Punta Nópolo that is good for camping. A better campsite is rocky **Playa Juncalito** south of Nópolo, backed by the majestic Sierra de Gigante.

LA PAZ AREA BEACHES

Beachaholics, you have arrived. Without question, Baja's most beautiful beaches are located in the southern zone from La Paz to Cabo San Lucas on the Sea of Cortez. These are the ultimate in desert beaches—treeless, stark, dune-like, with blinding white sand washed by striking blue sea. If you like this kind of clean beauty, you will agree that Waikiki and Acapulco have nothing on the beaches that follow.

Playa Pichilingue—This series of small sand beaches near the ferry terminal north of La Paz attracts locals and day-tripping sunbathers. The shallow bay makes this a pleasant sailing destination for a lunch stop, but the pebbly sand, especially at low tide, and lack of shade detract from the already bland setting.

Facilities: Restaurants with bathrooms. *Camping:* Not recommended. *Swimming:* Pleasant. *Windsurfing:* Fair.

Getting there: Follow Carretera Pichilingue north of La Paz for 12 miles; take the ferry terminal turnoff and follow the dirt road to the right.

Puerto Balandra—Balandra occupies a tranquil cove north of La Paz, but campers and picnickers like it too well. Its sands meander among many beachside rock formations that create wonderful hide-'n-seek crevices good for reading, resting or romancing.

Facilities: None. *Camping:* Good. *Swimming:* Good. *Snorkeling:* Good around the rocks. *Windsurfing:* Good.

Getting there: From the Pichilingue ferry building 12 miles north of La Paz, follow the main road around the beachfront restaurants where it turns to gravel after about four miles. Continue past a sign reading "Balandra-Tecolote" and take the left fork at the dunes to the beach.

Playa Tecolote—A cleaner, wider, much longer beach than Balandra, Tecolote faces the open sea with a few scattered *palapas* for shade and camping. Strong wind and stronger waves kick up along these shores. Wild and unprotected, Tecolote is backed by sandy prairie containing a few lone ranchos.

Facilities: None. *Camping:* Good, but often windy. *Swimming:* Good. *Snorkeling:* Good around rocks to north and south. *Windsurfing:* Good.

Getting there: About 15 miles from La Paz north of Pichilingue ferry terminal. Dirt road from the terminal leads to Puerto Balandra and continues north for about half a mile, turning to sand and veering left at thatch-roofed rancho for the beach.

Punta Arena de la Ventana (★)—Overlooking spirited Bahía de la Ventana, Punta Arena is a four-star beauty of a beach that is surprisingly unvisited. Lovely dunes and miles of isolated beach curving around an old lighthouse lie just southwest of a secluded resort hotel.

Facilities: Supplies in nearby San Juan de los Planes. *Camping:* Great. *Swimming:* Good. *Snorkeling/diving:* Around Isla Cerralvo offshore. *Windsurfing:* Good. *Fishing/boating:* Good. Check hotel about boat rentals.

Getting there: Take paved Highway 286 from La Paz to San Juan de los Planes, continuing along gravel road about seven miles to marked Hotel Las Arenas turnoff. This washboard sand track squeezes through cactus forest (no go for RVs), opening onto clay road that leads to beach.

Ensenada de los Muertos (★)—A tiny fishing community shares camping space with RVs at this end-of-the-road bay. Soft dunes slope down to the pebbly shores of the sheltered Bahía de los Muertos. A long, lovely sand beach embraces the bay, where porpoises play and windsurfers skim among the cool reflections of safely anchored vessels.

Facilities: None. Supplies in nearby San Juan de los Planes. *Camping:* Good. *Swimming:* Good. *Snorkeling:* Good off rocks to the south. *Windsurfing:* Good. *Fishing:* Good. Ask about renting boats at fishing camp. *Shell-collecting:* Scattered small shells.

Getting there: Take Highway 286 to San Juan de los Planes, proceed past Hotel Las Arenas turnoff, continue directly to Ensenada de los Muertos where road ends.

LOS BARRILES AREA BEACHES

Punta Pescadero (★)—This remote rock-strewn beach, with its old hotel perched on a promontory overlooking the sea, is a lovely refuge among tidepools and cliffs. Pretty sections of beach weave in and out of rocks, continuing north to the town of El Cardonal and Boca de Álamo.

Facilities: Hotel. *Camping:* Best north of hotel. *Swimming:* Good, but requires dodging rocks. *Snorkeling/diving:* Good around rocks, hotel rents gear. *Fishing/boating:* Good, hotel rents boats.

Getting there: There's an airstrip north of hotel. Driving is trickier. Take Las Barriles turnoff from Transpeninsular Highway, veer left at Palmas de Cortez Hotel and continue for eight bone-rattling miles along extremely rough washboard road. Not recommended for RVs or big campers.

Los Barriles—This windy, wild, white-sand beach on open sea has a well-established community of trailer parks and good hotels, catering especially to windsurfers. With a small village at the entrance, the beach stretches for miles to the south along the Bahía de las Palmas.

Facilities: Small supply stores. *Camping:* Good. *Swimming:* Good. *Windsurfing:* Sporting magazines have praised this beach as one of

Baja's top windsurfing locales. Sailboards are for rent at the Hotel Playa Hermosa. *Fishing/boating:* Excellent. Boats for rent at hotels.

Getting there: In Los Barriles, 70 miles south of La Paz.

LA RIBERA TO SAN JOSÉ DEL CABO BEACHES

This 55-mile stretch of unpaved coastal road covers some of Baja's most marvelous secluded beaches—so many that I only have space here for the best. The drive is a fascinating journey in itself (see "Sightseeing" section in this chapter), rough but quite passable by conventional car. The whole area is a happy hunting ground for skinny-dippers, if you're willing to go off the beaten track. Be careful not to get your car stuck in the sand and be aware that beaches can be very windy in winter months.

The Coastal Rural Road (El Camino Rural Costero) begins at the turnoff from the Transpeninsular Highway for La Ribera, some 80 miles south of La Paz. The first eight miles of road are paved; the rest is washboard gravel. The following beaches appear in order as you drive south toward San José:

Punta Colorada a n d **Punta Arena**—The site of a fine old fishing resort, Punta Colorada has a rather rocky beach that smooths into lovely white sand as it slides south toward Punta Arena. Circuitous sandy tracks off the main coastal road will lead you to various sections of beach. Avoid the track leading to the Punta Arena lighthouse, which is part of a military base and is off-limits for swimming or camping.

Facilities: Hotel. *Camping:* Good south of hotel. *Swimming:* Good. *Windsurfing:* Good. *Fishing/boating:* Excellent. Rent boats at the hotel.

Getting there: About seven miles south of La Ribera on coastal road, turn at Hotel Punta Colorada sign.

Playa El Rincón (★)—Remote and not much used, this gorgeous beach extends from a secluded guest house called El Rincón to a point beyond a lone ranch house south of Punta Arena. The isolated beach is open to the blaze of the desert sun, especially ruthless because the Tropic of Cancer crosses Baja's western coast right here. Nude sunbathing is possible.

Facilities: Hotel. *Camping:* Good south of guest house. *Swimming:* Good. *Windsurfing:* Good. *Shell-collecting:* Good.

Getting there: South of Hotel Punta Colorada along sandy coastal road, continue past ranch facing dry fountain and past cultivated palm grove to sandy turnoff onto beach.

Cabo Pulmo (★)—One of the sweethearts of Baja campers, divers and windsurfers, Cabo Pulmo spreads its generous and pristine sands along a big, active cove where RVs, tents and vans settle in with a long, contented sigh. Usually the beach is quite breezy, with consistent side-shore winds that serious windsurfers love. Offshore, unique finger reefs extend into 15 to 80 feet of water, a diver's paradise.

Facilities: Open-air restaurant behind the beach. *Camping:* Great. *Swimming:* Excellent. *Snorkeling/diving:* Terrific around offshore coral reefs. Spearfishing is forbidden. *Windsurfing:* Excellent and very popular. *Fishing:* Good.

Getting there: About 20 miles south of La Ribera along sandy coastal road past Las Barracas.

Los Frailes (★)—Like the feminine counterpart of the more rugged Cabo Pulmo, this shapely white beach on gentle Bahía Los Frailes draws its share of campers and boaters to its sheltered cove.

Facilities: None. *Camping:* Excellent spot. *Swimming:* Great. *Snorkeling/windsurfing:* Good. *Fishing:* Good.

Getting there: About 25 miles south of La Ribera along sandy coastal road, just past Cabo Pulmo.

Fig Tree Beach (Playa Higuera) **(★)**—Several miles south of a gravel road heading inland toward the main highway stands a startling fig tree with enormous multiple trunks. Its wood is bleached silver like prehistoric bones, bent toward the ground in supplication; and its huge leafy head is permanently blown toward the road by perhaps a century of sea wind. Just beyond the tree is a savage-looking beach lashed by waves and half hidden among muscular rock formations, resembling a set for *King Kong*.

Facilities: None. *Camping:* Good, rocks provide a fine shelter. *Swimming:* Rough surf, for daredevils only.

Getting there: About 35 miles south of La Ribera along sandy coastal road, just past gravel junction and Rancho San Luis.

Playa Anónima (★)—About four miles before the coastal road ends near San José, you pass widening hills of sand that obscure a nameless and glorious beach. Steep dunes give some wind-breaking shelter to campers and descend toward a drop-off at the shoreline, which is pounded by vigorous surf. The beach itself is extremely wide, clean and solitary, facing open sea.

Facilities: None. *Camping:* Good. *Swimming:* Strong swimmers only, beware of stinging jellyfish. *Windsurfing:* Good winds, possible beyond rough surf. *Fishing:* Boats for hire in nearby Puebla La Playa.

Getting there: About 50 miles south of La Ribera along the sandy coastal road. The sandy turnoff is not marked. You may have to search for it. It leads to a wide clearing that opens onto the beach.

SAN JOSÉ DEL CABO TO CABO SAN LUCAS BEACHES

The development that began in 1973 with the opening of the Transpeninsular Highway is turning into a boom along this 20-mile strip of scenic beaches. The sampling of beaches here includes those still accessible despite all the new development.

Hotel Beach (Playa Hotelera)—This wide, beautiful beach extending along San José del Cabo's seaside tourist zone faces the rigors of the open sea and is guarded by a procession of slick hotels. It is best for sunbathing and strolling. At its eastern end stands a freshwater lagoon. To the west it merges with Playa Costa Azul, reputedly a good surfing beach.

Facilities: Restaurants here. *Camping:* Not recommended; try the trailer park nearby. *Swimming:* Not recommended; current too rough. *Boating:* Small boats for rent to explore the lagoon.

Getting there: Located in San José del Cabo.

Playa Palmilla—This cozy, protected beach, wedged between outcroppings of rock at Punta Palmilla south of San José, is a rustic haven for pelicans, chickens and rickety fishing shacks. The sand continues west around the rocks to a more beautiful beach fronting the Hotel Palmilla.

Facilities: Restaurant; all amenities in nearby San José del Cabo. *Camping:* Too cramped. *Swimming:* Safe and calm, good for children. *Snorkeling:* Good among the rocks; gear for rent on beach. *Windsurfing:* Good, calm yet breezy. *Fishing/boating:* Good. Catamarans and *pangas* for rent.

Getting there: Turn off Transpeninsular Highway about seven miles south of San José del Cabo at entrance to Hotel Palmilla, veer left before entering hotel grounds, descend to beach.

Playa Bledito (Tequila Cove)—This is another bathtub cove, marvelous for swimming, with fluffy sand curving around an attractive trailer park called Cabo Real. A big recreation *palapa* stands ready for parties up on a hill; hammocks and *palapa* shelters line the shore. The friendly, festive atmosphere here turns the beach into a summer camp for adults.

Facilities: Bathrooms, showers. *Camping:* Very good, small fee. *Swimming:* Delightful. *Snorkeling:* Good around rocks. *Windsurfing:* Good. *Fishing:* Good.

Getting there: Turn off Transpeninsular Highway north of Cabo San Lucas near Km. 19.5 at gate with sign for Cabo Real.

Playa Bahía Chileno—This long beach on sparkling Bahía Chileno has two sections: one is wide open and slightly untamed, with beautiful sand but a rocky shore that discourages swimming. A more inviting section of beach directly fronts the hotel, with more manicured, shady sands maintained for the hotel guests.

Facilities: Hotel. *Camping:* Very good on bluff overlooking the wilder beach. *Swimming:* Rough among rocks, better closer to hotel. *Snorkeling, windsurfing, fishing:* All good.

Getting there: North of Cabo San Lucas, turn off Transpeninsular Highway at Km. 14, "Accesso Público" sign for entrance to camping beach, Km. 15 for entrance to hotel beach.

Playa Bahía Santa María—Considered one of the finest diving and snorkeling spots in the Los Cabos vicinity, this small fairy-tale bay is cupped between two protective cliffs and teems with marine life. The bay also provides safe anchorage for boats. The translucent water laps at a pearly crescent of pebbly sand.

Facilities: Hotel here. *Camping:* Not recommended. *Swimming:* Lovely. *Snorkeling:* Excellent, terrific visibility. *Windsurfing:* Possible, though this bay is ripple-free calm.

Getting there: North of Cabo San Lucas, turn off Transpeninsular Highway at Km. 11.5, "Hotel" sign. Park at Twin Dolphin Hotel and take walkway off service road down to beach.

Shipwreck Beach (Playa Barco Varado) (★)—For sheer drama, this beach is the most breathtaking along this strip. The rusty wreckage of a Japanese freighter juts out of the rocks that split the beach's personality in two—one side bustling with campers, the other an introspective, empty sickle of sand swinging up toward a rocky point that bears a distant lighthouse. Waves crash on the sprawling sands, which are open to the sea.

Facilities: None. *Camping:* Great here. *Swimming:* Use caution. Camp-ing side is more sheltered. *Snorkeling:* Good around rocks bearing freighter. *Surfing/windsurfing:* Good. *Fishing/boating:* Tops.

Getting there: Turn off Transpeninsular Highway just north of Cabo San Lucas at Km. 8, near *vado* (dip in the road) sign.

Playa Vista del Arcos (★)—This hidden beach, with patches of sand threading through a whole metropolis of giant rocks, offers a stunning vista of Land's End and the famous Cabo arch. Passionate waves crash among the rocks, which provide enough privacy to permit nude sunbathing.

Facilities: None. *Camping:* Great and quite secluded. *Swimming:* Risky. Wade in tideline only.

Getting there: Turn off Transpeninsular Highway north of Cabo San Lucas at Km. 5, across from Los Arcos Restaurant. Vicious road. Four-wheel drive only, or walk in.

CABO SAN LUCAS BEACHES

Playa Medano (Rafa's Beach)—This wide, white, curvaceous beach, two miles of exquisite sand and tide, explains at once the backbone of Cabo's popularity. Medano is Cabo's main public beach and *the* people-watching beach of Baja Sur. The shining sands teem with tourist life, the primeval rocks off Land's End rise in the distance and elegant Bahía San Lucas bobs with sailboats and yachts.

Facilities: Restaurants, aquatic sports center. *Camping:* Too much action here, try the ridge overlooking the northeast end of the beach. To get there, take sand road next to Cabo Cielo RV Park (Km. 4 off Transpeninsular Highway) and turn toward the sea just past the cemetery. *Swimming:* Wonderful. *Snorkeling:* Too congested, better at Land's End. *Windsurfing:* Very good. *Fishing/boating:* Tops. Boat rentals available.

Getting there: Take Transpeninsular Highway to sandy turnoff across from Pemex station at northern edge of Cabo San Lucas, continue about a quarter-mile out to beach.

Playa del Amor (Love Beach) (★)—So called because it's secluded, this two-part beach winds among huge rock formations and straddles the Sea of Cortez and the Pacific Ocean. One beach, tucked snugly among the cliffs facing Cabo San Lucas, hugs a sapphire cove. This is Baja's most southerly beach on the Sea of Cortez, reachable only by boat. Beyond the sheltering rocks lies a connected beach whose windy openness matches the wild breakers foaming on its shores. This is Baja's most southerly beach on the Pacific Ocean, accessible from the beach next door (Playa Solmar). The romance of this dual beach attracts so many visitors that it's seldom as private as you would hope.

Facilities: None. All amenities available in nearby Cabo. *Camping:* Best on roomier Pacific beach. *Swimming:* Good on Sea of Cortez side, too rough on Pacific. *Snorkeling/diving:* Excellent around rocks on Sea of Cortez side. Fine diving near Needle Point rock, with "sand falls" created by sand sliding down underwater slopes of over 100 feet. *Fishing/boating:* Boats available at Cabo marina.

Getting there: By boat from the marina or Playa Medano, or on foot from Playa Solmar by climbing over monstrous rocks (safest and easiest at low tide, wear good tennis shoes).

Playa Solmar—This magnificent beach at Land's End spreads out like a vast desert at the feet of two big resort hotels. The sand is hewn into a steep dropoff by the mauling waves of the Pacific. To the east tower fantastic rocky citadels carved by the wind into faces, totems, animals, macabre abstractions. Beyond these rocks is Playa del Amor.

Facilities: Hotels. *Camping:* Not recommended. *Swimming:* Dangerous. *Fishing/boating:* Good. Fishing boats for rent.

Getting there: Follow Hotel Solmar signs from the marina.

TODOS SANTOS AREA BEACHES

Between Cabo San Lucas and Todos Santos on Highway 19, there are at least a dozen sandy turnoffs leading to huge, lonely Pacific beaches with explosive waves that surfers love. The best of these wilderness beaches are just south of Todos Santos.

Playa Punta Lobos—This long open Todos Santos beach extends south from the faded Sierra de la Laguna to windy Punta Lobos, where fishermen gather. Go see the "boat surfing": to avoid being sucked back by the big surf, fishing *pangas* bob among the whitecaps until just the right wave surges up, then rev their engines and catch the crest of the wave, racing all the way to shore and onto the beach in a spray of sand.

Facilities: None. Hotel, groceries, restaurant in town. *Camping:* Good, but wide open. You'll need shelter. *Swimming:* Very dangerous. *Fishing/boating:* Good. Rental *pangas* for whale watching.

Getting there: Turn off Highway 19 just north of Km. 54 and follow dirt road past airstrip for about a mile out to beach.

Playa San Pedrito (★)—This lovely beach summons up images of Polynesia with its dramatic promontories that break the rushing Pacific winds, its palm-fringed cove and its reed-lined lagoon near the sea. The shady solitude makes a welcome campsite or hideaway for discreet nude sunbathing.

Facilities: None. Supplies in nearby Todos Santos. *Camping:* Excellent. Small fee charged by landowners. *Swimming:* Signs warn against swimming near cliffs. You can safely swim in center of beach, away from threatening currents. *Surfing:* Just enough wave action for belly-boarding.

Getting there: Take Highway 19 to sand turnoff near Km. 57 across from the Campo Experimental Forestal (CIFNO), a botanical research center and garden. Bear south on turnoff and continue for a few miles into shady palm grove along a warped clay road.

Playa El Estero—Locals call this famous surfing beach El Pescadero after the nearby fishing village. Even more confusion surrounding its name has arisen since landowners opened an RV park here called San Pedrito and fenced off the old access road. But even though they now have to pay to use it, surfers still swarm to this windy, open strand where pounding waves gnaw away at the beach each winter and make swimming ill-advised.

Facilities: Full-service RV park and restaurant. *Camping:* Good but mostly unsheltered. *Swimming:* Risky. *Surfing:* Prime surfing spot, best from December to February.

Getting there: Follow Highway 19 to the village of El Pescadero. Well-signed entrance for San Pedrito RV Park is at Km. 60 marker.

Playa Los Cerritos—This crescent beach facing the open sea and guarded on one side by cliffs is probably the most beautiful and popular in the area. Soft dunes roll back from the shore.

Facilities: Palapa hut for shelter near northern cliffs. *Camping:* Good. *Swimming:* Dangerous near cliffs. Stick to the middle of the beach, safe even for children. *Surfing:* Modest waves. *Fishing:* Good.

Getting there: Turn off Highway 19 at Km. 64 about eight miles south of Todos Santos, follow dirt road 1.5 miles to beach.

Trailer Parks

All have hookups and bathrooms unless otherwise stated.

GUERRERO NEGRO TRAILER PARKS

Benito Juárez Trailer Park (Transpeninsular Highway, Km. 5, adjacent to Hotel La Pinta) is a simple roadside park (no hookups).

SANTA ROSALÍA TRAILER PARKS

San Lucas RV Park (off Transpeninsular Highway, nine miles south of Santa Rosalía) occupies a serene shore (no hookups).

MULEGÉ TRAILER PARKS

Jorge's Trailer Park (Transpeninsular Highway, a half-mile south of Mulegé) is an attractive park near the river.

Nearby is the rather luxurious **Villa María Isabel RV Park** (Transpeninsular Highway, 1.5 miles south of Mulegé).

The cushiest park along the Bahía Concepción is **Posada Concepción** (Transpeninsular Highway, 20 miles south of Mulegé).

LORETO TRAILER PARKS

Tripui (Transpeninsular Highway, Puerto Escondido turnoff, south of Loreto) has everything from restaurant, pool and tennis courts to tents with bunk beds. The region's most deluxe RV park. Near the beach.

LA PAZ TRAILER PARKS

Oasis Los Aripez (Transpeninsular Highway, Km. 15, ten miles north of La Paz) is a self-contained seaside campsite; older **El Cardón** (Transpeninsular Highway, Km. 4; 2-00-78) has a pool.

LOS BARRILES TRAILER PARKS

Playa de Oro (Transpeninsular Highway, Los Barriles turnoff, toward north end of beach) is an attractive seaside park.

SAN JOSÉ DEL CABO TRAILER PARKS

Brisa del Mar (Transpeninsular Highway, Km. 30) is a veteran 90-space RV park on Playa Costa Azul at the edge of town.

CABO SAN LUCAS TRAILER PARKS

The best are **Vagabundo Trailer Park** (Transpeninsular Highway, about three miles north of Cabo) and **Cabo Cielo** (Transpeninsular Highway, about four miles north of Cabo), next to the beach.

TODOS SANTOS TRAILER PARKS

San Pedrito RV Park (Transpeninsular Highway, Km. 60) is a new beach park featuring a restaurant, pool and hot showers on the beach.

Travelers' Tracks

Sightseeing

GUERRERO NEGRO AND VIZCAÍNO DESERT AREA

Just north of Guerrero Negro, the Transpeninsular Highway passes the 140-foot tall **Eagle Monument,** marking the 28th parallel of north latitude, the dividing line between Baja Norte and Baja Sur. This point marks the change from Pacific to Mountain Time. Turn your watch ahead one hour if you're driving south.

A side road leads into **Guerrero Negro**, site of thousands of salt evaporation ponds and a world leader in salt production. Aside from whale watching at nearby Scammon's Lagoon, there's little of tourist interest here. The town's thriving, well-ordered downtown, however, reflects a level of progress and prosperity not prevalent in many other Baja communities.

From here, the Transpeninsular Highway cuts through the **Desierto de Vizcaíno** (Vizcaíno Desert). For nearly 90 miles, the tortured landscape yields only spiny vegetation and brittle shrubs. Midway along this road, at the farming community of Ejido Vizcaíno, is a turnoff for the wild **Vizcaíno Peninsula**.

Continuing southeast on the Transpeninsular Highway, the march of the cactus finally gives way to an apparent mirage: a forest of date palms spreading into the parched hills. The highway curves over a pond where subterranean water bubbles up, feeding the charming oasis city of **San Ignacio.** Wander around the shady town square and visit the majestic old **Misión San Ignacio,** built by Dominican missionaries in 1786. With its four-foot-thick walls of lava stone, the church is refreshingly cool and wonderfully preserved. Nearby cave paintings in the **San Francisco de la Sierra** provide a glimpse into one of Baja's earliest Indian societies. The best way to visit these hard-to-find paintings is with a guide. See Jorge Fisher on the square at a tiny grocery marked "Primero Consupa and Tourist Información." His family leads trips to these sites at reasonable rates.

Back en route across the desert, the highway continues toward lava fields dominated by three volcanic cones known as **Las Tres Vírgines** (The Three Virgins). Dried out by the harsh heat, the old girls last coughed up a puff of smoke in 1857.

SANTA ROSALÍA

The highway hairpins down through steep rocky terrain until the blue Sea of Cortez flashes into view and a cliffside road winds into Santa Rosalía. On the outskirts stands the rusty, blackened shell of a 19th-century **copper smelter** that arches right over the road. Several little locomotives—used 100 years ago to carry ore out of the mountains—are perched on the cliffs like part of some ancient Disneyland ride.

Downtown Santa Rosalía is filled with evidence of the town's French founders. In addition to the many small shoulder-to-shoulder painted houses with plant-strewn balconies, you'll find the graceful white **Palacio Municipal** (main plaza), the elegant **Hotel Francés** (Mesa Norte) and a handful of surviving **French colonial houses** in the hillside residential zone. The central church, **Iglesia Santa Bárbara** (Calle Obregón and Calle Callel), was designed by A. G. Eiffel (creator of the Eiffel Tower) and made from prefabricated iron shipped here in pieces. An intriguing museum, **Museo de Historia,** (located just off Calle Francesco next to the IMPECSA warehouse) highlights the region's mining and smelting history.

Several miles south of Santa Rosalía, a rough dirt turnoff leads to one of Baja Sur's most intriguing and least-explored attractions: its ancient **cave paintings** in the mountainous desert at San Borjita and La Trinidad. Magical drawings of animals, children and, it is hypothesized, women's sexual organs cover the massive roofs of caves. This area is only accessible by 4-wheel drive. For information about how to reach the caves or secure a guide, contact the Delegado Municipal in Mulegé (Calle Madero; 3-02-48).

MULEGÉ

About 40 miles south of Santa Rosalía stands the lovely oasis at Mulegé. A date-palm jungle crowds around the town and the lazy **Río Santa Rosalía** (also called Río Mulegé), which runs out to the Sea of Cortez. At the river's mouth rises a hat-shaped lookout mound called **El Sombrerito.**

Upstream from the village just south of the plaza stands **La Misión Santa Rosalía de Mulegé,** a well-maintained Jesuit mission. Founded in 1705, the stone-and-mortar church occupies a cool bluff that commands a lovely view of town. A *mirador* behind the mission gives a grand perspective of the oasis, plus a reservoir and dam.

A hill on the other side of town is crowned by old **El Carcel** (federal prison). The colonial jail, dating back to 1842, used to house prisoners on an honor program, allowing them to work in the outside world by day and return behind bars at night. The prison is being turned into a museum and arts and crafts center.

LORETO

After following the beautiful **Bahía Concepción** for about 25 miles, the highway proceeds for 60 miles more into the foothills of the craggy

Sierra de la Giganta. Suddenly, the road widens into proud, freshly laid boulevards on the outskirts of **Loreto**. Then, as you enter town, they dwindle into the dusty, cracked lanes of a typical old Mexican village, which Loreto still remains despite government efforts to turn it into Baja's Cancún.

Home of the "Mother of the Californias," the oldest mission in Baja, Loreto was once capital of the entire peninsula. Its 17th-century church just off the plaza, **Nuestra Señora de Loreto**, was founded in 1697 and served as the axis of military and civil rule in Baja. After weathering both an earthquake and a hurricane, the building is still in decent shape, although the ancient oil paintings inside have been eaten away by time and, one historian told me, bat urine.

Next door to the mission is the **Museo de los Misiones** built in 1973, one of the few museums in Baja, containing the story of Baja's history, colonial art and religious paintings.

A rough side road off the Transpeninsular Highway just south of the Loreto junction leads some 20 miles inland to **Misión San Javier**, the best preserved of Baja's Jesuit missions, founded in 1699. Four-wheel drive only.

LORETO TO LA PAZ

Now you enter a long, 225-mile-long yawn before you awake in the sultry tropics of Baja's southernmost playground. On the way there, you speed over an agricultural plain fed by underground springs around bustling, dusty **Cuidad Constitución**. With a population of 45,000, it is the second largest population center in the state of Baja Sur. Continue through flat mesa land the color of sawdust and ash, along a trajectory of dusty blacktop headed for La Paz, Baja Sur's capital city.

LA PAZ

Once renowned for its lustrous gray pearls, La Paz now enjoys fame for its shell-pink and violent-purple **sunsets,** some of the most passionate in Mexico.

These sunsets are best viewed from anywhere along the shady **malecón** (sea walk), which follows the bayside Paseo or Avenida Alvaro Obregón, La Paz's main drag. The friendly town square, **Plaza Constitución**, is downtown at Calle Cinco de Mayo and Avenida Revolución. Across from the plaza, **Nuestra Señora de la Paz** (La Paz Cathedral) stands on the site of a Jesuit mission built here in 1720.

From shore you'll see distant **El Mogote**, a skinny peninsula poking into **Bahía de La Paz**. Farther north, the island of **Isla Espíritu Santo** was once a center for gray pearl cultivation before the oyster beds were wiped out by a mysterious disease in the 1940s. Nearby **Isla Partida** is the site of a sea lion colony.

You can survey the area's history at the modern **Museo Antropológico** (Calle Cinco de Mayo and Calle Altamirano; 2-01-62).

For an interesting side trip, take lonely Highway 286 south of La Paz. It roller-coasters down into an immense plain that seems to project to infinity and accounts for the name of the main farming town, **San Juan de los Planes** (St. John of the Plains). Side roads amble north to the fishing villages of **El Sargento** and **La Ventana,** and to some beautiful unspoiled beaches.

LA PAZ TO SAN JOSÉ DEL CABO

From La Paz, the Transpeninsular Highway continues south for about 115 miles to San José del Cabo, a prominent tourist town. En route the road passes the late, great mining town of **El Triunfo,** once a silver center like neighboring **San Antonio.**

Next comes the beach community of **Los Barriles,** which launches a rough but scenic road to enchanting **Punta Pescadero.**

A junction farther south points toward the coastal village of **La Ribera,** the source of a rustic road that weaves along about 55 miles of beautiful desert coastline past ranchos, remote hotels, one little restaurant, herds of shy goats and cows, arroyos, cactus and glorious empty white sand beaches. In 1984 this magical road was improved and dubbed **El Camino Rural**

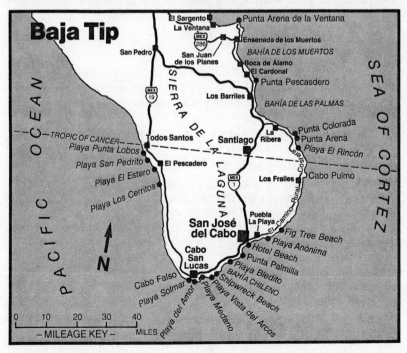

Costera (The Rural Coastal Road) (★)—safe for any car. Don't miss it. Back on the Transpeninsular Highway south of the La Ribera turnoff, another junction leads to the farming town of **Santiago,** the unlikely custodian of southern Baja's only **zoo.** Just a mile past Santiago's plaza and church, you come upon a dusty, well-kept colony of cages where you can wander among roadrunners, snakes, monkeys, jaguarmundis, toucans, foxes and more.

When you return to the main highway, watch the roadside for a giant concrete ball sliced with a latitude line (23.5° north)—you've just arrived at the **Tropic of Cancer.** From here on down to the capes, the action gets very hot indeed.

SAN JOSÉ DEL CABO

The neat coastal town of San José del Cabo is split between the old downtown village and the new seaside hotels. In town, stop by the **main plaza** with its church, **Nuestra Señor de San José,** built in 1940 but originating in the Jesuit mission founded here in 1730 and later sacked by rebellious Indians. A curious mosaic over the church entrance shows angry Indians dragging a bound priest toward a fire to burn him for his heresies— his attempts to halt polygamy among the tribes.

At the eastern end of the hotel zone, there's a placid freshwater estuary, **Estero de San José,** where roving buccaneers renewed their water supply 400 years ago while waiting for galleons to rob. Now this oasis is home to 200 species of birds.

CABO SAN LUCAS

The last 20 miles of the Transpeninsular Highway roll through fast-developing coastline studded with hotels and future condos. Our brave highway putters out right near the **main plaza** in the village of Cabo San Lucas, where the sights get pricey.

Of course, the famous Land's End Arch, **El Arco,** costs nothing to look at from shore, but most people like to boat out and through the rugged natural portal eroded by wind and waves.

Another interesting, no-cost sight is the old lighthouse, **Faro de Cabo Falso,** high on the dunes south of Cabo San Lucas overlooking Cabo Falso. You need a dune buggy or 4-wheel drive to visit this spot.

TODOS SANTOS

Highway 19 pushes north from Cabo San Lucas along a sparsely inhabited strip of surf-pounded coastline to the oasis town of **Todos Santos,** site of a short-lived Jesuit mission destroyed by an Indian revolt in 1734. About 15 miles southeast of Todos Santos, near the inland village of Las Burreras, the **Sierra de la Laguna** provides plenty of wilderness where you can rub elbows with puma and deer and camp in mountainous forests. For information about hiking trips and horse rentals, check at the Todos Santos Inn (Calle Obregón 17, Todos Santos).

Shopping

NORTHERN BAJA SUR SHOPPING

The first place to buy any serious tourist trinkets is Mulegé. One of its bigger shops is **Mulegé Curios** (Calle Moctezuma near the entrance of town), which carries seashells, jewelry and stuffed iguanas. For tropical fashions and pottery try **Ana's** gift shop at the Las Casitas Hotel (Calle Madero 50).

In Loreto, there are craft and souvenir shops along thd strip, **Calle Salvatierra,** leading from the old mission. One of the nicest, located near the mission, is **El Alacrán**, featuring Mexican handicrafts and printings.

LA PAZ SHOPPING

Now you can take out your travelers checks and give yourself some slack. Many shops line the waterfront boulevard, Avenida Alvaro Obregón. Downtown, off **Calle 16 de Septiembre**, are alleys full of Oriental shops where you can take advantage of Baja's status as a duty-free zone.

For quality ceramics and especially fine reproductions of Aztec art, stop in at **Bazar del Sol** (Avenida Alvaro Obregón 1665).

Soko's (Avenida Alvaro Obregón and Calle 16 de Septiembre) is more of a Mexican bazaar. It's got the biggest selection in town of Taxco silver, leather, hats, sandals and chess sets.

For festive Mexican dresses and jumpsuits, wooden figures and other handicrafts, check out **Tienda de Artesanías de Baja California** (Parque Cuauhtémoc and Avenida Alvaro Obregón).

Watch artists at work spinning pots at the **Centro de Arte Regional** (Calle Chiapas between Calle Legaspi and Calle Encinas). This family-run workshop sells both ceramics and baskets.

Another workshop, in threads and cloth, resides in a little metal building south of town called **The Weaver** (Calle Abasolo across from the Conasupo). This weaving factory turns out tablecloths, shirts, rugs, dresses and bedspreads.

Now cruise into the heart of town and spend some time at the colorful **Central Mercado** (Calle Revolución and Calle Degollado). This covered bazaar has clothes, sandals, and guitars, as well as baked goods and colorful mounds of fruits and vegetables. A second market (Calle Bravo and Calle Prieto) has similar offerings.

SAN JOSÉ DEL CABO SHOPPING

Amid the haphazard T-shirt shops that dominate the shopping scene are a few select stores. The village's nicest boutique is **La Casa Vieja** (Boulevard Mijares 27; 2-02-70), featuring fine jewelry, Cuernavaca rugs and designer beachwear.

For souvenirs, **Curios México** (Calle Zaragoza, across from Aramburo) offers a potpourri of pre-Columbian-style ceramics, sandals, sombreros, blankets, lacquered parrots and shells.

For fresh fruits, vegetables and local color, shop the village's **Mercado Municipal** (off Calle M. Doblado behind the Tres Estrellas de Oro bus station). The beautiful produce is shipped down from northern Baja's rich San Quintín Valley.

CABO SAN LUCAS SHOPPING

Since Cabo has become a jet-set destination, curio shops have multiplied. Prices are elevated to match demand. Bargaining works best at the **open-air market** on the marina—a block of covered stalls stacked with jewelry, leather and baubles, as good as anything at the boutiques.

The major curio jungle in town is Calle Hidalgo. One of the biggest shops along this strip is **The Boutique** (Calle Hidalgo 10), featuring hand-blown glassware, Taxco silver and clothing.

See the fascinating **Rostros de México Ethnic Art Gallery** (Avenida Lázaro Cárdenas). Its name means "Faces of Mexico" and this one-of-a-kind shop features antique ceremonial masks from one of the world's largest collections. Marvelous wooden faces of animals, scorpions, devils and spirits cover the walls.

Up the street, **El Lugar** (Avenida Lázaro Cárdenas, next door to the Mar de Cortez Hotel) has a terrific assortment of Mayan-style statues from the Yucatán, plus masks, fossils and vases.

Cabo's newest and largest shopping center, **Plaza Aramburo** (Calle Zaragoza and Avenida Lázaro Cárdenas) contains several dozen upscale shops and galleries.

On Playa Medano, the Hotel Hacienda features its own **Plaza Mayor,** a colonial-style arcade with shops offering jewelry, clothing, handicrafts and Oriental jade.

Nightlife

MULEGÉ AND LORETO NIGHTLIFE

Baja boogeying is meager until you get to Mulegé. Here, the major nocturnal events are the Mexican fiestas, with spicy buffets and some of the best mariachi music in Baja. These parties are held on various weeknights at local hotels: the **Hotel Serenidad** two miles south of Mulegé on Transpeninsular Highway; 3-01-11), **Las Casitas Hotel** (Calle Madero 50; 3-00-19), and **Hotel Terraza** (Calle Zaragoza; 3-00-09). Hotel Serenidad also has weekly pig roasts.

For life after dark in Loreto, try the disco or one of the bars at the **Presidente** (Boulevard Misión de Loreto, Playa Nópolo; 3-07-00).

LA PAZ NIGHTLIFE

The **Pelicanos Bar** (upstairs at the Los Arcos Hotel, Avenida Alvaro Obregón 498; 2-27-44) has a fine sunset view. The low lights and casual classiness attract both locals and tourists.

Even more low key, with a European coffeehouse feel and parachute-draped ceilings, **Kabuki's Club** (Calle Independencia 78) has good local singers and a selection of coffees and snacks.

No nighttime lineup would be complete without **La Terraza Restaurant** (Hotel Perla, Avenida Alvaro Obregón; 2-07-77)—the best spot for meeting locals or tourists. Drinks with complimentary chips and hot sauce are served in the bar section, where a tropical group sings on weekends.

The happening hangout for the disco crowd is **La Cabaña**, the upstairs club at Hotel Perla (Avenida Alvaro Obregón; 2-00-77). The live music and wild dance floor pack 'em in. Mafioso types guard the door. Dim lighting enhances the pickup aura. Cover charge.

Other nightspots to sample: **Okey Laser Club** (Avenida Alvaro Obregón and Callejón La Paz; 2-31-33), the newest video-disco with 20 televisions, two bars, three dance floors, confetti, balloons and a partridge in a pear tree (cover charge); and **El Rollo** (Hotel Palmira, Km. 2.5 on the road to Pichilingue; 2-40-00), a big, carpeted disco with flashing light shows (cover charge).

SAN JOSÉ DEL CABO NIGHTLIFE

Start with a banana margarita or something equally exotic at the **Lobby Bar El Oasis** in the Posada Real (Zona Hotelera; 2-01-55), a friendly and smart-looking meeting ground. The lounge is built around an island-bar and features live music on weekends.

At the east end of the beach is the classy **Anuiti** (Zona Hotelera next to the Presidente; 2-01-03), a big restaurant-bar on the shores of the Estero de San José. From its outdoor patio you can watch the birds on the water.

Outside of these local lounges, San José claims only one glamorous nightspot: **Cactus Disco** at the Presidente (Zona Hotelera; 2-02-11), a big, multitiered club with a large dance floor and a light show on the ceiling. Cover charge.

Pancho & Lefty's (Boulevard Mijares, just south of City Hall; 2-02-66) is a *palapa*-style, down-home boogin' joint featuring old-time rock n' roll, live on weekends. Biggest bar and longest happy hour in town. Satellite television for videos and sporting events.

CABO SAN LUCAS NIGHTLIFE

A hulking New York-style disco, **The Oasis** (Avenida Lázaro Cárdenas) offers a driving beat and giant video screen. Cover charge for men only. You can fuel up amid a gaggle of tipsy gringos at the **Giggling Marlin** (Avenida Lázaro Cárdenas across from the marina). Signs at the entrance of this popular restaurant-bar gleefully announce, "Perfect English broken here," and the waiters will all speak it better than you by the time you leave. The happy hour lasts all afternoon, and the margaritas are potent.

Estela's By the Sea (Playa Medano) is another popular *palapa*-style bar with a hip cactus garden containing auto parts. Inside there's recorded jazz and a bright bay view.

Despite these choices, I believe the best nightlife in Los Cabos revolves around the deluxe hotel bars with views. Inside Cabo itself, the **Whale Watcher's Bar** at the Hotel Finisterra (Playa Solmar; 3-00-00) tops the list for a sunset cocktail. The only way you can improve the cliffside scenery— moon rising over the rocky pinnacles, the sand and sea toasty-gold with the day's last light—is to try a coco loco. Mariachis nightly.

Another terrific view-bar: the **Mermaid Lounge** at the Hotel Cabo San Lucas (Transpeninsular Highway, Km. 15) is a spacious terrace bar suspended on a cliff among rugged stone pillars with a spectacular view of Bahía Chileno. Mariachis warm the scene.

The more casual **La Cantina Bar** at the Clarion Hotel (Transpeninsular Highway, Km. 4.5; 3-00-44) has an equally fabulous view, looking out past three tiers of cliffside swimming pools toward the famous arch and rocky headlands of Land's End.

Baja Sur Addresses and Phone Numbers

MULEGÉ

Bank—Bánamex, Calle Zaragoza
Hospital—Local clinic, Calle Madero (2-02-44)
Laundromat—Lavamática, across from Las Estellas bus station on
  Calle Doblado
Police—Delgado Municipal, Calle Madero (3-02-48)
Post Office—On the main plaza
Tourist Information—The tourist booth in Santa Rosalía serves both
  towns (off the Transpeninsular Highway next to Balneario Selene
  Restaurant, across from the Pemex station)

LA PAZ
Bank—Bánamex, Calle Arreola and Calle Esquerro (2-10-11)
Hospital—Hospital Salvatierra, Calle Bravo and Calle Licenciado de Verdad (2-15-93)
Laundry—Laundromat Yoli, Calle Cinco de Mayo and Calle Rubio (2-10-01)
Police—Calle Belisarío Domínguez (2-66-10)
Post Office—Corner of Calle Constitución and Calle Revolución (2-03-88)
Tourist Information—Secretario de Turismo, on the *malecón* at Calle 16 de Septiembre (2-59-39)

SAN JOSÉ DEL CABO
Bank—Banco Serfín or Bancomer, both on Calle Zaragoza
Hospital—2-00-13
Police—Palacio Municipal, Boulevard Mijares (2-03-94)
Post Office—Off the main plaza across from the church
Tourist Information—Palacio Municipal, Boulevard Mijares (2-03-77)

CABO SAN LUCAS
Bank—Bánamex, Calle Hidalgo and Calle Cinco de Mayo
English-speaking doctor—Dr. Alberto Acosta, in the office across from the Hotel Mar de Cortez, Avenida Lázaro Cárdenas (3-01-27)
Hospital—3-04-80
Police—Across from The Oasis disco (3-00-57)
Post Office—Calle Moreles
Tourist Information—Viajes Plaza Travel Agency in the main plaza, Avenida Lázaro Cárdenas and Calle Hidalgo (3-02-55)

CHAPTER SIX

Northwest Coast

Stark, dry and flaring with sunlight, the great Mexican northwest mirrors the Baja Peninsula just a hundred miles west across the Sea of Cortez. The deserts, beaches and dunes of each could be cousins. But unlike raw, unruly Baja, this 600-mile-long coast proudly flaunts its progress and enjoys the spoils of human cultivation. Rivers yoked by mighty dams have fattened the once-wilting deserts, turning them into the country's richest land. Irrigated plains bloom with cotton and cane. Ranches produce top-grade steak-on-the-hoof (menus often proudly specify "Sonora beef"). Mineral deposits of every ore ripple through the Sierra Madre, where ancient Indian tribes still lead lives undisturbed by modern ways.

For the traveler, this region offers a casual introduction to the West Coast of Mexico, more famous for its fast-lane resorts to the south. Although the northwest coast lacks glamour, it has its own sunburned persona, characterized by the rousing *ranchero* ballads and *norteño* tunes played on frisky accordions. Some of Mexico's tallest *mestizos* stride through the cow towns in their boots and stetsons, obviously influenced by their neighbors to the north. An optimistic energy charges the agricultural boomtowns.

From the U.S. border at Nogales all the way south to Culiacán, Mexico 15, which becomes a coastal highway at Guaymas, roars with traffic. American weekenders pour down in RVs to bask in the dry, Mediterranean-desert climate. But most of the time the road is mobbed with cargo trucks that lumber through the cactus-studded land, many bound for the United States, bulging with the bounty of the range.

Sonora, Mexico's second biggest state, dominates the northwest. Its prairielike Sonora Desert pushes north into Arizona and New Mexico. Near the stubby land link between Baja and the mainland, the dusty Desierto de Altar (Altar Desert) is marbled with ancient lava fields and volcanic ranges. Farther south around Guaymas the great Sierra Madre Occidental erupts from the eastern plains. Its harsh peaks, shot through with fat veins of metals, made the area wildly rich in centuries past. In fact, though its silver mines are now played out, northern Sonora leads the nation in copper and graphite mining and continues to harvest scores of exotic ores.

To the south in the state of Sinaloa, the parched landscape softens with unexpected palm groves, shaggy shade trees and velvety valleys—a forecast of the exuberant Mexican tropics. But Sinaloa's vegetation includes more than the top-of-the-line tomatoes churned out by the ton. Million-dollar fields of poppies and marijuana lie in the rumor-shrouded inland valleys of the Sierra Madre. Sinaloa is legendary as one of Mexico's big drug trafficking and racketeering kingdoms. But you're unlikely to witness its shady side out on the beaches.

Nor will you see many of this area's Indians. Only small pockets of these spirited hunters and fishermen are left: the Seris around Bahía Kino, the Yaquis around Guaymas, the Mayos near Navojoa and Los Mochis, the Tarahumaras in the Sierra Madre east of the Río Fuerte Valley. Similar to some of the United States' southwest plains' Indians in their ritual dances, animistic spiritualism and use of rattles and drums, Mexico's desert tribes also suffered abuse at the hands of intruders. The Spanish enslaved the Indians for labor in the fields and mines. Ensuing Indian revolts watered the stolen lands with blood. Not until the 20th century did land reform laws return some tribal territory to its original caretakers. And many tribes still refuse, 400 years after the Spanish arrived, to mingle with modern Mexican society.

Up north, the first beach community of any size is Puerto Peñasco, known among gringos as Rocky Point. This popular little port town claims fine beaches, good fishing, succulent shrimp and mind-boggling dunes.

South of here, in the ancestral heartland of the Seri Indians, stands Bahía Kino. About an hour's drive west of Hermosillo, this quiet beach resort on a beautiful bay was named for Father Eusebio Kino, a Jesuit who built 25 missions in the desert that have now turned to dust.

The seaport of Guaymas to the south embroils you in a congested big city atmosphere, although it's set amid wizened, cactus-prickled hills. Nearby, the pretty bayside resort of San Carlos compensates with its water sports and fine marinas.

Just south of the Sinaloa state line, a fertile valley fed by the Río Fuerte surrounds the well-organized town of Los Mochis and the nearby deepwater port of Topolobampo. The beaches in this area lack charisma, but Los Mochis has one singular attraction: it is the pushoff point for the exciting Copper Canyon railroad trip into the Sierra Madre (see "Copper Canyon By Rail" section in this chapter).

The next stop is booming Culiacán, capital of Sinaloa. Several gray sand beaches stripe the nearby coast, but this is no place to linger. With some 300,000 people, traffic-choked avenues and smoke-spewing factories, Culiacán spells out loud and clear "industrial town—pass on through."

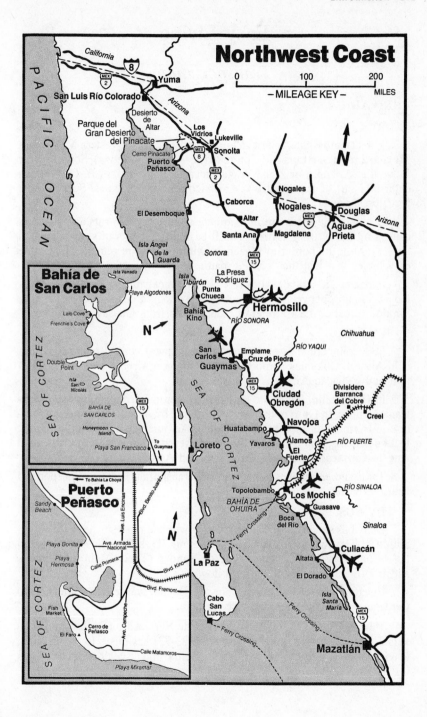

Northwest Coast

0   100   200
– MILEAGE KEY –   MILES

PACIFIC OCEAN

California
Yuma
San Luis Río Colorado
Arizona
Desierto de Altar
Parque del Gran Desierto del Pinacate
Los Vidrios
Lukeville
Cerro Pinacate
Puerto Peñasco
Sonoita
Nogales
Nogales
Caborca
Douglas
Arizona
El Desemboque
Altar
Agua Prieta
Santa Ana
Magdalena
Isla Ángel de la Guarda
Sonora
La Presa Rodríguez
Isla Tiburón
Punta Chueca
Hermosillo
Bahía Kino
RÍO SONORA
Chihuahua
RÍO YAQUI
San Carlos
Guaymas
Emplame
Cruz de Piedra
Ciudad Obregón
Divisidero Barranca del Cobre
Creel
Navojoa
Huatabampo
Álamos
RÍO FUERTE
Yavaros
El Fuerte
Loreto
Topolobambo
Los Mochis
RÍO SINALOA
BAHÍA DE OHUIRA
Guasave
Boca del Río
Sinaloa
Culiacán
Altata
El Dorado
La Paz
Isla Santa Maria
Cabo San Lucas
Ferry Crossing
Ferry Crossing
Ferry Crossing
Mazatlán

SEA OF CORTEZ

Bahía de San Carlos

Isla Venado
Playa Algodones
Lalo Cove
Frenchie's Cove
Double Point
Isla San Nicolás
BAHÍA DE SAN CARLOS
Honeymoon Island
Playa San Francisco
To Guaymas

SEA OF CORTEZ

Puerto Peñasco

To Bahía La Choya
Sandy Beach
Playa Bonita
Ave. Luis Encinas
Blvd. Benito Juárez
Ave. Armada Nacional
Playa Hermosa
Calle Primera
Blvd. Kino
Blvd. Fremont
Fish Market
Ave. Campeche
El Faro
Cerro de Peñasco
Calle Matamoros
Playa Miramar

SEA OF CORTEZ

Easy Living

Transportation

ARRIVAL

BY CAR

You can cross the American border and enter northwestern Mexico via **Mexico 2** from San Luis Río Colorado (near Yuma, Arizona), Sonoita (near Lukeville, Arizona) or Agua Prieta (near Douglas, Arizona). Or you can enter this part of the country via **Mexico 15** from Nogales, Sonora (near Nogales, Arizona).

A few of the roads are in mediocre condition, with ruts and potholes caused by heavy truck traffic. You'll be fighting fleets of slow trucks all the way from the border to Mazatlán, with many grim reminders en route of vehicles that lost the "passing battle." Pass with care.

In contrast to Suicide Alley (the cheerful nickname for the strip of Mexico 15 running between Nogales and Guaymas), a beautiful new section, **Sinaloa 1**, called La Carretera Costera, runs from Guasave to Culiacán.

BY AIR

Five commercial airports serve the northwest coastal region: Hermosillo Airport, Guaymas Airport, Ciudad Obregón Airport, Los Mochis Airport and Culiacán Airport.

In **Hermosillo**, flights are provided by Aeroméxico, Noroeste and Mexicana Airlines. In **Guaymas**, service is offered by Aeroméxico and by Noroeste in Hermosillo. In **Ciudad Obregón**, Aeroméxico has the only flights. In **Los Mochis**, you can book flights on Aeroméxico and Aero California. And in **Culiacán**, it's Aero California and Aeroméxico once again.

Taxis and *collectivos* (vans) provide transportation from all airports to nearby towns.

BY BUS

Daily bus service connects all major towns and most smaller beach communities. The two major northwest lines are **Tres Estrellas de Oro** and the second-class **Transporte Norte de Sonora** (TNS). Main bus stations and information numbers are as follows:

Puerto Peñasco: TNS (Boulevard Benito Juárez and Calle Lázaro Cárdenas; 3-20-19) is the only service here.

Hermosillo: Central de Autobuses de Hermosillo (Boulevard Transversal about one mile from downtown; 3-33-73) has buses to Bahía Kino, leaving from Transportes de la Costa de Hermosillo (Avenida Plutarco Elías Calles 99; 2-21-94).

Bahía Kino: Buses to and from Hermosillo stop at the Pemex station outside Old Kino and along Boulevard Mar de Cortez in New Kino to drop off and pick up passengers (just wave).

Guaymas: Transportes del Pacífico (2-05-75), Tres Estrellas de Oro (2-12-71) and TNS (2-70-07) are located in two downtown stations (Calle 12a and Calle 14a Sur). Local buses to San Carlos leave from Calle 19a and Calle Yáñez near the central market.

Los Mochis: Tres Estrellas de Oro (Calle Obregón 61 Poniente; 2-17-57) has local buses to Topolobampo, leaving from the corner of Calle Obregón and Calle Allende.

Culiacán: Transportes del Pacífico (2-33-36), Tres Estrellas de Oro (3-28-36) and TNS (3-56-64) are all located at the main station (Boulevard Leyva Solano and Calle Aquiles Serdán). Local buses leave from here for the beach towns of Altata and El Dorado.

BY TRAIN

A thorough train system operates along the Pacific coast. Station locations are as follows:

Puerto Peñasco: Ferrocarril del Pacífico (Calle Serdán and Calle Ferrocarril; 3-26-10, reservations: 7-23-86, in Mexicali).

Hermosillo: Ferrocarriles Nacionales de México (Ticket office: Boulevard Transversal and Calle Manuel González; 3-87-01. Train station off Mexico 15, one-and-a-half miles north of downtown; 4-38-29).

Guaymas: There's passenger service from Empalme, a town six miles south of the city.

Los Mochis: Ferrocarril el Chihuahua Pacífico (Avenida Bienestar; 2-08-53) is a first-class train that runs through the Copper Canyon. Vista is a second-class train that makes the same run (see the "Copper Canyon by Rail" section in this chapter).

BY BOAT

Regular passenger-vehicle ferry service runs to and from southern Baja California for Guaymas and Topolobampo.

In Guaymas, tickets for the overnight trip to Santa Rosalía may be purchased at the **Muelle Patio** ferry terminal (off Avenida Serdán, 2-33-93). Onboard accommodations include seats (salon class) and bunks (*turista* class).

In Topolobampo, overnight ferries push off for La Paz from the ferry terminal at **Atracadero de los Transbordadores** (just past the shrimp boat harbor; Tel. in Los Mochis: 2-03-21). There are three classes to choose from.

For all ferry trips, you should make reservations from eight to fifteen days in advance.

CAR RENTALS

At Hermosillo Airport, you will find booths for **National** (4-09-36), **Hertz** (4-16-95) and **Budget** (4-38-05). At Guaymas Airport, you can rent from **Budget** (2-14-50) and **Hertz** (2-10-00). At Los Mochis Airport, try **National** (2-53-60) and **Hertz** (2-11-22). At Culiacán Airport, you can rent wheels from **Hertz** (2-19-99), **National** (3-68-58), **Budget** (3-99-66) and **Avis** (4-40-87).

PUBLIC TRANSPORTATION

Most northwestern coastal towns can be navigated quite easily on foot. For long jaunts there are taxis.

Hermosillo, Guaymas and Culiacán have municipal bus systems.

Hotels

The northwest coast is not saturated with hotels. Rooms fill up fast in small resorts on weekends and holidays.

PUERTO PEÑASCO HOTELS

The most popular lower-range hostelry, with good reason, is the **Motel Señorial** (Calle Tercera 81; 3-20-65). A block from the main beach, this 70-room quasi-colonial-style hotel surrounds a courtyard often jammed with jeeps and vans. The hotel has a good restaurant and comfortable medium-sized rooms with phones, televisions and picture windows. The newer upstairs rooms, along a sweeping balcony, cost more but have air-conditioning. Budget.

On the outskirts of town stands the little **Motel Mar y Sol** (Sonora 8 between Sonoita and Peñasco, Km. 94; 3-31-90) with 20 rooms and flower-sprinkled grounds. Among its amenities are a pleasant restaurant and bar, with entertainment in the evening. The tile-floored rooms, with air-conditioning, ceiling fans, double beds and colorful furnishings, add a touch of domestic cheer. Budget.

If you'd like to soak in a cliffside jacuzzi or swing at a video-disco hewn from the rocks, the 44-room **Hotel Viña del Mar** (Vine of the Sea) (Calle Primero de Junio and Boulevard Malecón Kino; 3-36-00) is your vacation castle. Set on a promontory overlooking the sea in the Old Town section, the inviting Viña del Mar spills down the hillside and features a restaurant, bar, cafeteria, pool with swim-up bar and lovely rooms with dark-beamed ceilings, phones, wood fixtures, ocean views and Spanish red-tiled roofs. Moderate.

BAHÍA KINO HOTELS

This obscure resort has surprisingly costly accommodations, all located in New Kino.

The 14-room **Kino Bay Motel-Trailer Park** (the far north end of Boulevard Mar de Cortez; 2-02-16) sports completely remodeled rooms with modern kitchenettes (including microwaves) and air-conditioning. The rooms face breezy, parklike grounds across from the bay. Budget.

A more expensive option is the fancier, beachside **Posada Santa Gemma** (Boulevard Mar de Cortez; 2-00-26). Its 14 split-level stucco bungalows all contain an upstairs bedroom and balcony, downstairs bath with additional bedroom, full kitchen and white-brick dining area around a cozy fireplace—an ideal set-up for a family. Moderate.

The **Hotel Posada del Mar** (Boulevard Mar de Cortez, near the south end of New Kino; 2-01-55) is the only true hotel in town. Looking out over the bay, the hotel features a raised network of brick walkways that connect a pool, wading pool, restaurant-bar and 48 rooms, all with bay views and patios. The rooms, however, are suffering from neglect, towels are threadbare, and there is little front desk service. Budget.

GUAYMAS–SAN CARLOS HOTELS

Most people prefer to stay in San Carlos near the beach action, but Guaymas also has some good, less expensive hotels.

GUAYMAS HOTELS

Right in the heart of Guaymas, near the central market and bus station, stands the clean, economical **Motel del Puerto** (Calle Yáñez 92; 2-34-08). The drab cement-block exterior is enlivened by cheerful orange balconies twined with vegetation. The 72 small rooms, all with air-conditioning, include compact desks, brick-base nightstands and brightly tiled baths. Ask for a ground-floor room; the stairs are remarkably steep. Budget.

Directly on Playa Miramar about a mile north of Guaymas, you can enjoy reasonable family-style accommodations at the 11-room **Leo's Inn** (North Playa Miramar; 2-13-37). More like a home than a hotel, Leo's has a bright living-room-like lobby with overstuffed chairs, bamboo-frame sofas and breezy terrace from which you can watch the sunset over Bahía Bacochibampo. The more expensive beachfront rooms are flooded with light and have pale wicker furniture and air-conditioning. The interior rooms are darker, with antique furniture and tiles—all comfortable and clean. The management is exceptionally friendly. Budget.

Undoubtedly the finest hotel in the whole Guaymas–San Carlos area is the stately, 125-room **Hotel Playa de Cortés** (Bahía Bacochibampo, take Colonia Miramar exit off Mexico 15; 2-01-35). Built back in 1935, the hotel rests in a beautiful rolling garden by the sea, fragrant with fruit trees and budding vines that drop their petals on the pool and patio furniture. The yawning dining rooms and majestic old lobby hold antiques and oil paintings that create the mood of a museum. The spacious rooms and bungalows repeat this theme, with colonial-style dark furniture, heavy curtains and king-sized beds. Many have fireplaces. Moderate.

SAN CARLOS HOTELS

For families and groups, a bungalow or apartment may be the best deal. **Teta Kawi Trailer Park** (Carretera San Carlos, east end; 6-02-20) rents out some dandy little studios set back from the trailers and facing the sea, with kitchenettes, air-conditioning, two double beds, simple furnishings and front terraces with roomy leather rockers. Each accommodates up to four people. Budget.

At the **Shangri-La Trailer Park** (end of the Carretera San Carlos; 6-02-35), a more weathered little colony of cabañas crouches on a hill over-looking Bahía de San Carlos. These basic units have delightful balconies sporting rustic log furniture where you can cool your morning coffee in a sea breeze. Each cabaña comes with a kitchenette and small corner hearth with gas heater. Budget to moderate.

If you prefer a straightforward room in an inn, the 24-unit **Motel Crestón** (Carretera San Carlos next to the San Carlos Diving Center; 6-00-20) offers modest accommodations around a shady pool and patio. The medium-sized rooms smell of bug spray (which didn't stop a *cucaracha* from hiding in the shower), but they look otherwise clean and comfortable, with air-conditioning, warm color schemes and throw rugs on the floor. Budget.

The glamour stop on the bay, with roots stretching back to the beginnings of San Carlos, is the venerable **La Posada de San Carlos** (Carretera San Carlos, west of the country club; 6-00-15). Set in a garden with its own patch of beach, this 150-room complex is a jumble of buildings, from flat-topped bungalows to seven-story tower. The simplest rooms are spacious and brightly decorated, while the suites are more somber, with sofa beds, kitchenettes and wind-freshened balconies. All rooms are air-conditioned. At your service are two swimming pools, three restaurants, cavernous disco and gift shop—an all-in-one stop where you can remain pleasantly cocooned. Budget.

LOS MOCHIS–TOPOLOBAMPO HOTELS

You would not want to set up housekeeping at the **Hotel Beltrán** (Calle Hidalgo and Calle Zaragoza; 2-07-10), but it's adequate for a no-frills over-night stay. Right in the heart of downtown Los Mochis, this three-story hotel consists of 53 small rooms crammed together along the hallways. Each has a dusty mirror, dilapidated air-conditioner and tiny double bed. Noisy traffic outside the window. Budget.

If you can afford to leap out of the budget range, go for some class at the nearby **Hotel Santa Anita** (Avenida Leyva and Calle Hidalgo; 5-70-46), with 130 uninspired but comfortable rooms and a lovely downstairs restaurant. Moderate.

Topolobampo has only one hotel—a nice one, albeit on the expensive side, as befits its cruise-line character. Enjoy the illusion of luxuriously sailing the bay at the boat-shaped **Yacht Hotel** (set on a cliff behind Topolobampo, reached by the marked turnoff southwest of the Pemex plant en route to town; 2-38-62). Its 20 charming rooms contain thick blue carpets, bamboo chairs and beds as broad as Bahía Ohuira. The restaurant and bar belong to the yacht-shaped section. Below is a rocky beach with crumbling dock. Moderate.

CULIACÁN HOTELS

Culiacán is swamped with hotels. A few options:

The musty **El Mayo** (Boulevard Madero and Calle Noris; 5-22-20) won't thin out your wallet much and may bore you into a good night's sleep. The 50 rooms are small, dark and not too handsome (mine had a hole in one wall), with two puddinglike beds, but let's give them an "A" for television and air-conditioning. They get a "D" for chilly receptionist and creaky elevator that you almost need an elevator to step up into. Budget.

For more spit and polish, try the American-style **Hotel San Marcos** (Calle Carrasco 44 Norte; 3-78-76). This five-story downtown rectangle is completely middle class, from the fold-out sofas to the built-in closets. The 100 cool, carpeted rooms flash with chrome, formica and elevated televisions. Moderate.

Restaurants

Terrific seafood from the Sea of Cortez, particularly plump jumbo shrimp, fills restaurants all the way south. Sonora's prime beef and delicious produce heighten the menus as well.

PUERTO PEÑASCO RESTAURANTS

The best restaurant here, located in the Old Town, is the family-style **Costa Brava Restaurant** (Boulevard Kino and Calle Primero de Junio; 3-31-30). With several attractive rooms decked out in red tablecloths and decorative ceiling fans, the Costa Brava sports a touch of style absent in most of Puerto Peñasco's eating spots. The exotic menu includes Mexican dishes and seafood: *pescado Costa Brava* (fish with ham and cheese), flaming shrimp with brandy and a regal seafood combination—octopus, shrimp, clams and flounder in a spicy tomato stew. Moderate.

Another neighborhood favorite, the simple **La Cita Café** (Calle Primero de Junio, near the Pemex station; 3-22-70) welcomes you with an authentic Mexican flair, including very modest decor and a jukebox packed with romantic Latin ballads. The menu is limited, offering Mexican dishes, steaks, chicken, sandwiches and seafood. The Mexican-style shrimp, in a buttery broth of onions and tomatoes, is delicious. Budget.

If you want action, step out to **Restaurant La Curva** (Boulevard Kino and Calle Comonfort; 3-34-70). Senior citizens jam the joint, and they have quite a time here. In decor, La Curva consists of tables set side-by-side, the better to pack 'em in. Free nachos come with dinner. The substantial menu is Americanized: Mexican pizza, stuffed potato skins, grilled chicken and hamburgers. But a number of Mexican dishes are offered also, including the popular shrimp quesadillas. Budget.

For breakfast, the terrace of Hotel Viña del Mar's coffee shop, **La Gaviota** (Calle Primero de Junio and Boulevard Malecón Kino; 3-36-00), can't be beat, either for good food or stunning views. On the rocks below swarm hundreds of gulls and pelicans, and from the docks shrimp boats head out to sea against the backdrop of Sandy Beach. Both Mexican and American breakfasts are served. Moderate.

BAHÍA KINO RESTAURANTS

In New Kino, the best atmosphere and worst service go hand-in-hand a t **Pepe's Pulpo** (Boulevard Mar de Cortez, across from the Kino Bay Motel-Trailer Park). Overlooking the bay, this cheery, bright restaurant serves fish, shrimp, lobster and some meat dishes. Lunch and dinner only. Moderate.

Also in New Kino, **El Pargo Rojo** (Boulevard Mar de Cortez 1426; 2-02-05) is a popular, lively spot, with guitar music in the evening. This small establishment, draped in fishing nets, specializes in shrimp cooked numerous ways, from kabobed to *camarón relleno* (shrimp stuffed with cheese and ham). Moderate.

In Old Kino you'll find **The Marlin** (Calle Tastiota, across from the Islandia Marina; 2-01-11), the kind of seafood house you go to strictly for the food. Its specialties are broiled lobster and all kinds of shrimp. Budget.

For both food and atmosphere, Old Kino's best restaurant is the warm, inviting **La Palapa del Pescador** (Calle Tastiota and Calle Yavaros; 2-01-40). The fish and shrimp are superb. Moderate.

GUAYMAS–SAN CARLOS RESTAURANTS

Good restaurants fill Guaymas and the resort of San Carlos.

GUAYMAS RESTAURANTS

You'll find stylish dining at the downtown **Restaurant Del Mar** (Avenida Serdán and Calle 17a; 2-02-26). Arched brick windows, heavy colonial tables and chairs and tortoise-shell light fixtures convey a night-on-the-town mood. Service is gracious and quick. The menu includes a good selection of wines, salads and seafood. Excellent coffee. Moderate.

Like an eccentric lady with years of charm etched into her face, **Las Playitas Restaurant-Bar** (Calle Varadero, en route to Guaymas Naval Base; 2-27-27) smiles through over two decade's worth of accumulated decor, still lively and full of fun. Varnished log tables and chairs, glass balls and blowfish, walls encrusted with thousands of shells, painted sombreros and Japanese lanterns—it's a rustic fantasyland that makes dining a fiesta.

Bands entertain in the evenings. Choose from a huge array of meals: Mexican food, barbequed steaks, Chinese dinners, creamed clams, curried shrimp and vegetarian plates. Budget.

Los Charros Grill (Avenida Abelardo Rodríguez 166), just off the *malecón,* is the lively *in* spot in town. It evokes Old México, with high-backed carved chairs and piñatas hanging from the ceiling. Steaks and Mexican dishes are featured and mariachis provide the entertainment. Moderate.

You can eat in style on antique tables made from railroad ties, surrounded by gardens and sparkling linens, in the dining rooms of the **Hotel Playa de Cortés** (Bahía Bachochibampo, Colonia Miramar exit from Mexico 15; 2-01-35). The Old World charm includes attentive waiters who have served here for 30 years and wandering mariachis who soak you in sweet romantic ballads. The dinner menu changes nightly, with a choice of seafood, Mexican dish or meat—all equal to the ambience. Moderate.

SAN CARLOS RESTAURANTS

A great easy-going spot known for its breakfasts, **Rosa's Cantina** (Carretera San Carlos) consists of scattered picnic tables in two cool dining rooms. A colorful mural of old San Carlos wraps around two walls, and egg cartons cover the ceiling. You place your order at the window, choosing from a lineup of egg dishes, sweet rolls, pecan pie and all the coffee you can drink. For lunch, specialties include tortilla soup, *frijoles charros* (spicy beans with ham and cheese) and a hearty vegetable-beef stew called *cocido.* Budget.

There are several fine seafood restaurants in San Carlos, all of similar quality and atmosphere. Here are the top three:

The semiposh **Terraza Bar-Restaurant** (Carretera San Carlos, Km. 5; 6-00-39) combines carpeted bar with candle-lit restaurant, just across from the bay. To the beat of live organ music from the bar, you can enjoy an assortment of seafood, salads, poultry and meats. Try the juicy, exotic Greek-style fish. Moderate.

A shell's throw from the Terraza is the ever-popular weekend hangout **El Paradise** (Carretera San Carlos; 6-05-42). This seafood restaurant features a dimly lit dining room and another bright, bustling room designed for families. In the bar, behind swinging saloon doors, a rowdier crowd swills beer and tequila. Paradise has a busy menu, too, with soups, salads, steaks, shrimp and lobster in every style, and good but salty deviled crab. Moderate.

If you have a good day at sea and want to turn your catch into dinner filets, have them fixed at **La Roca Restaurant** (Carretera San Carlos; 6-01-60). Some fishermen who invited me to dinner brought a bagful of cleaned *dorado* that the chef lightly fried, then served with lettuce, tomatoes and limes. A huge batch of french fries, odd onion rings (entire onions deep-fried) and a round of margaritas completed a very satisfying meal. Naturally, La Roca has a full menu of seafood to order, plus a romantic cliffside view overlooking the bay. Add guitar music and beautiful songs and the magic is complete. Moderate.

LOS MOCHIS–TOPOLOBAMPO RESTAURANTS

In Los Mochis, 24-hour **El Taquito** (Avenida Leyva and Calle Juan de la Barrera; 2-81-19) resembles a Mexican Denny's. With padded booths, uniformed waiters and good, friendly service, the downtown restaurant looks as lively at midnight as at breakfast. You can order everything from club sandwiches to shrimp rancheros, *bistek milanesa* to corn flakes. Budget.

Topolobampo's only really good sit-down restaurant is the **Yacht Hotel Restaurant-Bar** (Los Mochis-Topolobampo road, turnoff southwest of the Pemex plant at the sign; 2-38-62). Set in a yacht-shaped building overlooking Bahía Ohuira, the restaurant is freshened by sea breezes and occasionally plagued by invasions of sand fleas. Fresh seafood, seasoned by live music, is the key attraction. Try the seafood platter, with shrimp, a heavenly fish filet and crabmeat baked in the shell. The spicy tortilla soup, loaded with cheese, avocado and chilies, will warm your ears. Moderate.

CULIACÁN RESTAURANTS

Culiacán is swamped with hotels. A few options:

The eating's inexpensive, quiet and tasty at the restaurant in the **El Mayo** hotel (Boulevard Madero and Calle Noris; 5-22-20). Sandwiches, seafood, chicken, meat and Mexican meals are served. Similar fare is offered in more elegant surroundings at the downstairs restaurant of the **Hotel San Marcos** (Calle Carrasco 44 Norte; 3-78-76).

Try the riverfront area for good, inexpensive seafood. **El Acuaducto** (Avenida Los Niños Héroes 446) is a particularly pleasant open-air spot, with excellent *frijoles charros* and *camarones rancheros*.

The Great Outdoors
The Sporting Life

CAMPING

Many unspoiled camping beaches dot this area. The problems are lack of shelter, thin sand and *jejenes* (sand fleas) in the early mornings and late afternoons.

From November through March, the northwest coast can be chilly and windy. Late winter dust storms blinded me in Puerto Peñasco, and rain storms turned my umbrella inside out in Bahía Kino. Pack a good tent, warm clothes and all-weather gear.

For camping supplies in Puerto Peñasco, try Jim-Bur Shopping Center (Boulevard Benito Juárez, just south of the train tracks). In Guaymas, try **MZ** (Mercado Zaragoza) (Calle 10a and Avenida Serdán).

SWIMMING

The Sea of Cortez can be nippy in the winter but warms up from late March through October. Stingrays hover offshore. To scare them away, shuffle your feet in the sand as you go out for a swim. If stung, seek medical attention at once.

FISHING AND BOATING

The Sea of Cortez is one of the world's premier fishing holes. Corbina, yellowtail, sierra, dorado, marlin and sailfish, plus shrimp, crabs and oysters fill the bays and estuaries of this region.

In Puerto Peñasco, sportfishing charters can be arranged near Pelican Point at El Faro Sociedad Cooperativa de Producción Turística and across the street from **J. J.'s Cantina** (3-27-85). For *panga* rentals, inquire at your hotel or ask at the Bahía de la Choya boatyard. For more information about local fishing, write to the **Cholla Bay Sportsmen's Club** (4922 West Hubbell, Phoenix, AZ 85035).

In Bahía Kino, commercial fishing is a mainstay. You can rent a *panga* on the beach at Old Kino. Unfortunately, there is no commercial charter service. For more information, visit the **Club Deportiva Bahía Kino** (end of Calle Cadiz, New Kino; 2-01-51) or write the club (Apartado 84, 83340 Bahía Kino, Sonora, Mexico).

For the Guaymas–San Carlos area, the big sportfishing action is centered in San Carlos. To arrange fishing trips, try **San Carlos Diving Center and Charter Boats,** locally known as "Gary's Place" (Carretera San Carlos near the country club; 6-00-49) or the **Sociedad Cooperativa Tetabampo de Pesca Deportiva** (Boulevard de la Marina; 6-00-11).

In Topolobampo, Bahía Ohuira is a fine place to toss a line since there are so few tourists. You can rent a *panga* near the road entering town. For more information, inquire at the **Club de Náutico** (Yacht Club, across from the ferry terminal).

About 55 miles east of Los Mochis, **La Presa Miguel Hidalgo** (Miguel Hidalgo Dam) in the town of El Fuerte has some of the best freshwater large-mouth bass fishing in the world.

SKIN DIVING

Diving territory galore lies off the northwest coast, but few outlets rent gear. In San Carlos, the northwest's richest diving center, equipment rentals, excursions and instruction are provided by **San Carlos Diving Center and**

Charter Boats (Carretera San Carlos; 6-00-49) and **Cortez Sea Sports** (Boulevard de la Marina; 6-02-30). You can fill your tanks at the San Carlos Marina. For a huge selection of diving gear in Guaymas, try **MZ** (Mercado Zaragoza) (Calle 10a and Avenida Serdán).

WINDSURFING

There's little surf along this coast, protected as it is by the Baja Peninsula, but the bays are fine for windsurfing. In Puerto Peñasco, you can rent windsurfing gear in Bahía de la Choya at the boat yard or the **Cholla Bay Sportsmen's Club** (J. J.'s Cantina). In San Carlos, **Club Med** (6-01-66) offers lessons and equipment rentals to guests or one-day visitors.

HUNTING

The northwest inland wilds shelter numerous doves, ducks, geese, deer, jack-rabbits, goats, pigs, rams and mountain lions.

HORSEBACK RIDING

These broad empty beaches make for good riding, but the rental outlets are relatively few. In Puerto Peñasco, check at the **Cholla Bay Sportsmen's Club** (J. J.'s Cantina), Bahía de la Choya . In San Carlos, try the **San Carlos Country Club** (Carretera San Carlos; 6-00-07). Horses are also for rent near **Club Med** (6-01-66) across from Playa Algodones.

GOLF

In San Carlos, there's an 18-hole course at the **San Carlos Country Club** (Carretera San Carlos; 6-03-39). Golfing in Los Mochis is popular at the **Los Mochis Country Club**. Arrange through your hotel.

TENNIS

In San Carlos, courts are available at **San Carlos Country Club** (Carretera San Carlos; 6-02-26) and **Hotel Posada de San Carlos** (Carretera San Carlos west of the country club; 6-00-15). In Los Mochis, **Hotel Las Colinas** (Carretera Internacional and Boulevard Macario Gaxiola) has one court. You can also make arrangements through your hotel to play at the **Los Mochis Country Club**.

Beaches

PUERTO PEÑASCO BEACHES

Some 25 miles of beaches and dunes surround Puerto Peñasco.

Sandy Beach—Located a mile or so south of the gringo community of Bahía de la Choya, this may be the best beach north of Mazatlán. It lives up to its name with lovely, grainy sand (about an 8 on a scale of 10), sloping into soft dunes that are often packed with American vans, dune buggies and tents. The sand runs for miles to the south in a soft curve, fusing with beaches close to town. Just north of Sandy Beach, sand mazes lead off to a steep, fantastic, sand-smothered hill where three-wheel All-Terrain Cycles (ATCs) buzz at breakneck speeds.

Facilities: Bathrooms; stores; horses. *Camping:* Excellent, for a fee. *Swimming:* Excellent. *Snorkeling/diving:* Good off Pelican Point at southwest end of road through Bahía de la Choya. *Windsurfing:* Very good; equipment for rent in Bahía de la Choya. *Fishing/boating:* Rent sailboats and skiffs at Bahía de la Choya. *Shell-collecting:* Best spot is north of Bahía de la Choya along beaches at the foot of Cerro Prieto (Black Mountain).

Getting there: Sandy Beach is about ten miles northwest of Puerto Peñasco by the sand road. From Sonora 8 (leaving Puerto Peñasco), take turnoff at directory sign across from tire shop. Cross the train tracks and pass rows of curio shops. Road forks: veer left for Sandy Beach, right for Bahía de la Choya. Or take Avenida Luis Encinas from Puerto Peñasco to the junction road to Bahía de la Choya.

Playa Hermosa and **Playa Bonita**—Two major municipal beaches flow into one another and are nearly indistinguishable. Playa Hermosa begins near Puerto Peñasco's old port and the circular sea drive where everyone gathers on Sundays. Its powdery grayish sand and soft dunes, tattooed with tire tracks, roll for about a mile along open sea and turn into Playa Bonita, which continues for another few miles to Sandy Beach.

Facilities: All amenities in town. *Camping:* Not allowed on beach; try at the trailer park. *Swimming:* Good. *Windsurfing:* Good. *Fishing/boating:* Fishing around distant reefs and surf-fishing are both good. Check around port for skiff rentals. *Shell-collecting:* Lots of small shells along high tideline.

Getting there: For Playa Hermosa, take Calle Nacional west in Puerto Peñasco, cross the railroad tracks and continue to the circular sea drive above the beach. For Playa Bonita, take Calle Nacional west and follow signs to Playa Bonita Trailer Park.

Playa Miramar—This succession of small, narrow beaches at the southern end of Puerto Peñasco extends several miles south to the elegant beach community of Las Conchas. Backed by low condominiums and trailer parks, the sand tumbles down to a rocky tideline foaming with waves.

Facilities: Amenities in town. *Camping:* Not permitted. *Swimming:* Good when water is calm; watch out for rocks near shoreline. *Snorkeling:* Good around rocky points. *Fishing/boating:* Good surf-fishing.

Getting there: From Puerto Peñasco, take Avenida Campeche to sandy Calle Matamoros, which runs parallel to the beach.

BAHÍA KINO BEACHES

Ten miles of continuous beaches stretch from the estuary at the southeast end of Old Kino to Cerro Prieto (Black Mountain—many mountains in Mexico bear this name) at the north end of New Kino, where the paved road ends. Farther north lie remote, lonely beaches that seem light years from the rat race.

Playas Kino Nuevo (New Kino Beaches)—A five-mile ribbon of yellow-gray sand, somewhat littered in parts, follows New Kino's main drag—Boulevard Mar de Cortez—along the bay. Lovely, distant hills rise behind the sparkling waters where dolphins sometimes play. This gently curving beach proceeds for over 80 miles beyond Caverna del Seri RV Park and Cerro Prieto, where it becomes rockier and is interspersed with headlands.

Facilities: Restaurants and shops. *Palapa* umbrellas along the sand offer shade. *Camping:* Good. *Swimming:* Good, safe and gentle. *Snorkeling:* Good around offshore islands and rocks north of Cerro Prieto. *Windsurfing:* Good all along the bay. *Fishing/boating:* Good.

Getting there: Follow Mexico 16 into New Kino; enter the beach anywhere along Boulevard Mar de Cortez.

Playas Kino Viejo (Old Kino Beaches)—Around the village of Old Kino, the beach is dingy, gray, trashy with bones and smelling of fish. But to the south, around the Condominios Jacquelynn and the estuary (Laguna de la Cruz), white, shapely dunes offer a fine view of Isla Alcatraz. The estuary at the far southern end of the beach flows serenely into the sea around a shell-washed point backed by an abandoned trailer park.

Facilities: Restaurants and stores. *Camping:* Good south of town, but no shelter. *Swimming:* Good. *Windsurfing:* Good. *Snorkeling/diving:* Good around nearby Isla Alcatraz and other offshore islands. *Fishing/boating: Pangas* for rent in Old Kino. Good fishing in the bay. The estuary yields clams and crabs. *Shell-collecting:* Terrific around the estuary: thousands of *turritellas* and many smaller shells.

Getting there: For the road to the estuary and southerly beaches, take Mexico 16 east of Pemex station, turn right onto the first sand road you see; go for about two miles and bear right at fork. Pass Condos Jacquelynn and proceed about a quarter-mile to the estuary.

Playa Las Dunas de San Nicolás and **Punto Kino** (★)—Do you want a lonely beach that stirs your soul to new depths of introspection and gives you appreciation for the sight of a human face? Try this hidden cove some 30 miles southeast of Bahía Kino, where no sign of civilization mars the desert landscape except for some empty tar-paper shacks on a hill above the sea. This windy virgin beach wanders for half a mile between two rocky outcroppings, and behind it rise naked, sinuous dunes that offer protection from the strong sea breezes. (This beach has no official name. Locals refer to the area as the northern dunes.)

Facilities: None. *Camping:* Good; complete privacy. *Swimming:* Good on calm days. *Fishing/boating:* Good.

Getting there: From Bahía Kino, take Mexico 16 east toward Hermosillo for about 20 miles, then turn right onto Calle 36a Sur (no signs, look for junction with paved road). After about four miles, turn right onto dirt road past sign for San Nicolás. Proceed along the dirt road for about 12 miles till surroundings turn arid. Veer right through mountains toward emerging dunes, park near tar-paper shacks and walk through the desert down to beach.

GUAYMAS–SAN CARLOS BEACHES

The locally popular Playa Miramar is on Bahía Bacochibampo west of Guaymas, but the best beaches are around Bahía de San Carlos.

Playa San Francisco—This rocky sand beach runs parallel to the Carretera San Carlos for most of the length of the tourist strip—a couple of miles—and is covered with beautiful colored stones along the tideline.

Facilities: Restaurants and stores. *Camping:* Not permitted. *Swimming:* Good. *Snorkeling:* Good around the offshore islands. *Windsurfing:* Good beyond the rocks. *Fishing/boating:* Good; rent boats at San Carlos Marina. *Shell-collecting:* Few shells, but scores of pretty rocks (called *piedras pintadas* or "painted stones") in earth tones, striped like abstract art, translucent or as creamy as marble.

Getting there: From Guaymas, take Mexico 15 about five miles north to San Carlos turnoff and continue eight miles into Nuevo Guaymas. The beach runs along Carretera San Carlos.

Playa Algodones (Cotton Beach)—Yes, it's almost as white as cotton. One of the loveliest sandboxes north of Mazatlán, this beach with its curvaceous dunes is also called "Catch-22 Beach" after the movie filmed here. Home to a pueblo-style Club Med, the beach meanders east for about a mile along Bahía de San Carlos to a spit of sand linked to a rocky island.

Facilities: Club Med (members only or day passes for visitors). A beautiful new marina has just been developed, and new hotels are not far behind. Full facilities in nearby San Carlos. *Camping:* Very good. *Swimming:* Very good. *Snorkeling:* Good around offshore island past Club Med. *Windsurfing:* Excellent spot for windsurfing; there is always good wind. Lessons available at Club Med. *Fishing/boating:* Rent in San Carlos or inquire at Club Med.

Getting there: From San Carlos, follow right fork of Carretera San Carlos near Bánamex, then follow Club Med signs. After the dunes appear, take first left onto a dirt road to beach parking.

Lalo Cove and **Frenchie's Cove**—These small, rocky beaches west of San Carlos embrace protected coves within walking and swimming distance of one another. Both are noted for good snorkeling, best during the summer after the winter seaweed that darkens the water disappears.

Facilities: None. All amenities in nearby San Carlos. *Camping:* Good, fairly isolated. *Swimming:* Good. *Snorkeling:* Good around rocky points and offshore reefs. *Windsurfing:* Good. *Shell-collecting:* Scattered shells, better rocks.

Getting there: For Lalo Cove, take Carretera San Carlos from San Carlos toward Club Med, turn left at the Playa Algodones billboard onto the dirt road, continue onto the road curving left, then bear right to sandy clearing. For Frenchie's Cove, continue slowly on bumpy dirt road, bearing left until you come to the clearing above the beach.

SOUTH OF GUAYMAS BEACHES

Several little-known beaches trim the coastline as you head south. The sand quality drops to about a 3, powdery and dingy, which may account for the seclusion you encounter here.

Playa Huatabampito—This long, grayish sand beach rolls along the open sea, backed by weathered holiday cottages and low dunes. You can drive for miles on its dark, hard-packed sand along the tideline. Huatabampito is the weekend playground of people from nearby Huatabampo, Navojoa and Ciudad Obregón.

Facilities: Restaurants. Stores in Huatabampo 12 miles away. *Camping:* Fair, if you can stand the sand fleas. *Swimming:* Good. *Fishing/boating:* Good. *Shell-collecting:* Some butterfly clam shells.

Getting there: Follow Mexico 15 south of Navojoa and take turnoff for the farming town of Huatabampo. Before entering Huatabampo, take the marked turnoff for Yavaros near the Pemex station and follow right fork to Huatabampito.

Playa Las Bocas and **Playa Camahuiroa**—These two beaches are almost identical in their layout and mood. With grayish sand spreading along miles of gentle sea and thrown-together vacation bungalows slumping along the low dunes, Las Bocas and Camahuiroa offer a holiday getaway for city dwellers from Navojoa and Los Mochis.

Facilities: Restaurants and grocery stores. Full amenities in the towns of Navojoa and Los Mochis. *Camping:* Fair and reasonably private. *Swimming:* Good. *Windsurfing:* Good. *Fishing/boating:* Good. Local fishermen rent *pangas. Shell-collecting:* Some butterfly clams.

Getting there: For Las Bocas, proceed about 25 miles south of Navojoa on Mexico 15 to gravel turnoff after Km. 115 and continue along the gravel road for ten miles to the beach community. For Camahuiroa, continue south of Las Bocas turnoff along Mexico 15 and turn right after the "Luis Camahuiroa" sign. Proceed ten miles on the gravel road to the beach community.

LOS MOCHIS–TOPOLOBAMPO BEACHES

Playa Las Animas (also called Playa Baviri or Maviri) is the only beach accessible by road in the immediate Topolobampo area. If you need a place to camp or relax while waiting for the ferry to Baja, try this spot. Otherwise it's not attractive enough to warrant a visit. Far superior is:

Playa Santa María (★)—Many of the best hidden beaches in Mexico lurk on the shores of remote islands. In this case, Topolobampo's real beauty of a beach (certainly hidden from the average motorist) is the desert island of Santa María out in Bahía Ohuira. This island is 99 percent pure pillowy sand, with dunes drifting nearly a mile across, from shore to shore. According to the shrimp boat captain who brought me here, parts of the old movie *Mayflower* were filmed on Isla Santa María. Most of the time it belongs strictly to fishermen. Las Copas, another island closer to Topolobampo, also has lovely beaches.

Facilities: None. *Camping:* Terrific, but remember your bug repellent. *Swimming:* Lovely. *Snorkeling:* Best off of Roca de Farallones in Bahía Ohuira. *Fishing/boating:* Mullet, pargo, cabrilla, corbina and manta ray are all available. *Pangas* for rent in Topolobampo. *Shell-collecting:* Scattered shells in dunes.

Getting there: The island is about ten miles from Topolobampo, an hour away by shrimp boat or half hour by motorized *panga*. Rent a *panga* at inlet near entrance to the town.

SOUTH OF LOS MOCHIS BEACHES

Several obscure Mexican beach resorts are tucked along the coast between Guasave and Culiacán.

Playa Las Glorias—The little holiday community of Las Glorias, west of the agricultural town of Guasave, has about five miles of grayish sand beach with steep dunes at the northern end. Las Glorias' special distinction is its wealth of colorful clam shells. Nearby is the fishing village of Boca del Rio, on an estuary, and beyond lies another long beach, Buena Vista.

Facilities: Restaurants. All amenities in Guasave. *Camping:* Good, very private. *Swimming:* Good, safe, shallow—great for children. *Windsurfing:* Good. *Fishing/boating:* Rent a *panga* from the fishermen at Boca del Río or around the Estero La Pithaya east of the Las Glorias dunes. This estuary is rich in clams. The estuary around Boca del Río has mangrove roots encrusted with oysters. *Shell-collecting:* Starfish and many exquisite butterfly clam shells tinted purple, yellow, rust and blue.

Getting there: Take Mexico 15 to the turnoff for Guasave (El Centro), go through town to the Pemex station and turn right at the monument. Continue about 25 miles along paved Highway 153 to Boca del Río turnoff, where the road leads to the town of Las Glorias and the beach.

Playa Altata and **Playa El Tambor**—An hour's drive northwest of Culiacán through tropical sugar cane country brings you to the popular fishing village of Altata. Its main calling card is seafood. Dozens of open-air restaurants lie along the long, damp, muddy beach (sand of about a lowly 1 in quality), one of the least inviting I've seen. Much nicer is the sandy, secluded beach at El Tambor just beyond the quaint fishing village of Dautillos, about a half-hour drive from Altata. Here you feel the call of the tropics in the thickening vegetation and clumps of palms that sway behind eight miles of sand.

Facilities: Restaurants. *Camping:* Good and very private at El Tambor. *Swimming:* Good. *Snorkeling/diving:* Around offshore islands (Isla de Tachichilte and Isla de Altamura) north of El Tambor. *Fishing/boating:* Boats can be rented at the nearby village of Dautillos. Fishing is especially good around offshore islands. *Shell-collecting:* Starfish and pastel butterfly clams.

Getting there: For Playa Altata, take the Altata turnoff from Mexico 15 north of Culiacán onto paved Sinaloa 30 (also known as 280). Continue for about 30 miles to Altata. For El Tambor, take the marked turnoff from Sinaloa 30 on the approach to Altata and proceed north for about 12 miles along the hard-packed *terraza* road, bearing left to get to beach.

Trailer Parks

All have full hookups and bathrooms unless otherwise noted.

PUERTO PEÑASCO TRAILER PARKS

Playa Bonita RV Park (on Playa Bonita; 3-25-96) has 245 spaces, a restaurant, store, laundry and the best beachfront situation.

Playa Miramar Trailer Park (Calle Matamoros and Final Avenida Campeche; 3-25-87) has 105 spaces, laundry, satellite hookups and a boat ramp.

Playa de Oro Trailer Park (just up the beach from Miramar on Calle Matamoros; APDO 76) offers 300 spaces, laundry and clubhouse.

BAHÍA KINO TRAILER PARKS

Caverna del Seri RV Park (end of Boulevard Mar de Cortez in New Kino; 2-00-98) has 28 spaces on the beach, a restaurant and a boat ramp.

Islandia Marina Trailer Park and Cabins (Calle Guaymas, across from the Marlin restaurant; 2-00-80) faces the bay and features a boat launch, rustic cabins and shower facilities.

GUAYMAS–SAN CARLOS TRAILER PARKS

Las Playitas Trailer Park (four miles from downtown Guaymas on Calle Varadero past the boat yard; 2-27-27) overlooks Bahía Guaymas and has 100 spaces, pool, bungalows and restaurant-bar.

Quiet **Escalante Trailer Park** (Colonia Miramar across from La Bocana Restaurant; 2-48-22) has 64 spaces, a laundry and a beach across the street.

Among San Carlos' many trailer parks, **Teta Kawi** (Carretera San Carlos; 6-02-20), with 132 spaces, stands out for its cable television, jacuzzi, laundry and bungalows.

One of the biggest trailer parks in Mexico is the **Shangri-La** (end of Carretera San Carlos; 6-02-35), with 325 spaces on a hillside, a pool, restaurant-bar, cabañas and a small private beach.

Travelers' Tracks
Sightseeing

NOGALES TO SANTA ANA

From the orderly town of Nogales, Arizona, you enter disorderly, festive **Nogales**, Sonora, founded in 1880 and chockful of shopping arcades.

Traffic-clogged Mexico 15 continues down to the small city of **Magdalena**. The attractive main plaza (at Calle Abasolo and Calle Hidalgo) enshrines the bones of Father Eusebio Francisco Kino known as the "Conquistador of the Desert," the stalwart Jesuit who founded 25 missions in the northwest plains and died here in 1711. A monument in his honor stands in the plaza across from the renovated 18th-century Franciscan temple of **Santa María de Magdalena**.

SANTA ANA TO PUERTO PEÑASCO

About ten miles south of Magdalena near Santa Ana, Mexico 15 intersects with Mexico 2, which veers northwest toward Puerto Peñasco. Potholes and gravel spewed up by truck brigades plague this route, which passes through the agricultural city of Caborca into the rugged **Desierto de Altar** (Altar Desert).

This barren stretch is punctuated by cactus and lava beds from a volcanic region to the west. Mexico 2 continues northwest beyond Sonoita to the refreshing, verdant town of **Los Vidrios** and the **Parque del Gran Desierto del Pinacate**—a national park centered around the 4,000-foot Cerro del Pinacate, an extinct volcano rising from an old lava flow 45 miles long and 30 miles wide. Here, among the lunarlike perforations and ash cones, American astronauts trained for their first moon mission. You can camp around Pinacate and explore the area's 2,000 craters. A rough road leads into the park from Los Vidrios.

Backtracking to Sonoita, it's a smooth 65-mile drive south on Sonora 8 to the seaside resort of Puerto Peñasco. En route, you can sidetrack to the desolate, dramatic **inland dunes** (★). About 50 miles south of Sonoita, turn right at a sign reading "Dunas—10 km." A sand road winds inland toward the phantomlike dunes through a black lava field rimmed by towering sierra. If you don't have a 4-wheel-drive vehicle, park at the edge of the meadow where the sand begins to deepen. Walk onto voluptuous, Sahara-like drifts of sand, stippled with coyote tracks and steeped in silence. This vast dune zone continues for seven or eight miles to the sea.

The town of **Puerto Peñasco** at the end of Sonora 8 appears small and sleepy but actually occupies both sides of the railroad tracks. **Old Town,** on the rocky point (Cerro de Peñasco) where the town first sprang up, contains a commercial fishing harbor and fish market along the windy *malecón.* A good ten miles north of town, off Sonora 8, lies the carefree, sandy-trailed gringo village of **Bahía de la Choya.** South of town is its direct opposite, the elite **Las Conchas** community, with security gate and white-domed beach chalets owned largely by Americans.

SANTA ANA TO BAHÍA KINO

Back at the Santa Ana junction, continue south on Mexico 15 through drab desert terrain. About 75 miles down the road, the desert softens into an irrigated valley as you approach **Hermosillo,** the prosperous capital of Sonora. It owes its success to **La Presa Rodríguez** (Rodríguez Dam) one of Mexico's largest, built east of town to harness the Río Sonora. Hermosillo is crowded, commercial and not very scenic. Watch for the turnoff for Mexico 16 to Bahía Kino.

BAHÍA KINO

About 70 miles from Hermosillo, as you approach **Bahía Kino,** Mexico 16 meets a junction. The paved road curves north into New Kino, while an unpaved turnoff at the Pemex station heads into the poor fishing village of Old Kino. There you can wander among street-corner bonfires and wet laundry, check out the **fish markets** along the bay and smoky shacks selling ironwood carvings, or drive south to languid **Laguna de la Cruz,** where the shelling is good.

Back on the paved roadway, the asphalt breezes into New Kino and turns into cottage-and-condo-lined **Boulevard Mar de Cortez,** with a beautiful view of the bay. The boulevard follows the contours of the beach for about six miles, then deadends at a hulking red hill called **Cerro Prieto.** From here, a gravel road curves around the hill and meanders off to miles of wild untrodden shores.

The New Kino area features several sights, including offshore Isla Tiburón and the local **Museo de los Seris** (Seri Indian Museum) (★), a small cream-colored building at Boulevard Mar de Cortez and Calle Progreso. Inside, displays document the life and times of the local Seri Indians, from the pelican-plume garb of yesteryear to tightly woven baskets, their toys, cave paintings and elegant animal sculptures—probably the finest made in Mexico today. Unfortunately, there are no English translations describing the displays.

Isla Tiburón (Shark Island) was the ancestral home of the Seris. One of Mexico's largest islands, 29 miles long and about 45 minutes from Kino by boat, it contains remnants of Seri villages on its shores and huge colonies of land tortoises.

For a first-hand look at the Seris and their handicrafts, take an excursion to the village of **Punta Chueca**, about 18 miles north of New Kino via a gravel road. The marked turnoff for this road is off Boulevard Mar de Cortez near the Posada Santa Gemma Hotel. You arrive at a destitute seaside pueblo of small cement-block houses built by the government, with no water, electricity or garbage collection. Many Seris camp outside the houses, living amid trash-piled yards and bony dogs. As tourists drive up, the Indians descend upon them with their beautiful baskets and carvings, eager to make a sale. There's a bigger community of Seris farther north at the town of **El Desemboque**, a long, rough drive suited for trucks or 4-wheel drive only.

GUAYMAS–SAN CARLOS

From Bahía Kino, there's a shortcut to **Guaymas**: follow Mexico 16 east for about 35 miles and take the marked turnoff. This side road joins Guaymas-bound Mexico 15 about 55 miles away.

Surrounded by sun-parched craggy mountains, overlooking **Bahía Guaymas**, Guaymas is one of Mexico's finest seaports and shrimping centers. Decades of discarded oyster shells have acted as landfill and built up the bayside contours of the town. Though it's as old as the native Guaymenas Indians for whom Spanish explorers named the area in 1535, the town is rather colorless and drab. The downtown **Plaza de Pescador**, a tribute to the city's main industry, features a giant bronze fisherman with a mammoth fish underfoot. Up the street is the white-domed 18th-century **Catedral de San Fernando** (between Calle 24a and Calle 25a).

Heading north from El Centro on Mexico 15, you pass fancy Colonia Miramar, an upscale suburban neighborhood with its own beach on Bahía Bacochibampo. The 50-year-old, villa-style **Hotel Playa de Cortés**, a local institution, presides over sprawling gardens and an antique-filled lobby—stop in for a look.

About 12 miles farther north off Mexico 15, the resort of **San Carlos** is filled with hotels and condos lying along **Bahía de San Carlos**. The town is dramatically backed by the barren, 2,000-foot Sierra de Bacochibampo,

(Text continued on page 164.)

Copper Canyon By Rail

Some call it "the world's most scenic railroad," others the Eighth Wonder of the World. Take a break from the beach and see for yourself. Two trains leave Los Mochis every morning for the Copper Canyon (Barranca del Cobre), Mexico's Super-Grand Canyon, a chasm so big that four Grand Canyons could fit inside it.

You'll be heading into the high, cool Sierra Madre aboard the Ferrocarril el Chihuahua Pacífico. The 572-mile railroad winds through breathtaking gorges, river valleys and mountain villages en route to Chihuahua, 14 hours away. If you're mainly after scenery, buy a ticket only as far as Creel, a town just eight hours west of Los Mochis.

Almost as soon as the train begins its panting ascent and intricate switchbacks, you realize this railroad is quite an engineering feat. Completed in 1961 after 90 years and $90 million, it crosses 39 bridges and penetrates 86 tunnels, all carved out of canyons that sometimes plunge more than 6,000 feet.

To enjoy the roller-coaster ride, plant yourself between cars with your camera and try to capture the thrill of the track dropping away to the shining Río Fuerte and the train inching across the dizzying, 335-foot-high Chinipas Bridge. You spiral through old mining country glistening with creeks and apple orchards. Sometimes the cliffsides are so close you could prick your finger on a cactus sprouting from the rocks.

Then, darkness blots everything out as the train rumbles into a tunnel. As you ascend, the evergreens thicken and sting your nose with minty pine, mingled with the fragrance of burning wood. The dark, stoic faces of Indians peer up from the stations.

This is Tarahumara Indian territory. In fact, this part of the mountain range is called the Sierra Madre de Tarahumara after the nearly 50,000 Indians

living in caves, ranches and villages throughout these mountains. The Tarahumaras weave simple baskets and carve crude little animals out of pine bark, but their real strength is as long-distance runners.

At the longest stop of the ride—the Divisidero Barranca del Cobre—everybody pours off the train for 15 minutes and rushes to the railing that over-looks the magnificent Barranca del Cobre. In this multihued, mile-deep gorge, light and shadow play off the rippling slopes and bleached pinnacles. Little citadels of rock bathed in coppery iridescence reach into the blue sky. The gorge seems to drop into a chilly, bottomless abyss—though, in fact, the base of the canyon teems with subtropical foliage.

The next big stop is the hamlet of Creel, a good place to stay and explore a few days before returning to the coast.

Getting there: Train tickets (very reasonable) are available an hour in advance of the early morning departures at the Chihuahua al Pacífico Railway Station in Los Mochis (Avenida Bienestar; 2-08-53). Two trains are available: the regular, crowded vista train and the new luxury train. Children 5 to 12 pay half fare. Autos or trailers may be shipped by rail on the Vista train. Or you can park your car in an enclosed garage in Los Mochis until you return. Inquire at the Hotel Santa Anita (Avenida Leyva and Calle Hidalgo; 5-70-46).

Hotels in Creel: Creel's best hotel, with a mountain-lodge atmosphere, is the 36-room **Motel Parador de la Montaña** (Avenida López Mateos 44; 6-00-75). Moderate.

Just across from the train station on the other side of the tracks is the less expensive but still attractive **Hotel Nuevo** (right behind La Tiendita Super; 6-00-22). Budget.

Excursions from Creel: Arrange to explore the Sierra Madre de Tarahumara by horseback or guided bus tour at the **Motel Parador de la Montaña** (Avenida López Mateos 44; 6-00-75) and the **Hotel Nuevo** (across from the railway station; 6-00-22).

which include a well-known pair of peaks called **Tetas de Cabra** (Goat Teats). Half-a-dozen uninhabited **rocky islands** dot the bay: La Ventana, Honeymoon Island, San Nicolás, Catalina, Isla Venado, San Pedro Nolasko and San Pedro Mártir. Abundant sealife—whales, porpoises, sea lions and manta rays—flocks to the Guaymas Trench, a 5,000-foot-deep underwater canyon formed when the Baja Peninsula broke away from the continent and slid west. Cortez Sea Sports (Boulevard de la Marina; 6-02-30) offers cruises for island-exploring and whale-watching (from January to April), plus river trips through the Sierra Madre.

GUAYMAS TO LOS MOCHIS

South of Guaymas down to Mazatlán is a low-priority recreational zone. The **Sierra Madre** shadowing the highway is a hunter's paradise, but the coast is a relative wilderness, with mousy gray beaches weaving south for over 200 miles.

Along Mexico 15 just south of Guaymas at the pueblo of **Cruz de Piedra**, a huge **Yaqui Indian reservation** stretches 50 miles to the Río Yaqui just north of Ciudad Obregón. This property was deeded to the Yaquis after a big uprising in the late 1920s.

Dominating the fertile **Yaqui Valley**, the boomtown of Ciudad Obregón enjoys rich cotton production because of a network of dams that tap the Río Yaqui. Another agricultural oasis surrounds the smaller city of Navojoa. The 40-mile strip between these two towns is known as "Mexico's Bread Basket" because of its wheat production and flour mills. Founded by the Mayo Indians, Navojoa serves mainly as the pushoff point for visiting the restored colonial city of **Álamos**, 30 miles east on Highway 19. Full of extravagant old haciendas renovated by *norteamericanos*, this former silver capital is considered a national monument.

LOS MOCHIS–TOPOLOBAMPO

Just south of the village of Estación Don, you enter the state of **Sinaloa**. The next big town, harnessing the Río Fuerte to moisten its sugarcane fields, is fertile **Los Mochis**. Built by American entrepreneur Benjamin Johnston in 1893, the town is laid out as neat as a Mondrian painting. From Los Mochis, the famous Ferrocarril el Chihuahua Pacífico train departs for the **Copper Canyon** in the Sierra Madre. Along this railway route lies the colonial town of **El Fuerte**, founded in 1504 as a Spanish silver outpost.

Twelve miles west of Los Mochis is the developing port of **Topolobampo**, first conceived by an American dreamer named Albert Kinsey Owen as a modern utopia. Topolobampo's best sights are the **desert islands** out in Bahía Ohuira: Las Copas, Isla Santa María and Roca de Farallones, with its sea lion colony.

Also be sure to view **Topolobampo harbor**—the world's third-deepest natural bay—from the various points around town (including the

Topolobampo church). The bay, which leads to the Sea of Cortez, is a shimmering spectacle, with dolphins playing in the distance.

SOUTH OF LOS MOCHIS

Now the landscape changes visibly from desert to subtropics. When Mexico 15 crosses the Río Sinaloa, large shade trees suddenly shoulder the sun and vegetation creeps across the land. Flocks of white birds soar over fields of tomatoes against the misty foothills of the Sierra Madre. An overflow of greenery refreshes the thirsty eye.

For a better look at Sinaloa farmland, the side road (Sinaloa 30, also known as 280) to the beach town of **Altata** takes you through about 30 miles of sugarcane fields and waving palms, over lazy tropical rivers and lagoons, past stands selling coconuts and through fields of corn.

Another road (Sinaloa 293) on the northwestern outskirts of Culiacán goes to the agricultural town of **El Dorado** near the sea. Trucks bulging with ripe tomatoes sway down the highway. A sweet ketchuplike smell fills the air as you pass tomato processing plants. Postcard images of Old Mexico—tumbledown shacks, horse-drawn carts, murmuring streams where barefoot children play, sleepy cows—sprinkle the roadside.

Shopping

PUERTO PEÑASCO SHOPPING

Shell doodads, terra cotta vases and ironwood sculptures are for sale here. The best variety of curios fills the stalls along the sand road to Bahía de la Choya. One well-stocked shop is **Mariner Curios** (take a left off the Bahía de la Choya road just west of the train tracks).

In the **Jim-Bur** (Boulevard Benito Juárez, just south the the train tracks) shopping center are two excellent shops: **El Vaquero** (3-22-77) carries shoes, belts, buckles, baskets and seashell items at reasonable prices. Next door is **El Gift Shop**, with a nice selection of ceramics, wood carvings and weavings, as well as knickknacks made from seashell.

Americans are allowed to bring home fresh seafood from Mexico. If you don't catch it yourself, buy it fresh at the open-air **Fish Market** in the Old Town along the *malecón*. The chipped tile stalls and cracked coolers brim with squid, red snapper, giant flounders and shrimp in assorted sizes. The little pink shrimp are sweet, the bigger brown ones hearty, but the jumbo blues are nectar in a shell, sold by the five-pound bag for half what they cost in the United States.

BAHÍA KINO SHOPPING

Those polished sculptures of marlin and eagles that you see in every Mexican resort originate here with the Seri Indians. The Seris still carve them in a distinctive style, but most pieces are imitations turned out by Mexican craftsmen.

The difference shows in the detail and lines of the finished piece. Mexican works are labored and intricate; Seri carvings are graceful and minimal, almost abstract. While Mexicans use motor-driven tools, the Seris reportedly still carve their sculptures by hand. Both use ironwood, *palo fierro*, a rock-hard mesquitelike wood from the Arizona and Sonora deserts.

The carvings are all of native desert and marine animals: dolphins, turtles, seals, roadrunners, whales, sharks, pelicans. The sculpting art, always part of Seri culture, was revived in 1961 by Jose Astorga of El Desemboque, "the father of Seri artists."

The best place to buy true Seri sculptures is the Seri village of **Punta Chueca** north of Kino. The prices aren't cheap and the Indians don't bargain much. They know the value of their work, which is sought out by collectors, but they will trade or give discounts for bright blouses and skirts.

Old Kino is full of stalls selling Mexican-made sculptures, in the **market area** and along the dirt road from the main highway out to Islandia Marina. Pieces are sold from homes, too.

For a variety of handicrafts, the only game in town is the **Azteca Gift Shop** (Boulevard Mar de Cortez between Calle Halifax and Calle Quebec, New Kino; 2-00-09).

GUAYMAS–SAN CARLOS SHOPPING

GUAYMAS SHOPPING

Downtown Guaymas has one of the best little shell shops in northern Mexico, **La Casona** (Calle 24a 3; 2-01-99). There are seashells from Mexico, Australia, the Philippines and other countries, painted and carved into collages, earrings and lamps. You'll also find gorgeous black pearl necklaces, silver vases and more.

From here, cruise on up several blocks to Guaymas' **Mercado Central** (Avenida Rodríguez between Calle 19a and Calle de Alemán). Refresh yourself with a creamy fruit *licuado*, and amble through the aisles lined with clothes, vegetables, sandals and toys.

For fresh seafood, drop by the earthy little **Pescadería Castro** (Boulevard Sánchez Tabuda; 2-78-30). Lobster, snails, crabs, shrimp, scallops, octopus, manta ray and salted shark are heaped in a fantastic disarray, buzzing with flies. Those who may be put off by the sight should remember that restaurateurs buy here.

SAN CARLOS SHOPPING

The **Elite Rock Shop** (Carretera San Carlos; 6-00-03) is a small museum of semiprecious stones, arrowheads and shells. A giant petrified ammonite snail shell that yawns in one corner dates back 200 million years or so. In a more reasonable price range, there are delicate fossils of prehistoric fish and *ca-ca* (sí, just what you think), dolomite clocks, bone chess sets, pre-Columbian reproductions and lovely pearl jewelry.

Just up the road is the well-stocked **Sagitario** (Carretera San Carlos across from the Country Club; 6-00-90), with floor-to-ceiling crafts: Taxco silver, black Oaxaca pottery, Guanajuato ceramic tiles, rugs, masks, clothes and *santos* sculptures (wooden saints) from Guerrero.

Next door is the roomier **Puerta de Sol Gift Shop** (Carretera San Carlos and Paseo Vista Hermosa 158). Here you can browse through aisles of ceramics, metal art, glassware, Christmas ornaments, jewelry and clothing.

For clothes and leather goods, I recommend **Mic-Mac Bazar** (Carretera San Carlos near marina entrance; 6-05-85). Jumpsuits, jackets, hand-knit sweaters and leather purses fill the racks.

Nightlife

PUERTO PEÑASCO NIGHTLIFE

The hordes of young Americans who pour down to Rocky Point have encouraged a mild proliferation of discos. About the rowdiest hangout is the gringo-saturated **J. J.'s Cantina** in Bahía de la Choya (across from the Pemex station). Otherwise known as Cholla Bay Sportsmen's Club, J. J.'s is a cement-floored, outdoorsy pub where the drinks are served in plastic cups and the interior decorator was probably a fisherman with a hangover.

Tourists also like the bar at the **Motel Señorial** (Calle Armada Nacional; 3-20-65), which is noisy, dark and crowded and sometimes features live music. The **Hotel Viña del Mar Bar** (Calle Primero de Junio and Malecón Kino; 3-36-00) offers a *más suave* atmosphere—nice for a quiet drink, with a sea view.

For dancing, head down the cobbled drive from the Viña del Mar Bar to the hotel's compact, cavelike disco, **Rocky-O** (Calle Primero de Junio and Malecón Kino; 3-36-00). Rock hits boom out while videos dance along the walls. Cover, open weekends only.

BAHÍA KINO NIGHTLIFE

In Old Kino the only nightlife is the *palapa* bar and disco at the **Marlin** (Calle Tastiota; 2-01-11) on Friday and Saturday nights.

In the retirement community of New Kino, most folks retire early. One exception is the Wednesday night Mexican fiesta and the Friday night country and western festival at the *palapa*-style **Caverna del Seri Restaurant-Bar** (end of Boulevard Mar de Cortez at the trailer park, built directly against the rocky hill; 2-00-98). A very reasonable sum buys you a tasty meal and a hearty side dish of local music and dance. The seniors who pack the tables join in the fun, waltzing cheek-to-cheek as the *cerveza* moves them. Check for changing activities.

GUAYMAS–SAN CARLOS NIGHTLIFE

Guaymas has more discos while San Carlos has more bars.

GUAYMAS NIGHTLIFE

Charles Baby Disco (Avenida Serdán 107) bills itself as "a place for young hearts," and indeed, these mirrored walls reflect mostly teenage peach fuzz and braces. Twinkle lights glitter floor to ceiling to the pulse of American rock. Weekend cover.

A more sophisticated nightspot is the **Casanova Video-Disco** in the Hotel Armida (Avenida Serdán and Carretera Internacional; 2-30-50). Resembling a converted warehouse, this club features a giant video screen and elevated dance floor. Cover.

SAN CARLOS NIGHTLIFE

Nights in San Carlos begin at happy hour, usually running between 4 and 7 p.m. The **Terraza Restaurant-Bar** (Carretera San Carlos, Km. 5; 6-00-39) whips up mighty stiff margaritas and live organ music around a semi-circular bar and a cozy dance floor. Nearby, friendly spirits flow at the informal **Restaurant-Bar El Paradise** (Carretera San Carlos; 6-05-42), especially on weekends.

You get a panoramic view with a Latin accent at **Restaurant-Bar El Yate** (in the hills behind the San Carlos marina, take the dirt turnoff past the marina; 6-03-11). The harbor lights shine below to the strains of recorded music.

Stella's (Carretera San Carlos 246) is the late-night party destination. Dance to recorded rock music under the large *palapa* dome.

Prefer more of the *tranquilo* spirit? Take a two-hour **sunset cruise** around Bahía de San Carlos aboard a comfortable charter boat. The San Carlos Diving Center and Charter Boats (Carretera San Carlos; 6-00-49) and La Sociedad Cooperativa de Tetabampo de Pesca Deportiva (Boulevard de la Marina; 9-16-22) offer cruises.

LOS MOCHIS–TOPOLOBAMPO NIGHTLIFE

Aside from late-night taco stands, Topolobambo's evening social life centers around the boat-shaped **Yacht Hotel Restaurant & Bar** (located on a cliff behind Topolobampo, reached by the marked turnoff southwest of the Pemex plant en route to town; 2-38-62), which features a romantic quartet and organ music in the bar.

Inland in Los Mochis, you can shake a leg at **Scorpio's Discotheque** and the adjoining **Bar Las Bugambilias** at the Hotel Florida (Calle Ramírez and Avenida Leyva; 2-12-00) or just sip something cool at the **Hotel Santa Anita Restaurant-Bar** (Avenida Leyva and Calle Hidalgo; 2-00-46), which usually has live entertainment.

The young crowd hangs out at **Fantasy** (Avenida Leyva and Calle Cárdenas; 2-00-24) in the Plaza Inn. This is the hot disco in town, with large video screens dwarfing the dance floor. Cover.

Beyond this, the coastal nightlife fades into an after-dinner drink and bedtime gossip.

Northwest Coast Addresses and Phone Numbers

PUERTO PEÑASCO

Bank—Bánamex and Bancomer, both on Avenida Benito Juárez
Hospital—ISSSTE (Social Security Hospital), Calle Simón Morua and Calle Juan de la Barrera (3-21-10)
Laundry—Laundromat Liz, Calle Altamirano and Calle Simón Morua
Police—3-26-26
Post Office—Boulevard Fremont and Calle Coalhuila
Tourist office—Located in the Jim-Bur shopping center

BAHÍA KINO

Bank—Bancomer, in Old Kino, on Calle Llavaros
Hospital (Clinic)—Reachable by CB Radio, Channel 4, Old Kino
Police—Reachable by CB Radio, Channel 4, Old Kino
Post Office—Calle Eusebio Kino, Old Kino
Tourist office—No local tourist office; try Club Deportivo Bahía Kino at Calle Tampico and Calle Guaymas in New Kino (2-00-24)

GUAYMAS

Bank—Bánamex, Calle 20a and Avenida Serdán
Hospital—2-01-22
Laundry—Lavandería Lavamática, Calzada Moreno 96
Police—2-00-30
Post Office—Avenida 10 between Calle 19a and Calle 20a (2-01-04)
Tourist office—Calle 22a between Avenida Serdán and Avenida Rodríguez (2-29-32)

SAN CARLOS

Bank—Bánamex, Boulevard Estrada at the fork in Carretera San Carlos
Clinic—24-hour emergency medical service (6-01-01)
Laundry—Lavandería, across from the police station, Carretera San Carlos (6-00-13).
Police—Carretera San Carlos (6-00-04)

CHAPTER SEVEN
The Mexican Riviera

Where the Tropic of Cancer crosses the Pacific Coast just north of Mazatlán, Mexico's lushest tropical zone begins. About 950 miles of fabulous beaches—some of the world's best—sweep south along the Pacific in a riot of palm groves and highrise hotels collectively known as the Mexican Riviera.

Few coastal landscapes rival the steamy beauty of this stretch. Its luxurious resorts—Mazatlán, Puerto Vallarta, Manzanillo, Ixtapa-Zihuatanejo and Acapulco—embrace brilliant bays full of sailfish and placid lagoons where white herons glide, all backed by the miragelike majesty of the distant Sierra Madre Occidental.

Six states comprise the Mexican Riviera: Sinaloa, Nayarit, Jalisco, Colima, Michoacán and Guerrero.

While agriculture-rich Sinaloa, semiarid and irrigated, is only subtropical, little Nayarit is the West Coast's true gateway to the tropics. It's the nation's premier producer of tobacco and a big supplier of tropical fruits, corn, coffee and peppers.

Fertile Jalisco, west of Mexico City, gave birth to many elements of the classic Mexican image: the tequila-drinking *charro* (Mexican cowboy), the Mexican hat dance, the brassy and elaborately dressed mariachis. Puerto Vallarta and neighboring Guadalajara, capital of Jalisco, still boast the best mariachis in Mexico.

Tiny tropical Colima next door contains Mexico's only active volcano, a smoking crater called El Fuego, and the best black-sand beaches in Mexico thanks to its volcanic past.

In the beautiful state of Michoacán, spangled with rivers, lakes and mountains, some 150 miles of formerly inaccessible beaches are now reachable by a new corridor of highway.

Mountainous Guerrero, a state with a turbulent bent, has a reputation for illegal activities. It also houses rich silver deposits and the gold mine beach resorts of Acapulco and Ixtapa-Zihuatanejo.

171

Indian tribes roamed these states long before the Spanish conquest, and some still do today. The Cora Indians of Nayarit were saved from Spanish invasion by their forbidding Sierra del Nayar stronghold, where the remaining thousand Coras maintain their ancient customs and dress. They continue to worship the Morning Star, take peyote and paint themselves black for rituals.

The isolationist Huichol Indians of Jalisco also escaped Spanish domination because of their remote headquarters in the Sierra Madre. The tribes' famous consumption of peyote involves an annual pilgrimage to the northern desert where the peyote cactus grows. Bitter peyote buttons are eaten even by Huichol children to celebrate the cycles of planting and harvest, summon the rain god and petition for divine blessings.

The more adaptable Tarascans, known as talented artisans, thrive in Michoacán, with some 80,000 believed to populate the area surrounding Lake Patzcuaro and the plateau of Tarasca. Many speak Spanish and have adopted Christian practices without giving up their own deities. To survive, they fish and hand craft everything from lacquerware to guitars.

Unfortunately, you may get only passing glimpses of these mountain-dwelling peoples as long as you stick to the coast. Aside from these tribes, the Mexican Riviera has little traditional culture. But whatever the coastal towns may lack in historical architecture, museums and glorious pasts, they make up for in seafood, shopping, nightlife and the great outdoors.

A good paved highway running the length of the coast makes exploration inviting. While it is certainly Mexico's most developed piece of coastline, well-steeled for tourist invasions with hotels and shopping malls, the central West Coast is also packed with off-the-beaten-track surprises and adventures.

Tucked in between every big name resort are dozens of secluded fishing villages with beaches unknown to most foreigners and nearly untouched by tourism. Many wait at the end of bone-crunching gravel roads often ill-marked from the highway and shunned by the average sensible driver. Most have few facilities but make terrific campgrounds, with fresh, home-cooked seafood at beachfront cafés for half the resort restaurant price.

The easy-going residents welcome the sight of a new face. Mexican families from nearby inland towns roll in now and then to romp in the tide. But most often days pass in a drowsy blur of bird song, waves and breeze-ruffled foliage. It is a minor miracle that so much beauty has not been incorporated into the master plans of developers. The choicest beaches remain unspoiled—spots like Novillero, Chacala, Maruata and Tenacatita, and even better-known towns like San Blas, Rincón de Guayabitos, Playa Azul and Pie de la Cuesta.

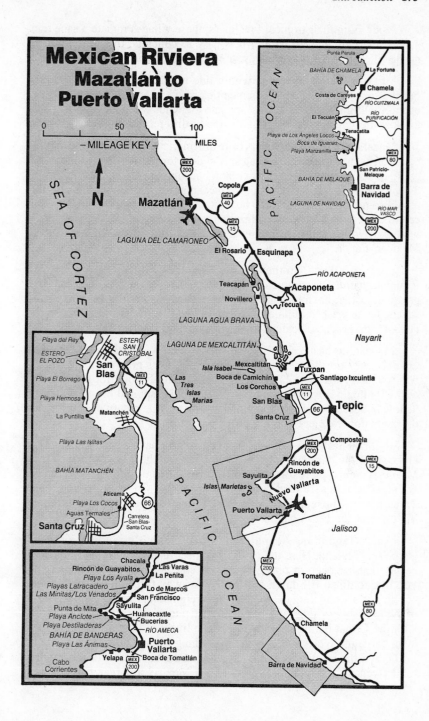

Mexican Riviera
Mazatlán to Puerto Vallarta

Aside from their tropical loveliness, these villages radiate a sane tranquility and closeness to nature. It is easy to conclude that these, not the hustle-filled Riviera playgrounds, are the real Pacific paradises.

Many of these villages are within side-trip distance of the big resorts. For the sake of excitement and amenities, you can headquarter yourself in one of the Big Five cities and escape into the wilds when the highrises start to close in. Each resort offers a distinctly different kind of visit.

Mazatlán has long been a favorite of American West Coast tourists because of its proximity to the States. It's ideal for families and students because of its relatively inexpensive hotel accommodations. Best known as a sportfishing mecca, Mazatlán also has an air of masculine grandeur that attracts outdoor types. With the heavy tourist action and best beaches concentrated at one end of town, Mazatlán remains very much its own city—a busy port with a huge shrimping fleet and an old downtown area full of Mexican flavor.

Puerto Vallarta, on the other hand, oozes with a more coquettish, feminine charm. The commercialism and time-sharing hustle can become oppressive at times, but for lovers of the picturesque, it is a heaven of cobble-stone streets, white-washed buildings, balconies, red-tiled roofs and cliff-side restaurants. Its beaches, boating trips and shopping take up any slack.

Manzanillo has very little charisma as a city—strictly a no-frills port town. Named for the *manzanillo* (chamomile) trees growing there when it was founded back in 1522, the town was a push-off point for the conquest of the Philippines by Captain Miguel López Legaspi and his crew. Today, its lovely beaches and self-contained resorts provide plenty of comfort and diversion for travelers seeking peace and quiet.

Highrise flash and fishing village quaintness have a beautiful marriage i n Ixtapa-Zihuatanejo. Ixtapa is a computer-hatched, government-made, Miami Beach-type resort carved from 16 miles of palm-soaked coast. Blessedly, it's situated five miles from the old seaside pueblo of Zihuatanejo, whose narrow alleys and beachfront cafés remain intimate. Visitors get the best of both worlds.

As for legendary Acapulco, it's still Mexico's gaudiest and most glamorous funland. Here the mountains meet the bay in a flush of natural beauty that has been inspiring decadence since the 1930s. Whether or not you like to disco till dawn or elbow your way through bikini-jammed beaches, it's fascinating to see what the foreign thirst for escapism has made of this ex-fishing village and pirate-stormed port, once a great center of trade with the Orient dating back to 1597. The lively old town has some great hotel bargains. Water sports cover everything from regatta races to marlin hunts, and the weather remains divinely in the 80s. Beneath the carefree tourist veneer, the romantic blood of old Mexico still runs deep.

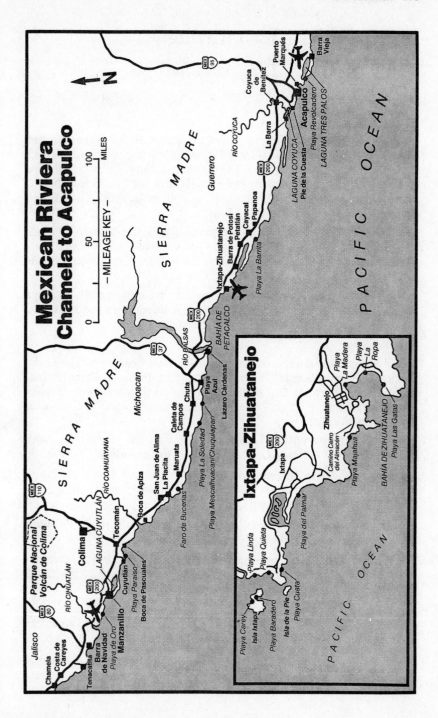

Mexican Riviera
Chamela to Acapulco

– MILEAGE KEY –

0   50   100

MILES

Easy Living

Transportation

ARRIVAL

BY CAR

Probably the busiest gateway from the United States to the Mexican Riviera is at Nogales, Sonora (near Nogales, Arizona) where **Mexico 15** leads south directly to Mazatlán. Other common entry routes are **Mexico 45** from Ciudad Juárez (bordering El Paso, Texas); **Mexico 85** from Nuevo Laredo (near Laredo, Texas), joining Mexico 40 to the south; and **Mexico 40** from Reynosa (near McAllen, Texas).

All these routes connect with Mexico 15 at the coast. Mexico 15 winds along the coast from Guaymas to a point just south of Tepic, where it turns into **Mexico 200**, which weaves its way through most major destinations along the central and southern Pacific Coast.

A newer section of Mexico 200 now runs from Manzanillo to Playa Azul. There are no gas stations in this stretch, a distance of some 150 miles. Fill your tank in Manzanillo before embarking.

BY AIR

Five commercial airports serve the major West Coast resorts along the Mexican Riviera: Mazatlán International Airport, Puerto Vallarta International Airport, Playa de Oro International Airport (located about 25 miles north of Manzanillo), Ixtapa-Zihuatanejo International Airport and Acapulco International Airport.

Mazatlán International Airport: Mazatlán is served by Aeroméxico, Mexicana Airlines, Delta Airlines and Alaska Airlines.

Puerto Vallarta International Airport: Airlines flying into Puerto Vallarta include Aeroméxico, Alaska Airlines, Mexicana Airlines, Delta Airlines, American Airlines, and Continental Airlines.

Playa de Oro International Airport: Manzanillo is served by Aeroméxico and Mexicana Airlines.

Ixtapa-Zihuatenejo International Airport: This area is served by Aeroméxico, Mexicana Airlines, Continental Airlines, Western Airlines and Delta Airlines.

Acapulco International Airport: Airlines servicing Acapulco include Aeromar, Aeroméxico, Mexicana Airlines, Delta Airlines, American Airlines, Continental Airlines and Eastern Airlines

Taxis and vans provide transportation from the airports into town or to nearby destinations.

BY BUS

Regular bus service connects all major resorts and most towns along the Mexican Riviera. The major lines for this section are **Tres Estrellas de Oro, Transportes del Norte, Transportes del Pacífico** and **Transportes Norte de Sonora** (TNS) (with service to points north). Information numbers and main bus stations are as follows:

Mazatlán: Calle Río Tamazula and Carretera Internacional Norte, depot for Tres Estrellas de Oro (1-36-80), Transportes del Norte (1-23-35) and Transportes del Pacífico (2-05-77).

San Blas: Calle Sinaloa, off main plaza (5-00-43).

Rincón de Guayabitos: Avenida Emiliano Zapata 1 (Tel. 25).

Puerto Vallarta: Depots for Transportes del Pacífico (Calle Insurgentes 282; 2-56-22); Tres Estrellas de Oro (Calle Insurgentes 210; 2-10-19); TNS (Avenida Madero 343; 2-16-50).

Barra de Navidad: Avenida Veracruz 228 (7-02-65).

Melaque: Calle Gómez Fariez 251 (7-02-43).

Manzanillo: Avenida Hidalgo and Calle Vicente Suárez, depot for Tres Estrellas de Oro (2-01-35), TNS (2-04-32) and Autobuses de Occidente (2-01-23), which has buses to small nearby towns.

Playa Azul: Avenida Independencia (6-00-48).

Lázaro Cárdenas: Avenida Lázaro Cárdenas 1810, depot for Tres Estrellas de Oro (2-04-26), Autotransportes Galeana (2-02-62) and TNS (2-04-26).

Zihuatanejo: Paseo del Palmar (4-21-75).

Acapulco: Avenida Cuauhtémoc and Calle Magallones (5-25-08).

BY TRAIN

Mazatlán and Manzanillo can be reached by train. In Mazatlán, **Ferrocarriles del Pacífico** (just off Mexico 15 on the southern outskirts of town at Calle Esperanza; 1-28-70) has four trains daily, two from Nogales and Mexicali, two from Guadalajara and Mexico City. In Manzanillo, **Ferrocarriles Nacionales de México** (Calle Juárez, 2-00-40), has first- and second-class trains from Guadalajara every morning.

BY BOAT

Cruise ships love the Mexican Riviera. These sparkling floating palaces can be seen docked at all major resorts. Mazatlán, Puerto Vallarta and Acapulco are favorite ports-of-call, especially for ships out of San Francisco and Los Angeles. The cruise lines that offer frequent journeys along the Pacific Coast include **Carnival Cruise Lines** (525 Northwest 87th Avenue, Miami, FL 33179; 800-327-9501), **Princess Cruises** (2029 Century Park East, Los Angeles, CA 90067; 213-553-1770), **Holland American Line Westours** (300 Elliot Avenue West, Seattle WA 98119; 800-426-0327), and

Admiral Cruises (1220 Biscayne Boulevard, Miami, FL 33132; 800-327-0271). Admiral Cruises also offers "cruise and drive" luxury voyages with transportation for your vehicle on board.

There is also regular passenger-vehicle **ferry service** from La Paz to Mazatlán, with salon, tourist, cabin and deluxe accommodations on board. Ferries arrive and depart from the **Muelles Transbordador** (Prolongación Calle Carnaval; 2-53-78). Advance reservations (1-70-20) are strongly recommended, as it's difficult to get a booking.

Although presently suspended, ferry service between southern Baja and Puerto Vallarta is scheduled to resume.

CAR RENTALS

All major resorts offer car rentals. Widely available jeeps are a favorite in the tropics. The airports serving the towns of Mazatlán, Puerto Vallarta, Manzanillo, Ixtapa-Zihuatanejo and Acapulco have a variety of rental companies, most of which charge similar rates. Most big hotels have car rental booths in their lobbies.

At the Mazatlán airport, try **National** (2-40-00), **Avis** (2-14-87), **Budget** (2-63-63) and **Auto Arrendadora** (3-46-33).

You can rent a car at the Puerto Vallarta airport from **Avis** (2-11-12), **National** (2-12-26), **Hertz** (2-04-53), **Budget** (2-01-88), **Quick** (2-14-42), **Auto Travis** (2-23-24) and **Dollar** (2-55-15).

At the Manzanillo airport, look for **AMMSA** (3-04-19), **Avis** (3-15-90), **Budget** (3-14-45) and **National** (3-06-11).

Serving the Ixtapa-Zihuatanejo airport are rental companies including **Avis** (4-22-48), **Hertz** (4-25-90), **Budget** (4-21-48), **Dollar** (4-23-14) and **Fast** (4-22-48).

At the Acapulco airport, take your pick from **Hertz** (4-13-53), **National** (4-40-90), **Saad** (jeeps only, 4-50-70), **Avis** (4-16-33), **Budget** (4-82-00) and **Dollar** (4-29-30).

BICYCLING AND MOTORBIKING

Tooling around on a two-wheeler is an exciting way to get to know a town. In Mazatlán, mopeds are for rent all over the Zona Dorada. Try **Gabby's Rentals** (Avenida Camarón Sábalo and Calle Río Ibís) and **rental stands** in front of the Hotel Aristos and Hotel Costa de Oro (both on Avenida Camarón Sábalo).

Puerto Vallarta's cliffside drives make good cruising ground for mopeds, available at **Moto-Rent** (Calle Perú 1204).

In Ixtapa, rent bicycles and mopeds from **Mr. Moto** in the La Puerta shopping area (Paseo Ixtapa).

Mopeds can be rented in the Manzanillo area from **Renta Una Mota** on Mexico 200 near Hotel Charles, between Manzanillo and Santiago.

In Acapulco, mopeds are a smart way to zip around the crowded Costera. Try the **rental outlet** in front of the Hotel Acapulco Tortuga (Playa Condesa, Avenida Costera Miguel Alemán; 4-88-89).

PUBLIC TRANSPORTATION

All towns, even most small ones, have taxis. Arrange the fee in advance. Bigger towns have thorough local bus service.

In Mazatlán, buses ply the beachfront strip from the downtown market through the Zona Dorada to the northern beaches. The streets swarm with charming little three-person cars resembling golf carts called *pulmonias* (meaning "pneumonia" because they're wide open): a great way to get around. Or try the larger red trucks that can seat ten people.

Puerto Vallarta has a bus line running from the airport to Playa de los Muertos.

Downtown Manzanillo has northbound buses from the *zócalo* and train station for beaches such as Playa Azul and Playa Miramar.

Between Ixtapa and Zihuatanejo, buses run regularly.

In Acapulco, buses circulate along the Costera between Playa Caleta and Puerto Marqués. Buses for Pie de la Cuesta stop near the *zócalo* in front of Sanborn's. Balloon-covered carriages called *calandrias* sway down the main boulevard, drawn by clopping horses and offering slow and romantic sightseeing by day or night.

Hotels

MAZATLÁN HOTELS

The priciest hotels tend to be concentrated along the beach in the Zona Dorada, while the economical spots are clustered along the *malecón* (sea walk) and toward the Olas Altas end of town.

For a great bargain, whether you're planning to stay 3 days or 30, settle in at one of the many modest furnished apartments scattered around the Zona Dorada. One of my favorites is the **Apartamentos Fiesta** (Calle Río Plata and Calle Ibís; 3-53-55), a family-run complex built around a big, walled garden full of whistling parrots and chuckling lizards, three blocks off the beach. Of the 11 apartments, the better ones have kitchenettes, living rooms with sofas usable as beds, medium-sized bedrooms with overhead fans and clean baths. Budget.

At the other end of town in the old Olas Altas area, two of the city's original inns—the Hotel Belmar and the Hotel Freeman—are still popular with bargain hunters. The pricier **Hotel Belmar** (Avenida Olas Altas 166; 5-11-11) is practically a historical monument. Its painted tiles, old bullfight posters and dark-wood interior date back nearly to the turn of the century, when the Belmar was Mazatlán's number one hotel. Its 250 rooms, new and old, are all air-conditioned and have phones. Older rooms are a fascinating mishmash of styles: an old carved bed next to a crate for a bedside stand, an exquisite antique mirror alongside a rusty metal chair. The newer rooms are more modern, with wood-paneled walls, shag carpets and seafront balconies. Budget.

Just up the street, the 12-floor **Hotel Freeman** (Avenida Olas Altas 79; 1-21-14) caters to groups, especially students. Never mind that the room phones have cracked dials and the furniture is scruffy; this is a good buy for your money. The Freeman provides great views, balconies, ceiling fans and clean baths. Budget.

If staying near the beach isn't an absolute must, you might try the downtown area, which has many reasonable hotels near lots of inexpensive restaurants. The **Hotel Central** (Calle Belisarío Domínguez 2 Sur and Calle Ángel Flores; 2-18-88) is a clean walk-up in El Centro, completely air-conditioned, with phones in all 67 rooms. These rooms are low-ceilinged, with small double beds, little wooden desks, views of nearby plazas and fresh baths. Budget.

In the Zona Dorada at the north end of town, one of the prettiest middle-range hotels around is the **Hotel Plaza Gaviotas** (Calle Bugambilias 100; 3-43-22). Situated on a quiet side street amid a screen of vegetation, the 66-room Plaza Gaviotas is built around a central pool and shady garden with adjoining coffee shop. Stores and the beach are a block away. The rooms are spacious and colorful, with lots of light, air-conditioning and phones. Parking available. Moderate.

Farther south, along the *malecón*, is the slightly weathered, motel-style **Hotel Aqua Marina** (Avenida del Mar 110; 1-70-80). Its 100 rooms, bar and restaurant are spread among several two-story buildings around the pool and parking area. The beach is just across the street. The comfortable rooms all have balconies facing the sea, dark curtains and faded doors. Moderate.

A less expensive place on the same lively beachfront is the yellow-and-white **Las Brisas Hotel** (Avenida del Mar 900; 3-66-99). Its 50 medium-sized rooms are clean and air-conditioned, but the worn furniture and yellow-and-orange-striped walls are not especially inviting. The balconies overlooking the sea and the quiet back garden with pool add an upbeat note. Budget.

More expensive and luxurious, the 423-room **Hotel Playa Mazatlán** (Playa Las Gaviotas; 3-44-55) dominates the most popular beach in the Zona Dorada, offering access to all water sports. The spacious rooms come with air-conditioning, phones and balconies offering breezy sea views. A favorite of families, the hotel features a heated pool and delightful terrace restaurant. Moderate.

Moving south down the *malecón*, you will find a more intimate sophistication at the eight-story **Hotel Hacienda** (Avenida del Mar and Calle

Flamingos; 2-70-00). Polished steps lead up to a sun-swept lobby, with a pool and patio tucked behind the restaurant. The 95 rooms have beautiful views of the beach, balconies, air-conditioning, color televisions, marble-tiled baths and carpeting. Check out the rooftop solarium with synthetic grass carpet and *palapa* umbrellas. Moderate.

Probably the city's finest hotel is the stately, modern **Hotel Camino Real** (Punta Sábalo; 3-11-11). Set on beautifully landscaped cliffs at the quiet northern end of the hotel zone, the 170-room Camino Real looks out through waving palms to its own private beach. Like other hotels in the Camino Real/Westin chain, this one is a small village containing *palapa*-style bars, restaurants, tennis courts and pool. The attractive rooms are large and air-conditioned, with color televisions, subdued coloring, carpets, seating area and servibars. Some rooms have balconies. Deluxe.

TEACAPÁN AND NOVILLERO HOTELS

In Teacapán, the only hotel is the five-room **Trailer Park and Motel Oregon** (Calle Reforma 50; 55). Set on shady grounds near the beach, these little bungalows are quite comfortable, with screened doors and windows (this is bug country), tile floors and rather elegant onyx-tiled baths. Budget.

In Novillero, there are several little seaside hotels. The best is the yellow **Hotel Playa Novillero** (Playa Novillero; 3-03-65), on a sand road near the beach. Its 39 rooms are fresh and plain, with tile floors and shuttered windows that have a view of the pool. Some rooms have air-conditioning, others ceiling fans. Budget.

SAN BLAS HOTELS

For a minor tourist stop, the town has a surplus of hotels. Unfortunately, none are beachfront.

Two of the least expensive and most individualistic are El Bucañero and Los Flamingos, both in one-time mansions near the port. The cheaper **Hotel El Bucañero** (Calle Juárez 75; 5-01-01) is a crumbling old pirate's retreat with a stuffed crocodile in the lobby and the buccaneer's creed of freedom etched on the wall. The 33 rooms—comfortable but stuffy despite ceiling fans—are built around a courtyard and have high beamed ceilings, double beds and slightly leaky baths. Budget.

Up the street is the **Hotel Los Flamingos** (Calle Juárez 163 Oriente; 5-04-48), a century-old hacienda built around a courtyard as lush as a little jungle, with a stone well, vine-smothered columns and tiled outer patio used as a veranda. The 25 rooms include some big, colonial ones with steep ceilings and vast shuttered windows, plus much smaller rooms that tend to be a little depressing, with chipped walls and shabby furniture. Budget.

A neat, friendly, family-style inn just across the street from the sea is the **Hotel Posada del Rey** (Calle Campeche; 5-01-23). Its 13 small rooms are all gathered around a small pool and brick patio. Each has a brick ceiling, overhead fan, tile floor and compact bath. Budget.

The best class-act hotel in town is the amiable **Hotel Las Brisas** (Calle Cuauhtémoc 106 Sur; 5-01-12), inhabiting a three-story building, with brick patios lit by yellow lamps and brightened by bougainvillea and smiling management. The 32 attractive rooms feature sliding glass doors, ceiling fans, pigskin chairs and two double beds. There is a large gift shop and very good restaurant. Moderate.

RINCÓN DE GUAYABITOS AREA HOTELS

In the town of La Peñita, just north of Guayabitos, the basic 20-room **Hotel Siesta** (Calle Lucio Blanco; 4-01-22) offers a pool and small outdoor cooking areas. The rooms are pleasantly rustic with lots of brick, deep-red bedspreads and swinging saloon doors. Budget.

If you want to set up housekeeping for a bit, try the friendly 18-unit **Bungalows El Delfín** (Retorno Ceiba and Calle Cocoteros, Rincón de Guayabitos; 4-03-85). Just steps from the beach, El Delfín has two-to-four person apartments, all with roomy kitchens, balconies, ceiling fans and bare bulbs. Below are shady grounds around a pool. Budget.

The area's best medium-range hotel is the attractive 92-room **Hotel Peñamar** (Avenida Sol Nuevo and Calle Jacarandas, Rincón de Guayabitos; 4-02-25), a couple of blocks from the beach. There's an ample patio, two pools, a restaurant-bar and parking. The more expensive rooms have marble floors, bamboo closets and air-conditioning—bare but comfortable. The cheaper rooms are small, with noisy fans. Budget.

For more luxury, head for the cool, blue **Hotel Fiesta Mar** (Avenida Sol Nuevo and Loto; 4-03-46). It's set up resort-style, with a large pool, upstairs disco, restaurant and alfresco lobby-bar showing movies on a jumbo video screen. The 36 rooms feature air-conditioning, royal-blue carpet, sliding glass doors and double beds mounted on tile frames. Breakfast is included. Moderate.

In the village of San Francisco to the south, there's a wonderful beachfront hideaway up a hillside about a mile out of town. **Club de Playa Costa Azul** (★) (Mexico 200, Km. 118, San Francisco) consists of 40 lovely white villas and suites set among towering palms. Each little villa radiates a romantic sparkle, with blue and white furnishings, kitchenette, high ceilings with fans, brightly tiled sunken tub, lots of light and great ocean views. Restaurant and pool. A fabulous value. Budget.

PUERTO VALLARTA HOTELS

The best low-cost hotel for your money in town may be the **Hotel Marlyn** (Avenida México 1121; 2-09-65). Located at the mellow northern end of the old town, across from the Parque Hidalgo, the 36-room Marlyn provides pretty patios on all four floors, with fresh and ample rooms featuring wicker lamps, red- tile floors, ceiling fans and, in some cases, sea views.

A family-style side-street hotel south of the Río Cuale, inexpensive and very popular with young travelers, is the 50-room **Hotel Posada de Roger** (Calle Basilio Badillo 237; 2-08-36). Roger's resembles a quaint little guesthouse built around an overgrown garden, with a rooftop pool and brick pathways. Some rooms are small and dark, with skimpy windows. Ask for one of the bigger rooms, with ceiling fan and cobbled bath. Budget.

On the beach on the north end of the *malecón* is **Hotel Rosita** (Paseo Díaz Ordaz 901; 2-10-33), with an uninviting exterior, but pleasant courtyard, pool, gardens and restaurant. Its 90 modest rooms and 20 suites have brick walls and ceiling fans. Budget.

Another old establishment, pricier and better maintained, is the 1940s-era **Hotel Encino** (Calle Juárez 122; 2-00-51), right next to the Río Cuale. The white, five-story building contains two restaurants, two bars, a rooftop pool and a sundeck. The air-conditioned rooms are cheerfully decorated with pigskin chairs and tables, sofas and thick curtains, and each has a phone and balcony. Budget.

A good seaside buy with all the trimmings, the five-story **Hotel Oro Verde** (Calle Rodolfo Gómez 111; 2-15-55) offers luxury-hotel amenities at middle-class prices. Set directly on Playa de los Muertos, it offers a restaurant, two bars and a swimming pool. Its 135 generous rooms and 28 suites have air-conditioning, servibars, double beds, sliding glass doors, sea views, terraces and phones. Moderate.

Seekers of an old-fashioned interlude will enjoy the cozy, colonial-style **Hotel Los Cuatro Vientos** (Calle Matamoros 520; 2-01-61) up in the old town. This charming little 16-room hacienda, smothered in a passionate scarlet vine called *flamado de amorado* (flame of love), sits among the hills away from the sea and has some lovely views of the village's red-tile roofs. One of Puerto Vallarta's first hotels, built in 1956, it has been converted into a bed-and-breakfast. The rooms are very simple: small, with one double or two twin beds, fan, wicker chairs and arched brick ceiling. Budget.

Enclosed inside a stone wall next to the Río Cuale, the pretty **Hotel Molino de Agua** (Calle Ignacio L. Vallarta and Calle Aquiles Serdán; 2-19-57) also faces the beach. Its parklike grounds are sprinkled with white brick cabins connected by stone pathways, with fountains, caged parrots and monkey, hibiscus, willows and ferns. The cabins and new seafront buildings contain patios, wicker and dark-beamed ceilings. Budget.

One of the liveliest hotels in town is the tropical beachfront **Hotel Playa de Oro** (Paseo de las Garzas 1; 2-03-48). This 450-room resort, next to the marina and ferry terminal, features steep thatched roofs and palm-filled gardens that house numerous restaurants, bars, whirlpool bath and giant pool. The beach is lined with *palapas* for shade, and all sorts of water sports are available. The big, comfortable rooms come with balconies or terraces facing the garden or sea, two double beds, servibars, phones and air-conditioning. Deluxe.

The premier high-life hotel in town is the 250-room **Camino Real** (Mexico 200, 1.5 miles south of town; 2-55-55), on its own crescent of sand, Playa de las Estacas. This beautiful resort stands on sloping, shady grounds, with pool and swim-up bar, tennis courts, first-class restaurant and donkey polo. The plush rooms have gorgeous sea views, primitive paintings, servibars, phones, television and air-conditioning. Deluxe.

YELAPA HOTELS

It's worthwhile to stay overnight at this isolated beach community to get a taste of its real personality. Accommodations are rustic. You can stay at the village's only official hotel, **Hotel Lagunita,** or at one of the private jungle palaces up in the hills overlooking the beach. The Lagunita, built in the 1960s, has 45 *palapa*-style huts along the cliffs near the boat landing. These wide-open cabins have bamboo beds with mosquito nets, bare bulbs lit by generator and bathrooms out in the back. Budget.

CHAMELA TO BARRA DE NAVIDAD HOTELS

This stretch of beaches north of Manzanillo contains many wonderful, nearly unheard-of hotels.

In Chamela, you'll find the best of two worlds: an indoor-outdoor "camping club" on Playa Chamela called **Villa Polinesia** (Mexico 200, Km. 72; 22-39-40 in Guadalajara). The club contains villas, several delightful *palapa* "tree-house" rooms overlooking the ocean and 35 small A-frame cement "tents" with electricity, built-in cushioned slabs for beds and a tiny screen for fresh air. Two thatched restaurant-bars, communal baths and showers, a trailer park with 16 sites and a sandy clearing for tent-camping are all part of the complex, with miles of beach at your doorstep. Budget.

Many times more glamorous, the 3,700-acre **Hotel Plaza Careyes** (Costa de Careyes, Playa Careyitos; 7-00-50) is a vast Mediterranean villa surrounded by palms and set on a small, private crescent beach. A one-and-a-half hour drive from Manzanillo, two-and-a-half from Puerto Vallarta, this complex is a pueblo unto itself, with an airstrip, pharmacy, gift shops, tennis courts, car and horse rentals and snorkeling gear. The 90 comfortable rooms sport adobe walls, Indian wall hangings, ceiling fans, hot tropical color schemes and balconies scattered with bougainvillea blossoms. Deluxe.

My favorite get-away-from-it-all hotel along this coastline is a rugged hilltop resort, six miles off the highway, constructed from rich native *guayabillo* wood. **El Tecuán** (★) (Playa El Tecuán, 30 miles north of Manzanillo in Melaque; 7-01-31. For reservations: Garibaldi 1676, Guadalajara, Jalisco, 44100, México; 16-00-85) combines the mood of a fountain-filled hacienda and rough-hewn lodge, offering spectacular views of the Pacific and glassy Laguna Fortuna. Its rooms gleam with exotic appeal, from the beamed entryways to the tropical bedspreads. There's also air-conditioning, phones, pool, tennis courts, bikes, horses, canoes, landing strip, galleon-style restaurant and miles of virgin beach. Unbelievably priced. Moderate.

Another resort with every amenity and lots of activity is the big **Fiesta Americana Los Ángeles Locos** (Mexico 200, Km. 20 on Bahía de Tenacatita; 7-02-20). Sitting right on lovely Playa Los Ángeles Locos, the four-story pueblo-style building flames with vivid red, orange and purple color schemes within. Each room has air-conditioning, phone, satellite television, rug, sofa and giant bed. It has recently instituted an all-inclusive rate, which includes all meals, social activities and sports, such as tennis, horseback riding, scuba diving, windsurfing, sailing and fishing. Moderate.

The low-key resort zone of San Patricio-Melaque has a handful of reasonable hotels, the best of which is the giant old beachside **Hotel Melaque** (Avenida Miguel Ochoa López, Bahía de Melaque; 7-00-01). This long, boxy inn has a windswept upstairs restaurant and oceanfront pool—the consummate 1950s-style family hotel. Its medium-sized rooms have ruffled bedspreads, formica desks and balconies with bay views. Moderate.

BARRA DE NAVIDAD HOTELS

A good choice is the 20-room, friendly **Hotel Delfín** (Calle Morelos 23; 7-00-68), shaded by palms and a gnarled *ule* tree and sheltered behind a white wall scalloped with blue waves. There's a key-shaped pool, breakfast café and view of the nearby lagoon from top-floor balconies. The clean rooms feature sunny bedspreads, flowery curtains and ceiling fans. Budget.

Across the street, half drowned in a dense and wonderful garden, the seasoned **Sands Hotel** (Calle Morelos 24; 7-00-18) sits next to the tranquil lagoon with a giant swimming pool and open-air restaurant. The 43 small rooms and bungalows include fans, rather low ceilings and erratic decor—you're paying for the setting rather than your quarters. Budget.

Barra's four-star hotel—with a marina, tennis courts, swimming pool, restaurant and small boutique—is the posh, 100-room **Hotel Cabo Blanco** (Pueblo Nuevo; 7-01-03). Shaped like a pueblo and painted in pale ochre tones, the hotel is set away from the village on peaceful grounds, with comfortable rooms containing both air-conditioning and ceiling fans, phones and glossy tile floors. Moderate.

MANZANILLO HOTELS

This area excels in self-contained resorts, some quite glamorous. There are many modest hostelries, too.

If being near the beach isn't mandatory and your dollar count is low, check out the regal downtown **Hotel Colonial** (Avenida México 100; 2-10-80), dating back to the 1940s. It's a showcase of hand-painted tiles, wrought-iron chandeliers, stained-glass windows and carved staircases. The rooms are clean and quaint yet somber, with frilly dark bedspreads, old black phones and thick windows looking out onto the busy street. Budget.

Prefer to stay near the sea? The modest **Parador Marbella** (Mexico 200, Playa Azul; 3-11-03) occupies a secluded section of beach and features a restaurant, pool and parking. Its 20 newly refurbished rooms have balconies or small terraces, white brick walls and overhead fans. Budget.

To the south, in the Las Brisas area, another low-cost beach-chalet is the simple, three-story **Hotel Star** (Avenida Lázaro Cárdenas 1313; 2-05-09). Its 46 rooms, with or without kitchens, include desks, low ceiling fans, cramped tile baths and pictureless walls. Bungalows accommodate up to four people. Budget.

Bigger and cushier, the old five-story, 107-room **Hotel Playa de Santiago** (Bahía de Santiago; 3-07-27) is a pleasant, clean facility. The rooms have phones, ceiling fans and seaside balconies. Downstairs are the pool, restaurant, mini-golf course and tennis courts. Moderate.

Billing itself as "the passionate pink hotel by the tropical sea," **La Posada** (Colonia Las Brisas, Avenida Lázaro Cárdenas 201; 2-24-04) is small, well staffed and warmly domestic. Palms, yellow lanterns and stone footpaths fill the grounds, as do many cats and kittens. The main sitting room, where delicious breakfasts are served, is a charming melange of posters and artifacts. Set on the beach around a pool, the 24 comfortable rooms have brick walls, ceiling fans and heavy wooden doors opened by giant skeleton keys—La Posada's trademark. Deluxe.

Right next door are 40 stylish condo-apartments, ideal for groups, at the modern **Condominio Club Roca del Mar** (Colonia Las Brisas, Avenida Lázaro Cárdenas; 2-19-90). Pool, boutique, restaurant and beautiful gardens surround this complex of two-bedroom, two-bath condos. All have maid-service, air-conditioning, coppery kitchens, dining rooms with modern art, baths with rock walls and skylights, and terraces. Moderate.

The all-white **Las Hadas** (Península de Santiago, 3-00-00. Mailing address: P.O. Box 15, 28200 Manzanillo, Colima, reservations: 1-800-228-3000), at first glance resembles a full-blown vision from the *Arabian Nights*. With its chalky domes, ice cream spires, Arabic arches and Eastern statuary, it is an exotic hybrid of the Moorish, the Mediterranean, the Mexican and the Disneyesque. This 230-room Xanadu was built in the late 1960s. Set in a cove on Manzanillo Bay, where dainty white luxury tents billow along its private beach, the resort spills down a vegetated hillside. The golf course, tennis courts, disco, restaurants, beautiful rooms with marble baths and ocean views, and private villas with individual pools, all make Las Hadas ocean views, and private villas with individual pools, all make Las Hadas a nice package. The special effects, from its Byzantine lanterns to the twin stone fairies at its entrance, make this place magic. Deluxe.

PLAYA AZUL AND LÁZARO CÁRDENAS HOTELS

Playa Azul's best is the big **Hotel Playa Azul** (Avenida Venustiano Carranza; 6-00-24), just a block from the beach. You're buying ambience here. The 80 simple rooms surround a delightful patio and garden shading a big pool. Rooms are clean but time worn, with scruffy wooden desks, ceiling fans and tiled patios lined with plants and rocking chairs. Budget.

Nearly as nice and less expensive, the 30-room **Hotel María Isabel** (Avenida Madero; 6-00-30) occupies a quiet side street several blocks from the beach. It's a squarish double-decker building with pool, patio and small restaurant-bar. For the price, the double rooms are the best deal in town, with freshly painted walls, overhead fans and louvered windows. Budget.

In nearby Lázaro Cárdenas, take a respite from the sand and surf at the attractive green downtown **Hotel María Margarita** (Calle Corregidora 79; 2-11-31). It has a restaurant-bar, air-conditioning, parking and boutique. The 49 rooms are small but neat and warm, with color televisions, phones, small refrigerators, carpets and marble baths. Moderate.

The budget-minded traveler's choice in Lázaro Cárdenas is the compact, popular **Hotel Veronica** (Avenida Javier Mina; 2-02-54), also downtown. There are 13 fresh, small rooms with red-tile floors, ceiling fans, bare walls and little balconies. Downstairs is an attractive restaurant-bar.

IXTAPA-ZIHUATANEJO HOTELS

You can choose from three areas here: Ixtapa has the posh mega-hotels; Zihuatanejo has budget hotels and guest houses; the beaches south of Zihuatanejo, La Ropa and La Madera, have medium-range hotels with spectacular ocean views.

North of Ixtapa at Playa Linda, the family-style **Hotel Playa Linda** (Carretera Playa Linda; 4-33-81) has 250 plain, white rooms on the beach. Bunk beds and washstands constitute the main decor, but rooms are air-conditioned. Tennis courts, pool, playground, restaurants and trailer park complete the facility. Moderate.

In Ixtapa, the one hotel in a reasonable price range is the 108-room **Posada Real** (Paseo de las Palmas; 4-23-41). This middle-class inn has two pools, restaurant and air-conditioning. The brightly decorated rooms have phones, sitting areas and built-in dressers with desks. Half of them overlook the beach. Deluxe.

For those looking for both seclusion and luxury, the **Camino Real** (Playa Vista Hermosa; 4-33-00) is the spot. Set on its own cove, there is nothing else in sight but this magnificent Mayan-looking structure climbing the hillside. All rooms have attractive balconies with tables, potted plants and chaises longues. Ultra-deluxe.

If you want to go first class, my recommendation is the 256-room **Krystal Ixtapa** (Paseo Ixtapa; 4-26-18). Outside it's just another highrise rectangle stuck in a palmy garden, but inside the lobby and restaurants are breezy and beautiful, opening onto a lagoonlike pool and patio on the beach. The rooms are all-American standards, with king-sized beds, air-conditioning and terraces looking out to sea. Ultra-deluxe.

The oldest and one of the least expensive caravansaries in Zihuatanejo, **Hotel Tres Marías**, gives you two locations to choose from. The older hotel (Calle La Noria 4; 4-21-91), nestled in plants, is across a wooden footbridge that spans the lagoon; its small, clean rooms have tiny step-up baths, cement floors and bare bulbs. The other, El Centro branch (Calle Juan Alvarez 52; 4-29-77), attached to a restaurant, has similar rooms brightened by balconies. Budget.

The best in town is the 75-room **Hotel Zihuatanejo** (Calle Agustín Ramírez 2; 4-26-69), tucked on a cobbled side street. The small rooms all have fans, air-conditioning, phones, small balconies, filmy white curtains and lots of light. The hotel has a pool and pretty restaurant on the premises. Budget to moderate.

South of the village, curving around the bay, in the Zona de Hoteles, the charming, colonial-style **Hotel Irma** (Playa La Madera; 4-20-25) overlooks Playa La Madera. Dating back to the early 1960s, the Irma attracts lots of repeat business with its breezy hillside restaurant, swimming pools and 75 cozy rooms dominated by double beds swathed in mosquito nets and balconies facing the beach. Moderate.

The ultimate view of the bay can be seen from the nearby cliffside **Hotel Catalina Sotavento** (Playa La Ropa; 4-20-32), another old Zihuatanejo standby. The Sotavento claims 70 airy rooms, each with wicker furnishings, phone, fan, sombreros posing as lampshades and one entire screened wall facing an enormous patio slung out over the hillside like the deck of a ship. A long staircase winds down to the beach and hotel restaurant. Moderate.

For elegant intimacy, the 17-room beachfront **Villa del Sol** (Playa La Ropa; 4-22-39) enjoys a reputation as the find of this area—with *très chic* prices. The rooms are wonderful re-creations of Old Mexico, built in two or three tiers with terraces and beamed ceilings. No phone, television or other intrusions of civilization are allowed, except a touch of classical music at its posh thatched restaurant. There is one tennis court. Deluxe.

If such lodgings suit your aesthetics but not your pocketbook, check out the less expensive and lovely Mediterranean-style **Villas Miramar**

(Playa La Madera; 4-21-06), whose 12 spacious units have a similar pueblo atmosphere with more contemporary touches. Moderate.

PIE DE LA CUESTA HOTELS

This peaceful village is full of bargain seaside guesthouses within half-an-hour of Acapulco by car or bus.

Years ago I first stumbled on the delightful old **Hotel Puesta del Sol** (★) (Playa Pie de la Cuesta; 3-76-74), undergoing a long-deserved spruce-up under new management. This palm-shaded villa, built in the 1930s by a famous bullfighting family, now has a sparkling swimming pool, freshly laid tennis courts, inviting alfresco restaurant-bar, television room and expanded parking. Its simple beachside bungalows, most still being renovated, have ceiling fans, rustic furnishings and quaint pull-chain showers. Some have kitchenettes. Smaller rooms in the main villa are attached to an upstairs terrace. Very hospitable. Budget.

At the other end of the village near the air base, the fresh, whitewashed **Bungalow Coral** (2-38-09) has even less expensive accommodations, with a pool and small restaurant. The 16 clean little rooms are carpeted and feature ceiling fans and hot-water showers. Budget.

Little **Tres Marías** (Playa Pie de la Cuesta; 3-61-50) has eight small, nicely kept rooms, four on the lagoon side and four on the beach, as well as a restaurant. Budget.

Midway between these two hotels, the new pueblo-style **Ukae Kim** (Playa Pie de la Cuesta 356; 5-10-98) suggests that Pie de la Cuesta may be moving toward resorthood. Its debonair little restaurant-bar, pool and Mediterranean-style rooms with elevated entry salons and tiled terraces make this the village's most citified place to stay. Rooms have ceiling fans and mosquito netting; most are oceanside, with a few on the lagoon. Moderate.

ACAPULCO HOTELS

Surprisingly low-cost hotels fill the old sections of Acapulco around Caleta and the *zócalo*, with prices rising as you move southeast down the Costera.

Two of the least expensive yet livable no-frills hotels near the *zócalo* are the **Hotel Sutter** (Calle Teniente José Azueta 10; 2-02-09) and the **Hotel Fiesta** (Calle Teniente José Azueta 16; 2-00-19). I stayed at the 28-room Sutter during my first visit to Acapulco and enjoyed the protective warmth of the Sutter family, as well as the basic comforts of a medium-sized room, with louvered windows, ceiling fan and cold-water shower. The 36-room Fiesta, just up the street, is run by the same family and has similar rooms—including little balconies and painted wood furniture—at even lower rates. Both budget.

In the same neighborhood, move up a notch to the more expensive and charming colonial-style **Hotel Misión** (Calle Felipe Valle 12; 2-36-43), located inside a walled courtyard near the bay. Balconies run along the two top floors of this 200-year-old compound, and excellent meals are served in the patio. The small rooms radiate good cheer, with white brick walls, ceiling fans, hand-painted tiles and red stone floors. Budget.

For a low-cost hotel closer to the action along the Costera, try the **Hotel Acapulco Diana** (Calle Francisco Pisero 58; 4-73-73). From here, it's a one-block walk to Glorieta Diana and Acapulco's best beaches. The pleasant yellow-and-white building houses a small pool, restaurant-bar and 53 simple rooms with air-conditioning, phones, beautiful marble floors and terraces. Budget.

More costly, but with more atmosphere, the **Hotel Los Flamingos** (Avenida Adolfo López Mateos; 2-06-90) is an old seaside institution within walking distance of Playa Caleta. Nestled in thick tropical foliage on a hillside, the 46-room pink hotel features bright, medium-sized rooms with lovely terraces, light-filled picture windows, tile floors, small refrigerators and rather scruffy desk-dressers. Budget to moderate.

Another original, famous for its views of the Quebrada high divers, is the 1930s-era **Hotel El Mirador** (La Quebrada 74; 3-16-25), one of Acapulco's oldest. This 133-room resort clings to a cliffside in the old Caleta district. Part of its Hollywood glamour lives on in its restaurant-bar and nightclub. The somewhat cramped rooms, all named for indigenous fish and animals, have stone walls and floors, small dressers and beds, phones, air-conditioning and balconies. Moderate.

You'll find a breathtaking view of Old Acapulco at the cliffside **Hotel Casablanca Tropical** (Cerro de la Pinzona 195; 2-12-12). Another of Acapulco's oldest lodgings in the Caleta district, the Casablanca has a well-scrubbed blue-and-white exterior. Its lobby bar, top-floor restaurant and poolside snack bar offer smashing vistas. The 120 basic rooms are a little worn, with phones, air-conditioning and breezy terraces that overlook the bay. Moderate.

Moving east onto the busy coastal drive, you may begin to see jeeps emblazoned with the name **Hotel Sands** (Avenida Costera Miguel Alemán 171; 4-22-60). This 94-room, reasonably priced favorite (which rents jeeps)—a homely six-story rectangular building across the street from the beach—has a *palapa*-fringed pool area. Its sunny rooms have air-conditioning, carpets, phones and patios. Moderate.

Those with slimmer funds can try the nearby lowrise **Sol-i-Mar** (Calle Cañonero Bravo 5; 4-13-56). This motel-like inn, overshadowed by highrises, occupies two sides of the street, each half with its own pool. The small, carpeted rooms offer single beds, old wooden dressers and air-conditioning. Some of the city's flashiest discos are minutes from your door. Moderate.

An older hotel with a youthful spirit, the 18-floor, beachfront **Fiesta Americana Condesa Acapulco** (Avenida Costera Miguel Alemán; 4-28-28) is always a hotbed of activity, with a jammed lobby and a lively flow of people to and from the Costera. The completely refurbished, air-conditioned rooms are comfortable, decorated in soft tones, with bamboo furnishings, carpets, seating area, tubs in the bathrooms and balconies. Deluxe.

One of my favorite beachside hotels is the renovated **Acapulco Ritz** (Avenida Costera Miguel Alemán; 5-75-44). A modern Mexican colonial theme runs throughout the hotel. The pale blue lobby is full of painted ceramics, whimsical wall murals and overstuffed furniture. The cheerful pastel rooms, divided into sitting and sleeping areas, have huge beds, private balconies, servibars, phones and cable television. A bar, coffee shops and restaurant complete the facilities. Moderate to deluxe.

You'll get a large, comfortable room and excellent service, as well as the use of a stunning pool-and-garden oasis at the **Hyatt Continental** (Bahía de Acapulco; 4-09-09). Rooms, many with private balconies and ocean views, have marble baths, attractive rattan furniture and bright decor. For a full-service resort at the center of beach activities, shopping, restaurants and nightlife, the price is surprisingly reasonable. Deluxe.

The honeymooner's dream hotel is the blushing-pink hillside **Las Brisas** (Carretera Escénica 5255; 4-15-80). You'll see its famous pink jeeps all over Acapulco. Pink hibiscus float on the 150 small pools inside the charming walled *casitas* (little houses). Breakfast is delivered daily through an opening in the wall. All villas have servibars and wet bars, gardens, small rooms with immense beds, big marble tubs, air-conditioning and exquisite views of the bay. At the top of the hill is a wedding chapel, at the foot a private beach club with a big natural seawater pool and water sports facilities. Deluxe.

Just southeast of neon-lit Acapulco, a 16-story Aztec pyramid rises out of a 240-acre palm grove. This is the great-grandame of resorts, with two golf courses and an eternity of silky beach, the 1,000-room **Acapulco Princess** (Playa Revolcadero, 4-31-00. Mailing address: P.O. Box 1351, Acapulco, Guerrero; call 1-800-223-1818 for reservations). The marble-floored atrium-lobby remains wide open day and night, filled with legions of guests and gawkers. Beyond the sparkley boutiques and corridors connecting adjacent buildings lies a network of manmade lagoons and tropical gardens. Stone walkways (where you may come upon a pink flamingo or scuttling crab) lead to seven restaurants and innumerable bars. There are lagoonlike swimming pools, tennis courts, horses for rent, a nightclub with volcanic rock walls and beautiful air-conditioned rooms with seaview terraces that let you scope the coast halfway down to Guatemala. Ultra-deluxe.

Restaurants

MAZATLÁN RESTAURANTS

The shrimp capital of Mexico, Mazatlán specializes in fine seafood to fit every budget.

In the old waterfront section of town, **Copa de Leche** (Avenida Olas Altas 33; 2-57-53), also called Antojitos El Farol, is a comfortable indoor-outdoor café where locals gather for Sunday beer and dinner, relaxing in leather chairs under a shady awning. Meat dishes are the specialty. Budget.

In the heart of downtown Mazatlán, you'll find immaculate, air-conditioned **Doney** (Avenida Cinco de Mayo and Calle Mariano Escobedo; 1-26-51). Situated in a renovated old house with domed brick ceiling and stately columns, Doney has been feeding Mazatlán since 1959. The menu covers everything from hamburgers to seafood to Mexican dishes. Budget.

The coastal drag that runs for miles along the *malecón* bristles with inexpensive little family-style restaurants. A good one is **Karnes En Su Jugo** (Avenida del Mar 550; 2-13-22), serving delicious Mexican chopped beef with a bowl of gravy, onions, radishes, bacon and beans. The interior design is ranch-style with beamed roof and paneled walls. Budget.

The **Rocamar Restaurant-Bar** (Avenida del Mar and Calle Río Tamazula; 1-60-08) is another *malecón* café with indoor-outdoor seating and seafood specialties. Try *camarones Rocamar*, broiled shrimp seasoned with pepper and smothered in cheese and bacon strips. Budget.

Of the city's best-known seafood restaurants with a genuine Mexican ambience, the least expensive is **Mamucas** (Calle Simón Bolívar 404 and Cinco de Febrero; 1-34-90). This popular side-street hangout in the old town has formica tables, air-conditioning and loaded menus. Choose from squid *mata indios* (Indian-killer squid), *mariscos explosivos* (explosive seafood) and the house specialty, *parrillada de mariscos* (grilled seafood for two). Budget.

Another seafood favorite, **El Marinero** (Avenida Cinco de Mayo and Paseo Claussen; 1-76-82) has net-draped ceilings and looks out at the sea through shell-curtained windows. Lunch and dinner include frogs' legs, quail, all types of oysters, seafood platters with everything from scampi to a gooey, rich seafood Newburg. Moderate.

Some say the best seafood restaurant in town is the giant *palapa*-style **Tres Islas** (Avenida Camarón Sábalo between the Holiday Inn and the Hotel Caravelle; 3-59-32). Sea breezes and wandering mariachis make this a delightful spot for lunch or dinner. Everything's good: red snapper, chicken in *mole* sauce, oysters Rockefeller, seafood platter for two. Moderate.

For bringing in the morning, the **Terraza Playa** (Hotel Playa Mazatlán, Playa Las Gaviotas; 3-44-55) is hard to beat. Big and inexpensive (though part of a deluxe hotel), this terrace café has brightly tiled tables shaded by thatched umbrellas, with the beach right at your elbow. Service is quick, tables are packed, food is tops—omelettes, French toast, *huevos Mexicanos* or *rancheros*—à la carte or buffet. Lunch and dinner also served. Budget.

The old **Restaurant Olas Altas** (Boulevard Centenario 14; 1-31-92) is another great breakfast spot, fresh and never crowded, although this used to be *the* restaurant in town before the tourist zone moved north. It's very cheerful, with shiny black tile floors, green-and-white tables and a fine view of the rocky beach. Good meals and the town's best coffee. Budget.

El Shrimp Bucket (Avenida Olas Altas 11; 1-63-50), a Carlos Anderson creation, is probably the *número uno* eatery in Mazatlán. It's always full of gringo families gobbling up the famous breaded shrimp served in a terra cotta "bucket." Located in the old Olas Altas district, the restaurant occupies a large courtyard lit with Chinese lanterns inside the La Siesta Hotel. Dinner includes everything from bean pot soup to ten varieties of shrimp. Breakfast and lunch served, too. Moderate.

Mazatlán's *primo* restaurant, many claim, is the elegant **Casa de Tony** (Calle Mariano Escobedo 111; 5-12-62), situated on a secluded side street in the Olas Altas area, between Calle Ángel Flores and Calle Constitución. Choose between romantic courtyard dining around a large fountain, or one of the three indoor rooms, with piano accompaniment flowing throughout. Service is impeccable. There's a nice selection of beef, seafood and Mexican specialties. Deluxe.

SAN BLAS RESTAURANTS

For seafood, the town's best is **La Isla**, also known as Tony's (Calle Paredes Sur and Calle Miguel Mercado Poniente; 5-04-07). A sea motif dominates this small, attractive restaurant—nets, shells and shark jaws cover the walls. People flock here for Tony's fish and shrimp. Lunch and dinner only. Budget.

Torino Bar and Grill (Calle Paredes Sur 13; 5-01-01) is another good option for seafood, chicken or barbequed shrimp. It's lively and warm, with heavy colonial high-backed chairs, red curtains and wrought iron. Budget.

Cheerful, colonial-style **Restaurant McDonald's** (Calle Juárez 36) is no relation to the yellow-arches chain, but does serve hamburgers. With tile floors, wrought-iron doors, stone urns and breezy ceiling fans, McDonald's is about the most pleasant breakfast spot in town and cooks up good seafood, too. Budget.

For more class, try the **Restaurant-Bar El Delfín** (Hotel Las Brisas, Calle Cuauhtémoc 106 Sur; 5-01-12). The split-level dining area curves around a planter, and its soft yellow lighting catches the glow of dangling painted parrots. The menu includes chef's salad, steak and shrimp in white wine. Moderate.

(Text continued on page 196.)

A Feast of Tropical Fruits

Produce markets in the United States, for all their waxed red apples, robust naval oranges and ripe bananas, seem downright bland and miserly compared to the exuberant, juicy exotica overflowing in Mexico's *mercados*. You've seen mangos and papayas, no doubt, but never this big, this ripe or this cheap. Bananas sometimes grow to a foot long.

And how about *guayabas, mameys* or *guanabanas*? *Tamarindos* and *chirimoyas*? *Zapotes* and *jovitos*? Sorry, no translations available. Unique to the tropics, these fruits are waiting to discovered, squeezed, sipped in cold drinks and eaten in heaping fruit plates available all over Mexico.

Fresh fruits grow wild along the West and East coasts. Ragged thatched stalls along roadsides sell pineapples, papayas, rainbowed mangos and chilled coconuts. The tops of coconuts are lopped off with a machete and the cold milk inside sipped through a straw—a nectar surely ranking with any refreshment of the gods. Fresh-squeezed orange juice (*jugo de naranja*) is as plentiful as beer.

In fact, the streets and markets positively glitter with myriad juices in the form of *aguas frescas* (fruit juice and sweetened water), served ice cold from giant glass jars in plastic bags poked with straws. On a hot day, with sweat pouring down your face and your throat as parched as sand, you will

want to bolt down gallons of tangy *agua de sandia* (watermelon), *melon* (cantaloupe), *jamaica* (a red flower) and *chía* (lemonade swirling with tiny dark seeds). *Que rico!*

Then there are the marvelous desserts. Fruit *paletas* (popsicles), peddled by wandering vendors with battered refrigerated carts, aren't just fruit-flavored but chockful of fruit. *Paletas de coco* bristle with shredded coconut; *paletas de fresa* are lumpy with strawberries. Rainbows of flavors, from *ciruela* (plum) to *durazno* (peach), are available at festive *paleterías* (popsicle stands) in every town. A chain called La Flor de Michoacán has the biggest and best assortment.

You haven't really lived until you've sipped a fruit *licuado*, Mexico's answer to the malt. Milk, ice, sugar (or honey) and the fruit of your choice are tossed into a blender. The result is a creamy pastel confection as filling as ice cream and as sensual as an elixir of love. Mango and papaya *licuados* can hardly be topped, unless you blend the two.

Many tropical fruits spice Mexican recipes in adventurous ways that add a citrus rush or a pungent sweetness. Raisins and sometimes fried bananas go into *mole* sauce, whose 30 ingredients include chocolate and peanuts. *Atole* is a corn liquor flavored with honey and puréed pineapple. And where would tequila be without *limones* (limes)?

Go ahead and be tempted. Remember to wash any fresh fruit well before happily gorging yourself. You're in for a fabulous treat.

RINCÓN DE GUAYABITOS AREA RESTAURANTS

The place everybody talks about is **Restaurant Hilda** (Calle Esteban Baca Calderón 8, La Peñita; Tel. 34), a friendly hole in the wall serving breakfast all day. It's good home cookin'. The Americanized menu includes eggs, steak, flour burritos, bacon-lettuce-and-tomato sandwiches and fresh corn ice cream on a stick. Budget.

In Rincón de Guayabitos, you can order a tasty pizza at the casual **Restaurant-Bar Los Reales** (Avenida Sol Nuevo and Calle Huanacaxtle; 4-01-77). Thoroughly Americanized, with hamburgers and some seafood, this restaurant nevertheless has the slow service, ceiling fans and background music of many a Mexican café. Budget to moderate.

Just up the street, the old brick-columned **Restaurant Villa Nueva** (Retorno Ceiba; 4-03-70) is part of the trailer park by the same name and is the best of many beachfront restaurants lining Playa Guayabitos. The menu offers seafood (delicious garlic shrimp), meat, chicken, frogs' legs, soups and breakfasts. Budget.

Salvadore's (Calle Tabachines and Retorno Tabachines; 4-03-57), in La Misión hotel, has both the atmosphere and the cuisine. Romantic violin music and ocean breezes complement delicious seafood and Mexican dishes. (The skewered shrimp with carrots, onions and bananas is wonderful). Moderate.

PUERTO VALLARTA RESTAURANTS

For food and friendliness, **Ándale** (Calle Olas Altas 425; 2-10-54) is tops. Compared to the animated downstairs bar, the upstairs restaurant is a little oasis of calm, with lanterns, a plethora of brick arches, glass-topped tables and standup wooden menus. Choices include fetuccine with scallops, baked fish, hamburgers, brandy-laced cappuccinos, plus garlic bread and pre-meal popcorn. Moderate.

One of the oldest restaurants in town, with a terrific beachfront atmosphere, is the *palapa*-roofed **El Dorado Restaurant** (Calle Amapas 156; 2-15-11). The yellow leather chairs, heavy bamboo beams and bright tablecloths are freshened by sea breezes blowing in off Playa de los Muertos. Salads, seafood, Mexican meals, crepes and varied breakfasts are served. Budget.

On the *malecón*, **Carlos O'Brien's** (Paseo Díaz Ordaz; 2-14-44) lives up to the zany, raucous reputation of all Carlos Anderson restaurants. Fire hats and lifesavers, old typewriters and LPs clutter the walls. The bar and upstairs balcony are known for being pickup grounds. Everything from Barbarian Omelettes to Fish Smellington packs the menu. Budget.

One of my favorite breakfast stops is **Las Palomas** (Paseo Díaz Ordaz 107; 2-36-75), right on the *malecón*. Its long open windows, high beamed ceiling, Mexican handicrafts and paintings of European royalty give the restaurant a hacienda air. I strongly recommend the shrimp omelettes. There's also lobster, red snapper, chicken parmesana and crepes. Moderate.

Another charming getaway, ideal for coffee and dessert, is the **Franzi Café** (Isla Río Cuale Local 33). Spilling into a garden on the Río Cuale, this brick-floored café with potted flowers on the tables serves fabulous coffees, from *Flamante Intriga* (Flaming Intrigue, with rum and crema chantilly) to *Café Héctor* (galliana and Kahlua). Quiche, gazpacho and full meals are also served, with live jazz featured during the high season. Budget to moderate.

For a jungle lunch with a freshwater swim, visit **Chino's Paradise** (take the marked turnoff from Mexico 200 about one mile inland from Playa Mismaloya). This romantic, thatch-roofed Tarzan palace is set amid waterfalls and crystalline pools. Meats and seafoods served. Bring your swimsuit. Moderate.

A panoramic view comes with your meal at air-conditioned, seventh-floor **El Panorama** (Hotel La Siesta, Calle Ortiz de Domínguez and Calle Miramar; 2-18-18). Gentle lighting, crisp tablecloths and crystal, potted trees and background jazz set the mood for a chic repast. The specialties of the house are flaming entrees, from shish kabob to pepper steak. Moderate.

Sr. Chico's (Calle Púlpito 337; 2-35-70) sits high on a hill overlooking the bay, another uplifting spot to toast the stars and twinkling village lights. The restaurant ambles onto several covered terraces, with hanging plants and live guitar music by which to eat your savory barbequed chicken, frogs' legs, pork ribs, crab-meat crepes and shrimp Shanghai. Moderate.

Around sunset there's no place better than **Tequila's** (Calle Galeana 103; 2-57-25), overlooking the *malecón*. Mexican dishes are featured. Moderate.

You get a tad more glamour, Mexican-Polynesian style, at **El Set** (Hotel Conchas Chinas, Mexico 200, Km. 2.5; 2-03-02). Nestled on a beachside cliff, this restaurant-bar glows with amber lights, splashy tablecloths and the sheltering arms of manzanilla trees and palms. Live music accompanies your dinners of seafood, spare ribs, soups and salads. Moderate to deluxe.

A truly spectacular restaurant, perched like a bird's nest on a cliff overlooking the cove at Boca de Tomatlán, the *palapa*-style **Chee Chee's** (Mexico 200, Km. 18; 2-46-97) is actually an entire bamboo-and-thatched-roofed complex. Shops and bars trip dramatically down the hillside along a winding stairway that ends at a swimming pool and the cliff-edge restaurant-bar. Here you can take a dip and choose from the mobile menu: a cartful of meals, including lobster, shrimp, red snapper and meat shish kabobs. A lunch or dinner must. Moderate.

Getting back down to earth, the snazziest restaurant in town, with some of the best food, is **Le Bistro** (Isla Río Cuale; 2-02-83). Set on the river, this open-air restaurant with antiques, brass bar and vine-tangled columns resembles some Greco-Victorian greenhouse, overflowing with greenery and featuring background jazz. The menu offers escargot, Cuban black bean soup, spinach salad, four kinds of crepes, jumbo shrimp, ten different coffees and some great dessert drinks. Moderate.

If you're with someone you want to impress, take him or her to the sophisticated **Place Vendôme** (Centro Comercial Plaza Vallarta; 2-44-48) for fine French cuisine. With grand piano music and rose buds on every table, Place Vendôme presents the talents of a former chef from Maxime's in Paris. The mouth-watering menu includes vichyssoise, crawfish crepes, scallops au gratin and burgundy escargots. Moderate to deluxe.

YELAPA RESTAURANTS

This beach community south of Puerto Vallarta is packed with open-air restaurants. The best two eating spots are in the village overlooking the water, along the trail to the waterfall. **El Tule** is a small *palapa*-roofed restaurant with about ten wooden tables. Salads, steaks, grilled chicken, shrimp shish kabob and baked fish are served. Right next door, the bigger thatch-roofed **Yacht Club** is a little fancier, with bamboo bar, small stage for live music and dance floor. Mexican food, seafood and meat are on the menu. Lunch and dinner only. Both budget.

BARRA DE NAVIDAD RESTAURANTS

For breakfast, the restaurant in the **Hotel Tropical** (Avenida López de Legaspi 96; 7-00-20) is a sunny seaside stop. The elevated restaurant looks out on the beach behind a screen of coconut palms. To the rhythm of the waves, you can enjoy egg dishes, hot cakes, French toast, *chilaquiles* and other goodies, plus lunch and dinner. Moderate.

A well-known restaurant just doors away, **Corales Restaurant-Bar** (Avenida López de Legaspi 146) is open for lunch and dinner. Enclosed behind bamboo shutters, with country-western music wafting along the sea breeze, Corales provides tasty seafood and salads, plus filet mignon, stuffed avocado and a house specialty called *piña coral*, with shrimp and octopus in cheese fondue stuffed in a pineapple. Highly recommended. Moderate.

Nearby stands a giant, *palapa*-style family restaurant with blue-and-white-checked tablecloths, caged parrots, the clink of beer bottles and the savory smell of fried fish. **Restaurant Pancho** (Avenida López de Legaspi 51; 7-01-76) serves Mexican meals and seafood under its steep palm roof while diners listen to the ocean surf. Budget.

Another good seafood bet on the lagoon side of town is the **Restaurant Eloy** (Calle Yucatán 47; 7-03-65). Here the breezes are gentler than on the sea, and the setting sun reflects the pink of the tables and chairs inside. You receive warm attention from the Eloy Marín Básquez family, which makes a rousing seafood combination dish of octopus, scallops and shrimp in a secret garlic sauce. Paella is also prepared for big groups. Budget.

On the far side of the lagoon, reachable by *panga*, stands a row of rickety restaurants known for their excellent seafood. The oldest and reputedly best of these is **Restaurant Dona Concha** (Isla Colimilla), serving fresh crawfish, oysters, clams, crab and hot chile lobster. Budget.

For upscale ambience, try the **Restaurant Acuario** (Hotel Cabo Blanco, Pueblo Nuevo/Puerto Navidad; 7-01-03). A vine-trellised section stands next to the pool, with a palm tree growing through the ceiling. Nearby, an enclosed section offers candlelight dining. The food is quite tasty—seafood, steaks, and the best flan I've ever eaten. Moderate.

MANZANILLO RESTAURANTS

A prime breakfast spot, **Juanito's** (Mexico 200, Km. 14, in Santiago; 3-13-88) is a cheerful pueblo-style restaurant with outdoor picnic tables and an interior mural of a happy beach scene. You can order scrumptious omelettes, hot cakes, French toast, plus sandwiches and chicken for lunch and dinner. Budget.

To reach **El Oasis** (Calle Delfín near Club Santiago, Santiago; 3-09-37) just drive up to the gate for Club Santiago and tell them where you're going. At the breezy patio section under the palms or the fan-cooled seating area where bands entertain during the high season, breakfasts come in American, continental or Mexican style. Lunch and dinner also served. Budget.

The best breakfasts in Manzanillo are served at the **Hotel La Posada** (Colonia Las Brisas, Avenida Lázaro Cárdenas 201; 2-24-04). The big open-air sitting room overlooking Playa Azul—crowded with shells, posters, driftwood and leather chairs—provides a rich Mexican setting for your first meal of the day. For a set price you may order excellent French toast, omelettes, hot cakes, bacon, juice and delicious coffee. Budget.

For Old World dining, I love eating at the downtown **Colonial Restaurant-Bar** (Hotel Colonial, Avenida México 100; 2-10-80). From the vast arched windows with wooden grillwork to the heavy beamed ceiling and wrought-iron chandeliers, everything here is Spanish colonial to the hilt. The thronelike chairs may be missing a few knobs, but it's still an elegant place to nibble your breaded shrimp, octopus in its ink and broiled lobster. Budget.

You're sure to be well fed at **Carlos 'n Charlie's** (Mexico 200, Boulevard Costera, between Manzanillo and Santiago, Km. 6.5; 3-11-50). This little restaurant, part of the Carlos Anderson chain, has a picnic mood, with folding chairs, a ceilingful of stuffed animals, and lively waiters. Oysters are the specialty, plus lobster, Mexican food and barbeque chicken with real biscuits. Dinner only. Budget.

A local beachfront favorite in the Las Brisas area, **Willy's** (Avenida Lázaro Cárdenas; 2-24-15) serves fine French food on informal pigskin tables under colorful globe lights and a bamboo ceiling. A guitarist provides background music that mingles with the percussion of the waves. Ocean breezes waft through arches framing the beach and ocean, making it a great spot for sunsets. The unique menu includes seafood, homemade pâté, duck à l'orange, apple pie and *profiterol*, a decadent ice cream pastry. Moderate.

One of the oldest and most popular tourist restaurants is the classy **Ostería Bugatti** (Mexico 200, Crucero Las Brisas; 2-15-13), specializing in Italian food. This romantic, air-conditioned restaurant-bar has high brick ceilings lit by yellow lanterns. A wandering minstrel strums from table to table. As the evening wears on, people gather round the grand piano for late-night cocktails. Meals include Sonora beef, pasta dishes, seafood and salads. Moderate.

PLAZA AZUL AND LÁZARO CÁRDENAS RESTAURANTS

In Playa Azul, your best bet is the restaurant at the **Hotel Playa Azul** (Avenida Venustiano Carranza; 6-00-24). The tables and chairs, surrounded by plants and color television, give the indoor section a comfortable, middle-class air. Seating continues outdoors in a palm-shaded patio. You can have nine different breakfasts (from dietetic to captain's) plus lunch and dinner. Budget.

Open-air restaurants crowd the Playa Azul beachfront, all serving good, low-cost seafood—the cheapest lobster I've seen anywhere, plus seafood cocktails, shrimp, oysters, langostinos (crawfish) and chilled coconuts. Locals recommend **Los Tres Enramadas** (end of Calle Lázaro Cárdenas). Budget.

In nearby Lázaro Cárdenas, you can get a fancier meal at the air-conditioned **Restaurant María Goretti** (Hotel María Margarita, Calle Corregidora 79; 2-39-35). The green carpets and wall murals give the restaurant a classy look. For breakfast there's a buffet; lunch and dinner emphasize international cuisine. Moderate.

IXTAPA-ZIHUATANEJO RESTAURANTS

IXTAPA RESTAURANTS

Every big hotel in Ixtapa has its share of chic restaurants, none cheap. The shopping malls also give you some good choices.

For a laid-back beachside meal, there's sprawling *palapa*-style **Carlos 'n Charlie's** (Playa del Palmar; 4-33-25), guaranteeing a good time and decorated in a crazy manner with flying horses, low straw chairs and a popcorn machine. The specialties are barbequed meals and Mexican dishes. Everything's tops. Budget to moderate.

Villa de la Selva (Paseo de la Roca, up the hill from the Camino Real) is set in a flowery jungle overlooking the sea, perfect for starlight dining.

This lovely indoor-outdoor restaurant with green awnings and bamboo furniture was once the vacation home of former Mexican President Luis Echeverría. Dinners include sauce-smothered seafood dishes and flaming café royal. Moderate to deluxe.

For a magic carpet ride to Morocco, this area's most fabulous restaurant (worth skipping breakfast and lunch for) is **Bogart's** (Paseo del Palmar; 4-26-18). Beyond the torches and turbaned doorman at the arched entrance is a dazzling tribute to the movie *Casablanca*. Humphrey Bogart's photos fill the dim Arabic bar. The long dining hall is furnished totally in white and lit by a lavender florescence in the fountains and elongated pool. To top it off, a pianist plays "As Time Goes By" on a white grand piano amid the aromas of duck Shanghai, lobster bisque Oman, Persian crepes and Caribbean lobster. Dinner only. Moderate to deluxe.

Superb "haute" Mexican cuisine is served at the Camino Real's **Las Esferas El Méxicano** (Playa Vista Hermosa; 4-33-00). The service and presentation are equal to the food, with huge ceramic domed dishes concealing such offerings as *cabrito* (baby goat), rabbit in tangy chili sauce and duckling in pumpkin-seed sauce. Rolls and toasted tortillas are served with avocado and chili butters. The dessert tray cannot be ignored. Deluxe.

ZIHUATANEJO RESTAURANTS

Locally popular and attractive, **Restaurant Garrobo's** (Calle Juan Alvarez 52; 4-29-77) is a big, neat seafood house tucked behind a screen of vegetation on the ground floor of the Hotel Tres Marías. Paella, *tiritos de pescado* (marinated fish strips), steaks and flan with Kahlua are served. Budget.

Restaurant Elvira (Paseo del Pescador; 4-20-61) is a small, comfy café on the *malecón*, freshened by sea breezes and serving tasty breakfasts as well as beef, chicken and seafood. Budget.

The open-air restaurants down on beautiful Playa La Ropa serve very good meals. The giant **La Perla** (4-27-00) has slow service but excellent breakfasts and seafood under its big *palapa* roof, with wooden tables and chairs sunk in the sand. Down at the southern end of the beach, the attractive little wood-and-tile **La Gaviota** enjoys an excellent reputation for its fresh seafood, including shrimp *empanadas* and abalone. Budget.

Going up in price, the hilltop **Kon-Tiki Restaurant-Bar** (Carretera Playa La Ropa; 4-24-71) offers a lovely view of the bay. You can dine on its picnic-style terraces or in its more formal indoor area, with flickering candles and romantic lanterns. The menu's specialty is pizza, plus stuffed peppers, chop suey and more. Lunch and dinner only. Budget to moderate.

Known for its seafood, the **Canaima Restaurant-Bar** (Paseo del Pescador; 4-20-03) is a popular spot on the *malecón* in town, facing the beach. Ceiling fans spin overhead, and low-hanging lamps cast a warm glow on the tables and decorative bronze sculptures. Shrimp and *carne asada* are featured. Budget to moderate.

On a downtown corner stands a small castle-like building with some of the best food in town. **El Castillo** (Calle Ejido 25; 4-38-50) was once a *bodega* (wine cellar) and a tortilla factory, and is now jazzed up with black metal lanterns, stylish window-guards and colonial furniture. The management is attentive and the menu broad, with everything from lentil soup to scampi tempura, pepper steak and fresh barracuda in season. Dinner only. Moderate.

One of Zihuatanejo's best-known and oldest restaurants is the elegant, mission-style **La Mesa del Capitán** (Calle Nicolás Bravo 18; 4-20-27), founded in 1975 by an Englishman and his Mexican wife. The interior, with warm lanterns and arches, opens onto a pretty patio where water splashes down rocks forming the back wall. Wandering mariachis and a pianola provide romantic music. Tasty barbeque ribs, lobster and exotic seafood dishes are served. Moderate.

PIE DE LA CUESTA RESTAURANTS

With its many little seafood restaurants, Pie de la Cuesta is a popular dining alternative to more costly Acapulco. Some of the better spots include the **Hotel Puesta del Sol** restaurant with an international menu of wienerschnitzel, baked chicken, spaghetti, smoked pork chops and fish; and **Tres Marías**, one of the oldest and best-known in the village, serving red snapper and all kinds of shrimp. Both located on Playa Pie de la Cuesta, both budget.

One of the most pleasant spots in town is the restaurant at hotel **Ukae Kim** (Play Pie de la Cuesta 356; 5-10-98). Dining is in a courtyard smothered in foliage, not far from the beach. Salads and seafood are featured. Moderate.

ACAPULCO RESTAURANTS

This all-night town has quite a few 24-hour restaurants. Most are along the main drag, Avenida Costera Miguel Alemán. For a quick take-out taco or eat-and-run sandwich, check out **Lonchería Chavelis** (Calle Iglesias and Avenida Costera Miguel Alemán), a great little tropical food stand near the *zócalo*. Always crowded, with hanging bananas and pineapples, the *lonchería* also serves terrific fruit *licuados*. Budget.

Coffee aficionados should head for the tiny and cozy **Pastelería-Cafetería Viena** (Avenida Costera Miguel Alemán 715-A near the Glorieta Diana; 4-25-51). Resembling a little European bakery, this air-conditioned café with lace-covered tables serves very rich coffees, pastries, hot sandwiches and breakfasts. Budget.

Another tempting breakfast spot is **100% Natural** (Avenida Costera Miguel Alemán 13a). It offers American and Mexican meals and specializes in huge *licuados*. Next door is **Aca Taco,** *the* place to have a late night snack. *Tacos al pastor* (meat carved from a spit) are the rage here.

Combine people-watching with a low-cost breakfast at the outdoor sidewalk café **La Flor de Acapulco** (Plaza Juan Alvarez; 2-50-18), right on the fountain-filled *zócalo.* You can fork up fluffy omelettes, fruits and toast at umbrella-shaded tables. Or take a seat inside for a hearty lunch or dinner. Budget.

The downtown area is a treasure trove of budget-priced seafood houses. One of the best is **Amigo Miguel** (Calle Benito Juárez 31; 3-69-81), a bright, tile-floored restaurant on a triangle of land pointing toward the *zócalo.* Choices include breaded oysters and *ceviche.* Open for lunch and dinner.

Another good seafood joint, **Mariscos Pipo,** has three locations (Calle Altimirante Brentón 3; 2-22-37, Avenida Costera Miguel Alemán, Playa Condesa; 4-01-65 and Carretera Aeropuerto; 4-60-36). They are easy-going, popular with locals and fan-cooled, with sea-theme decor, serving seafood cocktails, tuna fish stew, grilled octopus, shrimp and more. Lunch and dinner. Budget.

Well off the tourist track in a working-class neighborhood, **Restaurant Tlaquepaque** (Colonia Vista Alegre, Calle Uno, Lote 7; 5-70-55) draws locals almost strictly. Here in a softly lit courtyard full of potted plants, you can feast on the city's heartiest *pozole* (a corn stew full of pork and chicken, seasoned with limes, oregano, onions and avocado—out of this world!) or other Mexican dishes. Lunch and dinner only. Budget.

Back in the Old Town, the time-honored American-style **Sanborn's** (Avenida Costera Miguel Alemán 209; 2-61-68) is a department store whose restaurant lets you eat in super-clean, air-conditioned comfort with the *Los Angeles Times* or *Mexico City News* from the magazine department. It may not be authentic Mexican, but it serves the world's best *crepas con cajeta* (crepes with caramel sauce), plus good breakfasts. Lunch and dinner aren't as good and are overpriced. Budget to moderate.

Enjoy a home-cooked Argentinian meal every Tuesday afternoon in the patio of the **Hotel Misión** (Calle Felipe Valle 12; 2-36-43). You'll eat out under the trees on picnic tables with one of downtown Acapulco's old families as your hosts. The outdoor grill sizzles with half-a-dozen types of meats (sausage, tripe, beef filet, tenderloin steak, spare ribs, pork). Exotic salad dishes, combining beans, mushrooms, eggplant and hearts of palm, plus pastry and coffee, complete this delicious lunch. Moderate.

The *turistas* love **Mimi's Chili Saloon** (Avenida Costera Miguel Alemán; 4-25-49) for its rock music, fun crowds, hamburgers, burritos, nachos, and, of course, chili. This is decidedly informal, with a sawdust-covered floor, chattering parakeets, and drinks served in huge chamber pots. Moderate.

For top-notch barbeque chicken and ribs, step out to cozy **D'Joint** (Avenida Costera Miguel Alemán 1070; 4-37-09). It's an entertaining little two-story joint, with red, blue and gold exterior, confetti all over the floors and a lantern-encrusted ceiling that earns the restaurant its self-appointed name of "upstart junkyard." The menu comes on a paper bag. Dinner only. Moderate.

Elegance and freshly made pasta come with the territory at **Dino's** (Avenida Costera Miguel Alemán, Playa Condesa; 4-00-37), the primo Italian restaurant in town, overlooking the busy *costera*. Opened in 1957, this second-floor restaurant combines fettucine alfredo, veal parmigiana and other classics with a charming villa-terrace ambience. Lunch and dinner only. Moderate.

Probably *the* favorite eating and meeting spot in Acapulco is **Carlos 'n Charlie's** (Avenida Costera Miguel Alemán 999; 4-00-39), open for dinner only. This was the original link in the Mexico-wide chain of Carlos Anderson restaurants, opened in 1970 and still going strong. Decorated with hanging paraphernalia and strings of lights along the balcony railing, this lively upstairs restaurant with adjacent video bar is almost always packed. And the food is always good, whether it's chicken curry, broiled swordfish or huge breaded shrimp. Moderate.

Among the many theme restaurants in town, the big beached galleon housing **Black Beard's** (Avenida Costera Miguel Alemán 101; 4-25-49) is the most entertaining. In your deckside booth overlooking Playa Condesa, you receive a wooden menu rimmed in rope with selections of lobster, Indonesian kabobs, chicken, and apple pie. There's a host of tropical drinks, rogueish pirates at your service and navigational maps adorning the tabletops. Both food and service are excellent. Moderate.

Pepe & Co. (Calle Hernán Cortel, Playa El Morro; 5-20-51) boasts a beachfront location, *palapa* roof, cane chairs, huge hanging basket-lights and the soothing tones of ocean surf and piano music. An international menu is served, including baby shark tacos. Moderate.

Treat yourself to a Disneylike vision of Old Mexico at the hillside **Los Rancheros** (Carretera Escénica 38; 4-19-08), open for lunch and dinner. Looking out over the bay at the southeast end of Acapulco, this split-level ranch house shines with old Spanish and Chinese lanterns, gaily painted columns, wagon wheels and ceiling fans. Juicy beef and chicken fajitas (stir-fried meat strips with green peppers, onions, tomatoes and spices) are the house specialty, along with other Mexican plates. Moderate.

A first-class restaurant with the city's most mouth-watering Mexican food is **La Hacienda** (Acapulco Princess Hotel, Playa Revolcadero; 4-31-00), open for dinner only. A Mexican *charro* (cowboy) with a rifle greets you at the door of this lovely wood-beamed steakhouse, and mariachis serenade you at your table. The cuisine focuses on Sonora beef—try the savory, slim-sliced *La Sábana de Res*, the house specialty. Reservations recommended. Deluxe.

Without question, the most stunning restaurant in town, with a 360° view of the bay and mountains, is the hilltop **El Campanario** (Fraccionamiento Condesa, Calle Paraíso; 4-88-31), open for dinner only. Resembling a huge restored monastery, this restaurant was actually built from scratch in 1985. Its many tiers and terraces, with domed brick ceilings and hand-carved rafters, overflow with plants, colonial furniture, softly lit fountains and vine-clad columns. Excellent continental fare is served, from Creole gazpacho to shrimp fried in coconut. Reservations recommended. Deluxe.

The Great Outdoors

The Sporting Life

CAMPING

Despite the highrise jungle that marks this touristy stretch of coastline, there are many excellent camping beaches both near the big resorts and in between. Camping supplies and sporting goods can be found at the following places:

Mazatlán: Plaza Ley Supermercado (Mexico 15 south, near the bus station) and Deportes Estrella (Calle Serdán 2421; 2-07-63).

La Peñita: Supermercado Lorena (Avenida Emiliano Zapata).

Puerto Vallarta: Conasupo (Calle Uruguay near the Pemex station) and Super Sports (Avenida México 1106; 2-48-30).

Manzanillo: Conasupo (Calle Juárez, two blocks north of the downtown zócalo) and Deportes del Puerto (at two locations: Calle Juárez 16; 2-26-70, and Avenida México 414; 2-01-13).

Lázaro Cárdenas: Conasupo (Avenida Melchor Ocampo).

Zihuatanejo: Mercado Municipal (Paseo de Cocotal).

Acapulco: Three giant supermarkets along Avenida Costera Miguel Alemán—Comercial Mexicana (2-16-19), SuperSuper (5-30-23) and Gigante (5-13-08)—and Deportes Patos (Calle Galeana 4; 2-25-42).

SWIMMING

The water temperature along the Mexican Riviera is warm enough for swimming all year round and is especially inviting in spring and summer. Watch out for stingrays and stinging jellyfish.

FISHING AND BOATING

Mexico's Pacific coastline swarms with fish, some 600 varieties: red snapper, dolphin (*dorado* or *mahimahi*), mackerel, sea bass, grouper, tuna, bonito, cabrilla, yellowtail, as well as big game species like marlin, sailfish, swordfish and shark.

In Mazatlán, one of the sportfishing capitals of the world, some 5,000 billfish are hooked every year. The season for striped marlin is November to May; for sailfish, black and blue marlin, it's May to November.

Over a dozen sportfishing fleets line the sportfishing docks behind Cerro de Crestón (Summit Hill). Try **Bill Heimpel's Star Fleet** (2-38-78) or **Mike's Sportfishing Marina, Flota Faro** (2-28-24).

Catamarans and mini-motorboats can be rented in Playa Gaviotas and Playa Sábalo in the Zona Dorado.

Sportfishing, especially for sailfish and marlin, is good and less expensive out of San Blas than the bigger resorts. Local fishermen rent *pangas* and act as guides. Arrange trips around the Aduana Building near the port or through your hotel.

In Rincón de Guayabitos, you can rent *pangas* in front of the **Paraíso de los Pescadores (Fisherman's Paradise) Trailer Park** (Retorno Ceibas, Lote 1 and 2) on Playa Guayabitos.

Marlin and sailfish season in Puerto Vallarta runs from November through May. You can rent *pangas* and cabin cruisers at the **Progreso Turístico Vallartense** (Paseo Díaz Ordaz and Calle 31 de Octubre, in front of Hotel Rosita; 2-12-02).

To rent *pangas* in Barra de Navidad, try the lagoon dock at the Cooperativa Lanchera on Calle Morelos. For larger boats, inquire at the **Hotel Cabo Blanco** (Pueblo Nuevo/Puerto Navidad; 7-01-68).

Some of the deep-sea fishing operations in Manzanillo include **Lori Fleet** (Avenida Constitución 19; 2-16-53) and the **Sociedad Cooperativa de Prestación de Servicios Turísticos Manzanillo** (Avenida Niños Héroes 597; 2-10-31).

The relatively untapped waters around Ixtapa-Zihuatanejo are a sportfisherman's delight. Fishing trips can be arranged through the **Sociedad Cooperativa de Servicios Turísticos de Lanchas Teniente José Azueta** (at the entrance to the municipal pier in Zihuatanejo; 4-20-56). Here you can also arrange boat trips to Ixtapa and nearby Playa Las Gatas. Catamarans can be rented at the municipal beach. For cabin cruiser rentals and fishing supplies, try **La Rapala** (Calle Juan N. Alvarez 34; 4-38-55).

In Acapulco, sailfishing is good all year round, while marlin take the bait best in February and March. Boats are for rent along the Malecón de Pescadores (Fisherman's Dock) in front of the *zócalo* downtown, at the **Sociedad Cooperativa Primero de Junio** (Avenida Costera Miguel

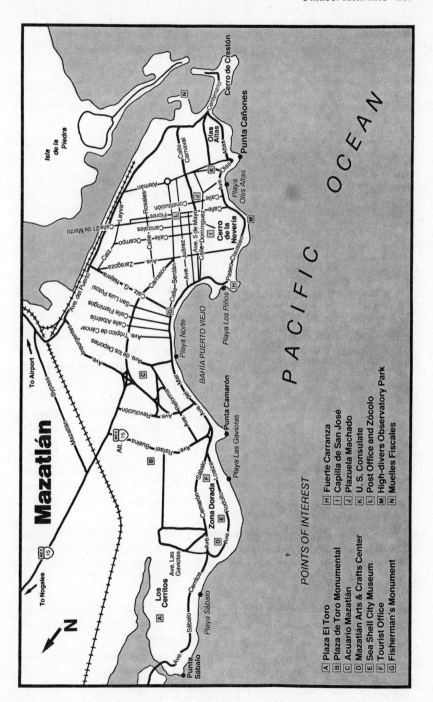

Mazatlán

To Nogales

To Airport

PACIFIC OCEAN

Cerro de Crestón

Punta Cañones

Olas Altas

Cerro de la Neveria

Isla de la Piedra

BAHIA PUERTO VIEJO

Playa Norte

Playa Los Piños

Playa Las Gaviotas

Punta Camarón

Zona Dorada

Los Cerritos

Punta Sábalo

Playa Sábalo

Playa Olas Altas

Centenario

Calle Carnaval

Aleman

Rosales

Leyva

Calle 21 de Marzo

Constitución

Flores

Canizales

Ocampo

Zaragoza

Ave. del Puerto

San Luis Potosi

Calz.-G.-Nájera

Calle Flamingos

Calle Albatros

Ave. Trópico de Cáncer

Ave. de los Deportes

Ave. del Mar

Ave. Revolución

Ave. Palomo

Ave. Rafael Buelna

Ave. Camarón Sábalo

Ave. Rodolfo Loaiza

Ave. Las Gaviotas

Ave. Sábalo Cerritos

Calle Olas Altas

Ave. Olas Altas

Calle

Calle

Calle Domínguez

Ave. 5 de Mayo

Calle Juárez

Calle Serdan

Carrasco

Paseo Clausson

Bypass

Mazatlán

POINTS OF INTEREST

A Plaza El Toro
B Plaza de Toro Monumental
C Acuario Mazatlán
D Mazatlán Arts & Crafts Center
E Sea Shell City Museum
F Tourist Office
G Fisherman's Monument
H Fuerte Carranza
I Capilla de San José
J Plazuela Machado
K U. S. Consulate
L Post Office and Zócolo
M High-divers Observatory Park
N Muelles Fiscales

Alemán 211; 2-10-99). Deep-sea charters also available through **Z-Mare** (2-00-19). For less expensive *panga* rentals, try the **Sociedad Cooperativa de Producción de Servicios Turísticos de Caleta y Caletilla** (Playa Caleta; 3-00-66).

There's very good freshwater fishing, especially for catfish, at nearby Laguna Coyuca in Pie de la Cuesta (eight miles north of Acapulco) and Laguna Tres Palos (15 miles south of Acapulco). Motorized *pangas* are for rent at both lagoons.

SKIN DIVING

Excellent diving sites dot the Mexican Riviera, with good facilities in the resort areas for both experienced divers and beginners. These southerly Pacific waters are generally warm and clear, not requiring a wet suit.

In Mazatlán, for diving trips and lessons, try **Scorpio's Diving Center** (Caravelle Hotel, Avenida Camarón Sábalo; 3-02-00).

Puerto Vallarta, a diver's paradise, has several shops. The best in town is **Chico's Dive Shop** (Paseo Díaz Ordaz 772; 2-18-95), with equipment rentals, lessons and tours. Other good shops are **Paradise Divers** (Avenida Olas Altas 443; 2-40-04) and **Aquarama** (Hotel Marsol, Calle Francisca Rodríguez 103; 2-13-65).

In Barra de Navidad, you can rent diving equipment at the **Sands Hotel** (Calle Morelos 24; 7-00-18). You can buy snorkeling gear at two shops in town, **Creaciones Gloria** (Calle de Legaspi) and **Curiosidades Al Faro** (Calle de Legaspi).

Ixtapa-Zihuatanejo has lessons and equipment rentals on Isla Ixtapa and Playa Las Gatas. Playa Las Gatas has the best-equipped dive shop in the area: **Carlo Diving**. Lessons are also available from Owen Lee, author of *The Skin Diver's Bible*. (For information write to him at Playa Las Gatas, Apartado 81, Zihuatanejo, Guerrero; 4-35-32). In Zihuatanejo around the marina, a good source of diving gear and lessons is the **Escuela de Buceo Casa del Mar** (Paseo del Pescador 20-6; 4-21-19). In Ixtapa, scuba lessons are given during the high season at the **Club de Playa del Palmar** (Playa del Palmar, next to Carlos 'n Charlie's).

In Acapulco, you can rent equipment and take scuba lessons through **Divers de México** (Avenida Costera Miguel Alemán 100; 2-13-98) and **Hermanos Arnold** (Avenida Costera Miguel Alemán 205; 2-18-77).

SURFING AND WINDSURFING

Here on the open Pacific it's prime surfing country. Windsurfing is good, too, along more protected shores. The availability of surfboards and sailboards, however, is limited. Bring what you need.

In San Blas, you can rent surfboards at **Team Banana** café on Playa Las Islitas south of town.

In Puerto Vallarta, you can learn to windsurf at the **Krystal Vallarta** (Avenida de las Garzas; 2-14-59) and the **Hotel Las Palmas** (Carretera al Aeropuerto, Km. 2.5; 2-06-50), both of which have windsurfing schools and rent sailboards.

Barra de Navidad has surfboards and sailboards for rent at the **Hotel Cabo Blanco** (Pueblo Nuevo/Puerto Navidad; 7-01-68), or in nearby Los Ángeles Locos de Tenacatita, at the **Hotel Fiesta Americana** (Mexico 200, Km. 20; 7-02-20).

In Manzanillo, try the **Restaurant Oasis** (Calle Delfín, Club Santiago; 3-09-37) for surfboards. To rent sailboards, try **Viento Marino** (Hotel Roca del Mar, Colonia Las Brisas, Avenida Lázaro Cárdenas; 2-19-90).

In Ixtapa-Zihuatanejo, you can find windsurfing equipment (and lessons, during the high season) on Playa La Ropa or at **Carlo Diving** (Playa Las Gatas).

Surfing is prohibited in Bahía de Acapulco because of the number of swimmers.

WATERSKIING

In Mazatlán, try **Caravelle Beach Club** (Caravelle Hotel, Avenida Camarón Sábalo; 3-02-00) and **Los Sábalos** (Avenida Rodolfo Loaiza; 3-53-33).

Acapulco has the best waters and facilities for this sport. Glassy Laguna Coyuca in nearby Pie de la Cuesta is lined with ski clubs like the **Club Cadena**, **Barefoot Ski Club** and **Tres Marías** (all located along the nameless main road) that rent boats and skis. In Bahía de Acapulco, you can take ski lessons and rent equipment at the **Club de Playa/Restaurant-Bar Colonial** (Avenida Costera Miguel Alemán 130; 3-70-77).

HUNTING

The hillsides, swamps and lagoons surrounding many Mexican Riviera resorts are full of wildlife, including migratory Canadian ducks and geese, mallards, canvas-backs, speckled pintails and teals, white-wing doves, blue pigeons, tree ducks, quail, wild deer, rabbits and wildcats.

HORSEBACK RIDING

You can rent horses in Mazatlán at the **Hotel Playa Mazatlán** (Playa Las Gaviotas; 3-44-55).

In Puerto Vallarta, horses are for rent around Playa de los Muertos and at various ranches in the area. Puerto Vallarta also has a zany beach sport called "donkey polo." Six to twelve ornery burros are mounted by hotel guests with mops and brooms, used to swat a volleyball through a folding chair. To play this game you usually need to be a hotel guest, but in the scuffle an outsider might slip in a quick ride. Check at the **Krystal Vallarta** (Avenida de las Garzas; 2-14-59) and the **Camino Real** (Mexico 200, Playa Las Estacas; 2-00-02).

The Barra de Navidad area has horse rentals at **Hotel Fiesta Americana** (Mexico 200 north of Barra de Navidad, Km. 20, Playa Los Ángeles Locos de Tenacatita; 7-02-20). In Manzanillo, try **Club Maeva** (Mexico 200, between Manzanillo and Miramar; 3-05-95).

You can find horses for rent in Acapulco on Playa Revolcadero in front of the **Acapulco Princess Hotel** (4-31-00).

In Pie de la Cuesta, horses can be rented at **Hotel Tres Marías** on Playa Pie de la Cuesta.

GOLF

Golf courses are located as follows: **El Cid Resort** (Avenida Camarón Sábalo, Mazatlán; 3-33-33); **Club Campestre** (Carretera Internacional, Km. 1195, Mazatlán; 2-57-02); **Los Flamingos Club de Golf** (Mexico 200, Km. 145, north of Puerto Vallarta; 2-27-03); **Club Santiago** (Avenida Carrizales, Santiago; 3-04-12); **Club de Golf Palma Real** (Boulevard Ixtapa, Ixtapa; 4-22-80); **Acapulco Princess Hotel** (4-31-00) and the **Pierre Marqués** (4-20-00), both on Playa Revolcadero south of Acapulco; and the **Club de Golf Acapulco** (Avenida Costera Miguel Alemán, Acapulco; 4-07-81).

TENNIS

You'll find tennis courts at the following places: **El Cid Resort** (Avenida Camarón Sábalo, Mazatlán; 3-33-33); **Raquet Club Las Gaviotas** (Calle Ibís, Fraccionamiento Gaviotas, Zona Dorado, Mazatlán; 2-76-44); **Camino Real** (Mexico 200, 1.5 miles south of town; 2-55-55); **John Newcombe Tennis Club** (Costera Vallarta, Km. 2.5, Puerto Vallarta; 2-48-50); **Club de Tenis Vallarta** (Fraccionamiento Aramara, Puerto Vallarta; 2-27-67); **Club Santiago** (Avenida Carrizales, Santiago; 3-04-12); **Club Maeva** (Mexico 200, between Manzanillo and Miramar, Manzanillo; 3-05-95); **Club de Golf Palma Real** (Boulevard Ixtapa, Ixtapa; 4-32-45); **Alfredo's** (Avenida del Prado 29, Acapulco; 4-00-04); **Club de Golf Acapulco** (Avenida Costera Miguel Alemán, Acapulco; 4-07-81); and **Hyatt Continental** (Bahía de Acapulco; 4-09-09).

Beaches

Dozens of splendid tropical beaches line this coast, most with good sand (averaging an 8 on a scale of 10) and many seldom visited by outsiders. Here are some of the best:

MAZATLÁN BEACHES

Mazatlán offers miles of beaches to the north and along its *malecón*.

Playa Los Cerritos—To my taste, this is the top Mazatlán beach. Cleanest and least crowded of the area's beaches, it lies on the northern outskirts of town past the Zona Dorada and most of the hotel hubbub and stretches for miles along open sea. Thick white sand is backed by rolling dunes and washed by crashing waves.

Facilities: Hotels, restaurants and trailer parks. *Camping:* Good, especially in the northern section. *Swimming:* Waves can be strong, use caution. *Snorkeling/diving:* Good around Isla de los Venados, Isla de los Pájaros and Isla de los Chivos, all best-reached from Playa Sábalo to the south. *Surfing/windsurfing:* Good surfing spots north of Camino Real. Windsurfing is better in smoother waters to the south. *Fishing/boating:* Surf-fishing is good for mackerel or mullet. Boats for rent at beaches to the south.

Getting there: Off Avenida Sábalo Cerritos. The beach stretches from Hotel Camino Real north to Punta Cerritos.

Playa Las Gaviotas and **Playa Sábalo**—These two popular beaches flow into one another and are barely distinguishable. Both front the busy hotel strip in the Zona Dorada. The beaches themselves are only medium size with moist, dark sand. A walking *mercado* of vendors sells everything from straw hats to kites. Just offshore are three uninhabited islands: Venados, Pájaros and Chivos.

Facilities: Hotels, restaurants. *Camping:* None. Try Isla de los Venados across the bay. *Swimming:* Excellent. The best in town. *Snorkeling/diving:* Good around the three offshore islands. Locals also dive for oysters around Punta Camarón and sell their take in the afternoons here. *Surfing/windsurfing:* Surfing is good on either side of Punta Camarón, distinguished by Valentino's Disco, and at Punta Lupe. Windsurfing is good off both beaches. *Fishing/boating:* Surf-fishing is good from the beach. You can rent sailboats, catamarans, canoes and mini-motorboats.

Getting there: Off Avenida Camarón Sábalo or Avenida Rodolfo T. Loaiza in the Zona Dorada, between Punta Camarón and Punta Sábalo.

Playa Isla de los Venados—For a lovely view of Mazatlán, spend a day on this quiet, clean island beach just ten minutes from the mainland by boat. The sand is white and scattered with shells. Around the rocky southern tip is another small, secluded beach (hidden enough for nude sunbathing). Beach parties are common during the high season. Otherwise, this island belongs to the deer, goats, mice and raccoons.

Facilities: Restaurant. *Camping:* Very good. *Swimming:* Excellent. *Snorkeling/diving:* Good around the rocky point at the southern end of the beach. Rent snorkeling equipment at the nearby restaurant. *Surfing/windsurfing:* Good for windsurfing. *Fishing/boating:* Good. Rent *pangas* at the restaurant. *Shell-collecting:* Good small shells around rocky point: conches, olive shells, cowries, keyhole limpets.

Getting there: Amphibious boats leave regularly from Playa Gaviotas and Playa Sábalo. Arrangements can be made at hotels El Cid and Las Flores.

Playa Norte—This is Mazatlán's longest and widest beach, following most of the *malecón* for six miles, from Punta Camarón to El Mirador (lookout) tower, where high divers perform in the afternoons. The sand is thick and cream colored, dotted with little *palapa* restaurants where you can seek shade and sample fresh coconut juice or a seafood cocktail.

Facilities: Restaurants, hotels. *Camping:* Not recommended. *Swimming:* Good, with brisk waves. *Surfing/windsurfing:* Surf is better north and south of here. Windsurfing is the best possibility. *Fishing/boating:* Surf-fishing is good. Small boat rentals in high season.

Getting there: Along *malecón* on Avenida del Mar.

Playa Olas Altas—This is the original beach of old Mazatlán, running past comfortable, seasoned cafés on the *malecón*. Named for its high waves (*olas altas*), this beach attracts young surfers despite its rocky, capricious shoreline, which changes dramatically with the tide.

Facilities: Old hotels, restaurants, shops. *Camping:* Not recommended. *Swimming:* Very good. *Surfing/windsurfing:* Good surf. Try Punta Cañones in front of the Hotel Freeman. Windsurfing possible, too. *Fishing/boating:* Surf-fishing is good, no boats for rent.

Getting there: Along Avenida Olas Altas.

Playa Isla de la Piedra (Stone Island) (★)—A favorite Sunday hangout for Mexican families, Isla de la Piedra has more than ten miles of silvery, palm-lined beaches, as yet unsullied by big-time tourism. This won't last long, however; a massive plan to develop hotels, shopping centers and recreation facilities is already underway. *Palapa* restaurants overrun the shore near the boat landing, but a short walk takes you beyond the excitement to virgin shoreline which juts out opposite the busy docks of Mazatlán's harbor.

Facilities: Restaurants. *Camping:* Great. *Swimming:* Terrific, especially for kids. *Snorkeling/diving:* Good off northern point (Cerro de los Chivos) and southern point (Cerro del Cardón). *Surfing/windsurfing:* Good surf off Cerro del Cardón. Windsurfing is better along the beach. *Fishing/boating:* Excellent. *Pangas* for rent.

Getting there: By boat from docks off Avenida Emilio Barragán (Avenida del Puerto) on port side of Mazatlán.

Playa Novillero (★)—Several hours south of Mazatlán by car, this is one of the longest continuous beaches in the country—about 55 miles. This seemingly endless silvery beach on open sea, wonderful for beachcombing and solitude, is far nicer than the ones at the tropical villages of Teacapán to the north and fuses with those of Los Corchos to the south. Lined with open-air restaurants and waving palms, the beach serves the 300-person fishing village of Novillero.

Facilities: Restaurants. *Camping:* Excellent. *Swimming:* Great, especially for kids. Shallow shoreline. *Snorkeling/diving:* Good around Isla Isabel (a two-hour boat-ride offshore) and Isla San Bernardino. *Surfing/windsurfing:* Conditions are good for windsurfing. *Fishing/boating:* Good. *Pangas* for rent on shore. *Shell-collecting:* Sand dollars, butterfly clams, spiked clams (royal comb venuses), olive shells and other unusual gems. This undiscovered shore is not picked over. Shells are also plentiful on Isla Isabel.

Getting there: About 17 miles west of Tecuala on Nayarit 23.

SAN BLAS AREA BEACHES

San Blas and the coastline south of town are lined with beautiful, un-crowded beaches. Visit before sundown, when the sandfleas come out.

Playa del Rey—This beautiful virgin beach with soft, lovely sand stretches along open sea for some 12 miles on a peninsula just opposite the port of San Blas. An old lighthouse stands on a hill between the boat landing and the beach. Big breakers crash along the shore. Birds, iguanas and fruit trees inhabit the peninsula's narrow interior.

Facilities: None. Restaurants in town. *Camping:* Great, very isolated. *Swimming:* Good, best at north end of beach near jetty which softens breaking waves. *Snorkeling/diving:* Around Isla Tres Marías and Isla Isabel. *Surfing/windsurfing:* Best for windsurfing. *Fishing/boating:* Good. Rent boats in San Blas near Aduana Building. Excellent clamming, too. *Shell-collecting:* Butterfly clams and spiked (royal comb venus) clams.

Getting there: By boat from pier near Aduana Building.

Playa Hermosa and **Playa El Borrego**—These two long grayish-sand beaches, which merge into one another, lie just south of town on open sea and are backed by groves of coconut palms. The sand is silent and empty, except for the giant ghostly Hotel Playa Hermosa at the southern end, built in 1951 and falling into sad neglect. You can walk south for miles until you reach the Estero San Cristóbal at La Puntilla.

Facilities: All amenities in town. *Camping:* Good. *Swimming:* Very good. *Snorkeling/diving:* Around Islas Tres Marías and Isla Isabel. *Surfing/windsurfing:* Windsurfing good. *Fishing/boating:* Good. Rent boats in town. *Shell-collecting:* Tiny sand dollars, butterfly clams.

Getting there: South of San Blas. Enter through naval base or via sand road out to Hotel Playa Hermosa.

Playa Las Islitas—This series of silvery sand beaches south of San Blas is strung between rocky outcroppings, embracing Bahía Matanchén and stretching north to Estero San Cristóbal and La Puntilla. The southernmost section of sand curves into long, wide-open Playa Matanchén facing the bay for which it is named. Mexican families gather in droves on holidays, and surfers gravitate here for the renowned waves at Stoner's Point, some of the longest right-point breaks in the world.

Facilities: Restaurants. *Camping:* Good, but not much privacy. *Swimming:* Very good, in open sections. Avoid areas near the rocks with *Peligro* (Danger) signs. *Snorkeling/diving:* Around Islas Tres Marías and Isla Isabel. *Surfing/windsurfing:* Tops. Mile-long breaks start at Stoner's Point and roll in to the beach, where surfboards are for rent at Team Banana. *Fishing/boating:* Good. Rent boats in San Blas.

Getting there: South of San Blas on Bahía Matanchén.

Playa Los Cocos—The epitome of the tropics, this narrow strip of palm-lined beach is divided into sandy coves that curve along the coast for about a mile. The sea has eroded the cliffs overlooking the beach, where palm trees hover as though about to topple into the tide. Bamboo ladders lead from the beach up to the restaurant-lined cliffs.

Facilities: Restaurants. *Camping:* Good except that beach is narrow. Watch out for the incoming tide. *Swimming:* Great. Inlet from ocean forms a pool about mid-beach where kids like to play. *Snorkeling/diving:* Around Islas Tres Marías and Isla Isabel. *Surfing/windsurfing:* Windsurfing is the best possibility. *Fishing/boating:* Good. Boats available in Santa Cruz.

Getting there: South of San Blas past village of Aticama.

RINCÓN DE GUAYABITOS AREA BEACHES

These tropical beaches are too beautiful to go undeveloped for long, yet so far remain relatively unspoiled.

Playa Chacala a n d **Playa Chacalilla (★)**—Straight out of a South Seas fantasy, this is one of the Mexican Riviera's best-kept secrets, preserved by its relative inaccessibility. A bumpy cobbled road leads from the main highway north of Rincón de Guayabitos to this tiny, busy village with two beaches. The main, half-mile-long beach, Playa Chacala, and its adjoining mini-beach (Chacalilla, or "Little Chacala") both embrace a sparkling cove backed by a dense, cool grove of palms. The sand is clean, white and thick, bracketed by two spits of thickly vegetated land.

Facilities: Restaurants, primitive bathrooms. *Camping:* Beautiful. You have a vast palm grove for shade and shelter. *Swimming:* Marvelous, great for kids. *Snorkeling/diving:* Try the rocks off southern tip of land and the clear water off Playa Chacalilla. *Surfing/windsurfing:* Adequate surfing waves in summer, conditions good for windsurfing all year round. *Fishing/boating:* Good. You can also see lots of dolphins in the spring. No boats for rent. *Shell-collecting:* Tiny sand dollars.

Getting there: South of Tepic and west of Las Varas, marked turn-off from Mexico 200. Rough unpaved road, veering left at fork, leads six miles to beach. Chacalilla is less than half a mile north of the main beach on a powdery dirt road past the Chacala parking area.

Playa Rincón de Guayabitos and **Playa Los Ayala**—The first of these pretty beaches wraps around Bahía de Jaltemba, ending a half-mile to the south at a wave-washed hill. You can walk around the hill via a small rocky beach to Playa Los Ayala, a palm-backed continuation of Guayabitos. At the southern end of Ayala, there's a trail along a vegetated cliff leading out to a woodsy point and down to a beautiful little secret cove with a private beach (some call it Playa del Beso, or Kiss Beach), charming for a picnic, romantic swim or isolated camping.

Facilities: Restaurants. *Camping:* Too crowded at Guayabitos, more shade and hammock-space at Ayala. *Swimming:* Excellent, shallow with mild waves. *Snorkeling/diving:* Around Isla de Congrejo and Isla del Coral, plus Punta Raza at south end of Los Ayala. *Surfing/windsurfing:* Good for windsurfing. *Fishing/boating:* Glass-bottom boats leave from Guayabitos for tours of nearby beaches and offshore islands. Boats for rent. Fishing very good.

Getting there: At Rincón de Guayabitos. Los Ayala is just south of Guayabitos, at marked turnoff from Mexico 200.

Playas Latracadero, Las Minitas and **Los Venados** (★)—This strip of dreamy beaches fronts the little cobbled fishing village of Lo de Marcos. A long creamy sickle of sand, Playa Latracadero, curves south of the village and ends at a wooded hill called Banco de Carranza. The view of the beach from here is pure paradise: a fringe of palms with the pastel Sierra de Vallejo rising in the background, wave-lapped shore sprinkled with faded *pangas*, glistening rocks full of foamy tidepools and driftwood to the south. Just beyond these rocks, reachable by trail over the hill or by paved road, is little Playa Las Minitas, where the sand sparkles with golden lights because of metallic deposits from nearby cave-mines. You can walk to the caves during low tide past the rocky point south of Las Minitas, where waves crash and giant tidepools form. Just south of this area is another quiet little beach called Playa Los Venados.

Facilities: Restaurants are at Latracadero and Minitas. *Camping:* Good at southern end of Latracadero, more private at the smaller beaches. *Swimming:* Good, but with bigger waves and steeper dropoffs than beaches to the north. *Snorkeling/diving:* Around rocks off Banco de Carranza. *Surfing/windsurfing:* Surfable waves in summer, good windsurfing anytime. *Fishing/boating:* Good. *Pangas* for rent at Latracadero.

Getting there: South of Rincón de Guayabitos at village of Lo De Marcos off Mexico 200. For Las Minitas and Los Venados, go through Lo de Marcos and turn left at sign for *Mi Pequeño Paraíso*, follow the road to marked turnoffs for these beaches.

Playa San Francisco—Located in the little town of San Francisco, this beach has the poetry of a place you'd visit in a dream. The thick white sand drops sharply to a roaring sea, while just steps away is a mirrorlike lagoon with driftwood poking through the water, white herons gliding among the lilies and horses wading near the shore. The beach ends at a massive cliff topped by the home of former Mexican president Luis Echeverría. An abandoned palm-roofed hut, like some way station between dimensions, opens onto the other side of the cliff, where miles of **wild beach** (★) backed by primeval rocks rush out before you.

Facilities: Restaurants and hotel. *Camping:* Good and fairly isolated. *Swimming:* Expert swimmers only, steep dropoff. Try southern end of beach where water is calmer. *Snorkeling/diving:* Rocks around southern point. *Surfing/windsurfing:* Too rough. Big waves in summer, but steep dropoff makes for short ride. *Fishing/boating:* Good. *Pangas* for rent. *Shell-collecting:* Scattered fragments beyond cliff.

Getting there: South of Rincón de Guayabitos at the village of San Francisco off Mexico 200.

Punta de Mita—After miles of palms and flowers, the desertlike landscape surrounding this rocky, barren point is jarring to the eye. Its beaches, littered with white coral from an offshore reef, weave along crystalline, calm waters well-suited for snorkeling.

Facilities: Restaurants. *Camping:* Highly uncomfortable. The beach consists of virtual dunes of jagged white coral. *Swimming:* Good but watch out for coral bottom. *Snorkeling/diving:* Good around offshore rocks and reef. *Surfing/windsurfing:* Too many rocks for either. Best surfing one mile south at Playa Anclote. *Fishing/boating:* Good. *Pangas* for rent near restaurants. *Shell-collecting:* Few shells but lots of coral.

Getting there: South of Sayulita and west of Huanacaxtle. Proceed from Huanacaxtle for 13 miles along the paved Carretera La Cruz de Huanacaxtle-Punta de Mita.

Playa Anclote (Anchor Beach)—It's immediately evident from the surrounding signs that this is a surfer's beach. Playa Anclote is pretty and white, though rocky in parts. It is rimmed in shade trees and curves around a turquoise cove with long, smooth waves.

Facilities: Restaurants. *Camping:* Fair, with sheltering trees, but sand is jagged with coral. *Swimming:* Good, shallow and great for kids. *Snorkeling/diving:* Best around Punta de Mita to the north. *Surfing/windsurfing:* Known as a hot surfing spot, with the tallest waves from June through August. Boogie boards for rent at El Coral Restaurant. *Fishing/boating:* Good. Rent *pangas* south of restaurants. *Shell-collecting:* Interesting fragments and white coral.

Getting there: South of Punta de Mita and west of Huanacaxtle on Carretera La Cruz de Huanacaxtle-Punta de Mita. Turn at sign for El Coral.

Playa Destiladeras (★)—Talcum-powder silver sand extends for miles in either direction backed by smooth ochre-colored sandstone cliffs, making this one of the most elegant beaches north of Puerto Vallarta. A few residences dot the cliffs, a few open-air cafés dot the shore, but otherwise the beach is long and lonely. Sheltered to the north by the arm of land that is Punta de Mita, the sea here is clear, gentle and vibrant.

Facilities: Restaurants. *Camping:* Good. *Swimming:* Wonderful. *Surfing/windsurfing:* Windsurfing is good, surfing is better at Playa Anclote to the north. *Fishing/boating:* Good. Rent boats at Playa Anclote.

Getting there: South of Punta de Mita and west of Huanacaxtle on Carretera La Cruz de Huanacaxtle-Punta de Mita. Take turnoff at fork and beach sign.

PUERTO VALLARTA AREA BEACHES

Good municipal beaches and better ones to the south are some of Puerto Vallarta's main attractions.

Playa de Oro—The city's northernmost beach, starting right next to the marina and ferry terminal, extends to the downtown area past many of the big hotels, changing names to match them. It's most often referred to simply as Playa de Oro, like the Hotel Playa de Oro, the oldest hotel on this strip. It's wide and clean, lined in palms with grayish sand and lively surf—much nicer than Playa de los Muertos south of town but not as popular.

Facilities: Restaurants. *Camping:* Not recommended. *Swimming:* Good, though shore drops off rather sharply. *Snorkeling/diving:* Around Islas Marietas offshore. *Surfing/windsurfing:* Waves have enough oomph for boogie-boarding and sometimes more. Surfboards are for rent at the Hotel Krystal Vallarta. Windsurfing lessons are given at the Krystal and Hotel Las Palmas, where sailboards can be rented. *Fishing/boating:* Good. Mini-boats and catamarans for rent. Parasailing.

Getting there: In northern Puerto Vallarta off Mexico 200.

Playa de los Muertos (Playa del Sol)—This cluttered little beach was originally called "Beach of the Dead" after a battle between pirates and Indians. The city fathers tried to rename it "Beach of the Sun" but "Los Muertos" has stuck. Bronzed bodies, fried fish-on-a-stick and skateboarders crowd its sands during the high season. Lined with cafés and palms, it proceeds for a quarter-mile to a rocky point called El Púlpito.

Facilities: Restaurants and cafés. *Camping:* Not recommended. *Swimming:* Good, lively waves. Huge inner tubes for rent. *Snorkeling/diving:* Around Islas Marietas offshore. *Surfing/windsurfing:* Both are possible. *Fishing/boating:* Good, rent boats in town.

Getting there: Just off Calle Olas Altas.

Playa Mismaloya—Probably the area's most famous beach, Mismaloya is where *Night of the Iguana*, the movie that put Puerto Vallarta on the map, was filmed. On a hilltop above the white crescent beach, you can visit the jungle-shrouded ruins of the brick hacienda where Richard Burton and Liz Taylor cavorted between takes. The view from here and out at the rocky southern point is magnificent: the *palapa*-lined beach curves around a lovely blue bay bobbing with boats, and off to the north stand Los Arcos, a well-known set of rocky arches in the sea.

Facilities: Restaurants. *Camping:* Not recommended, it's pretty crowded. *Swimming:* Good. *Snorkeling/diving:* Excellent around nearby Los Arcos, which has been designated a state marine-life preserve. *Surfing/windsurfing:* Windsurfing is possible. *Fishing/boating:* Good. *Pangas* for rent.

Getting there: About eight miles south of Puerto Vallarta off Mexico 200 (Carretera Manzanillo).

Boca de Tomatlán—This picturesque little tropical village is the southernmost beach stop accessible by road before the highway veers inland for Barra de Navidad and Manzanillo. The Río Tomatlán empties into the sea here, forming a lazy swimming hole for children in this shallow, protected cove. Natives claim the village is built on an Indian graveyard, and you can find buried arrowheads, figurines and drawings among the rocks.

Facilities: Restaurants. *Camping:* Sand too coarse to be pleasant. *Swimming:* Good. *Surfing/windsurfing:* No surf, windsurfing is possible. *Fishing/boating: Pangas* for rent for fishing or trips to nearby beaches of Quimixto, Las Animas, Majaguitas and Yelapa.

Getting there: Off Mexico 200 south of Puerto Vallarta, a few miles past Mismaloya.

Playa Las Animas—This secluded beach south of Boca de Tomatlán forms a white crescent along a sparkling cove set between two rocky outcroppings. No roads lead here, but boats make regular runs from Puerto Vallarta. The hills behind the beach are filled with palm-fringed jungle and the houses of isolationists who call this lovely beach home.

Facilities: Restaurants (selling *raicilla*, a potent Indian liquor that can take away seasickness). *Camping:* Very good, after the crowds leave. *Swimming:* Lovely. *Snorkeling/diving:* Good around the northern rocks. Snorkeling gear for rent at restaurants. *Surfing/windsurfing:* Gentle waves best for windsurfing. *Fishing/boating: Pangas* for rent. Parasailing and waterskiing.

Getting there: By boat only, from Puerto Vallarta, Mismaloya or Boca de Tomatlán.

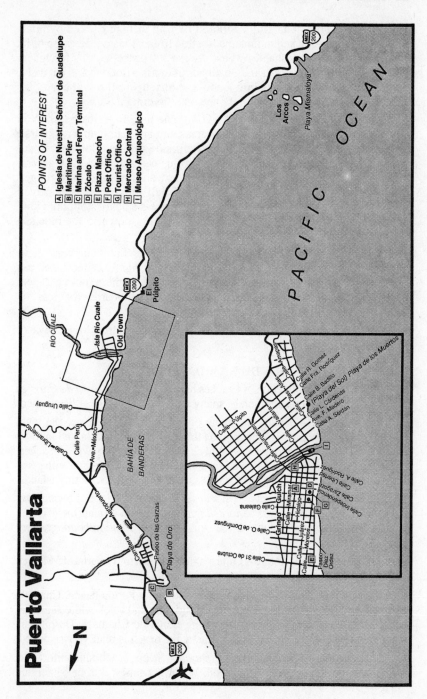

Puerto Vallarta

N

POINTS OF INTEREST

A Iglesia de Nuestra Señora de Guadalupe
B Maritime Pier
C Marina and Ferry Terminal
D Zócalo
E Plaza Malecón
F Post Office
G Tourist Office
H Mercado Central
I Museo Arqueológico

PACIFIC OCEAN

Los Arcos

Playa Mismaloya

MEX 200

RÍO CUALE

Isla Río Cuale

Old Town

El Púlpito

Calle Uruguay

Calle Libramiento

Calle Perú

Ave. México

Aeropuerto

Carretera

Paseo de las Garzas

Playa de Oro

BAHÍA DE BANDERAS

MEX 200

Calle R. Gomez
Calle Fra. Rodríguez
(Playa del Sol) Playa de los Muertos
Calle B. Badillo
Calle L. Cárdenas
Ave. F. Madero
Calle A. Serdán

Calle Púlpito

Calle A. Rodríguez
Calle Libertad
Calle Zaragoza
Calle Independencia
Calle O. de Domínguez
Calle 31 de Octubre

Gringo Gulch

Calle Galeana

Calle Miramar
Calle Juárez
Calle Hidalgo
Calle Morelos
Paseo Díaz Ordaz

Yelapa—This beautiful, secluded fishing village backed by mist-shrouded, jungle-cloaked mountains is a true tropical vision. Because of its isolation—it is only reachable by boat—some 500 peace-seeking foreigners have settled here in recent years. Boatloads of tourists flood in and out daily, turning its grainy beaches into a zoo and obscuring the real beauty of Yelapa. To enjoy it in its natural state, stay overnight.

The nearby waterfalls are just a 20-minute hike from the beach. You don't need a guide—just follow the beach south and climb up a rocky trail through the village. The trail ends in a cliffside café overlooking a pool fed by the waterfall. To see the source of this cascade, backtrack several hundred yards to the closest house, turn left and proceed on a rugged 15-minute hike up to a beautiful series of half-hidden pools that feed the waterfall. From this vine-twisted perch there's a heart-stopping view: an entire mountainside of sun-lit palms sweeping down to the blue sea far below.

Facilities: Restaurants. *Camping:* Possible, but you won't have much privacy. *Swimming:* Good. *Snorkeling/diving:* Excellent. You can rent snorkeling gear on the beach. Diving is best off northern rocks past boat dock. *Surfing/windsurfing:* Windsurfing good, sailboards for rent on beach. *Fishing/boating:* Good. *Pangas* for rent.

Getting there: By boat only, from Puerto Vallarta, Mismaloya or Boca de Tomatlán.

CHAMELA TO BARRA DE NAVIDAD BEACHES

This beautiful collection of beaches has been dubbed *Costa de Careyes* (Turtle Coast). Despite the hotels, many of the beaches are still untamed.

Punta Perula—This is the name of the rocky point below the town of Tomatlán where the highway rejoins the coastline after its inland journey from Puerto Vallarta. Around this point curve miles of empty white beaches, known as Playa Perula and Playa Fortuna, encircling the fishing village of La Fortuna and lovely Bahía de Chamela, which is dotted with tiny islands.

Facilities: Restaurants, stores. *Camping:* Good. *Swimming:* Good, with vigorous waves. *Snorkeling/diving:* Good around the offshore islands. *Surfing/windsurfing:* Good windsurfing. *Fishing/boating:* Very good. *Pangas* for rent.

Getting there: About 80 miles south of Puerto Vallarta off Mexico 200 via gravel turnoff.

Playa Chamela—A continuation of the Punta Perula beach, Chamela has steeper sand banks descending to the tideline and thick white sand that curves in a long, beautiful crescent along Bahía de Chamela. Despite the amenities in the nearby village of Chamela, the beach is relatively secluded.

Facilities: Stores nearby. *Camping:* Steep beach uncomfortable, try Villa Polinesia. *Swimming:* Good. Water is calmest during winter and spring. *Snorkeling/diving:* Around offshore islands. *Surfing/windsurfing:* Surf is up during the summer and early fall. Windsurfing good the rest of the year. *Fishing/boating:* Good. Ask at Villa Polinesia about boats. *Getting there:* Off Mexico 200 at Chamela.

Playa El Tecuán—This mysterious spot is windswept and solitary, on savage open sea. Miles of wide virgin beach stand empty except for the hilltop hotel and nearby Laguna Fortuna. To the north the beach snakes around a rocky point and sweeps on toward a fishing village. To the south a recreational development is in the works. The beach changes names several times, but the whole strip is part of El Tecuán: a fabulous walking beach with occasional *palapas* as your only shade.

Facilities: Bathrooms and showers near lagoon. *Camping:* Excellent. Beach shelters and camping facilities for rent at nearby hotel. *Swimming:* Not recommended. Rough waves. Try the northern end of beach near the point for more sheltered swimming. *Snorkeling/diving:* Around the rocks and islands off northern point. *Surfing/windsurfing:* Good surf from August to December. *Fishing/boating:* Good. *Pangas* for rent at the hotel. *Shell-collecting:* Northern point rich in vivid shells.

Getting there: South of Chamela off Mexico 200 at marked turnoff. Follow paved road about seven miles to hotel security gate, turn right onto dirt road and follow to beach.

Playa Tenacatita (★)—Another real gem. First you enter a dusty little village set in groves of banana trees, then pass a pond full of graceful herons and a dozing lagoon, and emerge at a kingdom of many wild, unhurried beaches. The seafront land forms a lovely sandy crescent on Bahía de Tenacatita, then juts out to the north into a small point flanked by two little beaches, Playa Mora and Playa Gris. En route back toward the highway, you pass a palm grove cut by a trail to another primitive beach, a continuation of Playa El Tecuán.

Facilities: Restaurants. *Camping:* Very good. *Swimming:* Very pleasant. *Snorkeling/diving:* Good in rocky cove around northern point at small, sheltered Playa Mora. An offshore coral reef has earned this area the nickname "The Aquarium." *Surfing/windsurfing:* Windsurfing good along the bay. *Fishing/boating:* Good. *Pangas* for rent. *Shell-collecting:* Some small shells at big open-sea beach that joins El Tecuán.

Getting there: South of El Tecuán off Mexico 200 at marked turnoff, follow dirt road about five miles to village beaches.

Playa Los Ángeles Locos (The Crazy Angels Beach)—This lovely sand beach with gentle waves embraces Bahía de Tenacatita. At the north end is an estuary that flows into the sea. Toward the southern end is a rocky formation. The beach winds north to Playa Tenacatita.

Facilities: Amenities in nearby hotel. *Camping:* Good. *Swimming:* Very good. *Snorkeling/diving:* Around rocks at northern end near the estuary. *Surfing/windsurfing:* Windsurfing good around the hotel. *Fishing/boating:* Good. *Pangas* for rent near estuary. *Shell-collecting:* Small butterfly clams.

Getting there: South of Tenacatita off Mexico 200, take the marked turnoff for Fiesta Americana, Los Ángeles Locos.

Boca de Iguanas and **Playa Manzanilla**—These two beaches fuse into one continuous arc of sand stretching five or six miles, backed by palms and low sand dunes. Boca de Iguanas is a wide-open beach rolling north around a rocky point into Los Ángeles Locos. To the south it becomes La Manzanilla, a lovely white ribbon of sand curving past a village of that name and ending to the south at a tree-covered hill. The long shallow tideline has hard-packed sand that's great for bicycling.

Facilities: Restaurants. *Camping:* Very good, on the beach or in the trailer park. *Swimming:* Very good. *Snorkeling/diving:* Around the southern rocks. *Surfing/windsurfing:* Good windsurfing. *Fishing/boating:* Good. *Pangas* for rent around village.

Getting there: South of Los Ángeles Locos off Mexico 200 at marked turnoffs for both beaches.

Playa Melaque and **Barra de Navidad**—These broad, merged beaches form a smashing four-to-five-mile semicircle along Bahía de Melaque past the towns of San Patricio-Melaque to the north and Barra de Navidad to the south. The rocky headland to the north is worth exploring. Palms and open-air restaurants vie for space along the thick, clean sand, and brisk breezes kick up the waves at sundown.

Facilities: Restaurants. *Camping:* Crowded but possible. *Swimming:* Safest swimming to the north around Melaque. *Snorkeling/diving:* Around rocks at northern point near Playa Melaque. *Surfing/windsurfing:* Some surf at Barra in October and November. Other times the bay is good for windsurfing. *Fishing/boating:* Good. *Pangas* for rent in Barra at the lagoon or cabin cruisers at the Hotel Cabo Blanco marina.

Getting there: Off Mexico 200 in Melaque and Barra de Navidad.

MANZANILLO BEACHES

From Barra de Navidad all the way to Boca de Pascuales south of Manzanillo, you'll find Mexico's finest black sand beaches.

Playa de Oro (★)—North of Mazanillo, this wild beach on the open sea is windy and unpeopled, with fine grayish sand, like the primeval haunt of a caveman. It weaves for miles among dramatic cliffs and rock formations, backed by low dunes.

Facilities: None. *Camping:* Fabulous, though it's often windy. *Swimming:* With caution. Beware of strong waves. *Surfing/windsurfing:* Boogie-boarding or windsurfing.

Getting there: About 20 miles north of Manzanillo off Mexico 200 via marked turnoff, 4.5-mile dirt road to beach.

Playa Miramar—One of Manzanillo's most popular beaches, this silvery runner of sand hugging Bahía de Santiago is the first one you see from the highway as you approach Manzanillo. The sand is white-over-black (when you scratch the surface it's clearly black underneath), rolling several miles north toward the Península de Juluapán and a quiet, rocky shore called La Boquita.

Facilities: Restaurants. *Camping:* Not recommended, not much privacy. *Swimming:* Very good. *Snorkeling/diving:* Around La Puntilla de Miramar. *Surfing/windsurfing:* Boogie-boarding and windsurfing. *Fishing/boating:* Good. *Pangas* for rent near La Boquita. *Shell-collecting:* Some clam shells down at La Boquita.

Getting there: North of Manzanillo off Mexico 200 across from Club Maeva, or in front of Club Santiago.

Playa La Audiencia—This small, popular beach hugs a private cove on the north side of the Península de Santiago opposite Las Hadas. Legend has it Hernán Cortés had an audience with the Indians of the area here. The beach curves for about a quarter mile between two rocky points, one topped by the fabulous *palapa*-roofed home of an American millionaire.

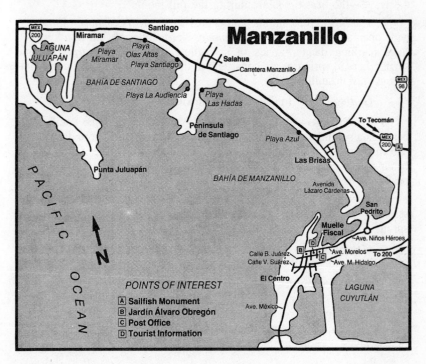

Facilities: Restaurants. *Camping:* At southern end. *Swimming:* Very pleasant. *Snorkeling/diving:* Around the rocky point. *Surfing/windsurfing:* Best for windsurfing. *Fishing/boating:* Good.

Getting there: North of Manzanillo off Mexico 200 via Las Hadas exit. Continue straight on cobbled road to beach.

Playa Azul—This long, wide, cornmeal-colored beach extends along Bahía de Manzanillo for several miles, from the commercial Las Brisas area north to the village of Santiago. Its northern zone faces rough waves on open sea, then curves south into gentler protected areas along the bay.

Facilities: Restaurants. *Camping:* Reasonable privacy north of Las Brisas. *Swimming:* Las Brisas area safest, rough waves to the north. *Surfing/windsurfing:* Try windsurfing.

Getting there: North of Manzanillo off Mexico 200, Las Brisas exit.

Playa Cuyutlán—The best black sand beach in Mexico: pick up a handful and you can count the rare sparkles of white. This long beach faces open sea south of Manzanillo in the town of Cuyutlán, home of the amazing *Ola Verde* (Green Wave). In April or May, monstrous 30-footers roll in, full of phosphorescent colors. A short *malecón* and rows of canvas beach chairs line the waterfront for viewing. Only chance determines if you'll see the wave—the best times are during the full moon.

Facilities: Restaurants and stores in town. *Camping:* Fine, but wide open and often windy. *Swimming:* Normally good, but watch for red flags marking danger zones in springtime. *Surfing/windsurfing:* Some surfing here in spring; more consistent to the south. *Fishing/boating:* Better out of Manzanillo.

Getting there: In Cuyutlán off Mexico 200.

Playa Paraíso—With miles of black sand along the blue Pacific, this beach is a southern continuation of Playa Cuyutlán, only more downhome and tropical. Thatch-roofed restaurants line the sand. Groves of palms and banana trees crowd around the little village, and a sleepy lagoon lies opposite the sea.

Facilities: Cafés. *Camping:* Good. *Swimming:* Depends on seasonal wave action, use caution. *Surfing/windsurfing:* Surf's up in spring. *Fishing/boating:* Good. *Pangas* for rent on beach.

Getting there: South of Cuyutlán along Colima 130, take marked turnoff, continue about five miles west.

Boca de Pasquales—Where the mouth (*boca*) of the Río Pasquales kisses the sea, this long and lonely black sand beach extends south along the Pacific for many miles. A lazy tropical fishing village of the same name is tucked among the palms, flanked by the sea and the river. The tempestuous waves here make this a surfer's paradise.

Facilities: Restaurants. *Camping:* Good but unsheltered. *Swimming:* Careful of high rollers. Watch for red flags warning against swimming; white flags give go-ahead. *Surfing/windsurfing:* A hot surfer's spot all year round. *Fishing/boating:* Good. *Pangas* for rent.

Getting there: About 25 miles south of Cuyutlán off Mexico 200, take Tecomán turnoff and follow paved road for eight miles.

MICHOACÁN TO PLAYA AZUL BEACHES

The coast of Michoacán is full of beautiful wild beaches. Because of the isolation, you should camp with caution or in groups. A sampling of the best spots:

Playa Faro de Bucerías—Clearly marked and built up to be a modest tourist recreation zone, this idyllic little white beach hugs a pretty blue-green cove between two rocky bluffs. There's a somewhat steep dropoff to the north, a smooth and gentler dropoff to the south near the lighthouse.

Facilities: Restaurants, showers and baths. *Camping:* Very good. *Swimming:* Best at southern end of the beach near the lighthouse. *Snorkeling/diving:* Around the rocks to the north. Diving gear for rent here. *Fishing/boating:* Good. *Pangas* for rent.

Getting there: About 10 to 15 miles south of La Placita off Mexico 200 at marked turnoff. A dusty road runs several miles to the sea. Follow right fork to parking area.

Playa Maruata (★)—Welcome to honeymoon camp. This romantic, secluded white-sand beach is tucked amid several big cliffs with surf surging up among the rocks and tall slender palms waving in the breeze. The beach itself is divided by a giant rock, with a shallow, open section to the north and a rocky, steep-shored cove to the south. A friendly, but rather primitive, little village lies a short way inland.

Facilities: Restaurants. *Camping:* Good. Stay near beachside settlement for safety. *Swimming:* Safe to the north in shallow area. *Snorkeling/diving:* Around rocks surrounding beaches. *Surfing/windsurfing:* Too many rocks for either.

Getting there: Off Mexico 200 in Maruata. Traveling south, turn left after Puente Maruata 1, make a U-turn to pass under the bridge, go through the village for about a mile to the beach.

Playa Caleta de Campos (★)—Another beautiful pair of beaches awaits you here. One curves along a calm cove at the foot of the hillside village. Beyond a rocky headland that defines the southern end of the sand there's an even better beach, reachable only by a long hike around the cliff—or, *más rapido*, by swimming around the rocks. This second beach, about a mile long, is utterly empty, palm-shaded and picturesque with jagged rocks; perfect for a picnic or discreet nude sunbathing.

Facilities: Restaurants. *Camping:* Sand is a bit rocky around cafés. Camping is better on second secluded beach, but do it in groups for safety. *Swimming:* Lovely. *Snorkeling/diving:* Around northern end of Punta Rompeolas. *Surfing/windsurfing:* Best surf during rainy season, June through September. At other times windsurfing is best. *Fishing/boating:* Good. *Pangas* for rent on beach.

Getting there: In Caleta de Campos off Mexico 200, 35 miles north of Playa Azul.

Playa La Soledad—This small, quiet beach with fine grayish sand stretches between two short, rocky points. A clump of palms shades the northern end where open-air restaurants snooze. Good for a little escapism and undisturbed camping.

Facilities: Restaurants. *Camping:* Good. Stay close to restaurants for safety. *Swimming:* Smooth and safe. *Snorkeling/diving:* Around the rocks at either end of the beach. *Surfing/windsurfing:* Surf is best during the rainy season, other times windsurfing is best. *Fishing/boating:* Good. *Shell-collecting:* Scattered sand dollars.

Getting there: South of Caleta de Campos off Mexico 200 at Playa La Soledad turnoff.

Playa Mescalhuacán (also known as Playa Chuquiapán or Playa Chuta) —This grand grayish-sand beach on open sea curves for miles to the south, vanishing into a grove of coconut palms. To the north stands a short rocky point. The shoreline is scattered with pebbles and several open-air cafés. There's some debate over what this neck of the sand is called. In Mexico, three names are always better than one.

Facilities: Restaurants. *Camping:* Good, relatively isolated. Stay near restaurants for safety. *Swimming:* Good. Open sea with shallow tideline. *Surfing/windsurfing:* Both possible. *Fishing/boating:* Good.

Getting there: South of Caleta de Campos along Mexico 200, Km. 35, marked turnoff at palm-tree sign.

Playa Azul—A favorite vacationland for Mexican families from nearby inland towns, this tranquil beach stretches along open sea in wide silver-gray belts of sand backed by palms and thickets of open-air restaurants. You can walk for beautiful breezy miles in either direction with few disturbances.

Facilities: Restaurants and stores are in town. *Camping:* Good. *Swimming:* Experienced swimmers only. Strong undertow. *Surfing/windsurfing:* Good surf. *Fishing/boating:* Good. *Pangas* for rent. *Shell-collecting:* Fragile sand dollars and clam shells.

Getting there: In Playa Azul off Mexico 200.

IXTAPA-ZIHUATANEJO BEACHES

Some 16 miles of beautiful beaches line this coastal strip.

Playa Quieta—A small, quiet beach with moist grayish sand and plenty of trees, Quieta serves the Club Med that dominates this part of the sea. An aquatic sports center offers club members every service, but *el público* is confined to splashing in the waves or taking boats to nearby Isla Ixtapa. Just to the south, **Playa Cuata** offers public watersports facilities on its tiny covelike crescent of sand.

Facilities: Restaurant and bathrooms nearby at Playa Cuata. *Camping:* Not permitted. Try the campground at Playa Linda to the north or Isla Ixtapa offshore. *Swimming:* Very good. *Snorkeling/diving:* Great around Isla Ixtapa. *Surfing/windsurfing:* Windsurfing looks good. *Fishing/boating:* Fishing good off breakwater. *Pangas* leave regularly for Isla Ixtapa about five minutes from shore.

Getting there: Northwest of Ixtapa along Carretera Playa Linda, take turnoff for Playa Cuata and bear right to public parking.

Playa Baradero and **Playa Carey**—These beaches lie on lovely Isla Ixtapa, a little wooded island off northern Ixtapa across from Playa Quieta that is a wonderful spot for a day's excursion, a picnic and some marvelous snorkeling. Deer, rabbits and birds are the only inhabitants. The best beaches are a short walk from the main beach where boats land. Playa Baradero occupies a pretty cove facing the mainland. On the opposite side of the

island is Playa Carey, even prettier and more private, with sloping coral-scattered sands and blue-green waters darkened by an offshore coral reef vivid with fish.

Facilities: Restaurants. *Camping:* Very good. *Swimming:* Excellent. *Snorkeling/diving:* Clear, beautiful snorkeling on the north side of the island at Playa Carey. *Surfing/windsurfing:* Windsurfing is possible. *Fishing/boating: Pangas* for rent on the beach.

Getting there: By boat from Playa Quieta.

Playa del Palmar—This long, gorgeous white beach on vigorous Bahía del Palmar is the one you see in all those "Ahhhh, Ixtapa" ads. Here the giant hotels crop up in increasing numbers, bikinied bodies from the chilly north come to toast, parasails billow in the blue skies and raging waves slash the shore. Watch out for sticky deposits of tar in the sand that can blacken your feet. The beach heads north out of the hotel zone into a virgin stretch culminating in a series of beautiful private coves.

Facilities: Restaurants. *Camping:* Not recommended. *Swimming:* Risky. Watch for flags posted in front of hotels, indicating swimming conditions. *Snorkeling/diving:* Best around Isla de la Pie or Isla Ixtapa to the north. *Fishing/boating:* No fishing, but you can rent catamarans.

Getting there: In Ixtapa off Mexico 200.

Playa Majahua—This small, isolated beach (known as the local nude beach) hides itself at the dead end of a coastal road north of Zihuatanejo. Backed by vegetated hills, a few lone palms and cactus, Majahua's lonely crescent of tarnished sand enjoys the surge of lively surf between two rocky outcroppings.

Facilities: None. Full amenities in Zihuatanejo nearby. *Camping:* Good. *Swimming:* Good. *Snorkeling/diving:* Try around southern rocks. *Surfing/windsurfing:* Both possible.

Getting there: From Zihuatanejo, follow Camino Cerro del Almacén north to where the road ends.

Playa La Ropa—Far lovelier than the cramped neighboring Playa La Madera and the crowded municipal beach in the village, La Ropa is this area's most beautiful beach and one of the best on the whole Mexican West Coast. Its white sand curves for over a mile between a rocky headland to the north and a hump of land to the west, beyond which lies Playa Las Gatas. The beach was named "La Ropa" (The Clothes) because years ago clothing from a wrecked Chinese ship washed up onto the shore. Palms and bougainvillea brighten the cliffs behind the beach, where several hotels are perched overlooking the bay.

Facilities: Restaurants, baths and showers. *Camping:* Campground Playa La Ropa, west of Hotel Sotavento. *Swimming:* Excellent. *Surfing/windsurfing:* Windsurfing good. *Fishing/boating:* Good. *Pangas* for rent on municipal beach.

Getting there: Southwest of Zihuatanejo in the Zona de Hoteles, enter where road ends or at any hotel or restaurant exit.

Playa Las Gatas—This pearly crescent beach embraces a sparkling cove inaccessible by road and thus relatively unspoiled. The shore is protected by the remains of an offshore breakwater built by an Indian king to keep the waters safe for his daughter. This rocky wall, visible from the beach, attracts marinelife and makes for fabulous snorkeling. "Las Gatas" (The Cats) refers to a local nonaggressive nurse shark with catlike whiskers.

Facilities: Restaurants. *Camping:* Good at less crowded southwestern end of beach. *Swimming:* Wonderful. *Snorkeling/diving:* Excellent. Rocky wall just offshore teems with sea life. Visibility is great. *Surfing/windsurfing:* Boogie-boarding good, sporadic surfable waves in winter and spring. *Fishing/boating:* Good fishing. *Shell-collecting:* No shells, but lots of white coral.

Getting there: By boat only. *Pangas* leave regularly from the municipal pier in Zihuatanejo.

SOUTH OF ZIHUATANEJO TO PIE DE LA CUESTA BEACHES

Lovely, undeveloped beaches cover the 150-mile coastline from Zihuatanejo south to Acapulco. Some of the best:

Barra de Potosí—This fishing village south of Zihautanejo rests on a wide, curving grayish-sand beach that runs for miles between two vegetated hills. A lazy lagoon (Laguna de Potosí) fuses with the sea at one end of the village, forming a muddy sand bar where *pangas* bake in the sun.

Facilities: Restaurants. *Camping:* Good, quite isolated. *Swimming:* Good. *Surfing/windsurfing:* Windsurfing possible. *Fishing/boating:* Good. *Pangas* for rent.

Getting there: South of the Ixtapa-Zihuatanejo Airport off Mexico 200, marked turnoff for Laguna de Potosí.

Playa La Barrita—Unhurried and often empty, this wide, graceful beach serves a tiny community of fishermen living in huts near a line of rustic restaurants. Facing open sea, the beach is located right off the highway and shaded by palms.

Facilities: Restaurants. *Camping:* Good, isolated, local anglers are very friendly. *Swimming:* Good. *Surfing/windsurfing:* Some surfable waves during the summer, windsurfing good all year round. *Fishing/boating:* Good. Locals will rent their *pangas. Shell-collecting:* Good. Scattered shells around rocky point at south end of beach.

Getting there: About 35 miles south of Zihuatanejo off Mexico 200, turn at signs for Restaurant Maritona or Las Peñitas.

Playa Papanoa—A long, handsome white beach on open sea, Papanoa covers some six miles of shoreline from the southern hills, where the Hotel Club Papanoa is perched, to a thick palm forest in an elbow of land to the north.

Facilities: Restaurants. *Camping:* Good, solitary. *Swimming:* Locals say it's safe, but use caution. *Surfing/windsurfing:* Windsurfing possible. *Fishing/boating:* Good. *Pangas* for rent.

Getting there: About 65 miles south of Zihuatanejo off Mexico 200, at marked turnoff.

Playa Pie de la Cuesta—The famous "sunset beach" where Acapulco visitors gather for the evening sky lights, Pie de la Cuesta (meaning Foot of the Hill) stretches for ten miles from a southern hill called El Rincón to a northern fishing village called La Barra. The beach is wide, white, palm-fringed and magnificent, with occasional dolphins leaping beyond the wild, foaming surf. The village of Pie de la Cuesta is wedged between the sea and beautiful Laguna Coyuca, framed in pale blue mountains. The paved village road ends at an air force base.

Facilities: Restaurants and stores. *Camping:* Good in or near the trailer parks. The beach can be dangerous at night, with wandering thieves and hungry dogs. *Swimming:* Very risky, fierce waves and undertow. Drownings and injuries occur here routinely. *Fishing/boating:* Good. *Pangas* for rent near southeastern end of beach. Very good cat-fishing in the lagoon.

Getting there: About eight miles north of Acapulco off Mexico 200 via marked turnoff.

ACAPULCO BEACHES

Both camping and surfing are prohibited on Acapulco beaches. Pollution in the bay is a real problem. Swim at your own risk.

Playa Caleta and **Playa Caletilla**—This pair of pretty, sheltered beaches in the old Caleta district was the original hub of Acapulco action back before highrises hit the strip farther east. Old hotels, alfresco restaurants and waving palms animate these strips of pebbly sand fronting a placid cove, still very popular with locals. A busy pier separates the beaches, where boats push off regularly for Isla La Roqueta just offshore.

Facilities: Restaurants, hotels, bathrooms and showers. *Swimming:* Good, though water is dirty from boat traffic. *Snorkeling/diving:* Excellent around nearby Isla La Roqueta. *Surfing/windsurfing:* Windsurfing possible. *Fishing/boating:* Very good. Launches for rent at pier. Small sailboats, paddleboats and kayaks for rent, too.

Getting there: In Caleta district of Acapulco.

Playa La Roqueta—Isla La Roqueta in Bahía de Acapulco, inhabited only by a few soldiers, has a narrow, modest beach strung between two wooded points facing the mainland. Its grainy yellow sand, backed by rocky bluffs, is packed with locals and tour-boat passengers on weekends.

Facilities: Restaurants and bathrooms. *Swimming:* Safe and shallow. *Snorkeling/diving:* Excellent around northern side of island, where diving schools operate from boats. *Surfing/windsurfing:* Windsurfing only. *Fishing/boating:* Good fishing. Kayaks for rent.

Getting there: By boat. All-day service from Playa Caleta.

Playa Hornitos and **Playa Hornos**—Another set of side-by-side beaches, these two mark the beginning of the curvaceous carpet of sand that hugs Bahía de Acapulco in one long, walkable stretch, all the way to the navy base at the southeast end of the Costera. Playa Hornitos (Little Ovens Beach) begins just east of El Fuerte de San Diego. It melts into Playa Hornos (Ovens Beach), wide and palm-lined, which runs up to Parque Papagayo. Some call this the "afternoon beach" because the sun favors this area toward the end of the day.

Facilities: Restaurants and bathrooms. *Swimming:* Usually safe, but watch for warning flags posted if the sea is rough. *Surfing/windsurfing:* Windsurfing possible. *Fishing/boating:* Good. Fishing pier; skiffs, small catamarans and paddle boats for rent.

Getting there: Along Avenida Costera Miguel Alemán just south of El Fuerte de San Diego.

Playa Papagayo (El Morro)—A continuation of Los Hornos, Playa Papagayo (Parrot Beach) runs past Parque Papagayo and widens into a beautiful, broad boulevard of sand that passes a natural formation in the sea called *El Morro* (The Rock). Hence, the beach's two names. It goes past a rocky point called Punta de las Brisas, where Mexican boys violate the local antisurfing rules and catch the tube waves that roll in during July and August, and during the full moon.

Facilities: Restaurants, bathrooms and showers. *Swimming:* Safe. Use discretion when waves are rough. *Snorkeling/diving:* Try around offshore rock, El Morro. *Surfing/windsurfing:* Windsurfing possible. *Fishing/boating:* Sailboats for rent. Parasailing.

Getting there: Along Avenida Costera Miguel Alemán in front of Parque Papagayo.

Playa Condesa—The hippest beach in town, this one is nevertheless not as pretty as many of the others. Long, steep and grainy, it slides down into tumultuous waves that make swimming chancy. But Condesa fronts the most glamorous strip of big hotels, and therein lies the secret of its success. Fashionable beach cafés and swinging bars line the sand. Vendors swarm everywhere, and young Mexicans on belly-boards provide great entertainment, doing double-flips into the waves.

Facilities: Restaurants and bathrooms. *Swimming:* Strong swimmers only, rough waves and undertow. *Surfing/windsurfing:* Windsurfing possible. *Fishing/boating:* Sailboats for rent. Waterskiing, parasailing.

Getting there: Along Avenida Costera Miguel Alemán west of Hotel El Presidente.

Playa Icacos—This fine little beach follows in the footsteps of Playa Condesa, albeit a bit more nonchalantly. Lots of beachfront seafood restaurants sink their tables in the sand in front of less expensive highrises. All water sports are available. The beach ends at a substantial naval base.

Facilities: Restaurants, bathrooms. *Swimming:* Watch for flags in front of the hotels indicating safe or rough water. *Surfing/windsurfing:* Windsurfing possible. *Fishing/boating:* Sailboats and rafts for rent. Parasailing, waterskiing.

Getting there: Along Avenida Costera Miguel Alemán, just northwest of the Hotel Hyatt Regency.

Puerto Marqués—From the cliffside road headed to the airport, the narrow bay at Puerto Marqués spreads out below you with unbelievable beauty, locked within two long green arms of land. Unfortunately, Puerto Marqués does not have much of a beach per se; instead, it's a fine family-oriented spot to swim and eat seafood. The half-mile beach, curving between a military base and a wooded hill, is so narrow the waves often lap at the sandy floors of the open-air restaurants jamming the shore. But the water is clean, clear and calm.

Facilities: Restaurants and bathrooms. *Swimming:* Delightful and unpolluted. *Surfing/windsurfing:* Windsurfing is good. *Fishing/boating:* Fishing good. Sailboats for rent.

Getting there: Southeast of Acapulco off the Carretera Escénica, take marked exit.

Playa Revolcadero—A beautiful, smooth satiny beach fronting the Pierre Marqués and Acapulco Princess luxury hotels, Revolcadero faces the open ocean where waves break in long, frosty tiers that look lovely but have a deadly undertow. You can amuse yourself here with horseback riding or wandering through the exquisite estate of the Princess.

Facilities: Restaurants and bathrooms. *Swimming:* Dangerous. Ferocious waves and current. *Surfing/windsurfing:* Body-surfing popular among daredevils.

Getting there: Southeast of Acapulco along Carretera Escénica in direction of airport, take marked turnoff.

Barra Vieja—This tranquil little fishing village, situated on Laguna Tres Palos, is far from the rush of Acapulco yet close enough for a day's excursion. The beach runs from Playa Revolcadero to the northwest along miles of open sea, with wide grayish sand backed by distant palm groves.

Facilities: Restaurants, bathrooms and showers. *Camping:* Good though unsheltered. *Swimming:* Not recommended. Steep waves, strong currents. *Fishing/boating:* Good. Launches for rent.

Getting there: Eighteen miles south of Acapulco off Mexico 200.

Trailer Parks

All parks listed have full hookups and baths/showers.

MAZATLÁN TRAILER PARKS

Bungalows/Trailer Park Playa Escondida (Avenida Sábalo Cerritos 999; 3-25-78), by far the loveliest park in town, has 200 spaces, a swimming pool, and rustic bungalows set in a quiet palm grove.

The 70-space **Mar Rosa Trailer Park** (Avenida Camarón Sábalo, just north of the Holiday Inn; 3-61-87) puts you directly on the beach.

Another pleasant park is the 179-space **La Posta Trailer Park** (Avenida Rafael Buelna 7; 3-53-10), two blocks from the beach. It has a pool, restaurant and party room.

TEACAPÁN TRAILER PARKS

Trailer Park/Motel Oregon (Calle Reforma 50; Tel. 55) is this tropical village's only park, with 19 spaces.

SAN BLAS AREA TRAILER PARKS

The best in town is the 100-space, shady **Los Cocos Trailer Park** (Avenida Teniente Azueta; 5-00-55), near the beach.

The **Playa Amor R. V. Resort** (Carretera San Blas-Santa Cruz) is just north of Playa Los Cocos, with 35 spaces.

RINCÓN DE GUAYABITOS TO BUCERÍAS TRAILER PARKS

Just north of La Peñita is lovely **La Peñita Trailer Park** (Mexico 200, Km. 92.5), which has a smashing view of the beach.

In Rincón de Guayabitos, trailer parks cater to fishermen, providing boat ramps and fish-cleaning tables. **Paraíso del Pescador** (Fisherman's Paradise, at Retorno Ceibas, Lote 1 and 2; 4-00-14) and **Villa Nueva Trailer Park** (Retorno Ceibas; 4-03-70) are right next door to each other on the beach.

Farther south in Lo De Marcos is the immaculate beachfront **Caracol Bungalows and Trailer Park** (Carretera Las Minitas; 12-49-37 in Guadalajara).

Just north of Puerto Vallarta in Bucerías is the chic beachfront **Bucerías Trailer Park** (Mexico 200, Km. 143).

PUERTO VALLARTA TRAILER PARKS

The best and most peaceful in town is **Laurie's Tacho's Trailer Park** (Camino Nuevo al Pitallal; 2-21-63), just across from the ferry terminal. It has a pool, restaurant and spaces for tent campers.

To be close to the downtown bustle, try the small tropical **Puerto Vallarta Trailer Park** (Calle Francia 143).

CHAMELA TO BARRA DE NAVIDAD TRAILER PARKS

In Chamela, the beachfront "camping club" **Villa Polinesia** (Mexico 200, Km. 72; 22-39-40 in Guadalajara) has R.V. spaces and A-frame cabañas for rent.

On a shady beach north of Barra de Navidad stands **Boca de Iguana Trailer Park** (Boca de Iguana, Mexico 200, Km. 16.5).

Closer to village life, right inside Melaque on the sea, is the **Melaque Trailer Park** (Calle Garranzas 51; 0-05-75).

MANZANILLO TRAILER PARKS

El Palmar Trailer Park (Crucero Las Brisas; 3-09-55) is a full resort, with 77 spaces, tennis courts, pool, laundry and market.

IXTAPA-ZIHUATANEJO TRAILER PARKS

Playa Linda Trailer Park (Carretera Playa Linda; 4-33-81), just north of Ixtapa, has 50 sites.

A new trailer park with friendly, English-speaking owners, is **La Ropa Trailer Park** (Playa La Ropa, at the end of the beach road), with only 20 spaces. They welcome tent campers and also rent hammocks.

ACAPULCO AREA TRAILER PARKS

The best trailer parks in the area are in the quiet fishing village of Pie de la Cuesta, eight miles north of Acapulco. Here you'll find palm-shaded **Acapulco Trailer Park**, one section on the beach and one on calm Laguna Coyuca, with laundromat, boat ramp and grocery store.

Just up the street is friendly **Quinta Dora Trailer Park** (Pie de la Cuesta; 3-93-94 in Acapulco) on the lagoon, with 23 sites, some reserved for tenters, and cold-water showers.

Travelers' Tracks
Sightseeing

MAZATLÁN

This sprawling port city of 400,000, one of the West Coast's top resorts, is 740 miles from the Arizona border on Mexico 15. Occupying a peninsula, the town rambles along a 15-mile coastal boulevard whose name changes five times from north to south.

First there's the fairly undeveloped **Los Cerritos** section along Avenida Sábalo Cerritos. Moving south, the boulevard becomes Avenida Camarón Sábalo and enters the **Zona Dorada** (Golden Zone), the heart of highrise tourist land. Mazatlán's bullring is located here: the **Plaza de Toro**

Monumental (Avenida Rafael Buelna near the junction with Mexico 15). Bullfights are held on Sundays from November through April. *Charreadas* (rodeos) occupy the bullring from May through October. Buy tickets at your hotel or through a travel agency.

Mazatlán's magnificent ten-mile *malecón* is paralleled by the waterfront boulevard, now called Avenida del Mar. This moderate hotel/restaurant zone culminates in the seaside **Fisherman's Monument**, a giant tribute to the city's principal industry and the sensuality of the tropics: a muscular fisherman stands next to a reclining, naked woman.

Here the coastal road becomes Paseo Claussen, passing **Bahía del Puerto Viejo** (Old Port Bay, where Mazatlán's original port was located) and, around a bend in the road, several lookout points along the *malecón*.

One of these points is an 18th-century Spanish fort, **El Fuerte Carranza,** located in the Casa del Marino near a favorite surfing spot (rocky Playa Los Pinos); another is the **High-Divers Observatory Park,** where skilled divers leap into the rocky sea below; the best lookout point is **Cerro de la Nevería** (Ice Box Hill), just off Paseo Claussen and Avenida Zaragoza, offering a great view of the whole town. In the late 1800s wealthy locals used to import ice from San Francisco and store it in the hill's tunnels to keep perishables chilled. Before that, during the 17th century, soldiers settled here to watch for marauding English pirates.

The *malecón* continues past a hillside cavern called **The Devil's Cave** and a proud, voluptuous bronze statue of **La Mazatleca,** a beautiful sea nymph rising out of a wave. In the next traffic circle stands a little bronze deer, Mazatlán's mascot ("Mazatlán" means "place of the deer" in Náhuatl, the indigenous tongue of the area). Now you're on Avenida Olas Altas, which loops past old seaside cafés and the veteran **Hotel Belmar.** This is where tourism began in the 1940s. At the end of Avenida Olas Altas, another traffic circle bears the **crest of Mazatlán**, with symbols of the state of Sinaloa, the city's shrimping industry (the biggest in Mexico), the spring Carnival (also the biggest in Mexico) and the Spanish conquest. A block farther on, the *malecón* ends.

The road, now Paseo del Centenario, continues up through a residential area, passing more lookout points. It emerges on the other side of the peninsula at **Cerro del Crestón** (Summit Hill), crowned by the second highest lighthouse in the world. The **Cerro de Crestón Lighthouse**, standing 515 feet above sea level and able to project its beacon 50 miles out to sea, can be visited by a footpath leading uphill from the end of the sportfishing docks. During the hot, 20-minute ascent, you'll have panoramic views of Mazatlán's harbor, the ferry terminal with its glamorous white carriers, and, to the south, the long, palm-lined beaches of **Isla de la Piedra** (Stone Island, which is actually a peninsula).

You can visit Isla de la Piedra by motorized launches from the harbor side of Mazatlán (dock and ticket offices are off Avenida Emilio Barragán or Avenida del Puerto near the Pemex station). Other pleasure-boat excursions include **harbor and bay cruises** on the *Yate Fiesta* (Calzada Joel Montés Camarena; 1-30-41); and trips to **Isla de los Venados** (Deer Island) aboard amphibious boats-on-wheels painted up like dragons and sharks, leaving from Playa Gaviotas and Playa Sábalo in the Zona Dorado.

North of the town's port area is **El Centro**, the heart of old Mazatlán, founded by the Spanish in 1531 though not incorporated as a town until 1806. Visitors often underestimate Mazatlán's charm because they seldom venture beyond the beach to explore the town's original core. This commercial-residential area—bounded by Avenida Olas Altas, Calle Rosales, Avenida Zaragoza and Calle Ángel Flores—is full of lovely squares, narrow streets and crumbling houses whose shuttered hearts beat with Latin music. The best place to start is the **zócalo** (between Calle 21 de Marzo and Calle Ángel Flores), with its charming bandstand. Across the street is the ornate **Mazatlán Cathedral**, built in 1890 and made a basilica in 1935, with blue-and-gold spires and a triple altar.

The oldest building in town is several blocks from the cathedral, the hillside **Capilla de San José** (Calle Canizales and Calle Uribe). Built in 1870 by Italian padres, this pretty whitewashed chapel has been beautifully renovated. From here, you can spread out and roam up tree-lined Calle Belisarío Domínguez and Calle Constitución to the secretive, leafy **Plazuela Machado**, the center of the old town.

Just up Calle Carnaval stands one of the architectural gems of this area: an abandoned opera house called **Teatro Rubio** (also known as Teatro Ángela Peralta in honor of the celebrated singer who died next door in 1883). Theatrical bas-relief faces stare from the upper facade and bougainvillea blossoms through fissures in the bolted doors.

Over on the port side of town, Mazatlán's favorite beer is being bottled at one of the country's biggest breweries. **Cervecería del Pacífico** (Pacific Brewery), Calle Melchor Ocampo and Calzada Gabriel Leyva; 2-79-66) was opened in 1900. For a plant tour, call the industrial relations department, Ext. 220.

Back near the *malecón*, **Acuario Mazatlán** (Avenida de los Deportes 111; 1-78-17; admission) displays 250 species of fish from all over the world in dozens of tanks.

When you've had enough of the sea, take a day trip 75 miles north of town via Mexico 40 to **Copola**, a spot once noted for its silver mining. You can roam the cobbled streets of this 400-year-old mountain village and visit its 16th-century church.

SOUTH OF MAZATLÁN

For a journey into the jungle, try a boat trip out of **Teacapán**. About 75 miles south of Mazatlán, this tropical fishing village sits amid dense plantations of *limones*, mangos and coconut palms. Mexico 15 takes you first past the town of **El Rosario**, with its 18th-century mission housing a grandly gilded altar, and the town of Esquinapa, where signs direct you to Teacapán. The village's estuary and lagoon flow into mangrove-choked waterways, flitting with butterflies and bugs. Plan your boat trip at the Trailer Park and Motel Oregon (Calle Reforma 50; Tel. 55).

Shortly before Mexico 15 crosses the Río Acaponeta, you enter the agricultural utopia of **Nayarit**, one of Mexico's smallest but greenest states. Lush countryside pads the route to the secluded fishing village of **Novillero**, with its infinite beach, via the farming town of Tecuala off Mexico 15.

Farther south lies the remote island village of **Mexcaltitán,** poetically nicknamed "The Venice of Mexico." Its only real resemblance to that historical city is that you must get there by boat. First, take Mexico 15 to Tuxpan. Continue on Nayarit 94 for about 20 miles on partly paved road. The last ten miles are increasingly rough and poorly marked. Turn right at the second water tower, proceed to a fork in the road, and there bear left. Five miles later the road ends at El Embarcadero, where you can park and catch a pole-driven *panga*, Mexico's answer to the gondola.

In five minutes you cross the shallow, muddy **Estero San Pedro** (also called Laguna de Mexcaltitán), where cows stand thigh-deep in water, nibbling tasty mangrove roots. From the boat landing on the other side, you can tour the little colonial-style island city on foot in less than half an hour.

The main street, fittingly called **Calle de Venecia** (Venice Street), is full of cracked stone houses, sweet-smelling *capiro* trees and friendly natives, mostly fisherfolk who have never left the island. The lovely main plaza boasts a stone bandstand, colonial lanterns and a small unnamed **museum** containing haphazardly arranged artifacts related to pre-Columbian tribes that inhabited the area some 3,500 years ago.

Legend has it that Mexcaltitán was actually discovered by the Aztecs before they moved east into the country's interior. They called the island Aztlán, "place of the herons," and created a circular, geometrically precise town representing their vision of the universe reflected in their calendar. Some say Mexcaltitán was the model for their great capital Tenochtitlán, later built where Mexico City now stands.

En route south to San Blas, it's just a five-mile detour from Mexico 15 on Mexico 16 to the lovely old colonial village of **Santiago Ixcuintla**. Dating back to 1570, Santiago has narrow, cobbled streets that wind among red-tile roofs and fruit stands stocked with the region's rich agricultural yield. You may glimpse brightly dressed Huichol Indians coming down to the market from the mountains. Don't miss the white plaza and the beautiful

18th-century **Iglesia del Señora de la Ascención,** full of chirping sparrows, on Calle 20 de Noviembre nearby.

Mexico 16 continues through verdant fields full of darting iguanas, yellow-and-black-winged birds and fuzzy-maned colts, to the quaint fishing villages of **Los Corchos** and **Boca de Camichín.**

SAN BLAS

The tropical mood increases as you head southwest to the picturesque port of **San Blas.** From the Mexico 15 turnoff onto Mexico 11, you slowly spiral down for 23 miles, dropping 1,000 feet through vine-smothered palm jungle toward the sea. Just before you enter town, a bridge over the Estero San Cristóbal (St. Christopher Estuary) marks the starting point for the popular **La Tovara River trip** (★). Motor-driven *pangas* go on half-day excursions into the shadowy lagoons and swamps around San Blas. Another push-off point, for a shorter trip, is at El Embarcadero on the road to Matanchén, southeast of town.

Each of the journeys takes you through channels hemmed and canopied in mangrove roots (pack insect repellent), with petals raining down from overhanging trees and turtles sunning themselves on shoreline rocks. The streams end at La Tovara, a crystal-clear pool fed by a mountain spring, perfect for a swim. Behind the pool is a pump that feeds San Blas with fresh water. A little "Tarzan house" was built in the treetops so that locals could spy on jaguars creeping out of the hills at night to drink at the spring.

At the approach to San Blas, past a cluster of open-air restaurants, a cobbled road winds up to **Cerro de San Basilio** (San Basilio Hill) and the 18th-century **Ruinas La Contaduria,** the ruins of an old fort and a Spanish church. This is where 70 families from Spain founded San Blas in 1768. The topmost ruin is an overgrown fort whose rusty cannons once fired at pirates. Here José María Mercado also defended San Blas from invading Spaniards during the Mexican War of Independence.

San Blas spreads out below like a storybook town in a palm grove. A short way down the hill stands **La Iglesia de Nuestra Señora del Rosario,** a massive stone shell shrouded in banana trees with the ghost of a cemetery buried in tumbled hunks of masonry. Henry Wadsworth Longfellow wrote a poem called "The Bells of San Blas" based on the chimes in this long-silent church.

The **main square** of old San Blas, where locals gather every night, is guarded by two equally surreal churches, side by side. **El Templo de San Blas,** circa 1810, is a dilapidated near-ruin with half its roof missing, no pews and ghostly statues resembling *campesinos* (farmers). The immense cathedral next door, aspiring to be grand, has been in the making for over 30 years. Named **La Apostólica Romana de San Blas,** it has pews but no roof yet—and no front doors. You can wander in and collect your thoughts under the moonlight. No one knows when it will be finished. These are both touching examples of Mexican faith—in *mañana*.

Up Calle Juárez stand the ruins of the 19th-century **customs house** and beyond that, the **old port**, once the bustling bailiwick of ships of trade, Spanish galleons and renegade pirate vessels. Across from the port is a spit of land with a hill, **Cerro de Vigía**, where the red-and-white **San Blas Lighthouse** was constructed in the 18th century.

SOUTH OF SAN BLAS

An unnumbered coastal highway connects San Blas with a string of fine beaches to the south. At the first stop, **Bahía Matanchén,** Padre Junípero Serra departed for Baja California in 1788 aboard the *Purísima Concepción*, built right here on the bay.

The main coastal road continues south to **Playa Matanchén** and on to the village of **Aticama**, oyster capital of Nayarit. Big succulent ones are prepared at a string of open-air restaurants along the village's rocky shoreline. From here, you pass **Aguas Termales** (Thermal Waters), a rocky pond where hot sulfuric waters bubble up from the ground every morning then recede in the afternoon. Nearby **Playa Los Cocos** is impossible to miss, with its coconut palms as dense as the Black Forest, followed up the road by the cobbled tropical pueblo of **Santa Cruz.** From here, the road veers northeast amid a fantasyland of lush vegetation and winds through hilly countryside up to the capital city of **Tepic.**

TEPIC TO PUERTO VALLARTA

The colonial town of Tepic, with 200,000 people, was founded in 1532. In addition to the flowery main square and old cathedral, an interesting stop is the **Museo Regional de Nayarit** (Avenida México 91 Norte; 2-19-00), which displays Meso-American pottery, jewelry, religious paintings and documentary photos.

At Tepic, Mexico 15 turns inland, and Mexico 200 begins as the coast highway. Mexico 200 follows the West Coast all the way south to the border of Guatemala. En route to Puerto Vallarta, you enter a rich region of beach communities around the poorman's resort town of **Rincón de Guayabitos,** very popular with families. About a mile north of Guayabitos is **La Peñita de Jaltemba** (known as La Peñita), a busy seaside town with shops, restaurants, banks and small hotels, serving as a sort of supply outpost for this area. In the fishing village of **San Francisco** (San Pancho), you can see the bizarre ruins of a once-lofty **Maritime Museum** (on a dirt road next to the village park) funded by former Mexican president Luis Echeverría.

PUERTO VALLARTA

It all began in 1963 with the filming of *Night of the Iguana* at Mismaloya Beach south of town. Elizabeth Taylor flew in to join the film's star, Richard Burton, and their love affair made red-hot headlines all over the world. Journalists' tales of the obscure tropical fishing village eventually launched a full-scale invasion of curious tourists. Now one of Mexico's top resorts, Puerto Vallarta has managed to maintain its original natural attractions. Located on **Bahía de Banderas** (Bay of Flags), Mexico's largest bay, the colonial-white town spills down surrounding hillsides to the sea and is backed by the Sierra Madre.

Puerto Vallarta is divided into five major sections. To the far north, still in the state of Nayarit, is the posh new community-in-the-making called **Nuevo Vallarta,** a playground of condos and villas where rich gringos can sail their yachts right up to their doorsteps just a shell's throw from the marina in Puerto Vallarta. South of here, after crossing the **Río Ameca,** you enter the state of **Jalisco** and Puerto Vallarta's northern city limits, containing the airport, marina, nearby **Plaza de Toros** (bullring) and highrise hotel zone. For tickets to bullfights and *charreadas* (rodeos), see a travel agency.

When Mexico 200 turns to cobblestones, the picturesque **old town** begins, full of boutiques and seaside cafés. Just beyond the trickling Río Cuale, which flows right through town, is the **Playa de los Muertos** vicinity, also heavy in hotels, restaurants and shops. South of here, along the cliffside coastal highway (Mexico 200) are Puerto Vallarta's most stunning view-restaurants, plus lovely beaches and chic hotels.

Old Puerto Vallarta is a fabulous walking town, from the breezy *malecón* to the lively *zócalo* along the seafront drive, **Paseo Díaz Ordaz.** The cobblestones are hard on your feet, so wear comfortable walking shoes. For a look at the residential neighborhood, hike up the steep winding back streets off the square. The upper Miramar area is known as **Gringo Gulch** because many foreigners bought homes here when Puerto Vallarta was first "discovered." As one local dryly sums up this wealthy enclave, "The rich Americans own the houses, the Mexicans take care of them."

At Calle Zaragoza 445 stands the **rambling villa** of the Gulch's most famous resident, Elizabeth Taylor, who comes but once a year to visit, usually in December.

Back down the hill on Calle Hidalgo at Calle Independencia, you'll find one of the town's architectural landmarks, the **Iglesia de Nuestra Señora de Guadalupe.** Noted for its unique crowned steeple (a model of the crown belonging to the Empress Carlota of Mexico), the little church was slowly built over a period of 33 years, from 1918 to 1951.

South of here, the Río Cuale is crossed by two little arched bridges (old and new) that have stairways leading down to **Isla Río Cuale.** This island houses shops, restaurants and the one-room **Museo Arqueológico,** which contains an interesting collection of pre-Columbian figures, musical instruments and crude Indian weapons.

Pleasure boat trips galore leave from Puerto Vallarta for the remote beaches and **fishing villages** of Yelapa, Quimixto, Boca de Tomatlán, Las Animas and Piedra Blanca. All trips begin at the main marina at the north end of town near the ferry terminal.

SOUTH OF PUERTO VALLARTA

As you're leaving town, just south of the village of **Boca de Tomatlán,** Mexico 200 turns inland for a long mountainous stretch. It snakes through the wooded foothills of the Sierra Madre and open farmland for the next 100 miles, re-emerging on the coast at isolated, dreamy **Punta Perula.** From here south to Barra de Navidad there's a long, lush swath of unspoiled beaches, some with wonderful uncrowded hotels and tiny villages.

Barra de Navidad, 140 miles south of Puerto Vallarta, is a pretty cobbled town on a sand bar sandwiched between the open sea and a placid lagoon, **Laguna de Navidad.** Village life remains unchanged here despite the steady flow of tourists who seek escape from civilization. Big families dine on the streets at rickety tables, parrots squawk from doorways and eaves, old men play cards until evening under the flowering trees. For a nice **side trip** out of town, take a *panga* at the Cooperativa Miguel López de Legaspi (lagoon end of Avenida Veracruz) to the palmy peninsula in the lagoon known as **Isla Colimilla.**

MANZANILLO

Mexico 200 proceeds from Jalisco into the little state of **Colima** south of the Río Cihuatlán and continues to the city of **Manzanillo** about 35 miles south of Barra de Navidad.

The Manzanillo area is confusing to the first-time visitor. From the airport to the downtown area, there's about 25 miles of seaside highway meandering through a hodge-podge of beaches, hotels and restaurants, with no real center. You pass through the small town of **Santiago** on Bahía de Santiago and, to the west, two tropically vegetated peninsulas—**Santiago** and **Juluapán**—both built up for the tourist trade. Farther along the highway there's a turnoff for the hotel-studded **Las Brisas** tourist zone, marked by a concrete sailboat in a *glorieta* (traffic circle). To the south, a stately white sailfish monument in another traffic circle commemorates Manzanillo's reputation as "Sailfish Capital of Mexico."

Bearing right toward El Centro, you enter the bustling warehouse district and port zone of the **San Pedrito** area. More port activity surrounds downtown Manzanillo, site of the Mexican Pacific Coast's biggest and busiest harbor. Sailors swarm through the streets, eyeing the local señoritas who promenade through the *zócalo* (public square), called **Jardín Alvaro Obregón,** on Avenida Morelos. This palm-filled plaza, famed for its old poinciana tree, is lined with wrought-iron benches and globe lights and features a fancy bandstand where musicians play on holidays.

SOUTH OF MANZANILLO TO PLAYA AZUL

Heading south of town, Mexico 200 degenerates into vicious potholes alongside the smelly **Laguna de Cuyutlán**, where a big thermoelectrical plant spews out plumes of smoke from a distant shore. Past this area, the road smoothes out again, with thick avenues of palms welcoming you back into the tropics. **Cuyutlán**, a small town about 20 miles south of Manzanillo (take marked turnoff from Mexico 200), is the site of the famous "Green Wave," a monstrous 30-footer that rolls up from the open sea to crash on the shore every spring.

An inland side trip through the mountains on Mexico 110, which meets the coast road just south of Cuyutlán, brings you to the 450-year-old capital city of **Colima**. This colonial town, about 50 miles northeast of Manzanillo, contains a 19th-century cathedral, the **Museo de las Culturas de Occidente** (Museum of Western Culture) (Calle 27 de Septiembre and Calle Niños Héroes), full of pre-Columbian artifacts, and an **antique car museum** (Calle Belisarío Domínguez 80), which houses more than 350 classic autos dating back to the early 1900s. About 25 miles north of Colima rise the misty peaks of its twin volcanoes, **El Nevado** (extinct and snow-topped) and **El Fuego** or Volcán de Colima (still rumbling and smoking), standing guard over Lago Carrizalillo.

South of the Mexico 110 intersection with the coast road, you pass through the busy agricultural town of **Tecomán**, the world's largest producer of oil-of-lemon extract and home to many copra-processing plants. When you cross the Río Coahuayana just north of Boca de Apiza, you leave the state of Colima and enter **Michoacán**.

Until 1985, this next part of Mexico 200 was nonexistent. Now 150 miles of freshly laid highway cut through mountains and jungle, crisscrossed by dozens of bridges and plagued in the rainy season with landslides. Just south of **San Juan de Alima**, a tropical beach town, a cliff-side *mirador* (lookout site) peers out high over Michoacán's virgin sands and whitecap-frosted sea. More than a dozen quaint fishing villages with hidden beaches dot the coastline down to the seaside resort of **Playa Azul.**

IXTAPA-ZIHUATANEJO

Still on Mexico 200, some 75 miles south of Playa Azul, sit the popular twin resorts of Ixtapa-Zihuatanejo. En route you pass **La Presa Morelos**, a big hydroelectric power plant harnessing the force of the Río Balsas and separating the state of Michoacán from **Guerrero.**

Passing more tiny seaside villages, you arrive in the charming old fishing town of **Zihuatanejo**, set on one of Mexico's most superb little bays, Bahía de Zihuatanejo. At the entrance to town is the **Plaza de Toros**, where bullfights are held in the high season. The hub of town is the **municipal pier** extending into the bay, a pleasant place to stroll when the fishermen bring in their afternoon catch. From this pier, the *Yate Fandango Zihua* leaves on bay cruises.

The town's ten square blocks of cobbled alleys, beachside cafés and small hotels can be explored in a few hours. About the only local claim to culture is the diminutive **Museo Arqueológico** (Avenida Cinco de Mayo; 4-23-43), where a potpourri of ancient and popular art fills two rooms.

South of town is a zone of cliffside hotels along marvelous **Playa La Ropa** and **Playa La Madera**. For a good overview of this whole area, drive along **Camino de Cerro del Almacén**, which winds up around the back of Zihuatanejo into the northern hills.

All the highrise luxury hotels are outside the village, confined to a long, open beach five miles north at **Ixtapa**. This made-from-scratch resort, initiated circa 1975, is a glorified American colony of wide boulevards and shopping malls. The government did a good thing to keep the sprawl in Ixtapa and preserve Zihuatanejo's quaint intimacy. The village's population, however, which has swelled from 5,000 to 38,000 since the mid-1970s, reflects inevitable growth and change ahead.

ZIHUATANEJO TO PIE DE LA CUESTA

Mexico 200 winds south through tropical terrain for about 150 miles toward Acapulco. A **lookout point** just past a spot called **Cayacal** provides a glorious view of the ocean and miles of empty beaches. Then the highway heads south over the Río Coyuca, through the town of Coyuca de Benítez and onto the turnoff for **Pie de la Cuesta**.

This steamy tropical fishing village is the home of the most ardent, dramatic **sunsets** on the Mexican Riviera. Its sun-bleached **cemetery**, thatched-roofed houses and massive beach guarded by mist-soaked mountains all contribute to the primitive ease that reigns here, just eight miles north of traffic-jammed Acapulco.

Aside from the sunsets, Pie de la Cuesta's premier attraction is palm-lined **Laguna Coyuca**, one of Mexico's most gorgeous lagoons. Covered skiffs can be hired anywhere in the village to cruise its waters. Rich in catfish, shrimp and bite-sized oysters clinging to the mangrove roots along its banks, the lagoon also nourishes an abundance of ducks, herons, pelicans, blackbirds and tropical swallows that soar above the wake of your boat to snap up small fish.

Floating among Laguna Coyuca's lilac water hyacinths are two sizable islands. **Isla Presidio** is rumored to contain an ancient Indian city buried in its center. Arrange to stop for lunch at inhabited **Isla Montosa**, named for its owner, a vigorous hombre said to have seven or eight wives. Complete your journey at the seaside village of **La Barra**, where the freshwater lagoon meets the salty, raging sea.

ACAPULCO

The eight-mile ride from Pie de la Cuesta to Acapulco follows sinuous, steep cliffsides with stunning views of the coastline. At night the mountains shimmer with distant lights and echo with peculiar bird calls that sound like someone whistling for a ride.

The northern approach to Acapulco, potholes notwithstanding, is just beautiful. Palms and trees with flaming blossoms frame the road. Before you, densely populated mountains ripple into a valley, and the city's lights become a twinkling galaxy by night. The traffic intensifies as you wind down into town, and your driving skills will be constantly tested by ruthless buses, suicidal taxis and oblivious pedestrians who stroll in the roadway amidst the screeching rubber.

Acapulco proper begins in the old westerly **Caleta** district, a peninsula of vintage hotels and older residential neighborhoods. Here you'll find the **Plaza Caletilla** (behind Playa Caleta, 5-85-40), where bullfights are held every Sunday. This area and **El Centro**, farther north around the *zócalo*, form the original nucleus of Acapulco that existed before the city exploded into a hedonist's happy hunting ground.

The main drag connecting the old town with the newer hotel strip is called **Avenida Costera Miguel Alemán**, or simply the **Costera**. This flashy, ten-mile-long boulevard follows the waterfront from the Caleta area into the highrise hotel zone. Beyond **Glorieta Diana**, a traffic circle which contains a bronze statue of Diana the Huntress, you'll encounter the heart of the tourist strip. At night, the Costera glitters like a million cheap baubles.

The Costera ends at a naval base, and the road continues southeast as the cliffside **Carretera Escénica** (Scenic Highway). This is a new boom area of boutiques, nightclubs, restaurants and some of the fanciest hotels in town—evidence that Acapulco continues to expand as it has since the 1940s. Along this drive you'll see the breathtaking bay at **Puerto Marqués**, the palatial Aztec-style **Acapulco Princess** and its more genteel cousin, the **Pierre Marqués** next door. The road—Mexico 200 again—goes on to the airport, secluded Laguna Tres Palos and fishing villages south to Puerto Escondido.

For sightseeing in town, one of the best-loved spectacles is the daring nightly sport of **La Quebrada cliff divers**. These young Mexicans, some bearing torches, plunge 150-feet into a chasm known as La Quebrada where the in-rushing tide forms a narrow channel of water. The show, held several times a day, is free on the public terrace next to the Hotel Mirador. Ringside seats are sold at the Mirador's La Perla Restaurant-Bar (La Quebrada 74, Caleta district; 3-11-55).

Offshore from nearby Playa Caleta is little **Isla La Roqueta,** an uninhabited island in the bay offering excellent snorkeling and swimming. The hilltop lighthouse provides a stunning view of Bahía de Acapulco. Glassbot-

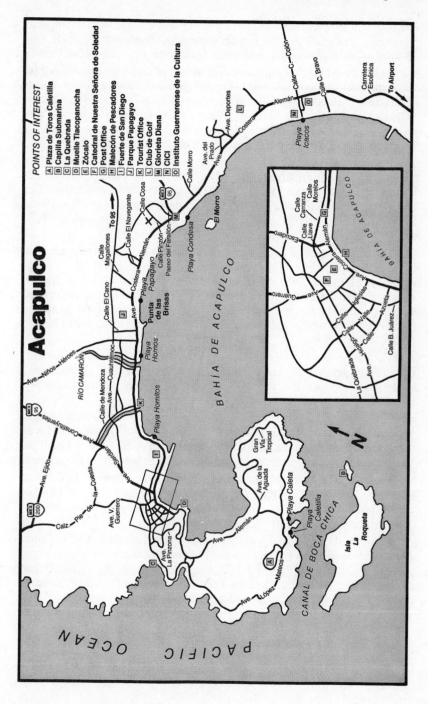

tom boats for Roqueta leave from the pier at Playa Caleta (3-00-66) regularly, making the circuit past the **capilla submarina** (submarine chapel), with an underwater statue of La Virgen de Guadalupe near the island.

Bahía de Acapulco **pleasure cruises** are offered by the ACA Tiki Catamaran & Supper Club (4-61-40) and Bonanza/Fiesta Cabaret Yachts (2-20-55), located at the Fiesta-Bonanza pier on the Avenida Costera Miguel Alemán; the less expensive *Yate Hawaiano* (Yate Hawaiano pier on the Avenida Costera Miguel Alemán; 2-40-11); and the *Trimaran Kon-Tiki* (pier below El Fuerte de San Diego; 4-65-70).

Farther west, where the Costera begins, Acapulco's fountain-filled *zócalo*, or **Plaza Juan Alvarez**, faces the sportfishing piers. At the foot of the square stands one of Mexico's most curious churches, the mosquelike blue-and-gold **Catedral de Nuestra Señora de Soledad,** built in the 1940s. This whole neighborhood, with family hotels and inexpensive cafés, retains a spicy Old Mexico flavor that's a treat to experience.

Dominating a hillside northeast of the *zócalo* on the Costera, the pentagonal-shaped **El Fuerte de San Diego** (Fort San Diego) (Calle Morelos and Playa Hornitos; 3-91-32) was built in 1616 to ward off pirate attacks. An earthquake destroyed the first fort in 1776. The current one was erected that same year. Inside, the fort houses the **Museo Histórico de Acapulco** (admission fee), where you can get a full rundown on the colorful history of old Acapulco.

Farther up the Costera, cool and shady **Parque Papagayo** (Avenida Costera Miguel Alemán and Avenida Cuauhtémoc), a well-groomed park on the bay, covers a full city block with botanical gardens, restaurant, aviary, artisans store, amusement park and small bullring.

Six dramatic fountains distinguish the entrance to the **Centro de Convenciones** (Avenida Costera Miguel Alemán; 4-70-50), with its Mayan decor and enormous stone sculpture. This modern open-air structure hosts theatrical and musical events, but simply strolling through it is a pleasure.

Down the Costera, the modest **Instituto Guerrerense de la Cultura** (Guerrero Institute of Culture) (Avenida Costera Miguel Alemán 7834; 4-23-90) holds forth on state culture, with an art gallery, small museum of Guerrero artifacts and gift shop on its premises.

Children will relish a day at the aquatic amusement park, **CICI** (Centro Internacional de Convivencia Infantil) (Avenida Costera Miguel Alemán and Calle Cristóbal Colón; 4-19-70; admission), including an assortment of water toboggans, a bullet-fast water slide, swimming pools, aquariums, crocodile lakes and a dolphin-and-seal show.

Shopping

The best resort shopping in Mexico can be found along the Mexican Riviera. Shop comparatively—the big hotels and tourist zones mark up items far more than the downtown markets.

MAZATLÁN SHOPPING

Shopping is excellent in Mazatlán.

The **Mercado Central** (Central Market), bounded by Calle Aquiles Serdán and Calle Benito Juárez, spans a full city block in downtown Mazatlán. Besides fruits and vegetables, you'll find inexpensive baskets, blankets, jewelry and ceramics.

The most expensive shopping area is the six-block **Zona Dorada** in northern Mazatlán. Let's start at the north end in the Spanish-style **Mazatlán Arts and Crafts Center** (Avenida Rodolfo T. Loaiza across from Hotel Los Arcos; 3-50-22). This mall bills itself as Mexico's largest shopping complex for handicrafts.

Next door in El Mercado is **Joyería Finissima**, with a nice selection of inexpensive jewelry. At **Plaza Maya** (Avenida Rodolfo T. Loaiza 411) you'll feel like you're exploring an ancient Mayan site while browsing through the native crafts.

Nearby is the monstrous, two-story **Sea Shell City** (Avenida Rodolfo T. Loaiza 407; 3-13-01). With hundreds of varieties of shell items, this store justifiably calls itself a museum. An immense upstairs fountain is composed entirely of shells in marine-life designs.

Two warehouses of Mexican souvenirs just doors away from one another are **The Tequila Tree** (Avenida Rodolfo T. Loaiza and Avenida Camarón Sábalo; 3-53-23) and the open-air **Mercado Viejo Mazatlán** (Avenida Rodolfo T. Loaiza 303; 3-63-63), which carry an enormous supply of clothes, curios and ceramics.

For a varied inventory, drop in at **Mr. Indio de Mazatlán** (Avenida Rodolfo T. Loaiza 311; 3-49-23), carrying brass, silver, decoupage, porcelain, ceramic and leather goods.

Get your fill of sombreros and straw goods at **The Basket** (Avenida Rodolfo T. Loaiza across from Hotel Playa Mazatlán; 3-00-31).

Two good, expensive jewelry stores in the same vicinity are **Artes de México** and **El Azteca** (also known as **Pardo's**, Avenida Rodolfo T. Loaiza and Centro Comercial de Rubino, Lote 7; 3-65-30).

For jazzy beachwear, I recommend **Designer's Bazaar** (two locations: a big store on Avenida Rodolfo T. Loaiza and a smaller one in the shopping arcade at the Hotel Playa Mazatlán). Both stock bright cotton dresses, skirts, skimpy tops and high fashion outfits by Vercellino Designs.

The leather goods section of the strip, at the southern end, features two excellent shops: **Rey Solomón** (Avenida Rodolfo T. Loaiza 201; 3-90-44), where you can find lined leather jackets, wallets and skirts; and **El Canelo** (Avenida Rodolfo T. Loaiza and Avenida Camarón Sábalo; 3-24-14, also downtown at Calle Ángel Flores 700; 1-21-81), with a great variety of purses, wallets, belts and specialty items.

For the freshest lobster, go down past the end of the sportfishing docks to the **Sociedad Cooperativa de Productos Pesquería "Eva Samano de López Mateos."** This lobster-fishing cooperative sells its catch for unbelievably low prices.

SAN BLAS SHOPPING

Basic necessities, like all-important bug spray, can be found around the main plaza. The **Mercado Central** (Avenida Batallón, San Blas) stocks fish, fruits, vegetables, even cheesecake and milkshakes. On the other side of the plaza, the **Huarachería de San Blas** (Calle Juárez) sells sandals and beachwear.

PUERTO VALLARTA SHOPPING

This is a shopper's Shangri-La—some say it has the best resort shopping in Mexico. The main shopping zones are along the *malecón* (Paseo Díaz Ordaz), Calle Juárez, Isla Río Cuale, Calle Insurgentes and Calle Lázaro Cárdenas, Calle Olas Altas, and in the boutiques in every big hotel. There's also a big **Artesania's Flea Market** at the north end of town near the cruise ship docks.

Starting along Paseo Díaz Ordaz, the **Plaza Malecón** (corner of Calle 31 de Octubre) is one of the bigger downtown shopping centers, selling leather goods, resort clothes and jewelry. The well-known **Huarachería Lety** chain features sandals in all colors.

At the other end of the *malecón* close to the Río Cuale is **El Pueblo Viejo de Vallarta** (Calle Morelos and Calle Agustín Rodríguez), a hacienda-style mall packed with craft boutiques.

The **Instituto de la Artesanía Jalisciense** (Calle Juárez and Calle Zaragoza; 2-13-01) is another big emporium presenting art objects from all over the state of Jalisco.

Not far away, near the new bridge over the Río Cuale, is the **Mercado Central** (Calle Miramar and Calle Agustín Rodríguez). This busy hive of open stalls is jammed with merchandise, from beach towels to wooden Aztec calendars, and vendors who are happy to haggle.

You could spend a whole day on **Isla Río Cuale**, wandering among the many shops where bargaining is recommended. Two exceptional ones are the **Katy Boutique** (across from the Franzi Café), with a smart selection of women's cotton resortwear; and **Gallery of Masks**, which presents startling wooden faces carved by Indians under the influence of peyote.

If you'd like to buy a beautiful handmade Mexican guitar, drop in at **Guitarras de Paracho** (Calle Libertad 282); for ceramic works of art in the Spanish style visit **Cosas y Cosas** (Calle Libertad 285; 2-69-60).

For unique ladies designer clothes, visit **Max**, at two locations (Calle Juárez 487; 2-34-75, and Calle Morelos 582; 9-13-22). The inventory includes oversized men's shirts, animal print pants, one-of-a-kind T-shirts and rough-hewn leather belts.

Probably the best selection of women's cotton clothes, in a rainbow of tropical colors, can be found at **Sucesos Boutique** (Calle Libertad and Calle Hidalgo; 2-10-02).

At **Visiones** (Calle Rodolfo Gómez 122; 2-19-82), you can find posters and marvelous reproductions of pre-Columbian pottery.

Two popular headquarters for inexpensive casual cottons, like jeans and workshirts, are **Ruben Torres** (Paseo Díaz Ordaz 592; 2-49-49) and **ACA Joe** (Paseo Díaz Ordaz 588), just steps apart.

Add a gleam of silver to your attire with very reasonably priced Taxco jewelry at **San Juan de Vallarta** (Calle Lázaro Cárdenas 271; 2-50-70).

Veryka II (Calle Ignacio Luis Vallarta and Calle Lázaro Cárdenas) has beautifully displayed weavings, ceramics and various objets d'art.

Since Puerto Vallarta is a magnet for artists, it's no surprise the town has had a boom in galleries. The biggest, oldest and best in contemporary Mexican art is **Galería Uno** (Calle Morelos 561; 2-09-08), which features bronzes, prints and oils by masters like Ruffino Tomayo, Francisco Zuniga and Manuel Lepe (Puerto Vallarta's best-known artist). The same owners run a smaller gallery, selling more decorative art, called **La Otra Galería** (Plaza Malecón, Paseo Díaz Ordaz; 2-47-35).

There are also several good folk art galleries. At **Sergio Bustamante** (Calle Juárez, between Calle Zaragoza and Calle Guerrero), you enter a fantasyland of bronze and ceramic animals from the whimsical studios of the Mexican artist for whom the shop is named.

The most magical craft shop in town, **Olinala, Galería de Artes Indigenas** (★) (Calle Lázaro Cárdenas 274; 2-49-95), is really more a museum. It specializes in vivid beaded masks and bowls made by the Huichol Indians, who have been crafting these items for 400 years. There are also wooden masks, lacquered boxes, opal and obsidian turtles and psychedelic yarn paintings. A nice service here is the descriptive literature given out about the works of art. A treat for folk-art lovers.

BARRA DE NAVIDAD SHOPPING

Barra de Navidad has quite a few T-shirt shops along **Calle López Legaspi** and stands selling coconut candies, sunhats and sandals. In nearby Melaque, the *mercado* area has shell jewelry and beachwear.

MANZANILLO SHOPPING

The Manzanillo area has relatively slim-pickin's for shoppers. The best places to pick up souvenirs are in **El Centro**.

Some of the better shops include **El Caracol** (Calle Juárez 33), a shell-oriented shop just off the *zócalo*; **Artesanías Nilba's Bazaar** (Calle Juárez 20; 2-22-36), a larger curio shop with ironwood sculptures and some leather; **Bazar María Lidia** (Avenida México 69; 2-25-65), with inexpensive onyx chess sets, windchimes and embroidered clothes. The **Mercado Central** (Calle Cuauhtémoc) concentrates mostly on fruits and vegetables. A breezy downtown mall called **Pasaje Oscarana** (between Calle Juárez and Avenida Morelos) carries clothing, books and shells.

In the Santiago area, there's the **Plaza Santiago** shopping mall (Mexico 200, between Manzanillo and Santiago), with a few boutiques. **Boutique D'Mario** (Local 8 across from Banco Mexicano Sómex, and another shop at Calle Balvino Dávalos 25 in El Centro) carries beachwear for men and women. **Boutique Grivel** (3-09-29) is a spacious shop full of jewelry, clothes, brass and blankets.

Across the street is **Conchas y Caracolas** (3-02-60), with an incredible array of items made from sea shells, as well as pieces of silver jewelry.

For a more elegant selection of handicrafts and clothes, try the little shopping mall in **Las Hadas** (Península de Santiago). Especially nice artwork and jewelry can be found at **Galería de Artesiles** (3-00-0).

IXTAPA-ZIHUATANEJO SHOPPING

Between the burgeoning boutiques in Zihuatanejo and the explosion of malls in Ixtapa, you have some heavy sprees ahead.

ZIHUATANEJO SHOPPING

Starting near Zihuatanejo's *malecón*, you'll find exquisite sarapes, hammocks, rugs, shawls and Zapotec weavings at **La Zapoteca** (Paseo del Pescador 9; 4-23-73). Another good store in this same building, specializing in masks from all over Guerrero, is **El Jumil** (Paseo del Pescador 9; 4-23-73). Right in front of El Jumil stands an open-air **shell market** on Playa Principal.

For designer beachwear, **La Fuente** (Calle Ejido and Calle Cuauhtémoc; 4-21-31) opens its thick double doors to a cool world of high fashion tropical attire and designer jewelry.

One of the best silver shops in town is **Alberto's** (two locations: Calle Cuauhtémoc 12 and Calle Cuauhtémoc 15; 4-25-51). You get a wide selection—rings, collars, bracelets—designed by Alberto himself with help from his seven children. He also does custom designs.

Right across the street is versatile **Sterling Silver** (Calle Cuauhtémoc 29; 4-31-24), with silver-plated gift items plus jewelry. For lovely silver jewelry at the most reasonable prices, visit **Pancho's** (Calle Nicolás Bravo 31; 4-39-76).

Two all-in-one shopping markets packed with stalls full of Mexican handicrafts include the **Flea Market** (Calle Ejido) and **Mercado Municipal Centro Artesanal** (Calle Catalina González).

IXTAPA SHOPPING

In Ixtapa, every hotel has its own boutiques. *Centros comerciales* (shopping centers) are sprouting like magic beanstalks along Paseo Ixtapa. These malls include Plaza IxpaMar, Los Fuentes, Los Patios, La Puerta and Los Arcos, built in nouveau-colonial or pueblo style, with hundreds of shops and fountains.

In the Plaza IxpaMar, **Ole** and **Calvin Klein** stock good men's and women's beachwear, and **El Amanecer** (4-23-70) carries Mexican folk art. In Los Patios, fashionable cotton outfits for him and her fill the spacious **Limoni-Bob Ore**, whose owner designs many of the clothes. Las Fuentes features a wonderful glassware shop called **Derfer**, selling handblown plates and wine glasses in a rainbow of hues. La Puerta shopping center offers excellent beachwear, jewelry and leather at **Boutique La Gaviota** (4-29-34) and **Aggie's Boutique** (4-30-25), elegant Mexican handicrafts at **Florence** (4-24-62) and good silver jewelry at **Creaciones Alberto's** (4-37-91). In nearby Los Arcos, get your fill of hip, bright Italian clothes at **Fiorucci.**

ACAPULCO SHOPPING

You can spend a fortune in Acapulco without half trying. The Costera is one unbroken line of sleek shops; every big hotel comes with its own private shopping complex; and even the beaches swarm with the temptations of roving vendors. Starting on the old side of town and moving southeast:

In the Caleta area, pueblo-style **Taxco El Viejo** (La Quebrada 830; 2-49-18) has silver galore.

El Centro around the *zócalo* is especially rich in jewelry stores. Several good ones are **Margarita** (Calle de la Llave 2; 2-52-40), by far the most lavish and most overpriced; the more reasonable and friendly **Platería Perlita** (Calle Jesús Carranza 12; 2-00-14); and the **Joyería Roberto** (Calle Jesús Carranza 12; 2-02-26), which offers discounts.

There's a great variety of jewelry, leather, shell knickknacks and hammocks at the **Mercado de Artesanía Noa Noa**, a sprawling bazaar on the Costera across from Playa Hornos.

Ready for more? Wander up the street along the canal to the labyrinthine **Mercado Central** (Calle Diego Urtado de Mendoza), a wonderland of sandals, mangoes, tropical fabrics, pottery, birds and fresh flowers.

If you wander into Parque Papagayo, stop by the big cool handicrafts market called **LADA** (Los Artesanos de Acapulco) at the Calle Sebastián El Cano side of the park (5-09-18).

A glittering split-level mall in front of the Acapulco Plaza Hotel along the Costera, the **Galería Acapulco Plaza**, includes familiar names like **Ocean Pacific, 10/10 Gallery** and **Calvin Klein** (with an emphasis on tropical sportswear). You'll find gorgeous designer dresses in silks and rayons, plus smart men's beachwear, at **Boutique Marietta** (5-98-61)—a great place for an eye-popping disco outfit.

Upstaging the Galería, though, is the new, modern **Plaza Bahía**, with more than 80 shops. This is where Acapulco residents do their shopping.

For moderately priced beachwear for men, women and children, the chain shop **Emil** has more than a dozen outlets in the Acapulco area. **Emil Centro** (Avenida Costera Miguel Alemán and Calle Escudero; 3-20-31) has just about everything you need for beach-bumming.

Just southeast of Glorieta Diana, another hot shopping zone begins. **Marbella Shopping Plaza** contains several shops selling sportswear as well as a contemporary sporting goods store.

If you like that famous polo logo, you can find all-cotton casual wear for about half the stateside cost at **Ralph Lauren** (Avenida Costera Miguel Alemán; 4-33-25).

Across the street is a ceramic and bronze zoo of storybook animals in all sizes from **La Colección de Sergio Bustamante** (Avenida Costera Miguel Alemán 711-B; 4-49-92).

You'll receive wonderful service along with a great choice of fruit-colored Girosol designer clothes at **Armando's Boutique** (Avenida Costera Miguel Alemán 144; 4-49-87). A kickier line of beachwear, including T-shirts, jogging outfits and bikinis, is sold at **Cocaine** (Avenida Costera Miguel Alemán 4055; 4-77-30), in front of Hotel Presidente.

Boutique windows flash with elegant but low-cost silver up and down the Costera. **La Paloma** (Avenida Costera Miguel Alemán and Calle Morro; 4-32-38) is home to a particularly smart collection of jewelry and gifts. A few doors down, **Platería Tlaxco** (Avenida Costera Miguel Alemán 1999-5; 4-89-27) lays out the goods in blinding rows, warehouse style. **Joyería Morse** (Avenida Costera Miguel Alemán 3845; 4-76-63) has a classy spread and is willing to bargain, and nearby **Van Cleef** (Avenida Costera Miguel Alemán 999-3; 4-10-21) sparkles with stylish earrings, plus an unbelievable pure gold chess set.

A couple of shopping malls surround Jackie 'O and Cat's Disco along the Costera. **Centro Comercial El Patio** is a collection of Old Mexico-style shops handling beachwear, Gucci designer bags, and naughty lacy lingerie. **Acapulco Gold Jewelry Factory** (4-54-89) provides friendly service, custom-made pieces and loose gems.

If you forgot your aerobics outfits at home, you can pick up a new one at **Dancin' Acapulco** (Avenida Costera Miguel Alemán 114-1; 4-78-01). Prefer to gaze at art? One of the city's most interesting galleries is **Esteban** (Avenida Costera Miguel Alemán 2010; 4-11-75), combining high-class Mexican crafts with fine art from all over the world.

No place can rival the glitter of **Felipe Zamora** (★) (Carretera Escénica; 4-34-10). Strung outside with dangling mirrors, this big hillside shop specializes in wonderful tropical hanging lamps made in a workshop behind the store. Every item here is unique: religious colonial art, tree-root tables and thronelike chairs carved with animals.

One of the ritziest shopping centers is the pueblo-style **La Vista** (Carretera Escénica next to Fantasy Disco), with restaurants, jewelry stores and clothing shops.

Nightlife

While exploring beaches all day, save some energy for the night. The Mexican Riviera seldom sleeps.

MAZATLÁN NIGHTLIFE

Discoing is Mazatlán's favorite evening recreation. By far the biggest night spot, with waiting lines on weekends, is **El Caracol Tango Palace** (Avenida Camarón Sábalo, Hotel El Cid; 3-33-33). This three-level disco, connected by spiral staircases to simulate the look of a snail shell, has five bars and a mammoth dance floor. It's almost uncomfortably cavernous; I got lost in there. Cover.

The hot new rage is a Disneyesque castle called **Valentino's Disco Club** (Avenida Camarón Sábalo; 4-17-17), perched on Punta Camarón. Dance on a plexiglass floor to the natural rhythms of surf and the artificial flash of lasers and strobes. Cover.

Sophisticated **Fandangos** (Avenida Camarón Sábalo 333-26; 3-73-63) is more upscale than most, with a red carpet and canopy leading to the door. Video screens and framed rock idols brighten the decor. Cover.

Another star on the disco scene is **Frankie Oh!** (Avenida del Mar 1300; 2-58-00), known for its laser shows. Large video screens and a hanging airplane hover over the dance floor. Cover.

The most stylish true nightclub—for straight sit-down entertainment and cocktails—is **La Guitarra** (Hotel Hacienda, Avenida del Mar and Calle Flamingos; 2-70-00). This basement club provides good live Mexican music and a variety of comedians and singers, attracting an older crowd of Mazatlán locals. A good grasp of Spanish helps. Cover.

For raucous late-night revelry on the beach, head for **Joe's Oyster Bar** (Hotel Los Sábalos, Calle Rodolfo Loaiza; 3-53-33). There's no inhibition and lots of spontaneity—more dancing occurs on tables than on the floor. Cover.

Relax with an exotic drink at sophisticated, hip **Chiquita Banana Beach Club** (Hotel Camino Real, Punta Sábalo; 3-11-11). Set in a series of chic bamboo-and-thatched huts overlooking the beach, the club features live tropical music, jazz and dancing.

SAN BLAS NIGHTLIFE

San Blas may not swing, but there is some entertainment to be found at night.

The dimly lit tavern attached to the **Hotel El Bucañero** (Calle Juárez 75; 5-01-01), enlivened with Mexican ballads, can get downright rowdy with singalongs, whistling and passionate outbursts—a great glimpse of Mexican sentimentality. Next door a youngish crowd gathers at **Lafitte Discotheque** (Calle Juárez 75; 5-01-01), a dank little hangout where occasional brawls break out. Cover.

A better dance hall, with live music and a spacious dance floor, is **Los Ponchos** (Avenida H. Batallon just past El Marino Inn; 5-03-63). It's a barn of a place frequented by the town's racier crowd.

For quieter surroundings, try the nice upstairs lounge of McDonald's Restaurant, **Mike's Place** (Calle Juárez 105). There's a balcony and live music during the high season.

Another upstairs lounge is **Mirador** in the Posada del Rey (Calle Campeche; 5-01-23), featuring satellite television and occasional live music.

PUERTO VALLARTA NIGHTLIFE

Puerto Vallarta has no dull nights.

One of the liveliest watering holes, where both locals and visitors fuel up for the evening, is little **Andale** (Calle Olas Altas 425; 2-10-54). People-watching crowds jam the semicircular bar, and owner Ángel Maranón of Spain is a warm, witty host sure to make you feel at home.

Brazz (Calle Galeana and Calle Morelos; 2-03-24) reportedly has the best mariachi music in town. This big attractive bar, which includes a restaurant, is arranged around a stage where an 11-man group blasts out Mexican classics audible up and down the *malecón*.

More relaxed live music prevails at **Zapata** (Paseo Díaz Ordaz 522; 2-47-48), an upstairs restaurant-bar with Mexican Revolution decor overlooking the *malecón*.

You can hear live jazz during the high season at the **Franzi Café** (Isla Río Cuale Local 33) on the banks of the Río Cuale and at **Mogambo Restaurant-Bar** (Paseo Díaz Ordaz 644; 2-34-76) on the *malecón*. Mogambo, with animal-skin-and-Persian-rug decor, has a grand piano and bass duet playing all year round.

Prefer a little salsa and samba? There's live tropical music nightly at the Polynesian-flavored **Mau-Mau** (Calle Corona 1; 2-52-65). This comfy upstairs club, with flower-print easy chairs and a lively dance floor, is a popular Mexican hangout.

The best lobby-bar entertainment graces the **Plaza Vallarta Hotel** (Playa Las Glorias; 2-43-60). In a glossy living room-style salon, a bilingual guitarist sings heart-melting ballads and Broadway hits that give Julio Iglesias a run for his money.

Everybody should attend a Mexican fiesta at least once. Many major hotels, like the **Hotel Playa de Oro** (Paseo de las Garzas 1; 2-03-48), host a Mexican night once a week. The most extensive (and expensive) is at **La Iguana** (Calle Lázaro Cárdenas 311; 2-01-05), twice a week. The mediocre Mexican buffet is offset by an open bar serving margaritas that make you stagger. Held in an outdoor arena strung with lanterns, the rousing show combines colorful folk dancing, a lariat act, the Mexican hat-dance, piñata-breaking and fireworks.

Discomania also reigns in Puerto Vallarta, from one end of town to the other. Celebrities tend to show up at the hillside **Capriccio** (Calle Púlpito 170; 2-15-93), one of the oldest and most popular spots. It's comfortable, with sofas and low stools, and excels in special effects: fire-engine whistles, a digital display unit flashing gibberish and fireworks outside the windows toward the wee hours. Cover. The elegant **Christine**, in the Krystal Vallarta Hotel (Avenida del las Garzas; 2-14-59), sports the latest in sound and light effects.

The chic **Sundance** (Calle Lázaro Cárdenas 329; 2-22-96) combines a night at the movies with the disco beat. It's the only disco I've ever seen with a built-in theatre projecting films while the action throbs around the dance floor—and the two don't interfere. Cover.

Along the *malecón*, slick new **Ciro's** (Paseo Díaz Ordaz 852; 2-49-87) features sci-fi lighting and multilevel seating, with pale tree branches against the dark walls. Cover.

My personal favorite is the glamorous **Friday López** (Hotel Fiesta Americana, Carretera al Aeropuerto, Km. 2.5; 2-20-10) on the north side of town. With both a live band and canned disco, this club offers some musical variety plus dancing that spills out all over the aisles. The palatial ceiling and arched windows flash with lights, balloons, sirens, smoke machines and party streamers as the night progresses into delightful pandemonium. Cover.

BARRA DE NAVIDAD NIGHTLIFE

This area is mostly early-to-bed, with a smattering of night-owl haunts.

The double-identity **Mar y Tierra** (Avenida López de Legaspi; 7-00-28) transforms from daytime restaurant to evening disco with a Latin-western beat. Its two dance floors flank a circular bar, and its bamboo back door opens onto the sea.

Aladino's Disco Club Internacional (Avenida Mazatlán; 7-00-18) attracts all ages. This *palapa*-roofed dancehall-in-the-round smells of spilled beer and vibrates to the pulse of rock, tropical and mariachi tunes. Weekend cover.

MANZANILLO NIGHTLIFE

The after-dark action here is mostly inside private resorts.

Socializing starts early at the 1950s-era **Bar Social** in El Centro (Calle Juárez 101). Locals crowd around the big round bar, with its red cash register and tireless television, for tasty *botanes* (snacks) of ceviche, guacamole and tacos with their afternoon drinks. Nights are quieter but still pleasant.

Bacho's Disco (Colonia Las Brisas, Avenida Lázaro Cárdenas Km. 2; 2-07-22) combines dancing and live entertainment, including Mexican comics and singers. Overlooking the beach, with low lighting and simple decor, Bacho's has a big local following. Cover.

More ambience and higher prices come with the flashing lights, balloons and videos at **Cartouche Disco** in Las Hadas (Península de Santiago; 3-00-00). If you're not a hotel guest, call for a pass. Cover.

Another resort nightspot, **Disco Club Fantasy** at Club Maeva (Mexico 200, between Manzanillo and Miramar; 3-05-95), has amphitheatre-style seating and is packed to the rafters during the high season. Non-guests should enter near the water slides after 10 p.m. Cover.

A spot that's popular on the disco scene, especially with the young set, is **Enjoy Disco** (Carretera Manzanillo–Aeropuerto, Km. 16.).

PLAYA AZUL–LÁZARO CÁRDENAS NIGHTLIFE

Playa Azul's nightlife consists of village musicians strumming their hearts out and serenading the moon. Nearby Lázaro Cárdenas has more action. **El Ejectivo** (Calle Nicolás Bravo 475; 2-03-71) is one of the fanciest clubs, with disco music and a live show, while **El Túnel** (Calle Matamoros 508; 2-09-13), in the Hotel Internacional, is a true strobe-lit disco, attracting young flashdancers. Both have cover charges.

IXTAPA-ZIHUATANEJO NIGHTLIFE

Ixtapa has the big glitter, Zihuatanejo has the coziness. Starting in the village, a relaxing nook for an after-dinner game of backgammon is **La Cabina del Capitán**, upstairs from La Mesa del Capitán Restaurant (Calle Nicolás Bravo 18; 4-20-27). This small, amber-lit bar was made from the cabin of an old galleon.

On the beach, lively **Bananas** (Paseo del Pescador, near the basketball court) is the place to hang out, watch the passers-by and enjoy the beat of rock music.

Another appealing downtown stop is **Gitano's** (Calle Cinco de Mayo and Calle Nicolás Bravo), set in an open-air garden with live band and dancing.

The most popular hangout in Zihuatanejo is **Coconuts** (Calle Agustín Ramírez 1; 4-25-18). Tucked inside white-brick walls and framed in palms and flowering trees, this old restaurant-patio bar attracts a mix of people, from surfers to movie stars. Open only during the high season.

South of town on Playa La Madera down winding stairs from the road, the cavelike **Disco Ibiza** (Carretera Playa La Ropa; 4-23-09) faces the sea with molded arches and a brisk little dance floor.

Across the street you'll find the romantic **Bay Club Bar & Grill** (Carretera Playa La Ropa), with a fantastic view of the town and the bay, as well as live dance music.

In Ixtapa, most hotels contain discos. Besides these, there are two standouts. Posh **Joy Disco** (Paseo Ixtapa and Paseo de las Garzas) features tiered seating around the sunken dance floor. Then there's the Star Wars of discos, **Christine** (Paseo Ixtapa, in the Hotel Krystal complex; 4-26-18), with the most spectacular light show on the entire Mexican Riviera. Computer-controlled flashers, lasers and celestial beams criss-cross the elegant club, which has three huge video screens. Even the dance floor blinks in an intricate grid like a computer chip. Dance in those rays and you'll feel like an instant celebrity. Cover charge at both.

To escape the hubbub, drop in next door at **Cheers** (Galerías Ixtapa). This lounge surrounds a television with padded booths where people watch movies and music videos. Casual and friendly.

ACAPULCO NIGHTLIFE

No city does it better than Acapulco after dark. The Costera lights up like Coney Island, people dress to the nines and the best nightlife in Mexico turns on, from transvestite shows to videotheques.

Start down around the *zócalo* at **Tabares y Las Ostras** (Plaza Juan Alvarez), a dark upstairs bar where bikini-clad waitresses spin around on roller skates while a pianist thumps out tunes.

Across from El Fuerte de San Diego, the **Restaurant Club Colonial** (Avenida Costera Miguel Alemán 130) presents a fine water-skiing show with human pyramids, clown shenanigans and barefoot skiing under speeding spotlights. Cover charge at restaurant or watch free from the harbor.

Across the street, near Hotel Las Hamacas, the Spanish-style **El Fuerte** (Avenida Costera Miguel Alemán 239; 2-61-61) features two flamboyant flamenco shows nightly. Cover.

The brightly lit **Restaurant-Bar Tropicana** (Avenida Costera Miguel Alemán) on Playa Hornos has the best open-air tropical dancing in town.

The big *palapa* roof vibrates with live salsa music, attracting a largely Mexican crowd. Meals also served.

A classier tropical joint, also with live salsa and a late-night comedy show, festive **Nina's** (Avenida Costera Miguel Alemán on Playa Condesa; 4-24-00) has all-night dancing under a balloon-encrusted ceiling and an open bar. Local hangout. Stiff cover charge.

Videos pop up in every bar, but probably the ultimate is **Cheers Videotheque** (Hotel Acapulco Ritz, Avenida Costera Miguel Alemán; 5-75-44), a smart new disco (one of the few with no cover) flashing with giant video screens and televisions. Big pick-up spot.

Two other lively spots on the Costera are **Disco Beach** (Playa Condesa), for discoing under the stars, and **Paradise** (Playa Condesa; 4-59-88), which swings with a live band, dancing waiters and patrons boogying in their bikinis.

Amid all the push-and-shove, **Pepe & Co.** (Calle Hernán Cortel, Playa El Morro; 5-20-51) on the beach, offers a relaxing sanctuary. The upstairs piano bar overlooking Playa El Morro couldn't be more romantic.

For children, there's **Grand Prix** (Calle Enrique Navigante, one block off the Costera; 4-67-89), a combination go-cart track, skating rink and video game center.

Don't miss the all-male revue at **Gallery Show Bar-Discotheque** (Avenida de los Deportes 11; 4-34-97), the best female impersonations I've ever seen. In extravagant costumes, these Mexican performers imitate top American and Latin stars with real finesse. Cover. The attached disco, **Peacock Alley,** is a flashy gay cruising ground.

The big-time discos, all on the southeastern side of town, are so numerous it's impossible to name them all. Most open late and don't come to life until midnight, then party 'til dawn. All charge a hefty cover, enforce a dress code (no jeans, shorts or sneakers at many), and sometimes turn away single guys but welcome single women and couples.

A quick rundown on your choices: Just before Glorieta Diana, you'll find **Cats** (Calle Juan de la Cosa 32; 4-72-35), an elegant spot, quieter and less crowded than most; **Midnight** (Calle V. Yáñez Pinzón 12; 4-82-95), lively, with a youngish crowd; and **Jackie 'O** (Centro Comercial El Patio, Avenida Costera Miguel Alemán; 4-82-95), small, somewhat intimate, pseudo-exclusive.

Near Glorieta Diana, there's **Eve** (Avenida Costera Miguel Alemán 115; 4-47-77), big and sophisticated, with a terrace behind the dance floor; and **Le Dôme** (Avenida Costera Miguel Alemán 4162; 4-11-90), an older disco-in-the-round specializing in wild parties. Most popular with the young set, is **News** (Avenida Costera Miguel Alemán 12; 4-59-02), where you can expect the latest in sound and light effects.

Toward the south end of the Costera are **Boccaccio's** (Avenida Costera Miguel Alemán 5040; 4-19-01), older and casinolike, a crowded yet romantic fiesta of mirrors; **Baby 'O** (Avenida Costera Miguel Alemán 22; 4-74-74), a chi-chi Acapulco institution resembling a cave, with outstanding light show, couples only; and **Magic** (Avenida Costera Miguel Alemán across from Baby 'O; 4-88-15), the most crowded in town, with exclusive entry attracting rich young locals.

I've saved the best until last. The highway heading south toward the airport takes you to cliffside **Fantasy** (Centro Comercial La Vista, Carretera Escénica; 4-67-27), a luxury disco with a fabulous view of Acapulco and a spectacular laser system that shoots beams across the bay.

Acapulco's red light district, **La Zona Roja**, between calles Agua Blanca and Malpaso, has its own seedy charm. You can see the dancing ladies take it all off at the **Tivoli** (Calle Malpaso) or you can join the tour buses that unload at the tamer **La Huerta** (Calle Malpaso; 2-01-18), a *palapa*-roofed disco where the girls browse for business in bikinis and animal-skin tights.

Mexican Riviera Addresses and Phone Numbers

MAZATLÁN
Bank—Bánamex, Avenida Camarón Sábalo, Zona Dorada, and at Calle Ángel Flores and Calle Benito Juárez, El Centro
Consulates—American Consulate, Circumnavigación 6 Poniente (5-22-05); Canadian Consulate, Calle Albatrós 705 (3-73-20)
English-speaking doctor—Dr. Gilberto Robles (1-29-17)
Hospital—Sanatorio Divinia Providencia, Calle Galeana Poniente 22 (2-40-11)
Laundry—Lavandería El Sábalo, Calle Ibís and Avenida Camarón Sábalo
Money Exchanges (Casas de Cambio)—Along Avenida Camarón Sábalo, Zona Dorado
Newsstand—Avenida Camarón Sábalo, kiosk in front of Bing's Ice Cream
Police—Calle Belisarío Domínguez (1-39-19)
Post Office—Calle Benito Juárez near Calle Ángel Flores, across from the *zócalo*
Tourist office—Avenida Rodolfo T. Loaiza 100 in Zona Dorada (3-25-45), in front of Hotel Los Sábalos

SAN BLAS
Bank—Bánamex, Calle Juárez 26
Hospital—Centro de Salud, Calzada Hildago (5-02-32)
Money Exchange (Casa de Cambio)—Calle Juárez and Avenida Batallón
Police—5-00-28
Tourist office—Presidencia Municipal, main plaza, 5-00-05

LA PEÑITA AND RINCÓN DE GUAYABITOS AREA
Bank—Bancomer, Avenida Emiliano Zapata 22, La Peñita
Hospital—Hospital Escuela, Dr. Reynaldo Saucedo, Calle África in San Francisco (south of Rincón de Guayabitos)
Laundry—LavaSol, Calle Cristóbal Colón Oriente, La Peñita
Police—in Compostela, nearest big town to the north (7-04-91)
Post Office—Plaza Cívica, Avenida Sol Nuevo, Rincón de Guayabitos; Avenida Emiliano Zapata 43, La Peñita
Tourist office—Plaza Cívica, Avenida Sol Nuevo, Rincón de Guayabitos

PUERTO VALLARTA
Banks—Banpaís, Paseo Díaz Ordaz 688
Consulates—American Consulate (2-00-69) and Canadian Consulate, (2-00-69)
Hospital—Centro Médico Quirúrgico, Basilio Badillo 365 (2-43-95)
Laundry—Lavandería Hildas, Calle Febronio Uribe, next to Hotel El Conquistador; or Lavandería Elsa, Calle Olas Altas 385 in old town
Police—2-08-84
Post Office—Calle Morelos 444 in old town
Tourist office—Presidencia Municipal, Calle Juárez near Plaza Aquiles Serdán (2-02-42)

BARRA DE NAVIDAD-MELAQUE AREA
Bank—Banco Mexicano Sómex, Calle Sinaloa 33, Barra de Navidad
Hospital—Centro Salud, Avenida Veracruz and Calle Zacatecas, Barra de Navidad
Police—7-03-99
Post Office—Calle Guanajuato 100, Barra de Navidad
Tourist office—Hotel Melaque, Bungalow 10, Melaque (7-01-00)

MANZANILLO
Bank—Banco Serfín, Calle Morelos 146, El Centro; or Banco Mexicano Somex, Mexico 200, between Manzanillo and Santiago
Hospital—Hospital Civil, Glorieta San Pedrito (2-00-29)
Laundry—Lavandería Toni's, Mexico 200, between Manzanillo and Salahua, Km. 11
Police—2-10-04
Post Office—Calle Cinco de Mayo and Calle Juárez, El Centro
Tourist office—Palacio Municipal, Calle Juárez (2-10-02) or, for federal tourism, Calle Juárez 244, 4th floor (2-20-90)

PLAYA AZUL-LÁZARO CÁRDENAS
Bank—Bánamex, Avenida Lázaro Cárdenas 1646, Lázaro Cárdenas; only American dollars changed here
Hospital—2-26-42
Laundry—Plaza Tabachines, Lázaro Cárdenas
Police—2-18-55

Post Office—Calle Nicolás Bravo, Lázaro Cárdenas or Avenida
Madero, Playa Azul

IXTAPA-ZIHUATANEJO
Bank—Bánamex, Calle Cuauhtémoc 4, Zihuatanejo
Hospital—Centro de Salud, Cinco de Mayo (4-20-88)
Laundry—Lavandería Darbet-Catalín, Calle González and Calle
Galeana, Zihuatanejo
Police—4-20-40
Post Office—Calle Catalina González 7, Zihuatanejo
Tourist office—Paseo del Pescador 20 (4-22-07)

ACAPULCO
Bank—Bánamex, Avenida Costera Miguel Alemán 211, near the
zócalo; Banco Serfín, Avenida Costera Miguel Alemán 51
Bookstore/newsstand—Sanborn's, Avenida Costera Miguel Alemán 209
(2-61-68)
Consulates—American Consulate (representative at 5-66-00) and Can-
adian Consulate (representative at 5-66-21)
Hospital—Hospital General, Avenida Ruiz Cortines (5-22-01)
Laundry—Lavandería Caleta, Calle 2a 8 (2-41-84)
Police—5-08-10
Post Office—Avenida Costera Miguel Alemán 125, near the *zócalo*
Tourist office—Avenida Costera Miguel Alemán 187, Playa Hornos
(5-22-84); Tourist Assistance Bureau, Centro de Convenciones,
Avenida Costera Miguel Alemán 4455 (4-61-36) and Pie de la Cuesta
(3-01-23)

CHAPTER EIGHT
Southwest Coast

Hardly anybody notices Mexico's southwest coast. But seekers of serenity, read on.

Overshadowed by the hot-shot resort belt from Mazatlán to Acapulco, this 900-mile shoreline, as unobtrusive as an orphan child, quietly connects the country with the Guatemala border. Probably fewer travelers venture down this way than to any other part of Mexico. Those who do home in on the growing fishing villages of Puerto Escondido—beloved old discovery of vagabonds—or Puerto Ángel. From here, a day's drive puts you in Guatemala, several days' drive cross-country lands you in the Yucatán. The southwest coast is usually thought of in these terms—as a springboard for farther shores, not a destination in itself.

Until recent years, the coastal highway (Mexico 200) along this route ambled through mud and riverbeds not yet spanned by bridges. Now, the road winds smoothly all the way to Tapachula.

So what's down here, south of the disco border and the bikini zone? Stunning beaches and heavenly nooks, stagnant marshes and tepid lagoons and, in between, a future Cancún.

Below Acapulco the shoreline is known as Costa Chica (Little Coast), the southern end of the state of Guerrero, where green promontories and wind-swept fields lie along the sea. The foothills of the Sierra Madre march down into the states of Oaxaca and Chiapas, then ripple up as the Sierra de Miahuatlán behind Puerto Escondido and Puerto Ángel. Wild, open beaches and dreamy bays sprinkle the coast all the way down to the Isthmus of Tehuantepec, the narrowest part of mainland Mexico, as homely as a bog. Strategically vital, the isthmus links the Pacific and the Gulf of Mexico, only 140 mountainous miles apart, and it is crossed by railroad. Bordered by brackish inland lagoons and the flame-tongued smokestacks of Salina Cruz, this area contains the bulk of Mexico's Pacific coast oil industry.

Chiapas grows lush and green to the south, with mist-shrouded mountains straddled by rainbows. Yet the coast deteriorates disappointingly here.

A dull region of mud flats squats on the Mar Muerto—the Dead Sea, a king-sized stagnant puddle, almost totally landlocked, with swampy brown beaches and haggard villages—one of the most joyless places in all Mexico. In the final stretch before the border, the luxuriant Sierra de Soconusco rears up and rescues the coast with some tropical backbone.

From December through April, days are balmy and nights are cool. Late summer brings the rainy season, when side roads can be mucky and landslides sometimes occur.

To encourage the gods to smile on the neglected southwest coast, the government has arranged the sacrifice of a virgin fishing village called Santa Cruz Huatulco, east of Puerto Ángel. All around this tiny town, workers are busy creating a super-resort to rival the jet-set splendors of Cancún. FONATUR, the government's tourist development sharpshooters, singled out this coastal wilderness precisely because nothing is here—except a string of inaccessible pearly coves along scalloped bays collectively called Bahías de Huatulco.

This coastline was also chosen because the area desperately needs an economic shot in the arm. Oaxaca and Chiapas, which dominate the southwest coast, are two of Mexico's poorest states.

Yet these states are some of Mexico's richest in Indian cultures. Indians are more concentrated in the mountains than on the coast. Oaxaca claims 16 distinct indigenous groups, including the Zapotec and Mixtec Indians, founders of civilization in this area. The state of Chiapas, a cornerstone of the Mayan culture, still is home to thousands of Mayan descendants, including the last tribe of pure Mayans, the jungle-dwelling Lacandón Indians.

As you enter the southwest coast from the north via Guerrero, be a little extra cautious. In the mid-1970s, this state was the scene of a revolutionary uprising against then-President Luis Echeverría. Some 10,000 soldiers raided the hills to snuff out the guerrillas, and the army has haunted Guerrero ever since. The state remains a drug-trafficking and gun-smuggling route. At checkpoints along the roads, soldiers may search your car.

Everybody's favorite destination along the southwest coast is Puerto Escondido. The hippie-revival climate that for years made this fishing village a backpacker's kingdom is giving way to a whole new mood. Where longhairs once slung their hammocks among the palms, packed hotels are sprouting and turning the town into a slick tropical resort. The beaches and coves are as gorgeous as ever.

True escapists have fled that scene for the endless siesta at Puerto Ángel, just 50 miles east. Another classic fishing village fated for hoteldom, Puerto Ángel lounges on a pretty bay, attracting streams of wanderers to its hillside guest houses.

About 30 miles away lies Santa Cruz Huatulco, focal point of the new Bahías de Huatulco tourist zone, which includes nine adjoining bays and

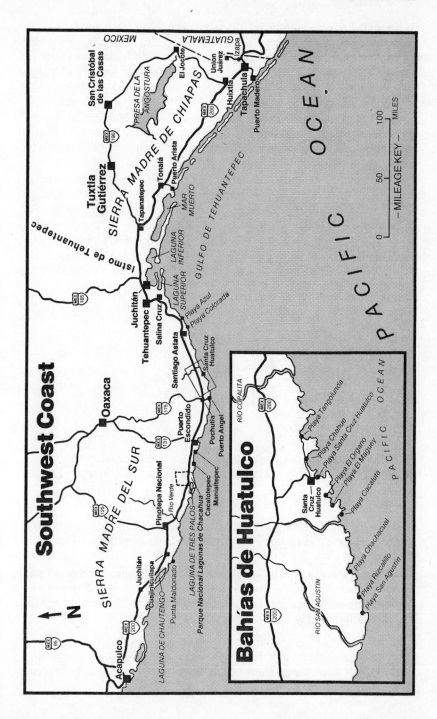

20 unspoiled coves along Oaxaca's rocky shores. An international airport is now operating, roads have been completed and resorts opened. The government projected a total of 25 years—with the mid-1980s as a starting point—to turn the area into a pot of gold. Just consider: in only 15 years, Cancún went from a handful of bamboo huts to the sleekest resort in the Republic.

Big industrial Salina Cruz, about 85 miles east of Huatulco, is a booming port rimmed in craggy, desolate hills. Windy dunes stack up along some beautiful, seldom-visited beaches west of town—the only real reason to visit.

South of the Isthmus of Tehuantepec, the rustic coastal resort of Puerto Arista fronts open ocean and provides a refreshing counterpoint to the stagnant shoreline of the nearby inland sea. Despite its nice wide beach, the village usually resembles a tropical ghost-town.

About 150 miles south, at the foot of an extinct volcano, the fertile, busy frontier city of Tapachula buzzes with commerce. South of Tapachula are the West Coast's most southerly beaches at easy-going Puerto Madero, a bedraggled seaside pueblo.

Easy Living
Transportation

ARRIVAL

BY CAR

Mexico 200 follows the southwest coast from Acapulco all the way south to Tapachula. It connects all towns in this section, some via paved side roads.

BY AIR

Three commercial airports serve the southwest coast: Puerto Escondido Airport, Bahías de Huatulco Airport, Salina Cruz Airport and Tapachula Airport.

Serving **Puerto Escondido** are Aerovías Oaxaqueñas and Mexicana Airlines. **Huatulco** has Aeroméxico and Mexicana Airlines. **Salina Cruz** is served by Aerovías Oaxaqueñas, which flies to and from Oaxaca. **Tapachula** has flights via Aeroméxico.

BY BUS

Bus lines connect all major towns along the southwest coast and offer frequent daily departures. Some of the bigger companies include **Estrella**

del Valle, Oaxaca Pacífico and **Ómnibus Cristóbal Colón.** Stations and information numbers are as follows:

Puerto Escondido: Terminal Estrella del Valle/Oaxaca Pacífico (Avenida Miguel Hidalgo; 2-00-50).

Pochutla (near Puerto Ángel): Estrella del Valle/Oaxaca Pacífico/ Lineas Unidas (Avenida Lázaro Cárdenas; 4-01-38).

Salina Cruz: Ómnibus Cristóbal Colón (Avenida Cinco de Mayo 412; 4-00-49).

Tapachula: Ómnibus Cristóbal Colón (first class—Calle 17a Oriente and Calle 3a Norte; 6-28-80; second class—Calle 11a Poniente and Calle Central Norte; 6-31-83).

BY TRAIN

Passenger trains pass through Salina Cruz and Tapachula.

In Salina Cruz, the **Ferrocarril Trans-Istmo** (Avenida Ávila Camacho and Calle Tuxpan; 4-09-68) carries people aboard second-class cars across the Isthmus of Tehuantepec to and from Coatzacoalcos. In Tapachula, **Ferrocarriles Nacionales de México** (Calle Central Sur; 5-20-85) has slow-moving trains for Ixtepec and Veracruz–Mexico City.

BY BOAT

Exploration Cruise Lines (1500 Metropolitan Park Building, Olive and Boren streets, Seattle, WA 98101, 206-625-9600) offers one of the few luxury cruises to the southwest coast. Its destination is Puerto Escondido.

CAR RENTALS

In Puerto Escondido, airport rentals are provided by **Budget** (2-03-12) and **Hertz** (2-00-35). Huatulco service is unreliable, but occasionally there is a representative of **Avis** (6-49-82) at the airport and **Budget** (4-00-84) at the Posada Binniguenda. At Tapachula Airport, try **AutoRenta del Sur** (6-26-40) or **Auto-Renta Exclusivas** (6-50-60).

PUBLIC TRANSPORTATION

You can take most southwest coastal towns in stride—they're small enough to walk around without the help of buses. Salina Cruz and Tapachula do have municipal buses, but for the few sights there, taxis serve best.

Hotels

Puerto Escondido and Puerto Ángel have the best range of hotels. East of there, the inns thin out until Tapachula.

PUERTO ESCONDIDO HOTELS

From November through May, you may have to hunt for a room, but during the rest of the year reservations are readily available.

For basic, but clean and safe lodgings near the beach, the **Posada Carrizalillo** (Bahía Carrizalillo; 2-00-77) is a good option. Its ten rooms have kitchenettes and ceiling fans. Budget.

Moving up the comfort scale, look downtown near the market for economical hotels—again, a five-minute walk from the sea. The best of the bunch, friendly three-story **Hotel Luz del Ángel** (Calle Porfirio Díaz; 2-01-51) houses 16 fresh pink rooms with ceiling fans, tile floors and balconies with sea views. Budget.

Down on the beachside promenade, the least expensive of the seaside inns is the plain **Hotel Roca Mar** (Avenida Alfonso Pérez Gasga 601; 2-03-39). Its 15 medium-sized rooms enjoy the basic comforts, from overhead fans to clean cement-floored baths with cold-water showers. Budget.

Stay right on the beach in style without dishing out a stylish sum at the tangerine-colored, modern **Hotel Las Palmas** (Avenida Alfonso Pérez Gasga; 2-02-30). Like the best haciendas, this inn surrounds a shadow-drenched garden with a central well. A walkway winds down to an alfresco restaurant-bar facing the bay. The 40 small rooms stack up in a three-story building, with all-glass front walls, tiled tubs and ceiling fans. Budget.

The snazzy **Hotel Santa Fé** (Calle del Morro; 2-01-70) punctuates the out-of-the-mainstream juncture between Playa Marinero and Playa Zicatela. Built in elegant colonial style, the comfortable hotel offers 30 fan-cooled rooms with picture-book Mexican trimmings: red-tile floors, cedar and mahogany doors and window casings, hand-painted washbasins, handwoven bedspreads and ceramic lamps. Some have balconies; most face the sea. There's also a restaurant, pool and boutique. The town is just ten minutes away on foot. Moderate to deluxe.

If it's atmosphere you're after, the 20-room **Hotel Paraíso Escondido** (Calle Unión 10; 2-04-44), three blocks off the beach, oozes villa charm from every pore. The reception desk people can be snobby, but the wonderland of lamps, grillwork, stone angels, paths, ponds, even a tiny chapel, soon warms away that initial chill. Walls decorated with painted animals enliven the rooms, and balconies look out over the hotel gardens. With the whimsy come a pool, air-conditioning and restaurant-bar. Moderate to deluxe.

Farthest from town, and in an area planned for more hotels and condominiums, is the **Best Western Posada Real** (Boulevard Benito Juárez; 2-01-33), on Playa Bacocho, not far from the airport. Rooms are unimaginative and in need of sprucing up, but the public areas are delightful, particularly the beach, lower level pool, bar and restaurant. Moderate.

PUERTO ÁNGEL HOTELS

Guest houses for the small spender dimple the hillsides of Puerto Ángel. Here the atmosphere of yesteryear's hippie communes lives on, with guitar music, tangle-haired children, homemade yogurt and, occasionally, the pungent fumes of marijuana.

Accordingly, the accommodations often resemble crash pads. For example, one of the better guest houses, **Casa de Huéspedes Gundi y Tomás** (up a marked dirt trail off Calle Frente al Sector Naval) has eight rooms for rent, but most are concrete cells with bare-mattressed beds, mosquito nets and open fretwork in the walls for ventilation. The screened downstairs rooms and a separate section of the hotel offering rooms with private baths are much more comfortable (and worth the extra price). Budget.

The two main 1960s-revival institutions of the area, each unique and magical, are Casa Gloria and La Posada Cañón Devata. Rustic, hillside **Casa Gloria** (north end of Playa Zipolite, about two miles from town) invites escapists to sleep in a palm-sheltered hammock overlooking a beautiful beach. The owner, Gloria Esperanza, opened this beachfront inn and its thatched vegetarian restaurant in 1976. Besides hammocks, little huts are also for rent. There is no electricity and no running water. Outhouses, a well for bathing, purified drinking water and a place to lock your valuables are provided. Budget.

You can have all the pleasure of living in a treehouse at the picturesque **La Posada Cañón Devata** (near Playa Panteón in town). For sheer charm and comfort, it's the best place to stay in Puerto Ángel. This multilevel guest house of wood and stone climbs up a forested hillside thick with banana trees and palms. Ten unique rooms—all screened and including private baths, double beds, beamed ceilings and painted tiles—are nestled along a brick pathway swirling with gold, white and striped butterflies. The path continues up to a big vegetarian restaurant and meditation chapel at the very top of the hill. All over the grounds you'll see statues, shells, polished log furniture, parrots and imaginative oil paintings by artist Mateo López, who co-owns the hotel with his hospitable wife, Suzanne. Budget.

A hillside inn at the entrance to town, the gold-and-white **Hotel Soraya** (Calle Virgilio Uribe across from the main pier) provides parking and 32 rooms overlooking the beautiful bay. This is the best alternative if you don't like the commune scene and the Devata is full. The big rooms have two double beds, ceiling fans or air-conditioning and airy terraces. Budget.

Highest geographically and pricewise is **Hotel Ángel del Mar** (Domicilio Conocido, on the hilltop overlooking Playa Panteón; 6), with a commanding view of the bay. Rooms are clean, simply furnished and feature balconies. Budget.

BAHÍAS DE HUATULCO HOTELS

The selection is still sparse in this newly developing area. Other than the huge Club Med on Bahía de Tangolunda, there are only two choices. There's the colonial-style **Posada Binniguenda** (Avenida Benito Juárez; 4-00-84), with tile floors, banana trees and overflowing pots of ferns and flowers. This in-town lodging has 74 pleasant rooms, many with balconies facing the tree-shaded pool. Moderate.

Much more upscale, on Bahía de Tangolunda, is the new **Huatulco Sheraton Resort** (Paseo de Tangolunda; 800-325-3535). The grandiose marble entrance, with soaring ceiling and enormous woven rugs, is almost as impressive as Bahía de Tangolunda itself. The 340 rooms are equally sumptuous, with natural wood and marble features. Guests can swim in the pool or along the expansive sandy beach, rent boats and eventually play golf and tennis. There are several restaurants and bars and all the services of a full-scale resort. Deluxe.

SALINA CRUZ HOTELS

Given Salina Cruz's less than scintillating personality, you're probably better off out at Playa La Ventosa (about five miles from downtown). But there's only one decent seaside hotel out there, the rundown-looking **Posada de Rustrián** (Bahía La Ventosa). Its 26 rooms are crackerboxes, cramped but clean, with bare bulbs and ceiling fans that whirl up a hurricane. Budget.

If you opt to stay downtown, you might try the **Hotel Magda** (Calle Cinco de Mayo 43; 4-01-07), the local family inn. Holy pictures bless the lobby walls, and 24 plain rooms surround the courtyard. Another option is the **Hotel Jacarandas** (Calle Manuel Ávila Camacho; 4-07-59). It's a bit run-down, but adequate, with air-conditioning, television and minibars. Both budget.

A highway oasis for travelers en route to beach destinations is **Hotel Calli** (Carretera Cristóbal Colón, Km. 790; 5-00-85) in Tehuantepec, just nine miles north of Salina Cruz. The 100 rooms are clean and ultramodern. Budget.

PUERTO ARISTA–ARRIAGA HOTELS

You're severely limited here. The beachfront **Hotel Bugambilias Arista** (Boulevard Mariano Matamoros), after several years of construction, has only a few rooms available. These have ocean views and air-conditioning, but the hotel's construction clutter and noise are annoying. Budget.

Try the friendly, pastel **Hotel-Restaurant Agua Marina** (Boulevard Mariano Matamoros) for a stripped-down room with standing fan. Across the shady brick lane, you'll find digs a notch up in looks and cost at the **Hotel-Restaurant Puesta del Sol** (off Boulevard Mariano Matamoros). Both budget.

Nearby in Arriaga, mid-way between Salina Cruz and Tapachula and only 20 miles from Puerto Arista, are two good hotels: near the *zócalo* is the motel-style **Ik-Lumaal** (Calle 1a Norte 7; 2-11-64), with 39 large rooms. On the highway, with more charm (and highway noise), is **El Parador** (Carretera Arriaga–Tapachula, Km. 46; 2-01-99), looking incongruously like a resort on a city *malecón*. The spacious rooms have air-conditioning, phones and television; and there is an attractive restaurant and bar. Both budget.

TAPACHULA HOTELS

Downtown near the main square, you can't go wrong at the comfortable **Hotel Fénix** (4a Avenida Norte 19; 5-07-55). Its parking area faces an interior garden. The rooms tend to be cramped, with double beds, ceiling fans, worn furniture and phones, but the price shouldn't cramp anyone's style. Budget.

You will pay more for the comparative luxury of the hilltop **Hotel Loma Real** (Mexico 200, Km. 244; 6-14-40), one of the town's oldest and best hotels. A standard among businessmen, the Loma Real features 86 rooms carpeted in royal blue with leather easy chairs, executive desk ensembles, phones, air-conditioning and big cable color televisions. There's also a pool and restaurant-bar. Moderate.

If you want to enjoy a first-class stay, indulge in the lovely **Hotel Kamico** (Prolongación Central Oriente, Carretera a Guatemala; 6-26-40). Its 92 quiet rooms radiate from a well-tended garden containing a pool, patio and restaurant-bar. The ample rooms are painted in warm autumnal tones and feature king-sized beds, terraces, televisions, phones and air-conditioning. Moderate.

PUERTO MADERO HOTELS

If you insist on staying near the sea, there's only one hotel out here and it's not exactly a looker. The **Hotel-Restaurant San Rafael** (Calle Tercera Poniente, southern end of the main drag; Tel. 5) is a big, sea-worn building slouching over the wave-dashed shoreline. Its 16 rustic rooms, half with private baths, sport dried-out calendars on the walls, floor fans and buckets in the bathrooms if water lines are broken. Budget.

Restaurants

PUERTO ESCONDIDO RESTAURANTS

Most restaurants are clustered along the main promenade, Avenida Alfonso Pérez Gasga.

At the west end of the pedestrian mall stands a large, tile-roofed restaurant with classical music and dirty tablecloths. That's **La Palapa**

(Avenida Alfonso Pérez Gasga 513), where the service is slow but the seafood is good. Budget.

A side street leads you down to the big, golden, bamboo-and-palm **Restaurant-Bar El Dorado** (Calle Marina Nacional). Inside, its vine-smothered bamboo windows give a lovely view of the bay. The decor here is casual: plastic chairs, striped tablecloths, fresh flowers on the table. The menu covers meats, chicken, seafood, cheese fondue and a fetching special-ty called "octopus in love." The waiters, though, tend to be rude. Budget.

Back on the pedestrian thoroughfare, walk a few blocks down to the simple **Restaurant San Ángel** (Avenida Alfonso Pérez Gasga; 2-00-25), a small *palapa*-roofed building next to Tanga's Sport, with no outstanding elements of style. The flair is in the kitchen, from which you can order seafood, meat and chicken dishes. Try the *camarones al ajillo*, spicy garlic shrimp seasoned with a chile sauce. Budget.

If you crave pizza and greasy Italian delights, try the lively **Ostería del Viandante** (Avenida Alfonso Pérez Gasga), a polished gringo hangout enveloped in garlic fumes. Though *palapa*-roofed and reasonably priced, the Ostería exudes a classy twinkle with its blond wood touches and beachfront vista. You can stuff yourself with rich pizzas, salad, spaghetti, lasagna and, of course, espresso and cappuccino. Dinner only. Budget to moderate.

Speaking of cappuccino, just a few doors away stands the closest thing to a real coffeehouse in town, the two-story **Il Cappucino** (Avenida Alfonso Pérez Gasga). Upstairs is for watching people on the street below, downstairs for sipping in peace. Breakfasts, mixed drinks, juices, coffees. Budget to moderate.

Better cappuccino can be had at the hip, garden-style **Banana's** (Avenida Alfonso Pérez Gasga), a cafeteria-snack bar at the east end of the tourist strip. Rock music pounds out at all hours, catering to the surfer and backpacker crowd. Breakfast is the house specialty: omelettes, *frittata* (eggs, ham, onion and potatoes), fruit, salads, sandwiches, juices, crepes. Moderate.

Vegetarians, you're in luck, and carnivores may decide to convert after a meal at beautiful, breezy **Restaurant Santa Fé**, in the Hotel Santa Fé (Calle del Morro, south end of Playa Marinero; 2-01-70). Classical music wafts through the windows, and broad white columns support the *palapa* roof. You can enjoy specialties like baked tofu or fettuccini alfredo, plus salads, baked fish, avocado soup, Mexican dishes, omelettes and granola. Moderate.

Serene, secluded **Coco's Restaurant and Bar** (Boulevard Benito Juárez, on Playa Bacocho; 2-01-33) is set back amid shadowy palms like some Polynesian idyll, and it has an entire beach to itself. It is part of the Best Western Posada Real, whose cross-shaped pool faces the restaurant.

Now You're On Mexican Time

A phrase you often hear in Mexico is *muy tranquilo*. No translation is necessary; tranquility and relaxation are just what you came for, and Mexico's coasts certainly excel in the easy-going good life. But one thing you have to accept in the bargain is the Latin view of time.

Mexican life seems to roll along to the beat of a different drum. Time moves more slowly than it does north of the border.

Take the siesta, for example. This two-to-three hour break in the middle of the day lets workers escape from their labors to eat their main meal and rest up for the evening's work. Travelers love the idea of the siesta, until they face the locked-up shops and offices, the barred church doors or the tardy taxis. But why get upset? Why not take a siesta yourself? Business begins again in the evening, and *mañana*, as Mexicans would say, is another day.

Mexicans relish a more natural pace and hate to rush. The stereotype says that the sultry climate induces a sensuous languor, but in truth Latins perceive time in a more cyclical way than gringos do. To them, all things occur in their proper hour and to be late for an appointment is merely part of being *tranquilo* and *muy informal*.

Many Mexicans think gringos are, in fact, *un poquito* mechanical in their zest for punctuality. They picture a world of clocks to punch, buttons to press, automatic coffee machines, computerized banking, burglar alarms and impersonal fast-food chains, everything inhumanly efficient.

When you cross the border, think of it this way: you are entering a timeless zone. Enjoy it and make it the time of your life.

Under the *palapa* roof and dangling starfish, red-clothed tables and chairs form long, neat rows. The menu includes shrimp cocktails, octopus in its own ink, soups, fowl and filet mignon. The *huachinanga* (red snapper) is particularly recommended. Lunch and dinner only. Moderate.

PUERTO ÁNGEL RESTAURANTS

One of the few enclosed restaurants here—though its windows are flung open and sea breezes whisk through—is the hillside **Restaurant Soraya** at the Hotel Soraya (Boulevard Virgilio Uribe). It's crisp and clean, with upbeat *ranchero* music and plaintive romantic ballads. This pleasant nook serves hot cakes, eggs, *pozole*, tamales, enchiladas and instant coffee. Budget.

En route to Playa Panteón, the large, *palapa*-roofed **Restaurant Beto's** (Camino a la Playa Panteón) loafs along the dusty roadside, blinking with Christmas lights at night. Only a few lonely tables occupy its cavernous floor, but the seafood is excellent: fish, lobster, shrimp, plus chicken and beef. Budget.

Directly on Playa Panteón, the raised **Restaurant-Bar Bricio y Cordelia** was once a part-time disco and still may be the only local restaurant big enough for a football game. A fresco of Mayan scenes and a whimsical oceanic underworld decorate the walls. Sea breezes blow through the pebbled columns. Seafood soup, lobster salad, shrimp and Mexican dishes spice up the menu. Friendly management. Budget.

At the serene **La Tortuga** in the Hotel Ángel del Mar (Domicilio Conocido; 6) you can enjoy sea breezes wafting through the four enormous arches that frame the bay view. Specialties are fish and shrimp, either fried or cooked in garlic. They also serve a variety of soups, salads, tacos, enchiladas and quesadillas. Moderate.

Start your day with granola and fresh-ground coffee at the **Restaurant Cañón Devata** in La Posada Cañón Devata (just west of Playa Panteón). The treetop restaurant, set with huge wood-slab tables, looks the part of the organic dining hall. Fruit salads, sandwiches and vegetarian meals are served. Budget.

Out at Playa Zipolite, the beachfront is peppered with open-air cafés serving fried fish and cold beer. Two restaurants more tuned in to the homesick vagabond's tastes share the far western end of the beach. A spacey cosmic sign points up the hill to **Restaurant Lo Cósmico**, a simple, *palapa*-roofed place specializing in crispy crepes filled with cheese, ham, fruits, chocolate, rum and caramel. On an adjoining hill is the old **Shambala Restaurant,** connected to Casa Gloria, exuding the hushed Buddhist quality of a tropical temple. Vegetarian pizza is prepared during the high season, plus *bodis* (brown rice with vegetables and cheese) and 12 different salads. Both budget.

SALINA CRUZ RESTAURANTS

The downtown area has some very respectable restaurants.

A block from the main square, you can dine with Clark Gable at the upstairs, colonial **Villa Florencia** (Calle Guaymas and Avenida Cinco de Mayo). Its walls are papered with old Hollywood photos. Take a table on a balcony and polish off soup, chicken or spicy *pescado a la veracruzana* (fish with onions, olives and tomatoes). Dinner only. Budget.

Down the street at **Restaurant Aloha** (Calle Wilfredo Cruz 13-A; 4-03-00), Hawaiian masks stare from lacquered palm trunks while fiery *telenovelas* (soap operas) burn up a television in the corner. The other entertainment is the menu, including oyster soup, fish stuffed with shrimp, paella, Mexican chicken, cheesecake, wine—just reading it is filling. Budget.

A nice little breakfast niche just off the square is air-conditioned **Vito's** (Calle Acapulco 18). The walls hold an interesting collection of circus and theatrical images. The menu emphasizes light dishes like sandwiches and omelettes. Budget.

On the western outskirts of town, the polished new **Hawaii 03 Restaurant-Bar** (Mexico 200 at Calle Lomas de Galindo; 4-23-91) has a Howard Johnson's neatness in its air-conditioning, brick walls and golden lanterns. The giant menu runs the gamut from *ceviche* to chicken to pork chops to seafood to mixed drinks and wine. Budget.

PUERTO ARISTA RESTAURANTS

Along the brief main street snooze many *palapa*-roofed restaurants that stay open even when business is down to 15 tumbleweeds for every tourist.

Toward the entrance to town, **Restaurant El Dulcito** (Boulevard Mariano Matamoros) serves spicy breakfasts, seafood cocktails, *mojarra* (a local fish), shrimp and eggs. El Dulcito lies under a monstrous *palapa* roof and offers a sunny view of the beach. Budget.

Up the street you can also eat well at two smaller seafood restaurants attached to guest houses. **Restaurant Agua Marina** and **Restaurant Puesta del Sol** stand catty-corner to each other across a brick walk off Boulevard Mariano Matamoros. Both budget.

TAPACHULA RESTAURANTS

Big, shady Parque Central Hidalgo, the central square, is rimmed in fetching indoor-outdoor cafés serving inexpensive meals and snacks. At one end stands **Capistrano Parque** (Portal Pérez and 6a Avenida Norte), a friendly spot spilling out onto a patio with grillwork furniture. The menu covers everything from eggs to tacos to *hamburguesas*. At the other end of the strip stands the more polished **Los Comales** (Portal Pérez, corner of 8a Avenida Norte), with a busy chrome-and-formica indoor section. The menu marches through fruits, ice creams, seafood, eggs, Mexican dishes, sandwiches and cappuccinos. Both budget.

Just across the street from Los Comales, lively and tropical **La Parrilla** (8a Avenida Norte 20; 6-25-88) stays open 24 hours a day and offers bargain meals. When I stopped there, its *comida corrida* (meal of the day) featured soup, rice, a meat entree, beans, dessert and a soft drink for slightly more than a dollar. You can order everything from beef brochettes to cheese sandwiches a la carte. Budget.

For more elegant dining, both the **Hotel Loma Real** (Mexico 200, Km. 244; 6-14-40) and the **Hotel Kamico** (Prolongación Central Oriente, Carretera a Guatemala; 6-26-40) have attractive restaurants open for all meals. In the Loma Real, the view is pleasant and the service excellent. The fish *veracruzana*, cooked with tomatoes, chilis, onions and bay leaf, is highly recommended, as is *sopa de tortilla* (tortilla soup), and for dessert, the scrumptious flan Loma Real. Moderate.

PUERTO MADERO RESTAURANTS

It's a bit of a culinary wasteland out here, but you can munch on fresh seafood and enjoy the crash of the waves at **Restaurant San Rafael** (Calle Tercera Poniente; Tel. 5). Ask for the mullet eggs. Budget.

Or saunter up the street to a thatch-roofed restaurant-in-the-round sizzling with barbequed beef on the charcoal grill. Open only at night, **El Kiosko** (Calle Tercera Poniente 3; Tel. 26) virtually disappears by day, leaving no trace of its bright tables and juicy broiled meals or icy fruit juices. Budget.

The Great Outdoors

The Sporting Life

CAMPING

Isolated beach camping on the southwest coast is good as far east as Salina Cruz, when the coastal terrain takes a turn for the marshy and the beaches start looking like quicksand. Many southwest beaches are windy and offer little protection.

You can restock your groceries and other supplies in Puerto Escondido at **Super del Puerto** (Calle Miguel Hidalgo and Calle Oaxaca; 2-01-57); in Pochutla (a sizeable market town near Puerto Ángel) at **Conasupo** (Avenida Lázaro Cárdenas) or the **main market** (downtown along Avenida Lázaro Cárdenas); in Salina Cruz at **Mercado Central** (Avenida Cinco de Mayo and Calle Guaymas); and in Tapachula at **Conasupo** (8a Avenida Norte near the *zócalo*).

SWIMMING

The swimming is delightful in coves around Puerto Escondido and Puerto Ángel, becoming considerably wilder off open-sea beaches farther down the coast. Some reports claim sharks are attracted to the warm waters and rich feeding grounds off Salina Cruz, Puerto Arista and Puerto Madero, but locals insist attacks are almost unheard of and the undertow poses more of a threat than the occasional fin.

FISHING AND BOATING

The good fishing typical of the northern Pacific Coast continues along the southwest coastline. You'll find deep-sea fishing facilities in Puerto Escondio and Puerto Ángel.

In Puerto Escondido, ask about renting *lanchas* (skiffs) at the **Sociedad Cooperativa de Servícios Turísticos "Punta Escondida"** (Avenida Marina Nacional) or check with fishermen on the main town beach, Playa Principal. Also inquire at **La Casa del Pescador** (Avenida Miguel Hidalgo and 3a Calle Poniente).

Inquire about renting *lanchas* in Puerto Ángel at the office of the **Capitania del Puerto** (Boulevard Virgilio Uribe and Avenida Principal, on the main beach south of the concrete pier). On Playa Panteón, you should negotiate with a fisherman.

SKIN DIVING

The crystal coves of Puerto Escondido and Puerto Ángel make for fine diving. In Puerto Escondido, the **Hotel Santa Fé** (Calle del Morro; 2-01-70) runs a diving school. For snorkeling gear, check **Deportimundo** (Avenida Marina Nacional).

In Pochutla, the market town east of Puerto Ángel, try **Deportes Jaimes** (Avenida Lázaro Cárdenas 74) for snorkeling gear.

SURFING

As one of the West Coast's biggest surfing centers, Puerto Escondido hosts two **annual surfing tournaments** on Playa Zicatela every November: one for adults and one for children in the eight-to-nine year range. For surfing gear, check at the **Surf Shop** (Avenida Alfonso Pérez Gasga; 2-02-86).

TENNIS

The only places you can swing your racket along this coast are in Puerto Escondido and at the Bahía de Tangolunda resorts in Huatulco. In Puerto Escondido try the **Posada Real** (Boulevard Benito Juárez; 2-01-33); and in Huatulco, try **Club Med** or the **Sheraton**.

Beaches

PUERTO ESCONDIDO BEACHES

Camping is not permitted on beaches in and around Puerto Escondido.

Playa Bacocho—At the northwestern end of Puerto Escondido, this long beautiful beach sweeps west for miles along the open sea. Its silent white sands weave among eroded, primal rock formations, with one covelike area sequestered between vegetated hills. Scattered driftwood, roaring surf and tree-covered cliffs give this beach a wild Oregonian air.

Facilities: Restaurant. *Swimming:* Not recommended: there are rough waves and an undertow. *Fishing/boating:* Check at municipal beach for skiff tours and fishing boat rentals.

Getting there: Take Mexico 200 northwest toward the airport and follow signs for the Best Western Posada Real. Proceed through a new *fraccionamiento* (neighborhood) to a road that winds down to the hotel, restaurant and beach.

Playa Carrizalillo—This is actually a pair of small, cloistered beaches separated by a rocky outcropping. The smaller beach, covered with shards of white coral from an offshore reef, hides in the shadow of a hill from which trickles a freshwater stream where locals wash their clothes. The bigger beach has smooth white sand, turquoise water and stronger waves. These two are the most private sandy nooks in the area.

Facilities: None on the beach. On the cliffs above is a trailer park with bathrooms; nearby restaurant. *Camping:* Campsites at trailer park. *Swimming:* Good at both beaches. Be careful of sharp coral. *Snorkeling:* Good around offshore coral reef.

Getting there: Take Mexico 200 about half a mile northwest of town and turn left at Avenida Miguel Hidalgo onto a dirt road proceeding past the old airport. Go right at the trailer park sign and continue veering right till the road enters the grassy plateau of the park. Trails lead down the cliffside to the beach.

Puerto Angelito—This popular, crystalline inlet almost lives up to its "port" title on those afternoons when the tourist boats come bobbing in from the main strand. Here, the beach consists of a series of little coves shaped by crescents of rocks—all lovely snippets of sand lapped by calm, bright waves. The main cove often brims with splashing children, families picnicking under the shade trees and snorkelers snooping offshore among the rocks.

Facilities: Restaurant with bathrooms. *Swimming:* Excellent, bathtub-calm, perfect for kids. *Snorkeling:* Fair visibility, and some coral; watch out for boats. Good oyster diving off of the southeastern rocks. *Fishing/boating:* Tour boats come and go all day from Playa Principal, where fishing boats are for rent.

Getting there: Take Mexico 200 northwest of town about half a mile to Calle Miguel Hidalgo at the old airport, turn left and continue to the billboard, turn left again and continue down the dirt road to the beach. It's about a 15-minute walk from town.

Playa Principal—This lovely palm-fringed beach, the center of village action, runs parallel to the town's main drag and wraps itself around a calm blue bay. To the northwest a lighthouse balances on a point, around which the beach continues to smaller coves. To the southeast, the beach rolls past a brackish lagoon to wilder shores. Vendors, beachcombers and surfers shuffle through the sands, and skiffs line the shore.

Facilities: Restaurants and groceries. *Swimming:* Lovely, calm with nice waves. *Snorkeling:* Try around the rocks near Playa Marinero. *Fishing/boating:* Skiffs for rent.

Getting there: Located off Avenida Alfonso Pérez Gasga in Puerto Escondido.

Playa Marinero—A continuation of Playa Principal, this ample white beach begins just southeast of the lagoon. Treeless, broad and less heavily trafficked, it begs you to sunbathe on it. The surf picks up around a clump of rocks, gaining momentum beyond the hefty point that marks the start of Playa Zicatela.

Facilities: Restaurants. *Swimming:* Good, but watch for currents toward the southern end. *Snorkeling:* Try around the rock formation (Punta Marinero). *Surfing:* Kid's stuff here.

Getting there: Walk from Playa Principal or off the east end of Avenida Alfonso Pérez Gasga.

Playa Zicatela—Said to be one of the best surfing beaches in the world by devotees, this ten-mile shag carpet of sand disappears to the south along the open sea, pausing at a rocky point called Punta Zicatela. With so little out here besides boards and waves, the empty beach seems totally untouched. A sandy road traces some residential developments along the beach for a short distance, then fades, leaving just low dunes and big breakers. It's beautiful for walking by day, but because of its isolation don't go alone and, most emphatically, do not walk out here after dark.

Facilities: Restaurant. *Swimming:* NO! Signs warn of the danger of riptides here, and even if you can't see them, trust the surfers—very mean waves break farther out. *Surfing:* This is the kingdom come of West Coast beaches, known for its long, 20-foot beach breakers ("the Mexican Pipeline"), especially good in July, August and September.

Getting there: Take Mexico 200 just southeast of the center of town and turn right onto Calle del Morro. This dirt road leading to Hotel Santa Fé continues south along the beach. It's also a ten-minute walk southeast from Playa Principal.

PUERTO ÁNGEL BEACHES

Playa Zipolite—A couple of miles west of town, this long white beach is the toast of offbeat travelers from all over the world. Amazingly, wealthy tourists have not discovered it yet. It slumbers in its innocence along the open sea, lined with sagging thatch-roofed restaurants and a crude guest house or two, backed by humble green hills and spotty palms. Curving for about a mile between two cliffs, the beach ducks discreetly around the eastern hill to form its own **Playa del Amor**—a secluded beachlet where skinny-dipping is not uncommon. (Don't be surprised to see nudity anywhere along Zipolite.) Toward the opposite end of the beach, where a couple of peace-and-love restaurants bring back the 1960s, the rocks form a natural cove where the swimmers go in with nothing but shells on. Zipolite may be the freest nude beach in Mexico, and no one seems to mind.

Facilities: Restaurants; nearby picnic spot. Toilets. *Camping:* Anywhere, except in front of the navy outpost at the eastern end. *Swimming:* Not advised along the main stretch, which is slashed by rough surf. Try instead at Playa del Amor's cove or the sheltered area at the west end of the beach near Casa Gloria. *Surfing:* Strong waves, wrong breaks—head west to Puerto Escondido. *Fishing/boating:* Try surf-fishing and line-fishing off the rocks around Playa del Amor. *Shell-collecting:* Oodles of *turritellas* tumble in the tideline toward the eastern end and are all over Playa del Amor.

Getting there: Follow the dusty road through town toward Playa Panteón; then, at the sign for Hotel Ángel del Mar, veer right, away from the arrow. A bumpy dirt lane proceeds for two miles to a fork—go right to the village and main beach.

Playa Panteón—This pretty little beach luxuriates in the clear, calm waters of Bahía de Puerto Ángel, protected by a rocky bluff to the south and enlivened by friendly neighborhood seafood joints that march their tables and chairs out onto the buff-colored sand. To the east, an arroyo and a navy base separate Panteón from the main beach in town.

Facilities: Restaurants. *Camping:* Much too public and cramped. *Swimming:* Delightful, but watch out for prickly sea urchins that roll up in the tide. *Snorkeling:* Good around southern rocks and the small offshore island. *Fishing/boating:* You can rent skiffs here or on the main beach next door to haul up snapper, bonito, grouper and *mero.*

Getting there: Take the dirt road through Puerto Ángel over the arroyo to the beach.

Playa Principal—Right in town, this lazy beach moseys along placid Bahía de Puerto Ángel with the dusty village rooftops rising behind it. A long cement pier pokes into the water, trimmed in colorful bobbing skiffs, which bake to bleached skeletons on the shore. A short *malecón* traces the curve of the beach, passing thatch-roofed restaurants in the shade of palms.

Facilities: Restaurants. *Camping:* Not recommended. *Swimming:* A little greasy from boat traffic—better at Playa Panteón. *Snorkeling:* Better at Playa Panteón, where the water is clearer and less clouded by boats. *Fishing/boating:* Good off the pier. You can also rent skiffs on the beach.

Getting there: Right off main street in Puerto Ángel.

Playa de Estacahuite—This hidden cluster of beaches just southeast of town offers privacy and many extras: bejeweled waters, pebbly white sand and craggy rocks impervious to the pummeling of waves. The spot also has big, hungry horseflies that bite like tiger sharks and take the icing off an otherwise very nice cake. But once you're in the water, nothing will bother you.

Facilities: Restaurants and a *palapa* shelter. *Camping:* Not recommended. *Swimming:* Excellent—calm and perfect for kids. *Snorkeling:* Good, especially around the rocks. *Fishing/boating:* Better in town off the main beach.

Getting there: Follow Mexico 175 out of town toward Pochutla for about a quarter of a mile to sign reading "Club de Playa." Turn right and descend the rocky road to the beach.

Playa de la Mina (★)—This brief, mysterious, isolated beach has the distant quality of a South Seas atoll or some tiny primeval remnant in Bali. Emerging from the black shadows of a dense palm grove, the white sand fans out past a stream to the sloping shore and inrushing waves. A pyramidal rock formation topped with gnarled trees and cacti acts as the jagged centerpiece of the beach. Caves and arches in the rock draw in the sea, which swirls, foams and spins, then exits in a panic. Though hard to get to, this beach is nevertheless well worth visiting.

Facilities: None. *Camping:* Not permitted; this is part of private property. *Swimming:* Not recommended: strong waves and steep dropoff.

Getting there: Take Mexico 175 north of Puerto Ángel toward Pochutla for about five miles. The dirt-road turnoff is not marked; look for a "30 kph" sign (30 kilometers per hour) on your right and turn directly onto a road half buried in a horrendous trash heap. Set your jaw and forge ahead till you find a clear space to park (the road gets unnavigably rocky ahead—don't try it in a standard car). Walk for about half a mile to the wooden gate, climb it if it's not open, cross the bridge and follow the trail past the well down to the beach.

SANTA CRUZ HUATULCO AND BAHÍAS DE HUATULCO BEACHES

The tiny fishing village of Santa Cruz Huatulco is the pushoff point for over a dozen beautiful beaches along the Bahías de Huatulco. Few have any facilities; most offer good swimming, snorkeling and camping, with the sand quality at an 8 or 9. All except Chahue, Tangolunda and Santa Cruz Huatulco are reachable only by boat out of Santa Cruz Huatulco. Because this area is constantly changing as tourist facilities grow, the beach descriptions here are purposely brief. From west to east:

WEST OF SANTA CRUZ HUATULCO BEACHES

The biggest of the Huatulco beaches, and the farthest from Santa Cruz, **Playa San Agustín** has at least a mile of gorgeous white sand facing wind-sculpted rocks and islands where iguanas, ducks and pelicans roost. **Playa Chachacual** and **Playa La India** are yin-yang complements on their own bay. The larger Chachacual rolls its sands to the tide in a challenging, straightforward line, while the smaller La India curls shyly off to the side around an exquisitely clear turquoise cove.

Facing a Caribbean-bathtub bay, **Playa Rizcalillo** shimmers along warm, gemlike water, with cool sands disappearing into a Oaxacan forest of cactus and low tropical foliage—absolutely idyllic. **Playa Cacaluta** shines broad and white, but its steep drop-off makes swimming risky. Lush, lovely **Playa El Maguey** forms a semicircle of dazzling sand along aquamarine waters.

Playa El Órgano and **Playa La Entrega** are small beaches in gentle coves framed by sheltering headlands just west of Santa Cruz Huatulco. Narrow, grainy **Playa Santa Cruz Huatulco,** the least impressive of the beaches, picks its way past open-air cafés along a turbulent bay crowded with fishing boats.

Getting there: Take Mexico 200 about 30 miles east of Puerto Ángel to the marked turnoff for Bahías de Huatulco. A paved road through little Crucecita leads to the turnoff to Santa Cruz Huatulco beach. From there you can hire a skiff through the Cooperativa Tangolunda to explore the distant secret coves. Strike a bargain with the boatmen and set up your own itinerary. Ask at any beachfront restaurant about renting a *lancha.*

EAST OF SANTA CRUZ HUATULCO BEACHES

Sculpted, dunelike **Playa Chahue,** just minutes from Santa Cruz Huatulco, contains nothing but a small trailer park and dive shop facing the low, sparkling surf—excellent for camping. **Playa Tangolunda,** the most perfect of the bay beaches and the site of several new resorts, is a heavenly string of sandy nooks (I counted five) linked into a long white crescent guarding a peaceful bay where little islands and pinnacles speckle the water—it's tailor-made for diving.

Getting there: For Chahue, take Avenida Benito Juárez east from Santa Cruz Huatulco beach for about a mile. Turn off at the sign for Chahue Trailer Park. Continue northeast on this road for a mile or so to Tangolunda.

SALINA CRUZ BEACHES

Playa La Ventosa, five miles east of Salina Cruz, is the closest to town, but much finer beaches lie to the west, such as:

Playa Colorada (★)—En route to Salina Cruz from the west, this is the first in a row of splendid, secluded beaches rolling east from Bahía San Diego past Bahía Mazatán. Named for a nearby rust-colored lagoon (*colorada* means "red" in Spanish), this gorgeous windy beach strikes out from cactus-spotted dunes in a wild, barren curve to distant hills. The dunes provide a breathtaking vista of the beach and vivid sea silver-tipped with whitecaps. Fishermen occupying nearby shacks say sea turtles crawl ashore here by the thousands during May near the San Diego lighthouse.

Facilities: None. *Camping:* Excellent and private, though quite windy. *Swimming:* Good, but waves swell to threatening size during the period of the full moon. *Snorkeling/diving:* The offshore rock attracts lots of sealife, locally known for its huge oysters and red clams. *Fishing/boating:* The super-friendly fishermen will take you out in their *lanchas*. *Shell-collecting:* Clam shells and loads of what the locals call *conchas chinas* (pink murex shells)—a gold mine.

Getting there: Take Mexico 200 west of Salina Cruz for about 40 miles and turn at the blue road sign for Playa Colorada. A bumpy dirt road winds about 1.5 miles past stagnant Laguna Colorada through a forest and up a hill overlooking the beach.

Concepción Bamba—A short distance east of Playa Colorada, this chalky, sun-bleached beach lies low behind a solitary, aloof point protruding into Bahía de Bamba. The sand is guarded by two rocky jetties, one crashed by angry sapphire waves from the open sea. Softer surf washes the protected cove. Against the blank backdrop of the cliffs, the sea is a stunning palette of icy pastels. Back in the hills sleeps a mud-and-thatched village.

Facilities: None. *Camping:* Good, but no shelter from the blazing sun. *Swimming:* Very nice in sheltered cove. *Snorkeling:* Clear water, try inside of the jetties. *Fishing:* If a *lancha* owner comes along, you can probably rent his boat. *Mojarra, huachinango* and mullet can be caught.

Getting there: Take Mexico 200 about 30 miles west of Salina Cruz to marked turnoff just before the bridge. Follow the dirt road for about a mile through a huge boulder field, veering left toward the sea. Right tracks take you up into the village.

Playa Azul—Desolate, wind-blown and beautiful, this powdery grayish beach is surrounded by desertlike dunes that swell along the open sea for miles. A tiny fishing community guards the royal-blue tossing waves. Don't run screaming to shore if you see a dark fin cruising among the diving pelicans. It's probably just a *tonina* (a harmless dolphinlike fish with a dorsal fin, common in these parts), resembling a playful shark. But be polite and let the *tonina* finish his lunch before you go back for a swim.

Facilities: Restaurants. *Camping:* Very good; two little *palapa* shelters offer some protection from the wind. *Swimming:* Good; lively but safe waves. *Snorkeling/diving:* Good around the western rocks. *Fishing/boating:* Mullet and *mojarra*. Skiffs for rent.

Getting there: Take Mexico 200 about 12 miles west of Salina Cruz to marked turnoff for "Balneario Playa Azul." Follow the bad dirt road to beach.

PUERTO ARISTA BEACHES

Puerto Arista—The big seaside getaway for residents of Chiapas, Puerto Arista is a dubious oasis on a dud shore full of mudflats and swampy sand. After going without a decent beach since before Salina Cruz, you're grateful for these familiar tropical trappings: the coconut husks and sleeping dogs, the slumping *palapas* and lighthouse nestled in palms, and especially that long silver-gray bullet of a beach, shooting 20 miles in both directions on the roaring sea with pelicans brushing their wingtips on the waves.

Facilities: Restaurants; bathrooms and showers. *Camping:* Nice and quiet except during Christmas and Easter seasons. *Swimming:* At your own risk. Rough, open sea has swift channels that sweep you seaward, plus sharks—nonattacking, locals insist, but who can read the mind of a shark? *Surfing:* Possible. I met two American surfers who tried it, but waves have short breaks and dark forms chased their boards. *Fishing:* This is not a fishing village, but if you can get hold of a boat there's *mojarra*, mullet and *pargo* out there.

Getting there: Take Mexico 200 to marked turnoff south of Tonalá, follow the paved road about ten miles southwest to the beach.

PUERTO MADERO BEACHES

Playa Puerto Madero and **Playa San Benito**—These rocky shores, some forming breakwaters against the surging brown surf, breed narrow beaches with dark, volcanic-black sand. At the southern end of town past the lighthouse, Playa Puerto Madero loops around open sea and fronts a quiet cove behind the lighthouse. A more attractive beach, Playa San Benito, sweeps the northern edge of town. Beginning near a small sandy cemetery, its gray sand, backed by *palapa* houses, curves for several miles along open sea.

Facilities: Restaurants; full facilities in Tapachula about 15 miles away. *Camping:* Possible at both beaches. *Swimming:* Dangerous currents near town. Safe off cove around lighthouse or near protective rocks at cemetery end of San Benito. Stay close to shore; sharks reportedly lurk here. *Fishing:* Shark fishing; also lots of shrimp.

Getting there: From Tapachula, proceed southwest on Mexico 225 for about 15 miles to the village. Follow the main road past the naval base out to the lighthouse for Puerto Madero beach; go in the opposite direction to the sandy road for San Benito.

Trailer Parks

All trailer parks have hookups and baths unless stated otherwise.

PUERTO ESCONDIDO TRAILER PARKS

Carrizalillo Trailer Park (also known as **Puerto Escondido Trailer Park**, on Bahía Carrizalillo; 2-00-77) covers an open field dotted with scattered trees and overlooking a quiet beach. The park has 150 spaces, a pool and area for tent camping.

El Neptuno Trailer Park (Avenida Alfonso Pérez Gasga) faces the town beach with 30 spaces and 40 bamboo shacks shaded by palms.

BAHÍAS DE HUATULCO TRAILER PARKS

Chahue Trailer Park (Playa Chahue) offers bathrooms and a snackbar. Campers compete with cows and chickens for the stark campsites.

Travelers' Tracks
Sightseeing

ACAPULCO TO PUERTO ESCONDIDO

This 250-mile, six-hour drive follows the coast up into the foothills of the **Sierra Madre**, then back to the coast along Mexico 200. From Acapulco, you head east through dwindling coconut groves into fields of corn. After the turnoff for the coastal Laguna de Chautengo, the road weaves its way to the tongue-twisting village of **Cuajinicuilapa**, founded by Mexico's earliest black population in 1562. Current inhabitants are descendants of African Bantu tribesmen and slaves from Zanzibar imported by Spanish nobles to work their land.

At a point just before Mexico 200 leaves the state of Guerrero, the turnoff for **Punta Maldonado** leads some 18 miles southwest to a rocky, windblown point where a lighthouse crowns a bluff and the shoreline sweeps northwest for miles.

Lively **Pinotepa Nacional** welcomes you to the state of Oaxaca, with its tropical market and old church across from the plaza milling with white-garbed Amusgo Indians. To the southeast past the Río Verde lie the jungly Lagunas de Chacahua, part of the **Parque Nacional Lagunas de Chacahua** (Chacahua National Park), a 50-square-mile government preserve for coastal flora and fauna. From here, the road drops gradually out of the dry mountains and strikes ocean again at the beach settlement of Cacalotepec.

About ten miles shy of Puerto Escondido, the shadowy **Laguna Manialtepec** glides among dense mangrove roots around a bird-filled island out to a remote beach (**Playa La Barra**) facing the sea. You can drive directly to the lagoon (off Mexico 200) and rent a covered boat for a two-hour trip to La Barra and back.

PUERTO ESCONDIDO

As you enter Puerto Escondido, you see signs of its inevitable growth: the new international airport, the handsome, rose-brick promenade (**Avenida Alfonso Pérez Gasga**) replacing the dusty main street of years past, the seaside inns and Italian restaurants. Founded as a coffee exportation center in 1925, this languorous hamlet had only 3,000 people 40 years later. Today, the population has shot up to 30,000, thanks to tourism.

This lush green town tumbles down dusty bluffs to the sea. For a bird's eye view, climb the wide white stairway leading up from Avenida Alfonso Pérez Gasga to the hillside **Plaza Independencia**, a small square with wrought-iron benches overlooking the bay. Better still, hike over to **el faro**, the cliffside lighthouse, via the winding Camino al Faro off Avenida Alfonso Pérez Gasga for a delightful vista of the whole bay.

You can make arrangements for **trips to the northern lagoons** of Manialtepec and Chacahua through Agencia de Viajes García Rendón (in the Posada Real, Avenida Benito Juárez; 2-04-58).

PUERTO ÁNGEL

The 45-mile ride from Puerto Escondido takes you through high-and-dry scrub terrain to the market town of **Pochutla**, a sort of supply depot for its seaside satellite, Puerto Ángel. From the Pochutla junction, the Mexico 175 turnoff corkscrews for about six miles down to the little fishing village, passing some secret beaches on the way. You can see the whole town on foot in a leisurely afternoon. Saunter along the brief **malecón** that passes the concrete pier and the naval base along the bay, then pick your way around the muddy arroyo flowing out of the hills and hike toward the hillside **cemetery**, whose cheerful pastel headstones overlook Playa Panteón (Cemetery Beach).

A more rigorous hike from here up to the Hotel Ángel del Mar will put **Bahía de Puerto Ángel's** bright splendors at your feet. En route, stop in at the enchanting **La Posada Cañón Devata**, a woodsy guest-house-in-the-trees whose resident painter, Mateo López, has captured the whimsy of Puerto Ángel on his canvases.

PUERTO ÁNGEL TO SALINA CRUZ

Once again the highway curves inland along plummeting cliffs with unknown wave-kissed coves far below. You snake through vegetated hills and the green **Sierra Madre Sur,** splashed with fields of tomatoes, corn, watermelons, limes, mangoes and coconut groves.

Yellow and white butterflies tumble from the thickets, and sunburnt foliage lining the roadside seems to wave you on to that magical spot just 30 miles ahead, **Santa Cruz Huatulco.** The government's FONATUR signs

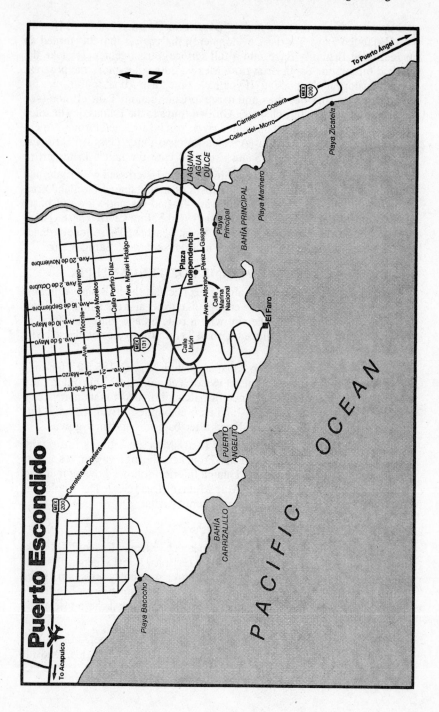

rear up on the highway, announcing "Desarrollo Turístico Bahías de Huatulco" (Huatulco Bays Tourist Development), the project that has turned an
insignificant fishing village into a full-service tourist center. Do take the
marked turnoff for Santa Cruz from Mexico 200 and explore the progress
so far—history in the making. If you have time, take a boat tour of the surrounding bays and beaches and drive to Chahue and Tangolunda (see
"Beaches" section in this chapter). **Guided tours** to the Bahías de Huatulco
tourist development and its unspoiled coves can be arranged through Agencia de Viajes García Rendón (Avenida Alfonso Pérez Gasga, Puerto Escondido; 2-01-14), at Playa Santa Cruz and with the hotels in the area.

The next 90 miles cover coastal highlands criss-crossed with rivers and
pueblos. Here and there, you get glimpses of mountainous farmland crin-
kling out in an emerald quilt to the wave-frosted sea and views of misty
shoreline shooting off like a comet's tail toward **Salina Cruz.** These visions
are the last hurrah for Mexico's West Coast beaches. These lonely dunes
and dazzling bays vanish into soggy mudflats south of Salina Cruz.

SALINA CRUZ AND THE ISTHMUS OF TEHUANTEPEC

You know you're nearing Salina Cruz because the hills shrivel up, the
hovels endemic to industrial life emerge like trolls and the smokestacks of
a fuming oil refinery haze the sky with a rude orange glare. The port of
Salina Cruz, on the wind-whipped **Gulf of Tehuantepec,** is not blessed with
looks. Move on.

From Salina Cruz, Mexico 200 merges with Mexico 185 for a ten-mile
jog due north to the major isthmus town of **Tehuantepec.** This old tropical
city, sunk like a dream in a jungle of palms, is famed for its matriarchal
society of Indians, the Tehuanas, and their elaborate festival costumes that
include remarkable bonnets designed after babies' baptismal gowns.

The next town along the road (now Mexico 190) is industrial
Juchitán—a spot with zero charisma. From here the highway curves around
the lifeless Laguna Superior and Laguna Inferior, followed by the mudflats
and enervated villages along the **Mar Muerto** (Dead Sea). The whole area
has a bad case of beach blues until Puerto Arista.

PUERTO ARISTA TO TAPACHULA

Right after the little town of Tapanatepec, where Mexico 200 breaks
from Mexico 190, you enter the state of Chiapas, a real change of scene.
The listless, windy landscape of the isthmus gradually stirs, shifts and
heaves up into the glistening shoulders of the verdant **Sierra Madre de
Chiapas.** South of sleepy Tonalá lies Puerto Arista, with its here-to-eternity
beach (see "Beaches" section in this chapter).

For the next 150 miles the highland-tropical landscape—misted hills
in ever-fading bluish tiers, palms and farmland, sugar cane fields, roadside
reeds, cattle ranches—beckons you into thriving **Tapachula.** This center

of commerce for the whole southwest agricultural zone is also a major conduit of traffic to and from Guatemala. To the north hovers the extinct volcano **Tacana**, 20 miles beyond Unión Juárez. Across the border rises a sister volcano, **Tajamulco.**

Even closer, north of Tapachula off Mexico 200, are the scattered ruins of **Izapa**, dating back 1,000 years to an Olmec-Mayan culture. Marked by a pyramid sign, a small ceremonial site standing on the roadside contains reconstructed pyramids, a sacrificial stone and hieroglyphics.

A more secretive site a mile or two south of here (back in the direction of Tapachula) is concealed on the opposite side of the road, reached by a path through a cocoa plantation. There's no sign; if in doubt, ask locals about **las esculturas escondidas** (the hidden sculptures). Children may lead you to a green field ringed in eroded stelae and chipped figures of a smiling frog and a tree of life. Beyond an unexcavated hill near a fast-running stream, a fantastic stone cobra rears up out of the banana trees with a man in its mouth. No doubt many more riches here wait to be unearthed.

You can also dip into local history at Tapachula's little **Museo de Antropología** (Parque de Exposiciónes, Mexico 225, Km. 2). The museum houses a fine collection of Mayan pieces, including a ritualistic urn with the original paints on its totemic faces and a turquoise-studded skull.

Shopping

The slow southwest coast is a drought for shoppers. Puerto Escondido has the only worthwhile stores.

PUERTO ESCONDIDO SHOPPING

The pedestrian section of **Avenida Alfonso Pérez Gasga** bustles like an open-air shopping mall. Shops sell T-shirts, beachwear, hammocks, blankets and other bits of Mexicana. Vendors and jewelry craftsmen spread their wares near the Hotel Las Palmas.

Platería Bambu (Avenida Alfonso Pérez Gasga), the nicest shop in town, specializes in silver and brass, with all sorts of jewelry, goblets and trays, masks and ceramics. Check out the tiny wooden surfboard pendants inset with mother-of-pearl.

Another good-sized shop, **Charly's Bazaar** (Avenida Alfonso Pérez Gasga near corner of Calle Marina Nacional), is filled with rock music and inexpensive beachwear: bikinis, shorts, cotton dresses, batik-print T-shirts, sashes and scarves.

For odds and ends, fruit and veggies, blankets and bargainable artisan's treasures, stroll downtown to the chaotic **central market** (starting at Avenida Oaxaca and Avenida Miguel Hidalgo).

Nightlife

There's not much cooking after hours in these climes. Figure out 25 ways to do nothing and bask in them. Or try:

PUERTO ESCONDIDO NIGHTLIFE

Puerto Escondido has a couple of erratically open nightspots where you can sweat out your Saturday night fever. The **Macumba Disco-Bar** (Avenida Alfonso Pérez Gasga 46; 2-04-48) is a casual *palapa*-roofed club with a patio overlooking the main beach and a small elevated dance floor.

For more serenity, enjoy an evening drink at the *palapa*-roofed restaurant-bar **La Estancia** (Avenida Alfonso Pérez Gasga), where a solo guitarist entertains amid the white-and-green tables and plants. The nicer hotels in town all have attractive restaurant-bars, too. Try the **Hotel Santa Fé** (Calle del Morro; 2-01-70), the **Hotel Las Palmas** (Avenida Alfonso Pérez Gasga; 2-02-30) and the **Best Western Posada Real** (Avenida Benito Juárez; 2-01-33).

PUERTO ÁNGEL NIGHTLIFE

There's even less hopping down here. Nightlife means strumming guitars and making journal entries. The favorite late-night spot (post-10 p.m.) for cold drinks and gossip is the **Restaurant El Árbol** (Boulevard Virgilio Uribe, across from the beach). It's just a glorified shack with a cement floor, but there's reggae music and a cool breeze blowing in off the bay.

Southwest Coast Addresses and Phone Numbers

PUERTO ESCONDIDO
Bank—Bancomer, Avenida Alfonso Pérez Gasga (2-03-37)
Hospital—Centro de Salud, Avenida Alfonso Pérez Gasga 409 (2-01-11)
Laundry—Lavandería Automática del Puerto, Avenida Miguel Hidalgo (2-04-33)
Newspapers and magazines—Papelería y Regalos Aquario, Avenida Alfonso Pérez Gasga; and Paperback Shack, Avenida Alfonso Pérez Gasga
Police—Plaza Independencia, off Avenida Alfonso Pérez Gasga (2-01-11)
Post Office—Mexico 200 near the westernmost turnoff for Avenida Alfonso Pérez Gasga
Tourist office—Delgado Estatal de Turismo Costa, Avenida Alfonso Pérez Gasga 900 (2-01-75)

PUERTO ÁNGEL-POCHUTLA
Bank—Bancomer, Avenida Lázaro Cárdenas and Calle Allende, in Pochutla
Hospital—Centro de Salud, Avenida Lázaro Cárdenas 75, in Pochutla (4-01-63)

Police—Palacio Municipal (4-01-35—municipal; 4-00-12—state), in Pochutla

Post Office—Calle Progreso, in Pochutla

Tourist office—Avenida Principal (continuation of Mexico 175, at the entrance to town in Puerto Ángel), rarely open

BAHÍAS DE HUATULCO

Bank—Bancomer, in Santa Cruz

Hospital—4-03-83; clinic (4-03-82)

Laundry—Lavandería Yinna, Calle Palma Real and Calle Gardenia, in Crucecita

SALINA CRUZ

Bank—Bánamex, Calle Guaymas near Avenida Ávila Camacho

Hospital—Hospital Rural, Avenida Ávila Camacho and Calle Tuxpan (4-01-10)

Laundry—Lavandería Anabel, Avenida Tampico

Police—4-05-23

Post Office—Avenida Ávila Camacho

TAPACHULA

Hospital—Avenida Norte 4a and Calle Poniente 19a (6-17-12)

Laundry—Lava Ropa, Avenida Central Norte 33 (6-35-25)

Police—6-19-96

Post Office—1a Calle Oriente and 9a Avenida Norte

CHAPTER NINE
Gulf of Mexico

Mexico's Gulf Coast packs more history into its three states and 1,000 miles of shoreline than any other coastal area of the country except the Yucatán Peninsula.

Here the nation's oldest known indigenous peoples, the Olmecs, founded their jaguar-worshipping civilization and carved their massive mysterious stone heads in the lowland jungles. From Olmec culture—the first to use a 365-day calendar—sprang all advanced civilizations in Mesoamerica, including the Mayas and Aztecs.

The death knell for Indian rule came in 1519, when Hernán Cortés and his band of conquistadors docked their galleons along the Gulf Coast. The Spanish first set foot in Mexico at a site they christened Villa Rica de la Vera Cruz (Rich Town of the True Cross), today the country's biggest port.

Centuries after the invaders harnessed Indian Mexico to the Spanish crown, the Mexican-American War of 1846-1848 began. Growing from skirmishes between Texas and the Gulf Coast state of Tamaulipas, the war, which bled Mexico of half its territory, then spread to Veracruz and points west.

The Gulf Coast has been the stage for many other dramatic, pivotal incidents in Mexican history: the forging of a new constitution in the wake of the revolution; the arrival of misguided Maximilian of France to rule a people who did not want him; and, at the turn of the century, the discovery of oil.

With its bottomless deposits of black gold, the Gulf Coast outshines most of the nation economically. First pumped in the rich state of Veracruz, oil was struck again in neighboring Tabasco in the mid-1970s. Immense gushers sent the nation's economy sky-high. The lowering of crude prices has taken the gleam off the oil bonanza, but petroleum remains one of Mexico's top two industries, matched only by tourism. Refineries and tankers lie along the southern Gulf, and Petróleos Mexicanos (Pemex) is headquartered in this region. Many boom towns, fueled with oil pesos, dot the area. The mushrooming industry is a source of national pride but does not offer much aesthetic appeal.

The Gulf Coast states of Tamaulipas, Veracruz and Tabasco share a common spirit of prosperity but are geographically quite different. Tamaulipas, part of the crusty, prairielike Northeast, contrasts with the mountainous, rainy abundance of Veracruz and the river-slashed jungles of Tabasco. Veracruz claims Mexico's highest peak, Orizaba, rising some 18,550 feet near the capital city of Jalapa.

The best season for visiting this area is November to April, when the weather is balmy. Summers can be oppressively humid, hot and rainy. *Nortes* (chill north winds and storms) sporadically sweep the Gulf from October to February.

This area is only a low-grade beach zone. The grayish sand and brownish Gulf waters, often sullied by oil waste, don't make an inviting combination. There are, however, about half-a-dozen surprisingly lovely tropical beaches between Matamoros and Villahermosa.

Among the Gulf Coast's other attractions are good fishing, fine seafood, great coffee and a sultry island tempo borrowed from the nearby Caribbean. The Gulf used to be a big tourist magnet before Cancún began to siphon off the sun worshippers. Its old towns still have a tang that the slick Americanized Caribbean playgrounds lack: the feeling of a weathered, well-settled area, full of character and roots reaching back to pre-Hispanic Mexico.

Starting up north at the American border near Brownsville, Texas, the busy city of Matamoros has a war-torn past but today enjoys a reputation as Mexico's friendliest, cleanest border town, with good shopping and a pleasant beach.

Farther south sits the dirty port of Tampico, an oil-boom city with a rowdy downtown full of sailors but a local beach and town square full of personality.

In the state of Veracruz, the town of Tuxpan alongside the Río Tuxpan is known for its tarpon fishing and its 20-mile-long beach, unfortunately infested with bloodthirsty bugs.

From the coast at Tuxpan, the highway ascends through the oil-boom town of Poza Rica to the charming mountain town of Papantla, a big vanilla center near the Totonac ruins of El Tajín. The present-day Totonacs are famed for their flying pole-dance.

At the small village of Gutiérrez Zamora a spur to the left leads to tiny seaside Tecolutla, which claims one of the Gulf Coasts's finest palm-lined beaches. Then the main highway returns to fabulous Veracruz. This historic port should not be missed—it's a hundred times more exciting than Cancún yet is often skipped because of its poor beaches. You'll hardly miss the

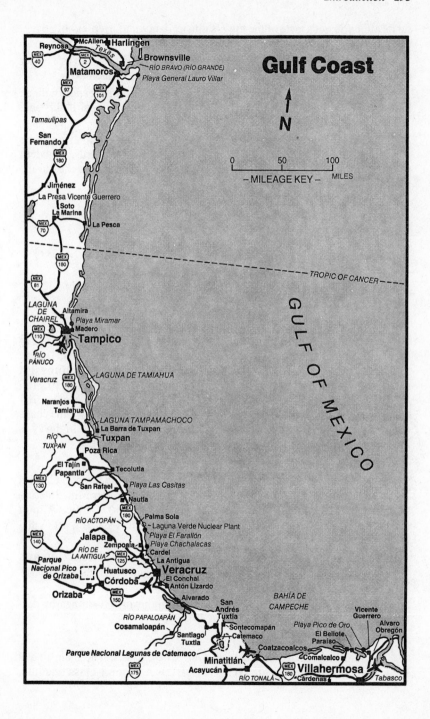

Gulf Coast

N

0   50   100
– MILEAGE KEY –   MILES

TROPIC OF CANCER

GULF OF MEXICO

Reynosa
McAllen
Harlingen
Texas
Brownsville
RÍO BRAVO (RÍO GRANDE)
Playa General Lauro Villar
Matamoros

Tamaulipas

San
Fernando

Jiménez
La Presa Vicente Guerrero
Soto
La Marina
La Pesca

LAGUNA
DE
CHAIREL
Altamira
Playa Miramar
Madero
Tampico

RÍO
PÁNUCO

Veracruz

LAGUNA DE TAMIAHUA

Naranjos
Tamiahua

LAGUNA TAMPAMACHOCO
La Barra de Tuxpan
Tuxpan
Poza Rica
RÍO
TUXPAN
El Tajín
Papantla
Tecolutla
San Rafael
Playa Las Casitas
Nautla

RÍO ACTOPÁN
Palma Sola
Laguna Verde Nuclear Plant
Playa El Farallón
Playa Chachalacas
Cardel
La Antigua
Jalapa
Zempoala
RÍO DE
LA ANTIGUA
Parque
Nacional Pico
de Orizaba
Huatusco
Veracruz
El Conchal
Antón Lizardo
Córdoba
Orizaba
Alvarado
San
Andrés
Tuxtla
BAHÍA DE
CAMPECHE
Vicente
Guerrero
Playa Pico de Oro
El Bellote
Paraíso
Álvaro
Obregón
RÍO PAPALOAPÁN
Cosamaloapán
Santiago
Tuxtla
Sontecomapán
Catemaco
Coatzacoalcos
Comalcalco
Parque Nacional Lagunas de Catemaco
Minatitlán
Acayucán
RÍO TONALÁ
Villahermosa
Cárdenas
Tabasco

sands after you get a taste of the town's music, dance and irrepressibly lively cafés.

To the south, the pretty mountain resort of Catemaco, known as a center of Mexican witchcraft, stands on ten-mile-long Lago Catemaco.

You can quickly pass through Coatzacoalcos, an ugly seaport with an industrial air, unless you want to check out its homely but spirited beach.

Continuing south, you enter the state of Tabasco and its rising capital, Villahermosa, gateway to the Yucatán Peninsula. Too commercial to be charming, the town is nevertheless graced with wide boulevards, a modern park with a unique Olmec sculpture garden and some lush beaches to the north.

Easy Living
Transportation

ARRIVAL

BY CAR

The most common points of entry into the Gulf Coast area are at Matamoros (near Brownsville, Texas) and Reynosa (near McAllen, Texas). From Reynosa, **Mexico 97** joins **Mexico 101/180** from Matamoros just north of the village of Francisco Villa. The highway continues as 101/180 for approximately 45 miles until the La Como Junction. There Mexico 101 heads west into the interior and Mexico 180 continues south down the coast, connecting all the major towns in this chapter. This two-lane highway is in reasonably good condition.

BY AIR

Five airports are located on the Gulf Coast: General Servando Canales International Airport (Matamoros), General Francisco Javier Mina International Airport (Tampico), Veracruz International Airport, Cantica Airport (Coatzacoalcos) and Capitán Carlos A. Rovirosa International Airport (Villahermosa).

Aeroméxico services **Matamoros** while both Aeroméxico and Mexicana Airlines fly to **Villahermosa**. Mexicana Airlines also serves **Tampico** and **Veracruz**.

Taxis and vans provide transportation from the airports to nearby destinations.

BY BUS

Regular bus service connects all Gulf Coast towns. The main line is the first-class **Autobuses de Oriente (ADO)**. A second-class bus line,

Transportes Frontera, connects United States and Mexican border towns. **Tres Estrellas de Oro** provides some service up north, but ADO predominates. Bus depots and information numbers are as follows:

Matamoros: The Central de Autobuses (Calle Canales between Calle Luis Aguilar and Calle Primera) is served by Tres Estrellas de Oro (2-24-25), ADO (2-01-81) and Transportes Frontera (2-31-75).

Tampico: The Centro de Autobuses (Calle Zapotal near Avenida Ejército Nacional) includes Tres Estrellas de Oro (13-41-31), ADO (13-41-82) and Transportes Frontera (13-48-67).

Tuxpan: There is an ADO depot (Calle Genaro Rodríguez 1; 4-01-02).

Papantla: The town has an ADO depot (Calle Benito Juárez 207; 2-02-18).

Veracruz: Central Camionera (Avenida Salvador Díaz Mirón and Avenida Xalapa) is served by ADO (37-55-22).

Catemaco: ADO (Calle Nicolás Bravo and Calle Aldama).

Coatzacoalcos: ADO (Calle Miguel Hidalgo 106; 2-04-40).

Villahermosa: ADO (Calle Lino Merino and Calle Mina; 2-14-46).

BY TRAIN

Matamoros, Tampico and Veracruz can be reached by the rail line **Ferrocarriles Nacionales de México**. Depots locations are: Matamoros (Calle Miguel Hidalgo; 2-02-55); Tampico (Avenida Héroes de Nacozari; 2-34-17); Veracruz (Plazuela Jesús García, end of Avenida Montesinos; 32-25-69).

CAR RENTALS

All major Gulf Coast towns have agencies where you can rent cars. The five airports serving these towns all have car rental booths.

In Matamoros, try **Dollar** (3-76-77), **Budget** (3-48-80), **Avis** (3-54-61), **Rally** (3-19-96) and **Fast** (6-01-00). In Tampico, rent from **Avis** (13-23-56), **Hertz** (13-66-55) and **National** (13-17-67). In Veracruz, your choices include **Dollar** (32-00-65), **Hertz** (32-40-21), **Auto-Renta** (37-08-64) and **Quick** (37-12-65). In Villahermosa, try **Hertz** (2-11-11), **Fast** (3-68-35), **National** (2-03-93) and **Dollar** (2-55-55).

PUBLIC TRANSPORTATION

In Matamoros, there are buses, *colectivos* (vans) and taxis throughout town, though you can walk to most places. Tampico has less consistent service, with *colectivos* and taxis, plus buses that leave for Playa Miramar from around the *zócalo*. Veracruz buses run regularly from the Plaza de la Constitución and Plaza de la República out to Playa Mocambo; there is good taxi service, too. In Villahermosa, buses and taxis are plentiful.

Hotels

MATAMOROS HOTELS

There is no shortage of hotels here, but budget choices are slim.

Pleasant and friendly, the **Hotel Roma** (Calle 9a No. 1420; 3-61-76) offers small rooms which are fresh and clean. The hotel also features room service. Budget.

Still within the budget range, the downtown **Autel Nieto** (Calle 10a 1508; 3-09-97) gives you a restaurant-bar and 85 huge, comfortable rooms with a pseudo-glamorous Las Vegas look: shag carpets, padded headboards, overstuffed chairs and fake-marble plastic doors. Budget.

The bright new star in Matamoros is the pretty pink **Hotel Plaza Matamoros** (Calle 9a and Calle Bravo Esquina; 6-16-02). Here a glass elevator rises over the four-story atrium, with an art-moderne black-and-white tiled restaurant below. Conveniently, it's situated a half-block from the new *mercado* and one block from the old. Moderate.

The town's oldest luxury inn, the 90-room **Hotel Ritz** (Calle 7a and Calle Matamoros; 2-11-90) has been remodeled and looks snazzy. The snug, carpeted rooms evoke the charm of a home bedroom, with rosy leather chairs, soft lighting and pastel walls, plus phones, air-conditioning and cable television. Moderate.

Matamoros' top luxury spot is the **Hotel del Prado** (Avenida Alvaro Obregón 249; 3-94-40). This 120-room facility offers large golden-toned guest accommodations furnished in Spanish colonial style, plus a swimming pool, landscaped gardens, restaurant and bar. Moderate to deluxe.

TAMPICO HOTELS

The downtown area is full of moderately priced hotels.

One of the few low-cost places to stay is the 60-room **Hotel Plaza** (Calle Francisco Madero and Calle de Olmos; 4-16-78). A bit dingy and shopworn but clean, the air-conditioned rooms are small and carpeted, with televisions and phones. Budget.

Right next door, the seven-floor **Hotel Colonial** (Calle Francisco Madero 210 Oriente; 2-76-76) guarantees an entertaining visit in its 150 small but nicely appointed rooms, which offer guests a movie list next to each cable television. The dark-wood furniture and brightly tiled baths add a finished touch. Budget.

Tampico's own little piece of Hollywood is its downtown, four-floor **Hotel Impala** (Avenida Salvador Díaz Mirón 220 Poniente; 12-09-90). Though quite friendly, the Impala favors chilly chandeliers and plastic plants surrounded by marbled mirrors. The 83 good-sized rooms are comfortable but garishly decorated, with 1950s-style furniture, phones and color televisions. Budget.

Tampico has two relatively inexpensive luxury hotels: the **Camino Real Tampico** (Avenida Hidalgo 2000; 3-88-11) is a comfortable resort in a tropical garden with 100 bright, modern guest rooms, a swimming pool, two restaurants and a bar. Moderate.

Posada de Tampico (Carretera Tampico–Mante, Km. 2.2; 3-30-50) is a palm-ringed resort on the north edge of town with 130 lovely pastel guest rooms, two restaurants, bar, swimming pool and tennis court. Moderate.

TUXPAN HOTELS

Three comfortable old downtown inns provide excellent choices. **Hotel Florida** (Avenida Benito Juárez 23; 4-02-22) has open-air halls and sitting areas as well as 73 rooms which offer views of the broad and lovely Río Tuxpan. Its unadorned rooms come with air-conditioners or ceiling fans, phones and simple wood furniture. Budget.

For the same money, you get color televisions and marble floors at the nearby **Hotel Plaza** (Avenida Benito Juárez 39; 4-07-38). Budget.

The most attractive of the three is the **Hotel Reforma** (Avenida Benito Juárez 25; 4-02-10), whose 100 rooms rise around a softly lit courtyard filled with potted palms and fountains. Rooms are medium-sized and modern, with phones and televisions. The third-floor doubles are the nicest rooms in town. Budget.

Impressive yet friendly is the resort-like **Hotel Tajín** (Km. 2.5 Camino A. Cobos; 4-22-60), set in spacious gardens along the banks of Río Tuxpan. Offering a panoramic view, 114 modern rooms, 49 bungalows, a restaurant, swimming pool and tennis court, it nevertheless is priced budget.

PAPANTLA HOTELS

Your best bet is the inexpensive **Hotel El Tajín** (Calle Núñez y Domínguez 104; 2-10-62), on a breezy hilltop overlooking the town. The simple rooms come with both air-conditioning and ceiling fans, phones, televisions and cheerful tiled furnishings. Some have balconies. Budget.

Another possibility is the fancier, moderately priced **Hotel Totonacapán** (Calle Olivio and Calle 20 de Noviembre; 2-12-18), but staying in nearby seaside Tecolutla is a better option.

TECOLUTLA TO VERACRUZ HOTELS

This seaside strip of highway has many pleasant hotels.

In the village of Tecolutla, the gracious old **Hotel Balneario Tecolutla** (Calle Matamoros; 5-07-63) rests invitingly amid a dense palm grove directly on the lovely beach. The handsome, cedar-beamed sitting room and restaurant open onto a patio and pool. The 72 rooms, plain but comfortable, come with ceiling fans, phones and sea-weathered furniture. Budget.

A cheaper option is Tecolutla's beachfront **Hotel MarSol** (Calle Aumas; 5-09-67). This white triple-decker hotel, built in 1950 and showing its age, has spacious fan-cooled rooms with double beds and sea views, basic but livable. Budget.

En route to Nautla, the pretty stretch of beach called Playa Paraíso has sprouted several comfortable inns, all budget priced. The best family spot, with a big pool and white air-conditioned bungalows set in a palmy garden, is **Hotel El Palmar** (Mexico 180 between Poza Rica and Nautla). The more economical, motel-style **Hotel Estrella del Mar** (Mexico 180, Km. 83.5; 5-03-14) has sparkling clean, rudimentary rooms with fans and an attractive restaurant-bar, but no sea views. The ritzier palm-shaded **Hotel Playa Paraíso** (Mexico 180 near San Rafael; 8-00-46) includes two pools, a restaurant-bar and 37 ample but worn rooms facing the sea, with small televisions.

On Playa Chachalacas, a popular beach north of Veracruz, 107 spacious rooms and villas make up the sprawling, government-run **Hotel Chachalacas** (Playa Chachalacas, Úrsulo Galván; 2-02-41, in nearby Cardel). Though the rooms need a paint job and tend to be colorless, their sea views add charm, and the grounds include an Olympic-sized pool and tennis courts. Budget to moderate.

VERACRUZ HOTELS

Veracruz is an undiscovered kingdom of old budget hotels. Those in El Centro on the lively Plaza de la Constitución are nearly relics, yet each is a fine place to stay. The best deal is the remodeled, 34-room **Hotel Prendes** (Avenida Independencia 1064; 31-02-41), built in 1926. Its substantial rooms, with air-conditioning and televisions, have balconies facing the *zócalo* and are in far better shape than rooms in nearby hotels. Budget.

A good second choice is next door at the **Hotel Colonial** (Calle Lerdo 105; 32-01-93), with 182 air-conditioned rooms, a sidewalk café, coffee shop, indoor swimming pool and solarium. Budget.

If you'd rather be close to the sea, the five-floor **Hotel Mar y Tierra** (Avenida General Figuerroa and Paseo del Malecón; 31-38-66) will put you right on the *malecón* with a view of the busy port. There are new and old rooms, all comfortable, with phone, air-conditioning, carpet, television and quaint touches. Budget.

For a hotel that is a minor empire, try the **Hotel Villa del Mar** (Boulevard Ávila Camacho; 31-33-66), right on the *malecón* south of El Centro. Its palm-shaded grounds contain rustic bungalows, tennis court, pool, restaurant, trailer park, playground and 81 good-sized air-conditioned rooms with color televisions and views of the Gulf. Budget to moderate.

Stay directly on the best beach in Veracruz at the inviting, classy **Hotel Playa Paraíso** (Calzada Ruiz Cortines 3500; 37-83-99), located in the nearby village of Boca del Río. Set in a fresh private garden, the Playa Paraíso offers modern air-conditioned suites and villas (or *casitas*, little houses).

All are super-roomy, warmly furnished and full of natural light. Pool and tennis courts. Moderate.

Right next door, bathed in tropical atmosphere and romance, the old **Hotel Mocambo** (Calzada Ruiz Cortines; 37-15-31) is an enchanted maritime fantasy. It features wooden mermaids, an immense carved steering wheel suspended from the lobby ceiling and layers of flower-filled patios cascading down the hill to the beach, connected by a walkway. The wonderful rooms look out on all this, offering honey-toned cedar chandeliers, color televisions and little refrigerators. A must to explore. Moderate.

For luxury at a bargain, try the **Hoteles Emporio Veracruz** (Paseo del Malecón and Calle Xicontencatl; 32-00-20). The completely remodeled eight-story hotel has 202 air-conditioned rooms with panoramic views of the city and bay. There's also a gourmet restaurant and three swimming pools. Moderate.

CATEMACO HOTELS

All hotels in this village are low priced and comfortable.

One of the cheapest, just off the main plaza, is the homely **Hotel Berthangel** (Calle Francisco Madero 1; 3-00-89), distinguished by its upstairs glass cafeteria. Everything is clean, but the 23 air-conditioned rooms are low-ceilinged and rather cramped. Budget.

On the other side of the plaza stands the town's pride, the old **Hotel Catemaco** (Calle Carranza 8; 3-00-45), as neon-lit as a movie marquee. In addition to its pool, parking lot and fine little restaurant, the hotel features large rooms that are the village's best, with paneling, color televisions and air-conditioning. Budget.

My preference, since Catemaco borders a lake, is a hotel with a view of that graceful spot. **Motel Posada Koniapán** (Avenida Malecón and Avenida Revolución; 3-00-63) fills the bill. Its two-story motel complex, tucked back amid quiet palms, holds 22 big, colonial-style rooms with either air-conditioning or ceiling fan and breezy balcony. Budget.

COATZACOALCOS HOTELS

Hotels are expensive and the sights few in this unappealing city. If you must stop here, two good choices are: **Hotel Varadero** (Calle John Spark 411; 2-63-88), a modern highrise near the beach with bland but fully equipped rooms and downstairs restaurant; and **Hotel Valgrande** (corner of Calle Miguel Hidalgo and Calle Morelos; 2-16-24), an oldish downtown hotel with smaller rooms but more old-fashioned character. Both moderate.

The best choice downtown is the **Hotel Margón** (Calle Zaragoza 302; 2-05-72), a three-story air-conditioned hotel just one block from the plaza. There's a good restaurant here and a pleasant lobby. Moderate.

VILLAHERMOSA HOTELS

This busy city has many reasonable but often crowded hotels. One of the least expensive is the somewhat rundown **Hotel Ritz** (Avenida Francisco Madero 1013; 2-16-11), about four blocks from El Centro. The small, dark rooms sometimes have no place to rest your suitcase except the closet, but they're air-conditioned and offer color televisions and restful double beds. Budget.

Not far away, right on the lovely downtown pedestrian mall, the much nicer **Hotel Madán** (Avenida Francisco Madero 408; 2-16-50) gives you 20 antiseptic but very comfortable carpeted rooms with more breathing space and air-conditioning. Budget.

The ritziest downtown hotel, also on the pedestrian mall, is the 68-room **Hotel Miraflores** (Calle Reforma 304; 2-00-54). Its modern rooms, though not especially attractive, have all the trimmings: phone, color television, air-conditioning. Budget.

The award-winning **Hotel Maya Tabasco** (Boulevard Adolfo Ruiz Cortínez 907 and Boulevard Grijalva; 2-11-78) is a contemporary five-story hotel with 160 large, comfortable rooms. Each is appointed with red carpets, colonial furniture, and blue-tiled baths. Very friendly staff. Moderate to deluxe.

Restaurants

MATAMOROS RESTAURANTS

Scattered around town are many Americanized restaurants charging in dollars, with menus in English and seemingly all offering frogs' legs, onion rings, hamburgers and turkey dinners with cranberry sauce.

One of the cheaper spots is the restaurant at the **Autel Nieto** (Calle 10a 1508; 3-09-97). Big and carpeted, right near the shopping zone, with uniformed waiters and a chiefly Mexican clientele, this is a good spot for breakfast. Budget.

Up the street is the family-style **Restaurant Louisiana** (Calle 8a and Calle Nicolás Bravo; 2-01-96), open for lunch and dinner only. With linoleum floors and fake fireplace, the Louisiana evokes the downhome flavor of bayou country. The servings are colossal: all meals—seafood, meat, Mexican dishes—come with french fries, onion rings, guacamole, beans and chips. Budget to moderate.

Two popular hangouts, open for lunch and dinner, are the sprawling gringoized **Restaurant-Bar U.S.** (Calle González 73 and Calle 5a; 3-78-19) and **The Drive Inn** (Calle 6a and Avenida Miguel Hidalgo; 2-00-22). The former, despite its good food and friendly service, is dark, windowless, soullessly elegant and ice cold (I wore a tablecloth throughout dinner to survive the air-conditioning). There's more real old-fashioned character at the incongruously named Drive Inn, open since 1916. Its crystal chandeliers, silky curtains and grand piano and violin music in the evenings evoke a musty romantic aura. Steaks and seafood complement the cheek-to-cheek dancing. Both moderate to deluxe.

TAMPICO RESTAURANTS

This sweaty port city bustles with downtown ice cream parlors (*neverías*) and cafés serving vanilla-flavored cappuccino and espresso. Tampico is the home of the famous *carne Tampiqueña*, a spicy broiled beef dish.

The favorite morning coffee stop of locals is the **Café y Nevería Elite** (Avenida Salvador Díaz Mirón 211 Oriente; 2-03-64), just steps away from the main plaza. This big, shiny café, with formica tables always packed, serves a great assortment of breakfasts (waffles, biscuits, eggs), other meals and ice cream specials. Budget.

Another great little coffee shop is the air-conditioned **Nevería Piter** (Calle Aduana 107 Sur; 2-42-67), serving coffees, desserts and *bocoditos* (tortillas filled with eggs, shredded meat, cheese or other fillings, popular for breakfast). Budget.

For seafood, everyone in town swears by **Restaurant de Mariscos Diligencias** (Calle Tampico Oriente 415, a block off Plaza de la Libertad; 14-12-79). Big, friendly, high-ceilinged and animated with painted octopus and sea life along its dusty outside walls, the Diligencias serves everything from spicy stuffed crab (pocked with shells) to fried fish eggs. Budget to moderate.

Most locals agree that Tampico's finest is the **Restaurant Jardín Corona** (Avenida Miguel Hidalgo 1915; 13-93-83). Quiet and proper, far from the noisy port, with crisp napkins and paneled walls, it serves seafood, steaks and its own *Tampiqueña*—thick and delicious, though not on the menu (just ask). Moderate.

TUXPAN RESTAURANTS

Restaurant Florida (Avenida Benito Juárez 23; 4-02-22) is one of several air-conditioned downtown restaurants with formica tables, tile floors and a view of the street. The menu includes eggs, tacos, spaghetti and tasty shrimp with seasoned rice. Budget.

Up the street is the similarly appointed **Restaurant del Hotel Plaza** (Avenida Benito Juárez 39; 4-07-38), clean and comfortable, with good breakfasts (including shrimp omelettes and cappuccino), soups, salads and Mexican dishes. Budget to moderate.

For a view of the Río Tuxpan, the attractive, globe-lit **Fisher's** (Calle Hernández, on the *malecón*; 4-02-71) offers indoor, air-conditioned dining and outdoor patio dining. The neon "Pizza" sign is deceptive; the menu also includes meat, chicken and rich seafood casseroles. Moderate.

(Text continued on page 306.)

Café Life in Veracruz

They say Veracruz has a rhythm like no other Mexican city. A little calypso, a dash of salsa, the cry of the crab vendor and the call of the ship's horn—exotic flavors spice the air with a special *joie de vivre*.

Some say it comes from a unique Afro-Caribbean influence, dating back to 1540 and the import of thousands of African slaves who intermarried with the Spanish and Indians. Others point to the feverish spring Carnival of Roman Catholic descent, an explosion of costumes, song and dance celebrated here since 1925. Whatever the source of this big port's party mood, amble down to the Plaza de la Constitución and see for yourself why Veracruz is considered Mexico's happiest town—especially after dark.

Toward dusk, the fountains (which often take a siesta by day) begin their splashy chorus. All along café-lined Los Portales, a wide columned breezeway running the length of the plaza, mariachis tune their trumpets and guitars. Strollers gather under the trees, their voices raised in political debate or hushed in good-humored gossip. *Jarochos*, natives of Veracruz, adore conversation. All the more reason to gravitate toward the cafés that ring the square, serving *café con leche,* seafood and beer. Oases of camaraderie, they are perfect little fan-cooled galleries for the all-night people-watching show to come.

Across the avenida at the Gran Café de la Parroquia, a marimba band strikes up a tropical melody on a wooden xylophone, joined by the festive ping of spoons on glass. People tap their glasses (no cups here) for attention. Ancient waiters shuffle over to pour milk into coffee from battered kettles—a time-honored custom at this old meeting ground.

Would you like a cigar? A letter-opener, newspaper, tiny dried fish for snacking? Perhaps a mammoth model ship that would fill your bathtub? Relax. The masses of vendors will come to you, peddling from table to table in endless orbit around the square. In their wake flows a stream of poor children and other unfortunates begging for leftovers—a sad sight amid all the gaiety.

The highlight of the evening is watching folk dancers perform to the music of a tropical band in front of the grand colonial Palacio Municipal, or City Hall. With frothy white skirts and heel-snapping boots, the dancers strut onto the stage. They do the *bamba*, *macumba*, *huapango* and *cumbia*, saucy native dances accented by the pluck of huge wooden harps. With enticing restraint, the women bow gracefully, whirl and act coy; the men, under white sombreros, stomp circles around them, whistle and grin. The courting ritual comes to a head with a comical body-slapping mosquito dance.

Then the band plays a round of Cuban *danzón* music, and the spectators drift back to the cafés, where the carnival of vendors and minstrels goes on, sometimes till dawn.

PAPANTLA RESTAURANTS

The very basic **Restaurant El Tajín** (attached to the Hotel El Tajín, Calle Núñez y Domínguez 104; 2-10-62) has a refreshing hilltop view and a brief menu offering eggs, steak, shrimp, tacos and cheese fondue. Budget.

The more pleasant **Restaurant La Terraza** (Calle Reforma near the *zócalo*, upstairs) has exactly the same menu but is open only for lunch and dinner. Overlooking the main plaza, it's fresh and cool, with a striped awning fending off the sun. Budget.

TECOLUTLA TO VERACRUZ RESTAURANTS

Nearly all the hotels along this strip have good, budget-priced restaurants attached.

VERACRUZ RESTAURANTS

Veracruz has great coffee and terrific seafood, including its own spicy *huachinango â la Veracruzana*—red snapper smothered in a tomato, onion and olive sauce.

The city's best-known institution is the bustling old **Gran Café de la Parroquia** (Avenida Independencia 1187), serving coffee as black as night and as strong as sin, widely acknowledged as the best in Mexico. Under the cracked tile arches, indoors and out on the covered veranda, Veracruz's movers and shakers sip *lechero*, a milky coffee that is positively addictive. Light meals are served, too. As a people-watching spot, La Parroquia is unsurpassed. Budget.

Where do Veracruzanos have their morning *gordas* and *picadas* (stuffed tortillas and topped tortillas, respectively)? At **El Samborsito** (Avenida 16 de Septiembre 700; 36-09-27), a little side-street café filled with humming machinery. The waitress presents a list on which you check off your choices. Try *picadas* with eggs and tomatoes. Breakfast only. Budget.

For traditional breakfasts, **Parador del Malecón** (Paseo del Malecón near Calle Gómez Farías; 31-39-44) has delicious juices, omelettes and cappuccinos. It also serves other meals. This breezy café looks out to the port, a short walk from the plaza. Budget.

Among the cafés that line the Plaza de la Constitución, **Restaurant-Bar Prendes** (Avenida Independencia and Calle Lerdo; 32-01-53) is a traditional seafood favorite, though it no longer lives up to its old reputation. It's best as a ringside seat for the nightly fiestas in the square. Lunch and dinner only. Budget to moderate.

Better seafood can be had at **Las Brisas del Mar** (Boulevard Ávila Camacho 3797; 37-46-66), south of El Centro along the *malecón*. Simple and to the point, with tile floors and ceiling fans, this seafood house has richly exotic selections like fish stuffed with eels. Budget to moderate.

The spacious, gracious **Garlic's** (Boulevard Ávila Camacho; 35-10-34) marches out a little of everything, from heavenly cheese fondue to crawfish gumbo. Fountains of greenery and cedar woodwork punctuate the 1950s-style decor, making this quiet seaside restaurant a gardenlike retreat. Budget to moderate.

For a full view of the port, the upstairs restaurant at the Hotel Emporio, **Tangerine** (Paseo del Malecón and Calle Xicoténcatl; 32-00-20) offers luxurious meals in carpeted, bamboo-furnished comfort. Excellent breakfasts. Moderate.

Another all-glass restaurant, lovely and candle-lit at night, **Tilingo Charlie's** (Hotel Emporio, Paseo del Malecón and Calle Xicoténcatl; 32-00-20) gives you a view of the twinkling harbor outdone only by its fine meats, chicken and seafood. Part of the Carlos Anderson chain, this lunch and dinner spot draws a chic crowd. Mariachis serenade every weekend. Moderate.

For the ultimate *huachinango â la Veracruzana*, visit **La Bamba** (Boulevard Ávila Camacho and Calle Emiliano Zapata; 32-53-55). This attractive waterfront restaurant with wave-splashed windows was named for a pirate who sacked Veracruz in 1683. The specialties include fried octopus, snail and red snapper (in season) or *róbalo*, gracefully deboned right at your table. Deluxe.

El Gaucho (Calle Cristóbal Colón, between Boulevard Díaz del Castillo and Calle Jara; 35-04-11) specializes in Argentine cuisine, with delicious pasta, shellfish and meat dishes. Moderate to deluxe.

CATEMACO RESTAURANTS

Lakeside dining is the order of the day here. Start with the giant, rustic **Restaurant-Bar La Ola** (Paseo del Malecón 1; 3-00-10), smack on the water. Under an immense woven-and-lacquered ceiling supported by columns swathed in vines, you can enjoy fresh *topotes* (sardines) and *mojarra* (sunfish) straight from the lake. Meats, breakfasts and other seafood served. Budget.

Up the street, the classier **La Suiza** (Hotel Siete Brujas, Paseo del Malecón; 3-01-57) resembles a blond-wood Swiss chalet, perhaps inspired by Catemaco's overstated reputation as "the Switzerland of Mexico." The bulging menu has everything from waffles to crab crepes. The nicest restaurant on the lake. Budget to moderate.

Inexpensive meals and good coffee are served at **Restaurant Villa del Carmen** (Paseo del Malecón; 3-02-38), one of many open-air restaurants along the water. Set amid shade trees, this café features an imaginative mural of a monkey family sipping soft drinks (inspired by the monkey-inhabited island in the lake). Budget.

The top eating spot in town is the **Restaurant Catemaco** (in the Hotel Catemaco, Calle Carranza 8; 3-00-45). Its fan-cooled comfort and awning-shaded patio make it a delightful place to dine, especially on Sunday evenings when the nearby plaza is teeming with strollers, gawkers and music. An unnerving menu selection, *carne de chango* (monkey meat), turns out to be specially prepared pork—not very good. Other meats, seafoods and malts are served. Budget to moderate.

COATZACOALCOS RESTAURANTS

Both the beachfront **Hotel Varadero** (Calle John Spark 411; 2-63-88) and the downtown **Hotel Valgrande** (Calle Miguel Hidalgo and Calle Morelos; 2-16-24) have good restaurants. Moderate.

VILLAHERMOSA RESTAURANTS

Get off to a good start at **Restaurant Oriente** (Avenida Francisco Madero 423; 2-11-01), on the edge of the downtown pedestrian mall. With checkerboard floor and cheerful service, this fresh little café is the perfect place for breakfast. Besides eggs and cereals, it serves sandwiches, chicken, seafood and steaks. Budget.

Another downtown winner is the sparkling, air-conditioned **Restaurant-Café Madán** (Avenida Francisco Madero 408; 2-16-50). Booths and carpet are part of its Americanized look. The menu features banana splits and hamburgers, plus Mexican dishes—and the food is good. Budget to moderate.

Though it looks strictly like a seafood house, **Restaurant-Bar Club de Pesca** (Avenida 27 de Febrero 812; 2-21-97) has assorted exotic species in its kitchen, like deer, crawfish and crab. This big, friendly downtown restaurant is decorated with Christmas lights and aquariums. Budget to moderate.

Out by the bullring on the south side of town, big bad **Carlos 'n Charlie's** (Plaza de Toros; 3-42-60) holds forth with the gags and charm typical of this Mexican chain: a bull's head in the bar wearing sunglasses, an amazing fully set table and chairs glued upside down to the ceiling, a tropical trio playing romantic tunes. The food, from spicy shrimp consommé to *sábana invierno* (thin filet covered with beans and cheese), is delicious. Budget to moderate.

Small but elite, **El Guaraguao** (Calle 27 de Febrero 947; 2-56-95) specializes in *empanadas pejelagarto* (empanadas filled with alligator fish) as well as other regional dishes from Tabasco. The few tables fill quickly in this popular spot, so go early or make a reservation. Moderate to deluxe.

The Great Outdoors
The Sporting Life

CAMPING

The Gulf Coast, with its scrappy beaches and petrol-soaked shores, isn't an ideal place to camp. But there are some beautiful exceptions to this rule (see "Beaches" section in this chapter). Spring is the best time to pitch a tent. Bugs and sand fleas are worst in the hot months, May through October, so pack repellent.

For supplies in Tampico, try the sprawling downtown **Mercado Hidalgo** (Calle Benito Juárez and Calle Francisco Madero). In Veracruz, find what you need at the lively downtown **Mercado Hidalgo** (Calle Hernán Cortés and Avenida Miguel Hidalgo) or the modern **Plaza Mocambo** mall (about five miles south of El Centro on Calzada Ruiz Cortines). In Villahermosa, the downtown **pedestrian shopping mall** (along Avenida Francisco Madero) and the **Tabasco 2000** complex (northwest end of Paseo Tabasco, past Boulevard Grijalva) should cover your needs.

SWIMMING

Because of the heavy petroleum industry and port activity along the Gulf Coast, the water tends to be dirty around bigger towns like Tampico and Veracruz. Watch where you swim. In spring and summer the water temperature is ideal.

FISHING AND BOATING

The Gulf has more than its share of game fish, from marlin to yellowtail. Tarpon (*sábalo*) is especially popular.

In Tampico, you'll find boat rentals at **Club de Regatas Corona** (Laguna de Chairel; 3-07-88) or **Club de Yates Tampico** (Avenida Miguel Hidalgo 3705-203; 3-25-85). Freshwater fishing is good in Laguna de Chairel (with boats for rent at the **Balneario Rojas** resort) and Laguna del Carpintero, both in town; and at La Presa Vicente Guerrero, a dam near Ciudad Victoria north of Tampico.

Tuxpan offers both gulf and river fishing. Boats and equipment are for rent at **Escuela de Buceo Deportivo Arrecife** (Avenida Independencia; 4-38-84).

In Veracruz, the **Club de Yates Veracruz** (Boulevard Ávila Camacho; 32-09-17) offers fishing information. To rent boats try the **Hostal de Cortés** (Boulevard Ávila Camacho; 33-00-65) or **Transportación Marítima Mexicana** (Avenida Independencia and Calle Cinco de Mayo).

Catemaco's fertile lake yields *mojarra*, *topotes* (sardines) and other freshwater species. Fishing boats are for rent along the *malecón* across from the **Hotel Siete Brujas**.

SKIN DIVING

Diving operations and water visibility are limited along the Gulf Coast. The sea life resembles the corals and tropical fish of the Caribbean, with the clearest water from April to October. In Tuxpan, **Escuela de Buceo Deportivo Arrecife** (Avenida Independencia; 4-38-84) rents equipment, gives lessons and arranges diving trips.

Veracruz has a dive shop, **Tridente** (Boulevard Ávila Camacho 165-A; 32-79-24), that offers lessons, equipment rentals and dive trips.

HUNTING

Around Tampico and Veracruz, there's an abundance of migratory white-wing doves, ducks, geese, deer and rabbits.

GOLF

In Tampico, check out the old **Club Campestre de Tampico** (Avenida Miguel Hidalgo, en route to Ciudad Mante). Veracruz offers a nine-hole course at **Club de Golf Villa Rica** south of town (El Conchal, Carretera Veracruz–Antón Lizardo 1351). Villahermosa's **Tabasco 2000** complex (northwest end of Paseo Tabasco, past Boulevard Grijalva) has a new 18-hole course.

TENNIS

Tennis courts can be found in Tampico at **Club de Regatas Corona** (Laguna de Chairel; 3-07-88). In Veracruz, try **Club de Golf Villa Rica** (El Conchal, Carretera Veracruz–Antón Lizardo 1351) and **Las Palmas Raquet Club** (off Prolongación Costa Verde, Colonia Jardines de Mocambo south of El Centro).

Beaches

Grayish-brown sand (a lowly 2 in quality) and brownish-gray water characterize these beaches. A Mexican traveler summed up the beach situation this way: "You can cover the whole Gulf Coast in three days." Here are a few nice beaches worth a pause and some lovelies worth a stay. But be forewarned: many facilities are pretty rustic.

MATAMOROS BEACHES

Playa General Lauro Villar—This isolated beach well east of town has dark sand hard-packed enough to drive on. Facing the open sea and dotted with *palapa* umbrellas, the sand runs for some 25 miles north (to where the vanished port of Bagdad once stood on the Río Bravo) and rolls intermittently south to Tampico for over 200 miles. A military base and a waterslide overlook the sand.

Facilities: Baths and showers, picnic area, restaurants. *Camping:* Good north or south of the restaurants. *Swimming:* Good. On holidays lifeguards man the towers. *Windsurfing:* Good. *Fishing/boating:* Boats for rent at restaurants. *Shell-collecting:* Scattered small shells.

Getting there: From Matamoros, take Avenida Lauro Villar (Mexico 2) east for about 25 miles.

SOUTH OF MATAMOROS BEACHES

Playa La Pesca—The rundown fishing village of La Pesca ends at this wide, lonely beach covered with crumbling shell fragments and overflowing garbage cans. A stalwart lighthouse stands guard, and a rocky jetty juts out alongside the beach, offering protection from the waves. This is a cousin of the beach at General Lauro Villar, miles to the north.

Facilities: Picnic tables, restaurant. *Camping:* Good. *Swimming:* Good. *Windsurfing:* Fair. *Fishing/boating:* Very good. Campo La Pesca, a fishing camp along the road into La Pesca, rents skiffs. *Shell-collecting:* Tons of small sun-bleached shells.

Getting there: Several miles east of village of La Pesca, which is 30 miles east on Mexico 70 from Mexico 180.

TAMPICO BEACHES

Playa Miramar—This popular beach, lined with thatched umbrellas and backed by a bleached seaside community, evokes a kind of tropical Coney Island mood. Sand fleas dance amid the seaweed, driftwood and spotty trash clutter the long, hard-packed shore. A vast jetty at the far south end fends off the sludge produced by nearby petrol plants. To the north Miramar fuses with solitary Playa Altamira, near the village of Altamira.

Facilities: Restaurants, baths and showers. *Camping:* Good (barring bugs). *Swimming:* Good, surprisingly clean. *Windsurfing:* Fair. *Fishing/boating:* Good. *Shell-collecting:* Small scallops, sand dollars and clams.

Getting there: Proceed east on Avenida Obregón through the seaside town of Madero past the oil refinery. Take the left fork through Pinar del Mar to the beach.

TUXPAN BEACHES

Playa Tuxpan—This 15-mile-long, super-wide beach with hard-packed sand is as crisscrossed as a runway with tire tracks and traffic. Yet it's clean and fairly unspoiled, facing open sea. Its one scourge is swarms of tiny black bugs (they do bite). At the south end is a small thatched settlement called Barra de Tuxpan, fronting the best part of the beach. To the north is an electricity plant, source of much truck traffic.

Facilities: Baths with showers, restaurants. *Camping:* Good toward the southern end (if you can stand the bugs). *Swimming:* Good; calm and shallow. *Snorkeling/diving:* Good around offshore islands and reefs. *Windsurfing:* Good. *Fishing/boating:* Good. Rent boats at restaurants. *Shell-collecting:* Many small scallops, some sand dollars.

Getting there: From Tuxpan, follow Avenida Miguel Hidalgo along the Río Tuxpan east to the beach.

TECOLUTLA TO VERACRUZ BEACHES

Playa Tecolutla—One of the Gulf Coast's loveliest beaches, this wide carpet of ash-blond sand spreads out at the feet of a charming seaside village tucked in a forest of palms. From the Río Tecolutla, the beach stretches 45 miles north to Tuxpan and 18 miles south to Nautla, interrupted by various rivers and dotted with shaggy *palapa* shelters.

Facilities: Baths and showers, restaurants. *Camping:* Good, but mosquitoes come out after dark. *Swimming:* Good. *Windsurfing:* Good. *Fishing/boating:* Very good. Ask at the restaurants about boat rentals. *Shell-collecting:* A sprinkling of scallops.

Getting there: In Tecolutla, off Mexico 180.

Playa Las Casitas—Much nicer than the beach at Nautla and just north of there, this wide grayish beach fronts a funky little resort village backed by a tumbled grove of palms. A few ragged *palapa* huts offer shade. Abandoned boats and deserted buildings, seaweed and toppled trees litter the sand.

Facilities: Restaurants. *Camping:* Good; fairly isolated. *Swimming:* Good. Shallow water, gentle waves. *Windsurfing:* Good. *Fishing:* Good.

Getting there: Off Mexico 180 several miles north of Nautla; take Las Casitas turnoff just north of Puente Nautla (Nautla Bridge).

Playa El Farallón (★)—As vast as a desert and almost as secluded, this dark-sand beach is backed by rolling, vegetated dunes and fertile green hills to the north. The sand spreads for miles along clean open sea. North of the beach, fortunately out of sight, is Mexico's only nuclear power plant, Laguna Verde.

Facilities: None. Nearest food and shops at Palma Sola. *Camping:* Good, though unsheltered and windy. *Swimming:* Good, but waves can get rough. Use common sense. *Shell-collecting:* Sand dollars.

Getting there: Off Mexico 180 north of Veracruz and Cardel. Take Campamento Farallón turnoff and follow "playa" signs along a rocky, unpaved road.

Playa Chachalacas—A favorite Sunday destination for Veracruzanos, this narrow grayish beach is the hub of a busy little seaside resort. Too many fiestas have left it junked up with beer cans and coconut husks. Facing open sea, the sand straggles past a long line of faded open-air cafés, widening to the south into a sand bar at the mouth of Río Actopán.

Facilities: Restaurants, baths and showers. *Camping:* Fair. *Swimming:* Safe near the beach, waves get strong farther out. *Windsurfing:* Good. *Fishing:* Good. Boats for rent near the river. *Shell-collecting:* Some scallops and bits of coral.

Getting there: North of Veracruz, turnoff from Mexico 180 at Cardel, eight miles to beach.

VERACRUZ BEACHES

Playa Mocambo—Of the various beaches in Veracruz, this southernmost stretch of dark sand offers the most attractive swimming and sunbathing choice. The excellent facilities, *palapa* shelters and background palms turn its otherwise mediocre shores into the city's favorite seaside spot. The fishing village of Boca del Río and its informal beach lie to the south.

Facilities: Baths, showers, dressing rooms, pools and restaurant. *Camping:* Fair, if you can get away from the commotion. *Swimming:* Fair; it's far enough from the port to be clean. *Snorkeling/diving:* Very good around outlying reefs and islands, especially an offshore undersea park called La Blanquilla.

Getting there: About five miles south of downtown Veracruz along Calzada Ruiz Cortines (or Boulevard Mocambo). Enter via driveway to Hotel Mocambo or other easterly roads off Cortines.

COATZACOALCOS BEACHES

Playa Coatzacoalcos—This long, drab beach is one of the most animated along the Gulf. The hard-packed sand encourages wheeled traffic. Cars weave among coconut stands, vendors, families, romping children, *palapas* and horse-drawn carts. An entire shantytown squats along the edge of the beach and is slated to be shoveled off someday and replaced by a modern *malecón*. The beach ends to the south at a jetty and surreal cement building honeycombed with empty rooms like an abandoned bomb shelter.

Facilities: Baths and showers. *Camping:* Fair, when the crowd clears. Sand fleas. *Swimming:* Not recommended. Gentle waves, but locals warn of holes beyond the tideline, and the water does not look clean. *Shell-collecting:* Occasional sand dollars and fragments.

Getting there: In Coatzacoalcos via any Gulf-bound street, like Calle Nicolás Bravo or Calle Allende.

VILLAHERMOSA BEACHES ·

Playa Paraíso—Appropriately named, this beautiful beach is the Gulf Coast's own little piece of paradise. Ten miles long, with sand almost white against a dark forest of towering coconut palms, it stands at the end of a very circuitous route north of the delightful tropical village of Paraíso. A large modernistic pavilion dominates the sand like a Latino Sydney Opera House, bouncing with salsa tunes on Sundays.

Facilities: Baths, showers, restaurant-bar and pool. *Camping:* Good, except for nightly mosquitoes. *Swimming:* Good; shallow. *Windsurfing:* Good. *Fishing:* Good. Launches for rent.

Getting there: About 65 miles northwest of Villahermosa off Mexico 180, just north of Paraíso. From Villahermosa, there are two routes: via either the village of Comalcalco or Vicente Guerrero. Avoid the horrible ruts of the latter route and use the former.

Playa Pico de Oro—This wide, empty, brooding beach backed by distant palms offers a hermetic alternative to the social scene at Paraíso. Weather-worn *palapa* shacks slump along the brownish sand, matched by the dishwater tones of the Gulf.

Facilities: None. *Camping:* Good. *Swimming:* Safe, but sometimes sullied by petroleum waste, evident in the blackened sand dollars along the shore. *Shell-collecting:* Scattered sand dollars.

Getting there: About 50 miles north of Villahermosa. Turn left off Mexico 180 at Alvaro Obregón; look for signs at the junction just past Vicente Guerrero, or ask locals.

Trailer Parks

All parks have hookups and bathrooms unless stated otherwise.

NORTH OF VERACRUZ TRAILER PARKS

Hotel Playa Paraíso Trailer Park (Mexico 180 near San Rafael; 8-00-46) is a lovely 42-space park sharing the hotel's pool, restaurant and beach.

Trailer Park Neptuno (Mexico 180, Km. 86.5, just north of Las Casitas) is a well-kept beachside park with restaurant and tent camping.

Restaurant Los Almendros, Sitio para Acampar (Mexico 180, Km. 82, north of Las Casitas) is a pleasant, palm-fringed restaurant-campground on the sea, open from November to June.

VERACRUZ TRAILER PARKS

Trailer Park Los Arcos (Mexico 180, south of town; 37-40-75) is a shady, 140-space beachfront court nestled in palms.

CATEMACO TRAILER PARKS

Solotepec Campground (Camino Catemaco–Laguna Solotepec, east of Hotel Playa Azul) is a lakeside retreat for tents and trailers.

Travelers' Tracks
Sightseeing

MATAMOROS TO TAMPICO

The border town of **Matamoros**, with its shady plaza and friendly markets and malls, is a pleasant introduction to Mexico. A major producer of cotton, the big town sits on the banks of the historic Río Bravo (the Río Grande on the Texas side) in a fertile plain.

Founded in 1765, the town was renamed for heroic Padre Mariano Matamoros, who was killed during the Mexican War for Independence with Spain in 1810. In the Mexican-American War of 1846, Matamoros lost half its ground to Texas. During the American Civil War, contraband goods were shuttled from its port to the South. To learn more about its war-torn past, stop by the **Casa Mata** (Calle Degollado Oriente and Calle Guatemala), a combination museum and fort featuring musty relics of the Mexican Revolution.

From Matamoros, Mexico 101/180 heads south through the broad, flat plains and scrub-covered prairie of the state of **Tamaulipas**, not unlike the landscape of the neighboring Lone Star State of Texas. North of San Fernando the highway branches, and Mexico 101 heads west toward the interior while Mexico 180 continues south down the coast. At Soto La Marina, a 37-mile paved side road takes you to the rather rundown sportfishing village of **La Pesca**, with its lonely, open beach.

En route south, Mexico 180 crosses the **Tropic of Cancer**, marked by a yellow roadside sphere, and enters lovely valleys and lush fields as it nears the river-fed surroundings of Tampico.

TAMPICO

About 375 miles south of Matamoros, **Tampico** is sometimes called the "New Orleans of Mexico" because its downtown port area on the **Río Pánuco** has the quaint, rundown, balcony-trimmed look of that city's French Quarter. There's charm, too, in Tampico's grandiose, palm-graced **Plaza de Armas** (Calle de Olmos and Calle Emiliano Carranza) with its massive rose-colored kiosk. You can also explore the city's friendly cafés and colorful **Plaza de la Libertad** (Avenida Salvador Díaz Mirón and Calle Benito Juárez) which looks down on the steaming portside **Mercado Hidalgo**, full of produce and cantinas. But Tampico is foremost a thriving petroleum center and port, not a tourist town.

Old Tampico was founded between 1533 and 1535 on an Huastec Indian site destroyed by Hernán Cortés ten years earlier. The town battled Indians, pirates and the elements until a Franciscan mission was established in 1560. The present-day neoclassical **Catedral de Tampico** (Plaza de Armas) was built again in 1931 with donations from a California oil tycoon.

Meanwhile, deep-water canals were dug for sea-going traffic, and the white-brick Victorian **Aduana Marítimo** (Customs House) was constructed in 1889 along the docks (end of Calle Benito Juárez). Aged but still elegant, the Aduana remains the heart of port activity, with bronze railings and arched verandas lying in stark contrast to the multi-ton freighters and yawning warehouses along the piers.

When petroleum was discovered near Tampico in 1911, the boom was on. Mexico's first petrol plant was built here. Shortly afterward, the country's first official airline, Mexicana (formed to protect oil company payrolls from bandits, the story goes), was also established here. With the birth of Tampico's industrial sister port near **Altamira,** a few miles north and directly on the Gulf, the Tampico area became a top commercial zone.

TAMPICO TO TUXPAN

When leaving Tampico, you can cross the roiling Río Pánuco either by toll bridge (inland, Mexico 70/80/180) or by ferry (Mexico 180). On its southern banks, the state of Veracruz begins.

Mexico 180 runs south and turns inland for about 65 miles as the countryside becomes greener. At the village of Naranjos there's a turnoff for **Laguna de Tamiahua.** A 25-mile bumpy dirt road leads to the tropical lagoonside village of **Tamiahua,** whose seafood restaurants and wealth of offshore islands attract Sunday visitors and divers. A rainbow of skiffs lines the town's concrete fishing pier. (You can rent them for fishing trips or tours.)

TUXPAN

Both a gravel road from Tamiahua and Mexico 180 from Naranjos lead to the picturesque riverside city of Tuxpan, located about eight miles inland from the Gulf. In town, the action revolves around vivacious **Parque Reforma** (Avenida Benito Juárez), where locals make the evening *paseo* (stroll) and gather on wrought-iron benches to socialize. On the edge of this square, the small **Museo Regional de Antropología y Historia** (in the Casa de la Cultura) houses artifacts from the indigenous Totonac culture and historic information about the state of Veracruz.

For the most scenic view in town, stroll down the palm-lined *malecón* along busy brown **Río Tuxpan,** all a-chug with battered shrimp boats. Skiffs tour the river during Semana Santa (Holy Week). The shrimpers dock to unload their haul at dusk right across from pretty **Parque Enrique Rodrigues Cano,** the riverfront plaza on Avenida Miguel Hidalgo, where the spare 18th-century **Catedral de Nuestra Señora de la Asunción** stands.

Two blocks east, Avenida Miguel Hidalgo runs past the rowdy **Mercado Central,** then moseys eight miles out to a never-ending beach that skirts lethargic **Laguna Tampamachoco,** a lagoon huddled amid many cafés.

PAPANTLA AND EL TAJÍN

About 35 miles south of Tuxpán, Mexico 180 passes through the industrial city of **Poza Rica** (Rich Well), a grimy oil-refining town of no interest to tourists. However, as you enter town, if you turn right just past the Hidalgo Monument (on the left) and the Pemex offices (on the right), there is a sign pointing to a shortcut to the one nearby attraction: **El Tajín**, the old sacred city of the Totonac Indians, who still live in the surrounding orchid jungles cultivating vanilla.

The ruins are about ten-and-a-half miles from this point; curve left along the road past the oil refinery until you arrive at the El Tajín Zona Archeológica on your left. There, vegetation pries through toppled carvings, and butterflies flit among half-excavated, well-preserved pyramids, such as the unique **Pyramid of the Niches**, whose 365 niches mark the days of the year. There are ten ancient, overgrown ball courts, where death was the loser's lot. A makeshift museum (admission) stands at the entrance. El Tajín marked the height of Totonac culture around 800 A.D., although some archeologists believe it was built as early as the fifth or sixth century by an earlier tribe.

Fifteen miles past Poza Rica on Mexico 180 brings you through dense jungle-cloaked hills to **Papantla**, whose name means "place of the birds" in the native Totonac tongue. This charming mountain town, Mexico's leading producer of vanilla, is best known as home of the Totonac *voladores*, the Indian "fliers" who dress as red birds and spin from a tall pole by a rope attached to their feet. Originally a rain dance, this ancient ritual involves five fliers, representing the four directions and the center of the universe. The dance is performed on weekends in the **Plazoleta del Volador** outside the town cathedral (across from the main plaza) and at the entrance to the ruins of El Tajín.

For a vivid history of the Totonacs, see the massive stone **Mural Homenaje a la Cultura Totonaca** facing Papantla's main plaza, Parque Israel C. Tellez, and the painted murals in the **Palacio Municipal**, on the plaza, done in the 1960s by Teodoro Cano.

TECOLUTLA TO VERACRUZ

Mexico 180 returns to the coast east of Papantla, where a spur road leads to the picture-postcard village of Tecolutla, and sweeps for 145 scenic miles to big, rambunctious Veracruz. En route, little beachfront hotels and holiday communities punctuate the lush landscape down to **Nautla**, a seaside hamlet with ragged restaurants lining its beach. Much farther south past Palma Sola on the lonely coast, the forbidding **Laguna Verde thermonuclear power plant** mars the view.

Just north of the **Río Actopán**, a brief side road off Mexico 180 goes to the minor Totonac ruins of **Zempoala** (not a must-see), where Hernán Cortés made his first native allies.

Much more fascinating is the jungle-shrouded village of **La Antigua** (★) south of Cardel and about 20 miles north of Veracruz. Drowsing on the northern banks of the **Río de La Antigua,** this half-forgotten pueblo stands on the spot where Cortés landed in 1519 and built his first house. The shadowy, roofless brick ruins of the old **Casa de Cortés,** vanquished by moss, roots and vines, are fabulous to see. They stand just off La Antigua's main square, near the old thick-walled **Parroquia de Cristo del Buen Viaje** (Church of Christ of the Good Trip). The toylike, whitewashed **La Capilla del Rosario,** a chapel about a block away, was built by the conquistadors in 1523. Village children will lead you to **La Ceiba,** the old riverside tree where Cortés secured his ships, then burned them to keep his men from turning back.

VERACRUZ

About 145 miles south of Papantla stands historic **Veracruz,** the oldest city in the Americas. Over 450 years after Cortés' arrival here, Veracruz is today Mexico's premier port, awash with sailors and merchant marines from every continent.

The greatest symbol of the port's victories and struggles is the **Castillo de San Juan de Ulúa** (end of Calle San Juan de Ulúa; admission), a massive fort built between 1535 and 1707 on a peninsula east of the harbor. Its bastions and parapets have helped shield the town against pirates, French invaders and American troops, and offer great views of the port. Its arteries of eroded stairs, dungeonlike rooms, cobbled plazas and arched breezeways keep boredom at bay.

Many fine old edifices surround the *zócalo* or **Plaza de la Constitución** (also called Plaza de Armas, between Avenida Independencia and Avenida Zamora). The decrepit **Catedral La Parroquia** (*zócalo*) is a monumental 18th-century basilica. The 19th-century **Aduana Marítima** or Customs House (Calle Landero y Coss) contains part of a wall from the old walled city. The tiny **Baluarte de Santiago** (Santiago's Fort) (Avenida Gómez Farías and Calle Canal) is the only remaining bulwark of the old wall.

About six blocks south of the *zócalo* stands shady, inviting **Parque Zamora** (bounded by Calle Rayón and Calle Doblado). Wander over to nearby **Mercado Hidalgo** (between Avenida Francisco Madero and Avenida Miguel Hidalgo at Calle Hernán Cortés) and browse the enchanting witchcraft stalls and rhythmical meat market, where the butchers beat their knives on chopping blocks to Latin tunes.

Take in some Mesoamerican history at the big colonial **Museo Cultural de la Ciudad** (Avenida Zaragoza between Calle Canal and Calle Morales; 32-84-10). The displays of old Veracruz artifacts and of Olmec and Totonec art badly need cleaning but are worth a look.

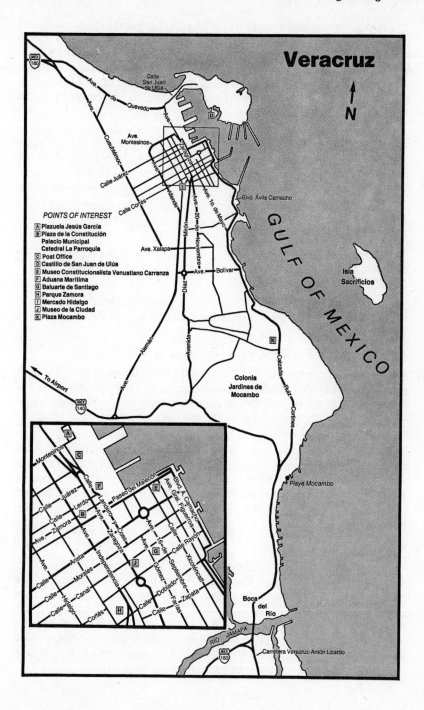

Veracruz

N

POINTS OF INTEREST

- A Plazuela Jesús García
- B Plaza de la Constitución
  Palacio Municipal
  Catedral La Parroquia
- C Post Office
- D Castillo de San Juan de Ulúa
- E Museo Constitucionalista Venustiano Carranza
- F Aduana Marítima
- G Baluarte de Santiago
- H Parque Zamora
- I Mercado Hidalgo
- J Museo de la Ciudad
- K Plaza Mocambo

GULF OF MEXICO

Isla Sacrificios

Colonia Jardines de Mocambo

To Airport

Playa Mocambo

Boca del Río

RÍO JAMAPA

Carretera Veracruz-Antón Lizardo

Along the hale and hearty *malecón* (following Avenida Insurgentes east and onto Boulevard Ávila Camacho), the yellow turn-of-the-century **Museo Constitucionalista Venustiano Carranza** (Paseo del Malecón) houses a lighthouse and museum dedicated to former Mexican President Carranza. A hulking statue of Carranza stands in the front yard. It was here at his residence that he met with fellow statesmen to hammer out the post-revolutionary Mexican Constitution.

Just across the street, tour boats push off from the *malecón* on **harbor cruises**, which include a running spiel on port sights sung out by the guide like a sailor's chant. Offshore you can see **Isla Sacrificios**, where the arriving conquistadors witnessed human sacrifices for the first time. Once a popular recreational spot, the island is now closed for ecological restoration.

South of Veracruz along Calzada Ruiz Cortines, the stately old **Hotel Mocambo** (37-15-31) is a rare gem of maritime design married to hacienda sprawl, right on Playa Mocambo.

Barely a mile south, the seaside village of **Boca del Río** lolls along lazy **Río Jamapa** and offers excellent seafood restaurants and a solemn dune-backed beach on the Gulf.

The same unmarked road continues south to **Laguna Mandinga**, serene and rimmed in mangrove roots, with rickety restaurants and skiffs for hire.

SOUTH OF VERACRUZ TO CATEMACO

South of Veracruz, Mexico 180 rambles down the coast past pineapple stands and dark-sand dunes. You will happen upon quaint seaside settlements, such as the tiny port of **Alvarado** located on the Río Papaloapán and Laguna de Alvarado. Stop by the old town square or stroll the rusty, restaurant-sprinkled harbor.

The highway plows inland into luxuriant misty hills, passing through **Santiago Tuxtla** and its prettier sister-city, **San Andrés Tuxtla.** This cool mountain town in the tobacco-rich San Andrés valley produces Mexico's finest cigars. An unpaved road off Mexico 180 just east of town leads eight miles south to 135-foot high **El Salto de Eyipantla** (Eyipantla Waterfall) in the jungle.

CATEMACO

Just beyond San Andrés Tuxtla lies the little resort of **Catemaco.** The town rests on shining **Lago Catemaco** with a mountainous backdrop that has earned it the exaggerated nickname, "The Switzerland of Mexico." **Boat rides** around the breezy ten-mile-long lake are lovely, taking in two monkey-crowded islands (**Isla de Agaltepec** and **Isla de los Changos,** where the University of Veracruz conducts simian research), a grotto called **El Tegal**, where it is said the Virgin of Catemaco appeared to a fisherman in 1710, and limpid shallows afloat with water hyacinths.

In town, the charming *zócalo* shows off the beautifully restored **Catedral de Nuestra Señora del Carmen**, dating back to around 1667 when Catemaco was founded.

The town is said to be Mexico's center for pre-Hispanic **witchcraft** (*brujería*). Here, witches (*brujos*, mostly men) and healers (*curanderos*) gather during the first week of March every year. Many *brujos* live in town and do inexpensive consultations (which may become sales pitches for very expensive talismans). An herb shop called **Casa de los Tésoros** (Calle Cuauhtémoc and Calle Zaragoza) posts a list of local witches.

North of Catemaco, along an extremely rocky road toward the Gulf, lies peaceful **Laguna de Sontecomapán**. Farther on lie two Gulf beaches, for high-clearance vehicles or tanks only.

SOUTH OF CATEMACO TO VILLAHERMOSA

As Mexico 180 wends its way southeast, industrial Mexico emerges around you in futuristic bridges, power pylons like mini-Eiffel Towers, four-lane freeways and the ubiquitous presence of Pemex signs pointing to petroleum plants and refineries.

Past big, heaving Coatzacoalcos on the Gulf, a Pemex-bred boomtown, and east of the Río Tonalá, the state of Veracruz gives way to the state of **Tabasco**. Mexico 180 veers inland, leaving behind a coast full of beach towns.

Save your wanderlust for the best: a beautiful unnumbered **coastal road** north of Cárdenas connects the beach communities of Paraíso, El Bellote and Pico de Oro, looping back to Villahermosa. This road passes tropical hamlets, lagoons, rustic port towns and groves of palms. Beware of the dangerous stretch along the return loop between Pico de Oro and Alvaro Obregón (Santa Cruz). It is crisscrossed with deep ruts that throw your steering out of control. Go slowly.

At **Comalcalco** (35 miles northeast of Villahermosa by paved road) small, overgrown ruins, distinctively built from fired bricks, are all that remain of this Mayan offshoot of Palenque.

VILLAHERMOSA

For another look at intriguing ruins, visit **Villahermosa**, an expansive petroleum center, lying 75 miles east of Coatzacoalcos. Its shining star is **Parque La Venta** (off Paseo Tabasco and Boulevard Grijalva), a beautiful park that weaves along La Laguna de los Illusiones, with bridges, lookout points, a columned *malecón*, a zoo and a most unusual **outdoor museum** (admission) that resembles a sculpture garden. Among the 30 Olmec stone monuments here, three massive heads, hauled from oil fields 100 miles northwest where they were discovered, stare eerily out of thickets of tropical foliage. Their original site, La Venta, was an Olmec ceremonial center dating back over 3,000 years. The Olmecs believed the head was a great source of power. Their 25-ton Negroid images, which some think link the Olmecs to African cultures, were hewn out of basalt dragged 100 miles from the nearest mountains.

Another must: the **Museo Regional de Antropología Carlos Pellicer Camara** (Malecón Carlos Madrazo; admission), one of Mexico's top museums. Poet Carlos Pellicer Camara organized its fine collection of Olmec, Totonec and Mayan artifacts. The museum also contains representative pieces form Aztec, Mixtec, Teotihuacén, Totonac and Zapotec cultures, as well as from the states of Colima and Nayarit.

Shopping

MATAMOROS SHOPPING

Along the entire Gulf Coast, Matamoros is the best place to shop. Prices are inflated but variety is good. Most shopping is concentrated in the downtown area and along Avenida Alvaro Obregón.

Mercado Juárez (Calle 10a and Calle Matamoros) is the newer crafts market, packed with blankets, onyx, clothes, sombreros and leather in dozens of shops and stalls. Check out the **Yerbería Santa Fé** and **Herbario Juárez**, both carrying incense, love herbs and luck perfumes. **Miranda Brothers Curio Shop** has leather saddles.

Pasaje Juárez (Calle Nicolás Bravo between Calle 8a and Calle 9a) is the old market, with many of the same curios as the new.

The **pedestrian mall** (running along Calle Abasolo for several blocks) is a big, paved shopping zone with record shops, shoe stores, pharmacies and clothing boutiques.

Cowboy boots and glassware are good buys along **Avenida Alvaro Obregón,** approaching the International Bridge. The warehouselike **Arti** (Avenida Alvaro Obregón; 2-27-62) fills a large, glass-fronted building with liquor and crafts.

Across the street, **Lali** (Avenida Alvaro Obregón 12, Edificio Rebeca) features a classy selection of ceramics and clothes.

Mary's Curio Shop and Liquors (Avenida Alvaro Obregón 26; 6-24-31) is another good crafts emporium.

The finest of all is **Barbara** (Avenida Alvaro Obregón 37; 6-54-56), a lovely two-story boutique with select (and expensive) ceramics, jewelry, crafts and fashions for men and women.

TAMPICO SHOPPING

About the only place to shop is dilapidated **Mercado Hidalgo** (along Calle Benito Juárez near the port). You pass oodles of stalls crammed with bizarre curios fashioned from seashells: altars, coaches, cars, earrings and boats in bottles. The covered *mercado* sells everything from stuffed crabs to enormous piñatas. A rough, colorful area.

TUXPAN SHOPPING

Tuxpan's sole shopping zone is its **Mercado Central** (Avenida Miguel Hidalgo and Calle Pipila), a pandemonium of bird cages, shell whatchamacallits, fruits and flowers.

PAPANTLA SHOPPING

The vanilla capital of Mexico, Papantla is the best place to stock up on real vanilla. You can buy extract by the gallon, fresh vanilla beans (a wonderful flavoring for coffee), zany little vanilla-bean sculptures of crosses, hearts and scorpions, and a sweet creme of vanilla liqueur. The **covered market** (Calle 20 de Noviembre and Calle José Azueta) sells vanilla in all forms. **Dulcería y Curiosidades La Josefina**, at the entrance to the market, is especially well supplied.

VERACRUZ SHOPPING

For such a grand town, the shopping is a letdown. The so-called **Mercado de Artesanías** (Avenida Landero y Coss and Avenida Insurgentes) consists of ticky-tacky knickknack stalls.

A better selection of curios can be found at **El Mayab** (Avenida Zaragoza 78; 32-14-35). **Silvett** (Avenida Zamora 32; 31-30-65) may be the best craft shop in town, with Taxco silver, erotic ceramic figures and leather goods, as well as some fine inlaid-wood wall pieces.

Take in some local flavor at big, seething **Mercado Hidalgo** (Avenida Francisco Madero and Avenida Miguel Hidalgo at Calle Hernán Cortés). It's got everything from hand-dipped candles to wedding tiaras to occult elixirs. Under the banner of *plantas medicinales* (medicinal plants), the magic shops are jumbled bowers of charmed soaps, dried hummingbirds and tarot cards.

SAN ANDRÉS TUXTLA–CATEMACO SHOPPING

San Andrés Tuxtla is said to turn out Mexico's premier cigars. They are sold by the wooden box at the downtown tobacco factory, **Matacapán Tabacos** (Avenida Constitución 8; 2-00-98), makers of Te-Amo brand cigars.

In keeping with the *brujería* tradition in Catemaco, **Casa de los Tésoros** (Calle Cuauhtémoc and Calle Zaragoza) sells medicinal herbs and other gifts.

VILLAHERMOSA SHOPPING

For browsing, the downtown **pedestrian mall** (along Avenida Francisco Madero) has attractive boutiques, though not many crafts. For indigenous art, try the **artisan's shop** at the Museo Regional de Antropología Carlos Pellicer Camara (Malecón Carlos Madrazo).

Nightlife

Gulf Coast nights are reasonably active in the bigger towns.

MATAMOROS NIGHTLIFE

This border town's many clubs come to life on weekends. An area called **Zonatur** (for Zona Turística), just north of the railroad tracks at Calle 6a and Calle Galeana, houses a fistful of bars and taverns with music and dancing.

One favorite hangout with live entertainment is **Mary's** (Avenida Alvaro Obregón 26; 6-24-31), attached to a gift shop by the same name. The scene is personal, with pigskin chairs and tables surrounding the stage and dance floor. Members of the audience sometimes get up and perform. Weekend cover.

Retire from the border-town shenanigans at cool, dark **Bar Jardín** in the Hotel El Presidente (Avenida Alvaro Obregón 249; 3-94-40), with easy chairs, video, and marimba music on weekends.

TAMPICO NIGHTLIFE

A hundred little back-alley taverns keep the sailors drinking all night in Tampico, but regular nightspots are harder to find.

For a pleasant evening drink on the veranda or in the slick, refurbished interior, stop by the historic **Restaurant-Bar Saloon Palacio** (Calle Aduana and Calle Ribera 401 Oriente, on the Plaza de la Libertad; 12-18-77). Until recently this was a wild seamen's cantina with swinging saloon doors. Founded in 1897, it was used as a rowdy movie set for *The Treasure of the Sierra Madre*. Even now, it attracts many mariners whose babble of languages, from Greek to Norwegian, recall the bad old days.

If you'd rather people watch than dance, the bustling Plaza de Armas stays up half the night. Just grab a ringside seat at the cheerful 24-hour **Café-Nevería El Globito** (Avenida Salvador Díaz Mirón and Calle de Olmos), at the corner of the square. This alfresco ice cream parlor serves the best fresh fruit drinks in town.

Just east of Tampico in the seaside town of Madero, a forgettable-looking little clapboard tavern called **Cheto's Las Glorias de Baco**, or Bacchus' Glories (Calle Emiliano Carranza east of the railroad tracks), serves 50 inventive drinks with a tropical flair (like *Naranjita*, made from oranges, sherbet and gin). In old machismo style, women are not allowed inside.

VERACRUZ NIGHTLIFE

The best nightlife here is free: music and socializing in the *zócalo* and Los Portales until all hours.

There are a fair number of discos and video bars, too. **Disco Plaza 44** (Plaza de la Constitución; 36-12-78), right on the square, is a select upstairs club with a middle-class dress code—no dirty shoes or sloppy clothes. Air-conditioned, carpeted and compact, it's built around a dance floor with video screen. The downstairs bar is actually much nicer, with three dimly-lit, quiet rooms and several televisions. Cover charge for the disco.

Peace and quiet, with good entertainment, prevail south of town along Mocambo Beach. The bamboo-appointed **Rainbow Bar** at the Hotel Playa Paraíso (Calzada Ruiz Cortines 3500; 37-83-99) swings to a lively combo but remains chic and low key. Next door at the splendid Hotel Mocambo, the **Bar Casablanca** (Calzada Ruiz Cortines; 37-15-31) is a cool, cavelike nook where you can enjoy a sea view and live Latin music, or take to the dance floor.

CATEMACO NIGHTLIFE

About the only things cooking here after sundown are river fish and **La Tortuga Nightclub** (Paseo del Malecón and Calle García Mantilla; 3-00-50), the first club in Catemaco. Located upstairs over La Luna Restaurant, easy-going La Tortuga has a lovely view of the lake, live romantic music and good dancing.

VILLAHERMOSA NIGHTLIFE

A good bit's stirring here after sundown. Take your choice of two good discos: **Studio 8** (Hotel Maya Tabasco, Boulevard Ruiz Cortines 907; 2-11-11) is a suave club for an older clientele, while **La Plataforma** (Excelaris Hyatt Hotel, Avenida Benito Juárez 106, Colonia Linda Vista; 3-44-44) is a hopping deluxe club that draws a younger crowd.

If a jazzy drink is enough action, saunter over to **Carlos 'n Charlie's** (Plaza de Toros; 3-42-60) and enjoy live tropical music amid bullfight decor. Check with the tourist department on seasonal bullfights at the neighboring bullring.

The most romantic place to relax after dark is **Los Guayacanes** (Malecón Carlos Madrazo; 2-92-85), a beautiful bamboo-roofed restaurant-bar attached to the Museo Regional de Antropología and overlooking the Río Grijalva.

Gulf Coast Addresses and Phone Numbers

MATAMOROS

Bank—Bánamex, Calle 6a on the *zócalo*
Hospital—Hospital Alvaro Obregón (3-94-15)
Police—2-00-08
Post Office—Calle 6a near Calle Iturbide (2-15-97)
Tourist Office—Puerta México, International Bridge (2-36-30)

TAMPICO

Bank—Bánamex, Calle Francisco Madero 403 Oriente
  Consulate—American Consulate, Avenida Miguel Hidalgo 2000 (3-22-17)
Hospital—Hospital General de Tampico, Boulevard Ejército Nacional
  1403 (3-09-32)
Laundry—LavaFacil, Avenida Salvador Díaz Mirón 724 Oriente
Police—2-11-57
Post Office—Calle Francisco Madero 309, Plaza de la Libertad
Tourist Office—Calle de Olmos 101 Sur-Altos, aross from Plaza de
  Armas (2-26-68)

VERACRUZ

Bank—Bancomer, Avenida Independencia 993 (31-00-95)
Consulate—American Consulate, Calle Benito Juárez 110 (31-01-42)
Hospital—Clínica de IMSS (32-96-97)
Laundry—Mar y Sol, Avenida Zamora 410
Police—38-06-85
Post Office—Plaza de la República (32-20-38)
Tourist Office—Palacio Municipal on the *zócalo* (32-99-42)

VILLAHERMOSA

Bank—Bancomer, Calle Benito Juárez 523, pedestrian mall (2-12-61)
Police—3-19-00
Post Office—Calle Saenz and Calle Lerdo (2-10-40)
Red Cross—3-35-93
Tourist office—Delegación Federal de Turismo (federal), Avenida
  Gregorio Mendez 718 (2-73-36); Dirección Estatal de Turismo (state),
  Avenida Retorno de Vía 5a, Number 104, the Tabasco 2000 complex
  (3-57-62)

CHAPTER TEN
Yucatán Peninsula

Real enchantment fills the Yucatán Peninsula. It's as though this hook of hot, jungle-clad land at Mexico's easternmost tip exists in a two-way time warp. The old brooding mysteries of the Mayan ancients, deep as a subterranean stream, haunt everything. At the same time, modern magic has turned the Caribbean coast into a kingdom of pleasure worship, born of a computer and as fizzy as uncorked champagne. You might say the Yucatán is where history meets hedonism.

This is one of the only spots in the world where you can explore the remnants of a great lost civilization and also get a mean tan. Gemlike waters wash the peninsula's eastern shore while white-hot Mayan pyramids rear up out of its shimmering inland fields. You can peer into a sacrificial well one day and dive for lobster in a translucent sea the next.

Ruins lovers tend to base themselves in the interior city of Mérida to tour famous sites like Uxmal and Chichén Itzá. But sea lovers head straight for the Mexican Caribbean. The coast and its islands make up an unparalleled mecca for divers and snorkelers. The fabulous reef system, a fantasyland of fish and undersea flora, darkens the water for miles just offshore. And contrary to what some may think, this coast is not one long, jangling tourist sprawl. The area south of Cancún, the major resort, has been designated a low-growth zone where the breathtaking beaches will always remain unspoiled.

Steamy weather also makes the Caribbean alluring. From May to October comes the rainy season, when fewer tourists visit. From November to April, temperatures hover at 80 to 95° and the area is cooled by luscious sea breezes. During autumn months, however, hurricanes pose an occasional threat. The most recent major storm, Hurricane Gilbert, struck with ferocious intensity in 1988, stripping away much of the coastal vegetation. While it will take years to replace the region's palm trees and flowering plants, most of the damaged buildings were repaired within months of the storm.

The peninsula's three states—Campeche, Yucatán and Quintana Roo—contain roughly 1,000 miles of coastline, bordering the Gulf of Mexico to the west and north, the Caribbean to the east.

The Yucatán's weak point is its landscape—much of the inland terrain is flat and tedious. Low-lying jungles cover the porous limestone topsoil, which erodes into gorgeous cool white sand but makes crop cultivation tough (so much so that thousands of beekeepers farm honey instead). Rain seeps through the limestone, creating underground rivers, some in explorable caverns. The peninsula is riddled with caves. The only surface rivers are in southern Campeche. In fact, the few continuous sources of water are *cenotes*, deep sinkholes formed when the weak limestone collapses to the water table, connecting these wells with the subsurface channels.

The Mayas built their Yucatán kingdom around *cenotes*. One theory about the mysterious demise of their civilization is that a prolonged drought dried up their water supply.

Recorded Mayan history spans more than a millennium, from 200 to 1500 A.D. Because of their beautiful sculpture and architecture, the Mayas have been called "the Greeks of the New World." Great traders, they plowed the coastal waters in huge canoes, using precious cocoa beans for currency. Their empire spread from southern Mexico and Guatemala into Honduras and El Salvador.

By 900 A.D. their culture was one of the most advanced in the world, with thriving cities throughout the Yucatán. They perfected a calendar as accurate as any in existence, discovered the use of the zero before the Arabs, constructed observatories for stargazing and carved a theory of evolution in stone 1,000 years before Darwin. Their writings no doubt contained more of their genius, but we shall never know about most of it. In the early 16th century, Spanish Friar Diego de Landa destroyed more than 2,000 Mayan codices—tantamount to burning a library of rare manuscripts—believing their message heretical to Christianity. Only three codices were preserved.

Advanced as they were, the Mayas practiced a ritual we now consider barbaric—human sacrifice. To appease the gods, virgins were tossed into "bottomless" wells and hearts were ripped from the breasts of prone victims. The Mayas worshipped Kukulkán (the plumed serpent who brought civilization to humanity, known as Quetzalcoatl among the Aztecs) and Chac-Mool, the rain god, who nourished their corn. Ceremonial centers like Uxmal, Chichén Itzá and Cobá, now the Yucatán's greatest ruin sites, formed the heart of their Mexican empire.

Oddly enough, the Mayas began to abandon their Yucatán cities just at their civilization's apex, around 900 A.D. No one knows exactly why. Some say a widespread epidemic drove them away, others that a drought, hurricane or earthquake struck.

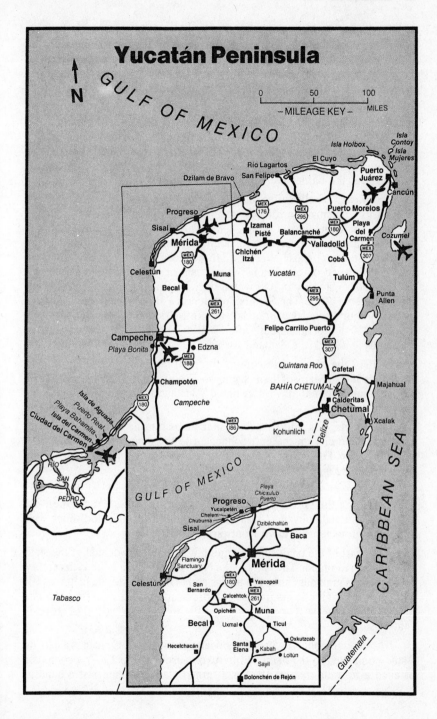

Yucatán Peninsula

N

GULF OF MEXICO

0   50   100
– MILEAGE KEY –   MILES

Isla Contoy
Isla Holbox
Isla Mujeres
El Cuyo
Río Lagartos
San Felipe
Dzilam de Bravo
Puerto Juárez
Cancún
Progreso
MEX 176
MEX 295
Puerto Morelos
Sisal
Izamal
Pisté
Balancanché
MEX 180
Playa del Carmen
Cozumel
Mérida
MEX 180
Chichén Itzá
Valladolid
MEX 307
Celestún
Muna
Yucatán
Cobá
Becal
Tulúm
MEX 261
MEX 295
Punta Allen
Campeche
MEX 188
Edzna
Felipe Carrillo Puerto
Playa Bonita
MEX 307
Quintana Roo
Cafetal
Champotón
BAHÍA CHETUMAL
Majahual
MEX 180
Campeche
Calderitas
Chetumal
Isla de Aguada
Puerto Real
Playa Bahamita
MEX 186
Xcalak
Ciudad del Carmen
Isla del Carmen
Kohunlich
Belize
RÍO SAN PEDRO

CARIBBEAN SEA

Tabasco

GULF OF MEXICO
Playa Chicxulub Puerto
Progreso
Yucalpetén
Chelem
Chuburna
Dzibilchaltún
Sisal
Baca
Flamingo Sanctuary
Mérida
MEX 180
Celestún
San Bernardo
Yaxcopoil
Calcehtok
MEX 261
Opichén
Muna
Becal
Uxmal
Ticul
Hecelchacán
Santa Elena
Oxkutzcab
Kabah
Loltún
Sayil
Bolonchén de Rejón

Guatemala

Or could their disappearance have hinged on their conquest by the war-like Toltecs from central Mexico? These great masters of human sacrifice (Chac-Mool, whose lap dish received fresh human hearts, is of Toltec origin) dominated Chichén Itzá until around 1200 A.D. After this the city-states collapsed. The great Mayan centers were in ruins by the time the Aztecs came to ascendancy.

The Mayas continued to live in large settlements, however, and still dominated the peninsula when the Spanish appeared. Not until 1542 did Conquistador Francisco de Montejo (El Mozo) begin the final campaign against the fierce Mayas, building the city of Mérida over the Mayan city of Tihó. But the battles were far from finished.

The Mayas rebelled time and again. They were crushed and subdued, escaped to Guatemala, or died by the thousands from Spanish-introduced diseases. The development of an *encomienda* (royal land grant) system of Spanish-held land absorbed the remaining Indians as serfs. Before the outbreak of the brutal Caste War of 1846 between landowners and Indians, the Mayas slaved on plantations where sisal or henequen (a rope-making fiber from the agave cactus, cultivated since Mayan times) made the Spanish landowners wealthy. The Spanish partied in Paris, brought back French wives and built exquisite little chateaux in Mérida. The Yucatán was one of Mexico's richest states until after World War II, when synthetic fibers drastically cut back the demand for sisal.

In 1917 the Mexican Revolution brought land reform and equality to the Mayas at last. Many of their customs—in housing, crafts and dress—still persist. Some 300,000 Mayas live in the Yucatán today, and Mayan is widely spoken in villages.

By vehicle, you will probably enter the peninsula at Ciudad del Carmen, an island city on the gulf connected to the mainland by a ferry and a bridge. Once a base for pirates, Carmen is now a major shrimping center (with lip-smacking seafood).

To the northeast lies the old port of Campeche, capital of the state of Campeche on the Gulf of Mexico. Founded in 1540, it's an open-air museum of ruined bulwarks, forts and remnants of the eight-foot-thick wall that once protected the town from pirate attacks.

The heart of the peninsula is shining white Mérida, capital of the state of Yucatán. Anointed "The Paris of the New World" during the 19th century because of its gracious European plazas and mansions, Mérida features folk dancing and music in its parks, complemented by the festive *huipiles* (embroidered dresses) and *guayaberas* (pleated men's shirts) of its residents.

The capital of the Mexican Caribbean vacationland, Cancún is a narrow island connected to the mainland by two causeways. In 1967, a computer hatched a formula that by 1973 had turned Cancún—then just a handful of fishermen's shacks—into Mexico's most expensive jet-set resort. The experiment worked beyond anyone's dreams.

Isla Mujeres (Island of Women) is the smallest Caribbean resort, just a few miles from Cancún yet eons from the razzle-dazzle. Escapists love its peaceful beaches and quaint village.

Isla Cozumel, originally a sacred Mayan site (its name means "island of the swallows"), was the Mayan equivalent of the Garden of Eden. It's still just that for skin divers, who flock to its fabulous Palancar Reef, one of the world's five greatest reef systems.

Chetumal, capital of the state of Quintana Roo, is a duty-free port on the border of Belize. Built in 1898 over an old Mayan town and rebuilt after a hurricane in the 1950s, Chetumal makes a pleasant stopover en route to lakes and ruins in the vicinity.

Easy Living

Transportation

ARRIVAL

BY CAR

Both **Mexico 180** and **Mexico 186** enter the Yucatán peninsula from the southwest, connecting the state of Campeche with neighboring Tabasco and Chiapas. You may also enter from the country of Belize via Chetumal. From a point directly north of the Belize border, Mexico 186 heads west across the bottom of the Yucatán Peninsula and **Mexico 307** shoots north toward Caribbean beaches. A good road system unifies the peninsula, connecting all major towns, ruins and mainland beaches.

BY AIR

Eight commercial airports serve the Yucatán peninsula: Ciudad del Carmen National Airport, Campeche National Airport, Licenciado Manuel Crescencio Rejón International Airport (in Mérida), Cancún International Airport, Isla Mujeres Airport, Cozumel International Airport, Playa del Carmen Airport and Chetumal International Airport.

Ciudad del Carmen National Airport: Ciudad del Carmen has flights on Mexicana Airlines.

Campeche National Airport: Aeroméxio has service to Campeche.

Licenciado Manuel Crescencio Rejón International Airport: Mexicana Airlines, Aeroméxico, Aeorcaribe, American Airlines, and Continental Airlines offer regular flights into Mérida.

Cancún International Airport: Service is provided by Mexicana Airlines, Aeroméxico, Aerocaribe, American Airlines, Continental Airlines, Northwest Airlines and United Airlines to Cancún.

Isla Mujeres Airport: At present there is no airline service to Isla Mujeres.

Cozumel International Airport: Mexicana Airlines, Aeroméxico, Aerocaribe, American Airlines, Continental Airlines and United Airlines all have flights to Cozumel.

Playa del Carmen Airport: At present there is no service to Playa del Carmen.

Chetumal International Airport: Aeromar provides flights to Chetumal.

Taxis and *combis* (vans) provide transportation from all airports to towns and nearby destinations.

BY BUS

Daily bus service connects all mainland cities and major ruins in the Yucatán. The key bus lines are **Autotransportes del Oriente (ADO)** and **Autotransportes del Caribe,** both with first- and second-class coaches. Local service is provided by **Autobuses de Progreso, Unión de Camioneros de Yucatán** and **Batty Bus.** Main information numbers and bus stations are as follows:

Ciudad del Carmen: ADO (Avenida Periferica).

Campeche: ADO (Avenida Gobernadores 289; 6-28-02).

Mérida: ADO (Calle 69a 554; 24-83-91); Autobuses de Progreso (Calle 62a 524; 24-89-91); Unión de Camioneros de Yucatán (Calle 69a 554; 24-90-55).

Cancún: ADO (4-13-78) and Autotransportes del Caribe (4-13-65), both at Avenida Tulum and Avenida Uxmal, Ciudad Cancún.

Playa del Carmen: ADO and Autotransportes del Caribe (both across from Plaza Central).

Chetumal: ADO (Avenida Héroes 172; 2-06-39), Autotransportes del Caribe (Avenida Insurgentes between Avenida Juárez and Avenida Belice; 2-07-41) and Batty Bus (Avenida Belice 172).

BY TRAIN

Regular rail service, by the line **Ferrocarriles Nacionales de México,** links Campeche (Avenida Héroes de Nacozari; 6-51-48) and Mérida (Calle 55a between Calle 48a and Calle 50a; 23-59-44) with the rest of Mexico.

BY BOAT

Cruise ships often anchor off Cancún and Cozumel as they voyage through the Caribbean. Companies that serve this area include **Carnival Cruise Lines** (5225 N.W. 87th Avenue, Miami, FL 33166; 800-327-7373),

Norwegian Caribbean Line (1 Biscayne Tower, Miami, FL 33131; 800-327-7030) and **Royal Caribbean Cruise Line** (903 South America Way, Miami, FL 33132; 800-327-4368).

There is also **ferry service** at several points on the peninsula, getting to and from Ciudad del Carmen, Isla Mujeres and Cozumel.

On the western approach to Ciudad del Carmen from Villahermosa along Mexico 180, you have no choice but to wait at two separate points for the often-slow ferries that connect this island city with the highway. The first crosses Río San Pedro, separating the states of Tabasco and Campeche. The second crossing is at the Laguna de Términos at Zacatal. The waiting lines tend to be long. Ferries don't operate at either crossing after dark on Sundays.

For Isla Mujeres, passenger ferries leave regularly from Puerto Juárez. Vehicle ferries push off from Punta Sam. Both embarkation points are just north of Ciudad Cancún. Crossings to and from the island are frequent and cheap, but lines may be long and schedules change. Check with the tourist department for the latest hours.

Cozumel is connected to the mainland by regular passenger ferries to and from Playa del Carmen, about 40 miles south of Cancún. Vehicle ferries, with highly erratic schedules, sail to and from Puerto Morelos, a village about 20 miles south of Cancún. The dock here was severely damaged during Hurricane Gilbert, however, and at this writing only one ferry a day—at 4:30 a.m.—was sailing. For current information, call the terminal in Cozumel (International Pier across from Hotel Sol Caribe; 2-08-49) or go directly to the Puerto Morelos terminal (no phone) and ask. The passenger ferry pier in the village of San Miguel de Cozumel, is also the base for on-again-off-again waterjet service (2-05-88) to and from Cancún. This waterjet leaves Cancún at the Playa Linda pier (Paseo Kukulkán, Km. 4; 4-42-11).

CAR RENTALS

All major Yucatán resorts offer car rentals. The airports serving Campeche, Mérida, Cancún and Cozumel all have booths charging similar rates. The downtown areas of many Yucatán cities have car rental agencies, as do the lobbies of big hotels in Mérida and Cancún.

In downtown Ciudad del Carmen, you'll find **Fast** (2-23-06) and **Auto-Rentas del Carmen** (2-23-76). At the Campeche airport, look for **Auto Rent** (6-27-14) and **Hertz** (6-48-55). For rentals at the Mérida airport, try **Hertz** (24-94-21), **Fast** (27-10-70), **Avis** (23-78-56), **Aquiladora Caribe** and **Rent-a-Matic Itzá.** At Cancún's airport, check **Budget** (4-02-04), **Hertz** (4-20-50), **National** (4-21-26), **Avis** (4-23-28) and **Econo-Rent** (4-18-26). Try **Hertz** (2-01-00), **Avis** (2-00-99), **Fast** (2-09-83), **Budget** (2-09-03) and **National** (2-15-15) at the Cozumel Airport. In downtown Chetumal, there's an **Avis** office at Hotel El Presidente (2-05-44).

BICYCLING AND MOTORBIKING

In Cancún, bikes and mopeds (*motos*) can be rented at various beachside hotels. Try the **Hotel Carrousel** (Paseo Kukulkán, Zona Hotelera; 3-05-13), **Casa Maya Hotel** (Paseo Kukulkán, Zona Hotelera; 3-05-55) and **Franky's** (next door to the Krystal Cancún, Paseo Kukulkán; 3-11-33).

For a small island like Isla Mujeres, *motos* are the perfect way to get around. Rental outfits are ubiquitous. Check out **Joaquín** (Avenida Juárez 7; 2-00-68), **Ciro's** (Avenida Matamoros 11; 2-01-02), **Kankín** (Calle Abasolo 15), **Kin-ha** (Avenida Rueda Medina next to the Pemex station; 2-00-86) and **Moto Rent Cárdenas** (Avenida Guerrero 105-A; 2-00-79).

On the island of Cozumel, *motos* are equally popular. **Ruben's** (Calle 1a Sur and Avenida 10a; 2-02-58) has a big assortment of bikes and scooters. So does **Rentadora Cozumel** (Avenida 10a; 2-11-20).

PUBLIC TRANSPORTATION

Good local bus systems and taxis galore make Yucatán cities very easy to navigate.

Campeche has regular buses around town circulating out of the market district (Avenida Gobernadores and Avenida Circuito), but most of the interesting sites can be seen on foot.

Mérida's city buses leave from around the main plaza, but this is another wonderful town for walking. Sightseeing is also fun via *calesa*, a 19th-century-style horse-drawn buggy, available around the main plaza (establish a price before taking off).

Cancún has a terrific bus system. Main routes are Avenida Tulum in Ciudad Cancún to the Zona Hotelera along Paseo Kukulkán. Some buses go as far down the beach as the Club Med. Others go to Puerto Juárez and Punta Sam for the Isla Mujeres ferries.

On Cozumel, buses run from San Miguel (in front of Las Palmeras Restaurant) to Laguna Chancanab and southern beaches.

Hotels

The Yucatán peninsula is blessed with many bargain colonial hotels and beachfront inns.

CIUDAD DEL CARMEN HOTELS

The inexpensive **Hotel Internacional** (Calle 20a 21 and Calle 31a; 2-13-44), just a block off the main plaza, has a boxy flophouse look outside but is domestic and comfortable within. Rooms come with air-conditioning or ceiling fans, a collection of worn furniture and battered French doors opening onto a parlor and upstairs balcony. Friendly and clean. Budget.

The more modern, 58-room **Hotel Zacarías** (Calle 24a 58-B; 2-01-21), just off the plaza, starts with a classy little gray-marble lobby and leads into two types of rooms. The small, fan-cooled quarters (the least expensive) have a dark, slightly downtrodden air. The air-conditioned rooms cost more but are brighter, more cheerful and better furnished. Budget.

Although it's one of the nicer lodging spots in town, the **Hotel Lli-re** (Calle 32a and Calle 29a-A; 2-05-88) is oddly outdated, from its transvestite shows to its plaid sofas backed by 1950s-style wood paneling. The rooms are spacious almost to a fault, with rather spartan furnishings, televisions, phones, servibars and air-conditioning. Bar and restaurant. Budget.

The city's finest hotel, built to accommodate the flow of Pemex traffic, is the four-story **EuroHotel** (Calle 22a 208; 2-10-30). With its fancy pool, lobby-bar, two restaurants, boutique, disco and 80 lovely carpeted rooms, EuroHotel has a big, solid presence spanning about half a block. The modern, air-conditioned rooms and suites are solidly furnished in subdued color schemes. Moderate to deluxe.

CAMPECHE HOTELS

Old hotels fill this old town, but they tend to be shabby.

On the southern approach to town about 25 miles from Campeche, the 76-room **Hotel Si-Ho Playa** (Mexico 180, Km. 35; 6-29-89) is the only seafront choice. Built over a roughhewn stone hacienda, the Si-Ho enjoys beautiful sea views from its restaurant and pool, with a waterslide into the gulf. The large, breezy rooms have terraces and heavy Spanish-style furniture. The suites are carpeted and contain servibars. Moderate.

In town, the best of the low-cost inns is the **Hotel López** (Calle 12a 189; 6-33-44), built around a narrow courtyard. Its 60 rooms are saved from being drab by the pink tile walls, high ceilings and colored tile floors. All are air-conditioned and have a fan and telephone. Good upstairs bar-restaurant. Budget.

For comfort, the old, 103-room **Hotel Baluartes** (Avenida Ruiz Cortines; 6-39-11) takes top billing. Modern and squarish, set in an unexciting parking lot with its back to downtown and its face to the *malecón*, the Baluartes has ample, gold-hued rooms with hanging wicker lamps, carpets, color televisions and big picture windows with views of the gulf. For extras, there's the restaurant-bar, nightclub, pool, café and terrace. Moderate.

For affordable luxury, the 119-room **Ramada Inn** (Avenida Ruiz Cortines 51; 6-22-33) should fill the bill nicely. With spacious rooms, modern decor and balconies overlooking the water, it has much to offer at a moderate price. The public amenities include a swimming pool, restaurant, bar, playground and even a popular disco. Moderate.

MÉRIDA HOTELS

The abundance of wonderful old hotels here makes the choosing almost painful.

If you're really strapped for funds, skip the antique inns and head straight for the downtown **Hotel Mucuy** (Calle 57a 481; 21-10-37), about three blocks from the Parque Hidalgo. This quiet, attractive, motel-style guest house has 22 small, sparkling rooms around a neat courtyard, with little wrought-iron desks, beds and doors. It's so well kept and fresh that everything shines. Ceiling fans cool the rooms. Very friendly management. Budget.

The delightful old colonial-style **Hotel Caribe** (Calle 59a 500; 24-90-22) occupies a balcony-laced 1876 building overlooking Parque Hidalgo. The lobby, which greets you with a displayed suit of armor and beamed ceiling, opens onto a courtyard restaurant. The 56 rooms are rather dark but comfy, with tiled floors, phones, air-conditioning or fans, simple furnishings, televisions and balconies. Rooftop pool. Budget.

Another former colonial home that has long functioned as a hotel, the 20-room **Posada Toledo** (Calle 58a and Calle 57a; 23-16-90) reeks of upper-class antiquity. Oil portraits and crystal chandeliers surround a sunny interior courtyard swimming in vines. Great sculpted doors open onto rooms that are surprisingly small, slightly gone to seed but still comfortable, frilly and full of antiques. Some are air-conditioned; others have fans. Budget.

You'll be equally charmed by the 54-room colonial **Hotel Colón** (Calle 62a 483; 23-43-55), with its own art deco *baño de vapor* (steam bath), including sunken pool and tiled massage slab (open to visitors for a fee), restaurant and bar. The rooms are less picturesque but comfortably equipped with air-conditioning, phone, carpet and old furnishings. Budget.

Since parking is difficult in Mérida, the 20-room **Hotel del Parque** (Calle 60a 497; 24-70-44) is an attractive choice for those with cars. Besides its roomy parking area, the hotel has small, sweet-smelling rooms with overhead fans, phones and views of Parque La Madre. It's plain but comfortable. Budget.

You can enjoy a colonial atmosphere and still get modern, stylish rooms at the downtown **Hotel Colonial** (Calle 62a 476; 23-64-78). Big, firm beds, phones, small televisions, air-conditioning and occasional colored windows brighten the accommodations. A pool, small bar and restaurant add to the conveniences. Budget.

Fresh and bright, the **Hotel María del Carmen** (Calle 63a 550; 23-91-33) is a modern six-story hotel located just a few blocks from the main plaza. With its marble-and-mirror lobby and friendly staff, this 94-room facility features a restaurant, swimming pool and other amenities. Moderate.

For easy living and a good locale, the 11-floor downtown **Hotel Mérida Misión** (Calle 60a 491; 23-95-00) is a complete resort in a hacienda package, with lobby-bar, restaurant, pool, disco and shops set amid potted plants, beamed ceilings, fountains, urns and columns. The Spanish influence disappears in the 150 carpeted, contemporary rooms with demure color schemes, phones, air-conditioning, color televisions and lovely views of the town. Moderate.

Also consider **El Castellano** (Calle 57 513; 23-01-00), a modern high-rise hotel with 170 rooms and a spacious lobby. The guest rooms are appointed with wrought-iron furniture, red-tile floors and potted plants.

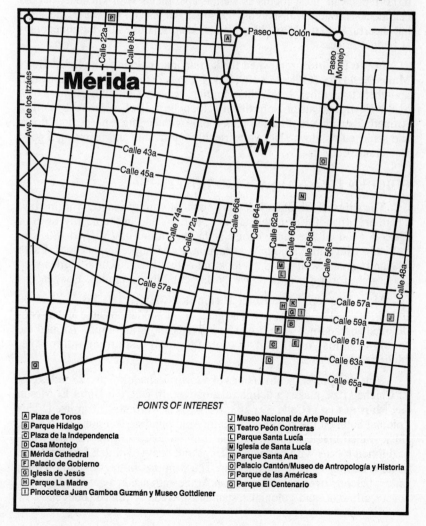

POINTS OF INTEREST

A Plaza de Toros
B Parque Hidalgo
C Plaza de la Independencia
D Casa Montejo
E Mérida Cathedral
F Palacio de Gobierno
G Iglesia de Jesús
H Parque La Madre
I Pinocoteca Juan Gamboa Guzmán y Museo Gottdiener

J Museo Nacional de Arte Popular
K Teatro Peón Contreras
L Parque Santa Lucía
M Iglesia de Santa Lucía
N Parque Santa Ana
O Palacio Cantón/Museo de Antropología y Historia
P Parque de las Américas
Q Parque El Centenario

Among the extra added attractions are restaurants, swimming pool and solarium. Moderate to deluxe.

GULF COAST HOTELS

All around Mérida along the gulf runs a string of little beach resorts, from Celustún to Progreso to Río Lagartos, with mostly run-down inns. These villages can best be explored using Mérida or another big town as your base, but if you want to stay overnight, here are a few possibilities:

In Progreso, **Tropical Suites** (Avenida Malecón and Calle 20a; 5-12-63) offers clean guest rooms as well as apartments with kitchenettes (and hammocks!). Budget. Just across the street and also on the water, the small but cheerful **Real del Mar** (Avenida Malecón and Calle 20a) has nine rooms at budget prices.

In Río Lagartos, renowned for its flamingo colonies, the faded **Hotel María Nefertity** (Calle 14a 109; Tel. 14, ext. 78) has the hotel scene tied up—there is no other. Inside the slumping, sea-eaten building stands a bust of the Egyptian Queen Nefertiti in a fountain full of melancholy turtles. Around this patio are 20 small pink rooms with ceiling fans, cement floors and screened windows. Not very friendly but livable and featuring a good restaurant. Budget.

CHICHÉN ITZÁ–VALLADOLID HOTELS

The ruins of Chichén Itzá may enchant you into an overnight stay. There are a handful of hotels around the ruins and in the nearby town of Pisté. A good middle-range choice is the **Pirámide Inn** (Mexico 180, Km. 5, Pisté), with a nice adjoining restaurant. Its 45 large, somber rooms with Mayan rugs and wall hangings look out onto a lovely central garden with pool, great for a dip after a sweaty day climbing pyramids. Budget.

More luxurious is the **Hotel Misión Inn** (Mexico 180, Pisté; 23-95-00 in Mérida), a 40-room facility. The guest accommodations here are air-conditioned and adorned with bright bedspreads and print drapes. Around the lovely grounds you'll find a swimming pool, restaurant and lounge. Moderate to deluxe.

You may prefer the diversions of a town. Valladolid, just 28 miles east of Chichén Itzá, makes a delightful stopover. In fact, the **Hotel El Mesón del Marqués** (★) (Calle 39a 203; 6-20-73) is worth a visit in itself. This colonial hotel on the *zócalo* in a century-old building lost none of its cool, thick-walled magic in the transition from hacienda to inn. To its 24 old-fashioned rooms with beamed ceilings and heavy wooden furniture, the hotel is adding 16 new guest rooms. The windows in the old section open onto a balcony overlooking the pool. At the entrance is a garden, fountain, lovely gift shop and colonial restaurant. Incredibly priced: budget.

The inexpensive but rather plain **Hotel San Clemente** (Calle 42 206; 6-22-08), located on the corner of the plaza, has 64 guest rooms as well as a restaurant and bar. Budget.

CANCÚN HOTELS

This glamour zone has many inexpensive hotels in Ciudad Cancún. The glitter strip hugs the beaches east of town.

The only real bargain hotel on the beach is **CREA Youth Hostel** (Paseo Kukulkán, Km. 3.2; 3-13-37), part of a nationwide Mexican chain. In addition to its enormous, fan-cooled dormitories with fabulous sea views and 612 beds, there's a campground in front of the beach and several air-conditioned villas with private baths for rent in the off season. Cafeteria, pool and bicycle rentals. Clean and friendly. Budget.

In Ciudad Cancún, the slightly hangdog **Hotel Yaxchilán** (Avenida Yaxchilán Lote 41-43; 4-13-24) has 18 passable rooms with ceiling fans or air-conditioning, cratelike furniture and small televisions. A decent base for beachbumming. Budget.

Better and more expensive than the above, but still the best little money saver in town, is the charming white pseudocolonial **Hotel Novotel** (Avenida Tulum 2; 4-29-99). The fancy rooms, with air-conditioning, televisions and phones, cost the most. But the cheaper rooms, out back behind the parking lot, are lovely lodgings with red-tile floors, fans, brightly tiled baths, dark-wood trim and great beds. Charming lobby café. Budget.

The more luxurious **Hotel Plaza Caribe** (Avenida Tulum and Avenida Uxmal; 4-13-77) presents a garish orange facade across from the downtown bus station. Surrounding its interior patio and pool are 120 bland rooms with air-conditioning, phones (on the blink at times), carpeting and marble washbasins. Moderate.

The best of the middle-range downtown hotels is the **Hotel-Suites Caribe Internacional** (Avenida Yaxchilán 36; 4-39-99), which offers free bus service to the beach. This glassy, six-story highrise contains a lobby-bar, poolside restaurant, hibiscus-filled garden and 80 attractive, air-conditioned rooms with tile floors and marble showers. Moderate.

Moving on to the beach, the oceanfront **Club Verano Beat** (Paseo Kukulkán 166; 3-07-22) looks like the least expensive hotel on the strip, youth-oriented and a good bet for apartmentlike quarters with patio and kitchenette. All spaces are air-conditioned, tiled and tropical-colored. You can enjoy the hacienda-style lobby-bar, quiet beach and private pier. Deluxe.

Overlooking Laguna Nichupté opposite the Caribbean, the plush **Hotel Club Lagoon** (Paseo Kukulkán, Km. 5.8; 3-11-11) emanates a whitewashed Mediterranean air. Its 89 small rooms have molded Arabic walls, orange-tile tubs, splashy decor and bright patios facing the calm lagoon.

Heavy on water sports, the hotel has its own marina, plus two restaurants and two bars, one in a striking pyramid. Deluxe.

Luxury on the ocean is the simplest way to characterize **Hotel Presidente** (Paseo Kukulkán, Lote 7; 3-03-30), a 294-room extravaganza. The good life is made even better here with a beachfront restaurant, swimming pool, waterfalls, tennis court and an adjacent golf course. The price tag, need I mention, is ultra-deluxe.

For big-time glamour, the **Hotel Krystal Cancún** (Paseo Kukulkán, Lote 9-A; 3-11-33) pulls out all the stops. Set on a beautiful stretch of beach, this highrise offers lagoonlike pools, full water sports, marvelous theme restaurants, Cancún's best disco and breakfast buffet, jacuzzi, sauna and tennis courts. The 325 big, tan-toned rooms feature rattan furnishings, easy chairs, televisions and queen-sized beds. Ultra-deluxe.

The spectacular (and spectacularly expensive) **Camino Real** (Punta Kukulkán; 3-01-00) goes one better, with a natural seawater pool fed by the Caribbean and a gently sloping pyramid design that meshes with the sun and sand. The usual assortment of bars, restaurants, nightspots, sea sports and swimming pools is enhanced by lush interior gardens. The 291 rooms have real native charm, with beautiful white marble floors, lovely terraces facing the sea, festive furnishings, gray marble tubs, color televisions and servibars. Cancún's best. Ultra-deluxe.

ISLA MUJERES HOTELS

Of the many low-cost hotels on the island, the cheapest is **Poc-na** (Calle Matamoros 91; 2-00-90), a pleasant youth hostel with neither age limits nor curfew. Located just a short walk from Playa Los Cocos, the rambling hostel contains mixed dormitories with woven-hemp bunks, tiny ceiling fans and small communal baths. There's an extra charge for sheets, towels, pillow and mattress. Restaurant-bar on the premises. Budget.

Just up the street stands the fresh, bright **Hotel Isleño** (Avenida Madero and Avenida Guerrero; 2-03-02), not far from the *zócalo*. Molded cement forms the closets and bedstands in the small white rooms, decorated by little more than cute overhead lamp-fans. There are several rooms per shared bath. Budget.

The **Perla Caribe** (Avenida Madero 2; 2-04-44) puts you right on the sea, with a small rocky beach behind its big blue-and-white facade. The little blue-and-white rooms come with ceiling fans or air-conditioning, balconies and plain decor. A new wing contains a cafeteria-bar and pool. Moderate.

True sea-worn atmosphere pervades the quaint **Hotel Rocamar** (Avenida Guerrero and Avenida Bravo; 2-01-01), facing a beach just across from the plaza. Its three floors, lined in stone seagull railings, contain slightly funky but very homey fan-cooled rooms (the ones with balconies are a sea-breeze heaven). The sea theme appears everywhere, in seashell lamps, giant fish hooks holding up the dressers and polyurethane washbasins inset with shells and seahorses. Budget.

For bungalows right on the island's nicest beach, check in at **Las Cabañas María del Mar** (Avenida Carlos Lazo 1; 2-01-79). There are five roomy cabañas, with outdoor patios and ceiling fans, plus eight smaller rooms in this garden-filled compound. The rooms are cheerfully set up with carved beds, little refrigerators and hammock-slung patios. Budget to moderate.

The three-story stucco **Posada del Mar** (Avenida Rueda Medina 15; 2-01-98) resembles a plain motel but has the island's best lodgings. The big white rooms enjoy bright views of the village beach and lighthouse, with phones, air-conditioning and fans, balconies and American-style furnishings. A lovely pool, garden and restaurant-bar add to the relaxation. Moderate.

For a secluded stay in a charming niche toward the south end of the island, visit **Maria's Kan-Kin** (Carretera al Garrafón; 3-14-20). Pretty and friendly, Maria's is a complex of five stucco-and-bamboo rooms set in a garden high above the ocean. Some rooms have air-conditioning, others fans; all have two double beds but are individually decorated. A restaurant, pier and beach complete the picture. Moderate.

At the north end of Isla Mujeres, on an island of its own, sits **Hotel Del Prado** (2-01-55). This 104-room luxury hotel provides such amenities as pool, bar and restaurant at deluxe prices.

COZUMEL HOTELS

Fancy hotels, many with scuba diving packages built into their prices, line the leeward side of the island. The modest inns are mostly in the village of San Miguel.

Hotel Pepita (Avenida 15a Sur 120; 2-00-98), a simple side-street hotel in town, has the best deal on rooms. About half the 30 units are air-conditioned; the rest have ceiling fans. All include small refrigerators, wooden desks, bare walls, two double beds and light pouring in from the central patio. Budget.

There's more panache and convenience at the slightly higher-priced **Hotel Mary Carmen** (Avenida 5a Sur 4; 2-05-81), half a block from the main plaza. Built around a central garden, with chandeliers in the lobby, the Mary Carmen offers 27 small, attractive carpeted rooms containing walnut-veneer furniture and air-conditioning. Budget.

Prefer a sea view? The most reasonable waterfront hotel is the whitewashed, motel-like **Hotel Vista del Mar** (Avenida Rafael Melgar 45; 2-05-45), right on the *malecón* in town. Its three floors all have lounging areas, and its 24 ample, bright rooms with balconies and compact refrigerators are so breezy the air-conditioning is hardly needed. Budget.

A nice compromise between luxury and practicality is the **Hotel del Mesón San Miguel** (Avenida Juárez; 2-02-33), the fanciest inn in the village yet still at a working-class price. Right on the *zócalo*, its easy-going lobby with overstuffed sofas and spacious, attractive restaurant set the tone for the 97 rooms. Roomy and casual, with terraces that overlook the square, they have carpets, air-conditioning and phones. Moderate.

Amid a welter of hotels catering to scuba divers, the picturesque, villa-like **Galapago Inn** (Carretera a Chacanab, Km. 1.5; 2-06-63) offers one of the best deals. Set around a fanciful patio, the upbeat stucco rooms blend painted tiles, pigskin furniture and natural light (some have balconies). All are air-conditioned, with refrigerators. Prices include three meals daily. Moderate to deluxe.

For extravagant effect, the **Hotel Sol Caribe** (Carretera a Chacanab; 2-07-00) takes the cake. Its enormous wooden-roofed lobby soars out over a tropical bar that features live music. Flower-cloaked trails curl around the pool and restaurants, boutique and disco, out to a hivelike highrise holding 220 rooms. The rooms are comfortable, with phones, air-conditioning, color televisions, servibars and carpeting or marble floors. Deluxe.

Some of the finest rooms on the island wait at the classy **Mayan Plaza** (Playa Santa Pilar; 2-04-12), a beachfront highrise at the north end of the island. All air-conditioned and carpeted, with lovely sea views and balconies, the 200 rooms have rich tapestry touches: wallhangings, brocade chairs, burlap-shaded lamps. The grounds include two pools, restaurant, shops and tennis courts. Ultra-deluxe.

The island's oldest luxury hotel, **El Presidente** (Carretera a Chancanab, Km. 6.5; 2-03-22) still has the most beautiful setting and finest all-around facilities. Shadowed in palms, facing a perfect snorkeler's cove, the hotel features a breezy *palapa* bar, outdoor restaurant and lobby bar with live music. The big tropical-colored rooms are delightfully bright, with sea views, air-conditioning and huge bathrooms. Deluxe to ultra-deluxe.

Plaza Los Glorias (Avenida Melgar, Km. 1.5; 2-19-37), one of Cozumel's brightest and newest hostelries, is a Mediterranean villa complete with pink balconies. In addition to a pool overlooking the ocean, this 163-room facility offers several restaurants and bars. Deluxe.

SOUTH OF CANCÚN HOTELS

The 40-mile stretch of coastal highway (Mexico 307) from Cancún to Playa del Carmen is quite undeveloped, aside from some overnighter guest houses around Puerto Morelos and several rustic bungalow complexes around Punta Bete.

The best of these is the charming, secluded **La Posada del Capitán Lafitte** (★) (Carretera Puerto Juárez–Tulum, Km. 60, Punta Bete), an escapist's beachside paradise about a mile off the main highway by dirt road. Under low palms and pink bougainvillea, 30 stone and wood cabañas face the turquoise sea, with ceiling fans, private terraces and battered dressers. The deceptively simple sandy grounds contain a dive shop, pool, restaurant-bar and *palapa* recreation room with television. Closed in October. Deluxe.

PLAYA DEL CARMEN HOTELS

This pretty beach town breeds unique little tropical inns.

For those short on funds, the **CREA Youth Hostel** (four blocks north of Avenida Principal, turn at the Autobuses Turismo and follow the signs) has big, clean dormitories plus several private cabañas for rent with air-conditioning and baths. Budget.

The Caribbean's own makeshift Taj Mahal is **House Benji's** (four blocks north of the plaza, on the beach), an India-style guest house featuring arched windows, built-in beds with portraits of gurus shining down, small niches with colored lights, a vegetarian restaurant, a sauna and yoga classes. Standard rooms are a bit cramped but still nice, with communal baths. Ask to see the special room with red bathtub and air-conditioning. Budget to moderate.

Like some whitewashed haven of shipwrecked souls on a half-forgotten isle, the **Blue Parrot Inn** (five blocks north of the plaza, on the beach) rests among the palms with a semi-Mediterranean laziness. Its nine rooms and one cement teepee share communal baths, all with ceiling fans, crude wooden furniture and fabulous sea views. Great little upstairs restaurant. Budget to moderate.

Want more amenities? The colonial-style **Hotel Molcas** (next to the ferry terminal; for reservations: Aviomar Cozumel, Avenida Rafael Melgar 13 in Cozumel; 2-04-77) is the local comfort station, with pool, dining room, bar and boutique. The 36 rooms are air-conditioned, with tiny balconies, dark Spanish furniture and little Tiffany lamps. Deluxe.

AKUMAL HOTELS

This lovely beach community is a little oasis of hotels, none inexpensive. You'll pay the fewest pesos at what appears to be a boring, sterile motel, the **Hotel Akumal Caribe** (Carretera Puerto Juárez–Tulum, Km. 104; 4-22-72 in Cancún), which actually houses 100 hot-blooded tropical rooms, all with air-conditioning, rattan furniture and sunny terraces. The hotel rolls out a red carpet with its pool, disco-bar, restaurants, dive shop and tennis courts. Moderate to deluxe.

For groups of up to seven people, look into the lovely, spacious **Las Casitas** (Playa Akumal; for reservations, contact: Apartado Postal 714, Cancún, Quintana Roo, México; 4-09-89 in Cancún). By far the finest accommodations at Akumal, these expensive "little houses" come with two bedrooms, ceiling fans, private stone patios, living and dining room, kitchens, two baths and tasteful, festive decor using Mexican handicrafts. Deluxe.

Just south of Akumal, on its own private beach, **Aventuras Akumal** (Carretera Puerto Juárez–Tulum, marked turnoff; for reservations, contact: Apartado Postal 1314, Cancún, Quintana Roo, México; 3-10-02) presents modern, upscale accommodations in pale shell tones and rich cedar trim, all air-conditioned. Each room bears a plaque with the name of a Mexican diver, and the diving focus is clear in the well-equipped dive shop. The hotel is a playground of rusty ballast-balls, ship's ropes and horns, nets and shells around its pool, restaurant and bar. Deluxe.

TULUM TO BOCA PAILA HOTELS

If you just want to see the ruins, the forlorn and solitary **Hotel El Crucero** (Carretera Puerto Juárez–Tulum, at the crossroads for the Tulum turnoff from Mexico 307) will do for an overnight stay (especially since it is the only place for miles around). Its 15 stripped-down rooms consist of ceiling fans, cold-water showers and two double beds. Restaurant next door. Budget.

The badly paved road from south of Tulum to Boca Paila is dotted with primitive but personalized bungalow inns. These beach camps with their palm-thatched cabins line the coast; but you have to like slumming it to tolerate the facilities (wells for washing, latrines, etc.), or lack of them.

Continue down the road several miles to the dreamy **Cabañas Chac-Mool** (★) (Carretera Tulum–Boca Paila), the best tropical hamlet of huts in these parts. Their 19 thatched heads probe the dense shade of the palms and stand out against the brilliant beach beyond. Each big round hut is softened with Mexican rugs and blankets, made enchanting with bamboo chairs and hanging beds. Wonderful communal bathrooms of roughhewn stone and a massive restaurant make this a truly beckoning retreat. Budget.

Farther along lie the dunelike, palm-spotted grounds of **Cabañas Arrecife** (Carretera Tulum–Boca Paila), where 13 varying cabañas are scattered inside a walled compound on miles of white beach. The bigger cabañas come with electricity, private baths, stone walls inset with shelves, front porches and shuttered windows. Smaller huts have only a bed and mosquito nets. Budget.

The weatherworn **Cabañas Tulum** (★) (Carretera Tulum–Boca Paila) rises out of the palms like a caricature. What is this big, well lit building, with 18 stone cabañas half sunk in drifts of sand, doing on this skinny jungle backroad? Just relaxing and waiting for people like you. It's one of those hip hangouts only the offbeat-elite really appreciate. There's erratic lighting, a good restaurant and a beach to make your heart sigh. Rooms are battered but tolerable, like mini-hurricane shelters. Budget.

The paved but pothole-studded road deteriorates to dirt as you continue to Boca Paila. Here the better of two luxurious fishing camps is the **Boca Paila Fishing Lodge** (Carretera Tulum–Boca Paila, reservations: P.O. Box 59, Cozumel, Quintana Roo, México; 2-00-53). This expensive mecca for bonefishing in the nearby lagoon has nine large, attractive cabañas, with electricity and baths, facing a heavenly beach. Good restaurant. Deluxe.

CHETUMAL AREA HOTELS

About 25 miles north of Chetumal on brilliant Laguna de Bacalar is a wonderfully peaceful spot to stay, the quiet **Hotel Laguna** (Mexico 307, Bacalar turnoff; 27-13-04 in Mérida). Its three-story turquoise-and-white facade, nestled in shade trees, reflects the jeweled sheen of the lagoon. The spacious pale-blue rooms, freshened by breezes and expansive terraces, have ceiling fans and shell lamps. A delightful pool, patio-bar and restaurant overlook the water. Budget.

In Chetumal there are many low-cost hotels for those passing through. The oldest in town and one of the least expensive is the motel-style **Hotel El Dorado** (Avenida Cinco de Mayo 42; 2-03-15), near the plaza. Its 27 rooms are air-conditioned and have been remodeled. Ask for an upstairs room with balcony. Budget.

A pleasant alternative is the higher-priced **Hotel Caribe Princess** (Avenida Alvaro Obregón 168; 2-09-00), a few blocks off the main drag. Its ugly concrete-molded exterior belies a comfortable, friendly interior of air-conditioned, plain rooms with carpets, phones and balconies. Budget.

Small but appealing, the **Hotel Principe** (Avenida Héroes 326; 2-47-99) features 48 bright rooms overlooking a garden. There is also a restaurant and bar at this budget-priced establishment.

In downtown Chetumal, classy **Hotel Del Prado** (Avenida Héroes 138; 2-05-44) has all the trimmings, like bar-disco and boutique, plus the best accommodations in town. Good-sized and air-conditioned, the 80 rooms come with color televisions, phones, small terraces and seating areas. An interior garden contains a pool and volleyball court. Deluxe.

Restaurants

A wild assortment of indigenous dishes awaits you in the Yucatán. From *pan de cazón* (baby shark in layered tortillas) to *cochinita pibil* (spicy baked pork wrapped in banana leaves) to *tinkinchik* (picante barbequed fish in *achiote* and orange sauce), you'll sample exotic concoctions dating back to the Mayas.

CIUDAD DEL CARMEN RESTAURANTS

Carmen revels in good coffee, with many outdoor cafés serving cappuccino and espresso. **Café Vadillo** (Calle 33a), which locals say has the best coffee in town, is one of a string of hole-in-the-wall cafés along the pedestrian walkway near the *zócalo*. The 24-hour **La Fuente** (Calle 20a;

2-06-66) enjoys a breezy view of Laguna de Términos, serving up coffee and ongoing *telenovelas* (Mexican soap operas) on its television. Both budget.

Shrimp are Carmen's specialties, and nowhere are they better prepared than at an unexciting little outdoor stand across from the ferry landing called **La Mesita (★)**, or The Little Table (Malecón de Puntilla). From morning till dusk, especially around midday, hungry faithfuls line up to sample the most mouth-watering seafood cocktails in Mexico. (I've never eaten better.) You can mix fresh shrimp, crab, oysters and snail (conch), served in a spicy sauce and a parfait glass. Budget.

For good standard fare, the **Restaurant-Bar El Kiosco** (Calle 33 and Calle 22; 2-30-46) offers quiet, pleasant surroundings, with potted palms and picture windows, inside the Hotel del Parque across from the *zócalo*. Eggs, chicken, seafood and Mexican dishes are on the menu. Budget.

The cheerful, smart **Vía Veneto** (inside EuroHotel, Calle 22a 208; 2-10-30), named for the famous café-lined street in Rome, practically beams with yellow chairs, tables, wicker lamps and floral carpeting. The ideal breakfast café, it serves a sumptuous morning buffet plus lunch and dinner. Moderate.

An attractive seafood house about six blocks from El Centro, **Pepe's** (Calle 27a 15; 2-22-09) serves exotic dishes such as filet of fish Rockefeller and shrimp in *salsa diabla*. Its air-conditioned comfort is enhanced by fresh flowers, wood-paneled walls and carpeting. Lunch and dinner only. Budget to moderate.

CAMPECHE RESTAURANTS

For cappuccino or espresso, the small and slightly shabby **Café Plaza** (Calle 8a 261; 6-23-28) makes a comfortable sit-down stop, right near the plaza. This carpeted, air-conditioned café serves sandwiches, breakfasts and Mexican dishes. Budget.

My favorite all-night café (open only from sundown to sunup) is the indoor-outdoor **Cafetería Le Jardín** (Hotel Baluartes, Avenida Ruiz Cortines; 6-39-11). Locals gather around the white wrought-iron tables and in the air-conditioned coolness to sip coffees, nibble pastries and lick ice creams. Budget to moderate.

Out in the suburbs, a casual little open-air restaurant called **Arteaga** (Avenida López Mateos 122; 6-41-62) dishes out spicy regional dinners. No menu—you just name your choice, be it *tamales colados* (hot chicken tamales in banana leaves), *panuchos* (crispy tortillas layered with chicken, avocado, chile and beans) or *pitaya* (lemon drink with seeds). Budget.

The downtown **Restaurant del Parque** (Calle 8a and Calle 57a; 6-02-40) attracts a lively local crowd. With colored lights and ceiling fans, it's breezy and upbeat, facing the well-lit Parque Principal. The menu is highlighted by seafood, assorted meats, salads and Mexican plates, but service is pokey. Budget to moderate.

The local seafood institution, **Restaurant Miramar** (Calle 8a and Calle 61a; 6-28-83), lights up an old colonial building full of romantic touches: black Spanish lanterns, golden glass doors laced with grillwork, beamed ceilings. Its atmosphere outshines its cuisine, which includes the popular *congrejo moro* (stone crab), fish soup, squid, and even hamburgers. Budget to moderate.

MÉRIDA RESTAURANTS

Mérida is a gourmet's promised land. Besides its Mayan dishes, there's Lebanese food such as hummus and tabouleh.

The classic coffeehouse and hangout of locals and tourists alike is bustling, high-ceilinged **Restaurant Express** (Calle 59a; 21-37-38). A delightful spot to nurse a coffee, watch the people pass in the Parque Hidalgo across the street or write postcards under the whirling ceiling fans, the Express also has good food, from yogurt to Mayan chicken. Budget.

Another leisurely breakfast spot is the outdoor **Cafetería El Mesón** (Calle 59a 500; 24-90-22), in the Parque Hidalgo. You can enjoy omelettes or enchiladas at umbrella-shaded wrought-iron tables on a brick patio. The only problem: an endless stream of hammock vendors and beggars. Budget.

El Louvre (Calle 59a between Calle 62a and Calle 61a; 21-32-71), just off the main plaza, is a noisy corner hashhouse, hot and crowded, with a reputation for inexpensive food, especially its *comida corrida* (meal of the day). Try, if you dare, the *huevos motuleños*, an untranslatable Yucatecan specialty: a mountain of eggs on tortillas drowned in tomato sauce, ham, beans, bacon and peas—i.e., scrambled leftovers. Locals love it. Budget.

Dine outside in a star-lit patio or an air-conditioned colonial salon at **Pórtico del Peregrino** (Calle 57a 501; 21-68-44), a sweet old-fashioned restaurant near the university. The menu covers seafood and meats, Yucatecan cuisine (try the lime soup) and delicious baked eggplant. Budget to moderate.

The widest range of Yucatecan dishes in town can be sampled at **Los Almendros** (Plaza de Mejorada; 21-28-51), about six blocks from Parque Hidalgo. This spacious, cheerful, turbulent restaurant, buzzing with employees in regional costumes, presents menus with photos and translations of all selections. *Pollo ticuleño* is particularly good. Lunch and dinner only. Budget.

Take a break and dip into some zesty Italian cooking at the charming **La Casona** (Calle 60a 434; 23-83-48). Occupying a fine old restored house with a lush interior garden near Paseo Montejo, La Casona serves homemade pasta, steaks, seafood and soups. Budget to moderate.

For a special splurge, French-accented **Le Gourmet** (Avenida Pérez Ponce 109-A; 27-19-70) has a classy, air-conditioned allure and a superb menu. An awning-covered portico introduces a series of carpeted dining rooms with cane-backed chairs and excellent service. Start with *mousse de alcachofa* (artichoke pâté) as an appetizer, then move on to shrimp stuffed with crab meat, chicken crepes or the winner, venison Le Gourmet-style. Moderate to deluxe.

My favorite restaurant in Mérida (I'm sure I'm not alone) is **Alberto's Continental** (Calle 64a and Calle 57a; 21-22-98). Shadowy and seductive, Alberto's dominates a beautiful white colonial building erected in 1727 over the rubble of a Mayan mound. Old statues, lamp-lit eaves and a courtyard full of antiques give it the air of an enchanted monastery, but the food is an earthy blend of Mayan, Mexican and Lebanese. Moderate to deluxe.

GULF COAST AND CHICHÉN ITZÁ RESTAURANTS

Except for those in Progreso, all the hotels listed in the corresponding "Hotels" section of this chapter have good, budget-priced restaurants attached. In Progreso, try the big, seafront **Capitán Marisco** (Calle 19a and Calle 12a; 5-06-39), with its central skylight, draped fishing nets and outdoor patio. All sorts of seafood are served. Closes in early evening. Budget.

CANCÚN RESTAURANTS

A whirl of glamorous restaurants with catchy themes sweeps the Cancún landscape, many in the grand hotels. It's like eating in Disneyland every night. Great fun, but expensive. Cheaper restaurants tend to be clustered in Ciudad Cancún.

The refreshingly clean, minimal, air-conditioned **Cafetería Pop** (Avenida Tulum 26; 4-19-91) has an American-style directness and a lengthy menu of breakfasts, sandwiches, Mexican meals and such. Popular businessman's hangout. Budget.

One of the nicest downtown sidewalk cafés is **Amigos del Mar,** or Sea Friends (Avenida Tulum and Calle Crisántemas; 4-11-99). You can dine on the fan-cooled, open-air patio or in an air-conditioned section behind glass, full of cushioned bamboo chairs and Tiffany lamps. The broad menu ranges from shrimp-stuffed avocado to lobster brochette. A good breakfast stop. Moderate.

For choice seafood, everyone's rushing to **El Pescador** (Calle Tulipanes 5; 4-26-73). It's a nondescript little indoor-outdoor joint on a side street, cramped, with scarlet tables, but the fish and shrimp are really great. Moderate.

Downtown, **Pericos** (Avenida Yaxchilán 71; 4-31-52), has more of the gaudy old Mexican rambunctiousness. Live marimba music bounces off the yellow globe lights and vibrates the thick walls of the quasi-colonial building. Dancers in big sombreros shimmy among the pigskin tables, and newlyweds drink from lewd-shaped glasses at the packed bar. Lunch or dinner choices range from juicy shish kabobs to filet mignon. Moderate.

The pink Victorian **Bombay Bicycle Club** (Paseo Kukulkán, Km. 6, near Playa Tortugas) is like a wholesome fern bar without the ferns, very deep in brass ceiling fans and stained glass. The huge menu has ribs, pizza, seafood and fine breakfasts, including an anything-goes omelette of your own making. Moderate.

If you like Victorian decor, you'll find genuine turn-of-the-century elegance at **Cancún 1900** (Centro de Convenciones, Paseo Kukulkán; 3-00-38). Red carpets, old photos, cane-seated chairs and gilded frames conjure up an old-fashioned world o f art nouveau luxury. Delicious inter-

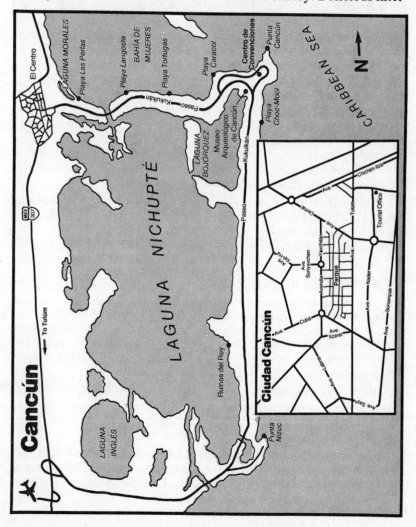

national foods are served, from fettuccine to Sinaloa steak. Great breakfasts. Moderate.

The ebullient **Carlos 'n Charlie's** (Paseo Kukulkán, Km. 5.5; 3-08-46) is a sprawling waterside restaurant, open and carefree, casting the glow of its yellow lanterns on Laguna Nichupté. Less manic than other restaurants in this nationwide chain, C 'n C's serves the same humorous "peep, moo, splash, crunch, slurp" menu of fine selections, from French onion soup to barbequed ribs. Lively disco-bar attached. Lunch and dinner only. Moderate.

Like its sister restaurant in Ixtapa, **Bogart's** (Hotel Krystal Cancún, Paseo Kukulkán, Lote 9-A; 3-11-33) is a torch-lit Arabic fantasy straight from the film *Casablanca*. A white grand piano churns out Bogie's theme song. Ceiling fans slowly revolve over thronelike wicker chairs, urns full of palms and delicate fountains. The sumptuous menu offers Middle Eastern delights, plus steaks and seafood (the red snapper and Musulman salad are superb). Moderate to deluxe.

The ultimate trendy, dazzling, multilevel, gardenlike **Blue Bayou** (Hyatt Cancún Caribe, Zona Hotelera; 3-00-44) is Cancún's first tribute to Cajun and Creole cooking. Gorgeously designed around a huge Mayan stela sleek with cascading water, the restaurant spans several floors made grander by vast windows and hanging plants. Live jazz filters over from the bar next door. New Orleans mint julips and gin fizzes top the menu. Tasty escargot, *filé* gumbo, jambalaya, *andouille* and crawfish *étouffé* are prepared by a French chef. Dinner only. Deluxe.

Quite different but equally glamorous is the **Mediterraneo Restaurant** (Hotel Presidente, Paseo Kukulkán, Lote 7; 3-03-30). Each of the five dining rooms presents the decor and gourmet cuisine of a Mediterranean country— France, Greece, Italy, Morocco and Spain. Dinner only; deluxe to ultra-deluxe.

ISLA MUJERES RESTAURANTS

The island is swimming with inexpensive restaurants. For breakfast, **Villa del Mar** (Avenida Rueda Medina Sur 1; 2-00-31) hits the spot. Its picture windows gaze out to the sweaty ferry docks, while inside it's clean and air-conditioned. With glass-topped tables and cushioned chairs, the café has no real character but serves a hearty selection of eggs, chicken, meats, Mexican meals and seafood. Budget.

Right next door, **Mirtita** (Avenida Rueda Medina Sur; 2-01-57) cooks up the best hamburgers and steaks in town. This easy-going waterfront restaurant-bar is air-conditioned with two dining areas as well as a small stage and dance floor for nighttime entertainment. Budget.

The almost unnoticeable **Lonchería Miramar** (Avenida Rueda Medina Sur, next to the ferry pier) slouches out over the water. *Palapa*-roofed and hemmed in red balcony railing, it's like a backwater stop for gondolas.

Some of the island's best seafood is served here, including *ceviche*, lobster, succulent garlic shrimp, plus chicken, eggs (and ask for fish tacos). Budget.

Just off the plaza, **Restaurant Gomar** (Calle Hidalgo; 2-01-42) is a popular meeting ground. Its hacienda-style patio and indoor dining room are fetchingly decked out in striped serape tablecloths, twirling fans and painted tiles. A cool screen of foliage shelters tables from the dust and sun. Good meals, including fresh seafood and meats, are served. Budget.

At night, **La Peña** (Calle Guerrero 5, just off the plaza) offers a breezy seaside picnic ambience under scattered *palapa* umbrellas, with a marimba band pinging out a blithe serenade to the stars. Savory pizza (vegetarian to seafood) is the house specialty. There's also chicken, chow mein and conch. Budget.

Ciro's Lobster House (Avenida Matamoros 11; 2-01-02) is one of the island's classier seafood houses, with an Americanized wood-paneled look and live music. But the food, from shrimp curry to lobster thermidor, needs a tune-up. Moderate.

The island's much-touted house of French haute cuisine is **Maria's Kan-Kin Restaurant** (Carretera al Garrafón; 3-14-20 in Cancún). I found the food very ordinary. In mood, it does excel: a charming *palapa*-roofed garden restaurant, with dangling seashells and shark jaws, soft lighting and hand-painted burlap menus offering king crab, lobster, shrimp and coconut mousse. Everything is marked in dollars—very overpriced. Moderate to deluxe.

COZUMEL RESTAURANTS

The island is drowning in great restaurants. **Ernesto's Fajitas Factory** (Zona Hotelera Sur, near Hotel Sol Caribe; 2-01-45) may be Cozumel's most distinctive eatery—an open, round *palapa* on the roadside, ringed in stools that are usually crowded with fajita fans. Fajitas are a kind of Tex-Mex taco with spicy beef, chicken or shrimp inside. You can also order all-American breakfasts, nachos and hamburgers. Budget.

In San Miguel, big tropical **Las Palmeras** (Avenida Rafael Melgar 27; 2-05-32) is the loveliest place for breakfast. Facing the passenger ferry pier, its open tile and brick interior is fanned by sea breezes that rustle its miniature gardens. Surprisingly prompt waiters bring you steaming omelettes, French toast, seafood, salads, Mexican meals and more. Budget.

Close by, the high-ceilinged seafront **La Portal** (Avenida Rafael Melgar 2; 2-03-16) offers all sorts of meals in a colonial-pirate atmosphere. Crossed swords and shields cover the tops of the arched windows; old-fashioned lanterns and grillwork stud the walls and doors. Especially good breakfasts. Budget.

Enjoy a cool drink or meal at the open-air **Plaza Leza** (Calle 1a Sur 6; 2-10-41). Its umbrella-shaded outdoor tables are sheltered by little shrubs, while the raised interior is top-heavy with Spanish-style furniture and travel posters. Mexican dishes dominate the menu. The Spanish omelettes and coconut ice cream with Kahlua are tops. Budget.

If you feel homesick or just want to catch the latest NFL game, **The Sports Page** (Avenida 5a Norte and Calle 2a; 2-11-99) is Cozumel's spotless, red-white-and-blue corner of Americana, with non-stop televisions showing the latest sports events. Walls and ceiling are plastered with football banners and team posters. Burgers and fries are big here, plus seafood, steak and excellent breakfasts. Budget to moderate.

Fish loll in the big aquariums that decorate the attractive, air-conditioned **Restaurante Acuario** (Avenida Rafael Melgar, in front of the Parque Quintana Roo; 2-10-97). This paneled, American-style restaurant on the water serves a wonderful array of seafood and meats. Try the king crab, flaming shrimp *acuario* or lobster. Lunch and dinner. Moderate.

Believed by many to be the island's best, **Pepe's Grill** (Avenida Rafael Melgar and Calle Adolfo Salas; 2-02-13) is a smart, slightly snobbish upstairs-downstairs restaurant on the *malecón*, shimmering with candlelight and live piano music. Such flaming specialties as shrimp jovial and brandy-laced drinks, light up the aisles like a magic show. Exotica like tomato stuffed with baby eels and conch chowder share menu space with delicious Mexican meals and meats. Dinner only. Moderate.

The rich, dark-wood **Morgan's** (Avenida 5a and Calle Juárez; 2-05-84), all in imported pine, resembles a West Indies townhouse, with outer veranda and patio, and lush island melodies lilting inside. Named for English pirate Henry Morgan, this chic, air-conditioned restaurant presents a treasure chest of entrees, from flaming crepes to Spanish *zarzuela* (seafood in tomato stew) to conch steak. Lunch and dinner. Moderate.

Top honors for elegance go to the upstairs waterfront **Café del Puerto** (Avenida Rafael Melgar 2; 2-03-16). Bamboo-and-gourd tropical lamps float from the natural straw ceiling and polish the coppery tile floor with soft lighting. The moonlit sea shines through the tall windows. A trio sings tender Yucatecan ballads as waiters serve sumptuous portions of seafoods and meats like *parriada mixta* (mixed seafood) and *langosta diabla* (lobster in a flaming pineapple). Dinner only. Moderate.

On the windward side of the island, have an escapist's breakfast or lunch at **La Tortuga Desnuda**, The Naked Turtle, (coastal highway, Playa Punta Chiquero, Km. 37). Thatched, open and denuded of interior decor, the Turtle faces the cove with arrangements of tables and chairs spilling onto a patio, where you can enjoy *ceviche*, fresh fish and cold beer. Budget.

PLAYA DEL CARMEN RESTAURANTS

Inexpensive **El Jardín** (Calle 5a Norte and Calle 2a Norte) is the local beach bum headquarters. With plaster roof, crude wood beams and plank floor, the little corner restaurant has a crooked, rickety charm but could use some fans to stave off the breathless heat. Very good breakfasts, chicken, seafood and salads are served. Budget.

Restaurant Yut Kun (across from the plaza) is Playa del Carmen's only Chinese restaurant, with everything from egg rolls to fried wonton. Tidy and compact, the restaurant extends from a plant-filled interior with ceiling fans to a cute porch with a view of the square and beach. Dinner only. Budget.

Next door, the tiny open-air **Charlie Boy Restaurant** (across from the plaza) specializes in snacks, milkshakes, hamburgers and vegetarian dishes. Very friendly. Budget.

The two fanciest spots in town sit side by side across from one another at the foot of the ferry landing. The restaurant at the **Hotel Playacar** (on the beach) has a lovely outdoor deck bathed in palm shadows and a wood-paneled indoor section with Spanish chairs and wandering Mayan minstrels. The menu ranges from seafood to pork. Across the street, the big, breezy dining room at the **Hotel Molcas** (on the beach), with serenading musicians, is air-conditioned in hot weather. Unusual entrees like Creole shrimp and beef kabobs are served. Both budget to moderate.

AKUMAL AREA RESTAURANTS

There are two fine spots to eat here, both moderate to deluxe. The informal, *palapa*-roofed **Lol-ha (Flor de Mar)** (Playa Akumal) parades its bamboo walls down almost to the tideline, where water that looks like turquoise cream laps at the shady sand. This, and the lovely morning breeze rustling its potted plants and maroon tablecloths, make Lol-ha the better breakfast spot. Besides tasty bacon and eggs, there's seafood, meat and chicken. Moderate to deluxe.

The natural dinner choice is **Restaurant Zacil** (Playa Akumal), a brief stroll from Lol-ha. Its cavernous *palapa* roof is alive with spinning fans, and its circular glassed walls look out to the beach and sea. Musicians entertain during the high season. You may choose from asparagus with French sauce, Caesar salad, steak, seafood and chicken. Budget.

At Playa Chemuyil, about six miles south of Akumal, the lively little **Restaurant-Bar Marco Polo** is a low-cost café-in-the-round whose bar stools are always full of interesting characters, and sometimes animals. I met fishermen, sailors, divers, a monkey, baby ocelot and coatimundi here one evening. The fish and chicken dinners are *muy sabrosas* (very tasty). Budget.

TULUM RESTAURANTS

There's nothing to work up an appetite over around here. **El Faisán y El Venado** (crossroads of Mexico 307 and the Tulum turnoff) is the freshest café, with formica tables and white tile floor. It serves good black coffee, seafoods and meats. The **Restaurant El Crucero** across the street is cheaper and serves tasty food, but it is not as nice. Both budget. Some small hotels to the south have restaurants, as well.

CHETUMAL RESTAURANTS

There are lots of choices here. Start with **Restaurant La Ostra** (Calle Efraím Aguilar 164; 2-04-52), a plain little side-street café, air-conditioned and clean, serving plain meals: eggs, seafood, Mexican dishes. Breakfast and lunch only. Budget.

A pleasant spot for breakfast or evening coffee, **Café Pérez Quintal** (Edifio 7 de Diciembre 4 and Calle 22 de Enero) is an open-air café set back amid white arches facing the tree-filled Parque Central. Delicious omelettes, seafood, sandwiches, fruit salads and meats. Budget.

For pizza, you cannot go wrong at popular, attractive **Sergio's Pizza** (Avenida Alvaro Obregón 182), where the excellent service is second only to the crisp crust. Air-conditioned but rather dark, with autumnal wall murals and paneling, Sergio's features a salad bar, cheese fondue, barbequed ribs and a respectable wine list. Lunch and dinner. Budget to moderate.

Restaurant Chez Farouk (Hotel Real Azteca, Calle Belice 186; 2-07-20) loses some of its gloss to the snorting downtown buses and sodden oil tanks in the neighborhood. But inside, with its imposing Spanish chairs and tile floors, it's quite inviting, as is the menu of seafood, Yucatecan dishes and Cantonese meals. Lunch and dinner. Budget.

The Cantonese influence appears again at the breezy seafront **Restaurant del Caribe** (Boulevard Bahía between Calle Esmerelda and Calle 22 de Enero; 2-06-28). With its wine racks and blond-wood chairs, this restaurant looks more European than Asian. Yet the menu lists chop suey, *tacos orientales* and *mariscada cantonesa* alongside seafood and pastas. Moderate.

About 25 miles north of Chetumal near Laguna de Bacalar, **Restaurant Cenote Azul** (turnoff from Mexico 307, Km. 34, Bacalar) is a junglelike, *palapa*-roofed restaurant hovering on the edge of the inky blue Cenote Azul. Caged toucans line the entryway, and wicker arches define the window openings. Besides seafood and barbequed sheep, ask for deer and wild boar (not on the menu). Breakfast and lunch only. Budget to moderate.

The Great Outdoors
The Sporting Life

CAMPING

Many marvelous camping spots lie along the Gulf Coast and Caribbean beaches. Developed resort areas on Cancún and parts of Cozumel are off-limits to campers, but that still leaves miles of beaches to the south, many with palm-shaded campgrounds right on the sea.

You can expect to deal with *muchos* mosquitoes and sandfleas, especially during the May-to-October rainy season. Bring repellent and mosquito nets.

Camping supplies and sporting goods can be found in Ciudad del Carmen at the **Conasuper** (Calle 20a and Calle 37a); in Campeche at **Superdiez** (Area Akim-Pech off Malecón Miguel Alemán near Avenida Francisco Madero); in Mérida at **Supermaz** (Calle 59a 514) and **Deporterama** (Calle 59a 508; 23-63-07); in Cancún at **Supermarket San Francisco de Asís** (Avenida Tulum next to Mercado Ku-huic); on Isla Mujeres at **Super Betino** (Avenida Morelos 5; 2-01-27); on Cozumel at the **Conasupo** (Ave-nida 10 in San Miguel); and in Chetumal at **Mercado Lázaro Cárdenas** (Calzado Veracruz and Segundo Circuito Periferico).

SWIMMING

For the most part calm and splendid, swimming in certain parts of the Caribbean can be tricky. Beware of riptides along the Cancún shoreline from the Hotel Camino Real to the Club Med. These sudden, strong currents can drag you out to sea. Don't panic or swim straight for shore. Instead, escape the current by swimming parallel to the shore, then swim in diagonally.

FISHING AND BOATING

Gulf waters swarm with tarpon (*sábalo*), and the Caribbean with sailfish, marlin, bluefin tuna (March through May) and kingfish and wahoo (May through September). Caribbean coast lagoons excel in fishing for bonefish and pompano. In addition to the following outlets, major hotels can arrange fishing trips:

In Ciudad del Carmen (whose Laguna de Términos is a tarpon heaven), make arrangements through the **Club de Pesca Nelo Manjárrez** (Calle 40a and Calle 61a; 2-00-73).

Make fishing arrangements in Campeche at the **pescadería**, or fish market, (end of Avenida Francisco Madero along the *malecón*) with the fishermen.

North of Mérida, a few miles west of the port of Progreso, **Servicios Acuáticos en la Península de Yucatán** (at the harbor in Yucalpetén) provides boats and fishing trips.

Cancún has a mind-boggling variety of facilities for lagoon fishing and deep-sea fishing. Try **Cancún Avioturismo** (Paseo Kukulkán across from the Casa Maya Hotel; 3-03-15), **Yacht Club Marina** (Paseo Kukulkán at Carlos 'n Charlie's; 3-13-04) and **Club de Pesca Pez Vela** (Paseo Kukulkán, Hotel Aristos; 3-09-92).

(Test continued on page 360.)

The Caribbean's Magic Gardens

On a good day you can see 250 feet into the depths of the Caribbean Sea. Far below shimmer the coral forests and multihued canyons that make the Yucatán's east coast one of the most spectacular diving sites in the world— second only, experts say, to the Great Barrier Reef in Australia.

People return year after year just to scuba or snorkel here, in an immense reef system that stretches some 250 miles from Isla Contoy north of Cancún all the way down to the speckled cays of Belize. These undersea zones resemble a silent, blossoming dream or dazzling hallucination. To dive is to enter another planet.

The reefs, though they look like inanimate rock, are actually living colonies of polyps that absorb food from the nutrient-rich Gulf Stream and have slowly grown into a coral jungle as complex as the Amazon. Finger coral, elkhorn, mountainous star, brain coral, purple leaf and orange tube, precious black coral with sepia age rings, plus green stinging coral and red fire sponges, which burn when touched, are a few of the species that bloom to towering heights on the ocean floor. Hewn into breathtaking landscapes, this coral world is dappled with vivid sea fans, treelike gorgonia, prickly sea urchins, sea whips and lush anemones.

Throughout this subterranean garden are brilliant schools of fish and myriad other sea creatures: gaudy parrotfish, candy bass, spotted scorpionfish camouflaged in the mottled sand, coral crabs skittering sideways like moving shards of reef, turquoise angelfish, fairy basslets, flamefish and starfish, colossal sea turtles and manta rays—an astonishing visual symphony rippling by, beautiful beyond belief.

But not all is harmonious beauty. Inside crevices, where you should never poke a prying hand, live moray eels, whose saw-toothed fangs hold decayed food particles that can fatally poison the eels' victims. And just off Isla Mujeres lie the bizarre caves of the sleeping sharks—the only place in the world where you can stroke a shark as it dozes in a stupor brought about by this area's low salinity.

Where are the tamer dive sites? For snorkeling on Isla Mujeres, El Garrafón is an exquisite sealife sanctuary. Nearby Manchones Reef provides calm depths for beginning divers, and El Dormitorio is a graveyard of 16th-century pirate ships. Cancún shares with Isla Mujeres a group of lovely shallow reefs (40-foot depths), including Cuevones Reef (full of small caves), fish-rich La Bandera Reef and the ornate reefs off Punta Nizac.

As for Cozumel, its riches surpass description. The most popular spots include the sea off shimmering Laguna Chancanab, La Ceiba Reef with its sunken plane, the precipitous Santa Rosa Wall, Columbia Reef with its mountainous columns and pinnacles, and the mighty Palancar Reef, six miles long and plunging 3,000 feet, containing easily half-a-dozen kingdoms of labyrinths, caverns and ravines.

South of Cancún, there's fantastic diving around Akumal, where objects from old Spanish galleons have been recovered, and great snorkeling in the lagoons at Xel-Há, where kaleidoscopic fish eat from your hand. Farther south, some 20 miles offshore from the village of Xcalak, stands the notorious Banco Chinchorro, whose jagged reefs have sent hundreds of ships to an early grave—a diver's happy hunting ground.

Strangest of all is to dive a *cenote*, the peninsula's perturbingly deep natural wells. With water as clear as liquid air, these wells are riddled with tunnels and caves where blind fish wriggle through the darkness.

On Isla Mujeres, sportfishing can be arranged through **Sociedad Cooperativa de Transportación Turística de Isla Mujeres** (Avenida Rueda Medina and Calle Madero; 2-02-74) or **Mexico Divers** (Avenida Rueda Medina near the ferry dock; 2-01-30).

On Cozumel, try **Club Náutico de Cozumel** (Recinto Portuario Banco Playa; 2-01-18), **Caleta Marina** (near Hotel El Presidente) or **Fantasía Divers** (across from Hotel Sol Caribe; 2-12-58). Fishing gear is sold at **Sportel** (Avenida 10a Sur 101; 2-02-65).

South of Cancún, you can plan fishing trips in Playa del Carmen through **Playacar Divers** (on Playa del Carmen near the ferry landing); in Akumal at **Kapaalua Dive Shop** (Playa Akumal); and at Playa Chemuyil's **dive shop**, directly on the beach.

South of Tulum, at Boca Paila, two fishing camps feature flats-fishing in Bahía Ascensión: **Boca Paila Fishing Lodge** (2-00-53 in Cozumel) and **Pez Maya Fishing and Beach Resort** (2-04-11).

For fishing around Chetumal, try skiff rentals at the villages of Xcalak, Bacalar or Calderitas.

Sailboats, kayaks, catamarans, motorboats, broncos and canoes are available at the Caribbean resorts. For information about pleasure cruises, see the "Sightseeing" section in this chapter.

In Cancún, there is a good selection of boats for rent at **Aqua-quin** (Hotel Camino Real, Zona Hotelera; 3-01-00), **Marina Playa Blanca** (Hotel Playa Blanca, Paseo Kukulkán; 3-03-44) and **Yacht Club Marina** (Carlos 'n Charlie's, Paseo Kukulkán; 3-13-04).

On Isla Mujeres, hobie cats and kayaks are for rent at **Mistral School** (Playa Los Cocos).

On Cozumel, there are sailboats and kayaks for rent at **Hotel El Presidente** (Carretera a Chancanab, Km. 6.5; 2-03-22) and **Sociedad Cooperativa de Servicios Turísticos** (municipal pier, San Miguel).

WINDSURFING

The waves along the gulf and the Caribbean won't support surfing, but are ideal for windsurfing. Sailboard rentals and lessons are widely available along the Caribbean.

In Cancún, nearly every beach has a marina offering windsurfing lessons. Try the **Caribbean Windsurfing School** (near Hotel Presidente, Playa Tortugas; 4-32-12) for daily instruction, with children's rigs available. For sailboards, try **Aquatours** (in front of Dos Playas Hotel, Zona Hotelera; 3-11-37), **Marina Mauna Loa** (Paseo Kukulkán; 3-00-72), **Club de Vela** (Hotel Playa Blanca, Paseo Kukulkán; 3-03-44) and **Cancún Deportes Acuaticos** (Hotel Calinda, Paseo Kukulkán; 3-16-00).

On Isla Mujeres, check at **Nautibeach Club** and **Mistral School** (both on Playa Los Cocos) for rentals and lessons.

On Cozumel, try **Hotel Cabañas del Caribe** (Playa San Juan; 2-00-72), **Hotel Villa Blanca** (Carretera a Chancanab; 2-07-30) and **Hotel El Presidente** (Carretera a Chancanab; 2-09-23).

SKIN DIVING

The Yucatán's Caribbean coast has the best skin diving in Mexico and some of the most fabulous underwater scenery in the world. Countless dive shops crowd the resorts and beaches (most hotels have their own). Some shops feature *cenote* and cave diving. Lagoon snorkeling is entrancing for beginners.

In Mérida, **Dive Mayab** (Molica Tours, Calle 58a and Calle 53a; 3-71-42) offers *cenote* diving in nearby archaeological zones.

In Cancún, a good place for instruction is **Scuba Cancún** (across from Casa Maya Hotel, Paseo Kukulkán; 3-10-11). Equipment and lessons are also available at **Neptuno Divers** (Club Verano Beat, Paseo Kukulkán 166; 3-07-22), **Aqua-quin** (Hotel Camino Real, Zona Hotelera; 3-01-00) and **Cancún Water Sports** (Hotel Calinda, Paseo Kukulkán; 3-16-00)

On Isla Mujeres, diving instructions and gear are provided by **Tienda de Buceo El Garrafón** (Carretera Garrafón, Km. 6), **El Cañon** (Avenida Rueda Medina 14; 2-00-60) and **Mexico Divers** (Avenida Rueda Medina and Avenida Madero; 2-01-31). Mexico Divers offers trips to the sleeping shark caves.

Cozumel, the *corazón* of Caribbean diving and home of the Palancar Reef, has more dive shops than restaurants. Some of the best are **Dive Paradise** (Calle 3a Sur 4; 2-10-07), **Discover Cozumel** (Avenida Rafael Melgar 23; 2-02-80), **Aqua Safari** (Avenida Rafael Melgar near Hotel Vista del Mar; 2-01-01), **Deportes Acuáticos** (Avenida Rafael Melgar and Calle 8a Norte; 2-06-40) and **Fantasía Divers** (in front of Hotel Sol Caribe, Carretera a Chancanab; 2-07-00). Fantasía is tops for diving lessons.

South of Cancún, you'll find gear and lessons in Playa del Carmen at **Playacar Divers** (in front of the ferry landing). On Playa Akumal, equipment is available at **Excursiones Akumal** and **Kapaalua Dive Shop,** which also provides cave and *cenote* diving. At **Aventuras Akumal** (off Mexico 307 just south of Playa Akumal), the Club of Explorations and Water Sports of Mexico (CEDAM) dive shop is a center for recovery of sunken treasure and runs trips to remote Banco Chinchorro. At crystalline Laguna Xel-Há to the south, snorkeling gear is for rent.

HUNTING

The Yucatecan jungles are full of wild boar, deer, turkeys, jaguars, pumas, ducks and rabbits.

GOLF

Golf courses are located just outside Mérida at the **Club Deportiva La Ceiba** (Mexico 261, about five miles north of town; 24-75-25) and in Cancún at **Pok-Ta-Pok Golf and Tennis Club** (Paseo Kukulkán, Km. 7.5; 3-08-71).

TENNIS

Most big resort hotels have their own tennis courts. You will also find courts in Mérida at the **Club Deportiva La Ceiba** (Mexico 261, about five miles north of town; 24-75-25); in Cancún at **Pok-Ta-Pok Golf and Tennis Club** (Paseo Kukulkán, Km. 7.5; 3-08-71) and **Paradise Beach and Racquet Club** (Zona Hotelera, next to Hotel Fiesta Americana; 3-14-03); and in Chetumal at the **Club Campestre** (Avenida López Mateos).

MISCELLANEOUS WATER SPORTS

Cancún offers a cascade of offbeat water sports, from jet-skiing to seaplaning. You can do some plain old waterskiing at **Hotel Club Lagoon Marina** (Paseo Kukulkán; 3-11-11) and **Gypsy's Marina and Aquatic Sports** (Paseo Kukulkán, Km. 10; 4-42-27). Seaplane rides, offering panoramic views of the coast, are available from **Avioturismo** (Paseo Kukulkán, Km. 5.5, Laguna Nichupté; 3-03-15). Jet-skis are for rent at **Marina Mauna Loa** (in the Mauna Loa Shopping Mall, Zona Hotelera; 3-00-72), where you can hitch your star to a motorized hang-glider. Balloon flights push off from **Wild Paradise** (Zona Hotelera; 4-53-92). And parasailing, giant water-wheels and aquabikes are available at **Cancún Deportes Acuáticos** (Hotel Calinda, Paseo Kukulkán; 3-16-00).

Beaches

Yucatán beaches start slowly, with pale little washes of sand along the Gulf of Mexico to the west and north, then build to a lovely crescendo along the Caribbean coast, with spots that rival the beauty of any beach in the world. The limestone-based sand, rating a true 10 among sands, is perfectly white, always cool—its particles retain no heat—and is as soft as eider down. The water glorifies the color blue in infinite translucent hues.

One blight lurking in Eden is a palm tree virus called "lethal yellowing" that is killing all the Jamaican tall palms in Quintana Roo. The disease began in Florida in the 1970s and somehow worked its way south, denuding Isla Mujeres and slowly snatching the shade in Cozumel and the whole Mexican Caribbean coast. A resistant breed of palm is being planted in some spots to reforest the beaches.

The region's second problem arrived in 1988 in the form of Hurricane Gilbert. This devastating storm, which whipped the entire seaboard, blew down countless trees, particularly palm trees along the coast and almond trees in Mérida. It also destroyed many of the flowering plants in Cozumel.

CIUDAD DEL CARMEN BEACHES

Playa Norte—The most popular of Carmen's beaches, this one starts at the north edge of town and stretches due east along the gulf for miles, to Puerto Real. Its white sand is mixed with pieces of shells, and blue-brown waters lap the shore where scattered *palapa* shelters shade the sand.

Facilities: Restaurant, *balneario* (bathing resort) with bathrooms. *Camping:* Private beyond the restaurants; grainy sand and aggravating chiggers make it uncomfortable. *Swimming:* Good. *Fishing:* Good. Tarpon, *huachinango*, mullet. *Shell-collecting:* Very good. You may find milky whelks, conches, spindles, cockles and tulip shells.

Getting there: Via Calle 26a from the *zócalo* in Ciudad del Carmen.

Playa Bahamita—This pretty, undeveloped beach outside town is an extension of Playa Norte to the east. The site of occasional holiday cottages and little picnic gazebos, Bahamita is generally quiet and empty except for hardy insects. Choked with shells, the strand is a perfect place to wander, particularly during the hurricane season (August to November) when the overactive sea rolls shells ashore in droves.

Facilities: None. *Camping:* Grainy sand and bugs make it uncomfortable. *Swimming:* Very good; calm clear waters. *Fishing:* Good. Tarpon, *huanchinango*, mullet found here. *Shell-collecting:* Superb. There are mint-condition snails, starfish, whelks, conches, cockles, spindles, chanks and tulips.

Getting there: About 12 miles east of Ciudad del Carmen along Mexico 180, various turnoffs.

Puerto Real—At the far eastern end of the island, this still beach rims a narrow point which holds the remains of an old ferry landing that was used before the present bridge was erected. The pebbly sand scraggles over platformlike rocks hairy with algae and washed by milky blue-green waters. On the western side of the point shine tidepools full of seaweed, shells and small fish.

Facilities: Restaurant. *Camping:* Uncomfortable on the shell-strewn shore. *Swimming:* Good along the beach; be careful around the rocks. *Diving:* Good around the point on the southern side of the island in an area called Cañon de Pirates. *Fishing:* Good, especially in Laguna de Términos for tarpon. *Shell-collecting:* Scattered small shells.

Getting there: About 23 miles east of Ciudad del Carmen along Mexico 180. Take the right fork in road opposite the Puente sign.

Isla de Aguada—On the other side of the bridge linking Ciudad del Carmen with the mainland, this "isla" is actually a fingerlike peninsula surrounded by sand. The gulf-side beaches roll north for about 50 miles, white and lonely, sharpened by pulverized shells but softened by gentle blue sea. The leeward shores on Laguna de Términos house a funky fishing village strewn with beer bottles, coconut husks and broken conch shells.

Facilities: Restaurants. *Camping:* Uncomfortable, with brittle sand and bugs. *Swimming:* Lovely. Shallow and calm. *Fishing:* Very good. Huachinango, tarpon, mullet here. *Shell-collecting:* Excellent. The tideline is a traffic jam of whelks, conches, cockles, olives, tulips, snails and spindles.

Getting there: About 25 miles east of Ciudad del Carmen on Mexico 180, eastern side of the bridge. Turn left after Restaurant Puente de la Unidad, park at the end of the road, hike out to the beach.

CAMPECHE BEACHES

Playa Bonita—The only strand worth mentioning in this area, this narrow beach on a small cove is a local weekend hangout. It's friendly but lacks beauty. Backed by a line of palms and a big recreational pavilion, the thin sand is littered with bottle caps and stones. A seaside trail leads south for several miles to a nicer, less accessible beach called **San Lorenzo.**

Facilities: Lockers, showers and baths, refreshments, *palapa* shelters. *Camping:* Unsafe. *Swimming:* Calm and gentle, but there is possible contamination from the nearby thermoelectric plant in Lerma.

Getting there: About eight miles south of Campeche on Mexico 180, marked turnoff.

MÉRIDA AREA BEACHES

Although the closest beach is over 20 miles from Mérida, this city is a good base from which to explore the surrounding Gulf Coast, whose modest beach towns are short on hotels.

Playa Celestún—Fronting a dusty fishing village full of zesty restaurants, this long white beach flows north along the Gulf of Mexico toward a natural sanctuary for flamingos. Along the village beach stand armadas of little fishing boats bristling with *jimbas* (cane poles) used to catch the local specialty, octopus. Hurricane season brings a brisk north wind; otherwise, the sand, sea and palms sway in a pleasant lull.

Facilities: Restaurants. *Camping:* Good north of the village. *Swimming:* Lovely, in opaque green water. *Diving:* Good around the vast Alacran Reef to the north. *Windsurfing:* Good. *Fishing/boating:* Great. To visit the flamingos, rent a fishing boat from fishermen in the village or at the bridge over the estuary. *Shell-collecting:* Small shells and big conches. The north end of the beach is best.

Getting there: About 60 miles west of Mérida on Mexico 281.

Playa Chuburna—This long, lazy beach slopes down from shrub-covered dunes crested by little beach houses and shady palms. Serving a sandy-trailed beach community, the narrow beach slides about 30 miles west along the gulf to the once-bustling port of Sisal where henequen was shipped by the ton. Don't attempt the roller-coaster sand road from Chuburna to Sisal in a standard car.

Facilities: Restaurants. *Camping:* Possible, but cramped and rather public. *Swimming:* Very good; beautiful turquoise water. *Diving:* Good around the Alacran Reef to the northwest. *Fishing:* Good. *Windsurfing:* Good.

Getting there: About 12 miles west of Progreso (35 miles northwest of Mérida) along Mexico 261.

Playa Chelem—Serving another holiday village, this beach scallops the gulf in neat scoops of shell-scattered sand and is overlooked by little stucco cottages. The fusion of the Gulf of Mexico and the Caribbean Sea here yields lovely blue water pocked with the stumpy remains of wooden piers.

Facilities: Restaurants. *Camping:* Cramped with no privacy. *Swimming:* Very pleasant. *Diving:* Good around the huge Alacran Reef to the northwest. *Windsurfing:* Good. *Fishing:* Good.

Getting there: About eight miles west of Progreso on Mexico 261, about 30 miles northwest of Mérida.

Playa Yucalpetén and **Playa Progreso**—Cut from the same cloth, these nice white beaches provide two kinds of lounging. Yucalpetén's tidy patch of sand has a *balneario* (bathing resort); speedboats and waterskiers from the nearby marina streak the blue-green waters. Progreso offers prettier sand, palms and restaurants, backed by a quaint ten-block *malecón*.

Facilities: Restaurants in Progreso; restrooms and showers in Yucalpetén; picnic areas at both. *Camping:* Not permitted in Yucalpetén; rather mosquito-plagued and public in Progreso. *Swimming:* Very pleasant. Clear, calm water. *Diving:* Good around the Alacran Reef to the northwest. *Windsurfing:* Good. *Fishing:* Good. Rent boats at the marina in Yucalpetén. *Shell-collecting:* Small scattered shells.

Getting there: About 25 miles north of Mérida along Mexico 261 to Progreso. Mexico 261 continues four miles west to Yucalpetén.

Playa Chicxulub Puerto—Just east of Progreso, this restful little beach launches a stretch of sand that wanders through coastal towns for about 50 miles, all the way east to Dzilam de Bravo. The same half-forgotten, careless air resides in all. Small vacation homes, patches of palms and sun-bleached skiffs line the narrow shores along an increasingly vivid blue gulf. The best beach areas east of Chicxulub Puerto are at **San Crisanto** and **Chabihau**, both tiny tropical villages.

Facilities: Restaurants, stores. *Camping:* Possible; best away from the private cottages. *Swimming:* Good; calm. *Windsurfing:* Good. *Fishing:* Good; skiffs for rent on the beaches.

Getting there: Chicxulub Puerto is about a mile east of Progreso on Mexico 27. San Crisanto is about 30 miles farther east, past Telchac Puerto, and Chabihau about four miles more.

NORTHEASTERN GULF BEACHES

A handful of minor, out-of-the-way beaches stipples the Gulf of Mexico north and northeast of Valladolid and Tizimín. This region, heavy in estuaries and marshy mudflats, has attracted huge pink flamingo populations. The beaches themselves are far less interesting and a bit remote.

Playa San Felipe—The gulf-side village of San Felipe has no mainland beach. However, an island beach by the same name is reachable by a ten-minute boat trip. The crumbly, thin sand curves around a soft point where the shallow water is a gorgeous foreshadowing of the approaching Caribbean.

Facilities: None. *Camping:* Uncomfortable sand; there's no shelter. *Swimming:* Excellent; ideal for children.

Getting there: In San Felipe, by boat from the main pier.

Playa Río Lagartos—Here again, the beach is not on the mainland but on the protective peninsula across the water at Punta Holohit. There are more than five miles of sand, which shifts from drab and narrow to broad and shell-packed, a beachcomber's heaven.

Facilities: None. *Camping:* Very private; no shelter. *Swimming:* Excellent. *Shell-collecting:* Great.

Getting there: In Río Lagartos, by boat from the shore.

Isla Holbox—This long, flat reef island hovering eight miles offshore at the junction between the Gulf of Mexico and the Caribbean Sea has fine, utterly secluded beaches swamped with shells. There's not much else aside from a wee fishing hamlet.

Facilities: Restaurant, small stores. *Camping:* The height of escapism. No shelter. *Swimming:* Excellent. *Shell-collecting:* Tops.

Getting there: By tiny vehicle and passenger ferry from Chiquila. There's no such thing as a schedule, so take your chances.

CANCÚN BEACHES

Some dozen pearly beaches trim the windward side of Cancún. The safest for swimming—the first four in this section—touch the gentle Bahía de Mujeres. The last two, which have some dangerous currents, face the open Caribbean. Narrow beaches with hotels line the glassy inner lagoons. Camping is not permitted on any Cancún beaches.

Playa Las Perlas—This is the most westerly beach, the first you hit coming from Ciudad Cancún, and one of the most natural beaches in the area. The hard-packed sand, like a diamond glaze tinted with shadows of surrounding trees, makes a tranquil picnic ground. A pier leads out over the exquisite water.

Facilities: Marina. *Swimming:* Lovely. Pool-like area perfect for kids. *Snorkeling/diving:* Excellent around offshore reefs. Diving gear for rent. *Windsurfing:* Good. *Fishing/boating:* Good. Boat rentals are available at the marina.

Getting there: Located in Cancún's Zona Hotelera, Paseo Kukulkán, Km. 2.5.

Playa Langosta—This sandy cove curves out to a small rocky point and widens into a fuller, softer beach at the feet of the Hotel Casa Maya. This part, scattered with *palapa* shelters, is protected by a small jetty.

Facilities: Restaurant, marina. *Swimming:* Very good. *Snorkeling/diving:* Good, especially around offshore reefs. Scuba school; diving gear for rent. *Windsurfing:* Excellent. Rentals and classes available. *Fishing:* Small pier to fish from. Boats for rent.

Getting there: Located in Cancún's Zona Hotelera, Paseo Kukulkán, Km. 5.

Playa Tortugas—Lovely and undeveloped, with powdery white sand, this beach could almost be in some backwoods fishing town. A few *palapa* shelters and a bamboo lifeguard stand shade the sand.

Facilities: Nearby restaurant. *Swimming:* Excellent. *Snorkeling/diving:* Excellent around offshore reefs. Snorkeling gear for rent at the café. *Windsurfing:* Good. *Fishing:* Very good.

Getting there: Located in Cancún's Zona Hotelera; take the marked turnoff from Paseo Kukulkán.

Playa Caracol—Beginning with a rustic picnic shelter and a fishing pier, this quiet satin beach gently loops along Bahía de Mujeres for about a mile to the Hotel Camino Real and a small lighthouse. This is the most easterly beach on the bay before the island makes a 90° turn around Punta Cancún and rolls south along the Caribbean.

Facilities: Nearby hotels and other services. *Swimming:* Beautiful. Calm water. *Snorkeling/diving:* Excellent. Reef zone at Punta Cancún with safe diving on the west side. Dive gear for rent. *Windsurfing:* Good. Sailboards for rent at Camino Real. *Fishing:* Good from pier.

Getting there: Located in Cancún's Zona Hotelera, Punta Cancún area. Take the Punta Cancún turnoff from Paseo Kukulkán. Proceed around the *glorieta* (traffic circle) past the Hyatt Regency and turn into parking lot past the "Archaeological Information" sign.

Playa Chac-Mool—By no means secluded or untouched by the Midas of tourism, this beach fronts many a hotel and condo but is none the worse for wear. A fabulous walking beach, it stretches from Punta Cancún for about five miles down to Playa del Rey. Its sugary-white sand gives you little white slippers as you step out of the crystal tide. The water burns so intensely blue it appears to be dyed. Up on a sandy dune, a reproduction of the rain god Chac-Mool surveys the scene.

Facilities: Bathrooms and showers, restaurants, stores. *Swimming:* Good, but stay close to shore to avoid the undertow. Watch for flags marking water conditions. *Snorkeling/diving:* Excellent, especially around the offshore reef. Dive gear for rent. *Windsurfing:* Good. Sailboards and lessons available. *Fishing:* Good. Boats for rent at the marina.

Getting there: Located in Cancún's Zona Hotelera, Paseo Kukulkán, Km. 13.

Playa del Rey—The southernmost beach on the island before Punta Nizuc, Playa del Rey starts with softly vegetated dunes sloping down into thick, virgin sand that runs along the turquoise sea. This long, unspoiled beach will give you a clue to how Cancún looked prior to its tourist buildup. Not for long, though. Flanked at both ends by construction, this beach will soon feel the crunch of Cancún's growing pains.

Facilities: None. Club Med at Punta Nizuc. *Swimming:* Rough; use caution. *Diving:* Very good off Punta Nizuc. *Windsurfing:* Good.

Getting there: Located in Cancún's Zona Hotelera, Paseo Kukulkán, opposite the Ruinas del Rey (old Mayan ruins).

ISLA MUJERES BEACHES

Playa Los Cocos—Isla Mujeres' most beautiful beach, with the most serene combination of velvety sand and bathtub sea I've ever seen, Los Cocos may be the best swimming (or lolling) spot on the whole coast. A continuation of the village beach that begins near the docks and wraps around a point, Cocos runs for half-a-mile along the island's northwesterly shore between Nautibeach and El Presidente. Its only lack is shade. The island's international set often bathes topless or suns bottomless here, something I saw in no other Caribbean resort.

Facilities: Restaurants. *Camping:* Too public. *Swimming:* Gorgeous. Shallow for half-a-mile out. *Snorkeling:* Good around El Presidente. Equipment for rent. *Windsurfing:* Excellent. Lessons and sailboards available. *Boating:* Kayaks, catamarans for rent.

Getting there: Northwest side of the island and village at the end of Calle Carlos Lazo.

Playa Lancheros—A less-visited, more secluded white sand beach near the southern end of the island, Lancheros has a protected section for gentle swimming. It also houses a turtle pen, which attracts daily rounds of Cancún tourists. Across the road and down a trail through the undergrowth lie the ruins of Mundaca the Pirate's hacienda.

Facilities: Bathrooms, restaurants. *Palapa* umbrellas for shade. *Camping:* None; permitted at a smaller beach just south of here. *Swim-*

ming: Lovely. *Snorkeling/diving:* Good, especially around the offshore reef. *Windsurfing:* Good. *Fishing:* Good.

Getting there: Along the road from the village to El Garrafón, marked turnoff.

El Garrafón—This snorkeling center has a mostly rocky beach. See the description in the "Sightseeing" section in this chapter.

COZUMEL BEACHES

This 30-mile-long island is crusted with beaches on both leeward and windward shores. Since the waters surrounding the island are part of an un-

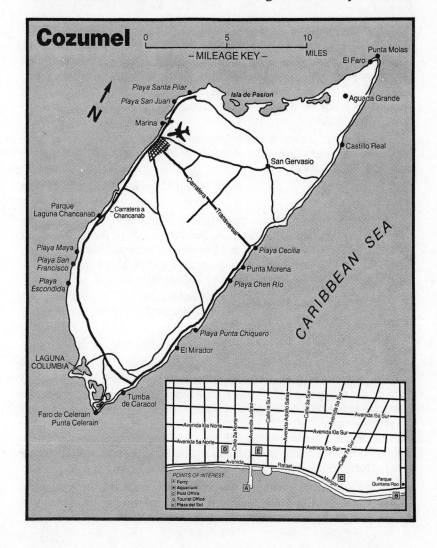

derwater natural park, shore fishing is not permitted. Some of the best beaches include:

Playa San Juan—Also called Playa Azul, this friendly, family-oriented beach covers the northern hotel strip from the Mayan Plaza Hotel to Puerto Abrigo. Its best section fronts the Hotel Playa Azul. Here windsurfers skim the soft waves, shade trees rustle and tiny black-and-yellow birds flit down to the local restaurant and perch on your chair.

Facilities: Restaurants. *Camping:* Not permitted. *Swimming:* Excellent; mild surf, perfect for children. *Snorkeling/diving:* Pleasant snorkeling; fair diving around Punta Norte. *Windsurfing:* Excellent. Sailboards for rent.

Getting there: Towards the northwestern end of Cozumel, turn off the paved road at Hotel Playa Azul.

Laguna Chancanab—This seaside crystalline lagoon, twinkling with colored fish, stands alongside a botanical garden and manmade beach with full facilities. The meadow of sand, small but lovely for sunbathing, faces the island's prime snorkeling turf just offshore—a giant jewel-box of tropical sea life.

Facilities: Bathrooms, showers, and restaurant. *Camping:* Not permitted. *Swimming:* Pleasant. *Snorkeling:* Superb. Dive shops here provide gear and classes.

Getting there: Six miles south of San Miguel, marked turnoff from the main coastal road.

Playa Maya—This quiet sandy beach, with a few *palapa* umbrellas and plastic reclining seats in the sand, lacks the sizzle of the more popular spots but exudes instead a feeling of dreamy relaxation. Backed by low-lying jungle, the beach forms scallops around soft points to the south. The sand is scattered with white coral and broken conch shells.

Facilities: Restaurant, bathrooms and showers. *Camping:* Not permitted. *Swimming:* Lovely. *Snorkeling/diving:* Very good; the dive shop rents equipment. *Windsurfing:* Good.

Getting there: About nine miles south of San Miguel, marked turnoff from the main coastal road.

Playa San Francisco—Cozumel's number one beach, San Francisco actually has two parts. The first is a little beach running along a mirrorlike piece of sea between two copses of shade trees, where narcissistic, bikini-clad sunbathers sip piña coladas. The second, just to the south and less visited, widens into a sandy pasture. Behind it lie the cooling shadows of a little woods dotted with rickety picnic tables and big *palapas*—a bucolic breeding ground for mosquitoes, which emerge after dark.

Facilities: Restaurant, bathrooms and showers at the northern beach. Restaurant at the southern beach. *Camping:* You can get away with it in the southern part. Bring repellent. *Swimming:* Glorious. *Snorkeling/ diving:* Excellent at both beaches. Great diving around the offshore reef. Gear for rent at the northern beach. *Windsurfing:* Good.

Getting there: For the northern beach, about nine and a half miles south of San Miguel, just past Playa Maya; take marked turnoff from the main coastal road. For the southern beach, about a mile farther south; take marked turnoff from main coastal road.

Playa Escondida (★)—In a hushed jungle at the end of a bumpy road, this secretive white beach flows out of the shadows and wanders for several miles along limpid and motionless water. Tin-and-thatched shacks half buried in shoreline vegetation send little smoke signals into the air as fish sizzle on outdoor grills. More of a sanctuary for natives than tourists, this may be Cozumel's best escapist beach.

Facilities: Restaurant. *Camping:* Not permitted. *Swimming:* Excellent. *Snorkeling/diving:* Excellent. Santa Rosa reef is right offshore. *Windsurfing:* Good. *Shell-collecting:* Abundant bits of white coral.

Getting there: About 12 miles south of San Miguel along the coastal road; marked turnoff.

Punta Morena—This pretty, wild beach on Cozumel's windward shore winds down from a small settlement of huts and palms where fishermen gather to barbeque fresh fish. Seaweed and interesting rock formations lie along the beach for about a half-mile. One sculpted rock, reached by a little wooden bridge, is called *Copa de Piedra* (the stone cup). An overhanging grotto with a sandy floor, called *Cueva del Amor*, is reached by crude rocky stairs.

Facilities: Restaurant. *Camping:* Good, but beware of the vicious sand flies. *Swimming:* The rocky shore is a bit rough, but try the natural seawater pool sheltered by rocks just south of the restaurant. *Snorkeling:* Good in sheltered areas.

Getting there: Along the windward road just south of Santa Cecilia, Km. 45.

Playa Chen Río—Another pretty beach in a cove protected by a wall of rocks, this crescent of sand slides along the somnolent turquoise water. Very quiet and private, with a few *palapa* umbrellas for shade.

Facilities: None. *Camping:* Very peaceful here. *Swimming:* Good. *Snorkeling:* Good.

Getting there: Along the windward road just south of Punta Morena, Km. 42.

Punta Chiquero (★)—The most beautiful beach on Cozumel's eastern coast, perhaps on the entire island, this primitive paradise awakens escapist yearnings. Protected by a touseled green headland, the sugar-white shore clings to a sheltered cove, then ventures south for a mile along the open sea. Cages holding parakeets dangle from the eaves of the quaint thatch-roofed restaurant, and playful coatimundis nuzzle their pointy noses into your sandals for attention.

Facilities: Restaurant. *Camping:* Good. *Swimming:* Good, but watch out for the rocky bottom. *Snorkeling/diving:* Very good, especially around the reef close to shore. Gear for rent at the restaurant. *Windsurfing:* Good.

Getting there: Off the windward road south of Chen Río, Km. 37.

SOUTH OF CANCÚN BEACHES

Put the highrises and discos behind you. Here's where the real hidden beaches begin. About 100 miles of low-profile, sultry, semi-primitive white beaches sweep the coastline from Cancún south to Boca Paila. The farther south you go, the wilder they get. Here are some of the most idyllic beaches on earth.

Punta Bete—This secluded beach zone fronts a series of rustic hotels, one named for Jean Lafitte, another a trendy colony of tents with all the trimmings. Sand and scattered palms fill the landscape. A dense scrub jungle toils behind the shore, encroaching on the mile-long road leading in from the highway.

Facilities: Restaurants, campground. *Camping:* Good at Camping Xcalacoco. *Swimming:* Very good. *Snorkeling/diving:* Very good. The dive shop at Capitán Lafitte rents gear.

Getting there: About 30 miles south of Cancún off Mexico 307. Take the turnoff for La Posada del Capitán Lafitte or El Marlin Azul and follow the gravel road about a mile to the sea.

Playa del Carmen—This wide, clean, gorgeous beach seems to rock to a tropical lullaby, soothing and unhurried, sweetened by the rustle of palms. The shore extends for miles both north and south of the ferry pier, where boats push off for Cozumel. An exotic little village offers outdoorsy amenities for the offbeat traveler.

Facilities: Restaurants, campground, stores. *Camping:* Heavenly, at La Ruina Campground. Watch out for mosquitoes after sundown. *Swimming:* Wonderful. *Snorkeling/diving:* Very good, especially around the offshore reef. Gear for rent at Playacar Divers. *Windsurfing:* Excellent. Sailboards and surfboards for rent at Playacar Divers. *Shell-collecting:* Bits of coral and seabeans (*cirripedios*) with crustaceans attached.

Getting there: About 40 miles south of Cancún off Mexico 307.

Playa Paamul—This rocky, palm-lined beach has an intimate feel; it is one of the least trafficked parts of this coast. Marvelous breezes sweep across the aquamarine cove, whose creamy-blue waters are darkened by offshore reefs. Rocky platforms intrude upon the cottony sand, but the area is all the more pleasant because it is tucked between two protective points.

Facilities: Restaurant. *Camping:* Trailer park, camping area; very pleasant. *Swimming:* Very good. *Snorkeling/diving:* Very good. *Windsurfing:* Good.

Getting there: About 55 miles south of Cancún, take the marked turnoff from Mexico 307, then follow dirt road about a mile to the beach.

Playa Akumal—The name means "place of the turtles" in Mayan, but there is nary a turtle in sight. Instead, a fair number of visitors wanders around a relaxed little tourist colony, which seems to have emerged almost organically among the palms. Through the fronds shines the opal-blue sea, and along its edge curves a mile-long splendor of sand—it's a dream come true.

Facilities: Restaurants, stores. *Camping:* Not permitted. *Swimming:* Sublime. *Snorkeling/diving:* Big stuff here. Dive shops offer gear, lessons, trips to offshore reefs and sunken ships, *cenote* diving. *Windsurfing:* Excellent. *Fishing:* Excellent, from dolphin to king mackerel. Ask about boat rentals at the dive shops.

Getting there: About 65 miles south of Cancún, there's a marked turnoff from Mexico 307.

Playa Aventuras—Beautiful in its own right, this beach lacks palm trees and is somehow left a little wanting despite its smattering of *palapa* shelters. Backed by a lowrise hotel and time-sharing complex at its northern end, the beach moves beyond a protecting point of land into a wilder open area, quite empty and isolated. A pier near the hotel accommodates boat traffic. Little globs of petroleum washing ashore can blacken your feet.

Facilities: Restaurant. *Camping:* Not recommended. *Swimming:* Excellent. *Snorkeling/diving:* Tops. Big offshore reefs. The dive shop has gear, classes and trips, and is national headquarters for Club of Explorations and Water Sports of Mexico (CEDAM). *Windsurfing:* Very good. Gear for rent at the dive shop. *Fishing:* Good. Cabin cruisers for rent at the dive shop.

Getting there: About 69 miles south of Cancún on Mexico 307, at the turnoff for Hotel Aventuras Akumal or Playa Aventuras.

Playa Chemuyil—The sign on the highway says "La Playa Más Bonita en el Mundo" ("The Most Beautiful Beach in the World"). It is no empty claim. Of all the beaches I have known and loved, this may be the bona fide Eden. Like a little palm plantation drenched in long shadows, pillowy white where the sun smiles through, with caressing breezes to turn the pages of your bestseller just at the crucial moment, Chemuyil leaves no want unmet. Thick jungle tumbles down from a southern point, and little screened jungle huts under the palms give camping a Congo edge with civilized conveniences.

Facilities: Bathrooms and showers; restaurant. Huts and hammocks. *Camping:* Ideal; small fee. One or two evening mosquitoes. *Swimming:*

Divine. *Snorkeling/diving:* Excellent. The dive shop rents equipment. *Windsurfing:* Very good. *Fishing:* Great. Boat for rent.

Getting there: Seventy miles south of Cancún on Mexico 307; watch for the famous sign.

Playa Xcacel—Another vision of loveliness, this fresh little beach faces the open sea with waves just strong enough for body-surfing. The thick white sand slopes down from a still palm grove to a row of *palapa* shelters. A shipwreck is visible from the shore. Great spot to escape the tourist flutter.

Facilities: Bathrooms and showers; restaurant. *Camping:* Excellent under the palms; small fee. *Swimming:* Lovely. Lively surf. *Snorkeling/diving:* Very good; best at the northern end. *Windsurfing:* Good.

Getting there: Seventy-one miles south of Cancún off Mexico 307.

Playas Tulum (★)—The site of the ruined Mayan fortress has only a minuscule patch of beach, but south of Tulum the beach runs wild for 15 miles down to Boca Paila on a pristine, still untamed peninsula. Random rustic hotels, fishermen's shacks, hidden *cenotes*, tangled jungle, furtive wild birds, lagoons and a flourishing mosquito population color this coast, explorable via a narrow, unpaved road. The long, silent beaches have a savage sort of timelessness that is almost mystical. Beyond the Boca Paila bridge to Punta Allen there's another 20 miles of solitary sand, jungle and palms. It is all set aside as an ecological reserve called Sian Ka'an ("beginning of heaven"), closed to future commercial development.

Facilities: Restaurants; two luxury fishing camps. *Camping:* Excellent, but bring insect repellent. *Swimming:* Wonderful. *Snorkeling/diving:* Good; bring your own equipment. *Windsurfing:* Good. *Fishing:* Excellent, especially flats-fishing in lagoons.

Getting there: About 80 miles south of Cancún along Mexico 307, take the marked turnoff for the Tulum ruins. From the ruins, continue on the road for Boca Paila south of the ruins. Almost any seaward turnoff leads to the beach.

Trailer Parks

All have bathrooms and hookups unless otherwise noted.

CAMPECHE TRAILER PARKS

Campeche Trailer Park (Calle 19a in the village of Samula, five miles south of Campeche) has 23 spaces in a quiet inland park.

CREA Youth Hostel (Avenida Melgar; 6-18-02) allows camping on its grounds (no hookups).

MÉRIDA TRAILER PARKS

Rainbow Trailer Park (Carretera Progreso, Km. 8, north of Mérida) has an overgrown, 100-space campsite full of fruit trees.

CHICHÉN ITZÁ TRAILER PARKS

Pirámide Inn and Trailer Park (Mexico 180, Km. 117, pueblo of Pisté) has 47 spaces near the ruins with use of Piramide Inn pool.

CANCÚN TRAILER PARKS

Mercoloco RV Park (five miles north of Cancún, Carretera Puerto Juárez–Punta Sam) faces a beach. Nearby **La Playa RV Park** has similar facilities.

CREA Youth Hostel (Paseo Kukulkán, Km. 3.2, Zona Hotelera) offers a grassy campsite overlooking the beach (no hookups).

PLAYA DEL CARMEN TRAILER PARKS

Camping Xcalacoco (five miles north of Playa del Carmen, turn off Mexico 307 at Marlin Azul sign) has beachside camping and cabins (no hookups). Open December through March.

Campground La Ruina (on Playa del Carmen) is a balmy beach-site containing a Mayan ruin, with hammocks and cabins for rent.

PAAMUL TRAILER PARKS

Trailer Park Paamul (off Mexico 307, on Playa Paamul) offers a lovely palm-filled campsite facing the beach and a rustic hotel.

CHETUMAL TRAILER PARKS

Cenote Azul Trailer Park (22 miles north of Chetumal off Mexico 307) is shady, friendly and near a huge *cenote* (no hookups).

Zaztal Yao Caanab (Sunrise on the Caribbean) Trailer Park (north of Chetumal in Calderitas, Carretera Yucatán) has 30 spaces on palmy grounds, with swimming off a nearby point.

Travelers' Tracks
Sightseeing

More ruins cover the Yucatán jungles than any other part of Mexico. Since this is a coastal book, the listings here focus on major ruins only. The same can be said for caves and *cenotes*. This grotto-riddled peninsula is a real spelunker's holiday, offering many more than the few underground sights included in these listings. For sightseers, there's also colonial splendor and Mayan lore alive in almost every village, and echoes of the past around every bend.

CIUDAD DEL CARMEN

About 110 miles northeast of Villahermosa via Mexico 180 and a ferry ride away, this tropical town on 23-mile-long Isla del Carmen enjoys a breezy, carefree existence amid wild groves of palms and banana trees. Separating the Gulf of Mexico and Laguna de Términos, Carmen is romantically linked to Old World pirates, who made the island their stronghold from 1558 to 1717. Rumor has it that treasures from galleons they sank are buried in surrounding waters.

Today, shrimping and, more recently, oil drilling keep Carmen busy. Its finest sight is the lush central square, **Parque Zaragoza** (Calle 22a and Calle 31a), with wooden gazebo, brick walkways, wrought-iron fencing and Spanish lanterns. In front of the square stands the region's main church, the cream-colored, elegant **Catedral del Virgen del Carmen**, for whom the town is named.

NORTHEAST OF CIUDAD DEL CARMEN TO CAMPECHE

Mexico 180 pushes northeast along sometimes bad stretches of road crumbling into the sea and through flat tropical terrain to the long Puente de la Unidad. This new bridge connects Isla del Carmen with a piece of the mainland called Isla de Aguada.

The highway continues through fishing villages up the coast, most notably Champotón where explorer Francisco de Cordoba, the first conquistador to die in Mexico, was killed in 1517. About 40 miles northeast (110 miles from Ciudad del Carmen), Mexico 180 enters the colonial port of Campeche.

CAMPECHE

Near the southern entrance to town on Mexico 180, a huge stone figure called **Monumento Resurgimiento** (Revival Monument) rises between the lanes—a torso with a torch held high for democracy, a Latin Statue of Liberty. This is the first of many monuments in a fabulously historic yet much-ignored city.

Capital of the state of Campeche, the port of Campeche originated as the Mayan village Ah-kin-pech, meaning "tick of the serpent." After the Spanish landed in 1517, the city became an important outlet for exotic woods used as dyes. As it grew and became more vulnerable to pirate attacks, a massive wall was erected in 1686 for the then-staggering sum of $3,300. The **Puerta de Mar** (Sea Door) and **Puerta de Tierra** (Land Door), a pair of massive stone portals at opposite ends of Calle 59a, are the most poignant remnants of the wall, which was torn down after several centuries to let the stifling city breathe again.

The waterfront area bounded by Circuito Baleartes and Avenida 16 de Septiembre was the site of the old walled city. It's charming to walk the narrow streets, alluringly lit at night with Spanish lanterns, and explore the ponderous *baluartes* (bulwarks) and pretty plazas. Start at the **Baluarte de San Carlos** (Calle 8a and Calle 65a), the first fort built in Campeche in 1676. Proceed down to the **Baluarte de la Soledad** (Calle 8a; 6-81-79), a fort converted into a tiny museum for ancient art from Isla de Jaina, a sacred Mayan burial ground 25 miles offshore. Unfortunately, you can't visit the island, but the delicate figurines excavated there are unmistakable.

The **Baluarte Santiago** (Calle 8a and Calle 49a; 6-68-29) is a fort now containing a lovely botanical garden, **Xmuch' Haltun**, full of hummingbirds and stone pathways. A few blocks back west stands the rambling **Parque Principal** in the shadow of the moldy 16th-century **Catedral de Campeche** (Calle 10a and Calle 55a). Go have a look at the amazing sarcophagus near the altar, encrusted with silver bells, angels, and a figure of Christ.

The town has one foot in heaven with its many churches. Another interesting one is old **Iglesia de San Francisco** (along the *malecón* at Calle Mariano Escobedo), where Hernán Cortés' grandson was baptized.

The **Museo de Campeche** (Calle 10a and Calle 63a; 6-14-24) occupies the former cathedral of San José. This hulking weather-streaked stone shell now shelters a display of artisans' work.

A better exhibition resides at the **Museo Regional de Campeche** (Calle 59a and Calle 14a), colonial home of the Spanish king's lieutenant in 1790. Its rooms, surrounding a central courtyard, contain contemporary art and a fine collection of Mayan artifacts, including outstanding jade masks from ancient tombs.

It's a short walk from here to delightful **Parque Alameda** (Avenida República and Calle 55a), a triangular garden just beyond the **Baluarte de San Francisco**. Walled in castlelike ramparts and posts, Alameda welcomes strollers with its molded benches and shade. **Puente de las Mercedes** at the north end is a small, white bridge guarded by snobbish stone dogs with their noses in the air.

For novelty, walk down Avenida 16 de Septiembre past the **Palacio de Gobierno** (Government Building) and **Congreso del Estado** (Congress Building), nicknamed "The Jukebox" and "The Flying Saucer," respectively, because of their sci-fi designs.

On the southern outskirts of town, the impressive **Fuerte de San Miguel** (ascend Carretera Escénica from Avenida Resurgimiento) leans out over a hillside and is rimmed by moats once filled with skin-seering lime. Dating from 1700, the fort now houses a **Museo Arqueología** that includes marvelous ship replicas, pirate lore and Mayan art. The view from the parapets alone is worth the trip.

About 35 miles southeast of Campeche off Mexico 188 lie the Mayan ruins of **Edzna**, a small gathering of ceremonial temples around a well-preserved acropolis, dating from 600 B.C. Though there are other ruins scattered around Campeche, these are the best and most accessible.

NORTH OF CAMPECHE TO MÉRIDA

There are two routes from Campeche to Mérida: the shorter route, partly along the coast (Mexico 180) and the longer ruins route (Mexico 261).

CAMPECHE TO MÉRIDA VIA MEXICO 180

The fast route from Campeche starts out as Campeche 24 for about 20 miles, then joins the Mexico 180 junction and heads inland. At the snoozing village of Hecelchakán, just off the highway, there's the rustic **Museo Arqueológico de Camino Real** (Calle 20a, on the *zócalo*) for Maya buffs. These five dusty, timeworn rooms trace the development of the Mayan culture with displays of artifacts, maps, stelae and a diorama.

About 15 miles north, the village of **Becal** is the fascinating center for weaving Panama hats from *jipijapa*, or shredded palm leaves, an art that began in the time of the Mayas. A few shops display the local handiwork and the **zócalo** even features a giant trio of concrete sombreros as a monument. What's intriguing is that all items are woven in manmade caves to keep the palm threads cool, moist and pliable. Nearly every backyard has its own cave. At the **home of Don Pastor Chuc** (Calle 30a 19, near the square), usually open to visitors, everyone in the family takes a turn in the backyard cave.

Mexico 180 continues into the state of Yucatán through a region of *cenotes*. You can sidetrack to an old henequen hacienda with a colonial museum at San Bernardo before arriving in Mérida, about 70 miles northeast of Becal.

CAMPECHE TO MÉRIDA VIA MEXICO 261

For the long ruins route from Campeche, often called Ruta Maya, follow Mexico 261 northeast of town. The first stop of interest, about 75 miles along, is **Bolonchén de Rejón**. This Mayan village, fed by nine deep wells, is renowned for its spectacular caves two miles south of the plaza. Hire a guide to tour the subterranean mazes.

Crossing the border into the state of Yucatán, Mexico 261 passes through small ruins at **Sayil** and **Kabah**. From the village of Santa Elena, consider some sidetrips: you can cut northeast via a side road to the pottery-making colonial town of Ticul, then proceed south to **Loltún**, site of the most famous caves used by the Mayas, dramatically illuminated with colored lights. Or go straight from Santa Elena to the ruins of Uxmal.

One of the peninsula's largest and best-preserved Mayan cities, **Uxmal** was once capital of part of the Puuc region of the Yucatán, inhabited from around 800 B.C. to 1200 A.D. Its name means "thrice built," but evidence shows some buildings were rebuilt five times or more. The ruins, covering about half a mile of flat jungleland, are easily toured in a few hours. The best structures are the **Temple of the Magician**, a steep pyramid with steps so narrow you have to climb them sideways to view the entire grounds from the top; the **Nun's Quadrangle**, four well-decorated buildings that the Spanish misinterpreted as a nunnery and others thought were luxurious quarters for the elite or for sacrificial victims before their bloody send-off; and the grand **Governor's Palace**, with its ornate upper friezes, probably the best existing example of Mayan architecture. Ruins are open daily (admission). There is a sound and light show at night.

From Uxmal, you can take another sidetrip to the isolated, immense caverns and underground streams at **Calcehtok**. Take Mexico 261 north to Muna, then veer northwest on Mexico 16, passing through Opichén to the hamlet of Calcehtok. Inquire about local guides and follow signs to the *grutas* (caves), about one and a half miles from town via dirt road. Bring a flashlight, wear good shoes and take a deep breath. Spiraling into these caves, amid hanging vines and muffled echoes, is like slipping into your own subconscious.

En route to Mérida, Mexico 261 passes by **Yaxcopoil** (admission), another grand old hacienda dating back to the 19th century. Henequen cactus still grow here and cattle graze on the grounds. About 30 miles more brings you at last to Mérida.

MÉRIDA

This beautiful colonial city of nearly 600,000, founded in 1542 by Francisco Montejo, is a walker's delight. Part of its charm rests in the slightly bohemian, highly romantic art-loving mood of the town, which shows in its many bookstores and nightly outdoor cultural events. Sundays bustle with bazaars, folk dancing and singing all over town.

Starting at the elegant **Plaza de la Independencia**, or main plaza (bounded by Calles 61a, 63a, 60a and 62a), you can wander amid the vendors and Sunday musicians or relax in the S-shaped Victorian love-seats (*confidenciales*) unique to the Yucatán.

Across the street is the colonial **Casa Montejo** (Calle 63a), built in 1549 and refashioned in 1984 into a bank. Walk in and enjoy the patio while imagining how the grandees lived when swaggering Spain grew fat on Mexico's riches. Check out the Montejo coat of arms at the entrance, featuring conquistadors crushing the heads of Mayas underfoot.

At the east side of the plaza looms the portentous **Mérida Cathedral** (Calle 60a), built on the site of a Mayan temple. Begun in 1561 and completed in 1598, the cathedral is considered one of Mexico's purest examples of 16th-century architecture. A relic called *El Cristo de las Ampollas* (Christ of the Blisters) has its own side altar. Legend says this cross was carved from a flaming tree that remained unscorched; the cross was merely blistered in a later fire that destroyed the church where it hung. Now there is an annual celebration in Mérida commemorating this miracle.

On the plaza's north face is the **Palacio de Gobierno** (Calle 61a), a veritable gallery of outstanding murals by the contemporary Yucatecan artist Fernando Castro Pacheco. The palatial second-floor **Hall of History** could have been lifted from Versailles.

Southwest of the *zócalo* you'll find the tiny 18th-century **Ermita de Santa Isabel** (wedged between Calle 66a and Calle 64a at the corner of Calle 77a), or traveler's chapel, where you can emulate tradition and pray for a safe trip. Its walled garden is full of Mayan sculptures.

Parque Hidalgo (Calle 60a and Calle 59a), also known as Parque Cepeda Peraza, is a busy little plaza just a block north of the main square. Besides hammock hawkers and a sidewalk café, there are two statues here: one of the heroic Father Hidalgo, who launched Mexico's War of Independence and one of General Cepeda Peraza, who fought with Benito Juárez against Porfirio Díaz in 1873.

Alongside this park rises the old **Iglesia de Jesús** (Calle 59a), a Jesuit temple where Mérida's blue bloods gather. Next to this church, peaceful **Parque La Madre** sheds its shade, with a marble mother-and-child replica of a French sculpture.

Also across from Parque Hidalgo, the **Pinocoteca Juan Gamboa Guzmán y Museo Gottdiener** (Calle 59a near Calle 60a) present a well-kept, starchy collection of old Yucatecan and European oil paintings, with a more contemporary sculpture gallery attached.

About six blocks east, the **Museo Nacional de Arte Popular** (Calle 59a and Calle 48a) pays a wonderful tribute to the wild Mexican imagination and handiwork of its *indígenas* with fine displays of jewelry, musical instruments, costumes, weavings and carvings from all over the republic.

Back around Parque La Madre stands the **Teatro Peón Contreras** (Calle 60a and Calle 57a), a half-block-long cultural center of Italian design, full of *fin de siècle* flourishes. Named for local poet José Peón Contreras, it stages many theatre and dance performances.

Parque Santa Lucía (Calle 60a and Calle 55a), the lively site of Yucatecan music and dance every Thursday evening, was a slave market and a terminal for horse-drawn carriages in centuries past. **Iglesia de Santa Lucía,** facing the park, was built in 1575, and served as a church for blacks and mulattos. Until 1821, its churchyard contained the municipal cemetery.

Just past the Parque Santa Ana, Calle 60a bends into the broad **Paseo Montejo**, named for the city's founding *padre*. This grand boulevard, speckled with sidewalk cafés and monuments, once imitated the Champs Elysees and was thick with French mansions—the spoils of rich henequen landowners who tried to give Mérida a Parisian accent. Sadly, these little castles are being replaced by modern construction.

The best remaining example is the phenomenal 19th-century **Palacio Cantón**, recently transformed into the excellent **Museo de Antropología**

y Historia (Paseo Montejo and Calle 43a; 23-05-57; admission). A top-notch collection of Mayan artifacts rests within the ornate walls of this former governor's residence. Exhibits cover all facets of Mayan life, including their grim practice of flattening the cranium of newborn babies. (There's a good bookstore here, too.)

The **Monumento a la Patria** (Monument to the Country), at the third *glorieta* (traffic circle) as you move north from the museum along the Paseo Montejo, presents a magnificent sculpture-in-the-round by Romulo Rozo, depicting the history of Mexico.

Another sculptural tour-de-force, the small **Parque de las Américas** (Paseo Colón between Calle 18a and Calle 22a), covers four square blocks with a different landmark at each corner, such as a serpent-entwined Mayan fountain and a Mayan-style open arcade. The park is planted with trees from every nation in the Americas.

Children will enjoy a visit to the woodsy, time-worn **Parque El Centenario** (Avenida de los Itzaes, bounded by Calle 65a and Calle 59a), about six blocks from the downtown area. There are refreshment stands, a zoo and a miniature train.

For bullfights, visit the **Plaza de Toros** (Calle 72a near Paseo Colón) during the December to April season. Advance tickets are available through travel agencies.

COASTAL SIGHTS NEAR MÉRIDA

A series of Gulf Coast fishing villages surrounds Mérida, all within an hour or two of town by paved road. **Celestún**, about 60 miles west of Mérida via Mexico 25 and Mexico 281, hovers at the edge of a **natural flamingo sanctuary**. It is reached by skiff at the bridge over Celestún's estuary. **Sisal**, about 30 miles from Mérida by Mexico 25, is a languid beach town which long ago was the major shipping port for local henequen.

Five miles north of Mérida on Mexico 261, the huge **Cordemex Plant**, where sisal fibers from the henequen plant are woven into carpets, offers tours. Then, five miles further north the highway leads to a turnoff for the ruins of **Dzibilchaltún**, the site of the longest continuously inhabited Mayan town in the Yucatán. The restored **Temple of the Seven Dolls**, whose crown is carved with stylized doll-like figures, is the one intact building. Minor scattered structures, a refreshing *cenote* and a small museum dot the area.

Mexico 261 continues north through smelly swampland into Progreso, an active port town of 30,000 where Mérida residents come to escape the stifling heat. Its pleasant **malecón**, lined with palms and rusty globe lights, runs along an appealing public beach, (which sustained heavy damage during Hurricane Gilbert).

A coastal highway, still Mexico 261, spreads out east and west of Progreso. Though one tropical village in this area looks pretty much like another, the ride along the gulf is fresh and picturesque. **Dzilam de Bravo,** at the end of the line to the east, is another gathering place of pink flamingos and the final resting place of the pirate Jean Lafitte, whose grave is on the beach.

EAST OF MÉRIDA

The most direct route to Chichén Itzá is via Mexico 180. But to catch some colonial sights along the way, go off on a tangent via Mexico 80 to the town of **Izamal,** where a 400-year-old fortress-like Franciscan convent and church edged in 75 yellow arches was built over the Mayan **Pyramid de Popolchach.**

CHICHÉN ITZÁ

About 75 miles east of Mérida, the famous ruins of **Chichén Itzá** cover seven square miles with temples, carvings and statues—the most impressive Mayan city in the Yucatán. It was occupied off and on from 450 A.D. to around 1200 A.D. Its name translates as "the mouth of the well of the Itzás," which refers to the tribe that founded the town and its enormous **Sacred Cenote.** The deep green well, its chalky limestone walls pocked with little grottoes and overhung with tangled vegetation, holds the bones of many men and children who were tossed to their deaths in sacrificial rituals. You can easily roam for a day through the jungles exploring these ruins, where fat iguanas sun themselves and butterflies boil through the torpid air. Afternoons are absolutely scorching; start early.

The highlight is **El Castillo,** a pyramid towering over 75 feet at the entrance to the grounds. During the spring and fall equinoxes, a snakelike shadow appears to ascend or descend the stairs, joining the feathered serpent head at the pyramid's base. This serpent-god, known among the Aztecs as Quetzalcoatl and among the Mayas as Kukulkán, was introduced by the Toltec tribe from central Mexico when they conquered Chichén Itzá. Their stone jaguars and eagles add a certain ferocity to the grounds.

The **Temple of the Warriors,** also known as Temple of the Thousand Columns, includes a flat-topped pyramid richly decked out in statuary. A vast field of pillars stand at attention at the temple's feet. A statue of **Chac-Mool,** containing a receptacle for the pulsating hearts of sacrificial victims, reclines on the altar.

The **Ball Court,** stretching longer than a football field, is bordered by superbly carved walls and templelike grandstands. Here teams played for their lives, trying to toss a ball through a stone hoop. If you look hard, you can see on the wall nearest the entrance an eroded carving of a team captain losing his head, the consequence of a bad day on the quadrangle. He kneels before an emblem of a skull, with plantlike snakes sprouting out of his neck. Every sound made on the ball court echoes and eerily resonates in the surrounding stands.

The **Astronomical Observatory**, also called El Caracol (The Snail) because of its spiral construction, has a crumbled stone dome where the Mayas are purported to have exercised their considerable astronomical skills. Next to it, the huge stone **Nunnery** intrigues visitors with mazes of narrow passageways and damp, pitch-black rooms where an occasional bat flaps out of hiding.

The ruins are open daily (admission). Vendors have set up shop nearby, turning Chichén Itzá into a well-stocked marketplace.

CAVES OF BALANCANCHÉ

Most people think of ruins as being above ground. But if you miss the **Grutas de Balancanché** (about five miles east of Chichén Itzá off Mexico 180; admission), you miss one of the most mysterious places of worship in the Chichén Itzá complex. The caves, shut up for over 500 years, were discovered in 1959 by a tourist guide. Today, a local guide takes small groups down into the electrically lit corridors, which narrow into passageways so tight and twisting you have to writhe through like a snake. Suddenly a wondrous chamber opens up, with a massive stalagmite rising from the floor like a mystic tree and sparkling stalactites encrusting the ceiling like leaves.

All around the chamber's base, carved faces stare up from Mayan pots, which are believed to be 1,000-year-old offerings to cave gods. Another crouch-down passageway leads to an underground pool as still as glass, with more pots glancing out of the crannies, one even sitting on its own small island in the water. The oxygen gets thin very fast, so the tour does not last long. Check schedules and arrive punctually.

VALLADOLID

Located 24 miles east of Chichén Itzá on Mexico 180, **Valladolid** is a quiet colonial town settled by upper-crust Spanish in 1543. Enraged Mayas massacred the settlers during the 19th-century War of the Castes. Today, what little action there is revolves around the pretty **zócalo** (bounded by Calles 42a, 39a, 41a and 40a) with its love seats and pattering fountain, and around the magnificent **Cenote Zaci** (Calle 36a between Calle 39a and Calle 37a). A small **regional museum** (3-21-07) hovers above the cavelike *cenote*. Its algae-speckled, blue-green waters plunge to nearly 400 feet, shadowed by a stalactite-studded cavern. Go for a swim or watch brave boys dive for tips from the overhanging precipice.

RÍO LAGARTOS

From Valladolid, Mexico 295 shoots north about 65 miles to **Río Lagartos** (Alligator River), a small Gulf Coast fishing village in a swampy region of lagoons. Although few alligators remain, the mudflats blush with hordes of pink flamingos. To see them, hire a boat in town (fishermen may wave you down as you drive along the waterfront). The two-hour trip takes you through islands in marshlands as soupy-green as a Louisiana bayou, rich in ducks, herons, pelicans and egrets. Finally you enter **Orilla Emal**, the muddy shallows where an estimated 15,000 flourescent-pink flamingos nest and feed, always gracefully taking wing before you get close enough for a photo. Their home grounds, a network of estuaries, extend west beyond San Felipe and east past El Cuyo. The best time to view them is early morning or late afternoon.

CANCÚN

This famous Caribbean resort, expected to house half-a-million residents by 1994, sprawls along a wiry island just 95 miles northeast of Valladolid via Mexico 180. Cancún actually consists of the mainland **Ciudad Cancún** and the island **Zona Hotelera** (Hotel Zone). Few sights in either sector can compete with its lily-white beaches and azure sea.

Specialty cruises revolving around pirate and carnival themes run frequently and are lots of fun. A few of the best include trips to Isla Mujeres aboard the glassbottom *Trimaran Manta* (Club Caribe Cancún Pier; 3-03-48) and the fishing yacht *Arandena* (Sunrise Marina, next to the Miramar Misión Hotel; 4-10-62); trips to Contoy Island via sailboat from Punta Sam (4-15-43) and aboard the air-conditioned *Discover Contoy Island* (3-14-88); a glassbottom yacht lagoon cruise aboard *Fiesta Maya* (3-03-89); or evening tropical cruises called Caribbean Carnival Night (Marina Playa Blanca; 3-06-06) or A Pirate's Night Adventure at Treasure Island (Playa Langosta Dock; 3-14-88).

Back on dry land, try a Wednesday bullfight at the **Plaza de Toros** (Avenida Cobá and Paseo Kukulkán, Ciudad Cancún), during the December to April season. Tickets are available at travel agencies.

The **Museo de Antropología de Cancún** (Centro de Convenciones, Paseo Kukulkán, Km. 10.9; 3-06-88; admission) houses a small collection of Meso-American artifacts. The displays give a good rundown on Mayan culture, especially sites in Quintana Roo.

Get out of the sun for a moment and explore the small, shady **aviary** at the Mauna Loa shopping center (Paseo Kukulkán, across from Centro de Convenciones), featuring all sorts of exotic birds.

At the south end of the island, the **Ruinas del Rey** (Paseo Kukulkán, about 12 miles from Ciudad Cancún) are local remnants of a Mayan city, named for a skeleton ("The King") found on top of the main pyramid. Iguanas and mosquitoes share this jungle site with overgrown foundations, columns and ancient rubble. Some say the tiny openings in the ruins suggest they were occupied by *aluxes*, bewitched Mayan pygmies about 18 inches tall.

ISLA MUJERES

Reached by ferry from Punta Sam or Puerto Juárez, this five-and-a-half-mile-long island about five miles north of Cancún was enchantingly named after statues of temple goddesses first seen by Spanish explorers in 1517. Almost nothing of the Mayan presence has survived the centuries. A charming fishing village with an active town square fills the island's northern tip. The hotels, restaurants and shops are concentrated here.

The ruined **hacienda of Mundaca the Pirate** (off Carretera Garrafón, across from Playa Lancheros) slowly decays in the island jungles, a rotting house and arched well that once watered the estate. The story behind the ruins far outshines the site itself: notorious Fermín Mundaca fell in love with an island beauty, quit his pirating days to build a hacienda and fabulous tomb for himself to impress her. For a while it worked. Then she jilted him and eloped with a penniless man.

El Garrafón (The Jug) (about four and a half miles from the village on the southwest end of the island) is an underwater national park glinting with tropical wonders, a magnet for snorkelers. On shore you can browse through a complex of shops. At the southern tip of the island, just past the old lighthouse, stands part of a crumbling **Mayan temple**. At sunset, its distorted double arch makes a highly dramatic frame for nearby land's end cliffs that drop down to the sea.

North of Isla Mujeres lies uninhabited **Isla Contoy**, a national park and bird sanctuary where people go to picnic, snorkel, explore and sun on a deserted beach. A dock and large pavilion featuring a display of indigenous marinelife constitute the park station on the island's leeward side. To arrange trips, see Sociedad Cooperativa de Transportación Turística de Isla Mujeres (Avenida Rueda Medina near the ferry dock; 2-02-74) or S.C.T.T. Adolfo López Mateos (Avenida Rueda Medina).

COZUMEL

Mexico's largest island, beautiful 28-mile-long **Cozumel**, predated Cancún as the Mexican Caribbean's prime getaway and remains the finest diving site in the country. Ferries to the island leave from Puerto Morelos and Playa del Carmen.

On the northwest side of Cozumel is its only town, San Miguel de Cozumel, a hive of boutiques and cafés buzzing around the broad seafront **Plaza del Sol** and extending about 12 blocks along a breezy **malecón**.

Toward the south end of the *malecón*, an **aquarium** (admission) presents closeup exhibits of the tropical marinelife in these waters. Here you can learn the names of the fish you may later meet while skindiving.

Farther south, **Parque Laguna Chancanab** (about five and a half miles south of San Miguel off the coastal road; admission) is unquestionably the gem of the island. The name Chancanab means "small sea" in Mayan, referring to the park's blue lagoon full of parrotfish, barracuda, sergeant majors, octopus and other colorful specimens. The lagoon's beautiful coral is dead, however, and experiments are being conducted to revive it. Visitors may not swim in the lagoon but can snorkel in the even more resplendent sea or roam through the park's **botanical gardens,** which contain over 2,000 species of plants from all over the world. The grounds also contain replicas of a Mayan house with backyard elevated farming and a small temple.

At the southern tip of the island, a dirt road turns off the paved highway toward the **Tumba de Caracol** a n d **El Faro Celerain** (Celerain Lighthouse). The tiny Caracol, a snail-like Mayan temple dating back to 1200 A.D., resembles a Disney mini-ruin crowned by a small square cupola. It's much too small even for the petite Mayas—maybe another haunt of the *aluxes,* those legendary Mayan pixies? The road continues to the antique lighthouse at **Punta Celerain,** land's end. If you speak some Spanish and the caretaker likes you, he may unlock the lighthouse and let you climb up for a wild, windy view of Cozumel. You can also negotiate for a boat ride on nearby **Laguna Columbia.**

The **windward shore** of Cozumel is the true escape route: undeveloped and mostly deserted, a coast of scrub jungle and barren beaches, rocks and crumbled ruins. You can drive it in a south-north loop from the leeward highway or cross the island via the Carretera Transversal (which originates in San Miguel as Avenida Benito Juárez) and begin your tour at the beach of Santa Cecilia.

En route, a side road off the Carretera Transversal leads inland to **San Gervasio,** Cozumel's best ruins. Less than spectacular, they consist of mediocre stonework nestled in ten acres of bug-bitten jungle.

Other minor ruins in the early stages of excavation dot the whole northern tip of the island. A 15-mile sand track, suited for motorbikes or jeeps only, squiggles north of Santa Cecilia along empty beach to **Punta Molas.** You pass the small ruined altar and vaulted fortress of **Castillo Real** along the way. Out at the point, a lighthouse shares sea winds with **Aguada Grande,** circular ruins of buildings on platforms.

The drive south along the paved windward highway is very refreshing. Just past Punta Chiquero, pause at **El Mirador** and gaze out from the rocky lookout point to the surging Caribbean.

For get-away-from-it-all **Robinson Crusoe cruises** and **glassbottom boat trips,** inquire at Hotel El Presidente (Carretera a Chancanab; 2-03-22) and Sociedad Cooperativa de Servicios Turísticos (municipal ferry dock, San Miguel).

SOUTH OF CANCÚN—PLAYA DEL CARMEN TO TULUM

Mexico 307, a good paved road through flat and uninspired jungle, runs along the Mexican Caribbean's best coastal strip. About 40 miles south of Cancún comes the first scenic village, Playa del Carmen, where the passenger ferry pushes off for Cozumel. One look at Carmen's palm-edged beaches and you need no other sightseeing spots.

About four miles south of Playa del Carmen, a marked turnoff leads to **Xcaret,** site of some tumbledown ruins and a jungle *cenote* with water

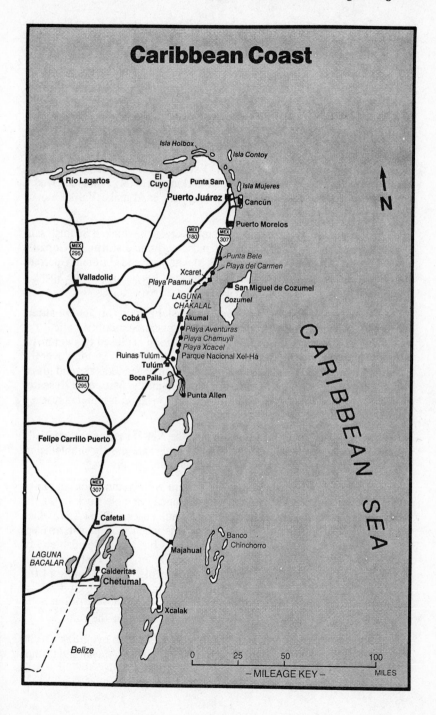

Caribbean Coast

so transparent it looks like a pale blue phantom on the rocks. Completely overhung with a cavernlike projection, the *cenote* appears as an enormous split in the earth. This fissure opens into a shadowy pool where you can swim in what may be the clearest water on earth.

Chakalal, a lovely turquoise-and-cream lagoon flowing into the sea, is about three miles past the beach of Paamul via the turnoff from Mexico 307 marked "Rancho Cuatro Hermanos." Near the west end of the lagoon stands a proud, boxy **Mayan temple.** Under the temple winds an underwater tunnel connected with an adjoining lagoon.

Another seldom-visited lagoon, **Yal-ku** is just north of Akumal, reached via a dirt road from the Akumal parking area. Its vivid green water, submarine caves and fish that nibble from your hand make Yal-ku a marvelous swimming and diving hole.

On luxurious **Playa Akumal**, where several shipwrecked Spanish sailors washed ashore in 1511, stands a handsome bronze **statue of Gonzalo Guerrero** dressed as an Indian, with his Mayan wife and children. Guerrero fathered the first Euro-American family and later fought against the Spanish when they tried to conquer the Yucatán.

About 72 miles south of Cancún, the crystal lagoons at **Xel-Há** attract everyone who ever wanted to don mask and flippers. Sometimes called "the world's biggest natural aquarium," the first lagoon is closed to swimmers, but the shallow seaside lagoon swarms with snorkelers exclaiming over the flashing rainbows of fish. There are rentals for dive gear, kayaks and glass-bottom boats. The entrance to the complex contains the **Museo de Rescates Subamáticos** (admission), a small museum showing crusty items rescued from shipwrecks by Mexican divers.

Across the highway from the lagoons, the **Xel-Há ruins** are gradually being dug out of the jungle. So far, these temples are mostly rubble heaps bearing faint frescoes. Nearby lies a leaf-strewn *cenote*.

The hot item down this way is the **Tulum ruins** (admission), a fabled fortress by the sea about 80 miles south of Cancún. People flock to see the well-preserved temples and fragmented walls dating back to 1200 A.D., which were still part of a thriving Mayan metropolis when the Spanish arrived. The conquistadors marveled that Tulum was as big as the Spanish city of Seville. It must have been artistically impressive, too, with scattered paintings and vivid murals whose colors are still visible in the **Temple of the Frescoes.** Tulum's trademark is the **Temple of the Descending God,** whose guardian, with his feet in the air and head pointed down, is a fitting deity for divers. The cliffside offers a very romantic view of the ruins.

The town of Tulum, just south of the ruins, is a drab eye-blink off the highway, with stores and a *palapa*-roofed church blending Mayan and Catholic traditions.

From the Tulum ruins, a largely unpaved road leads south for over 15 miles through shaggy rain forest to **Boca Paila**, and beyond this lonely point to the fishing village of **Punta Allen**. For *cenote* fans, cool clear **Cenote Salvaje (★)** hides deep in the jungle via a muddy trail inland from Rancho San Eric. With diving gear, you can explore its dropoffs into black abysses.

SOUTH OF TULUM TO CHETUMAL

About half-a-mile south of the Tulum ruins, a turnoff on the right from Mexico 307 leads to the powerful ruins of **Cobá** (admission). This paved road runs about 30 miles inland past jungle hamlets and hidden *cenotes* to the newest and biggest Mayan site in the Yucatán. It is also the least visited, the most mysterious and most beautiful.

Cobá's 80-square-mile territory is swallowed in undergrowth, with only a fraction of the ancient city presently uncovered. Believed to have been a center of commerce from 600 to 900 A.D., Cobá (meaning "wind-ruffled water") rests amid five lakes and resembles Guatemalan ruins in the Petén jungle. A network of *sacbes*, or ancient roads, radiates out from Cobá toward other settlements.

Trails wind through the rain forest to marked ruins, many mere rubble heaps. The most striking include the **Grupo de Cobá**, with a steep, crumbly pyramid near the site entrance, and the **Nohoch Mul** pyramid (located about a mile into the ruins), the tallest in northern Yucatán, rising like an island out of a sea of trees. There is a small village and good hotel on the edge of the ruins.

Mexico 307 veers away from the coast south of Tulum into low jungle. The only sizable town it passes is ho-hum Felipe Carrillo Puerto, named for the slain revolutionary governor of Yucatán who fell in love with an American journalist and wrote the classic Mexican love song "Peregrina" (Pilgrim) for her.

Laguna de Bacalar, about 25 miles northwest of Chetumal off Mexico 307, is called "The Lagoon of Seven Colors" and "The Place Where the Rainbow Is Born" It boasts pure, clear, placid water, streaked with flamboyant blues that resemble strips of satin. A *balneario*, or bathing resort, provides bathroom facilities, a restaurant and pier. Little open-air restaurants line the shore. **Fuerte San Felipe Bacalar**, built in 1729 to fend off pirate attacks, peers out from a hillside near the *balneario* and contains a small museum of regional artifacts.

The lakelike **Cenote Azul**, located off Mexico 307 at Km. 34 just south of Laguna de Bacalar, forms an immense circle edged in jungle growth. Its inert blue-black waters, the color of India ink, give you an eerie feeling as you swim out and peer down into unknown depths. A tropical restaurant with a menagerie of exotic birds overlooks the *cenote*.

Peaceful **Laguna Milagros**, little sister of Bacalar and about eight miles west of Chetumal off Mexico 186, lies fringed in lazy restaurants and grassy, palm-shaded shores.

Chetumal, capital of Quintana Roo, may come as a pleasant surprise. It is probably Mexico's nicest border town, on the edge of Belize. Throwing off its shady past as a smuggler's haven and its former isolation, the town has grown into a modern, attractive free port importing all sorts of foreign goods and exporting hardwoods from the peninsula's jungles.

At the end of busy, store-lined Avenida de los Héroes, the beautiful bayside **Plaza Cívica** and **Parque Central** have colored fountains, grand monuments and live folkloric performances on weekends. A lovely **malecón** curves along Boulevard Bahía, following the contours of the bay. A **balneario,** or bathing resort northeast of the square, provides facilities but no beach. In a town full of statues, the most arresting is the **Alegoría de Mestizaje** (Avenida de los Héroes near Avenida Mahatma Gandhi), a sculpted saga of the offspring of an Indian woman and a Spanish man.

Due east of Chetumal, about 20 miles offshore, lies **Banco Chinchorro**, the ship-eating shoal of reefs every diver dreams of exploring. Skiffs can be rented at the dozing pueblo of Xcalak, about 112 miles southeast of Chetumal (via Mexico 307 and a desolate unpaved coastal road).

For an interesting excursion west of Chetumal, follow Mexico 186 (the real thing) to a side road that tunnels through the jungle to the remote ruins of **Kohunlich**. Here most of the structures are just mounds half-consumed by vegetation, but deep in the palm forest stands a pyramid that served as a tomb, carved with huge and impeccably detailed masks of Mayan gods.

Shopping

Shopping in Mérida and in the Caribbean resorts (located in the duty-free state of Quintana Roo) is excellent. The bigger ruin sites have souvenir shops and swarms of vendors.

CIUDAD DEL CARMEN SHOPPING

There's not much to buy that isn't at the **Mercado Central** (Calle 20a and Calle 37a), a rousing indoor-outdoor market full of religious pictures, sombreros and clothes, plus fruits and vegetables grown to extremes—huge avocados, mammoth sweet potatos, fat carrots, giant bananas and bulging cabbages.

CAMPECHE SHOPPING

Not a great shopping town, Campeche does have a row of shops along Calle 8a peddling souvenirs. Two good ones are **Artesanía Típica Naval** (Calle 8a 259; 6-57-08), which carries bottled exotic fruits like *nance* and *maranón*, and **El Coral** (Calle 8a 255; 6-32-85), which has Mayan figurines.

Another collection of shops, **Exposición y Venta Permanente de Artesanías**, occupies the old Baluarte San Pedro (Avenida Circuito). Locally made crafts items—baskets and hats woven from *palma de jipijapa*, hammocks and indigenous dresses—are for sale.

The smelly **Mercado Municipal** (Avenida Gobernadores) is a labyrinth of indoor stalls tumbling with food, baby chicks, good luck soaps, handicrafts and posters of pop personalities and Jesus.

BECAL SHOPPING

This tiny village near the border between Campeche and Yucatán is the source of many Panama hats (no, they're not made in Panama!), plus other items woven from *jipijapa* straw. **Artesanías Becaleña** (Calle 30a 210-A), near the plaza, has good prices. Or you can buy directly from peoples' homes.

MÉRIDA SHOPPING

This first-rate shopping town specializes in *guayaberas*, pleated men's shirts native to the Yucatán; *huipiles*, beautifully embroidered dresses; hammocks, the best and brightest in the world; and Panama hats. The two main spending zones are the area along Calle 60a and the central market area.

CALLE 60 AREA

Let's start with a little class. Snazzy **Artesanía México** (Calle 59a and Calle 60a; 24-52-11) stocks toys, books, artistic postcards, gorgeous vases and smashing jewelry. Next door, **El Paso** (Calle 60a 501; 21-28-28) has bright batik blouses, handblown glass and wooden *santos* (statues of saints).

Georgia Charuhas' **Boutique Las Mariposas** (Calle 55a 499) may be Mérida's most fanciful extravaganza of women's fashions, based on old Creole designs.

Up the street, colonial-style **Fernando Huertas** (Calle 59a 511; 21-60-35) shines with unusual jewelry, sculptures and women's fashions displayed in antique armoires.

Nearby **Mercado Maya** (Calle 59a 509) presents native clothing, including *guayaberas*, plus assorted jewelry.

Talabartería Mérida (Calle 62a 492) has a good selection of leather goods, from wallets to suitcases.

Moving in the direction of Parque Santa Lucía, you'll pass several big curio emporiums. Friendly **Las Palomas** (Calle 60a) excels in silver and onyx chess sets. **Maya Artesanal** (Calle 60a 454) stocks ceramics, sisal articles and clothes.

A fascinating odds-'n-ends antique shop called **Ridecor** (Calle 60a 456-G; 24-59-59) features dusty religious art, colonial crucifixes, statues and paintings. Its owner, Manolo Rivero, also runs the **Galería Manolo**

Rivero (Calle 60a 456; 21-09-35), which showcases modern art from all over the world.

CENTRAL MARKET AREA

Here's where to get the best hammocks. If you buy from a street vendor, your selection is limited and you'll overpay. Instead, go straight to **Tejidos y Cordeles Nacionales** (Calle 56a 516-B; 21-33-68), a cooperative shop with over 10,000 hammocks to chose from. Colors? Every combination in the spectrum. The cotton ones are cheaper, but nylon is finer. All prices are by weight. You won't find a better deal anywhere.

The **Mercado Central** (Calle 65a and Calle 56a) rambles for at least a city block in a kind of bohemian madness. Hammock vendors will accost you; beggars and children will chase you down. Mosquito repellent, toothbrushes, bouquets of radishes and pyramids of grapes swell the outdoor aisles. The indoor stalls are packed with painted *huaraches*, sombreros, guitars and embroidered *huipiles* (native dresses). Upstairs hang hammocks and blankets. **Bazar de Artesanías Mexicanas** (Calle 56a) and **Curios Lucy** (Calle 56a; 23-74-91) are two big shops within the bazaar zone with good selections of curios.

A quieter place to browse, the government-run **Casa de las Artesanías** (Casa de la Cultura de Mayab, Calle 63a 503-A; 23-53-92) gathers Christmas ornaments, ceramic devils, painted urns, straw bags and crafts from all over Mexico under one roof.

CANCÚN SHOPPING

An easy place to drop a fortune, Cancún bubbles with boutiques and overflows with malls. Even tightwads will succumb to the local buying lust, especially for silver and tropical fashions. But there are no bargains. Ciudad Cancún shops charge as much as the *centro comerciales* (shopping centers) in the Zona Hotelera. Cancún is *the* most expensive resort in Mexico.

CIUDAD CANCÚN

Avenida Tulum, the main drag, is the hub of the shopping action. One of the better stores is **Las Casitas** (Avenida Tulum 37; 4-14-68), with a big but tasteful collection of clothing, leather, rugs, carvings, ceramics and jewelry.

For silver, you can't go wrong at **Alberto's** (Avenida Tulum 23), with exquisite designs, and **Charlie** (Avenida Tulum 1; 4-17-29), very friendly and willing to haggle a bit.

Among the city's shopping malls, **Plaza El Safa** (Avenida Tulum and Calle Crisántemas) has the most personality. Its foyer alone is worth a browse, decked in pointed arches, a frieze of pyramids and Egyptian bas-reliefs, with a bronze camel centerpiece. The mall's sassiest store is right at the entrance. **Strokes** (4-52-51) features unusual sequined clothes, painted silk and flamboyant jewelry.

Mercado Municipal de Artesanías Ki-huic (Avenida Tulum near Avenida Cobá) is the most overpriced circus in Cancún. Stalls sell silver jewelry, horsewhips, blankets and lace tablecloths in an open-armed aura that feels so Mexican, so much the bargainer's bailiwick. Shop around, or you will be stung. Two of the better shops are **Artesanías Xochimilco** (4-11-37), with artistic chess sets, Mayan statues and elegant boxes in marble, lapis lazuli and jade; and **Artesanías Cielito Lindo** (4-45-11), with cases of loose gems.

Shop in air-conditioned comfort at the two-story **Plaza México** (Avenida Tulum near Calle Agua), an enclosed mall full of glittering boutiques. **Platería México** has silver, copper and brass. The government-run **CASART** (4-35-06) carries Mayan idols, glassware and handcarved swans. **Fanny Boutique** features Christian Dior lingerie, plus sportswear, jewelry and silk. **Xochipilli** showcases huge clay replicas of savage animal gods.

ZONA HOTELERA

This empire of shopping malls keeps on growing, though you'd think the market had no room for more competition. One of the newest members of the mall elite is **Plaza Náutilus** (Paseo Kukulkán, Km. 3, next door to the 34-store Plaza Las Velas), distinguished by an egg-shaped outdoor aquarium. Its air-conditioned shops encircle a central café that features live organ music.

Still the plushest shopping arena, air-conditioned **Plaza Caracol** (Paseo Kukulkán, Km. 12) is also the most pleasant place to shop—clean and polished, a fusion of white marble and tinted skylights, run with American efficiency. Of the 63 shops within, try **ACA Joe** for cotton sportswear, **Margarita** (3-07-17) for spectacular jewelry, **Sybele** (3-17-38) for flashy men's and women's fashions, **Enny Cano** (3-13-39) for dreamy designer dresses and **Nouveau** (4-03-04) for leather boots and shoes.

Plaza Laguna and pink **Costa Blanca** (next door to one another near Plaza Caracol), are outdoor villa-style shopping centers selling beachwear, designer clothes, Mayan art and leather.

Plaza El Parian (off Paseo Kukulkán next to the Centro de Convenciones) has rounds of shops interspersed with outdoor cafés, so you can browse and rest. Its better shops include **Victor** (3-08-40) for antique jewelry and colonial religious art; **Anakena** (3-05-39) for Mayan temple rubbings and prints; **Fini** (3-12-60) for fine gold and silver; **Calvin Klein** (3-13-15) for hip sportswear; and **Asier** for beautiful leather goods.

Just across the street from the Centro de Convenciones, the **Mauna Loa Shopping Mall** affects a Polynesian air and boasts an aviary. This is the place for high-quality fashion shops, like **Roca-Mar** (3-14-60) for chic womenswear and imaginative jewelry; **Georgia Charuhas** (3-01-47) for frothy, romantic Victorian dresses (an ace spot to buy a wedding gown); and **Marcela de Cancún** for Mayan engravings on suede and smart leather goods (at inflated prices).

ISLA MUJERES SHOPPING

The village has scattered shops where costs tend to be more reasonable than in either Cancún or Cozumel.

Near the ferry landing, **Rachat & Rome** (Avenida Rueda Medina; 2-01-40) is the most upscale shop on the island. The sunset-pink building, carpeted and air-conditioned, has glass cases full of fine silver, pink coral and gold jewelry.

Off the plaza, **La Sirena** (Avenida Hidalgo and Calle Madero; 2-02-23) has a big inventory of masks, Mayan figures, T-shirts, blankets and papier-mâché items.

Down the street, you can observe an artist at work chipping designs in limestone at **Casa del Arte México** (Avenida Hidalgo 6). Besides these superb carvings, there are Mayan temple rubbings, batik clothing and images in ivory, obsidian and quartz.

The best shop may be **La Loma** (Avenida Guerrero 6), behind the plaza on the sea. It's a storehouse of treasures: coral jewelry, necklaces of old Mayan stones, lacquer trays, delicate knit sweaters and baby shoes.

COZUMEL SHOPPING

Shopping is terrific in San Miguel de Cozumel. Starting at the *zócalo* where it faces the *malecón*, several mega-shops hold court with catchalls of crafts. **Opus** (Avenida Rafael Melgar; 2-13-95) is one such, an air-conditioned zoo of brass animals, wooden toys, clowns, sunglasses and T-shirts. **Las Campañas** (Plaza del Sol; 2-07-72) is another curio outlet with good prices. The more sophisticated **Bali-Hai** (Avenida Rafael Melgar 8; 2-02-60) wows visitors with its expensive collection of brass buckles and tropical jewelry using shells, coins, tassles and seed pods.

Moving north along the *malecón*, posh **Casablanca** (Avenida Rafael Melgar 33; 2-11-77) resembles a colonial art gallery with cases and niches of Mayan art, jewelry and silver sculptures. **El Paso** (Avenida Rafael Melgar 21; 2-13-13), one of Cozumel's first shops, sparkles with silver and a big onyx collection.

Xaman-ek (Avenida Rafael Melgar 149; 2-00-40), named for the Mayan traveler's god, is a narrow, alleylike store packed with dangling birds and beasts in ceramic and leather.

Like its sister branch in Cancún, **La Casita** (Avenida Rafael Melgar 23; 2-01-93) carries a substantial array of fine crafts and lacy pastel dresses.

Bazaar Cozumel (Avenida Rafael Melgar 23; 2-00-85) is an artsy old shop with feather paintings, hand-painted tiles, modern wallhangings and Mayan figurines.

Los Cincos Soles (Avenida Rafael Melgar 27; 2-01-32) is my favorite, a wander-through complex of surprises, from wooden puzzles to papier-mâché fruits to a back gallery full of temple rubbings and antiques.

South along the *malecón* sprawls **Bazar del Ángel** (Avenida Rafael Melgar and Calle 3a Sur 25; 2-17-91), swamped with everything from horn-tipped visors to brassware.

Half a block from the plaza, **La Concha** (Avenida 5a Sur 141; 2-12-70) weaves a real spell with its fine tapestries, batiks, rugs from Guatemala and handwoven purses.

To take in some quaint tropical paintings by locals, stop by the minuscule **Galería de Arte Kin** (Calle 2a Norte; 2-01-35).

A vivid range of cotton designer clothes lines the racks at **Girosol** (Avenida 5a and Calle 2a; 2-14-72). Skirts and dresses are abstract patchworks of hot colors, the Girosol trademark.

A most unusual curiosity shop, **Antiques & Artifacts** (Avenida 10a and Calle Adolfo Salas) recycles old coins, fossils, guns, swords and sepia photographs.

You will find a thousand and one prizes at the **Mercado de Artesanías** (Calle 1a Sur and the *zócalo*) including silver-plated erotic figures and beautiful, rare shells.

The cruise ship terminal several miles south of San Miguel has a big complex of shops with pumped-up pricetags. **Caribia** (Carretera a Chancanab; 2-08-44) runs the whole gamut of beachwear and crafts.

SOUTH OF CANCÚN SHOPPING

PLAYA DEL CARMEN

You can pick up curios at small shops around the plaza.

Tucan Curios (across from the plaza) stocks embroidered bags, beachwear and assorted crafts. **El Bazar** (Calle 5a) combines fast-food inventory (soft drinks and toiletries) with handicrafts (onyx and straw bags). The nicest wares fill **El Cenote** (Calle 5a, a few steps up from El Bazar): Mayan statuary, intricate Aztec calendars in wood, miniature carvings, batiks and brass.

AKUMAL AND XEL-HÁ

Both these resort areas have limited shopping. Akumal has two shops with crafts and clothes near one another right on the beach. At the entrance to Xel-Há, there's a row of crafts shops with beachwear and blankets.

TULUM

Tulum has the best shopping along the coast south of Cancún. Stall after stall fills the parking area just outside the ruins, and haggling brings prices to very attractive levels. Silver, onyx, masks, blankets, hammocks—the full lineup can be found here.

CHETUMAL SHOPPING

Unless you plan to stock up on Danish ham, Planter's peanuts or Japanese calculators, most of the import shops along the Avenida de los Héroes won't interest you. But the **Mercado Municipal** (Avenida de los Héroes near Avenida Efraím Aguilar) probably will, especially on Sundays. Everyone who hasn't skipped off to one of the blue lagoons is here, fingering mounds of gaudy plastic jewelry or listening to cheap, pirated cassettes of Mexican hits. Clothes, hammocks, suitcases, dolls—a vibrant variety of sweet nothings make for a good spree.

Nightlife

Most of the Gulf side of the Yucatán, outside of Mérida, has fairly subdued nightlife. Along the Caribbean, however, sunset signals party time, with bars and discos flashing until dawn.

CAMPECHE NIGHTLIFE

The nighttime action in Campeche is concentrated in the town's two big hotels, side by side on the waterfront. **El Olones Centro Nocturno** (Hotel Baluartes, Avenida Ruiz Cortines; 6-39-11) is a rather exclusive looking club, with red carpeting, red leather chairs and muffled music pouring through its gates. If you prefer a more open place to chat over a *café con leche*, Hotel Baluartes has an all-night café, **El Jardín** (6-39-11) with charming outdoor seating and indoor air-conditioning.

Next door, the Ramada Inn features the city's main disco, **Atlantis** (Avenida Ruiz Cortines 51), where you can enjoy the pirate-galleon decor and a hit parade of sounds.

MÉRIDA NIGHTLIFE

This romantic city's best nightlife takes place outdoors in its many plazas and parks. Each night of the week, a different plaza highlights a new performance, including Yucatán serenades, folk dancing, nostalgic *trovador* ballads, classical concerts, local rock, poetry readings and dramas. This ongoing cultural festival is sponsored by the municipal government. Check at the tourist office (Calle 59a 412; 24-89-25) for schedules.

Soak yourself in sentiment at **El Trovador Bohemio** (23-03-85) and **Salón Piano Peregrina** (23-93-76), both on Parque Santa Lucía. These piano bars feature delightful singers of the moonlight-and-roses genre, Mérida's forte. El Trovador, apparently the more popular spot, is very dim and crowded, with more professional performances. Peregrina, however, gives a more varied show, with trios and bongos and old Mexican classics. The informality encourages the audience onto its dance floor. Cover at both.

Several places offer Mayan shows, with extravagant costumes and mock sacrificial rituals. The most elaborate is at **Los Tulipanes** (Calle 42a between Calles 43a and 45a; 27-20-09). This overpriced supper club under a giant *palapa* roof has its own *cenote*, where a human sacrifice is simulated. Nightly performances on a gaudily lit stage come with mediocre dinners—order the minimum. The dances are well done but a bit Las Vegas. Mosquitoes galore; wear repellent or you'll be somebody's dinner. Cover.

The rooftop **Nightclub Aloha** at the Hotel Montejo Palace (Paseo de Montejo 483-C; 24-76-44) features both a late-night dynamic floorshow and live dance music. Cover.

Pancho's Restaurant-Bar (Calle 59a 509; 23-09-42) looks small but actually extends back into a series of lantern-lit patios and a tree-filled garden where after-hours drinks are served. Despite the disco music, the mood caters to soft conversations. Even the dance floor is dark and intimate.

If you crave bright lights and chic pandemonium, Mérida has its discos. Go and get it at **Le Touch** (Hotel Mérida Mision, Calle 60a 491; 23-95-00) or **Zero** (Holiday Inn, Avenida Colón and Calle 60a; 25-68-77). Cover at both.

CANCÚN NIGHTLIFE

From deafening discos to hushed lagoonside bars, Cancún really struts its stuff after dusk. Night spots overrun the Zona Hotelera, where every big hotel has its lobby bar and disco. A few exciting places light up Ciudad Cancún, too.

CIUDAD CANCÚN

Bananas (Avenida Tulum 11; 4-07-91), a restaurant-bar that sparkles with twinkle lights, puts on the air of a swinging, overgrown Caribbean shack—with swings instead of barstools, in fact. Live music nightly and lots of chatter.

A block behind the main drag stands tropical-colonial **Restaurant-Bar Perico's** (Calle Yaxchilán 91; 4-31-52). With a marimba band, giant sombreros placed on customers' heads, an animated bar with saddles for stools and dancing in the aisles, there's never a dull moment.

At video-bar **Tropicanerías** (Avenida Tulum near Calle Claveles; 4-40-85), live tropical music alternates with disco, and the action doesn't really start till midnight. Dark and cellarlike but carpeted and comfortable, this air-conditioned club attracts a lot of the city's workers. Cover.

ZONA HOTELERA

There are too many discos to describe. Here's a sampling:

The Mining Company (Hotel Verano Beat, Paseo Kukulkán, Km. 1.6; 3-07-72) takes the prize for design. The interior is like a cave, glittering with gold speckles. Overhead beams, lanterns, flues of water and wooden bridges add to the somewhat claustrophobic aura of a mine. Surprisingly, it's very quiet with little action. Cover.

The more popular **La Boom** (Paseo Kukulkán, Km. 3.5; 3-13-72) is Mediterranean-moderne. Housed in a big white building by the lagoon, La Boom glints with exposed girders, carpets, mirrors, videos and a moving dance floor. Cover.

The latest spot for tapping your toes is **Extasis** (Paseo Kukulkan, next to Nautilius Mall). Here, not only do the dancers sway to the beat of the music, the dance floor actually moves up and down.

Palapa-style **Carlos 'n Charlie's** (Paseo Kukulkán, Km. 5.5; 3-08-46) has elevated dining and pierside dancing in its crowded bar on Laguna Nichupté, great for relaxing and people-watching.

For glamour and special effects, no disco can touch **Christine** (Hotel Krystal, Paseo Kukulkán; 3-11-33). A forest of plants under glass runs around the periphery, and overhead the ceiling is crusted with spinning, blinking, rolling spotlights as well as lasers and four video screens. Popular and expensive. Cover.

Another hotspot is **Aquarius** (Punta Kukulkán; 3-01-00), a swinging club at the Camino Real.

To retreat from the disco scene and enjoy an evening drink, try **Pancho Villa's Follies** (Paseo Kukulkán, Km. 6.5; 3-10-03). This lounge rests on the seafront just steps from Playa Tortugas. It has lovely outdoor and indoor *palapa*-roofed sections. Waiters in revolutionary garb, their chests criss-crossed with *bandoleras*, colored cigarette lighters as bullets, serve lunches and dinners as well as drinks.

Whatever you do, don't miss the outstanding **Ballet Folklórico** (Centro de Convenciones, Paseo Kukulkán; 3-01-99). A fabulous Mexican buffet supper precedes the performance as a live band entertains. The show presents indigenous dances from 11 regions of Mexico, with colorful costumes, high energy, humor and finesse. Expensive but worth it.

Keep in mind the Mexican fiestas held at many major hotels and the assorted night cruises available, some to Isla Mujeres. Any travel agency can give you the scoop on both possibilities.

ISLA MUJERES NIGHTLIFE

People come here to avoid noisy nightlife, so your choices are limited. The traditional hangout, with the most sun 'n sea flavor, is *palapa*-roofed **Buho's** (Avenida Lazo 1, on Playa Los Cocos). By day it's a restaurant, by night a tropical cantina with cement dance floor, tile-topped tables and disco music.

The meeting ground of the chic or would-be chic is the smart **Nautibeach** (Playa Los Cocos), also known as Nautibeach Le Club. Its sandy grounds surround a pool, wooden deck, bar, expensive restaurant, pier and beach *palapas*. On weekends all this becomes a disco. It's ideal for a sunset drink any night.

The closest thing to a true disco on the island is **Tequila** (Avenida Matamoros and Avenida Hidalgo; 2-00-19). Billed as a video bar and grill, it does serve meals but caters to the late-night dance-set, with an air-conditioned and carpeted interior, tavern-style bar, dance floor and giant video screen.

COZUMEL NIGHTLIFE

"Cozy" best describes the after-dark scene on Cozumel. There are several discos and various bars, but the proximity of things creates a neighborly atmosphere.

Beginning around San Miguel's main plaza, the **Café del Puerto** (Avenida Rafael Melgar 2; 2-03-16) offers an elegant elevated bar above its dining area. With a tropical bamboo theme, the place features live piano and organ music nightly.

Shift into recreational gear for a drink at the all-American **Sports Page** (Calle 2a and Avenida 5a Norte; 2-11-99). A television tuned eternally to the latest game and the bar's air-conditioned comfort make it a welcoming venue for game talk and beer.

Ever tried a floating disco? The **Pirate's Party** (2-05-88) aboard the well-lit *M/V Fiesta* (leaving from the municipal ferry dock) gives you an offshore tour of the island plus an open bar, live music, buffet and dancing.

Action central in these parts is a place called **Scaramouche** (Calle Adolfo Salas and Calle 11a Sur), a contemporary club which draws a lively crowd.

The other contender for disco king is **Maya 2000** (Hotel Sol Caribe, Playa Paraíso, Carretera a Chancanab; 2-07-00), where ancient Mayan design meets rock 'n' roll. Not just a disco, Maya 2000 has a rec room with pool tables, video games and a library of used paperbacks. The detached bar, set away from the small dance floor, gives you a fighting chance for privacy. Cover.

Quietude comes more naturally at the dramatic **Lobby Bar Chac-Mool,** also in the Hotel Sol Caribe (Carretera a Chancanab; 2-07-00). Under the soaring wing of a cantilevered roof, this patio bar spreads out beneath a replica of the Mayan god Chac-Mool and a series of cascading fountains. Mariachis and other musicians perform nightly.

Mariachis and live piano music also warm the halls of the lobby bar at **Hotel El Presidente** (Carretera a Chancanab, Km. 6.5; 2-03-22). For fresh air by the sea, have a nightcap at the hotel's long outdoor *palapa* bar under twirling ceiling fans.

SOUTH OF CANCÚN NIGHTLIFE

You can hang up your dancing shoes down here and call it a night long before the evening star has risen. A sprinkling of sleepy beach bars in Playa del Carmen, Akumal and Chemuyil barely keeps the coast awake between Cancún and Chetumal.

PLAYA DEL CARMEN

Just north of Playa del Carmen along Punte Bete, you'll find restaurant-bars at **La Posada del Capitán Lafitte** (off Mexico 307, Km. 60) and **El Marlin Azul** (off Mexico 307, Km. 61), two secluded beachfront inns.

The **Bar Hernán Cortés** at the Hotel Molcas (Playa del Carmen near the ferry terminal) is a fairly swank air-conditioned tavern with black leatherette chairs, conquistador decor and an elevated television broadcasting sporting events.

Sip rum with sand between your toes in the **Sailorman Pub** at rustic Cueva Pargo (four blocks north of the *zócalo*, on the beach). This bamboo bar with a Robinson Crusoe air has an upstairs balcony resembling a tree-house.

AKUMAL

During the winter high season, enough people fill the Hotel Akumal Caribe to bring to life its **Disco Hogot** (Mexico 307, Km. 104), an outdoorsy ramada with tropical music.

A more reliable spot for a seaside drink is the *palapa*-bar at **Aventuras Akumal** (off Mexico 307, Playa Aventuras).

CHEMUYIL

Restaurant-Bar Marco Polo (off Mexico 307, Playa Chemuyil) is a great little thatch-roofed watering-hole-in-the-round, wide open, right on the beach and often crowded. Try the "Chemuyil Special," a delicious blender drink of Kahlua, milk, rum, vanilla, coconut creme and ice served in half a gourd.

CHETUMAL NIGHTLIFE

It's slow. You can do some footwork at crowded **Antares Disco** (Boulevard Bahía near Calle Esmeralda), but if you're over 30 you'll feel every inch an oldster. All the teens in town congregate here. Cover.

Switch Bar in the Hotel Continental Caribe (Avenida de los Héroes 171; 2-11-00) mixes live Latin tunes and music videos in a mature environment where you can converse without shouting. Try the hotel's **Disco Focus** (2-10-80) for more action.

Yucatán Addresses and Phone Numbers

CIUDAD DEL CARMEN

Bank—Bánamex, Calle 24a and Calle 31a (2-12-77)
Hospital—Hospital Regional (2-03-06)
Police—2-02-05

Post Office—Calle 28a 58

CAMPECHE
Bank—Bánamex, Calle 10a 319-B (6-52-52)
Hospital—Hospital General (6-42-33)
Laundry—Lavandería Mágica 1, Superdíez (Área Akim-Pech, Malecón Miguel Alemán)
Police—6-23-09
Post Office—Avenida 16 de Septiembre and Avenida Ruiz Cortines (6-21-34)
Tourist Office—Turismo Estatal, Avenida Ruiz Cortines (6-60-68)

MÉRIDA
Bank—Bánamex, Calle 63a (23-70-72)
Consulates—American Consulate, Paseo de Montejo 453 (25-50-11) and Canadian Consulate, Calle 62a 3090 (25-62-99)
Hospital—Clínica Mérida, Avenida de los Itzáes 242 (23-92-21)
Laundry—Lavandería Automática, Calle 59a between Calle 72a and Calle 74a
Police—25-25-55
Post Office—Calle 65a and Calle 56a (21-24-68)
Tourist Office—Municipal Tourist Office, Calle 32a and Avenida de los Itzáes (25-30-33)

CANCÚN
Bank—Bánamex, Avenida Tulum, Ciudad Cancún (4-19-67)
Consulate—American Consulate, Avenida Cobá, Ciudad Cancún (4-24-11)
Hospital—Hospital Seguro Social, Avenida Cobá, Ciudad Cancún (4-18-20)
Laundry—Lavandería Alborada, Avenida Nader 5, Ciudad Cancún
Newspapers and books—Don Quixote, Avenida Tulum, Ciudad Cancún (4-12-94), plus three other locations
Police—2-19-84
Post Office—Avenida Xel-Há and Calle Sunyaxchen (4-14-18), Ciudad Cancún
Tourist Office—Tourist Information Center, near Centro de Convenciones, Zona Hotelera (3-04-47)

ISLA MUJERES
Bank—Banco del Atlántico, Avenida Juárez 5 (2-01-04)
Hospital—Centro de Salud, Calle Guerrero and Calle Morelos (2-01-17)
Police—Palacio Municipal, Avenida Hidalgo and Calle Morelos (2-00-82)
Post Office—Calle Guerrero and Calle López Mateos (2-00-85)
Tourist Office—Oficina de Turismo, Calle Guerrero 8 (2-01-88)

COZUMEL
Bank—Bancomer, Plaza del Sol, San Miguel (2-05-50)
Hospital—Medical Services Center, Avenida 20 Norte 425 (2-10-81)
Laundry—Lavandería Murrufo, Avenida 25a Sur 17 (2-02-48)
Police—2-00-92
Post Office—Avenida Rafael Melgar and Calle 7a Sur
Tourist Office—Secretaria Estatal de Turismo, Edificio Plaza del Sol,
2nd floor (2-09-72) or Infotur, Avenida 5a Norte between Calle 4a
and Calle 2a (2-14-51)

CHETUMAL
Bank—Bánamex, Avenida Juárez (2-27-10)
Hospital—Hospital General de la S.S.A., Avenida Andrés Quintana
Roo and Calle San José Sordía (2-19-77)
Laundry—Lavafacil, Segundo Circuito Periferico and Prologación
Héroes
Police—2-19-84
Post Office—Avenida Plutarco Elías Calles 2A (2-00-57)
Tourist Office—Palacio Municipal, 3rd floor, Parque Central (2-09-42)

Recommended Reading

HISTORY AND SOCIOLOGY

Calderón de la Barca, Frances. *Life in Mexico* (University of California Press, Berkeley, 1982). A huge tome of witty letters all about Mexico, written in 1840 by the Scottish wife of the first Spanish ambassador to Mexico.

Coe, Michael D. *The Maya* (Thames Hudson, 1980). A brief, solid summary of Mayan history, well-illustrated.

Crownover, Richard. *Erotic Mexico* (Phoenix Books, 1975). A colorful little guide to the romantic side of Mexico.

Díaz del Castillo, Bernal; translated by J.M. Cohen. *The Conquest of New Spain* (Penguin Books, 1963). Written by one of Cortés' soldiers, this classic account of the Spanish conquest of the Aztecs tells one of the great adventure tales of all time in simple language.

León-Portilla, Miguel (editor). *The Broken Spears* (Beacon Press, 1962). An Aztec version of the Spanish conquest.

Paz, Octavio; translated by Lysander Kemp. *The Labyrinth of Solitude* (Grove Press, 1961). An intense, probing analysis of Mexican thought and behavior by one of Mexico's foremost writers.

Reed, John. *Insurgent Mexico* (International Publishing, 1969). The famous journalist who covered the Russian revolution here captures the grit and glory of the 1910 Mexican revolution.

Riding, Alan. *Distant Neighbors* (Vintage Books, 1986). This bestselling portrait of Mexican society—past, present and future—offers fascinating insights into family life, politics, economics and psychology.

Simpson, Lesley Byrd. *Many Mexicos* (University of California Press, Berkeley, 1960). A fast-moving book of Mexican history.

FICTION

Fuentes, Carlos. *Where the Air is Clear* (Farrar, Straus & Giroux, 1971), *The Death of Artemio Cruz* (Farrar, Straus & Giroux, 1964), *The Old Gringo* (Harper & Row, 1985) and other novels. Any of the books by Mexico's most esteemed novelist promise great reading and astute insights into modern Mexico.

Greene, Graham. *The Power and the Glory* (Penguin Books, 1940). The brooding tale of a Mexican priest pursued by authorities during an anti-clerical purge in the 1920s.

Jennings, Gary. *Aztec* (Avon, 1980). A sensationalized, giant bestseller about the last days of the Aztec empire before the conquest, as told by an old Aztec to a Spanish chronicler.

Lawrence, D.H. *The Plumed Serpent* (Penguin Classics, 1985; first published in 1926). A rich, sensual depiction of the relationship between an Irish woman and two Mexican leaders who bring back the old Aztec gods to replace Christianity.

Lewis, Oscar. *The Children of Sanchez* (Vintage Books, 1963) and *A Death in the Sanchez Family* (Vintage Books, 1969). Novels about the hardships of a poor Mexican family.

Lowry, Malcolm. *Under the Volcano* (New American Library, 1947). A dark, classic novel about the last day in the life of an alcoholic British consul living in central Mexico.

Rulfo, Juan; translated by Lysander Kemp. *Pedro Paramo* (Grove Press, 1959). A slim, surreal novel about the thin line between life and death.

Traven, B. *Treasure of the Sierra Madre* (Hill & Wang, 1963), *The Bridge in the Jungle* (Hill & Wang, 1967), *The General from the Jungle* (Robert Hale, 1945) and others. Besides his famous adventure tale of gold and greed (*Treasure of the Sierra Madre*), this evasive author, who lived reclusively in Mexico, churned out many other novels set in southern Mexico, especially dealing with injustices to Indians.

PERSONAL COMMENTARY

Cannon, Ray. *The Sea of Cortez* (Lane Magazine and Book Co., 1966). Some say this book put Baja on the map. In glowing language, it presents a romantic, adventurous picture of a rich wilderness on a rich sea. Now out of print, but available in public libraries.

Flandrau, Charles Macomb. *Viva Mexico!* (University of Illinois Press, 1964). An absorbing, often amusing account of the author's sojourn at a coffee plantation in the mountains of Veracruz. Considered one of the classic books about Mexico, written in 1908.

Hoctor, Fred. *Baja Haha* (Backside Press, 1984). A comical grab-bag of character sketches and zany episodes that capture Baja's unconventional flair.

Huxley, Aldous. *Beyond the Mexique Bay* (Triad Paladin, 1984). A series of vignettes covering the Caribbean, Guatemala and central Mexico, written in 1934.

Lawrence, D.H. *Mornings in Mexico* (Penguin Books; first published in 1927). Vivid essays about Mexico written during Lawrence's residence there.

McMahan, Mike. *Adventures in Baja* (Stephens Press, 1983). A Baja veteran's humorous, personal rundown on the highlights of Baja.

Steinbeck, John. *Log from the Sea of Cortez* (Penguin Books, 1941). A book tracing the steps of Doc Ed Ricketts (of Cannery Row fame) as he collects marine animals for his biological supply business.

Stephens, John L. *Incidents of Travel in Yucatán* (Dover Publications, 1963). This two-volume study, first published in 1843, covers Stephens' groundbreaking explorations of Mayan ruins, with stunning etchings by Frederick Catherwood throughout both books.

UNUSUAL GUIDEBOOKS

Franz, Carl. *People's Guide to Mexico* (John Muir Publications, 1982). The classic vagabond guidebook: practical, funny and personably written in vignette-style—a pleasure to read.

Lewbel, George S. *Diving and Snorkeling Guide to Cozumel* (Pisces Books, 1984). A small guidebook full of enticing undersea photos and practical information about the reefs around Cozumel.

Miller, Tom. *World of the California Gray Whale* (Baja Trail Publications). Field guide to marine mammals of the Pacific.

Miller, Tom. *Angler's Guide to Baja California* (Baja Trail Publications, 1979). All about fishing Baja's waters.

Muller, Kal and García-Oropeza, Guillermo. *Mexico: Insight Guides* (Apa Productions, 1983). Part of an excellent series of lavishly illustrated source books, this one takes you through the history, customs and tourist highlights of Mexico with marvelous photographs.

Simon, Kate. *Mexico, Places and Pleasures* (Thomas Crowell, 1962). A selective guidebook full of the author's keen perceptions, lush and poetic in style.

Index

Abbreviations used in index for area chapters are:
(BN) Baja Norte; (BS) Baja Sur; (GM) Gulf of Mexico; (MR) Mexican Riviera;
(NWC) Northwest Coast; (SWC) Southwest Coast; (Y) Yucatán

Acapulco (MR), 171, 174; addresses and phone numbers, 261; beaches, 230–32; hotels, 189–91; map, 245; nightlife, 257–59; restaurants, 202–205; shopping, 251–53; sightseeing, 244–46; trailer parks, 234
Accommodations, 16. *See also* Hotels in area chapters
Address system, 17
Addresses and phone numbers. *See* Addresses and phone numbers in area chapters
Agencia Nacional de Viajes de la Comisión Nacional del Deporte, 16
Airline transportation, 7. *See also* Transportation in area chapters
Airports. *See* Transportation in area chapters
Akumal (Y), 359; hotels, 345–46; nightlife, 400; restaurants, 355; shopping, 395; sightseeing, 388
Álamos (NWC), 164
All-Terrain Cycles, 31
Altamira (GM), 316
Altata (NWC), 165
Alvarado (GM), 320
Alvaro Obregón (GM), 321
American Plan, 16
Animal life, 32–33, 34–35. *See also* Flamingos; Whale-watching; etc.
Aquariums (Y), 385
Architecture, 52–53
Arriaga (SWC), 270
Artifacts, and export, 9
Arts, 52–53, 56–58
Aticama (MR), 239
Auto clubs, 24–25
Automobiles. *See* Car rentals; Car travel; etc.
Aztec civilization, 38–39, 53

Bacalar (Y), 356
Bahía Bacochibampo (NWC), 161
Bahía Concepción area (BS): beaches, 117–18; restaurants, 108;

sightseeing, 129
Bahía de Banderas (MR), 240
Bahía de la Choya (NWC), 160
Bahía de La Paz (BS), 130
Bahía de los Ángeles (BN), 64; beaches, 82; hotels, 70–71; restaurants, 74; sightseeing, 88; trailer parks, 83
Bahía de los Muertos (BS), 104
Bahía de Puerto Ángel (SWC), 286
Bahía de San Carlos area (NWC), 141, 161
Bahía de San Quintín (BN), 87
Bahía de Santiago (MR), 241
Bahía de Todos Santos (BN), 84
Bahía de Zihuatanejo (MR), 242
Bahía del Puerto Viejo (MR), 235
Bahía Guaymas (NWC), 161
Bahía Kino (NWC), 33, 140; addresses and phone numbers, 169; beaches, 154–55; hotels, 144–45; nightlife, 167; restaurants, 148; shopping, 165–66; sightseeing, 160–61; trailer parks, 158
Bahía Matanchén (MR), 239
Bahías de Huatulco area (SWC), 264–65; addresses and phone numbers, 291; beaches, 281–82; hotels, 270; map, 265; sightseeing, 288; trailer parks, 285
Baja Norte (BN), 1, 61–93; addresses and phone numbers, 92–93; beaches, 78–82; history, 62, 64; hotels, 67–77; maps, 63, 85; nightlife, 90–92; population, 62; restaurants, 71–74; shopping, 88–90; sightseeing, 83–88; sports, 75–76, 78; trailer parks, 82–83; transportation, 65–66; weather, 3, 61, 75
Baja Sur (BS), 1, 61, 95–137; addresses and phone numbers, 136–37; beaches, 116–27; history, 95–96; hotels, 100–107; maps, 97, 131; nightlife, 134–36; restaurants, 107–11; shopping, 133–34; sightseeing, 128–34; sports, 111, 114–15; trailer parks, 127–28; transportation, 98–100; weather, 3, 95
Balancanché (Y), 383
Banks, 17–18

About the Authors

Rebecca Bruns, author of the original edition of *Hidden Mexico*, spent almost a year south of the border researching the book. Traveling in a 1978 Toyota, she drove nearly 20,000 miles along the coasts of Mexico. A onetime staff writer for the *New Orleans Times-Picayune*, she has traveled to 30 countries and written for the *Miami Herald, Los Angeles Times, Travel and Leisure, Islands,* and *Travel Holiday.*

Dave Houser, a former public relations executive, departed the traditional career path nine years ago to take up freelance travel writing and photography. Since then he has journeyed to more than 100 countries and "never once had time to look back." In 1984 he was named Photographer of the Year by the Society of American Travel Writers; the next year he was runner-up for the Travel Journalist of the Year award.

Jean Pierce Postlewaite first visited Mexico in 1963, flying in a single-engine plane to Puerto Vallarta, then just a sleepy fishing village with no paved roads. After a stint as a newspaper editor in London she served as managing editor for the Mobil Travel Guides and senior editor for the company's travel guide division. A member of the Society of American Travel Writers, Jean currently works as a freelance writer and editor.

Eleanor S. Morris, author of the *Guide to Recommended Country Inns of Arizona, New Mexico and Texas*, has published widely in newspapers and magazines throughout the country. When not traveling, which is rare, she is at home in Austin, Texas working on a novel.

About the Illustrator

Rob Harper is a San Francisco Bay Area artist whose paintings appear in several major collections. He traces his involvement with Mexico back to his great grandfather, who built a stone pier in La Paz for the Mexican government in 1898 and later settled in Mexico City.

ALSO AVAILABLE FROM ULYSSES PRESS